A TEXT BOOK OF

COMPUTER NETWORK

For

Semester - I

FINAL YEAR (BE) DEGREE COURSE IN ELECTRONICS / ELECTRONICS AND TELECOMMUNICATION / INDUSTRIAL ELECTRONICS AND ELECTRONICS AND COMMUNICATION ENGINEERING

Strictly As Per the New Revised Syllabus of
Dr. Babasaheb Ambedkar Marathwada University, Aurangabad
[2009-10]

G. R. PATIL
M.E. (Electronics),
Associate Professor in E & TC Department,
Army Institute of Technology,
Dighi, PUNE.

R. C. JAISWAL
M. E. (E&TC),
Assistant Professor, E&TC Department,
Pune Institute of Computer Technology
Dhankawadi, PUNE.

A. V. DHUMANE
M.E. Computer,
Assistant Professor, Comp. Engg. Department,
NBN Sinhagad School of Engineering
Ambegaon, PUNE.

NIRALI PRAKASHAN

COMPUTER NETWORKS - I (BE : E & TC - BAMU) ISBN : 978-93-83525-91-1

First Edition : October 2013

© : **Authors**

The text of this publication, or any part thereof, should not be reproduced or transmitted in any form or stored in any computer storage system or device for distribution including photocopy, recording, taping or information retrieval system or reproduced on any disc, tape, perforated media or other information storage device etc., without the written permission of Authors with whom the rights are reserved. Breach of this condition is liable for legal action.

Every effort has been made to avoid errors or omissions in this publication. In spite of this, errors may have crept in. Any mistake, error or discrepancy so noted and shall be brought to our notice shall be taken care of in the next edition. It is notified that neither the publisher nor the authors or seller shall be responsible for any damage or loss of action to any one, of any kind, in any manner, therefrom.

Published By : **NIRALI PRAKASHAN** Abhyudaya Pragati, 1312, Shivaji Nagar, Off J.M. Road, PUNE – 411005 Tel - (020) 25512336/37/39, Fax - (020) 25511379 Email : niralipune@pragationline.com	**Printed at** **Repro Knowledgecast Limited** **Thane**

DISTRIBUTION CENTRES
PUNE

Nirali Prakashan
119, Budhwar Peth, Jogeshwari Mandir Lane
Pune 411002, Maharashtra
Tel : (020) 2445 2044, 66022708, Fax : (020) 2445 1538
Email : niralilocal@pragationline.com

Nirali Prakashan
S. No. 28/25, Dhyari,
Near Pari Company, Pune 411041
Tel : (022) 24690204 Fax : (020) 24690316
Email : bookorder@pragationline.com

MUMBAI
Nirali Prakashan
385, S.V.P. Road, Rasdhara Co-op. Hsg. Society Ltd.,
Girgaum, Mumbai 400004, Maharashtra
Tel : (022) 2385 6339 / 2386 9976, Fax : (022) 2386 9976
Email : niralimumbai@pragationline.com

DISTRIBUTION BRANCHES

NAGPUR
Pratibha Book Distributors
Above Maratha Mandir, Shop No. 3, First Floor,
Rani Jhanshi Square, Sitabuldi, Nagpur 440012,
Maharashtra, Tel : (0712) 254 7129

BENGALURU
Pragati Book House
House No. 1, Sanjeevappa Lane, Avenue Road Cross,
Opp. Rice Church, Bengaluru – 560002.
Tel : (080) 64513344, 64513355,
Mob : 9880582331, 9845021552
Email:bharatsavla@yahoo.com

JALGAON
Nirali Prakashan
34, V. V. Golani Market, Navi Peth, Jalgaon 425001,
Maharashtra, Tel : (0257) 222 0395
Mob : 94234 91860

KOLHAPUR
Nirali Prakashan
New Mahadvar Road,
Kedar Plaza, 1st Floor Opp. IDBI Bank
Kolhapur 416 012, Maharashtra. Mob : 9855046155

CHENNAI
Pragati Books
9/1, Montieth Road, Behind Taas Mahal, Egmore,
Chennai 600008 Tamil Nadu, Tel : (044) 6518 3535,
Mob : 94440 01782 / 98450 21552 / 98805 82331, Email : bharatsavla@yahoo.com

RETAIL OUTLETS
PUNE

Pragati Book Centre
157, Budhwar Peth, Opp. Ratan Talkies,
Pune 411002, Maharashtra
Tel : (020) 2445 8887 / 6602 2707, Fax : (020) 2445 8887

Pragati Book Centre
Amber Chamber, 28/A, Budhwar Peth,
Appa Balwant Chowk, Pune : 411002, Maharashtra,
Tel : (020) 20240335 / 66281669
Email : pbcpune@pragationline.com

Pragati Book Centre
676/B, Budhwar Peth, Opp. Jogeshwari Mandir,
Pune 411002, Maharashtra
Tel : (020) 6601 7784 / 6602 0855

PBC Book Sellers & Stationers
152, Budhwar Peth, Pune 411002, Maharashtra
Tel : (020) 2445 2254 / 6609 2463

MUMBAI
Pragati Book Corner
Indira Niwas, 111 - A, Bhavani Shankar Road, Dadar (W), Mumbai 400028, Maharashtra
Tel : (022) 2422 3526 / 6662 5254, Email : pbcmumbai@pragationline.com

www.pragationline.com   info@pragationline.com

Preface...

It gives us great pleasure to bring out the book on **"Computer Network**. This text is designed to explain the various types of Networks in use today.

The book is written mainly for the compulsory subject of Final Year (BE) Students of Electronics, Electronics and Telecommunication, Industrial Electronics and Electronics and Communication course for the subject **"Computer Network"**. It is written strictly as per the revised syllabus of Dr. Babasaheb Ambedkar Marathwada University, Aurangabad.

Welcome to the world of Computer Networks-I. The world is getting networked today. It is making an impact on day-to-day of common man. Businesses and consumers are demanding more interactions with the network.

In view of this, it is necessary to have the fundamental knowledge of the Computer Networks.

This book gives the theoretical and practical knowledge of the different networks and networking technologies.

Unit 1 covers network topologies ISO-OSI model TCP/IP.

Unit 2 covers communication media, design issues, elementary protocol, switching.

Unit 3 covers routing algorithms, routing protocols, transport layer services and principles.

Unit 4 covers cryptography, DNS, security issues for intranet and internet.

Unit 5 covers IP addressing sub-netting, layer architecture, TCP/IP protocols.

Unit 6 covers ISDN IEEE 802.11, Advantages of digital network.

Nirali Prakashan put the book, what we thought of into reality. Our sincere thanks to Shri. Dineshbhai Furia, Shri. Jignesh Furia and Shri. M. P. Munde. The books could be completed in time, due to sincere and hard work of Nirali Prakashan's staff namely Mr. Malik Shaikh, Mrs. Prajakta, Mrs. Sonal and Miss Chaitali Takale. We thank them all.

Valuable suggestions from our esteemed readers to improve the text will be most welcome and highly appreciated.

Pune
Syllabus ...

1. **Introduction to Computer Networks**

   Objective components of Communication Networks, topologies, centralized and distributed networks, LAN, MAN, WAN, Broadcast vs Point to Point networks, Overview of network model: ISO - OSI and TCP/IP. Network design issues, layered architecture, interfaces and services, service primitives and relationships of services to protocols.

2. **Physical Layer & Data Link Layer**

   Communication Media: Twisted pair, coaxial cables, fiber optic cables, Wireless Communication. Design issues, framing, error detection and correction, CRC, Elementary protocols – stop and wait, Sliding window, Slip, bridges, circuit switching, message switching, packet switching network.

3. **Networks and Transport Layer**

   Virtual circuits, and datagram networks, circuit switching, and packet switching. Routing algorithms, routers and routing protocols. Congestion control. Transport layer services and principles. Connectionless v/s connection oriented services like UDP and TCP, QOS (Quality of Services).

4. **Application Layer**

   Introduction to Cryptography, Secret key and, public key algorithm, Security issues for Intranet and Internet, DNS (Domain name System), Electronic mail, World wide Web, Writing a web page in HTML.

5. **TCP/IP Protocol Suite**

   Layered Architecture, Protocol Stack., IP Addressing: Classes, static, dynamic (DHCP). Ipv4 v/s Ipv6, Sub-netting: masking and subnet masking. Protocols: Ping, FTP, telnet, http(www), SMTP, SNMP, Trace route, TFTP, BOOTP, DNS, NF S, RPC, ICMP, IGMP, ARP, RARP, etc.

6. **Digital Networks**

   Signal conversion, digital carrier systems, ISDN, SIDN Channels, DN Layers, SBS, Integrated Networks, IEEE CAN Standards, IEEE 802 standards, IEEE 802.11 standards for wireless networks.

***

Contents ...

1. Introduction to Computer Networks — 1.1 - 1.50

2. Physical Layer & Data Link Layer — 2.1 - 2.90

3. Network Layer & Transport Layer — 3.1 - 3.80

4. Application Layer — 4.1 - 4.174

5. TCP/IP Protocol Suite — 5.1 - 5.140

6. Digital Networks — 6.1 - 6.88

***

Unit I

INTRODUCTION TO COMPUTER NETWORKS

1.1 Data Communications

1. The purpose of data communication is to share the information.
2. The term Telecommunication includes Television, Telegraphy and Telephony etc. i.e. communication at a distance.
   (Tele = 'far' = 'at a distance').
3. Data communication is the exchange of data between two devices (computers, switch, hub, routers etc.) via. two types of media.
   (a) Wired media (coaxial, UTP, fiber cable).
   (b) Wireless media (IR, RF, Microwave).
4. For the communication of data between devices, devices must be a part of the communication system.
5. Communication system is made up of –
   (a) Software (programs).
   (b) Hardware (physical equipment).
6. The effectiveness of a data communication system depends on four fundamental characteristics.
   (a) Delivery
   (b) Accuracy
   (c) Timeliness
   (d) Jitter
7. **Delivery:** The system must deliver the data from correct source device to correct destination device.
8. **Accuracy:** The system must deliver the data accurately, (i.e. without altering the data).
9. **Timeliness:** The system must deliver the data in a timely manner, (i.e. without significant delay) i.e. Audio and Video data transmission should be done without significant delay i.e. real time transmission.
10. **Jitter:** The system must not have jitter. Jitter refers to the variation in the packet arrival time. It is the uneven delay in the audio and video data of real time transmission system. If video clip of 5 sec. duration has 2000 packets and if 1500 packets are delayed by 35 ms time, and remaining the 500 packets are delayed by 45 ms time, then uneven quality in the video is the result.

1.1.1 Components

1. Data communication system has the following five components:
   (a) Message.
   (b) Sender.
   (c) Receiver.
   (d) Transmission medium.
   (e) Protocol.

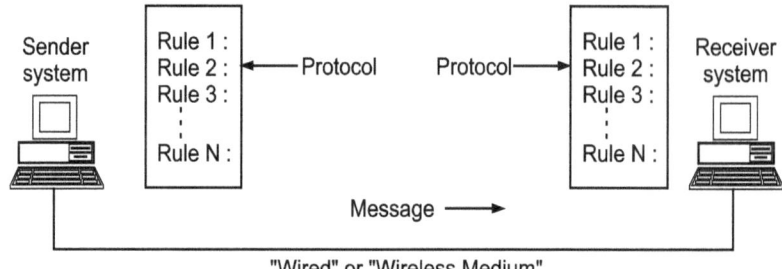

Fig. 1.1: Data communication system and its five components

2. **Message:** It is the information to be communicated. The data like text, numbers, pictures, audio and video information.
3. **Sender:** It is a transmitter, which sends the data message. It can be a computer system, workstation, telephone handset, video camera and network device like router etc.
4. **Receiver:** It is a device, which receives the data message. It can be a computer system, workstation, telephone handset, video camera and network device like router etc.
5. **Transmission medium:** It is a physical path by which a message travels from sender to receiver. There are two types of media:
   (a) **Guided:** For example, coaxial, UTP and fiber cable.
   (b) **Un-guided:** For example, IR, RF and microwave.
6. **Protocol:** It is a set of rules that governs data communications between sender and receiver.

1.1.2 Data Representation

1. The data message or information comes in different forms such as:
   (a) Text.
   (b) Numbers.
   (c) Images.
   (d) Audio.
   (e) Video.

2. The text can be in the form of unicode or ASCII code.
3. Numbers are represented by bit patterns like binary.
4. Images are represented by bit patterns. The image is composed of matrix of pixels (pictures elements), where each pixel is a small dot.

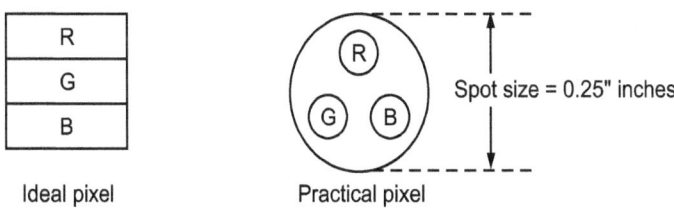

Fig. 1.2: Typical ideal and practical pixel

5. Theoretically, pixel is represented by an idealized rectangular area which is independent of its neighbouring pixels, in practice (or practically), each pixel has the shape of a "spot" which merges with its neighbours. If this 0.025 spot is viewed from sufficient distance, continuous image is observed.
6. **Pixel depth:** Number of bits per pixel is known as the pixel depth and determines the range of different colours that can be produced. For example,
(a) 12-bits = 4-bits for R
4-bits for G
4-bits for B
Yielding 2^{12} = 4096 different colours
(b) 24-bits = 8-bits for R
8-bits for G
8-bits for B
Yielding 2^{24} = 16 million different colours.
7. Also, there are several methods to represent colour images.
(a) RGB (Red, Green and Blue).
(b) YCM (Yellow, Cyan and Magenta).
8. Audio refers to the broadcasting or recording of the music or sound. The sound, music or voice is converted into electrical signal with the help of the transducer (i.e. microphone).
9. Video refers to the broadcasting or recording of the movie. The visible picture information is converted into electrical signal with the help of the transducer (i.e. video camera).

1.1.3 Data Flow

1. In data communication, the communication between two devices can be –
   (a) Simplex.
   (b) Half duplex.
   (c) Full duplex.

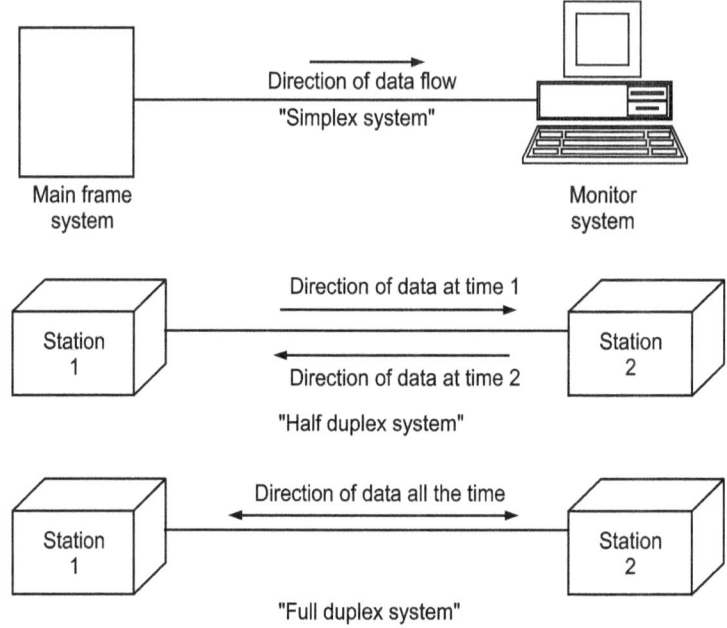

Fig. 1.3: Data flow (Simplex, half-duplex, full duplex system)

2. **Simplex system:** In this mode, the unidirection communication is done, for example, keyboards and monitors.
   Keyboard: Can only input.
   Monitor: Can only accept output.
3. **Half-duplex system:** In this mode, each station can both transmit and receive, but not at the same time. When one station is sending, other can only receive and vice versa. Walkie-talkies and Citizen Band Radio (CB) are the examples. The entire capacity of the channel can be utilized for each direction.
4. **Full-duplex system:** In this mode, both stations can transmit and receive simultaneously. For example, telephone network. When two people are communicating by a telephone line, both can talk and listen at the same time. Entire capacity of the channel is divided between the two directions.

1.2 Networks

1. Network is a set of devices (Nodes) inter connected by communication links.

2. A Node can be:
   - Computer.
   - Printer.
   - Networking component.
3. Most networks use **distributed processing,** in which a task is divided among multiple computer systems. (Instead of one single large computer system being responsible for all processes, different computer systems will handle different parts of the process).
4. **Network criteria:**
A network must meet the following criteria:
(a) Performance,
(b) Reliability,
(c) Security.
5. **Performance:**
Performance can be measured in the following ways:
(a) Transit time (time taken by the message to travel from one device to another).
(b) Response time (elapsed time between inquiry and response).
(c) Number of users.
(d) Type of transmission medium.
(e) Capabilities of the connected hardware.
(f) Efficiency of the software.
6. **Reliability:**
Reliability of the network is nothing but accuracy of delivery. The network reliability is measured by –
(a) The frequency of failure.
(b) The time taken by a link to recover from failure.
(c) Network's robustness.
7. **Security:**
Security includes system security and network security.
The following issues are there:
(a) Includes protecting data from un-authorised access.
(b) Protecting data from damage and development.
(c) Implementing policies and procedures for recovery from breaches and data losses.

1.2.1 Physical Structures of Networks

1. The study of physical structures of networks includes:
(a) Type of connection.
(b) Physical topology of network.

2. **Type of connection:**
- Generally, two or more devices are connected through links in a typical network.
- A link transfers a data from one device to other.
- There are two possible types of connections:
(a) Point to point connection.
(b) Multipoint connection.
- These connections are shown in Fig. 1.4.

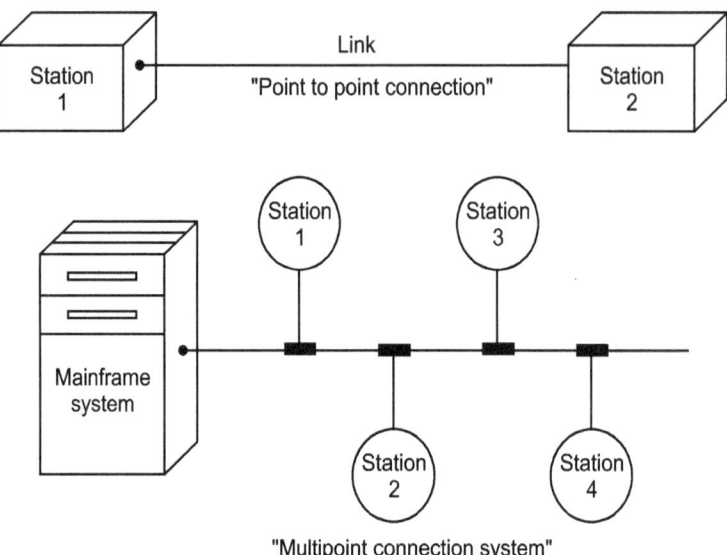

Fig. 1.4: Point and multipoint connection system

3. **Point to point:**
- This type of connection provides dedicated link between two devices.
- Entire capacity of the link is reserved for station 1 and station 2.
- TV remote and TV, establishes a point to point connection between them.
4. **Multipoint:**
- In this type of connection, more than two devices share a common single link.
- Capacity of link (or channel) is shared by following means:
(a) Spatially.
(b) Temporally.
- Thus, communication between two devices uses the connection, either point to point or multipoint.

1.3 Network Topology (Physical And Logical)

- The physical topology of a network refers to the configuration of cables, computers, and other peripherals.
- **Physical topology** should not be confused with **logical topology** which is the method used to pass the information between workstations.
- Every LAN has a topology, or the way that the devices on a network are arranged and how they communicate with each other.
- The way that the workstations are connected to the network through the actual cables that transmit data, and the physical structure of the network is called the **physical topology**.
- The **logical topology** is also called signal topology.
- The **logical topology** is the way that the signals act on the network media, or the way that the data passes through the network from one device to the next without regard to the physical interconnection of the devices.
- **Logical topologies** are bound to the network protocols that direct how the data moves across a network.
- The **Ethernet protocol** is a common **logical bus topology protocol**.
- **LocalTalk** is a common **logical bus or star topology protocol**. IBM's Token Ring is a common **logical ring topology protocol**.
- A network's **logical topology** is not necessarily the same as its physical topology. For example, twisted pair Ethernet is a **logical bus topology** in a physical star topology layout. While IBM's Token Ring is a logical ring topology, it is physically set-up in a star topology.

1.4 Network Topology (Physical)

1. The way, in which the connections are made, is called the topology of the network.
2. Network topology specifically refers to the physical layout of the network, especially the locations of computers and how the cable is run between them.
3. It is important to select the right topology.
4. Each topology has its own strengths and weaknesses.
5. The four most common topologies are:
   - (a) Bus
   - (b) Star
   - (c) Ring
   - (d) Mesh

1.4.1 Bus Topology

Bus topology is often used when network installation is small.

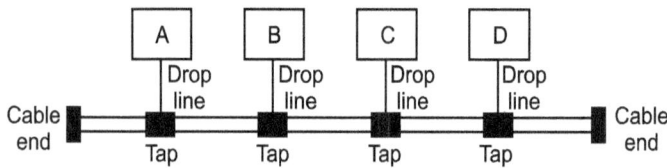

Fig. 1.5: Bus topology

Advantages:
1. Simple and reliable in very small network, easy to use and understand.
2. Least amount of cable required to connect computers, so it is less expensive.
3. Extension of bus is easy by joining cable and using BNC connector. So more computers can be connected.
4. A repeater can also be used to extend a bus, boost the signal and allow it to travel a longer distance.

Disadvantages:
1. Heavy traffic (network traffic) can slow a bus considerably, because any computer can transmit data any time, uses entire B.W. and interrupts each other instead of communicating.
2. Each barrel connector weakens the signal power.
3. It is difficult to troubleshoot bus. A cable break or loose connector will also cause reflections and bring down the whole network and network activity stops.

1.4.2 Star Topology

Star networks are used in concentrated networks, where the end-points are directly reachable from a central location. When network expansion is expected and when the greater reliability is needed, switch may be used.

Advantages:
1. It is very easy to modify and add new network without disturbing the rest of the network.
2. Center of a star network is a good place to diagnose network faults.
3. Single computer failure do not bring down the whole network.
4. With switch, you can use several cable types - UTP, STP, coaxial, fiber etc.

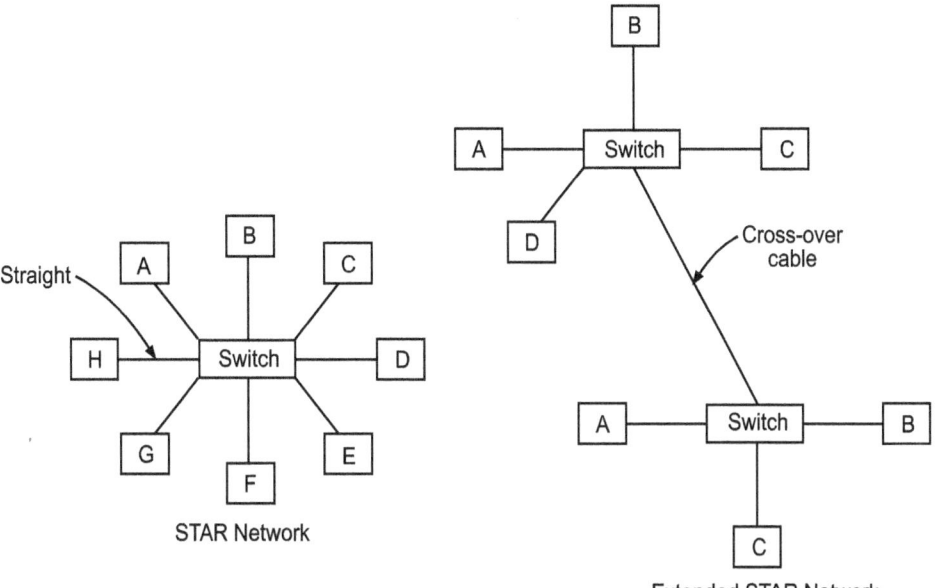

Fig. 1.6: Star and extended star topology

Disadvantages:
1. If central switch fails, the whole network fails to operate.
2. Cost is more than bus network because network cables must be pulled to one central point. Thus cable requirement increases.

1.4.3 Ring Topology

1. In ring network, each computer is connected to the next computer, with the last one connected to first.
2. Messages flow around the ring in one direction.

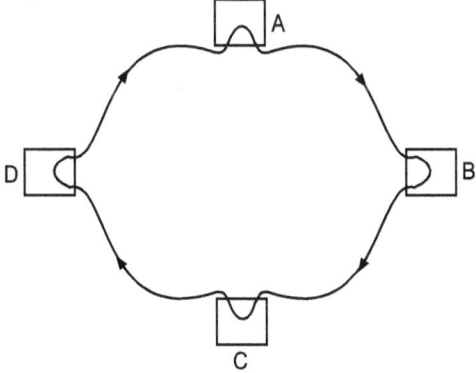

Fig. 1.7: Ring topology

3. Since each computer retransmits what it receives, signal loss problems are there.
4. There is no termination because there is no end to ring.

Advantage:
1. When more users are added, systems become slow but doesn't fail.

Disadvantages:
1. Failure of one computer on the ring can affect the whole network.
2. It is difficult to troubleshoot a ring network.
3. Adding or removing computers disturbs the entire network.

1.4.4 Mesh Topology

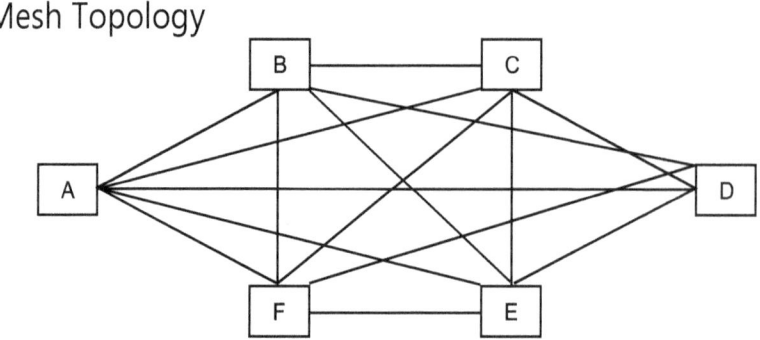

Fig. 1.8: Mesh topology

Each computer is connected to other with separate cable.

Advantages:
1. Guaranteed communication.
2. High channel capacity.

Disadvantages:
1. Difficulty of installation and reconfiguration.
2. Maintenance cost.

Network Classification

Interprocessor Distance	Processors located in same	Example
1 m	Square meter	Personal Area Network
10 m	Room	
100 m	Building	Local Area Network
1 km	Campus	
10 km	City	Metropolitan Area Network
100 km	Country	
1000 km	Continent	Wide Area Network
10,000 km	Planet	Internet

1. This is the classification of Networks depending upon the interprocessor distance. i.e. LAN, MAN, WAN and Internet etc.
2. But other types of networks are also available depending upon their role in Network systems such as:
   - **Client-Server Network and Peer-to-Peer Network.**
   - **Voice Networks.**
   - **Satellite Networks.**
   - **Integrated Networks.**
   - **Centralized Networks.**
   - **Distributed Networks.**
   - **Wireless Networks.**
   - **Broadcast and point to point Networks.**

1.5 Centralised Network

- The source data is located at central location.
- Other clients or terminals can access this centalized data.
- Following are the examples of the centralized networks.
   (1) Stock quotation and information system.
   (2) Bank credit card system.
   (3) Components distribution system.
   (4) ATM (Automatic Teller Machines) System.

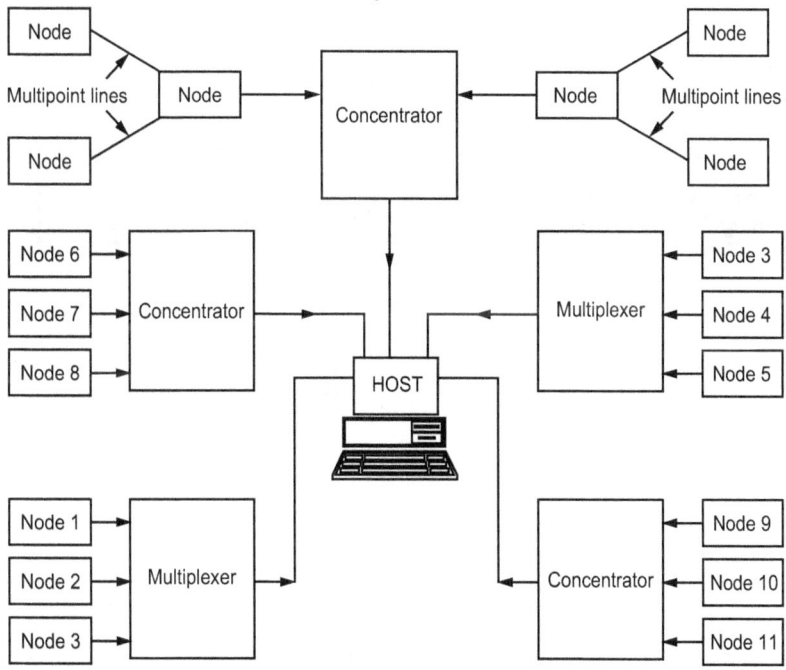

Fig. 1.9: Typical Centralized Data Network

- Centralized network can be a part of any complex network.
- In centralized network, different networks performing similar activities are linked.
- Tree topology is implemented in the centralized data network.
- In centralized network, cost effectiveness is achieved using concentrators and multiplexers.
- Nodes (also called as terminals) can be connected to central site directly or indirectly (i.e. through multiplexers and concentrators.

1.6 Distributed Computer Networks

1. A distributed computing system is immediate growth from centralized computer systems and client/server computer systems, as shown in Fig. 1.
2. Distributed computing is basically client/server computing.
3. Data is not located in one server, but in many servers.
4. These servers might be at different areas, connected by WAN links into enterprise networks that join the many standalone and autonomous computer systems in workgroups, departments, and divisions of an organization.

1.6.1 Centralized Network/Client-Server Network/ Distributed Computer Network

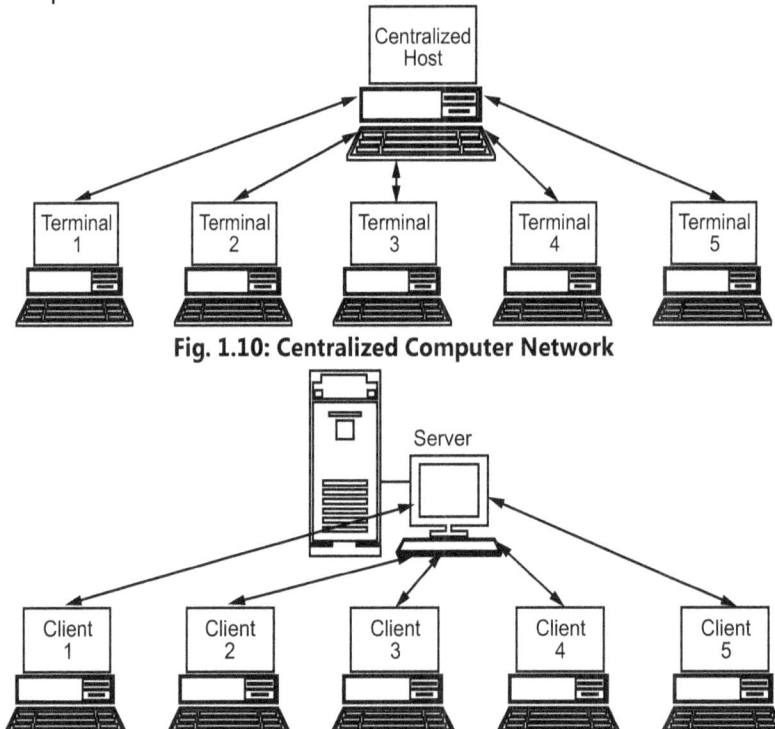

Fig. 1.10: Centralized Computer Network

Fig. 1.11: Client-Server Configuration

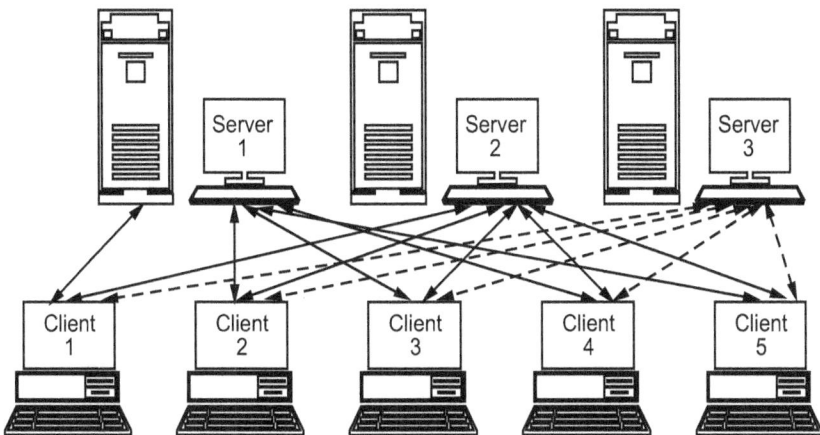

Fig. 1.12: Distributed Client Computing

5. Computer Networks built with Web technologies are also called as distributed computer networks. Distributed computer networks supports the Intranet and Internet.
6. Dynamic information provided by the Back-end database systems can be connected to these Web servers.
7. Web technologies add new features to distributed computing.
8. Web browsers like internet explorer, Netscape communicator, Netscape Navigator are universal clients that can connect with Web servers with any operating system.
9. A new trend is to build intranets in which all data is centralized on clustered servers that can handle the requests of many, many users at the same time so that organizations need powerful central processing systems.
10. A Distributed-computing environment is similar to a client/server environment, except that there are many servers and many clients who access any one of those servers at any time.

1.6.2 Advantages and Disadvantages of Distributed Computer Networks

1. The distributed computing model supports access to data already located at diverse sites.
2. Databases are replicated to other locations so that users at those locations can access data locally instead of using expensive WAN link to access centralized data at corporate places.
3. Distributing data in distributed computer networks provides protection from local network failure. If one site goes down, users can still access data at other sites.

4. In distributed computer networks Distributing data requires complex replication and synchronization over LAN or WAN links that requires more management and supervision. Skilled managerial activities are expected.
5. Next step is to have distributed systems built with TCP/IP protocols and Web technologies or network applications that promote distributed computing.
6. The target is to make the data computing as simple as possible.

1.6.3 Needs of Distributed Computer Networks
1. The network *platform* that supports a variety of multivendor products and TCP/IP protocol support due to its wide acceptance.
2. Real-time connection-oriented methods or communication systems are required to communicate with Servers.
3. Requirement and support of a directory naming service which keeps track of resources and information and where they are located.
4. Requirement and support of a time service to synchronize events among different servers that hold related information.
5. Requirement and support of database management systems that support advanced features such as *partitioning* and *replication* to provide the distribution of data and ensure the availability, reliability, and protection of that data.
6. Requirement and support of a *distributed file system* that operates in a peer-to-peer mode to allow users working at workstations to act as both clients and servers.
7. Requirement and support of Security features such as authentication and authorization, as well as trust relationships between systems so users can access multiple servers and databases without the need to prove their identity every time they access a remote resource.

1.7 Local Area Network (LAN)
1. Networks used to interconnect computers in a single room, rooms within a building or buildings on one site are called Local Area Network (LAN).
2. LAN transmits data with a speed of several megabits per second (10^6 bits per second). The transmission medium is normally *coaxial cables*.
3. LAN links computers, i.e., software and hardware, in the same area for the purpose of sharing information.
4. Usually LAN links computers within a limited geographical area because they must be connected by a cable, which is quite expensive.

5. People working in LAN get more capabilities in data processing, work processing and other information exchange compared to *stand-alone computers*.
6. Because of this information exchange, most of the business and government organisations are using LAN.

1.7.1 Major Characteristics of LAN

1. Every computer has the potential to communicate with any other computers of the network.
2. High degree of interconnection between computers.
3. Easy physical connection of computers in a network.
4. Inexpensive medium of data transmission.
5. High data transmission rate.

1.7.2 Components of LAN

1. Workstations:
- In LAN, a workstation refers to a machine that will allow users access to a LAN and its resources while providing intelligence on board allowing local execution of applications.
- It may allow data to be stored locally or remotely on a file server.
- Obviously, diskless workstations require all data to be stored remotely, including the data that is necessary for the diskless machine to boot up.
- Executable files may reside locally or remotely as well, meaning a workstation can run its own programs or those copied off the LAN.

2. Servers:
- A server is a computer that provides the data, software and hardware resources that are shared on the LAN.
- A LAN can have more than one server; each has its unique name on the network and all LAN users identify the server by its name.
- **Dedicated Server:** A server that functions only as a storage area for data and software and allows access to hardware resources is called a dedicated server. Dedicated servers need to be powerful computers.
- **Non-Dedicated Server:** In many LANs, the server is just another workstation. Thus, there is a user networking on the computer and using it as a workstation, but part of the computer also doubles up as a server. Such a server is called a non-dedicated server. Since, it is not completely dedicated to serving. LANs do not require a dedicated server since resource sharing amongst a few workstations is proportionately on a smaller scale.

- **Other Types of Servers:** In large installations, which have hundreds of workstations sharing resource, a single computer is often not sufficient to function as a server.

Some of the other servers have been discussed here under:
- **File Server:** A file server stores files that workstations can access and it also decides on the rights and restrictions that the users need to have while accessing files on LAN.
- **Printer Server:** A Printer server takes care of the printing requirement of number of workstations.
- **Modem Server:** It allows LAN users to use the modem to transmit long distance messages. Server attached to one or two modems would serve the purpose.

3. **Clients:**
- A client is any machine that requires something from a server.
- In the more common definition of a client, the server supplies files and sometimes processing power to the smaller machines connected to it. Each of the smaller machine is a client.
- Thus, a typical ten PC local area network may have one large server with all the major files and databases on it and all the other machines connected as clients.
- This type of terminology is common with TCP/IP networks, where no single machine is necessarily the central repository.

4. **Nodes:**
- Small networks that comprise of a server and number of PCs.
- Each PC on the network is called a node.
- A node essentially means any device that is attached to the network. Because each machine has a unique name or number (so the rest of the network can identify it), you will hear the term node name or node number quite often.

5. **Network Interface Cards:**
- The Network Interface card, or LAN adapter, functions as an interface between the computer and the network cabling, so it must serve two masters.
- Inside the computer, it controls the flow of data to and from the Random-Access Memory (RAM).
- Outside the computer, it controls the flow of data in and out of the network cable system.

- An interface card has a specialized port that matches the electrical signaling standards used on the cable and the specific type of cable connector.
- One must select a network interface card that matches your computer's data bus and the network cable.
- Token ring LANs require token ring NICs, Ethernet LANs require Ethernet NICs etc.
- The peripheral component interface bus (PCI) has emerged as a new standard for adapter card interfaces.
- It is advisable to use bus PCI-equipped computers and PCI LAN adapters wherever possible.
- Software is required to interface between a particular NIC and an operating system called **Network Interface Card Driver**.

6. **Connectors:**
- Connectors used with TP included RJ-11 and RJ-45 modular connectors in current used by phone companies.
- Occasionally other special connectors, such as IBM's Data Connector, are used.
- RJ-11 connectors accommodate 4 wires or 2 twisted pairs, while RJ-45 houses 8 wires or 4 twisted pairs.

7. **The Network Operating System:**
- The Network Operating System software acts as the command center, enabling all of the network hardware and all other network software to function together as one cohesive, organized system.
- In other words, the network operating system is the heart of the network.
- It can be client-server or Peer-to-Peer Network Operating System.

1.7.3 Advantages of LAN

1. The reliability of network is high because the failure of one computer in the network does not effect the functioning for other computers.
2. Addition of new computer to network is easy.
3. High rate of data transmission is possible.
4. Peripheral devices like magnetic disk and printer can be shared by other computers.

1.7.4 Uses of LAN

Followings are the major areas where LAN is normally used:

1. File transfer and Access
2. Word and text processing
3. Electronic message handling
4. Remote database access
5. Personal computing
6. Digital voice transmission and storage
7. Office automation
8. Factory automation
9. Distributed Computing
10. Fire and Security Systems
11. Process Control
12. Document Distribution.

1.8 Wide Area Network (WAN)

1. The term Wide Area Network (WAN) is used to describe a computer network spanning a regional, national or global area.
2. For example, for a large company the head quarters might be at Delhi and regional branches at Mumbai, Chennai, Bengaluru and Kolkata.
3. Here regional centers are connected to head quarters through WAN.
4. The distance between computers connected to WAN is larger. Therefore the transmission medium used are normally telephone lines, microwaves and satellite links.

1.8.1 Characteristics of WAN

Following are the major characteristics of WAN.

1. **Communication Facility:**
- For a big company spanning over different parts of the country, the employees can save long distance phone calls and it overcomes the time lag in overseas communications.
- Computer conferencing is another use of WAN where users communicate with each other through their computer system.

2. **Remote Data Entry:**
- Remote data entry is possible in WAN. It means sitting at any location you can enter data, update data and query other information of any computer attached to the WAN but located in other cities.
- For example, suppose you are sitting at Chennai and want to see some data of a computer located at Delhi, you can do it through WAN.

3. **Centralized Information:**
- In modern computerized environment you will find that big organizations go for centralized data storage.
- This means if the organization is spread over many cities, they keep their important business data in a single place.
- As the data are generated at different sites, WAN permits collection of this data from different sites and save at a single site.

1.9 Difference between LAN and WAN

1. LAN is restricted to a limited geographical area of few kilometers. But WAN covers large distance and operates nationwide or even worldwide.
2. In LAN, the computer terminals and peripheral devices are connected with wires and coaxial cables. In WAN, there is no physical connection. Communication is done through telephone lines and satellite links.
3. Cost of data transmission in LAN is less because the transmission medium is owned by a single organization. In case of WAN, the cost of data transmission is very high because the transmission medium used are hired, either telephone lines or satellite links.
4. The speed of data transmission is much higher in LAN than in WAN. The transmission speed in LAN varies from 0.1 to 100 megabits per second. In case of WAN the speed ranges from 1800 to 9600 bits per second (bps).
5. Few data transmission errors occur in LAN compared to WAN. It is because in LAN the distance covered is negligible.

1.9.1 Types of WAN
1. There are two types of WAN networks:
(a) Switched WAN.
(b) Point to point WAN.

2. The switched WAN is shown in Fig. 1.13.

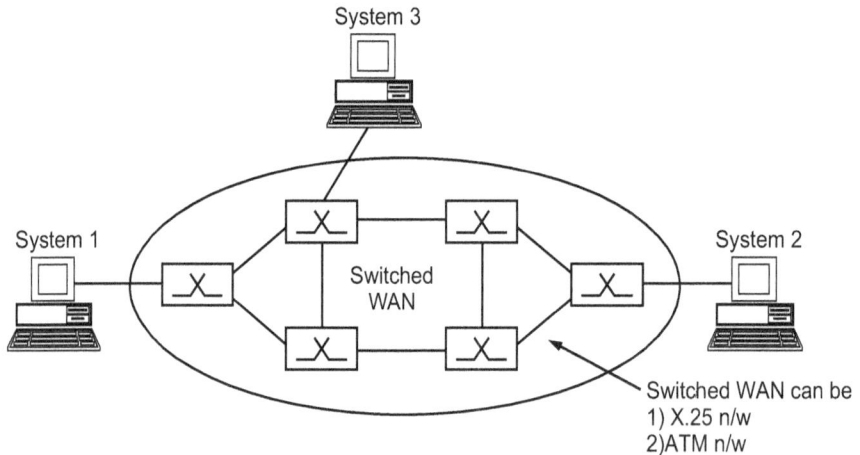

Fig. 1.13: Switched WAN

3. The point to point WAN is shown in Fig. 1.14.

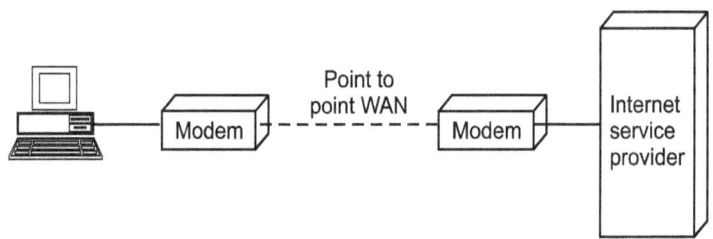

Fig. 1.14: Point to point WAN

1.10 Metropolitan Area Network (MAN)

1. A Metropolitan Area Network (MAN) is a bigger version of a Local Area Network (LAN) and usually uses similar technology.
2. A MAN can covers a group of corporate offices or a town or city, and can be either privately or publicly owned. A MAN can support both data and voice, and may be related to the local cable television network (CATV).
3. A MAN employs one or two cables, and does not contain switching elements, which simplifies the design.
4. A standard has been adopted for MANs called *Distributed Queue Dual Bus* (DQDB) and is defined by IEEE 802.6.
5. DQDB consists of two unidirectional buses (cables) to which all of the computers on the network are connected.
6. Each bus has a *head-end* that initiates transmission activity.

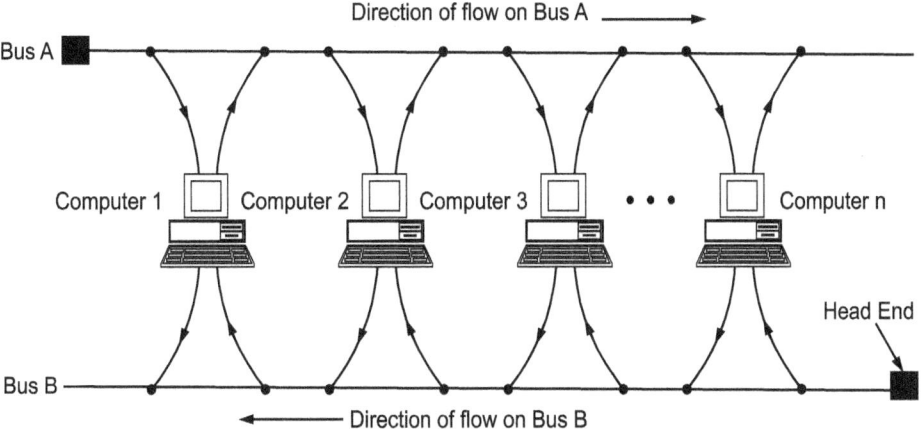

Fig. 1.15: Typical MAN network (also known as 802.6 DQDB network)

7. In the Fig. 1.15, traffic that is intended for a computer to the right of the source computer uses the upper bus, while traffic intended for a computer to the left uses the lower bus.
8. The network is based on fiber-optic cable in a dual-bus topology, and traffic on each bus is unidirectional, providing a fault-tolerant configuration.
9. Bandwidth is allocated using time slots, and both synchronous and asynchronous modes are supported.

1.11 Internet

- Internet is the extensive, worldwide computer network available to the public. An internet is a more general term for any set of interconnected computer networks that are connected by internetworking.
- The Internet, or simply the Net, is the publicly available worldwide system of interconnected computer networks that transmit data by packet switching using a standardized Internet Protocol (IP) and many other protocols.
- It is made-up of thousands of smaller commercial, academic, and government networks.
- It carries various information and services, such as electronic mail, on-line chat and the interlinked web pages and other documents of the World Wide Web.
- Hypertext is viewed using a program called a web browser which retrieves pieces of information, called "documents" or "web pages", from web servers and displays them, typically on a computer monitor.

- One can then follow hyperlinks on each page to other documents or even send information back to the server to interact with it.
- The act of the following hyperlinks is often called "surfing" or "browsing" the web. Web pages are often arranged in collections of related material called "web sites."
- Although the English word *worldwide* is normally written as one word (without a space or hyphen), the proper name World Wide Web and abbreviation WWW are now well-established even in formal English.
- Typical network schematic is shown in Fig. 1.16.
- Function of webserver is to host website (web pages).
- Function of proxy server is to provide internet connectivity to the different machines with private IP addresses.

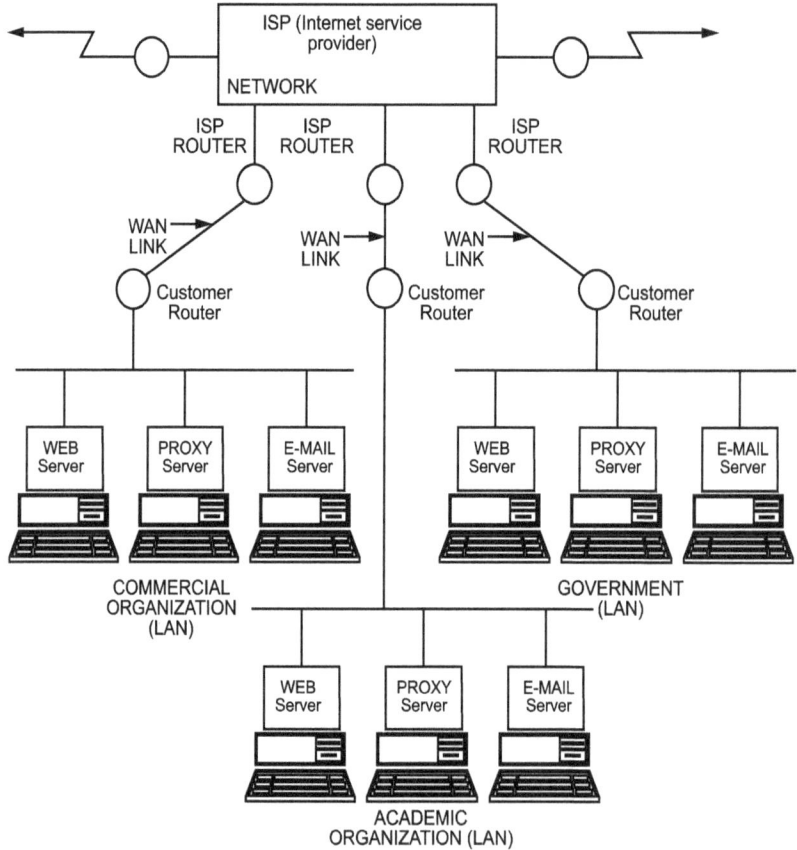

Fig. 1.16: Typical internet connection components

- E-mail server is used to provide different E-mail accounts for E-mail transactions.
- Thus, Routers are used to interconnect different LAN's to form Internet.
- Organization's **Router** and ISP's **ROUTER** are interconnected to form Internet.
- Customer router to ISP router link can be of –
   (1) Dial-up-line   (2) Leased line   (3) ISDN line etc.

- LAN Technology can be of –
(1) Ethernet (802.3 or CSMA/CD) Technology
(2) Token Ring (802.5) Technology
(3) Token Bus (802.4) Technology

- Thus, internet consists of the following groups of networks:
(1) **Backbones:** Large networks that exist primarily to interconnect other networks.
(2) **Regional networks:** Connecting for example, universities and colleges.
(3) **Commercial Networks:** Providing access to the backbones to subscribers and networks owned by commercial organizations for internal use that also have connections to the Internet.
(4) **Local Networks**, such as campus – wide university networks.

1.12 Broadcast Network vs. Point to Point Network

Broadcast Network :
1. Broadcast network has single communication channel that is shared by all the machines on the network. Short messages called packets in certain contexts, sent by any machine, are received by all the others. This packet is received and processed by every machine on the network. This mode of operation is called as broadcasting.
2. An address field within the packet specifies for whom it is intended. Upon receiving a packet, a machine checks the address field. If the packet is intended for itself, it processes the packet; if packet is intended for some other machine, it is just ignored.
   Example : LAN
3. It is normally a connection of hosts and repeaters.
4. Here if packet is not responded, then it will be lost.

Point-to-Point Network :
1. In contrast, point to point network consists of many connections between individual pairs of machines to go from the source to destination. A packet on this type of network may have to visit one or more intermediate machine.

2. Often multiple routes of different lengths are possible. So routing algorithms play an important role in point to point communication.

   Example : WAN

3. It is normally a connection of routers, called as subnet.

4. If two routers, that are not connected by a direct cable and wish to communicate, they must do it via other routers. A packet is sent from one to another via. intermediate router. The packet is stored there until required output line is free and then forwarded. A subnet using this principle is called as point to point store and forward or packet switched network.

1.13 Layered Task

1. The basic need/use/application of networking is to transfer the data from one system to another system.
2. It is not always data, it can be voice, video or data.
3. This is simply indicated in Fig. 1.17, that every system which is involved in the data communication process is represented by a stack of layers like:
   - Higher layers
   - Middle layers
   - Lower layers.

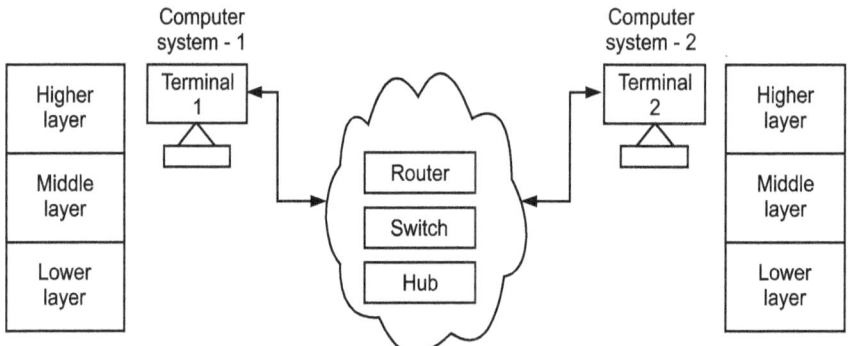

Fig. 1.17: Network communication system represented by stack of layers

4. The significance of each layer and related tasks can be explained with the simple example of sending a letter by one person, which is being received by other person as shown in Fig. 1.18.

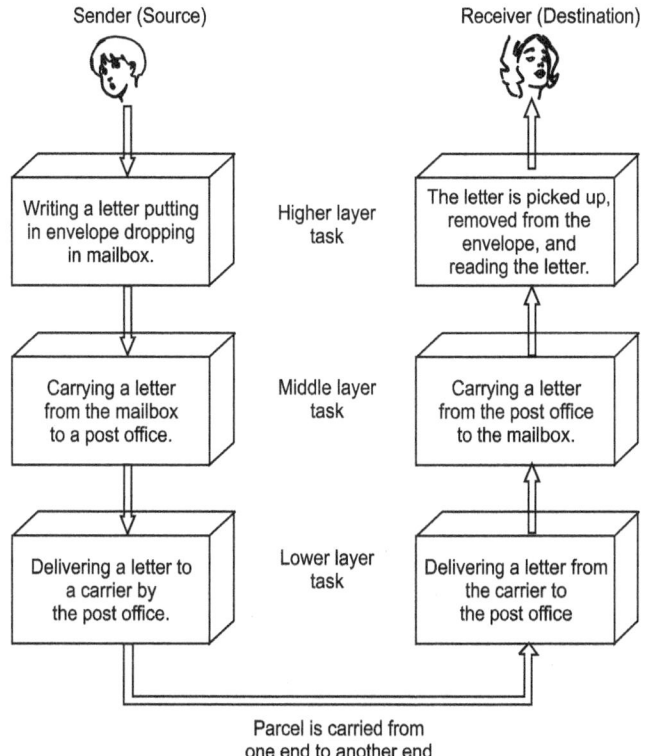

Fig. 1.18: Tasks involved [source to destination] in journey of letter

5. Thus, transporting of letter from source to destination or between sender and receiver is done by carrier.
6. Also each layer at the source (sender side) uses the services of the layer below it.
7. The higher layer uses services of the middle layer, middle layer uses the services of the lower layer and the lower layer uses services of the carrier.
8. Thus, in a data communication system, each system is represented by the stack of different layers. This reduces the design complexity in the networks.
9. This issue is discussed in detail, in the following sections.

1.14 Layered Network Architecture

1. To reduce design complexity, most networks are organized as a series of layers or levels. Each one built upon the one below it.
2. The number of layers, the name of each layer, the contents of each layer, and the function of each layer differs from network to network. However, in all networks, the purpose of each layer is to offer certain services to the higher layer.

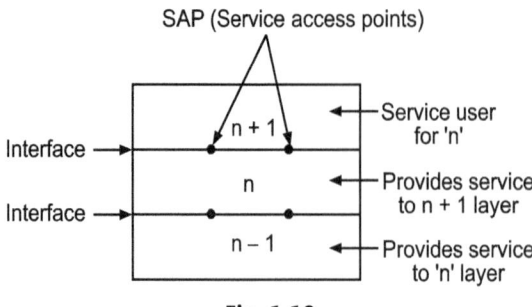

Fig. 1.19

3. The function of each layer is to provide services to the layer above it. The active elements in each layer are often called entities. Entity can be a software entity or a hardware entity.
4. The layered architecture concept redefines the way networks are conceived and creates significant cost savings and managerial benefits.
5. Instead of building a separate network for each service, user can have multiple services sharing a common core network.
6. Adding new services and managing the network infrastructure can be easy.
7. That is why the layered architecture concept will become increasingly important for the user.
8. It offers opportunities to reduce capital and operating expenditure by offering a smooth step-by-step migration to IP.
9. Key advantage is that network resources can be used more effectively in terms of simplicity and fewer equipment sites leading to lower total cost of ownership.
10. Also, the need for transmission connections in the network can, in many cases, be reduced by more than 50 percent.

1.14.1 Benefits of Layered Designs

1. Segmentation of high-level from low-level issues. Complex problems can be broken into smaller more manageable pieces.
2. Since, the specification of a layer says nothing about its implementation, the implementation details of a layer are hidden (abstracted) from other layers.
3. Many upper layers can share the services of a lower layer. Thus, layering allows us to reuse the functionality.
4. Development by teams is aided because of the logical segmentation.
5. Easier exchange of parts at a later date.

1.14.2 Downsides of Layered Designs

1. The trouble with layers of computer software is that sooner or later you loose the touch with reality. Layers are abstraction boundaries, and the more they encapsulate their works the more one is unaware of the application's inner works.
2. Layering is a form of information hiding. A "layering violation" occurs in situations where a layer uses knowledge of the implementation details of another layer in its own operations. At the limit this leads to changes to one layer resulting in changes to every other layer, which is an expensive and error prone proposition.
3. Layering can lead to poor performance. To avoid this penalty, in situations where an upper layer can optimize its actions by knowing what a lower layer is doing, we can reveal information that would normally be hidden behind a layer boundary.
4. The layers must be engineered at the outset, before the system is built.

1.15 Protocol Fundamentals

1. In computing, *a **protocol** is a set of rules which is used by computers to communicate with each other across a network.*
2. A protocol is a convention or standard that controls or enables the connection, communication, and data transfer between computing endpoints. In its simplest form, a protocol can be defined as the rules governing the syntax, semantics, and synchronization of communication.
3. Protocols may be implemented by hardware, software, or a combination of the two. At the lowest level, a protocol defines the behaviour of a hardware connection.

Typical Properties:

Detection of the underlying physical connection (wired or wireless), or the existence of the other endpoint or node:

- Handshaking.
- Negotiation of various connection characteristics.
- How to start and end a message.
- Procedures on formatting a message.
- What to do with corrupted or improperly formatted messages (error correction).
- How to detect unexpected loss of the connection, and what to do next.
- Termination of the session and/or connection.

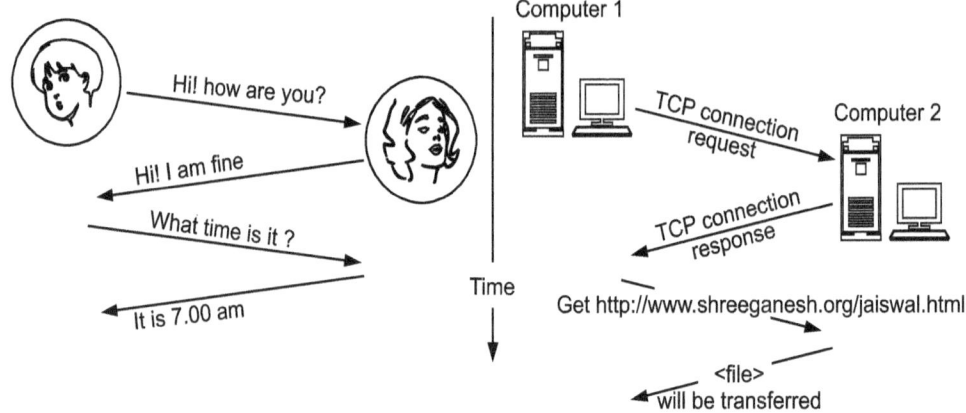

Fig. 1.20: Human protocol Vs. Computer network protocol

Importance of Protocols:

The protocols in human communication are separate rules about appearance, speaking, listening and understanding. All these rules, also called *protocols of conversation*, represent different layers of communication. They work together to help people successfully communicate. The need for protocols also applies to network devices. Computers have no way of learning.

1.15.1 Terms and Definitions

1. **Protocol:** Protocol is agreement between the communication - communicating parties on how communication is to proceed.

   Or

2. **Protocol:** Protocol is strict procedure and sequence of actions to be followed in order to achieve orderly exchange of information among peer entities.

   Or

3. **Protocol:** Protocol is a set of rules governing the format and meaning of the frames, packets or messages that are exchanged by the peer entities within a layer.

4. **Protocol stack:** A list of protocols used by a certain system, one protocol per layer is called a protocol stack.

5. **Interface:** Between each pair of adjacent layers, there is an interface. The interface defines which primitive operations and services the lower layers offers to the upper one.

6. **Network architecture:** A set of layers and protocols is called network architecture.

7. **Service:** Services and protocols are distinct concepts although they are frequently confused. Service is a set of primitives (operations) that a layer provides to the layer above it. The service defines what operations the layer is prepared to perform on behalf of its users, but it says nothing about how these operations are implemented. A service relates to an interface between two layers, with the lower layer being the service provider and the upper layer being the service user.

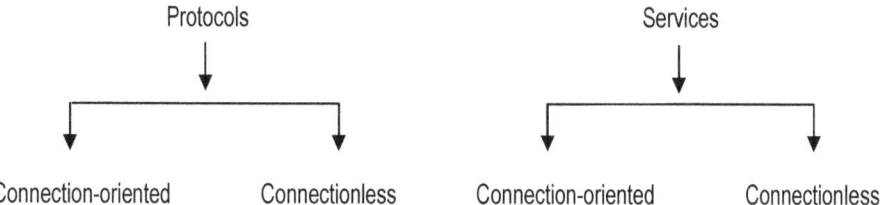

Layers can offer two different types of services to the layers above them.
1. Connection-oriented and
2. Connectionless.

1.16 Service Primitives and Relationship of Service to Protocols

- A service is formally specified by a set of primitives (operations) that define the service interface.
- The primitives differ for different services. As a simple example, a service may provide the following primitives:

1. **LISTEN:** Listen for an incoming communication request.
2. **CONNECT:** Make a communication request.
3. **RECEIVE:** Receive data of a communication.
4. **SEND:** Send data of a communication.
5. **DISCONNECT:** Disconnect or discontinue a communication.

We will discuss service primitives in more detail in our transport layer chapter.

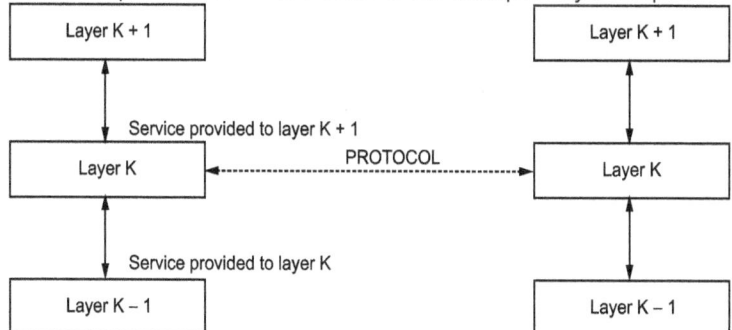

Fig. 1.21: Depiction of peers at level (Relationship between service and a protocol)

- As discussed before, each layer has specific functions and offers certain services to the layer above it.
- A service is a set of primitives (operations) that a layer provides to the layer above it.
- In the definition of services, we do not specify their implementation.
- The implementation is only visible to the provider of the service.
- A protocol defines the implementation of the service and is not visible to the user of the service.
- A protocol is a set of rules governing the format and meaning of the frames, packets, or messages within a layer and can be changed at will by entities, provided that they do not change the service visible to their users.

Connection-Oriented Service Vs. Connectionless Service

	Connection-Oriented Service	Connectionless Service
1.	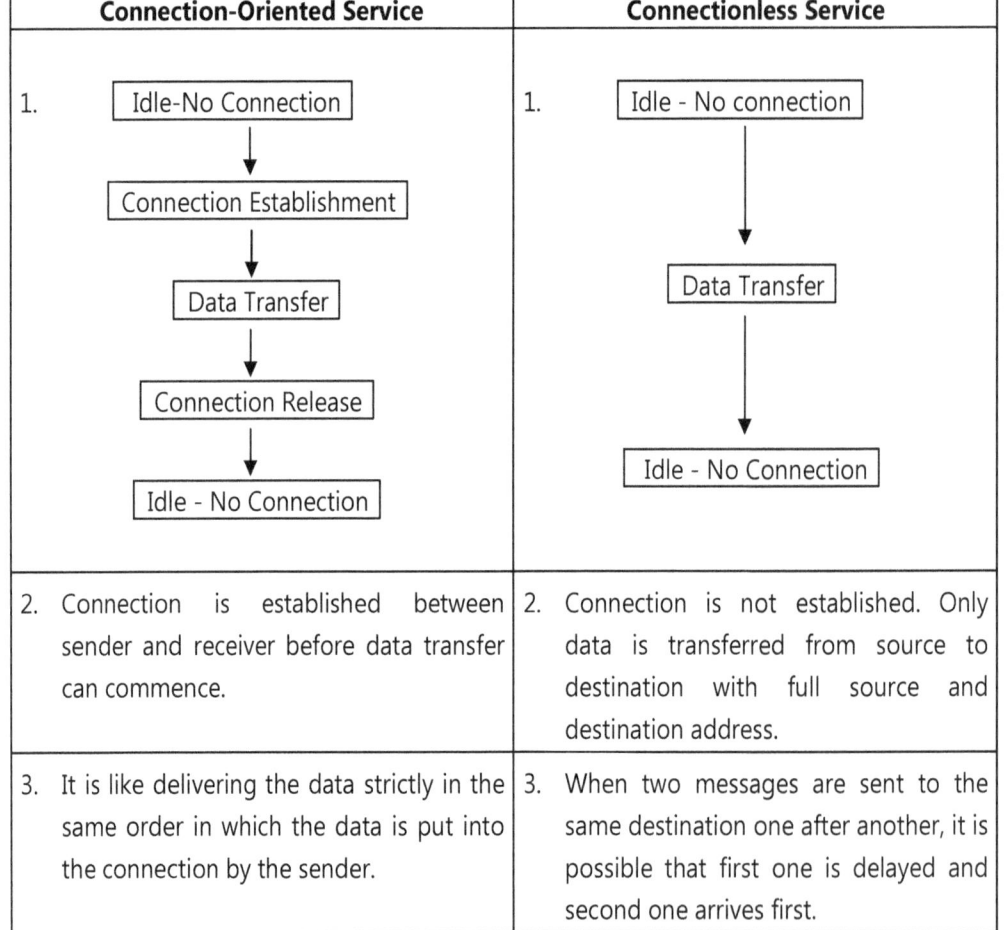	
2.	Connection is established between sender and receiver before data transfer can commence.	Connection is not established. Only data is transferred from source to destination with full source and destination address.
3.	It is like delivering the data strictly in the same order in which the data is put into the connection by the sender.	When two messages are sent to the same destination one after another, it is possible that first one is delayed and second one arrives first.

Connection-Oriented Service	Connectionless Service
4. It has provision for acknowledgements, flow control and error recovery.	4. Does not have such provisions.
5. Connection-oriented service is modelled after telephone system.	5. Connectionless service is modelled after postal service.
6. Example is a virtual circuit service like ATM network.	6. Example is a datagram service like INTERNET network.

1.17 ISO-OSI Reference Model

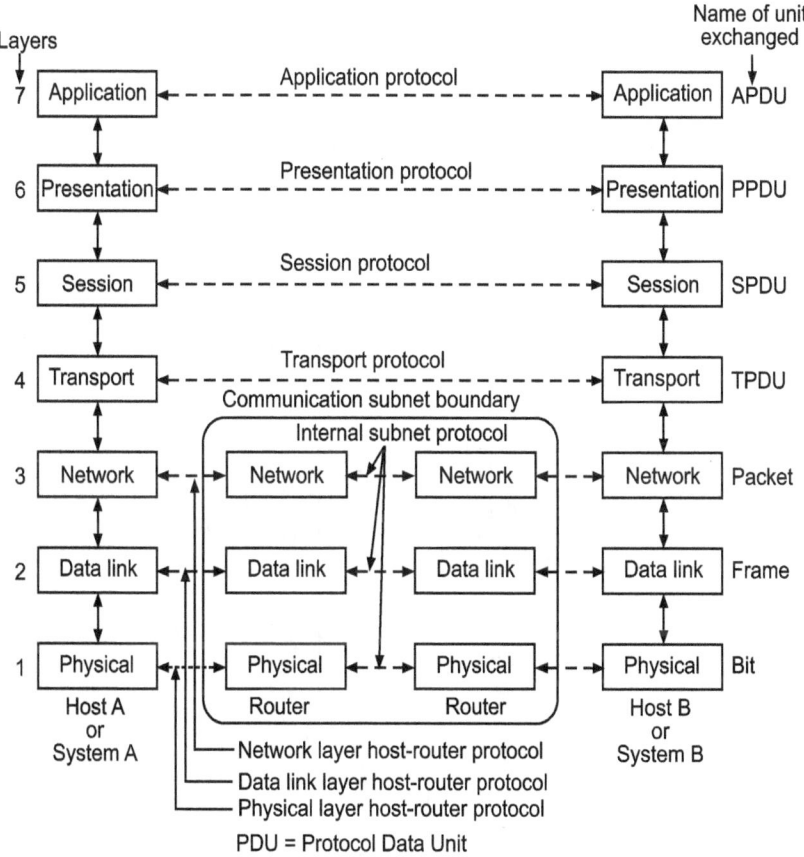

Fig. 1.22: The OSI reference model

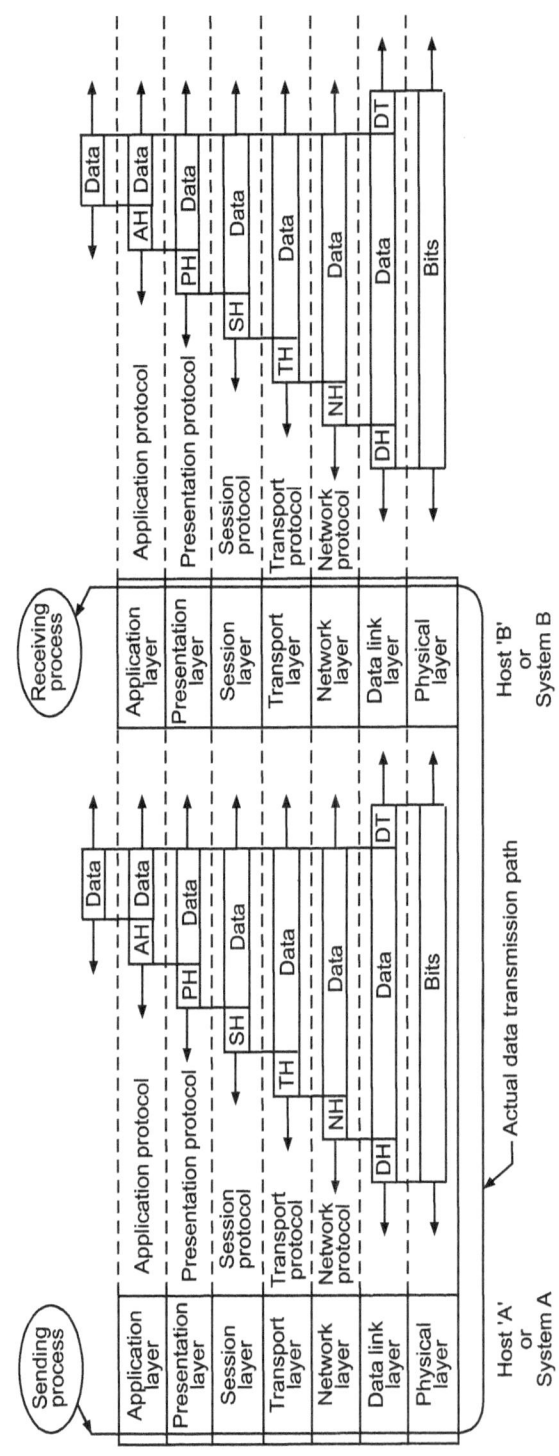

Fig. 1.23: Data communication between two systems is shown by OSI reference model

1. This model is based on a proposal developed by the International Standards Organization (ISO) as a first step towards International Standardization of Protocols used in various layers.
2. This model is called ISO-OSI (Open Systems Interconnection) reference model because it deals with connecting open systems that is systems that are open for communication with other systems.
3. OSI model has seven layers. The OSI model defines a layered architecture as pictured. The protocols defined in each layer are responsible for following:
(a) Communicating with the same peer protocol layer running in the opposite computer.
(b) Providing services to the layer above it (except for the top-level application layer).
(c) Peer layer communication provides a way for each layer to exchange messages or other data.
4. **Obviously, each layer does not have a physical wire running between it and its peer layer in the opposite system.** To send a message, a protocol must put the message in a packet that passes down to the next lower layer. Thus lower layer provides a service to higher layers by taking their messages and passing them down the protocol stack to the lowest layer, where the messages are transferred across the physical link.

1.17.1 Characteristics of the OSI Layers

1. The seven layers of the OSI reference model can be divided into two categories: upper layers and lower layers.
2. The **upper layers** of the OSI model deal with application issues and generally are implemented only in software.
3. The highest layer, the application layer, is closest to the end user. Both users and application layer processes interact with software applications that contain a communication component.
4. The term upper layer is sometimes used to refer to any layer above another layer in the OSI model.
5. The **lower layers** of the OSI model handle data transport issues. The physical layer and the data link layer are implemented in hardware and software.
6. The lowest layer, the physical layer, is closest to the physical network medium (the network cabling, for example) and is responsible for actually placing information on the medium.

Fig. 1.24 illustrates the division between the upper and lower OSI layers.

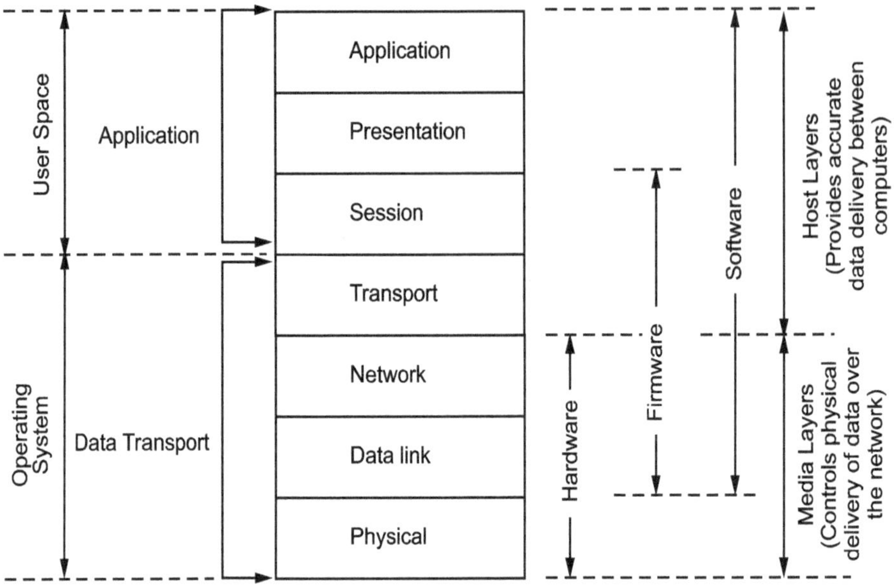

Fig. 1.24: Two sets of layers make-up the OSI layers

1.17.2 OSI Model Layers and Information Exchange

1. The seven OSI layers use various forms of control information to communicate with their peer layers in other computer systems. This **control information** (headers) consists of specific requests and instructions that are exchanged between peer OSI layers.
2. Control information typically takes one of two forms: headers and trailers.
3. **Headers** are prepended to data that has been passed down from upper layers.
4. **Trailers** are appended to data that has been passed down from upper layers.
5. An OSI layer is not required to attach a header or a trailer to data from upper layers.
6. Headers, trailers and data are relative concepts, depending on the layer that analyzes the information unit.
7. At the network layer, for example, an information unit consists of a layer 3 header and data.
8. At the data link layer, however, all the information is passed down by the network layer (the layer 3 header and the data) is treated as data.
9. In other words, the data portion of an information unit at a given OSI layer potentially can contain headers, trailers and data from all the higher layers. This is known as **encapsulation**.

Information Exchange Process:
1. The information exchange process occurs between peer OSI layers. Each layer in the source system adds control information to data, and each layer in the destination system analyzes and removes the control information from that data.
2. If System **A** has data from a software application to send to System **B**, the data is passed to the application layer.
3. The application layer in System **A** then communicates any control information required by the application layer in System **B** by prepending a header to the data.
4. The resulting information unit (a header and the data) is passed to the presentation layer, which prepends its own header containing control information intended for the presentation layer in System **B**.
5. The information unit grows in size as each layer prepends its own header (and, in some cases, a trailer) that contains control information to be used by its peer layer in System **B**.
6. At the physical layer, the entire information unit is placed onto the network medium.
7. The physical layer in System **B** receives the information unit and passes it to the data link layer.
8. The data link layer in System **B** then reads the control information contained in the header prepended by the data link layer in System **A**.
9. The header is then removed, and the remainder of the information unit is passed to the network layer.
10. Each layer performs the same actions: The layer reads the header from its peer layer, strips it off, and passes the remaining information unit to the next highest layer.
11. After the application layer performs these actions, the data is passed to the recipient software application in System **B**, in exactly the form in which it was transmitted by the application in System **A**.

1.17.3 OSI Layers in Detail

The following is a description of just what each layer does:
1. **The Physical layer** provides the electrical and mechanical interface to the network medium (the cable). This layer gives the data-link layer (layer 2) its ability to transport a stream of serial data bits between two communicating systems. It conveys the bits that move along the cable. It is responsible for making sure that the raw bits get from one place to another, no matter what shape they are in, and deals with the mechanical and electrical characteristics of the cable.

2. **The Data-Link layer** handles the physical transfer, framing (the assembly of data into a single unit or block), flow control and error-control functions (and retransmission in the event of an error) over a single transmission link; it is responsible for getting the data packaged and onto the network cable. The data link layer provides the network layer (layer 3) reliable information-transfer capabilities. The data-link layer is often subdivided into two parts – Logical Link Control (LLC) and Medium Access Control (MAC) depending on the implementation.
3. **The Network layer** establishes, maintains, and terminates logical and/or physical connections. The network layer is responsible for translating logical addresses or names into physical addresses. It provides network routing and flow-control functions across the computer-network interface.
4. **The Transport layer** ensures that data is successfully sent and received between the two computers. If data is sent incorrectly, this layer has the responsibility to ask for retransmission of the data. Specifically, it provides a network-independent, reliable message-independent, reliable message-interchange service to the top three application-oriented layers. This layer acts as an interface between the bottom and top three layers. By providing the session layer (layer 5) with a reliable message-transfer service, it hides the detailed operation of the underlying network from the session layer.
5. **The Session layer** decides when to turn communication on and off between two computers - it provides the mechanism that controls the data-exchange process and co-ordinates the interaction between them. It sets up and clears communication channels between two communicating components. Unlike the network layer (layer 3), it deals with the programs running in each machine to establish conversations between them.
6. **The Presentation layer** performs code conversion and data reformatting (syntax translation). It is the translator of the network, making sure that the data is in the correct form for the receiving application. Of course, both the sending and receiving applications must be able to use data subscribing to one of the available abstract data syntax forms.
7. **The Application layer** provides the user interface between the software running in the computer and the network. It provides functions to the user's software, including file transfer access, management and electronic mail.

Thus the OSI, or Open Systems Interconnection, model defines a networking frame-work for implementing protocols in seven layers. This can be summarized in Table 1.1.

Table 1.1

Application (Layer 7)	This layer supports application and end-user processes. Communication partners are identified, quality of service is identified, user authentication and privacy are considered, and any constraints on data syntax are identified. Everything at this layer is application-specific. This layer provides application services for file transfers, e-mail, and other network software services.
Presentation (Layer 6)	This layer provides independence from differences in data representation (For example, encryption) by translating from application to network format, and vice versa. The presentation layer works to transform data into the form that the application layer can accept. This layer formats and encrypts data to be sent across a network, providing freedom from compatibility problems. It is sometimes called the **syntax layer.**
Session (Layer 5)	This layer establishes, manages and terminates connections between applications. The session layer sets up, co-ordinates, and terminates conversations, exchanges and dialogues between the applications at each end. It deals with session and connection co-ordination.
Transport (Layer 4)	This layer provides transparent transfer of data between end systems, or hosts, and is responsible for end-to-end error recovery and flow control. It ensures complete data transfer.
Network (Layer 3)	This layer provides switching and routing technologies, creating logical paths, known as virtual circuits, for transmitting data from node to node. Routing and forwarding are functions of this layer, as well as addressing, internetworking, error-handling, congestion control and packet sequencing.
Data Link (Layer 2)	At this layer, data packets are encoded and decoded into bits. It furnishes transmission protocol knowledge and management and handles errors in the physical layer, flow control and frame synchronization. The data link layer is divided into two sublayers: The Media Access Control (MAC) layer and the Logical Link Control (LLC) layer. The MAC sublayer controls how a computer on the network gains access to the data and permission to transmit it. The LLC layer controls frame synchronization, flow control and error checking.
Physical (Layer 1)	This layer conveys the bit stream electrical impulse, light or radio signal through the network at the electrical and mechanical level. It provides the hardware means of sending and receiving data on a carrier, including defining cables, cards and physical aspects. Fast Ethernet, RS-232 and ATM are protocols with physical layer components.

Table 1.2: Application Oriented Explanation

ISO-OSI REFERENCE MODEL LAYERS	FUNCTIONS
Application Layer (Layer 7)	• Computer Applications like Word processor, Presentation Graphics, Spreadsheet, Database. • Network Applications like Email, FTP, Remote Access, Client-Server, Peer-to-Peer, Network management. • Internetwork Applications like WWW, Data Exchange, Email Gateways, Finance transactions, Conferencing.
Presentation Layer (Layer 6)	• Provides data formats, translations and code conversion. • Data compression and Data encryption. • Text/data (ASCII or EBCDIC). • Sound/Video (MP3, Wave, Mpeg, Quick time). • Graphics/Images (JPEG, Gif, BMP).
Sessional Layer (Layer 5)	• Network file System (NFS), X-Windows System. • Re-establishment of connection in case of failure. • Connection Permission Half-Duplex, Full Duplex. • Dialog control. • Synchronization. • Process to process delivery.
Transport Layer (Layer 4)	• Establishes reliable End-to-End transport connection. • Flow control, error control, connection control. • Data error detection, recovery for end-to-end connection.
Network Layer (Layer 3)	• Routing Algorithm (Routing). • Logical addressing. • Congestion Control Algorithm. • Internetworking.
Data Link Layer (Layer 2)	• NIC (Network Interface Card) Driver has LLC (Logical Link Control)-Framing, Flow Control, Error Control etc. • MAC (Media Access Control)-802.3, 802.4, 802.5 etc.
Physical Layer (Layer 1)	• Handles Voltages and Electrical Pulses. • Specifies Cables, Connectors and Media Interface Component.

1.18 Network Architecture

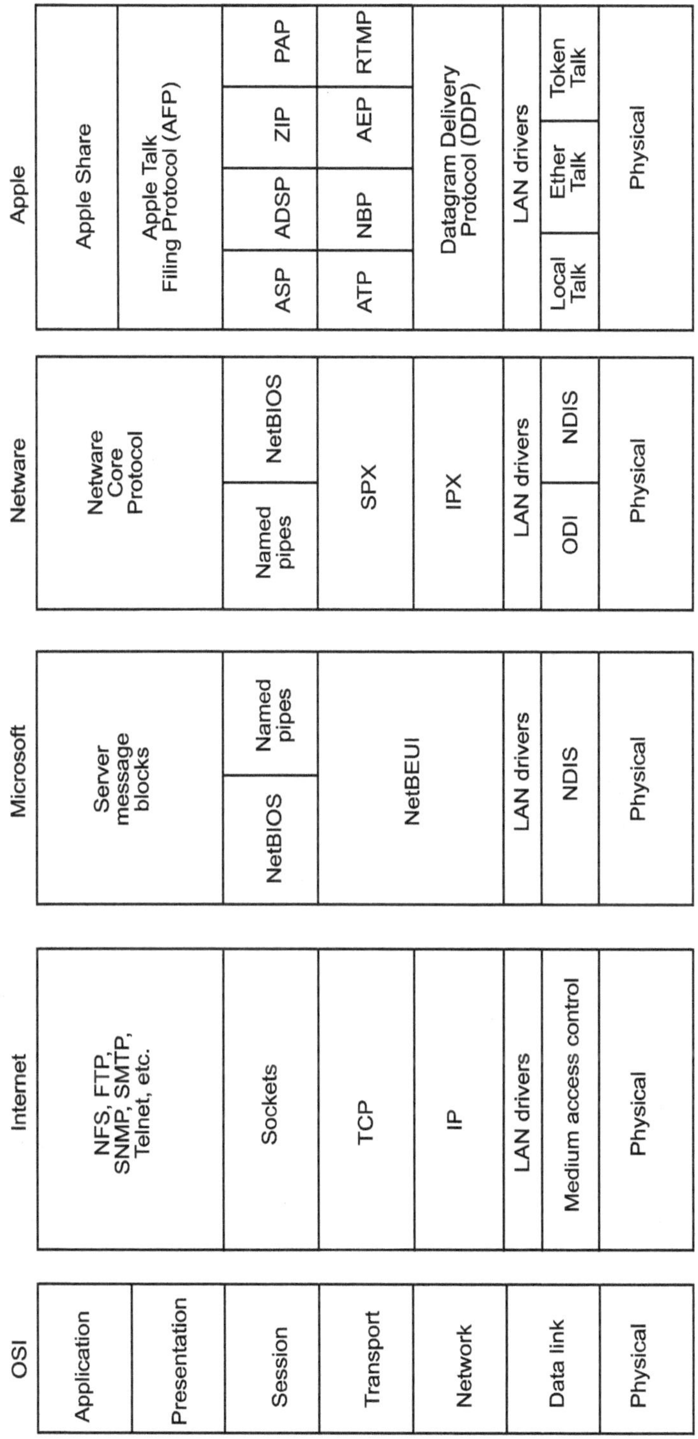

Fig. 1.25: Different network architectures

In computing, **network architecture** is the design of a computer network.

In telecommunication, the term **network architecture** has the following meanings:
1. The design principles, physical configuration, functional organization, operational procedures, and data formats used as the bases for the design, construction, modification, and operation of a communication network.
2. The structure of an existing communication network, including the physical configuration facilities, operational structure, operational procedures, and the data formats in use.
3. With the development of distributed computing, the term **network architecture** has also come to denote classifications and implementations of distributed computing architectures. For example, the application architecture of the telephone network PSTN has been termed the Advanced Intelligent Network.
4. There are variety of network architectures available such as:
- IBM's SNA (Systems Network Architecture)
- DEC's DNA (Digital Network Architecture)
- Apple's Network Architecture (For Macintosh OS)
- Microsoft's Network Architecture (For Windows OS)
- Novell's NetWare Network Architecture (For Netware OS)
- There are open architectures like the OSI (Open Systems Interconnection) model defined by the International Organization for Standardization.
- Internet Network Architecture. (Based on TCP/IP).
5. The OSI model has remained a model rather than a fully accepted international standard.
6. ISO OSI Model is there to discuss the Computer networks.
7. OSI protocols are not powerful as compared to TCP/IP so they are not used anywhere for practical applications.
8. TCP/IP is powerful protocol and used widely that's why it is also known as the Protocol of the Internet.

1.19 Introduction to TCP/IP
1. TCP/IP is a suite of protocols, also known as the Internet Protocol Suite.
2. It should not be confused with the OSI reference model, although elements of TCP/IP exist in OSI.

3. The Transmission Control Protocol and the Internet Protocol are fundamental to the suite, hence the TCP/IP title.
4. TCP/IP is a set of protocols developed to allow co-operating computers to share resources across a network.
5. A community of researchers centered around the ARPANET developed this TCP/IP.
6. The **Internet protocol suite** is the set of communication protocols that implement the protocol stack on which the internet and most commercial networks run.
7. The internet protocol suite like many protocol suites can be viewed as a set of layers, each layer solves a set of problems involving the transmission of data, and provides a well-defined service to the upper layer protocols based on using services from some lower layers.
8. Upper layers are logically closer to the user and deal with more abstract data, relying on lower layer protocols to translate data into forms that can eventually be physically transmitted.
9. The Transmission Control Protocol/Internet Protocol (TCP/IP) protocol suite is the engine for the Internet and networks worldwide.
10. Its simplicity and power has lead to its becoming the single network protocol of choice in the world today. In this chapter, we give an overview of the TCP/IP protocol suite.

| Application Layer |
| Transport Layer |
| Network Layer (or Internet Layer) |
| Layer 1 and Layer 2 (or lower layers) (or Network Interface Layers) |

Fig. 1.26: Typical four-layer TCP/IP Model

OSI-ISO Reference Model	TCP/IP Model
Application Layer (7)	Application Layer
Presentation Layer (6)	
Session Layer (5)	
Transport Layer (4)	Transport Layer
Network Layer (3)	Network Layer
Data Link Layer (2)	Layer 1 and Layer 2
Physical Layer (1)	

Fig. 1.27: 7-Layer OSI model and 4-layer TCP/IP model

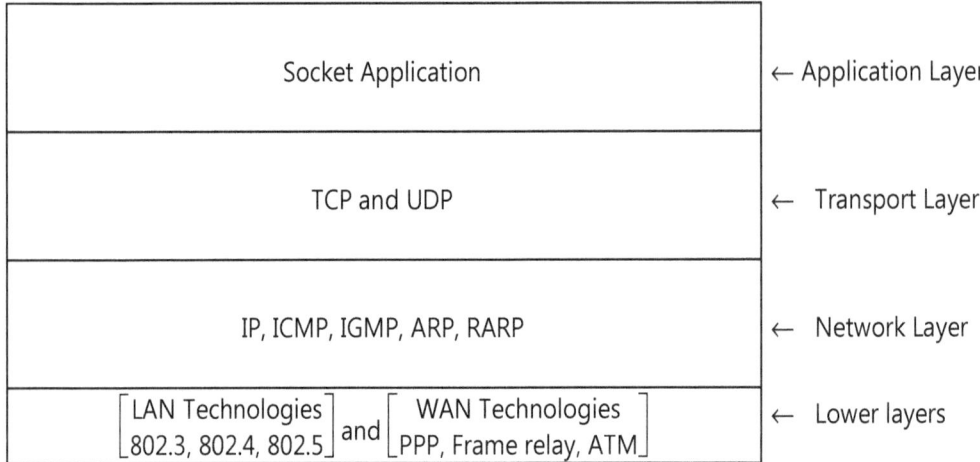

Fig. 1.28: TCP/IP 4 layers and main protocols

11. The main design goal of TCP/IP was to build an interconnection of networks, referred to as an Internetwork, or Internet, that provided universal communication services over heterogeneous physical networks.
12. The clear benefit of such an internetwork is the enabling of communication between hosts on different networks, perhaps separated by a large geographical area.

1.19.1 Layers in the Internet Protocol Suite Stack

1. The IP suite uses encapsulation to provide abstraction of protocols and services.
2. Generally a protocol at a higher level uses a protocol at a lower level to help accomplish its aims.
3. The internet protocol stack can be roughly fitted into the four fixed layers and are shown before.

Application Layer

1. This layer is broadly equivalent to the application, presentation and session layers of the OSI model.
2. It gives an application access to the communication environment.
3. Examples of protocols found at this layer are Telnet, FTP (File Transfer Protocol), SNMP (Simple Network Management Protocol), HTTP (Hyper Text Transfer Protocol) and SMTP (Simple Mail Transfer Protocol).

4. An application is a user process co-operating with another process usually on a different host (there is also a benefit to application communication within a single host).
5. The interface between the application and transport layers is defined by port numbers and sockets.

Transport Layer

1. The transport layer is similar to the OSI transport model, but with elements of the OSI session layer functionality.
2. This layer provides an application layer delivery service.
3. The two protocols found at the transport layer are **TCP (Transmission Control Protocol) and UDP (User Datagram Protocol)**.
4. Either of these two protocols are used by the application layer process, the choice depends on the application's transmission reliability requirements.
5. Transport layer provides the end-to-end data transfer by delivering data from an application to its remote peer.
6. Multiple applications can be supported simultaneously.
7. The most-used transport layer protocol is the Transmission Control Protocol (TCP), which provides connection-oriented reliable data delivery, duplicate data suppression, congestion control, and flow control.
8. **TCP** is a **reliable, connection-oriented** protocol that provides error checking and flow control through a virtual link that it establishes and finally terminates.
9. This gives a reliable service, therefore TCP would be utilized by FTP and SNMP File transfer and email delivery have to be accurate and error free.
10. **UDP** is an **unreliable, connectionless** protocol that provides data transport with lower network traffic overheads than TCP. UDP does not error check or offer any flow control, this is left to the application process.
11. SNMP uses UDP. SNMP is used to monitor network performance, so its operation must not contribute to congestion.

Network Layer or Internet Layer

1. This layer is responsible for the routing and delivery of data across networks.
2. It allows communication across networks of the same and different types and carries out translations to deal with dissimilar data addressing schemes.
3. Internetwork layer, also called the *internet layer* or the *network layer*, provides the "virtual network" image of an internet (this layer shields the higher levels from the physical network architecture below it).

4. Internet Protocol (IP) is the most important protocol in this layer.
5. It is a connectionless protocol that doesn't assume reliability from lower layers.
6. IP does *not* provide reliability, flow control, or error recovery.
7. These functions must be provided at a higher level.
8. A message unit in an IP network is called an *IP* datagram.
9. This is the basic unit of information transmitted across TCP/IP networks.
10. Other internetwork layer protocols are IP, ICMP, IGMP, ARP and RARP.
11. With the advent of the concept of Internetworking, additional functionality was added to this layer, namely getting data from the source network to the destination network.
12. This generally involves routing the packet across a network of networks, known as an internet.
13. In the internet protocol suite, IP performs the basic task of getting packets of data from source to destination.
14. IP can carry data for a number of different upper layer protocols; these protocols are each identified by a unique protocol number.
15. ICMP and IGMP are protocols 1 and 2, respectively.
16. Some of the protocols carried by IP, such as ICMP (used to transmit diagnostic information about IP transmission) and IGMP (used to manage multicast data) are layered on top of IP but perform internetwork layer functions, illustrating an incompatibility between the internet and the IP stack and OSI model.
17. All routing protocols, such as BGP, OSPF, and RIP are also really part of the network layer, although they might seem to belong higher in the stack.

Layers 2 and 1 (Network Access Layers)

1. The combination of data link and physical layers deals with pure hardware (wires, satellite links, network interface cards etc.) and access methods such as CSMA/CD (carrier sensed multiple access with collision detection).
2. Ethernet exists at the network access layer - its hardware operates at the physical layer and its medium access control method (CSMA/CD) operates at the datalink layer.
3. Network interface layer, also called the link layer or the data-link layer, is the interface to the actual network hardware.
4. This interface may or may not provide reliable delivery, and may be packet or stream oriented.
5. In fact, TCP/IP does not specify any protocol here, but can use almost any network interface available, which illustrates the flexibility of the IP layer.

6. The link layer is not really part of the internet protocol suite, but is the method used to pass packets from the network layer on two different hosts.
7. This process can be controlled both in the software device driver for the network card, as well as on firmware or specialist chipsets.
8. These will perform data link functions such as adding a packet header to prepare it for transmission, then actually transmit the frame over a physical medium.
9. The link layer can also be the layer where packets are intercepted to be sent over a virtual private network.
10. When this is done, the link layer data is considered the application data and proceeds back down the IP stack for actual transmission.
11. On the receiving end, the data goes up the IP stack twice (once for the VPN and the second time for routing).
12. The physical layer is made up of the actual physical network components (hubs, repeaters, network cable, fiber optic cable, coaxial cable, network cards, Host Bus Adapter cards and the associated network connectors: RJ-45, BNC etc).

1.20 TCP/IP and OSI Model

1. This chapter gives a brief comparison between OSI and TCP/IP protocols with a special focus on the similarities and on how the protocols from both worlds map to each other.
2. The adoption of TCP/IP does not conflict with the OSI standards because the two protocol stacks were developed concurrently.
3. In some ways, TCP/IP contributed to OSI, and vice-versa.
4. Several important differences do exist, though, which arise from the basic requirements of TCP/IP which are:
   - A common set of applications
   - Dynamic routing
   - Connectionless protocols at the networking level
   - Universal connectivity
   - Packet-switching
5. The main differences between the OSI architecture and that of TCP/IP relate to the layers above the transport layer and those at the network layer.
6. OSI has both, the session layer and the presentation layer, whereas TCP/IP combines both into an application layer.
7. The requirement for a connectionless protocol also required TCP/IP to combine OSI's physical layer and data link layer into a network layer.

1.21 Problems with OSI

1. OSI was a poor performer in implementation, and there are definite flaws in the protocols.
2. Flow control is a problem at *every layer* and error control must be implemented to all layers as well.
3. Network management is problematic and was actually omitted from the original OSI model.
4. Semantic confusion about the Presentation and Application layers created so many major headaches that data security and encryption were eventually taken out altogether.

OSI was killed off because:

- Early slow and bug-filled, unusable implementations ruined its public image.
- OSI was thought to originate with the European Community and the U.S. federal government.
- Its probable market for use was proprietary. TCP/IP was bundled as part of Berkeley UNIX and was free.
- OSI is full of almost bureaucratic levels of unnecessary complexity.
- The seven-layer model was somewhat arbitrary, and was basically done in an attempt to wrest control away from IBM's 7-layer SNA protocol to a world standard controlled by a neutral organization (the ISO) rather than by a single corporation, not to simplify actually using the model.

1.22 Problems WITH TCP/IP

Far from blameless, TCP/IP has some problems as well, the primary one being that it speaks only its own language:

- It can't be used to intelligently describe another type of protocol stack (like SNA).
- Its network layer is more of an interface than a true layer of its own.
- There is no distinction between the Physical and Data Link layers. This is a poor choice from an engineering standpoint.
- Many of the *original* protocol implementations hack with very limited usefulness and arbitrary constraints based on hardware limitations or on simplifying the coding task.

1.23 Similarities Between OSI and TCP/IP

Sr. No.	ISO OSI REFERENCE MODEL AND TCP/IP MODEL
1.	Based on a stack of independent protocols.
2.	Layers have roughly same functionality.
3.	Transport layer and below provide network-independent transport services.
4.	Layers above transport are application-oriented.

1.24 Comparison between OSI Model and TCP/IP

Sr. No.	ISO OSI REFERENCE MODEL	TCP/IP MODEL
1.	7 layer model.	4 layer model.
2.	OSI model is useful in describing networks, but protocols are too general.	TCP/IP model is weak, but protocols are specific and widely used.
3.	Model was conceptual, designers didn't know what functionality to put in the layers.	Model is practical, designers know the functionality of each layer and used in real world network.
4.	Model is general, and easier to replace protocols.	Model is not general, and difficult to replace protocols.
5.	Model had to adjust when networks didn't match the service specifications (wireless networks, internetworking).	Model need not require to adjust too much in this scenario.
6.	Model describe any type of network.	Model only describes TCP/IP which is not useful for describing any other networks (such as telephone networks)
7.	Network layer supports both connection-oriented and connection-less service.	Network layer supports only connectionless service.
8.	Transport layer supports only connection-oriented service.	Transport layer supports both connection oriented and connectionless service.

Sr. No.	ISO OSI REFERENCE MODEL	TCP/IP MODEL
9.	OSI introduced concept of services, interface, Protocols.	These were force-fitted to TCP/IP later. It is not easy to replace protocols in TCP/IP.
10.	In OSI, reference model was done before protocols.	In TCP/IP, protocols were done before the model.
11.	OSI: Standardized first, build later.	TCP/IP: Build first, standardized later.
12.	OSI took too long to standardize.	TCP/IP was already in wide use by the time.
13.	OSI becomes too complex.	TCP/IP is not general it's Ad hoc.
14.	OSI Flaws • Bad Timing. • TCP/IP already well-established in academia. • Bad Technology. • Complicated, controversial model. • Unbalanced layers. • Repeating functions. • Designed for communications, not computing. • Bad implementations. • Complicated to understand and implement. • Bad politics. • Seen as biased toward European telecom, European Community and U.S. government.	TCP/IP Flaws • Blurred lines. • Doesn't clearly distinguish between services (what a layer does), interfaces (how the layer communicates) and protocols (how the layer does what it does). • Too specific. • Model is only suited to describe TCP/IP, not other networks. • Protocols can be very specific, inflexible. • No distinction between physical and data link layers. • No description of transmission media, nor frame delimiters.

EXERCISE

1. Explain the components of data communication system?
2. How data is represented?
3. What is concept of pixel?
4. Explain data flow i.e. simplex, half-duplex and full-duplex system.
5. What is distributed processing?
6. What are different network criterias?
7. What are the different types of connections?
8. Explain the physical topology of network?
9. Write short note on:
   (a) Mesh topology
   (b) Star topology
   (b) Bus topology
   (d) Ring topology
10. Explain the following:
    (a) ISO-OSI reference model
    (b) TCP/IP model.
11. Compare and contrast OSI model Vs. TCP/IP model.
12. What are the different advantages of installing a network?
13. What are the different disadvantages of installing a network?
14. Write a short note on network topology.
15. Compare all network topologies.
16. Classify the different networks.
17. Write a short note on:
    (a) LAN
    (b) WAN
    (c) MAN
    (d) Internet

18. What is Network Layered Architecture?
19. What are the different benefits of layered design?
20. What are service primitives and relationship of service to protocols?
21. Compare connection oriented Vs. connectionless service.
22. Draw and explain ISO-OSI reference model.
23. Explain the function of each layer of OSI-ISO reference model.
24. List out the different network architectures.
25. Draw and explain TCP/IP network architecture.
26. Compare OSI model and TCP/IP model.
27. Compare broadcast and point to point networks?
28. Explain centralized and distributed networks.

***

Unit II

PHYSICAL LAYER AND DATA LINK LAYER

2.1 Communication Media

1. In computers, media refers to whatever medium is used to communicate data.
2. Media is usually the copper or fiber optic glass cables but data can also be sent through the air via electromagnetic frequencies such as infrared, micro waves or radio waves.
3. Media is important because it is often half the cost of the network.
4. **Important factors in determining media include:**

- Required speed.
- Distance.
- Ease of installation and maintenance access.
- Technical expertise required to install and utilize.
- Resistance to internal EMI (Electromagnetic Interference) inside the cable, especially the cross talk of parallel wires.
- Resistance to external EMI outside the cable.
- Resistance to other environmental hazards such as workers carelessly drilling into walls, fire and the weather.
- **Bandwidth**: It is the range of frequencies that the cable can accommodate. LANs generally carry data rates of 1 to 100 megabits per second and require moderately high bandwidth.
- **Attenuation characteristics:** Attenuation describes how cables reduce the strength of a signal with distance. Resistance is one factor that contributes to signal attenuation cost.

5. When data is sent across the network it is converted into electrical signals.
6. These signals are generated as electromagnetic waves (analog signaling) or as a sequence of voltage pulses (digital signaling).
7. To be sent from one location to another, a signal must travel along a physical path.
8. The physical path that is used to carry a signal between a signal transmitter and a signal receiver is called the **transmission medium**.
9. **There are two types of transmission media: guided and unguided.**

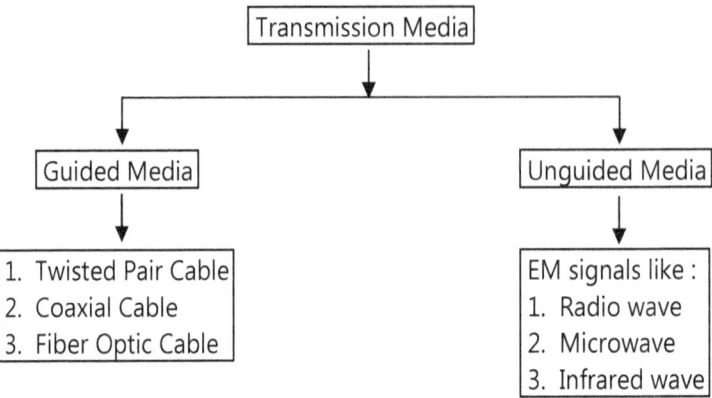

Fig. 2.1: Classification of transmission media

2.2 Guided Media

1. Guided media are manufactured so that signals will be confined to a narrow path and will behave predictably.
2. The three most commonly used types of guided media are **twisted-pair wiring, coaxial cable, and optical fiber cable.**
3. Each type is suited to specific applications and network topologies.

2.2.1 Unshielded Twisted Pair (UTP) Cable and Shielded Twisted Pair (STP) Cable

Unshielded Twisted Pair Cable (UTP)

1. Unshielded twisted pair has become the most popular network cabling media today.
2. Unshielded twisted pair cabling is used in a star or tree topology for Ethernet networks.
3. Maximum number of network devices is 1,024, with a maximum cable length of 100 meters for individual devices and a total distance of 500 meters of cabling between the farthest two devices, including links between data closets is possible using UTP cables.
4. The signal from a network hub can be repeated three times, giving you a maximum of four data closets.
5. The distance between closets can be extended by switching to a star bus topology and using fiber optic cable for links between closets.
6. **Twisted pair copper cable** is perhaps the oldest and certainly still the most commonly used transmission medium.

7. A twisted pair consists of two insulated copper cables, typically about 1 mm in diameter, twisted together to reduce electrical interference between adjacent pairs of wires (two pairs of parallel wires can act as a crude antenna).

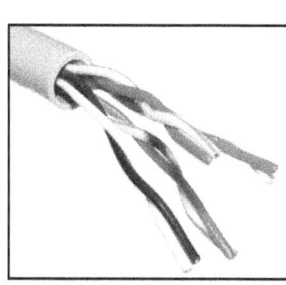

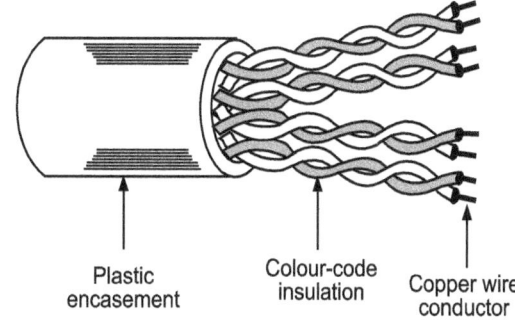

Fig. 2.2: Unshielded twisted pair cable

Fig. 2.3: Four pair UTP cable used in LAN (Local Area Network)

8. Twisted pair cable is still used in the public telephone system, specifically in the subscriber loop, the link from a domestic or business telephone subscriber to the local telephone exchange.
9. These links are good for several kilometers without amplification, but longer runs need repeaters.
10. The local subscriber loop is essentially an analog transmission medium, but twisted pair cables can also be used for digital transmission.
11. The data rate (or *bandwidth*) for twisted pair depends on factors such as the diameter of wire used and the length of the transmission line, but several megabits per second (Mbps) can be achieved over a few kilometers.
12. Low cost and ease of installation have kept twisted pair in widespread use both in the telephone system and in Local Area Networks (LANs).
13. The type of twisted pair cables used in LANs fall into two main categories as mentioned in points 14 and 15.
14. **Category 3** twisted pair cable is the type you will normally find connected to your domestic telephone outlet and consists of two insulated wires gently twisted together. Typically, four pairs are grouped together within a plastic sheath which serves both as protection and to keep the eight wires together.
15. **Category 5** twisted pairs, introduced in the late eighties, are similar to category 3 twisted pair but the difference is that category 5 consists of more twists per centimeter and Teflon-based insulation.

16. This results in a further reduction in crosstalk and a better quality signal over long distances, which makes them more suitable for high-speed data communication.
17. Both types are referred to as *Unshielded Twisted Pair* (UTP). A summary of the twisted pair categories is given below.

Category 1:
Used for traditional telephone voice communication (but not data) - most telephone cable used before 1983 were category 1.

Category 2:
Four twisted pairs - suitable for data rates of up to 4 Mbps.

Category 3:
- Four twisted pairs with three twists per foot - suitable for data rates of up to 10 Mbps.
- In the beginning of twisted pair technology, some networks were set-up utilizing spare pairs on existing phone systems or cabled with Category 3.
- These networks are only capable of 10Base-T (10 megabits per second) data transfer, and most of them set-up on spare pairs of existing phone wiring, run for slower than this speed.
- These networks have been obsolete for some time and cannot match the network speeds of today. New Category 3 should only be installed for phone systems.

Category 4: Supports data transmission of up to 20 Mbps.

Category 5:
- Four twisted pairs with a higher number of twists per foot than previous categories and Teflon based outer coating.
- Category 5 is generally accepted as the cable to install because of its higher transmission rate and better noise immunity.
- Testing of these cables assumes that only two pairs will be used - one to transmit (T_X) and one to receive (R_X).
- Falling costs in recent years have made category 5 twisted pair a more cost-effective option.
- The predominant type of twisted pair installed in the majority of commercial buildings is unshielded Category 5.
- It is most commonly used for 100 Base T Ethernet networks, giving data transfer rates of 100 megabits per second.

- In addition, the IEEE has approved a network standard for 1000 BASE T Ethernet networks (data transfer of 1,000 megabits per second) which can utilize most existing Category 5 cabling when it has been properly installed and certified.
- In addition to unshielded Category 5, there is also a shielded version, which provides some protection against electromagnetic interference.
- A typical application might be for a heavy manufacturing plant where interference from large electric motors could present a problem.
- For the vast majority of existing offices and smaller industrial plants, unshielded Category 5 is the most commonly found cable.

Category 5e:
- **Enhanced category 5** - more comprehensive testing is carried out on all four pairs to measure the effect of transmitting data, particularly with regard to crosstalk.
- This category is primarily intended for use in Gigabit Ethernet networks.
- Over the last several years, Category 5e has become the replacement for Category 5.
- There are two main types, known as "Little E" and "Big E", capable of 155 and 350 megabit transmission respectively.
- Although there are no network standards to support these speeds, the increased bandwidth does enhance this cable's ability to run gigabit Ethernet.
- With the price drop of Category 5e over the last few years, it has become the most common choice for new network installation.

Category 6:
- A proposed standard for cabling is having a transmission frequency of 200 MHz, with all components coming from one manufacturer (i.e. no "mixing").
- With the ever increasing speed of networks today, Category 6 is becoming more common in new office installations that demand reliable gigabit network speed.
- It is a viable choice today for a new network installation in a commercial space where the tenants plan to stay for an extended length of time.
- In addition, gigabit switches and network cards are also beginning to drop in price, so the cost of the hardware necessary to set-up a true gigabit network is becoming less expensive as well.

Category 7:
A proposed standard for cable is having a transmission frequency of 600 MHz using fully shielded cables, i.e. shielding is to be provided for both individual pairs and for the grouped pairs. A new connection type is also proposed.

18. The maximum recommended cable run for unshielded twisted pair is 100 meters.
19. UTP cables are terminated with RJ45 connectors, similar in design to the connectors used to connect telephones into a wall socket outlet (RJ11).
20. Twisted pair cables are most commonly used to connect workstations to hubs or MANs.
21. The standard connector for unshielded twisted pair cabling is RJ-45 connector.
22. RJ-45 is a plastic connector that looks like a large telephone-style connector.
23. A slot allows the RJ-45 to be inserted only one way.
24. **RJ stands for Registered Jack,** implying that the connector follows a standard borrowed from the telephone industry.
25. This standard designates which wire goes with each pin inside the connector.

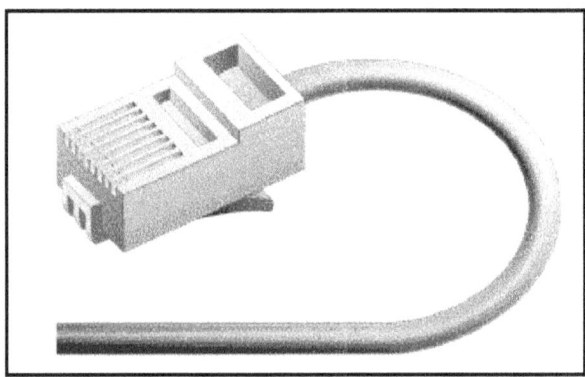

Fig. 2.4: RJ-45 Connector and UTP cable

Shielded Twisted Pair Cable

1. *Shielded Twisted Pair* (STP) cable was introduced in the 1980s by IBM as the recommended medium for their Token Ring network technology, and has a characteristic impedance of 150 ohms.
2. Each cable consists of two pairs, with each pair individually foil shielded, and an overall braided shield.
3. Because STP was specified by IBM, many users thought that it was required for reliable data transfer.
4. Since this is not in fact the case its popularity has declined due to:
- The high cost of the cable and connectors (much more complex than UTP).
- The increased bulk of cable and connectors compared to UTP.
- The increased time required for installation compared to UTP.

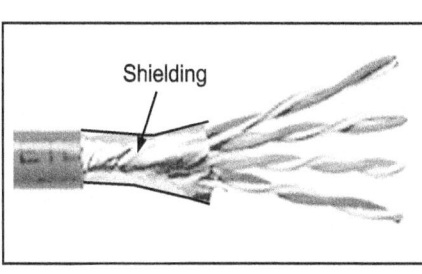 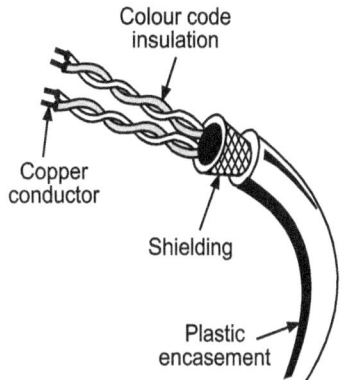

Fig. 2.5: Shielded twisted pair cable   Fig. 2.6: Typical two pair shielded twisted pair cable (STP cable)

Ground loops - These arise when the ground voltage at each end of a cable run is different, causing a current to flow in the cable's shield and creating a magnetic field, which induces current (noise) in the same cable that the shielding is designed to protect.

- The same cable length restrictions apply (100 meters maximum) as for UTP.
- STP is limited for data communication to IBM machines and Token Ring networks - there is no standard for STP or Ethernet, ISDN or analog telephones.
- Shielded twisted pair is now manufactured to the same standard as Unshielded Twisted Pair.

Thus following points summarize the features of STP cable:
- Speed and throughput — 10 to 100 Mbps.
- Average cost per node —Moderately expensive.
- Media and connector size — Medium to large.
- Maximum cable length — 100 m (short).

When comparing UTP and STP, keep the following points in mind:
- The speed of both types of cable is usually satisfactory for local-area distances.
- These are the least-expensive media for data communication. UTP is less expensive than STP.
- Because most buildings are already wired with UTP, many transmission standards are adapted to use it, to avoid costly rewiring with an alternative cable type.

Table 2.1: Categories of Unshielded Twisted Pair

Type	Bandwidth	Use
Category 1	< 1 MHz	Voice Only (Telephone Wire).
Category 2	1 MHz	Data to 4 Mbps (Local Talk) and Telephone, T_1 lines etc.
Category 3	16 MHz	Data to 10 Mbps (Ethernet), Telephone, 10Base-T, Token Ring, LAN applications.
Category 4	20 MHz	Data to 20 Mbps (16 Mbps Token Ring), 10Base-T, LAN application.
Category 5	100 MHz	Data to 100 Mbps (Fast Ethernet), 10Base-T, 100Base-T, LAN applications.
Category 5e	350 MHz	125 Mbps, Data Networks.
Category 6	550 MHz	Proposed standard for cable having a data rate of 200 Mbps, LAN applications.
Category 7	600 MHz	Proposed standard for cable having a data rate of 600 Mbps using fully shielded cables, LAN applications.

Some advantages of twisted pair wiring are as follows:
- Reasonable cost.
- High speed.
- Easy to add additional network devices.
- Supports large number of network devices.
- Telephone cable standards are mature and well established. Materials are plentiful, and a wide variety of cable installers are familiar with the installation requirements.
- It may be possible to use in-place telephone wiring if it is of sufficiently high quality.
- UTP represents the lowest cost cabling. The cost for STP is higher and is comparable to the cost of coaxial cable.

Some disadvantages of twisted pair are as follows:
- High attenuation (signal loss) limits individual runs to 100 meters.
- Susceptible to EMI/RFI (except shielded type).
- STP can be expensive and difficult to work with.
- Compared to fiber optic cable, all Twisted Pair cable is more sensitive to EMI. UTP especially may be unsuitable for use in high-EMI environments.
- Twisted Pair cables are regarded as being less suitable for high-speed transmissions than coax or fiber optic. Technology advances, however, are pushing upward the data rates possible with Twisted Pair. Cable segment lengths are also more limited with Twisted Pair.

2.2.2 Coaxial Cable

1. A coaxial cable consists of a central copper wire core, which is surrounded by an insulating material.
2. The insulator is surrounded by braided metal shielding which helps to absorb external electronic signals (noise) and prevents it from interfering with the data signal.
3. A plastic sheath protects the outer conductor. A durable plastic or Teflon jacket coats the cable to prevent damage. Fig. 2.7 diagram illustrates the basic construction of a coaxial cable.

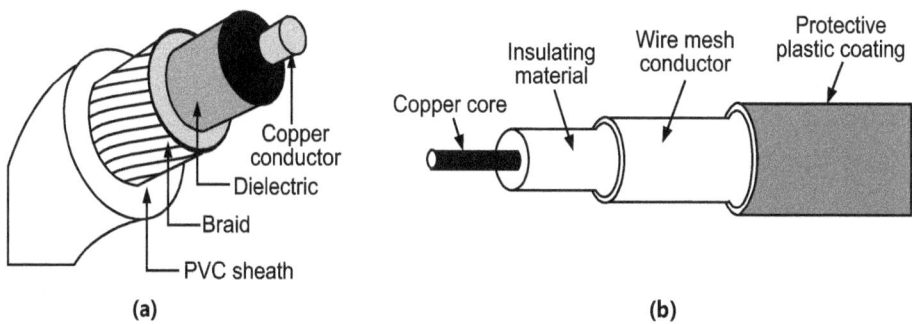

(a) (b)

Fig. 2.7: Coaxial cable construction

4. The construction and shielding of coaxial cable provides a high degree of immunity to noise, and coax can be used over longer distances (up to 500 meters) than twisted pair cable.
5. Coaxial cable runs are used to provide the network backbone cable segments in networks having a **bus topology**, and require a terminating resistor at each end of the cable in order to prevent interference due to signal reflection.
6. Coax has many desirable characteristics. It is highly resistant to EMI and can support high *bandwidths*.
7. Some types of coax have heavy shields and center conductors to enhance these characteristics and to extend the distances, so that signals can be transmitted reliably.
8. A wide variety of coax cable is available. You must use cable that exactly matches the requirements of a particular type of network.
9. Coax cables vary in a measurement known as the *impedance* (measured in a unit called the ohm), which is an indication of the cable's resistance to current flow.
10. The specifications of a given cabling standard indicate the required impedance of the cable.

11. Two types of coaxial cable can be used in computer networks:
- Thinnet or Cheapernet (also known as Baseband Coax - RG-58).
- Thicknet.

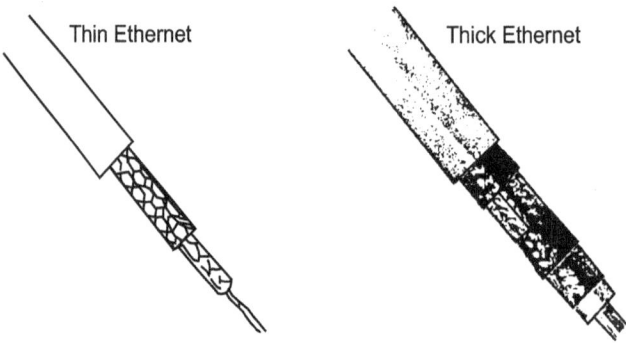

Fig. 2.8: Thin Ethernet and Thick Ethernet

12. Thinnet (10Base2) is so called because of the thin, inexpensive coaxial cabling it uses, and is fairly flexible, being 0.25 inches in diameter.
13. The IEEE specification refers to this type of cable as 10Base2, referring to its main specifications of 10 Mbps data rate, baseband transmission type, and 185 (nearly 200) meter maximum segment length.
14. The cable between computers must be at least 0.5 meters (20 inches) long.
15. An IEEE standard for Thinnet doesn't allow a drop cable to be used from the bus T-connector to a workstation.
16. Instead, the T-connector fits directly onto the network adapter card using a BNC connector.
17. **A Thinnet network** can support a maximum of 30 nodes per cable segment, and up to five segments can be connected using repeaters, of which three segments may be populated, allowing up to 90 nodes to be supported (based on the IEEE 802.3 specification).
18. **Thicknet cable** (also known as **Standard Ethernet**) is relatively rigid, being 0.5 inches in diameter.
19. The IEEE specification refers to Thicknet cable as 10Base5, referring to its main specifications of 10 Mbps data rate, baseband transmission type, and 500-metre maximum segment length.
20. Thicknet is generally used to provide the network backbone and can support up to 100 nodes per backbone segment.

21. The minimum cable length between connections (or taps) on a Thicknet cable segment is 2.5 meters (about 8 feet).
22. Thicknet cable has a data rate of 10 Mbps and can carry a signal for 500 meters before a repeater is required.
23. The grade of coaxial cable used will depend on where it is used.
24. Normal PVC coaxial cable is flexible, easy to work with, and may be used in exposed areas of offices, but because it gives of poisonous fumes when it burns, it is against the fire regulations in many countries for it to be installed in floor and ceiling voids which are also used to allow air to circulate around the building.
25. Thick coax was the transmission medium originally used by Xerox for their Ethernet network, although it was later replaced by thin coax.
26. Although still used in many networks, coaxial cable is gradually being replaced by fiber optic and UTP cable - fiber optic is normally used for the network backbone, while UTP is used to connect workstations to hubs or MAUs.
27. Following are some common examples of coaxial cables used in LANs, along with their impedances, and the LAN standards with which they are associated:

- RG-8 and RG-11 are 50-ohm cables required for use with thick wire Ethernet. (10Base5 - ThikNet).
- RG-58 is a smaller 50-ohm cable required for use with thin wire Ethernet. (10Base2 – ThinNet).
- RG-59 is a 75-ohm cable most frequently used to wire cable TV. RG-59 is also used to cable broadband 802.3 Ethernet.
- RG-62 is a 93-ohm cable used for ARCnet. It is also commonly employed to wire terminals in an IBM SNA network.

Some advantages of coaxial cable are as follows:
- Low cost due to less total footage of cable, hubs not needed.
- Lower attenuation than twisted pair.
- Good immunity to EMI/RFI or Highly insensitive to EMI.
- Supports high bandwidths.
- Heavier types of coax are sturdy and can withstand harsh environments.
- Represents a mature technology that is well understood and consistently applied among vendors.

Coaxial cable also has some disadvantages: They are as follows:
- Limited in network speed.
- Limited in size of network.
- One bad connector can take down entire network.
- Although fairly insensitive to EMI, coax remains vulnerable to EMI in harsh conditions such as factories.
- Coax can be bulky.
- Coax is among the most expensive types of wire cables.

2.2.3 Fiber Optic Cable

1. Data transmission over optical fiber has greatly increased over the last few years, although fiber to the desktop has not really caught on as expected.
2. However, fiber optic plays an important role in many networks.
3. In addition, it has some outstanding advantages over copper cabling for certain applications.
4. There are a number of network topologies and standards based on fiber optic, such as 10 BASE FL and FDDI, which apply mainly to the backbone cabling of very large facilities and campus environments.
5. The discussion will be limited here to the uses of fiber optic in star bus Ethernet network topologies.
6. When used as a link in a star bus topology, multi-mode fiber optic cable can transmit a maximum distance of 2,000 meters between all data closets, using a less expensive LED light source.
7. While single mode fiber can transmit up to 3,000 meters, it requires a more expensive laser light source.
8. By using fiber optic to link closets, it is possible to greatly extend the distance limitations in Ethernet networks using twisted pair only.
9. Fiber optic is an outstanding choice for linking buildings together.
10. In addition to the much greater distances possible, it is completely immune to over currents from lightning strikes and ground potential problems.
11. There is literally nothing metallic in a fiber optic cable to conduct current. It is an excellent choice for heavy manufacturing environments, such as a foundry, due to its immunity to EMI/RFI.
12. Finally, it is the best choice where data of a highly sensitive nature is being transmitted.
13. Fiber optic cable radiates no electrical signal at all, and the cable would be down for quite some time if someone tried to splice into it.

Construction of Optical Fiber:

- Optical fiber cable carries light signals instead of electric signal.
- Each fiber has inner core of either plastic or glass that carries light.
- The inner core is surrounded by cladding, a layer of plastic or glass that reflects the light back into core.
- Fiber optic cable can have single fiber or bundle of fibers at the centre of the cable. The refractive index of the core is relatively high.
- Refractive index is low. Cladding material is lossy.
- This entire optical core-cladding assembly is then coated with protective inner jacket and outer plastic jacket as shown in Fig. 2.9.

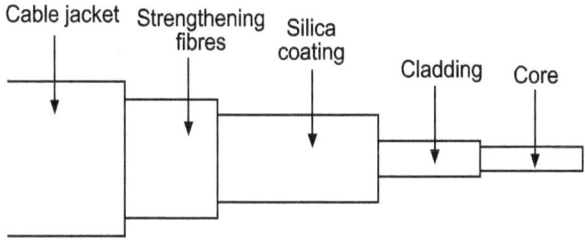

Fig. 2.9: Construction of fiber optic cable

The cross-section of a fiber illustrating the different layers is as shown in Fig. 2.10.

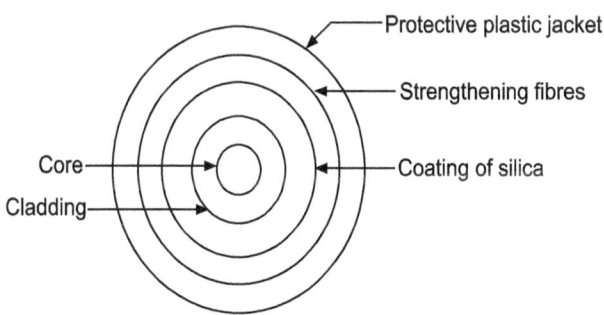

Fig. 2.10: A cross-section of a fiber illustrating the different layers

The core is surrounded by cladding surface and entire thing is coated with silicon oil and organic material like silica. External plastic jacket is to provide mechanical strength so that optical fiber is protected from mechanical wear and tear.

Typical optical fiber communication is shown in Fig. 2.11.

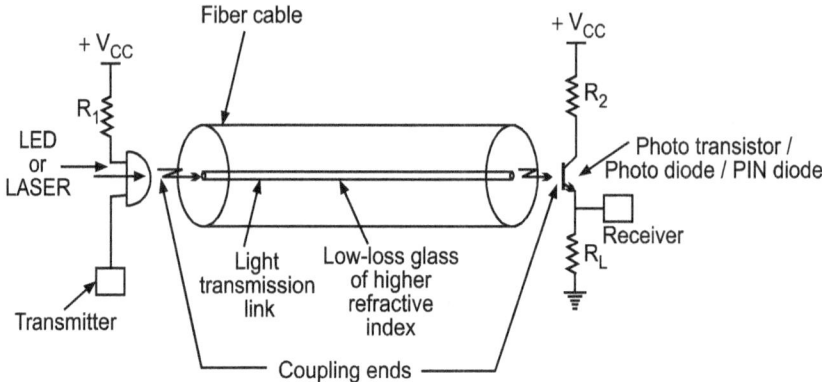

Fig. 2.11: Typical fiber optic communication system

The basic point-to-point fiber optic communication system consists of three basic units.
1. Optical transmitter unit
2. Fiber optic cable unit
3. Optical receiver unit.

Optical Transmitter Unit: The transmitter converts applied electrical, analog or digital signal into a corresponding light signal. The source of the light signal can be either a light emitting diode, or a solid-state laser diode.

Fiber Optic Cable Unit: Converted signal travels in the form of light from one end of fiber to other end of fiber. This is also called as **light transmission link.** If the distance between transmitter and receiver is in kilometers, then two or more fiber optic cables can be joined together.

Optical Receiver: The receiver converts the optical signal into the original electrical signal. This optical receiver uses the photodetectors like avalanche type photodiode or PIN type of photodiode (P type-Intrinsic-N type material is used).

Optical fibers can be classified in two ways as shown.

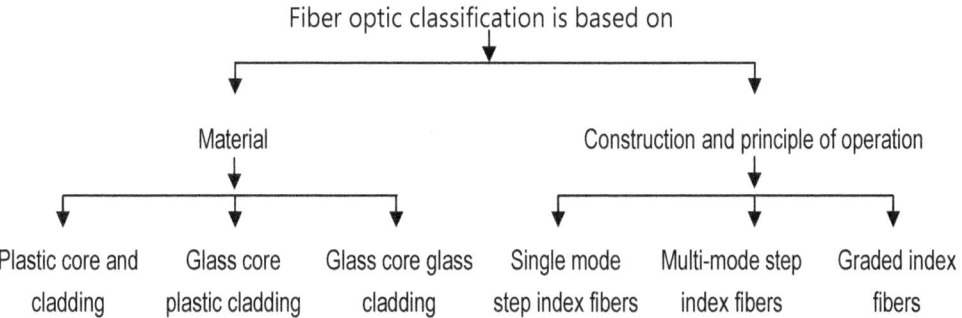

Plastic core and cladding: These type of fibers are more rugged than glass. They are less expensive. They provide high attenuation characteristics and can be used within a single building or a building complex. Less attenuation when exposed to external radiation.

Glass core with plastic cladding: These type of fibers are more effectively used in military applications.

Glass core and glass cladding: These type of fibers are least rugged and are more susceptible to increase in attenuation when exposed to external radiation compared to above both optical fibers.

Single mode step index fiber has following properties:
- Supports only one mode of operation.
- Use of LASER is must, as it makes power launching difficult.
- Fiber coupling is difficult due to less diameter size of core which is approximately ≈ 8 to 12 μm.

Multi-mode step index fiber has following properties:
- Supports hundreds of modes of propagation.
- LED can be used as optical transmitter, so power launching becomes easy.
- Fiber coupling is easy because moderate core diameter which is approximately ≈ 50 to 200 μm.
- In this fiber the pulse which is sent at transmitter end spreads in time, when it is received at receiver end. This pulse distortion is called as **intermodal dispersion**.

Graded index fiber:

- The intermodal dispersion of pulse is reduced in the graded index fiber due to its construction itself.
- Graded index fibers have larger bandwidth than step index fibers.

Construction of the monomode or single mode step index fiber is given in Fig. 2.12 (a).

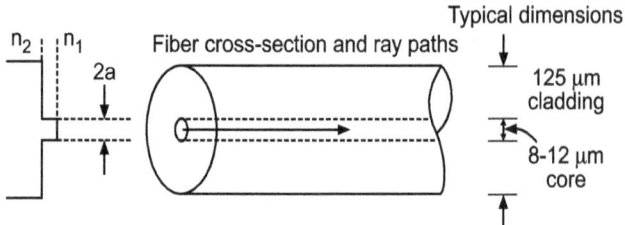

Fig. 2.12 (a): Monomode or single mode step index fiber

Construction of the multi-mode step index fiber is given in Fig. 2.12 (b).

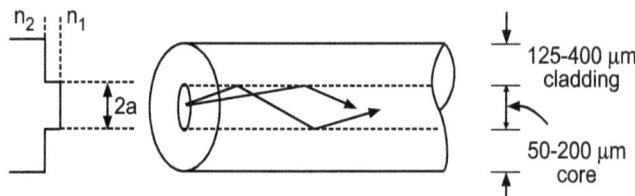

Fig. 2.12 (b): Multi-mode step index fiber

Construction of the graded index fiber is given in Fig. 2.12 (c).

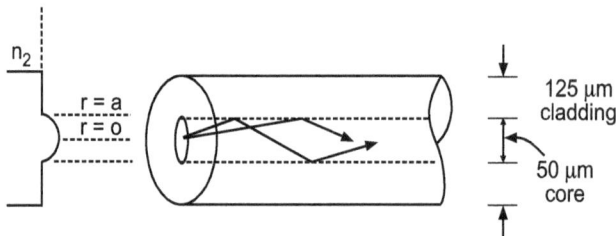

Fig. 2.12 (c): Graded index fiber

Thus fiber optic transmission line confines light energy within its surface and guides the light in a direction parallel to its axis.

In previous figures,
n_1 = refractive index of the core
n_2 = refractive index of cladding

Main advantages of fiber optic cable:
- High data rate and wide bandwidth.
- Immunity to EMI/RFI and lightning damage.
- No ground loops.
- Low attenuation (Low data loss).
- Longer distance - 2 and 5 km with multi-mode fiber and over 25 km with single mode fiber.
- Small cable diameter fits anywhere.
- Light weight.
- No sparks if cut.
- No shock hazard.
- Secure communication.
- Safe and easy installation.
- Low system cost.
- Longer life expectancy than copper or coaxial cable.
- Cable of the future.

Main disadvantages of fiber optic cable are as follows:
1. **Cost :** Despite the fact that the raw material for making optical fibers is abundant and cheap, optical fibers are still more expensive per meter than copper.
2. **Special Skills :** Optical fibers cannot be joined together as easily as copper. It requires additional training for person. Expensive precision splicing and measurement equipment are also required.
3. **Installation and Maintenance Cost :** Initial installation of the fiber optic system is more and maintenance is expensive.

Table 2.2: Summary of Cable Characteristics

Cable Type	Cable Cost	Installation Cost	EMI Sensitivity	Data Bandwidth
UTP	Lowest	Lowest	Highest	Lowest
STP	Medium	Moderate	Low	Moderate
Coax	Medium	Moderate	Low	High
Fiber Optic	Highest	Highest	None	Very high

- Thus choosing the correct type of cabling depends on what type of network you have or intend to have, the number of network devices used, expected future growth, the speed requirements of your applications and the physical layout of your facility.
- Make this decision with the assistance of a professional, licensed and insured network cabling company and a good information technology consultant.

Table 2.3: Characteristic comparison of guided media

Twisted Pair	Coaxial Cable	Fiber Optic Cable
1. It uses electrical signal for transmission.	It uses electrical signal for transmission.	It uses optical signal for transmission.
2. Affected by EMI and noise.	Less affected by EMI and noise.	Not affected by EMI and noise.
3. Bandwidth is low which is 3 to 4 MHz.	Bandwidth is high which is 300 to 400 MHz.	Bandwidth is very high which is 2 to 3 GHz.
4. Used for analog and digital transmission.	Used for analog and digital transmission.	Used for analog and digital transmission.
5. Supports low data rates up to 4 Mbps.	Supports high data rates up to 400 to 500 Mbps.	Supports very high data rates up to 3 Gbps.
6. Cost is very less.	Cost is moderate.	Very costly.
7. For long distance communication, repeaters are required after every 2 km distance.	For long distance communication, repeaters are required after every 1 km distance.	For long distance communication, repeaters are required after every 10 km distance.
8. Signal attenuation is more.	Signal attenuation is moderate.	Signal attenuation is least.
9. Installation is easiest.	Installation is less easy as compared to twisted pair.	Installation is difficult.
10. Signal to noise ratio is less.	Signal to noise ratio is moderate.	Signal to noise ratio is very high.
11. Crosstalk is more.	Crosstalk is moderate.	No crosstalk is present.
12. Losses like copper losses and radiation losses are present.	Losses like copper losses and radiation losses are present.	Losses like microbending and macrobending losses are present.

2.3 Unguided Media

2.3.1 Introduction

1. Unguided media are natural parts of the earth's environment that can be used as physical paths to carry electrical signals.
2. The atmosphere and outer space are examples of unguided media that are commonly used to carry signals.
3. **These media can carry electromagnetic signals** such **as microwaves, infrared light waves, and radio waves.**
4. Network signals are transmitted through all transmission media as a type of waveform.
5. When transmitted through wire and cable, the signal is an electrical waveform.
6. When transmitted through fiber-optic cable, the signal is a light wave: either visible or infrared light.
7. When transmitted through earth's atmosphere or outer space, the signal can take the form of waves in the radio spectrum, including VHF and microwaves, or it can be light waves, including infrared or visible light (for example, lasers).
8. Recent advances in radio hardware technology have produced significant advancements in wireless networking devices: the cellular telephone, wireless modems, and wireless LANs.
9. These devices use technology that in some cases has been around for decades but until recently was too impractical or expensive for widespread consumer use.
10. The next few sections explain technologies unique to unguided media that are especially of concern to networking.
11. There are a variety of wireless network media, each of which uses a different transmission protocol. Typically, a wireless network uses infrared light or radio transmissions to distribute data.
12. **Infrared networks** communicate by using beams of infrared light. They have a maximum range of 100 meters. Theoretically, they can transmit at 10 Mbps, but 1-3 Mbps is more typical.
13. **Narrow band radio networks** can cover an area up to 5,000 square meters at up to 4.8 Mbps. Their disadvantage is that they offer little security.
14. **Spread-spectrum radio networks** use multiple frequencies. These multiple channels provide network security. They can transmit data at up to 1 Mbps at a range of 800 feet indoors, though 300 kbps is more typical.
15. Some common applications of wireless data communication include the following:
- Accessing the Internet using a cellular phone.
- Establishing a home or business Internet connection over satellite.
- Beaming data between two hand-held computing devices.
- Using a wireless keyboard and mouse for the PC.

2.3.2 The Electromagnetic Spectrum

1. All electromagnetic waves travel at the speed of light (300,000,000 metres per second) in a vacuum, whatever their frequency (in copper or fibre), the speed drops to approximately two thirds of this value, and is slightly frequency dependent.
2. The relationship between frequency, wavelength and the speed of light (C) in a vacuum is given by:

$$F\lambda = C$$

3. Since C is a constant, if wavelength is known, then frequency can be calculated and vice versa.
4. Thus, a frequency of 1 MHz would give a wavelength of approximately 300 meters, and a 1 cm wavelength would give a frequency of approximately 30 GHz. The Electromagnetic Spectrum is shown in Fig. 2.13.

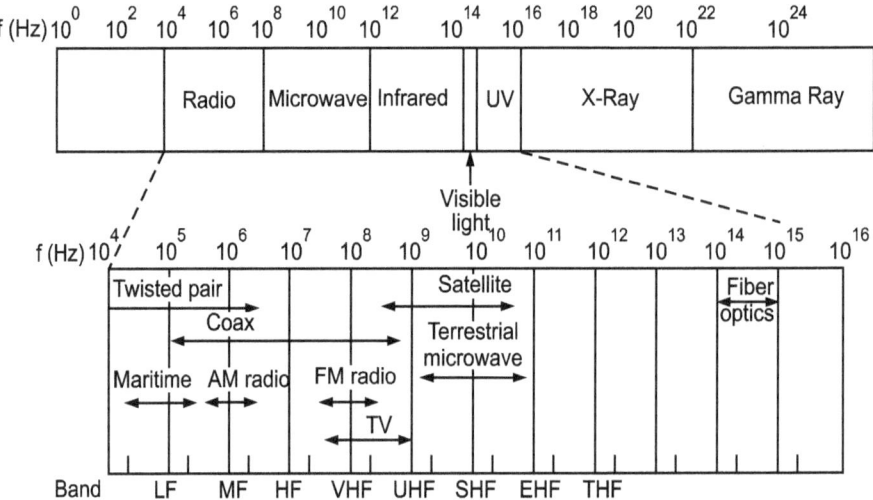

Fig. 2.13: The electromagnetic spectrum

5. The parts of the electromagnetic spectrum which can be used for transmitting information using amplitude, frequency or phase modulation are shown using a darker shading and include radio, microwave, infrared and visible light.

2.4 Radio Transmission

1. Radio waves are widely used for both indoor and outdoor communication because they are easy to generate, can travel over long distances, and can penetrate buildings easily.

2. Because they travel in all directions from the transmitter (i.e. they are omni directional), the transmitter and receiver do not need to be carefully aligned.
3. The properties of radio waves are dependent on frequency.
4. At low frequencies, they pass through obstacles well, but the power falls off sharply as the distance from the transmitter increases.
5. At high frequencies, radio waves tend to travel in straight lines and bounce off obstacles.
6. They are also absorbed by rain.
7. At all frequencies, they are subject to electromagnetic interference from electrical equipment such as electric motors.
8. The ability to travel over large distances means that radio transmissions can also interfere with each other, which is one of the main reasons why the use of radio transmitters is tightly controlled by governments.
9. In the very low to medium frequency bands, radio waves follow the ground, as illustrated below, and can be detected at distances of about 1000 kilometers. (Also called as Ground Wave Propagation)
10. Radio waves at these frequencies can easily pass through buildings and are subsequently widely used by terrestrial radio stations.
11. The relatively low bandwidth, however, means that they are not suitable for data communication.

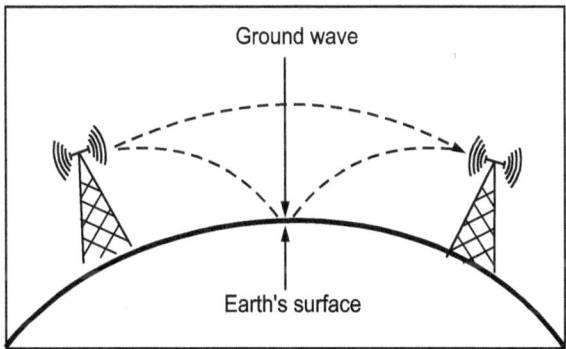

Fig. 2.14: Radio transmission using ground wave propagation

12. RF is part of electromagnetic spectrum that ranges from 3 Hz - 300 GHz.
13. Radio wave is radiated by an antenna and produced by alternating currents fed to the antenna.
14. RF is used in many standard as well as proprietary wireless communication systems.
15. RF has been used since long time for radio and TV broadcasting, wireless local loop, mobile communication, and amateur radio.

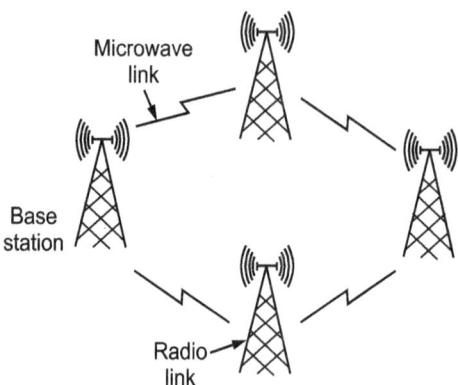

Fig. 2.15: Radio waves radiated by a Base Station's antenna

16. High (HF) and very high (VHF) frequency radio waves that reach the ionosphere, which is a layer of charged particles approximately 100-500 km above the earth's surface, are refracted by it and sent back to earth.

17. These bands are used by amateur radio operators to talk over long distances, and are also used for military radio communication.

18. **Radio waves** have virtually no distance limitations. However the radio waves are government regulated, expensive, and can be tapped into. This can be used across continents.

2.5 Microwave Transmission

1. At frequencies of 1 GHz and above, electromagnetic waves travel in straight lines and can be narrowly focused. Microwave is the upper part of RF spectrum. Because of the availability of larger bandwidth in microwave spectrum, microwave is used in many applications such as wireless PAN, wireless LAN, fixed broadband wireless access (wireless MAN), satellite communications, radar, and as backhaul in cellular networks.

2. A parabolic dish antenna can be used to focus the transmitted power into a narrow beam to give a high signal to noise ratio, and before the advent of optical fiber, some long distance telephone transmission systems were heavily dependent on the use of a series of microwave towers.

3. Because microwaves travel in a straight line, the curvature of the earth limits the maximum distance over which microwave towers can transmit, so repeaters are needed to compensate for this limitation. As a general rule, the higher the towers are, the further apart they can be.

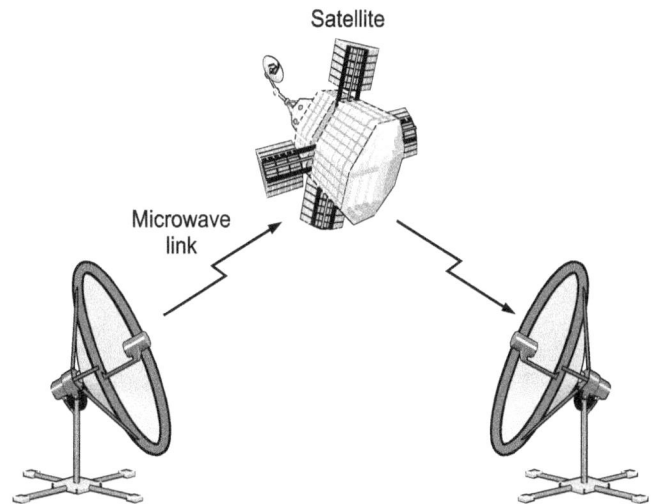

Fig. 2.16: Typical example of microwave link using dish antenna and satellite

4. At these higher frequencies, the transmitted waves do not easily pass through buildings.
5. In addition, however well focused the transmitter may be, some waves may be refracted by low-lying atmospheric layers, and will take longer to arrive at their destination than direct waves.
6. The delayed waves may therefore arrive out of phase with the direct waves and cancel out the signal. **This effect is known as multipath fading**.
7. Rain can also be a problem, as frequencies around 8 GHz are absorbed by water.
8. At higher frequencies, more expensive electronics are required, and transmissions can be subject to interference from radar installations and microwave ovens.
9. **Microwave does, however, have several advantages over fiber.**
10. Obstacles such as roads, railways and rivers may make laying cables difficult whereas these problems do not exist for microwave, and rights of way are not an issue.
11. Erecting simple towers or mounting antenna on top of tall buildings is usually far cheaper than laying several kilometers of cable.
12. Microwave also removes the need for reliance on telephone companies.
13. In addition, governments worldwide have set aside the frequency band from 2.400 GHz to 2.484 GHz for unlicensed transmissions, so use of these frequencies does not require a license, and is therefore popular for various forms of short range wireless networking.
14. **Microwaves** have a medium distance limitation and require line of sight. This is good between buildings or between satellites and satellite dishes. Weather and solar conditions may affect transmission.

15. Microwaves are used for long distance communication like cellular phones, garage door openers, and much more.
16. Microwave transmission is line of sight transmission. The transmitting station must be in visible contact with the receiving station.
17. This sets a limit on the distance between stations depending on the local geography. Typically the line of sight due to the Earth's curvature is only 50 km to the horizon! Repeater stations must be placed so the data signal can hop, skip and jump across the country.

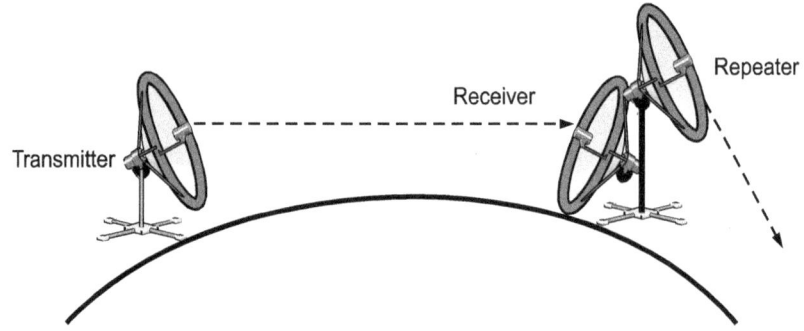

Fig. 2.17: Other example of microwave transmission

18. Microwaves operate at high operating frequencies of 3 to 10 GHz. This allows them to carry large quantities of data due to the large bandwidth.

2.5.1 Terrestrial Microwave Transmission

1. Communication is accomplished through line of sight parabolic dish antenna located on elevated sites.
2. Long distance communication is possible by using a series of relay stations.
3. The distance between the stations is dependent on the height above the ground.
4. Used for voice, television transmission, private communications and telephone networks. For example, emergency services, utilities etc.
5. Utilizes a wide frequency band, 2 to 40 GHz but is susceptible to attenuation and interference.
6. Attenuation can rise markedly in poor atmospheric conditions. For example, rain, but adversely affects the higher end of the frequency band, which is only used for short distance transmission.
7. Natural noise severely affects transmission frequencies below 2GHz.
8. Quick to install and overcomes the problems of laying cables in congested locations or over difficult terrain.

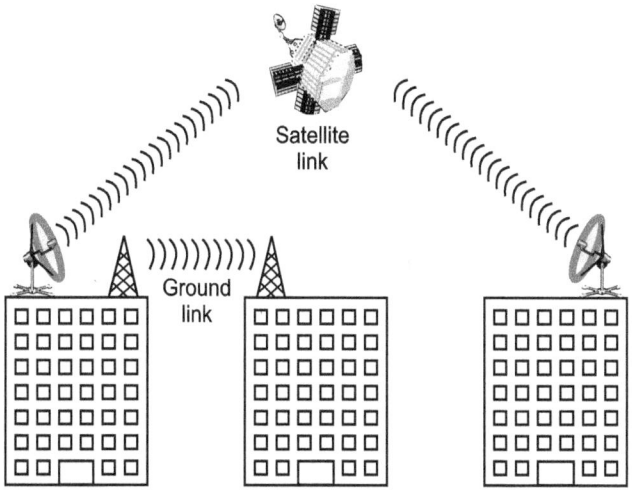

Fig. 2.18: Typical example of terrestrial and satellite microwave links

2.5.2 Satellite Microwave Transmission

1. Overcomes the line of sight problems of terrestrial microwave and can be used for point-to-point or broadcast transmission.
2. Uses an uplink and downlink frequency, a common frequency set is referred to as the 4/6 range which uses a downlink frequency of 4 GHz and an uplink frequency of 6 GHz.

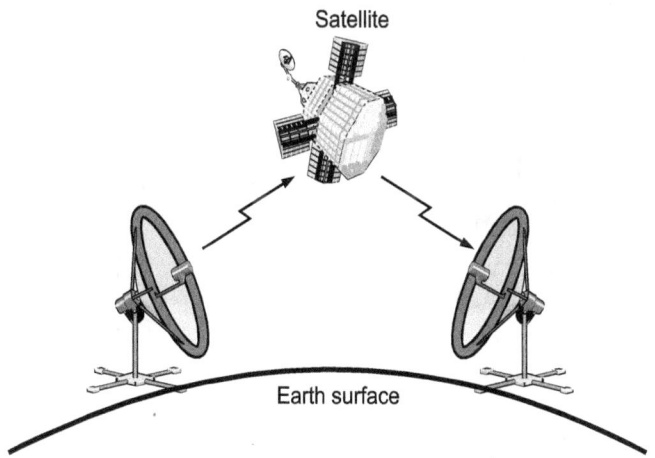

Fig. 2.19: Point-to-point link via satellite microwave

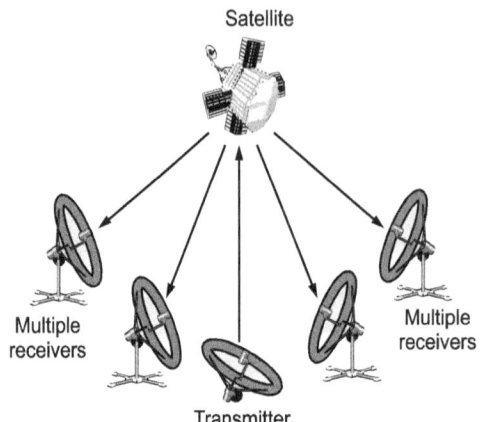

Fig. 2.20: Broadcast link via satellite microwave

3. Typical uses of satellite microwave - television distribution, long distance telephone transmission, private business networks for global organizations.
4. Suffers the same attenuation problems as terrestrial microwave.
5. Microwave transmitters and receivers, especially satellite systems, are commonly used to transmit network signals over great distances.
6. A microwave transmitter uses the atmosphere or outer space as the transmission medium to send the signal to a microwave receiver.
7. The microwave receiver then either relays the signal to another microwave transmitter or translates the signal to some other form, such as digital impulses, and relays it on another suitable medium to its destination.

Fig. 2.21 shows a satellite microwave link.

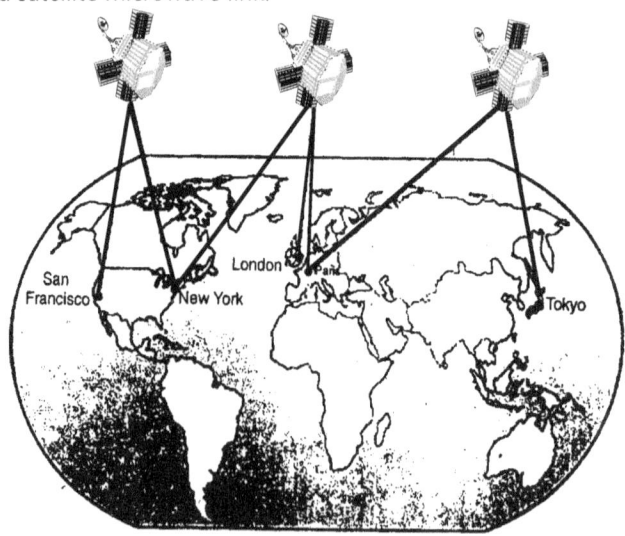

Fig. 2.21: Satellite microwave link for worldwide communication

8. Originally, this technology was used almost exclusively for satellite and long-range communication.
9. Recently, however, there have been developments in cellular technology that allow you to complete wireless access to networks, intranets, and the Internet.
10. IEEE 802.11 defines a MAC and physical access control for wireless connection to networks.
11. Used for TV distribution, long-distance telephone, and business networks.

Advantages:
(a) They require no right of way acquisition between towers.
(b) They can carry high quantities of information due to their high operating frequencies.
(c) Low cost land purchase: each tower occupies small area.
(d) High frequency/short wavelength signals require small antenna.

Disadvantages:
(a) Attenuation by solid objects: birds, rain, snow and fog.
(b) Reflected from flat surfaces like water and metal.
(c) Diffracted (split) around solid objects.
(d) Refracted by atmosphere, thus causing beam to be projected away from receiver.

2.6 Infrared Transmission

1. Unguided infrared waves are widely used for short-range communication. **Infrared** technology allows computing devices to communicate via short-range wireless signals. With infrared, computers can transfer files and other digital data bidirectionally. The infrared transmission technology used in computers is similar to that used in consumer product (television and VCRs) remote control units.
2. Used for very short line of sight transmission, remote car locking systems, wireless security alarms.
3. **Infrared** light is part of electromagnetic spectrum that is shorter than radio waves but longer than visible light. Computer infrared network adapters both transmit and receive data through ports on the rear or side of a device. Infrared adapters are installed in many laptops and handheld personal devices.
4. Its frequency range is between 300 GHz and 400 THz, that correspond to wavelength from 1 mm to 750 nm.

5. Infrared has long been used in night vision equipment and TV remote control.
6. Infrared is also one of the physical media in the original wireless LAN standard, that is IEEE 802.11. Infrared networks were designed to support direct two-computer connections only, created temporarily as the need arises. However, extensions to infrared technology also support more than two computers and semi-permanent networks.
7. Infrared use in communication and networking was defined by the IrDA (Infrared Data Association).
8. Using IrDA specifications, infrared can be used in a wide range of applications. For example, file transfer, synchronization, dial-up networking and Intranet (LAN).
9. However, IrDA is limited in range (up to about 1 meter). It also requires the communicating devices to be in LOS (Line of Sight) and within its 30-degree beam-cone. Infrared technology used in local networks exists in three different forms:

- IrDA-SIR (slow speed) infrared supporting data rates up to 115 kbps.
- IrDA-MIR (medium speed) infrared supporting data rates up to 1.15 Mbps.
- IrDA-FIR (fast speed) infrared supporting data rates up to 4 Mbps.

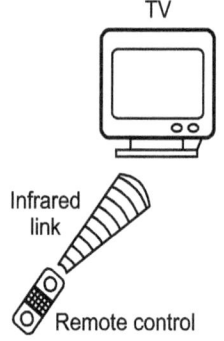

Fig. 2.22: TV remote control uses infrared

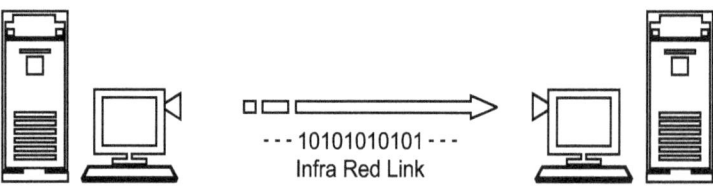

Fig. 2.23: Computer communication uses infrared

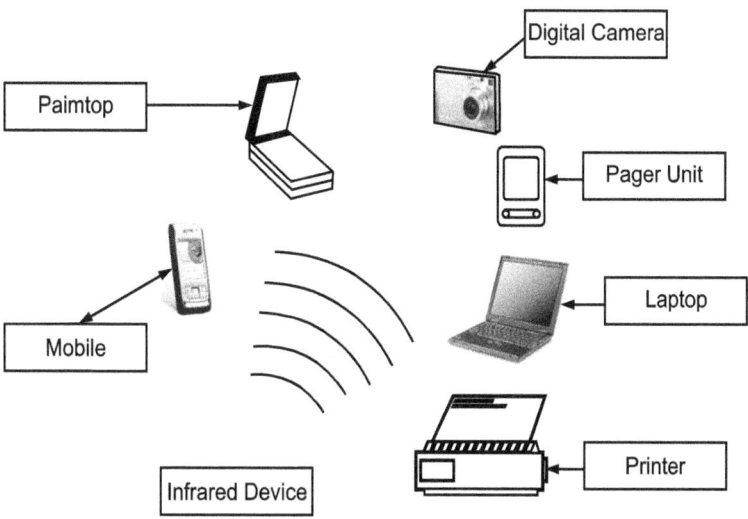

Fig. 2.24: Devices communicate using infrared

10. Infrared transmitters are (relatively) directional, cheap, and easy to manufacture. Infrared data and communication is a mode of communication that now plays an important role in wireless data communication. It suits the use of laptop computers, wireless data communication and other digital equipment such as personal assistants, cameras, mobile telephones and pagers.

11. The major drawback is that infrared waves will not pass through solid objects. The communication between the devices requires that each have a transceiver (a combination of a transmitter and a receiver) in order to communicate. This capability is provided by microchip technology. However, devices may also require further, specialized software allowing communication to be synchronized.

12. On the plus side, an infrared system in one room of a building will not interfere with similar systems in nearby rooms, and the possibility of eavesdropping is far lower than with radio-based systems. IR can be used over longer interconnections and has applicability to local area networks (LANs). However, the maximum effective distance is approximately 1 mile, with a maximum bandwidth of 16 Mbps.

2.7 Framing

When the bits of information is received from physical layer, data link layer entity identifies beginning and end of block of information i.e. frames with the help of special pattern placed by the peer entity.

The frames may be fixed length or variable length. The requirements of framing methods will vary accordingly.

In case of fixed length frames, a frame consists of a single bit followed by a particular length sequence.

Variable length frames required additional information for frame identification.

For example,

(i) Special characters to identify beginning and end of frame.
(ii) Starting and ending flags.
(iii) Character counts.
(iv) CRC Checking Methods (Checksum).

The first framing method uses ASCII characters DLE and STX at the start of each frame and DLE and ETX at the end of the frame. It is as shown in Fig. 3.2 (a), where DLE is Data Link Escape, STX is Start of Text and ETX is End of Text.

Fig. 2.25 (a): Character Framing

But then this framing method has a problem. Consider the case where the data to be transmitted contains the character DLE STX in which case wrong identification of start of frame will be made. Similarly, if DLE ETX occur it will trigger end of frame. This problem can be solved by stuffing (adding) another DLE whenever DLE occurs in the data sequence. This technique is called **character stuffing**. The stuffed DLE can be destuffed (deleted) by receiving DLL entity. It is shown in Fig. 2.25 (b).

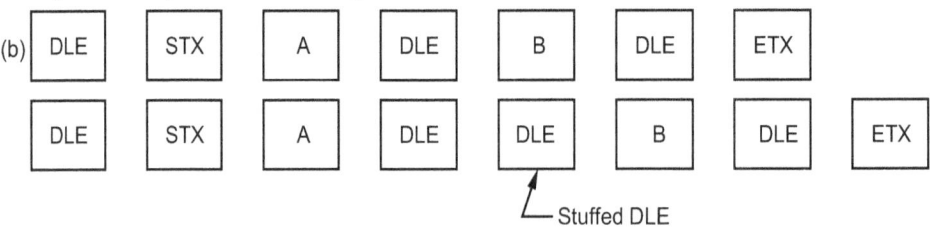

Fig. 2.25 (b): Character Stuffing

This method is suitable only for data containing ASCII or printable characters and not for arbitrary sized characters.

The second technique which is also called as bit stuffing allows arbitrary number of bits per character. At the beginning and end of each frame a special bit pattern 01111110 called as flag is used. Here also there is a possibility that the flag bits may occur in the data. The technique used to avoid this problem is bit stuffing. Whenever there are five 1's in data sequence, 0 is stuffed and at the receiving end it is destuffed.

Bit stuffing is shown in Fig. 2.26.

ORIGINAL PATTERN : (Data)
1111111111101111110111110

AFTER BITSTUFFING :
11111011111011011111010111110010

Fig. 2.26: Bit Stuffing

Five 1's followed by 11 will indicate an error.

If receiver looses synchronization all it has to do is scan for flag pattern.

The character count method employs count of number of characters in the frame to be placed at the beginning of each frame. The receiver will look into character count and extract those many character from the frame and hence it knows the end of frame also. Problem will come when the count is changed due to error in transmission. The synchronization will be completely lost. Even if we use checksum, there will be no way of identifying the start of next frame. Hence this method is not used much. It is shown in Fig. 2.27.

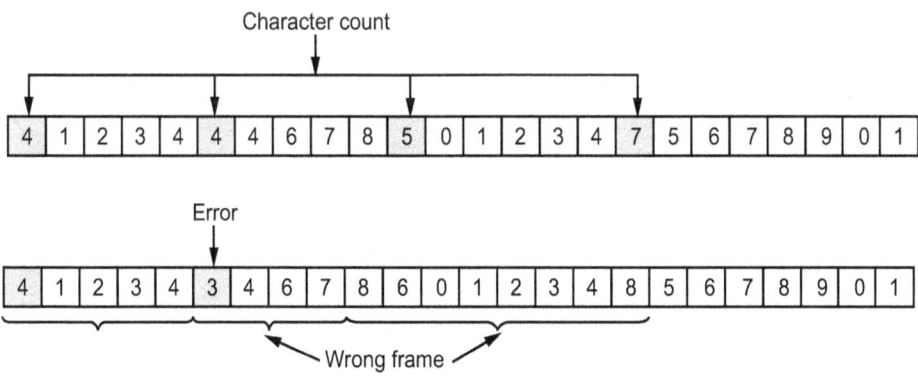

Fig. 2.27: Character count

In CRC based framing method, alongwith character count, CRC of count field is placed. Hence, the receiver examines four bytes at a time to see if CRC computed over first two bytes equals contents of next two bytes.

Many data link protocols use a combination of character count with other methods, for making it doubly sure that proper synchronization is achieved. For example, count of character is placed at the beginning of the frame and a flag is placed at the end of frame and may be checksum is also used. Count field is used to locate end of frdame and only if appropriate flag is present at the end of frame and checksum is correct, the frame is accepted.

2.8 Error Control

- It is an important function of DLL.
- Errors in transmission are going to occur due to noise or distortion in the channel even when the design is optimized.
- Some typical error rates are –
  - (i) For copper wire 10^{-6}.
  - (ii) For optical fibre 10^{-9}.
  - (iii) For wireless transmission 10^{-3}.
- Acceptability of bit error rate depends on the particular application. Applications requiring high reliability should have low bit error rate.
- Error rate performance can be improved by using error-control techniques.
- There are two types of error control techniques :
  - (i) **Automatic Repeat Request (ARQ) :** In this technique the incoming frame is tested for error. If error is detected, a retransmission request is made to the transmitter. A return channel is required for this. ARQ is used where bandwidth is more and delay in transmission can be tolerated.
  - (ii) **Forward Error Correction (FEC) :** Whenever error is dtected in the received frame, it is further processed to correct the errors. This technique is suitable where return channel is not available. It requires more redundancy and has complex procedure. It does not waste bandwidth as in the case of ARQ due to retransmission requests.

2.8.1 Introduction To Error Correcting Codes

(Readers can skip this section as it is covered in subject ITCT).

- A digital communication system must have higher data rate, minimum signal power, reliable transmission and minimum bandwidth requirement.
- The channel over which the transmission takes place is usually noisy and it will have limited bandwidth.
- If we have to keep the signal power minimum the signal to noise ratio will be lower. This will lead to increase in error probability (p_e), as it depends on E_b/N_0 ratio. Hence, reliability of the system suffers.

- Hence, in order to improve reliability for given E_b/N_0 ratio, we can use error control coding techniques.
- Error control coding techniques can correct errors, so that messages which are likely to go wrong in a noisy channel can be retrieved correctly at the receiver end.
- This is also known as Forward Error Correction (FEC).
- For a fixed value of error probability, it is also possible to reduce E_b/N_0 ratio (signal power) using error control coding.
- Since this technique tries to overcome channel noise it is also called **channel coding.**
- The error correcting codes are generated by adding redundancy to original message before transmitting it on a noisy channel. The channel encoder block in the transmitter does this as shown in Fig. 2.28.

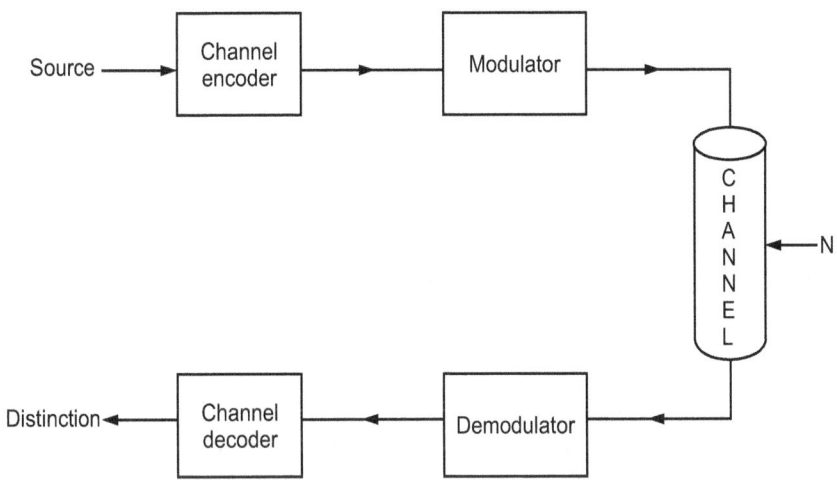

Fig. 2.28: Channel coding in communication system

- At the receiver we can recover the original message if the errors are within the limit as per the design of code. The channel decoder block does this recovery.
- A good error control coding technique should have –
  (i) Better error correcting capability.
  (ii) Faster and efficient method of coding and decoding.
  (iii) Maximum transfer of information in bit/sec. (or less overheads).
- If we try to increase error correcting capability, information rate will reduce and coding and decoding will also be slower. Complexity of design increases in order to achieve better coding technique. The addition of redundancy also increases the bandwidth requirement. Thus, reliability is at the cost of bandwidth and system complexity.

- Reliability can be increased by designing error detecting systems. In these systems, we add redundancy at the transmitter end in the message. The code is then transmitted. At the receiver end we will detect whether the code received is correct or not. If not, we request the transmitter to retransmit the code. The overheads required in this case are lower than that of FEC. This technique is called Automatic Repeat Request (ARQ).
- There are number of error correcting codes. They are classified as –
    (i)   Block codes.
    (ii) Convolutional codes.
- In block codes a block of k-bit message is encoded into n bits by adding n–k redundant bits.
- Convolutional codes are generated using a sliding window where, incoming message slides forward in the window. The window length is usually small and output code consists of encoder output corresponding to the message bits in the window.
- The memory requirement for linear block code encoder is more than convolutional code.

2.8.1.1 Basic Definitions

In digital communication, we use binary symbols (I/O) for transmission of message hence, we will be using the word bits instead of symbols in our discussion. But correct and general word should be symbols as a message may generate more than two types of symbols.

Let us first discuss some frequently used terms with coding.

1. **Word :** *It is a sequence of symbols.*

    e.g. Suppose we have a message consisting of 1010, then it is called a **message word.** Similarly, there will be code corresponding to this message called as **codeword.**

2. **Code :** *It is a set of vectors called as codewords or code vectors.*
3. **Parity bits :** *The bits which are added to the message bits are called parity bits.*
4. **Systematic code :** *Code in which codewords consists of message bits and parity bits separately is called systematic code.*
5. **Block codes :** *These are fixed length codewords generated from a block of message words.*
6. **Block code specification :** *The block code is specified in terms of number of code bits and number of message bits. If there are k bits in the message word and n bits are generated to form codeword, the block code is called (n, k) block code.*

7. **Code rate :** For an (n, k) block code the code rate is defined as the ratio of message bits and code bits (k/n). Code rate is always less than one.

8. **Parity check codes :** These are simplest possible block codes. These codes are generated by adding one bit to the message bits. They can be even parity check codes or odd parity check codes. Even parity check codes add 1 to message if number of 1's in message are odd and 0 if number of 1's in message are even.

   e.g.

Message	Code	Parity bit
100101	1001011	
110101	1101010	

   Similarly,

   Odd parity check codes

Message	Code	Parity bit
010011	0100110	
010001	0100011	

   If single error occurs in these codewords it can be detected at the receiver end.

9. **Weight of a codeword :** The number of non-zero symbols in a codeword is called weight of the codeword.

   e.g.

Codeword	Weight
10101	3
11110	4

10. **Hamming distance :** It is a number of symbols in which two codewords differ.

    e.g.
    $$c_1 = 10101$$
    $$c_2 = 11010$$

    Hamming distance between c_1 and c_2 is 4, denoted as $d(c_1, c_2) = 4$.

11. Minimum hamming distance between any two codewords of a code is called minimum hamming distance of that code. It is denoted as d_{min}.

12. **A linear code :** It is a code which has following properties.
    (i) The sum of any two codewords in the code will yield another codeword of that code.
    (ii) There is always all-zero codeword.
    (iii) The minimum hamming distance between any two codewords is equal to minimum weight of any non-zero codeword.

Example 2.1:

Consider following code.

$$C = \{000, 111\}$$

Solution:

It consists of the two codewords.

Weight of 000 is 0

Weight of 111 is 3.

Hamming distance between two codewords = 3.

Minimum Hamming distance of the code = 3.

It is a linear code since addition of the two codewords yield one of the codewords 111.

Example 2.2:

Consider a code.

$$C = \{000, 010, 001, 111\}$$

Codeword	Weight
000	0
010	1
001	1
111	3

Solution:

Minimum Hamming Distance = 1

It is not a linear code as addition of 001 and 010 does not yield valid codeword i.e. 011 is not a valid codeword of this code.

13. **Minimum Hamming distance (d_{min})** of a linear code is equal to minimum weight of the non-zero codewords in that code.

Consider a code C = {000, 010, 101, 111}

Codeword	Weight
000	0
010	1
101	2
111	3

Since, minimum weight of non-zero code is 1.

Minimum Hamming distance d_{min} = 1.

2.8.1.2 Matrix Description of Linear Block Codes

Consider an (n, k) block code in which there are k message bits (or symbols) and n code bits (or symbols).

Let the code bits be,

$$C = (c_1, c_2, c_3, \ldots c_n) \qquad \ldots (2.1)$$

Let the message bits be,

$$d = (d_1, d_2, d_3, \ldots d_k) \qquad \ldots (2.2)$$

For general case n bits of code C are generated by linear combinations of k message bits. This is called non-systematic code.

For a special case,

If $c_1 = d_1 \quad c_2 = d_2 \ldots c_k = d_k$

and c_{k+1} to c_n are generated from linear combinations of $d_1, d_2, \ldots d_k$ then the code is called systematic code. First k bits are message bits and (n − k) parity bits added to the message.

As we have seen in earlier section, any code C is a subspace of $GF(q^n)$ and any set of basic vectors S can be used to generate code space C = <S> by linear combinations of basis vectors. Hence, m can put all basis vectors in a matrix which is called generator matrix (G). This matrix is used to generate the codewords of C. If we have to generate the codewords of length n from k message bits we will need the generator matrix of the order k × n. Hence, we should have k basis vectors in the generator matrix. The code is generated by,

$$C = d \times G \qquad \ldots (2.3)$$

Now, if we have to generate systematic code we should have relationship between C and as below :

$$\begin{aligned}
c_1 &= d_1 \\
c_2 &= d_2 \\
c_3 &= d_3 \\
&\vdots \\
c_k &= d_k \\
c_{k+1} &= p_{11} \cdot d_1 \oplus p_{21} \cdot d_2 \oplus \ldots \oplus p_{k1} \cdot d_k \\
c_{k+2} &= p_{12} \cdot d_1 \; H \; p_{22} \cdot d_2 \oplus \ldots \oplus p_{k2} \cdot d_k \\
&\vdots \\
c_n &= p_{1n-k} \cdot d_1 \oplus p_{2n-k} \cdot d_2 \oplus \ldots \oplus p_{kn-k} \; d_k
\end{aligned} \qquad \ldots (2.4)$$

Hence the generator matrix will be,

$$G = \begin{bmatrix} 1 & 0 & 0 & \cdots & 0 & P_{11} & P_{12} & P_{1n-k} \\ 0 & 1 & 0 & \cdots & 0 & P_{21} & P_{22} & P_{2n-k} \\ \vdots & \vdots & \vdots & & \vdots & & & \\ \vdots & \vdots & \vdots & & \vdots & & & \\ 0 & 0 & 0 & \cdots & 1 & P_{k1} & P_{k2} & P_{kn-k} \end{bmatrix} \quad \ldots (2.5)$$

Thus, generator matrix G consists of two parts identity matrix I_k and Parity matrix P.

Order of I_k is k × k.

Order of P is k × n − k.

i.e. $\quad G = [I_k \ \ P] \quad \ldots (2.6)$

The generator matrix provides a concise and efficient way of representing linear block code i.e. a code can be written as,

$$C = dG \quad \ldots (2.7)$$

Thus, we need not store all codewors corresponding to all messages but we can generate them with the help of generator matrix which stores only few codewords.

Example 2.3:

Generate all codewords of (7, 4) Linear Block Codes (LBC) for following generator matrix.

$$G = \begin{bmatrix} 1 & 0 & 0 & 0 & 1 & 1 & 0 \\ 0 & 1 & 0 & 0 & 0 & 1 & 1 \\ 0 & 0 & 1 & 0 & 1 & 1 & 1 \\ 0 & 0 & 0 & 1 & 1 & 0 & 1 \end{bmatrix} \quad \ldots (2.8)$$

$$\underbrace{}_{I_k} \quad \underbrace{}_{P}$$

Solution:

We know that,

$$C = dG$$

Here, n = 7, k = 4.

Hence, there will be $2^k = 2^4 = 16$.

Message words we take each message word and multiply with G.

e.g. For message word d = [1 0 1 0]

$$C = [1\ 0\ 1\ 0] \times \begin{bmatrix} 1 & 0 & 0 & 0 & 1 & 1 & 0 \\ 0 & 1 & 0 & 0 & 0 & 1 & 1 \\ 0 & 0 & 1 & 0 & 1 & 1 & 1 \\ 0 & 0 & 0 & 1 & 1 & 0 & 1 \end{bmatrix} \quad \ldots (2.9)$$

$$[1 \cdot 1 \oplus 0 \cdot 0 \oplus 1 \cdot 0 \oplus 0 \cdot 0 = 1$$
$$1 \cdot 0 \oplus 0 \cdot 1 \oplus 1 \cdot 0 \oplus 0 \cdot 0 = 0$$
$$1 \cdot 0 \oplus 0 \cdot 0 \oplus 1 \cdot 1 \oplus 0 \cdot 0 = 1$$
$$1 \cdot 0 \oplus 0 \cdot 0 \oplus 1 \cdot 0 \oplus 0 \cdot 1 = 0$$
$$1 \cdot 1 \oplus 0 \cdot 1 \oplus 1 \cdot 1 \oplus 0 \cdot 0 = 0$$
$$1 \cdot 1 \oplus 0 \cdot 1 \oplus 1 \cdot 1 \oplus 1 \cdot 0 = 0$$
$$1 \cdot 0 \oplus 0 \cdot 1 \oplus 1 \cdot 1 \oplus 0 \cdot 1 = 1]$$
$$= [1\,0\,1\,0\,0\,0\,1]$$

Similarly, we can generate code for all message words which are given below.

Message word	Code word
0 0 0 0	0 0 0 0 0 0 0
0 0 0 1	0 0 0 1 1 0 1
0 0 1 0	0 0 1 0 1 1 1
0 0 1 1	0 0 1 1 0 1 0
0 1 0 0	0 1 0 0 0 1 1
0 1 0 1	0 1 0 1 1 1 0
0 1 1 0	0 1 1 0 1 0 0
0 1 1 1	0 1 1 1 0 0 1
1 0 0 0	1 0 0 0 1 1 0
1 0 0 1	1 0 0 1 0 1 1
1 0 1 0	1 0 1 0 0 0 1
1 0 1 1	1 0 1 1 1 0 0
1 1 0 0	1 1 0 0 1 0 1
1 1 0 1	1 1 0 1 0 0 0
1 1 1 0	1 1 1 0 0 1 0
1 1 1 1	1 1 1 1 1 1 1

From given generator matrix we can write code bits in a code word as,

$$c_1 = d_1$$
$$c_2 = d_2$$
$$c_3 = d_3$$
$$c_4 = d_4$$
$$c_5 = d_1 \times d_3 \times d_4$$
$$c_6 = d_1 \times d_2 \times d_3$$
$$c_7 = d_2 \times d_3 + d_4 \qquad \ldots (2.10)$$

Hence, the generator circuit for above code is shown in Fig. 2.29.

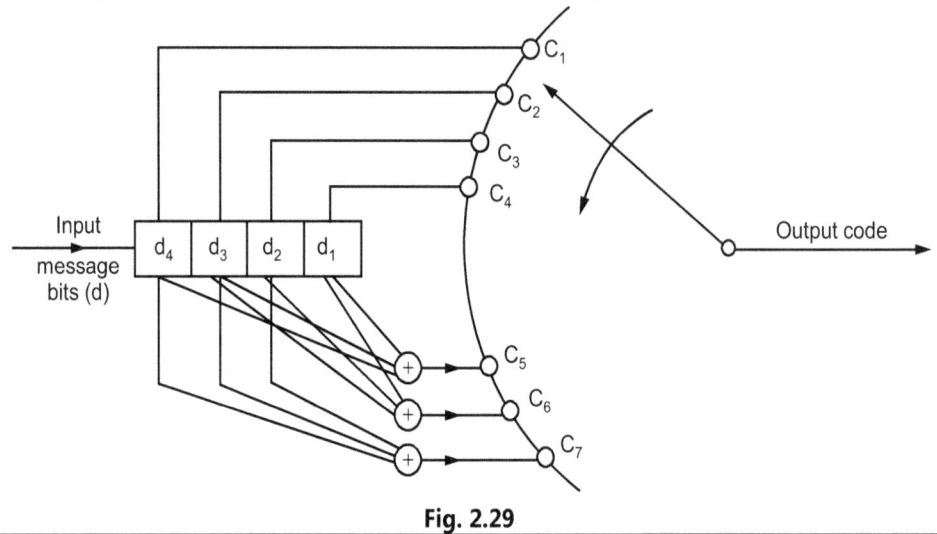

Fig. 2.29

2.8.1.3 Parity Check Matrix

We have seen that generator matrix is used to generate codewords from message words. These codewords will be transmitted through a noisy channel. At the receiver end we have to validate these codewords i.e. they are to be checked whether they are correctly received or not. If not the codewords should be corrected with the help of redundant bits that we have added at the transmitter end. For this, consider a matrix H called parity check matrix which is given by,

$$H = [P_T \ I_{n-k}]_{n-k \times n} \qquad \text{... (2.11)}$$

i.e. H consists of two parts. Transpose of parity matrix whose order will be $n - k \times k$ and identity matrix whose order will be $(n-k) \times (n-k)$.

It can be verified for any codeword C.

$$CH^T = 0 \qquad \text{... (2.12)}$$

i.e. if we multiply any codeword with transpose of parity check matrix H result will be zero-vector.

Thus, the received codeword at the receiver is multiplied with H^T and we get zero vector if the codeword is correctly received. But if multiplication results into non-zero codeword, there will be error in the received codeword.

Substitute C = dG in equation (2.12),

$$d \, G \, H^T = 0$$

Thus, for equation (2.12) to hold true we should have,

$$G \, H^T = 0$$

Now consider, $\quad G = [I_k \ P]$

and $\quad H = [P^T \ I_{n-k}]$

$$G^T = \begin{bmatrix} I_k \\ \overline{P^T} \end{bmatrix}$$

∴
$$H G^T = [P^T \ I_{n-k}] \begin{bmatrix} I_k \\ \overline{P^T} \end{bmatrix}$$

$$= P^T \ H \ P^T$$

$$= 0$$

∴
$$G H^T = 0$$

The process of coding and detection is shown in Fig. 2.30.

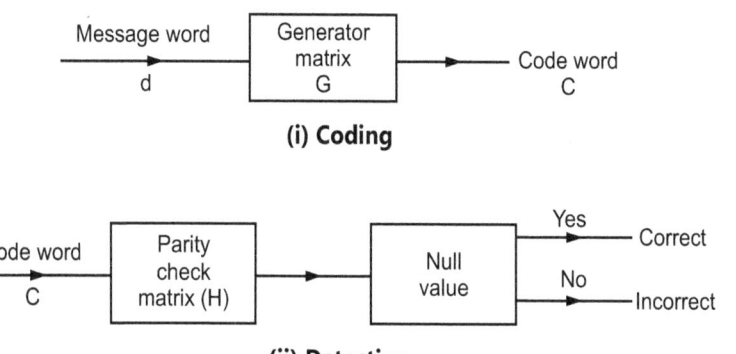

(i) Coding

(ii) Detection

Fig. 2.30

Example 2.4:

Consider a generator matrix given in example 2.3.

$$G = \begin{bmatrix} 1 & 0 & 0 & 0 & 1 & 1 & 0 \\ 0 & 1 & 0 & 0 & 0 & 1 & 1 \\ 0 & 0 & 1 & 0 & 1 & 1 & 1 \\ 0 & 0 & 0 & 1 & 1 & 0 & 1 \end{bmatrix}$$

Find parity check matrix and check whether following codewords are valid or not.

(i) 1 0 0 0 1 1 0

(ii) 0 1 0 1 0 1 1

Solution:

The given generator matrix is of the order 4 × 7.

Hence,
$$n = 7$$
$$k = 4$$

The parity matrix in the generator is,

$$P = \begin{bmatrix} 1 & 1 & 0 \\ 0 & 1 & 1 \\ 1 & 1 & 1 \\ 1 & 0 & 1 \end{bmatrix}$$

Now parity check matrix is given by,

$$H = [P^T \ I_{n-k}]$$

$$= \begin{bmatrix} 1 & 0 & 1 & 1 & 1 & 0 & 0 \\ 1 & 1 & 1 & 0 & 0 & 1 & 0 \\ 0 & 1 & 1 & 1 & 0 & 0 & 1 \end{bmatrix}$$

$$\therefore \quad H^T = \begin{bmatrix} 1 & 1 & 0 \\ 0 & 1 & 1 \\ 1 & 1 & 1 \\ 1 & 0 & 1 \\ 1 & 0 & 0 \\ 0 & 1 & 0 \\ 0 & 0 & 1 \end{bmatrix}$$

To check whether given codewords are valid are not we find CH^T.

(i) Given : $\quad C = [1\ 0\ 0\ 0\ 1\ 1\ 0]$

$$\therefore \quad CH^T = [1\ 0\ 0\ 0\ 1\ 1\ 0] \begin{bmatrix} 1 & 1 & 0 \\ 0 & 1 & 1 \\ 1 & 1 & 1 \\ 1 & 0 & 1 \\ 1 & 0 & 0 \\ 0 & 1 & 0 \\ 0 & 0 & 1 \end{bmatrix}$$

$$= [0\ 0\ 0]$$

Hence, given codeword is valid.

(ii) $\quad C = [0\ 1\ 0\ 1\ 0\ 1\ 1]$

$$CH^T = [0\ 1\ 0\ 1\ 0\ 1\ 1] \begin{bmatrix} 1 & 1 & 0 \\ 0 & 1 & 1 \\ 1 & 1 & 1 \\ 1 & 0 & 1 \\ 1 & 0 & 0 \\ 0 & 1 & 0 \\ 0 & 0 & 1 \end{bmatrix}$$

$$= [1\ 0\ 1]$$

Hence, given codeword is invalid.

2.8.1.4 Minimum Distance and H^T

- Hamming distance between two codewords is the number of positions in which their symbols differ.
- Hamming weight is number of non-zero elements in the codewords.
- The minimum distance d_{min} of a linear block code is the smallest distance between any pair of code vectors in the code.
- From the closure property of linear block codes the sum (or difference) of two codewords is another codeword.
- Minimum distance of a linear block code is the smallest hamming weight of the non-zero codeword in the code.
- Parity check matrix H and in turn generator matrix G is also related to minimum distance d_{min} of a code.
- Since $CH^T = 0$, the number of 1's in code vector C should be such that, corresponding rows of H^T add to zero i.e. corresponding columns of parity check matrix H must add to zero.

Consider the H^T discussed in earlier example.

$$H^T = \begin{bmatrix} 1 & 1 & 0 \\ 0 & 1 & 1 \\ 1 & 1 & 1 \\ 1 & 0 & 1 \\ 1 & 0 & 0 \\ 0 & 1 & 0 \\ 0 & 0 & 1 \end{bmatrix}$$

Now consider a valid code vector.

$$C = [1\ 0\ 0\ 0\ 1\ 1\ 0]$$

There are three non-zero elements at position 1, 5 and 6 and the sum of 1st, 5th and 6th row of H^T is,

$$\begin{bmatrix} 1 \\ 1 \\ 0 \end{bmatrix} + \begin{bmatrix} 1 \\ 0 \\ 0 \end{bmatrix} + \begin{bmatrix} 0 \\ 1 \\ 0 \end{bmatrix} = \begin{bmatrix} 0 \\ 0 \\ 0 \end{bmatrix}$$

- The number of non-zero elements in the code is 3. If you check other codewords in the (7, 4) code discussed earlier, the minimum number of non-zero elements is 3 which is nothing but minimum weight of that code and it is also minimum Hamming distance.
- Hence, the minimum distance of linear block code (d_{min}) is equal to minimum number of rows of H^T (or columns of H) whose sum is equal to zero vector.

2.8.1.5 Decoding of a Linear Block Code

Decoding is a process of detecting and correcting errors when messages in the form of codewords are transmitted on a noisy channel. The important question here is how many errors can we detect and correct. It will depend on the design of the code. The number of errors the code can correct or detect errors is called error correcting or detecting capability of that code.

A code contains certain number of codewords which are at some distance from each other which is specified in terms of Hamming distance.

e.g. Consider the following code.

Message word	Code word
0	0 0 0
1	1 1 1

There are two codewords in the code whose Hamming distance is 3.

When one of the codewords is transmitted the noise or distortion is likely to change some bits. e.g. when 0 0 0 is transmitted we might receive 0 0 1. As long as one codeword is not transformed into another codewords we can detect whether there was error in transmission or not. Thus, the number of errors that can be detected depends on minimum Hamming distance of the code, as it is the minimum distance between any two codewords.

i.e. if a code has Hamming distance d_{min} the number of errors that can be detected is,

$$\boxed{t_d \leq d_{min} - 1} \quad \ldots (2.13)$$

The number of errors that can be corrected also depends on minimum Hamming distance. When a codeword is received with error we have to find which codeword was actually transmitted? Obviously, the codeword nearest to the valid codewords will be the answer. But then the received codeword might be at same Hamming distance from two or more valid codewords. Hence, it is not possible to correct the code with this criteria. Also, if more errors occur, the received codeword will go near to another valid codeword which was not transmitted!

e.g. If 0 0 0 is transmitted and 0 1 0 is received we can make decision in favour of 0 0 0 as 0 1 0 is nearer to 0 0 0 than 1 1 1. But if 0 0 0 is transmitted and 0 1 1 is received we will make decision in favour of 1 1 1 as 0 1 1 is nearer to 1 1 1 than 0 0 0 which is not correct. Hence, this code cannot correct two errors. For error correction capability any two codewords in the code should be separated such that the number of errors (t_c) should result into a received word which is closest to original codeword and away from all other codewords. The condition for this is,

$$\boxed{t_c \leq \frac{d_{min} - 1}{2}} \quad \ldots (2.14)$$

This can be well understood using pictorial view. We can consider the codewords to be placed in spheres separated from each other as shown below.

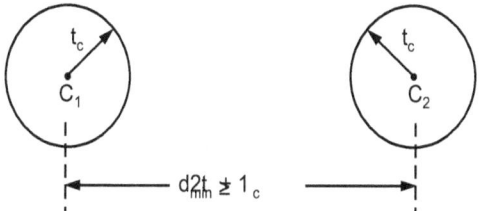

Fig. 2.31 (a): Decoding spheres

The sphere are of radius t_c, where, t_c is number of errors that can be corrected.

If t_c errors occur in code c_1/c_2, the new codeword will be within their spheres and remain nearer to the valid codeword. Hence, the minimum Hamming distance has to be greater than $2t_c + 1$.

If we consider the code C = {0 0 0, 1 1 1}. The codewords will be placed from other possible distortions as below on the vertices of a cube.

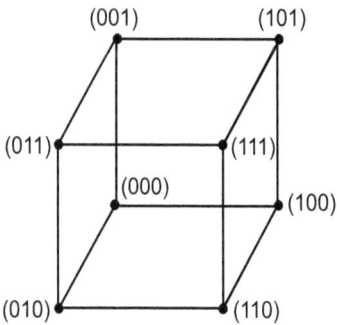

Fig. 2.31 (b): Decoding cube

If (0 0 0) is transmitted and (0 0 1) is received we find 0 0 1 is near to 0 0 0 than (1 1 1). Hence, we can make the correction in favour of (0 0 0).

But if (0 0 0) is transmitted and (0 1 1) is received we find (0 1 1) is nearer to (1 1 1) than (0 0 0), hence we cannot correct the two errors here. Thus, this code has error correcting capability of 1 error. This can be verified from the formula also. The code has $d_{min} = 3$.

$$\therefore \quad t_c \leq \frac{d_{min} - 1}{2}$$

$$\leq \frac{3-1}{2}$$

$$\leq 1$$

Note that, if 0 1 1 is received when 0 0 0 was transmitted, decision will be made in favour of 1 1 1, even though it is incorrect. Here, we assume that probability of occurrence of 2 errors is far less than that of 1 error.

Example 2.5:
Find the error correcting capability of code generated in example 2.4.

Solution:

Code word	Hamming weight
0 0 0 0 0 0 0	0
0 0 0 1 1 0 1	3
0 0 1 0 1 1 1	4
0 0 1 1 0 1 0	4
0 1 0 0 0 1 1	3
0 1 0 1 1 1 0	4
0 1 1 0 1 0 0	3
0 1 1 1 0 0 1	4
1 0 0 0 1 1 0	3
1 0 0 1 0 1 1	4
1 0 1 0 0 0 1	3
1 0 1 1 1 0 0	4
1 1 0 0 1 0 1	4
1 1 0 1 0 0 0	3
1 1 1 0 0 1 0	4
1 1 1 1 1 1 1	7

Since minimum weight of the non-zero codewords is 3.

$$d_{min} = 3$$

$\therefore$ Error correcting capability

$$t_c \leq \frac{d_{min} - 1}{2}$$

$$t_c \leq \frac{3-1}{2}$$

$$t_c \leq 1$$

If the code is such that there is ambiguity in deciding closest codeword, then it is called incomplete decoder. A complete decoder can decode every received word even if there are not more than t_c errors. They will make a good guess about the codeword.

There will be limit on maximum distance, on the code which will be,

$$d_{max} \leq n - k + 1 \quad \ldots (2.15)$$

where, k is number of message bits.

n is number of code bits.

This is called Singleton Bound.

2.8.1.6 Syndrome Decoding

Minimum Hamming distance d_{min} of a code decides error correcting capability of a code. Now, let us see how these errors can be corrected.

The generator matrix (G) is used at the transmitter to generate the code corresponding to message. The parity check matrix can be used to decode the received codeword.

- Let r be the received code vector.
- This code vector may or may not differ from transmitted code vector C.
- Let there be another vector e which will be called error vector defining the corresponding error pattern.
- Hence, $\quad r = C \oplus e \quad \ldots (2.16)$

If there is no error, e will be having all zero symbols. If there are some errors, then there will be that many number of 1's in the corresponding location.

i.e.
$$e_i = \begin{cases} 1 & \text{If an error has occurred in the } i^{th} \text{ location} \\ 0 & \text{Otherwise} \end{cases} \quad \ldots (2.17)$$

The received code vector is multiplied with H^T to get what is called syndrome vector. As we see if received codeword is same as transmitted codeword, this multiplication will result into 0 as $CH^T = 0$.

Since the received code vector is $1 \times n$ and H^T is of the order $n \times n - k$.

The syndrome vector will have $n - k$ bits.

Thus, $\quad S = rH^T \quad$ ... (2.18)

If $r = C$, S will all 0 vector.

If $r \neq C$
$$S = rH^T$$
$$= (C \oplus e) H^T$$
$$= C \cdot H^T \oplus e H^T$$
$$= e H^T \quad ... (2.19)$$

Thus, the syndrome depends on error pattern e.

Another property of the syndrome is that all error patterns that differ by a codeword have the same syndrome. Let us look into this.

Let there be k message bits.

Hence, there will be 2^k codewords $C_1, C_2, C_3, ... C_{2k}$.

Let there be some error pattern e which will also have 2^{k-1} distinct vectors $e_1, e_2, ... e_{2k}$.

$\therefore \quad e_i = e \oplus C_i \quad$ ... (2.20)

Set of vectors $\{e_1, e_2, e_3, ... e_{2k}\}$ is called coset of the code. There will be 2^{n-k} possible cosets of an (n, k) block code.

Now, $\quad e_i \cdot H^T = (e \oplus C_i) H^T$
$$= e H^T \oplus C_i H^T$$
$$= e H^T = S \quad ... (2.21)$$

Thus, each coset of the code is characterised by unique syndrome.

The vector having minimum weight in the coset is called coset leader.

A standard array is constructed using these coset leaders.

In the first row all valid codewords are written starting with all-zero codewords.

In second row we write vector e_2 which is not in first row as coset leader and then write the cosets $e_2 + c$ below each valid code vector. We continue this till all the cosets are listed.

e.g. $\quad C = \{0\,0\,0, 1\,1\,1\}$

Standard array :

Syndrome	Coset Leaders	n-tupes	
0 0	0 0 0	1 1 1	Code vectors
1 1	1 0 0	0 1 1	
1 0	0 1 0	1 0 1	Single errors
0 1	0 0 1	1 1 0	

The decoding procedure for a linear block code will be as below.
1. Compute $S = rH^T$, where, r is received code.
2. Identify the error pattern i.e. coset leader corresponding to the syndrome. let it be e.
3. Compute code vector.

$$C = r \oplus e$$

Example 2.5:

Decoding procedure for (7, 4) block code whose generator matrix is given in example (2.4).

$$G = \begin{bmatrix} 1 & 0 & 0 & 0 & 1 & 1 & 0 \\ 0 & 1 & 0 & 0 & 0 & 1 & 1 \\ 0 & 0 & 1 & 0 & 1 & 1 & 1 \\ 0 & 0 & 0 & 1 & 1 & 0 & 1 \end{bmatrix}$$

Also find the corrected codewords for following received word.

(i) 1 0 0 0 1 1 0   (ii) 0 1 0 1 0 1 1   (iii) 0 0 0 1 1 0 0

Solution:

Step I :

The given code has error correcting capability of 1. Hence, there will be $2^{n-k} = 2^3 = 8$ error single error patterns.

Step II :

The parity check matrix is given by,

$$H = [P^T \; I_{n-k}]$$

$$= \begin{bmatrix} 1 & 0 & 1 & 1 & 1 & 0 & 0 \\ 1 & 1 & 1 & 0 & 0 & 1 & 0 \\ 0 & 1 & 1 & 1 & 0 & 0 & 1 \end{bmatrix}$$

$$\therefore \quad H^T = \begin{bmatrix} 1 & 1 & 0 \\ 0 & 1 & 1 \\ 1 & 1 & 1 \\ 1 & 0 & 1 \\ 1 & 0 & 0 \\ 0 & 1 & 0 \\ 0 & 0 & 1 \end{bmatrix}$$

Step III :

We find syndrome vectors corresponding to each error pattern using,

$$S = e \, H^T$$

e.g. for error pattern 0 0 0 0 0 0 1 the syndrome will be,

$$S = [0\ 0\ 0\ 0\ 0\ 0\ 1] \begin{bmatrix} 1 & 1 & 0 \\ 0 & 1 & 1 \\ 1 & 1 & 1 \\ 1 & 0 & 1 \\ 1 & 0 & 0 \\ 0 & 1 & 0 \\ 0 & 0 & 1 \end{bmatrix}$$

$$= [0\ 0\ 1]$$

Following table gives all syndrome with their error patterns.

Error pattern	Syndrome
0 0 0 0 0 0 0	0 0 0
1 0 0 0 0 0 0	1 1 0
0 1 0 0 0 0 0	0 1 1
0 0 1 0 0 0 0	1 1 1
0 0 0 1 0 0 0	1 0 1
0 0 0 0 1 0 0	1 0 0
0 0 0 0 0 1 0	0 1 0
0 0 0 0 0 0 1	0 0 1

Note : If you observe above syndrome they are nothing but matrix H^T itself !
Thus, if there is single error in i^{th} bit. The syndrome will be i^{th} row of H^T !.

Step IV :

Once above table is ready we can now correct the errors in the received codewords.

(i)   r = [1 0 0 0 1 1 0]

∴   S = r H^T

         = [0 0 0]

Hence, there is no error.

∴   Corrected codeword

         C = r

(ii)   r = [0 1 0 1 0 1 1]

         S = r H^T

         = [1 0 1]

Corresponding error pattern from above table,

         e = 0 0 0 1 0 0 0 [Error in 4th bit]

(iii) Corrected codeword

$$C = r \oplus e$$
$$= [0\ 1\ 0\ 1\ 0\ 1\ 1] \oplus [0\ 0\ 0\ 1\ 0\ 0\ 0]$$
$$= [0\ 1\ 0\ 0\ 0\ 1\ 1]$$

$$r = [0\ 0\ 0\ 1\ 1\ 0\ 0]$$
$$S = r H^T$$
$$= [0\ 0\ 1]$$

∴ Error pattern is,
$$e = [0\ 0\ 0\ 0\ 0\ 0\ 1]$$

∴ Corrected codeword
$$C = r \oplus e$$
$$= [0\ 0\ 0\ 1\ 1\ 0\ 0] + [0\ 0\ 0\ 0\ 0\ 0\ 1]$$
$$= [0\ 0\ 0\ 1\ 1\ 0\ 1]$$

2.8.1.7 Introduction to Cyclic Codes

Cyclic codes are subclass of linear block codes. Generator matrix is used for generating linear block codes. Hence, for higher order codes we have to have large memory requirements and circuit becomes complex. Cyclic codes are linear block codes with an additional constraint. Cyclic codes are very easy to encode. Cyclic codes possess a well defined mathematical structure which makes them efficient in decoding.

Thus, cyclic codes are simple for implementation which is an important feature of cyclic code.

A binary code is said to be cyclic if it satisfies following two fundamental properties.

(i) **Linearity:** The sum of any two codewords in a cyclic code is also a valid codeword.

(ii) **Cyclic property:** A cyclic shift of bits in a codeword gives rise to another valid codeword.

As per the cyclic property if $(c_1, c_2, c_3, \ldots c_n)$ is a codeword, then,

$$(c_2, c_3, \ldots c_n, c_1)$$
$$(c_3, c_4, \ldots c_n, c_1, c_2)$$
$$\vdots$$
$$\vdots$$
$$(c_n, c_1, c_2, \ldots c_{n-2}, c_{n-1})$$

are all codewords in that code.

Example 2.7:

C = {0 0 0 0, 0 1 0 1, 1 0 1 0, 1 1 1 1} is a cyclic code.

As this code satisfies both linearity property and cyclic property.

Example 2.8:

C = {0 0 0, 0 1 0, 0 0 1, 1 0 0, 1 1 1} is not cyclic code. It satisfies cyclic property but does not satisfy linearity property.

2.8.1.8 Polynomials

Cyclic code can be represented in polynomial form. e.g. given a codeword of code C, $c_1, c_2, c_3, \ldots c_n$

We can write it as,

$$c(x) = c_1 x^{n-1} + c_2 x^{n-2} + c_3 x^{n-3} + \ldots + c_{n-1} x + c_n \quad \ldots (2.22)$$

In general, if $a_1, a_2, a_3, \ldots a_n$ are elements of GF(q) then a polynomial of these sequence of elements is expressed as,

$$p(x) = a_1 x^{n-1} + a_2 x^{n-2} + a_3 x^{n-3} + \ldots + a_{n-1} x + a_n \quad \ldots (2.23)$$

- If q = 2, coefficients $a_1, a_2, \ldots$ will be 1 or 0.
- a_1 is called leading coefficient.
- n − 1 is called degree of polynomial.
- If a_1 is unity, it is called monic polynomial.
- Let p[x] represent a set of polynomials in x with coefficients in GF(q). It is called a ring e.g. c[x] will be a set of polynomials of all valid codewords.

These polynomials satisfy first seven of eight properties that define a field.

e.g. addition or multiplication of two polynomials will result into coefficients in GF(q) only. Consider 2 polynomials.

$$a(x) = x + 1$$
$$b(x) = x^3 + x + 1 \text{ defined over GF(2)}$$

Then,

$$\begin{aligned}
a(x) + b(x) &= (x \oplus 1) \oplus (x^3 \oplus x \oplus 1) \\
&= x^3 \oplus [x \oplus x] \oplus [1 \oplus 1] \\
&= x^3 \oplus [1 \oplus 1] x \oplus [1 \oplus 1] \\
&= x^3 + 0x + 0 \\
&= x^3
\end{aligned}$$

$$\begin{aligned}
a(x) \cdot b(x) &= (x^3 \oplus x \oplus 1) \cdot (x \oplus 1) \\
&= x^3 \cdot x \oplus x^3 \cdot 1 \oplus x \cdot x \oplus x \cdot 1 \oplus 1 \cdot x \oplus 1 \cdot 1 \\
&= x^4 \oplus x^3 \oplus x^2 \oplus x \oplus x \oplus 1 \\
&= x^4 \oplus x^3 \oplus x^2 \oplus (1 \oplus 1) x \oplus 1 \\
&= x^4 \oplus x^3 \oplus x^2 + x + 1 \\
&= x^4 + x^3 + x^2 + 1
\end{aligned}$$

(A) Division Algorithm for Polynomials:

Consider two polynomials a(x) and b(x).
If divide a(x) by b(x) [b(x) ≠ 0]
We can write,

$$a(x) = q(x) b(x) + r(x) \quad \ldots (2.24)$$

where, q(x) is quotient.
    r(x) is remainder or residue whose degree will be less than b(x).

e.g. Let $a(x) = x^4 + x^2 + 1$
               $b(x) = x + 1$

```
              x³ + x²          ← q(x)
       ┌──────────────
x + 1  │ x⁴ + x² + 1
         x⁴ + x³
         ─────────
              x³ + x² + 1
              x³ + x²
              ─────────
                       1      ← r(x)
```

Note that in GF(2), $1 - 1 = 0$ and $0 - 1 = -1 = 1$, $1 - 0 = 0$ and $0 - 0 = 0$ which is equivalent to modulo-2 addition. Hence, the subtraction is equivalent to modulo-2 addition.

$$\therefore \quad \underbrace{(x^4 + x^2 + 1)}_{a(x)} = \underbrace{(x^3 + x^2)}_{q(x)} \cdot \underbrace{(x + 1)}_{b(x)} + \underbrace{1}_{r(x)}$$

A polynomial p(x) in p[x] is said to be reducible if p(x) = a(x) · b(x), where a(x) and b(x) are elements of p[x] and degree of a(x) and b(x) are smaller than degree of p(x).

A monic polynomial is a polynomial whose leading coefficient is one.

A monic polynomial which is irreducible and has a degree atleast one is called prime polynomial. Some examples of prime polynomials are x, $x + 1$, $x^2 + 1$, $x^2 + x + 1$, $x^3 + x^2 + 1$, $x^3 + x + 1$, etc.

(B) Representation of Cyclic codes using Polynomials:

We have seen that a codeword can be represented using polynomial as,

$$c(x) = c_1 x^{n-1} + c_2 x^{n-2} + c_3 x^{n-3} + \ldots + c_{n-1} x + c_n$$

e.g. if you are given a code word C = (1 0 1 1 0), it will be written as,

$$C = (1 \quad 0 \quad 1 \quad 1 \quad 0)$$

$$c(x) = 1 \cdot x^4 + 0 \cdot x^3 + 1 \cdot x^2 + 1 \cdot x + 0 \cdot x$$
$$\therefore \quad c(x) = x^4 + x^2 + x$$

We have seen that cyclic code satisfies cyclic property. We can verify that if c(x) is a code polynomial corresponding to a codeword then the remainder after dividing $x^i\, c(x)$ by $x^n + 1$ also represents a valid codeword.

e.g. $x^1 \cdot c(x) = c_1 x^n + c_2 x^{n-1} + c_3 x^{n-2} + \ldots + c_{n-1} x^2 + c_n x$ ... (2.25)

Divide $x^1 c(x)$ by $x^n + 1$ and find remainder.

$$\begin{array}{r} c_1 \\ x^n + 1 \overline{) c_1 x^n + c_2 x^{n-1} + c_3 x^{n-2} + \ldots + c_{n-1} x^2 + c_n x} \\ c_1 x^n + c_1 \\ \hline \text{Remainder} \quad c_2 x^{n-1} + c_3 x^{n-2} + \ldots + c_{n-1} x^2 + c_n x + c_1 \end{array}$$

The remainder represents the codeword

$$C_1 = (c_2, c_3, \ldots c_{n-1}, c_n, c_1) \quad \ldots (2.26)$$

which is a cyclic shifted version of original code word C. Similarly, you can verify that Remainder after divisior of $x^2 c(x)$ and $x^n + 1$ will give rise to another cyclic shifted codeword.

In general,

$$\text{Rem}\left[\frac{x^i \cdot c(x)}{x^n + 1}\right] = c_{i+1} x^{n-1} + c_{i+2} x^{n-2} + \ldots + c_n x^i + c_1 x^{i-1} + \ldots c_i \quad \ldots (2.27)$$

It is denoted as $c'(x)$.

i.e. $c^{(i)}(x) = x^i c(x) \bmod (x^n + 1)$ ... (2.28)

[Mod is a remainder after division operation].

2.8.1.9 A Method for Generating Cyclic Code

Theorem:

Cyclic code polynomial $c(x)$ can be generated using data polynomial $d(x)$ of degree $k - 1$ and a generator polynomial $g(x)$ of degree $n - k$ as,

$$c(x) = d(x) \cdot g(x) \quad \ldots (2.29)$$

where, $g(x)$ is $(n - k)^{th}$ order factor $x^n + 1$.

Proof:

Let $d(x)$ represent data polynomial of k message bits $d_1, d_2, d_3, \ldots d_k$ as,

$$d(x) = d_1 x^{k-1} + d_2 x^{k-2} + d_3 x^{k-3} + \ldots + d_{k-1} x + d_k \quad \ldots (2.30)$$

Now, consider the polynomial.

$$c(x) = d(x) \cdot g(x)$$

∴ $c(x) = d_1 x^{k-1} g(x) + d_2 x^{k-2} + \ldots + d_k g(x)$ ... (2.31)

Since $g(x)$ is $(n - k)^{th}$ order polynomial, $c(x)$ will be of degree $n - 1$ or less. i.e. degree of $c(x)$ will be atmost $n - 1$.

Now, we have to prove that this code is cyclic.

Let,

$$c(x) = c_1 x^{n-1} + c_2 x^{n-2} + \ldots + c_n$$

$$x\,c(x) = c_1 x^n + c_2 x^{n-1} + \ldots + c_n x$$

$$= (c_1 x^n + c_1) + (c_2 x^{n-1} + c_3 x^{n-2} + \ldots + c_n x + c_1) \quad \ldots (2.32)$$

Adding $c_1 \oplus c_2$,

$$= c_1(x^n + 1) + (c_2 x^{n-1} + c_3 x^{n-2} + \ldots + c_n x + c_1)$$

$$= c_1(x^n + 1) + c^{(1)}(x) \quad \ldots (2.33)$$

But,

$$x\,c(x) = x \cdot d(x)\,g(x) \quad \ldots (2.34)$$

Thus, from equations (3.33) and (3.34), we get,

$$x\,c(x) \cdot g(x) = c_1(x^n + 1) + c^{(1)}(x) \quad \ldots (2.35)$$

But $g(x)$ is a factor of $(x^n + 1)$ and if equation (2.35) has to hold good, $c^{(1)}(x)$ also has to be multiple of $(x^n + 1)$. But $c^{(1)}(x)$ is a cyclic shifted version of $c(x)$. Hence, the code $c(x)$ generated by multiplying $d(x)$ and $g(x)$ is cyclic.

Example 2.9:
Find generator polynomial $g(x)$ for a (7, 4) cyclic code and final codewords for following data words.
- (i) 1 1 0 0
- (ii) 1 0 1 0
- (iii) 0 1 1 1

Solution:

Given:
$$n = 7$$
$$k = 4$$

The generator polynomial should be of the degree $n - k = 3$.

The generator polynomial should be factor of $x^7 + 1$.

$$(x^7 + 1) = (x + 1)(x^6 + x^5 + x^4 + x^3 + x^2 + x + 1)$$
$$= (x + 1)(x^6 + x^5 + x^4 + x^3 + x^3 + x^3 + x^2 + x + 1)$$
$$= (x + 1)(x^6 + x^4 + x^3 + x^5 + x^3 + x^2 + x^3 + x + 1)$$
$$= (x + 1)[x^3(x^3 + x + 1) + x^2(x^3 + x + 1) + 1(x^3 + x + 1)]$$
$$= (x + 1)(x^3 + x^2 + 1)(x^3 + x + 1)$$

We have two polynomials of order 3, one of which can be selected as generator polynomial.

Let
$$g(x) = x^3 + x^2 + 1$$

Now, a code is generated using,
$$c(x) = d(x)\,g(x)$$

(i) 1 1 0 0

$$d(x) = x^3 + x^2$$
$$\therefore c(x) = (x^3 + x^2)(x^3 + x^2 + 1)$$
$$= (x^6 + x^5 + x^3 + x^5 + x^4 + x^2)$$
$$= x^6 + x^4 + x^3 + x^2$$
$$= 1.x^6 + 0.x^5 + 1.x^4 + 1.x^3 + 1.x^2 + 0.x + 0.x)$$
$$\therefore c = [1\ 0\ 1\ 1\ 1\ 0\ 0]$$

(ii) 1 0 1 0

$$d(x) = x^3 + x$$
$$c(x) = (x^3 + x)(x^3 + x^2 + 1)$$
$$= x^6 + x^5 + x^3 + x^4 + x^3 + x$$
$$= x^6 + x^5 + x^4 + x$$
$$= 1.x^6 + 1.x^5 + 1.x^4 + 0.x^3 + 0.x^2 + 1.x + 0$$
$$\therefore c = [1\ 1\ 1\ 0\ 0\ 1\ 0]$$

(iii) 0 0 1 1

$$d(x) = x + 1$$
$$\therefore c(x) = (x + 1)(x^3 + x^2 + 1)$$
$$= x^4 + x^3 + x + x^3 + x^2 + 1$$
$$= x^4 + x^2 + x + 1$$
$$= 0.x^6 + 0.x^5 + 1.x^4 + 0.x^3 + 1.x^2 + 1.x + 1$$
$$\therefore c = [0\ 0\ 1\ 0\ 1\ 1\ 1]$$

It can be observed from above example that the code generated is non-systematic code as message bits and parity bits are not in separate blocks.

Example 2.10:

Find generator polynomial for a (7, 3) cyclic code.

Solution:

Given: $\quad n = 7$
$\quad k = 3$

∴ The order of generator polynomial will be,
$\quad n - k = 4$

$g(x)$ will factor of $x^7 + 1$.

$$x^7 + 1 = (x + 1)(x^6 + x^5 + x^4 + x^3 + x^2 + 1)$$
$$= (x + 1)(x^6 + x^5 + x^4 + x^3 + x^3 + x^3 + x^2 + 1)$$

$$= (x + 1)(x^3(x^3 + x + 1) + x^2(x^3 + x + 1) + 1(x^3 + x + 1))$$
$$= (x + 1)(x^3 + x^2 + 1)(x^3 + x + 1)$$
$$= (x^4 + x^3 + x + x^3 + x^2 + 1)(x^3 + x + 1)$$
$$= (x^4 + x^2 + x + 1)(x^3 + x + 1)$$

∴ Generator polynomial of order 4 is,
$$g(x) = x^4 + x^2 + x + 1$$

(A) Systematic Cyclic Code :

In order to encode message sequence into systematic form it is necessary to have message bits and parity bits in separate block in the codeword.

Consider a message polynomial.

$$d(x) = d_1 x^{k-1} + d_2 x^{k-2} + \ldots + d_k \qquad \ldots (2.36)$$

Multiply above polynomial by x^{n-k}.

where,   n = Number of code bits
          k = Number of message bits

∴ $$x^{n-k} d(x) = d_1 x^{n-1} + d_2 x^{n-2} + \ldots + d_k x^{n-k} \qquad \ldots (2.37)$$

Divide equation (3.37) by g(x), we get,

$$\frac{x^{n-k} d(x)}{g(x)} = q(x) + \frac{p(x)}{g(x)} \qquad \ldots (2.38)$$

or

$$x^{n-k} d(x) = q(x) \cdot g(x) + p(x) \qquad \ldots (2.39)$$

Adding p(x) on both sides of equation (3.39), we get,

$$x^{n-k} d(x) \quad + \quad p(x) \quad = q(x) \cdot g(x) \qquad \ldots (2.40)$$
$$\downarrow \qquad\qquad\quad \downarrow \qquad\qquad \downarrow$$

Message bits   Remainder   Code
shifted by n – k   (k – 1) bits

where, q(x) will be quotient after division whose order will be k – 1 or less p(x) is remainder after division of the order n – k – 1.

Since q(x) is of order k – 1 or less and g(x) of order n – k, q(x) · g(x) will be code polynomial.

x^{n-k} d(x) represents d(x) shifted by n – k digits or the left side and since p(x) is of the order k – 1 it represents parity bits.

Thus, procedure for generating systematic cyclic code is as below.

(i) Write d(x) for given message bits.

(ii) Find $x^{n-k} \cdot d(x)$.

(iii) divide $x^{n-k} d(x)$ by g(x) and find remainder p(x).

(iv) Find $c(x) = x^{n-k} d(x) + p(x)$.

(v) Write codeword corresponding to c(x).

Example 2.11:

Construct a systematic (7, 4) cyclic code using generator polynomial $g(x) = x^3 + x^2 + 1$ for the messages.

(i) 1 0 1 0

(ii) 1 0 0 0

Solution:

Given:
$$g(x) = x^3 + x^2 + 1$$
$$n = 7,$$
$$k = 4$$
∴ $$d(x) = x^3 + x$$
∴ $$x^{n-k} d(x) = x^3(x^3 + x)$$
$$= x^6 + x^4$$

```
                    x³ + x² + 1
      x³ + x² + 1 ) x⁶ + x⁴
                    x⁶ + x⁵ + x³
                         x⁵ + x⁴ + x³
                         x⁵ + x⁴ + x²
                              x³ + x²
                              x³ + x² + 1
                                       1   ← p(x)
```

∴ $$c(x) = x^{n-k} d(x) + p(x)$$
$$= x^3(x^3 + x) + 1$$
$$= x^6 + x^4 + 1$$

∴ $$c = [1 0 1 0 0 0 1]$$

(ii) $$d = [1 0 0 0]$$
$$d(x) = x^3$$
$$x^{n-k} d(x) = x^3 \cdot x^3$$

$$
\begin{array}{r}
= x^6 \\
x^3 + x^2 + x \\
\end{array}
$$

$$
x^3 + x^2 + 1 \;\Big)\; \begin{array}{l}
x^6 \\
\underline{x^6 + x^5 + x^3} \\
x^5 + x^3 \\
\underline{x^5 + x^4 + x^2} \\
x^4 + x^3 + x^2 \\
\underline{x^4 + x^3 + x} \\
x^2 + x \quad \leftarrow p(x)
\end{array}
$$

$$
\begin{aligned}
\therefore \quad c(x) &= x^{n-k} d(x) + p(x) \\
&= x^3 \cdot x^3 + x^2 + x \\
&= x^6 + x^2 + x \\
c &= [1\;0\;0\;0\;1\;1\;0]
\end{aligned}
$$

(B) Parity Check Polynomial:

For linear block code we have seen that there is a generator matrix (G) and a parity check matrix (H) pair used at transmitter and receiver respectively.

A cyclic code can be specified by its generator polynomial g(x). There can be another polynomial called parity check polynomial h(x) such that,

$$[g(x) \cdot h(x)] \bmod [x^n + 1] = 0 \qquad \ldots (2.41)$$

or
$$g(x) \cdot h(x) = x^n + 1 \qquad \ldots (2.42)$$

(Analogous to $GH^T = 0$)

The parity check polynomial is of the order k and is specified as,

$$h(x) = 1 + \left(\sum_{i=1}^{k-1} h_i x^i \right) + x^k \qquad \ldots (2.43)$$

- Equation (4.21) shows that just like g(x), h(x) is also a factor of $x^n + 1$.
  e.g. for (7, 4) cyclic code let $g(x) = x^3 + x + 1$.

$$
\begin{aligned}
\therefore \quad x^7 + 1 &= (x + 1)(x^3 + x^2 + 1)(x^3 + x + 1) \\
&= (x^4 + x^2 + x + 1)(x^3 + x + 1) \\
\therefore \quad h(x) &= x^4 + x^2 + x + 1
\end{aligned}
$$

2.8.1.10 Decoding of Cyclic Code

The decoding process of cyclic code is same for both systematic and non-systematic cyclic codes.

Every valid codeword polynomial c(x) is a multiple of g(x). When this codeword is transmitted there may be some errors introduced hence the received codeword polynomial r(x) may not be same as c(x).

If received codeword is same as transmitted codeword then r(x) mod g(x) = 0. Otherwise it will be non-zero polynomial. Consider $\frac{r(x)}{g(x)}$. It can be written as,

$$\frac{r(x)}{g(x)} = q(x) + \frac{s(x)}{g(x)} \qquad \ldots (2.44)$$

where, q(x) is quotient polynomial and s(x) is remainder polynomial also called as syndrome polynomial.

Degree of q(x) will be k – 1 and that of s(x) will be n – k – 1.

r(x) can be written in terms of c(x) as,

$$r(x) = c(x) \oplus e(x) \qquad \ldots (2.45)$$

where, e(x) is an error polynomial decided by the bit error pattern in r(x).

$$\therefore \quad \frac{r(x)}{g(x)} = \frac{c(x) \oplus e(x)}{g(x)} \qquad \ldots (2.46)$$

$$= \frac{c(x)}{g(x)} \oplus \frac{e(x)}{g(x)} \qquad \ldots (2.47)$$

$$\therefore \quad \text{Remainder}\left[\frac{r(x)}{g(x)}\right] = \text{Rem}\left[\frac{c(x)}{g(x)}\right] + \text{Rem}\left[\frac{c(x)}{g(x)}\right] \qquad \ldots (2.48)$$

But Remainder after division of c(x) and g(x) will be zero.

$$\therefore \quad \text{Rem}\left[\frac{r(x)}{g(x)}\right] = \text{Rem}\left[\frac{e(x)}{g(x)}\right] \qquad \ldots (2.49)$$

Comparing equations (2.44) and (2.49), we can write,

$$s(x) = \text{Rem}\left[\frac{e(x)}{g(x)}\right] \qquad \ldots (2.50)$$

Equation (2.50) shows that the syndrome polynomial of error polynomial e(x) is same as received word polynomial.

Thus, the decoding process of a cyclic code will be as below.

If our aim is to only detect errors, then the received codeword polynomial is divided by g(x). If the remainder i.e. syndrome polynomial is zero, there will be no error and if it is non-zero then there will be error. If it is required to correct those errors, then the procedure will be,

    (i)   Prepare a table of error patterns and syndromes using relation (3.50).

    (ii)   Find syndrome after diving received word polynomial r(x) and g(x).

    (iii) Select the error pattern corresponding to the syndrome.

    (iv) Add error pattern to the received codeword.

Example 2.12:

Design (3, 1) cyclic repetition code and its decoding method. Find corrected codewords for –

    (i)   0 1 0

    (ii)   1 1 0

Solution:

Given: n = 3
k = 1

The generator polynomial g(x) order = 3 − 1 = 2.
Generator polynomial should be factor of $x^3 + 1$.
Now, $(x^3 + 1) = (x + 1)(x^2 + x + 1)$
∴ $g(x) = x^2 + x + 1$
Since, k = 1, there will be two message words 0 and 1.

(I) Coding:
(i) d = [0]
$$d(x) = 0$$
$$x^{n-k} d(x) = x^2 \cdot 0 = 0$$
∴ $$p(x) = 0$$
∴ $$c(x) = x^{n-k} d(x) + p(x)$$
$$= 0 + 0$$
$$= 0$$
∴ $$c = [0\ 0\ 0]$$

(ii) d = [1]
$$d(x) = 1$$
∴ $$x^{n-k} d(x) = x^2 \cdot 1$$
$$= x^2$$

To find p(x).

```
              1
x² + x + 1 ) x²
             x² + x + 1
             ─────────
                 x + 1   ← p(x)
```

∴ $$c(x) = x^{n-k} d(x) + p(x)$$
$$= x^2 + x + 1$$
∴ $$c = [1\ 1\ 1]$$

Hence, codewords are

Message	Code
0	000
1	111

(II) Decoding:
Since $d_{min} = 3$

Error correcting capability

$$t_c \leq \frac{d_{min} - 1}{2}$$

$$\leq \frac{3-1}{2}$$

$$\leq 1 \text{ error}$$

The error patterns will be,
    1 0 0
    0 1 0
    0 0 1

Find $s(x) = e(x) \mod g(x)$ for each error pattern.

(i)   For e = 1 0 0

$$e(x) = x^2$$

```
                  1
    x² + x + 1 ) x²
                 x² + x + 1
                 ─────────
                      x + 1  ← s(x)
```

$\therefore \quad s = [1\ 1]$

(ii)   For e = 0 1 0

$$e(x) = x$$

```
                  0
    x² + x + 1 ) x
                 0
                 ─
                 x  ← s(x)
```

$\therefore \quad s = [1\ 0]$

(iii)   For e = 0 0 1

$$e(x) = 1$$

```
                  0
    x² + x + 1 ) 1
                 0
                 ─
                 1  ← s(x)
```

$\therefore \quad s = [0\ 1]$

Hence, syndrome and error vector table will be as below.

Syndrome	Error Vector
1 0 0	1 1
0 1 0	1 0
0 0 1	0 1

Now, let us decode given received words.
(i)   r = 0 1 0

$$\therefore \quad r(x) = x$$

$$\begin{array}{r} 0 \\ x^2 + x + 1 \overline{\smash{)}\ x} \\ 0 \\ \hline x \leftarrow s(x) \end{array}$$

$$\therefore \quad s = [1\ 0]$$

This syndrome corresponds to $e = [0\ 1\ 0]$.

$$\therefore \quad \text{Corrected codeword } c = r \oplus e$$
$$= [0\ 1\ 0] \oplus [0\ 1\ 0]$$
$$= [0\ 0\ 0]$$

(ii) $r = 1\ 1\ 0$

$$\therefore \quad r(x) = x^2 + x$$

$$\begin{array}{r} 1 \\ x^2 + x + 1 \overline{\smash{)}\ x^2 + x} \\ x^2 + x + 1 \\ \hline 1 \leftarrow s(x) \end{array}$$

$$\therefore \quad s = [0\ 1]$$

This syndrome corresponds to $e = [0\ 0\ 1]$

$$\therefore \quad \text{Corrected codeword } c = r \oplus e$$
$$= [1\ 1\ 0] \oplus [0\ 0\ 1]$$
$$= [1\ 1\ 1]$$

2.8.2 Error Detecting Codes

Error detection system consists of encoding procedure similar to error correcting codes but at the receiver end the errors are detected by using pattern checking. The system has a provision of feedback which tells the transmitter to retransmit a message in error.

The number of errors that can be detected $t_d = d_{min} - 1$ where, d_{min} is minimum hamming distance of the code.

The parity check code discussed earlier is an example of error detecting codes. In case of even parity code, there are even number of 1's in the code. If the receiver detects odd number of 1's the received codewords is incorrect. This system will fail if there are even number of errors.

The effectiveness of an error detection code is measured by the probability that the system fails to detect an error. It depends on properties of communication channel.

Following are some examples of error detecting codes.

(i) Parity check code: A parity bit is added to the message such that number of 1's in the code becomes even in case of even parity and odd in case of odd parity. Errors can be detected by wanting number of 1's at the receiver end.

(ii) Two dimensional parity code: k information bits from m messages are arranged in m × k matrix form. Even parity of each row is calculated and stored in k+1th column and even parity of each of m columns is calculated and stored in m+1th row as shown in Fig. 2.32. If there are 3 or less errors anywhere in the matrix, error can be detected as atleast one row will fail the parity check. But some patterns with 4 errors cannot be detected as shown.

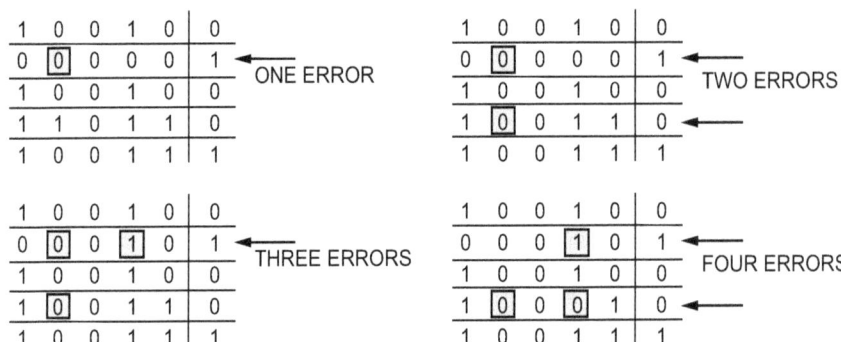

Fig. 2.32: Two dimensional parity code

(iii) Polynomial codes :
- They are used both in error detection as well as error correction as discussed earlier.
- Polynomial codes are easy to implement using shift register.
- Cyclic Redundancy Check (CRC) codes are used to generate check bits for error detection.
- As seen earlier the message, codeword and error vectors are represented in terms of polynomials with binary coefficient.
- The codeword is generated using

$$c(x) = x^{n-k} d(x) + p(x)$$

where,

$$p(x) = \text{Rem}\left[\frac{x^{n-k} d(x)}{g(x)}\right]$$

- Detection involves finding syndrome

$$s(x) = \text{Rem}\left[\frac{r(x)}{g(x)}\right]$$

- If remainder is zero, codeword is correctly received otherwise there will be error.
- Implementation of encoder and detector using shift register is already discussed.

2.8.2.1 Standardized Polynomial Codes

Three polynomials listed below are used as standard polynomials in many applications. They are –

$$\text{CRC-12} - x^{12} + x^{11} + x^3 + x^2 + x + 1$$
$$\text{CRC-16} - x^{16} + x^{15} + x^2 + 1$$
$$\text{CRC-CCITT} - x^{16} + x^{12} + x^5 + 1$$

Recently, CRC-8 and CRC-10 are also recommended for use in ATM networks. They are –

$$\text{CRC-8} - x^8 + x^2 + x + 1$$
$$\text{CRC-10} - x^{10} + x^9 + x^5 + x^4 + x + 1$$

Following two polynomials are also in use.

$$\text{CCITT-16} - x^{16} + x^{12} + x^5 + 1$$
$$\text{CCITT-32} - x^{32} + x^{26} + x^{23} + x^{22} + x^{16} + x^{12} + x^{11} + x^{10} + x^8 + x^7 + x^5 + x^4 + x^2 + x + 1$$

2.8.2.2 Error Detecting Capability of Polynomial Codes

As seen earlier syndrome s(x) is calculated by dividing r(x) with g(x). The error pattern e(x) is given by –

$$e(x) = r(x) \oplus d(x)$$
$$\therefore r(x) = d(x) \oplus e(x)$$
$$\therefore s(x) = \text{Rem}\left[\frac{r(x)}{g(x)}\right]$$
$$= \text{Rem}\left[\frac{d(x) + e(x)}{g(x)}\right]$$
$$= \text{Rem}\left[\frac{d(x)}{g(x)}\right] + \text{Rem}\left[\frac{e(x)}{g(x)}\right]$$
$$= \text{Rem}\left[\frac{e(x)}{g(x)}\right]$$

Thus, we can formulate g(x) that will not divide the given error polynomials.

e.g.

(i) To detect all single errors.

$$e(x) = x^i \qquad 0 \le i \le n-1$$

If g(x) has more than one term, it will not divide e(x).

(ii) To detect all double errors.

$$e(x) = x^i + x^j \qquad 0 \le i \le j \le n-1$$
$$= x^i (1 + x^{j-i})$$

As seen above, x^i is not divisible by $g(x)$. Hence, we should ensure that $1 + x^{j-1}$ is also not divisible by $g(x)$.

For this, $g(x)$ should be a primitive polynomial. Primitive polynomials have the property that, if degree of primitive polynomials is N then smallest value of m for which $1 + x^m$ is divisible by the polynomial is $2^N - 1$. Since $g(x)$ has degree n–k. It will detect all double errors if codeword has length less than or equal to $2^{n-k} - 1$.

The CRC-16 polynomial $x^{16} + x^{15} + x^2 + 1 = (x + 1)(x^{15} + x + 1)$ where, $x^{15} + x + 1$ is primitive. Hence, it can detect all double errors, if $n <= 2^{15} - 1 = 32767$.

(iii) To detect all odd numbered errors : If there are odd numbered errors, $e(x)$ will have odd numbered terms. Such polynomial does not have $x + 1$ as a factor. Hence, by selecting $(x + 1)$ as a factor, $g(x)$ we can detect all odd numbered errors.

(iv) To detect all burst errors. If a burst error of length L occurs starting from i^{th} bit position

$$e(x) = x^i \, b(x)$$

where, $b(x)$ is of degree L–1 representing burst-error pattern. To detect this error, $b(x)$ should not be divisible by $g(x)$. For this, $b(x)$ should have degree less than $g(x)$ i.e. n–k. Thus, we can detect a burst error of length less than or equal to n–k. we can also detect a burst error of length n–k+1, if error pattern does not match $g(x)$. Even we can detect some of the burst errors of length L > n–k+1.

All the CRC polynomials contain $(x + 1)$ as a factor. Hence they can detect all odd number errors. All single and double errors and all burst errors of length ≤ n – k.

2.9 Elementary Protocol

- Automatic repeat request is a combination of error detection and retransmission to ensure reliable data transmission.
- There are two basic types of ARQ protocols –
    (i) Simplex protocols.
    (ii) Sliding window protocols.
- Simplex protocols use stop-and-wait ARQ and sliding window protocols use Go-back-N ARQ and selective repeat ARQ.
- As shown in Fig. 2.33, the data link layer transmits information frames containing header and CRC alongwith payload. The receiving DLL entity checks for errors using CRC. Accordingly, a control frame is sent back to transmitting entity which includes acknowledgement (positive/negative). If positive Acknowledgement (ACK) is received, next frame can be transmitted. In case of Negative Acknowledgement (NAK) retransmission of previous frame (s) is made.

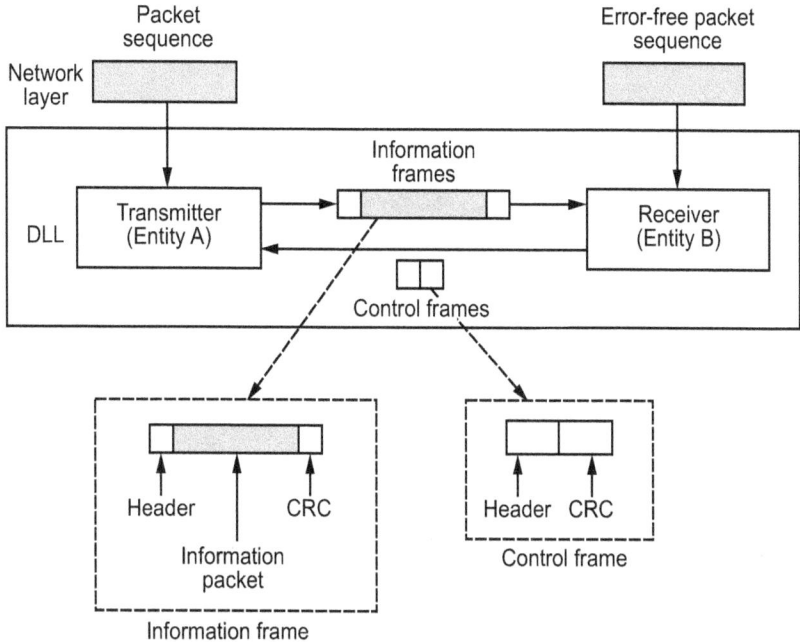

Fig. 2.33: Frame transmission in DLL

2.9.1 Stop and Wait ARQ (Simplex Protocol)

- In this technique transmitter (A) transmits a frame to receiver (B) and waits for an acknowledgement from B.
- When acknowledgement from B is received it transmits next frame.
- Now, consider a case where the frame is lost i.e. not received by B. B will not send an acknowledgement. A will wait and wait and wait ...... To avoid this, we can start a timer at A, corresponding to a frame. If the acknowledgement for a fame is not received within the time timer is on, we can retransmit the frame, as shown in Fig. 2.34 (a).

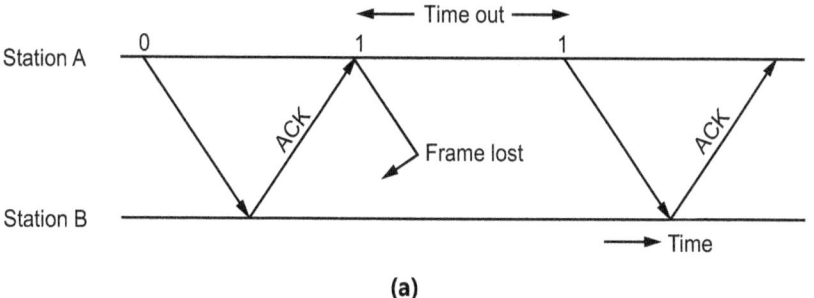

(a)

- Same thing can happen when frame is in error and B does not send acknowledgement. After A times out it will retransmit.
- There is another situation when some frame is transmitted but its acknowledgement is lost as shown in Fig. 2.34 (b).

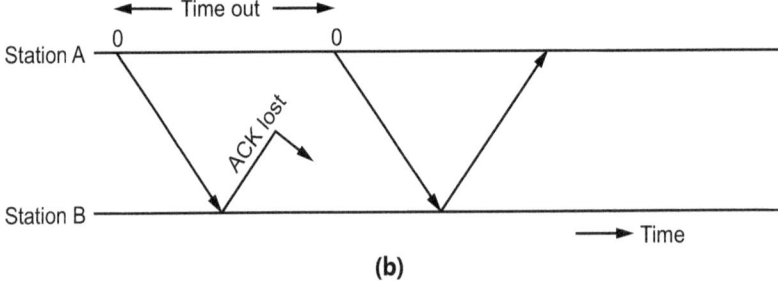

(b)

The time-out will send the same frame again which will result into accepting duplicate frame at B. For this, we have to bring in the concept of sequence number to fames. In case a duplicate frame is received due to loss of Ack, it can be discarded.

- A second ambiguity will arise due to delayed acknowledgement as shown in Fig. 2.34 (c).

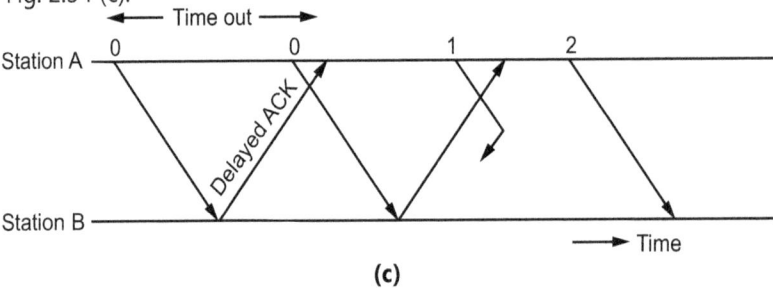

(c)

Fig. 2.34: Stop and Wait ARQ

As shown in figure, the acknowledgement received after frame 1 is transmitted would result into acknowledging frame 1 which is actually lost. We can give sequence number to acknowledgements so that transmitter knows the acknowledgement of which frame is received.

The acknowledgement number will be the number of next frame expected i.e. when frame 0 is received properly, we will be sending Acknowledgement number 1 as frame 1 is expected next.

Now, the next question is what should be the sequence numbers given to frame and acknowledgement. We cannot give large sequence numbers because they are going to occupy some space in frame header. Hence, sequence number should have minimum number of bits.

In stop-and-wait ARQ (simplex) protocol, one bit sequence number is sufficient. For this consider that frame 0 is transmitted the receiver receives and sends acknowledgement number 1. Now, Frame 1 is transmitted and sends acknowledgement for it since frame 0 is already received. We can use same number for next frame as shown in Fig. 2.35.

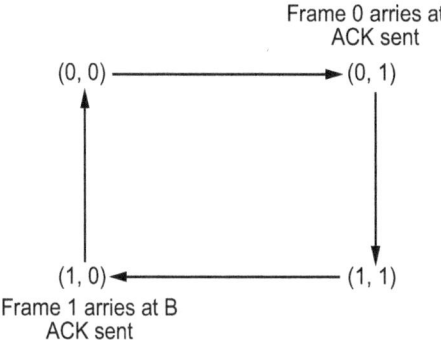

Fig. 2.35: Sequence number for stop and wait ARQ

This ARQ technique is used in IBM's Binary Synchronous Communication (BISYNC) protocol and XMODEM, a file transfer protocol for modems.

2.9.2 Sliding Window Protocol

- The stop-and-wait ARQ is inefficient.
- We can also use full-duplex transmission to transmit and receive from both sides called piggybacking i.e. we send information alongwith acknowledgement.
- The protocols known as sliding window protcols are robust in nature and perform well, inspite of garbled frames, lost frames or premature timeout's.
- In all sliding window protocols, each frame transmitted from transmitter has sequence numbers. They are part of sending window whose size is W_S (Number of frames).
- Each frame received at the receiver is kept in a buffer called receiving window. Its size is W_R (Number of frames).
- There are two soliding window protocols:
  (i) Go-Back-N ARQ.
  (ii) Selective-Repeat ARQ.

2.9.2.1 Go-Back-N ARQ

- Unlike stop-and-wait ARQ, in this technique transmitter continues sending frames without waiting for acknowledgement.
- The transmitter keeps the frames which are transmitted in a buffer called sending window till its acknowledgement is received.

- Let the number of frames transmitter can keep in its buffer be W_S. It is called size of sender's window.
- The size of window is selected on the basis of delay-bandwidth product so that channel does not remain idle and efficiency is more.
- The transmitter keeps on transmitting the frames in window (buffer), till acknowledgement for the first frame in the window is received.
- When frames 0 to $W_S - 1$ are transmitted the transmitter waits for acknowledgement of frame 0. When it is received the next frame is taken from network layer into the buffer i.e. window slides forward by one frame.
- If acknowledgement for an expected frame (i.e. first frame in the window) does not reach back and time-out occurs for the frame, all the frames in the buffer are transmitted again. Since there are $N = W_S$ frames waiting in the buffer this technique is called Go-back-N ARQ.
- Thus, Go-back-N ARQ pipelines the processing of frames to keep the channel busy.
- Fig. 2.36 (a) shows Go-Back-4 ARQ.

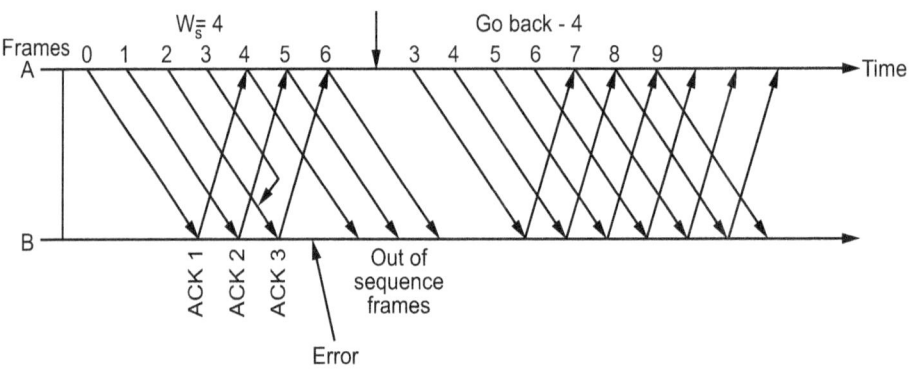

Fig. 2.36 (a)

- It can be seen that the receiver window size will be 1, since only one frame which is in order is accepted.
- Also, the expected frame number at the receiver end is always less than or equal to recently transmitted frame.
- What should be the maximum window size at the transmitter i.e. what should be value of W_S. It will depend on the number of bits used in sequence number field of the frame. On the face of it, it will look like to you as $W_S = 2^m$ i.e. if 3 bits are reserved for sequence number $W_S = 8$, but it will not ! For this consider following situation shown in Fig. 2.36 (b).

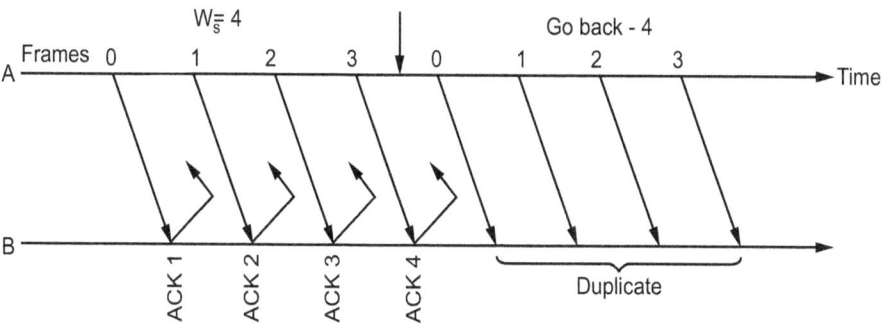

Fig. 2.36 (b)

i.e. if all the frames transmitted are acknowledged or their acknowledgement is lost. The transmitter will retransmit the frames in the buffer. The receiver will accept them as if they are new frames ! Hence, to avoid this problem, we reduce window size by 1 i.e. $W_S = 2^2 - 1 = 3$ i.e. make it Go-back-3. But the sequence number is maintained from 0 to 3. Now consider fig. 3.36 (c), where the acknowledgements of all the received frames 0, 1, 2 are lost but the receiver is expecting frame 3. Hence, even if we transmit 0, 1, 2 again they will not accepted as the expected sequence number does not match transmitted one. Hence, the window size should be $2^m - 1$ for Go-Back-NARQ.

- Go-Back-N can be implemented for both ends i.e. we can send information and acknowledgement together which is called **piggybacking**. This improves the use of bandwidth. Fig. 2.36 (c) shows the scheme.

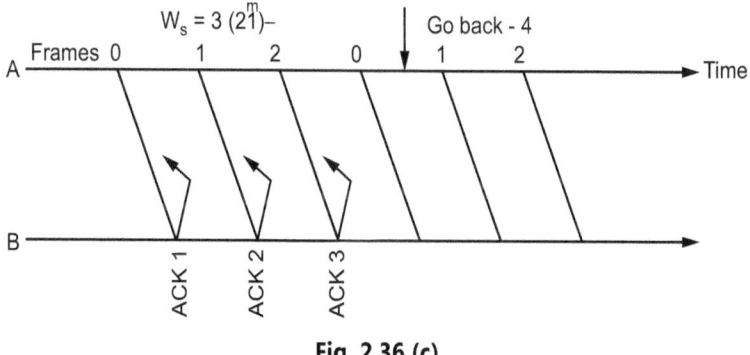

Fig. 2.36 (c)

Fig. 2.36: Go-back-N ARQ

Note that both transmitter and receiver need sending and receiving windows.
- Go-back-N ARQ is implemented in HDLC protocol and V-24 modem standard.

2.9.2.2 Selective Repeat ARQ

- Go-Back-N ARQ is inefficient when channels have high error rates.
- Instead of transmitting all the frames in buffer we can transmit only the frame in error.
- For this, we have to increase the window size of receiver so that it can accept frames which are error free but out of order (not in sequence).
- Normally, when an acknowledgement for first frame is received, the transmit window is advanced. Similarly, whenever acknowledgement for the first frame in receive window is sent it advances.
- Whenever there is error or loss of frame and no acknowledgement is sent, the transmitter retransmits the frame whenever its timer expires. The receiver whenever accepts next frame which is out of sequence now sends negative acknowledgement NAK corresponding to the frame number it is expecting. Till the time the frame is received it keeps on accumulating frames received in the receiver window. Then, it sends the acknowledgement of recently accepted frame that was in error. It is shown in Fig. 2.37 (a).

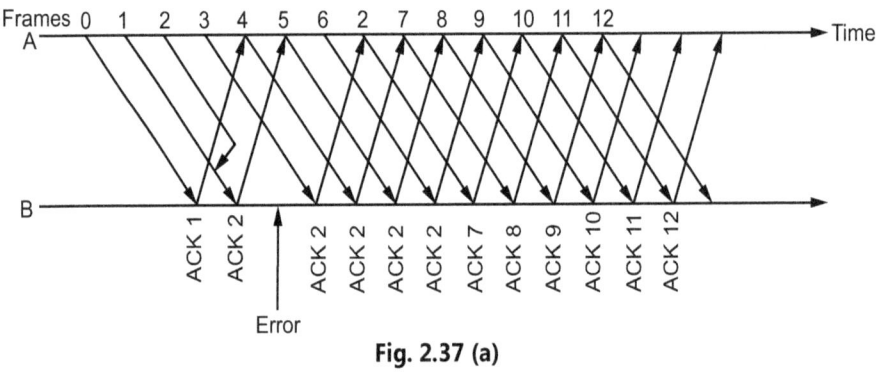

Fig. 2.37 (a)

To calculate the window size for given sequence numbering having m bits, consider the situation in Fig. 2.37 (b).

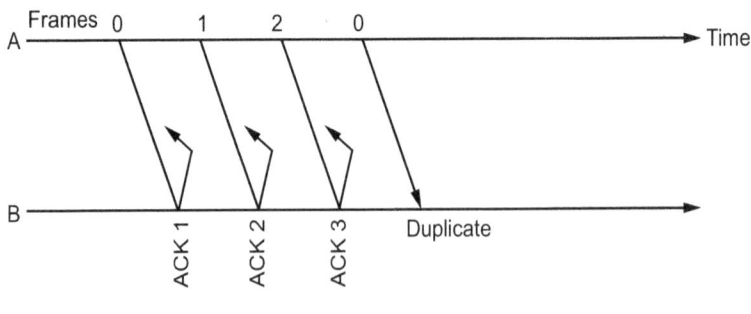

Fig. 2.37 (b)

Let us select window size for m = 2 as $W_S = 2^m - 1 = 3$. Let the frames 0, 1, 2 be in the buffer and are transmitted. They are received correctly but their acknowledgements are lost. Timer for frame 0 expires hence is retransmitted. The receive window is expecting frame 0 which it accepts as new frame but actually, it is duplicate !

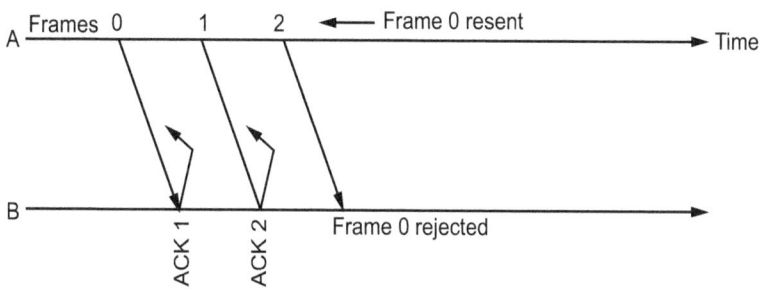

Fig. 2.37 (c)

Fig. 2.37: Selective Repeat ARQ

Thus, the window size at transmitter and receiver are too large. Hence, we select $W_S = W_R = 2^m/2 = 2^{m-1}$. In above case, $W_S = W_R = 2^2/2 = 2$. Sequence numbers for frames will be 0, 1, 2, 3. As shown in Fig. 2.37 (c). The transmitter transmits frames 0, 1. But because of lost acknowledgements, timer for frame 0 expires. Hence, it retransmits frame 0. At the receiver we have expected frames {2, 3}. Hence, frame 0 is rejected as it is duplicate and not part of receive window.

The selective repeat ARQ is used in TCP (Transmission Control Protocol) and SSCOP (Service Specific Connection Oriented Protocol).

2.10 Performance of ARQ Techniques

2.10.1 Stop-and Wait ARQ

Let $T_F \rightarrow$ Frame time

$T_P \rightarrow$ Propagation Delay (One way)

∴ Total time taken to transmitting one frame,

$$= T_F + 2T_P$$

(Neglecting acknowledgement time)

Efficiency or throughput is ratio of time of for one frame to the actual time taken to transmit the frame.

∴ $$\eta = \frac{T_F}{T_t} = \frac{T_F}{T_F + 2T_P}$$

Let R be the rate of transmission.

∴ Number of frame bits = $N_F = T_F \times R$

$$\eta = \frac{\frac{N_F}{R}}{\frac{N_F}{R} + 2T_P}$$

If errors occur the frames are to be retransmitted. Let p be the error probability of frame. Let $\overline{N_r}$ be the average number of retransmissions required to transmit a frame successfully,

∴
$$\overline{N_r} = \sum_{i=1}^{\infty} i \times p \text{ (i transmissions)}$$

$$= \sum_{i=1}^{\infty} i \times p_f^{i-1}(1-p_f)$$

$$= \frac{1}{1-p_f}$$

∴ Efficiency of Stop-and-Wait ARQ.

$$\eta = \frac{T_F}{(T_F + 2T_P) \times \overline{N_r}}$$

$$= \frac{T_F}{(T_F + 2T_P)} \times \frac{1}{1-p_f}$$

$$= \frac{T_F}{T_F + 2T_P} \times (1-p_f)$$

2.10.2 Sliding Window Protocol

If there is no error, W_S frames are successfully transmitted in time $T_F + 2T_P$.

Hence, the efficiency or throughput is given by,

$$\eta = \frac{W_S T_F}{T_F + 2T_P}$$

If rate of transmission is R.

∴
$$T_F = \frac{N_F}{R}$$

$$\therefore \quad \eta = \frac{W_s \times \dfrac{N_F}{R}}{\dfrac{N_F}{R} + 2T_P}$$

If there is an error in the frame Go-BACK-N and Select Repeat ARQ will have different throughput.

(i) Go-BACK-N ARQ :

The average number of retransmission required will be,

$$\overline{N}_r = \sum_{i=1}^{\infty} f(i)\, P_f^{i-1}\, (1-p_f)$$

$$f(i) = 1 + (i-1)k$$

where, k is number of frames retransmitted when error occurs.

$$\overline{N}_r = (1-k) \sum_{i=1}^{\infty} p_f^{i-1}(1-p_f) + k \sum_{i=1}^{\infty} i\, P_f^{i-1}(1-p_f)$$

$$= 1 - k + \frac{k}{1 - p_f}$$

Since, $\quad k = W_s$

$$\overline{N}_r = 1 - W_s + \frac{W_s}{(1-p_f)}$$

$$\therefore \quad \eta = \frac{W_s T_F}{\overline{N}_r (T_F + 2T_P)}$$

$$= \frac{W_s (1 - p_f)}{\left(1 + \dfrac{2T_P}{T_F}\right)(1 - p_f + W_s\, p_f)}$$

(ii) Selective Repeat ARQ :

Since this case is similar to stop-and-wait ARQ where we retransmit only one frame.

$$\overline{N}_r = \frac{1}{1 - p_f}$$

$\therefore$ Throughput $\quad \eta = \dfrac{W_s T_F}{(T_F + 2T_P)} \times (1 - p_f)$

2.11 Data Link Layer in Internet

- Wide-Area Networks are built from a point-to-point leased line. Internet is a wide area network using many point-to-point links.

  The point-to-point connection in internet can be of two types.

  (i) Two or more LANs are interconnected through routers on a leased line.

  (ii) Internet connection to many home users is provided through a dial-up line which is point-to-point link between Internet Service Provider and home user.

  For both leased line connection and dial-up connection a data link layer protocol is required to provide functions like framing, error control, flow control, addressing, etc.

  The two widely used protocols are:

  (i) Serial Line IP (SLIP).

  (ii) Point-to-Point Protocol (PPP).

2.11.1 Serial Line IP (SLIP)

- It is older internet protocol.
- It is simple.
- The frame consists of flag byte 0XC0 at the end of framing character stuffing is used in case XCO appears in pay load. The stuffed characters are 0XDB and 0XDC in place of 0XC0. If 0XDB appears, it is also stuffed.
- SLIP does TCP and IP header compression by removing them in case of recurrence.
- Drawbacks of SLIP are –

  (i) It supports only IP and no other network layer protocol.

  (ii) It does not implement error detection and correction.

  (iii) Both communicating devices should know each other's IP address in advance.

  (iv) No authentication is provided.

  (v) It is not an approved internet standard.

2.12 Bridges (Interconnecting LANS)

There are number of ways of interconnecting networks.
When two or more networks are interconnected at physical level, we use **repeater**.
At the MAC or Data Link Layer, it is **bridges** that interconnect the networks.
Routers are the devices which interconnect the networks at network layer.
At higher layers these devices are called gateways.
In local area networks because of shared medium, limited amount of traffic can be supported. Hence, if we have to increase the number of stations in LAN, there is limitation. The distance between two stations is also limited. A bridge can be used to interconnect multiple LANs instead of having them on single network.

Bridges are useful in the following situations:
1. Interconnecting LANs located in different buildings.
2. Interconnecting LANs of different types.
3. The LANs using different network layer protocols.

Fig. 2.38 shows interconnection of different networks using a bridge.

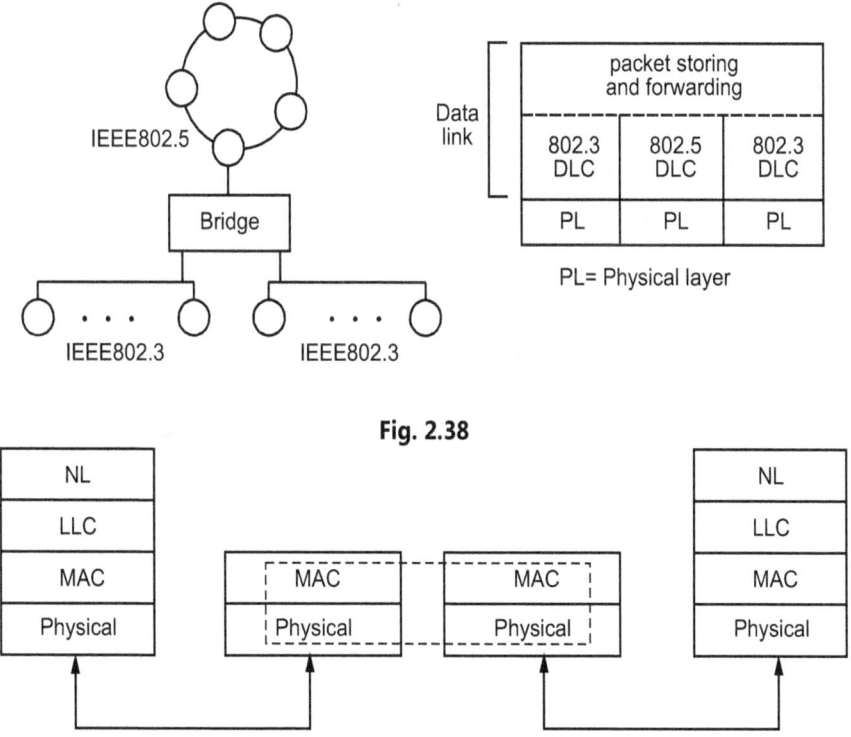

Fig. 2.38

Fig. 2.39: Bridges at MAC layer

Bridges work at MAC layer as shown in Fig. 2.39.

Bridges can examine the frame and packet headers-and control the flow of traffic. They can also filter the frames and hence are useful in implementing security.

Bridges have store and forward capability.

There are two types of bridges –
1. **Transparent bridges.**
2. **Source routing bridges.**

2.12.1 Transparent Bridges

They are used in ethernet LANs. They receive every packet transmitted on every attached LAN.

For each packet they store physical address of sender and port on which the packet was received.

When packet is received on any port, physical address of destination is found and the packet is forwarded to the specified LAN. If not found it is broadcast to all attached LANs.

Bridges have the capability of learning the address of destination's address.

They can also prevent loop in the topology.

2.12.2 Source Routing Bridges

They are used to interconnect token ring networks.

In source routing each station determines the route to the destination when it wants to transmit a frame. Additional routing information is put into the frame. This information is put only if two stations are in different LANs. The presence of this information is indicated by I/G bit in source address field. (It is made 1). The frame format for source routing is shown in Fig. 2.40.

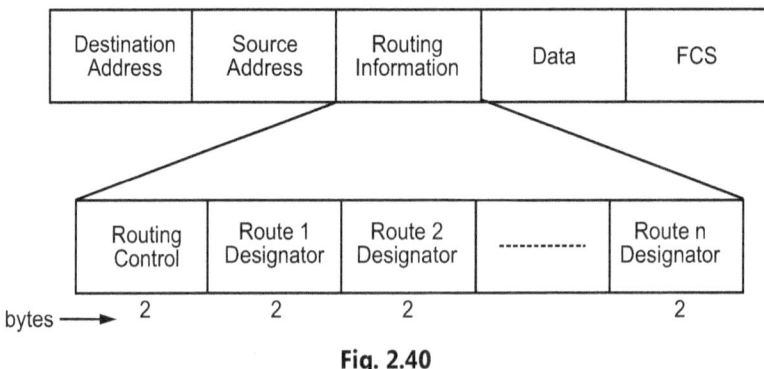

Fig. 2.40

Routing control field defines type of frame, length of routing information field, directions of route given by route designator (left to right or right to left) and largest frame supported over the path.

The route designator field has a 12 bit LAN number and 4 bit bridge number.

Following are points of comparison of the two types of bridges.
1. Transparent bridges are connectionless i.e. each frame is transmitted independently from all others. Source routing bridges are connection oriented as they determine the route using routing frames (discovery frames).
2. Transparent bridges are fully transparent to hosts, whereas source routing bridges are not.
3. Transparent bridges do not require network management, they configure themselves automatically. Source routing bridges require manual configuration.
4. Transparent bridges use spanning tree for routing. Source routing bridges use optimal routing.
5. Backward learning is used for locating destinations in transparent bridges. Source routing uses routing/discovery frames to find route to destination.
6. The failures in transparent bridges are handled by bridges themselves automatically. In source routing failures are handled by hosts.
7. Complexity of transparent bridges is in bridges, whereas source routing puts this complexity of implementation in hosts.

2.13 Switching Introduction

1. When multiple devices want to communicate with each other, then the simple solutions are:
- Mesh network formation.
- Bus network formation.

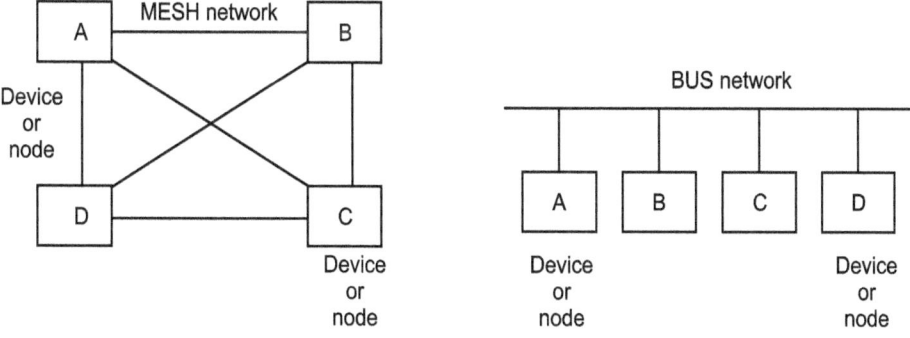

Fig. 2.41: Interdevice communication

2. When the above techniques are employed, it becomes impractical and wasteful when the network size increases.
3. Also network cost and maintenance becomes difficult for large network of devices.
4. Then the solution to the above problems is to use the switching system.
5. Typical use of switch and switching system is as shown in Fig. 2.42.

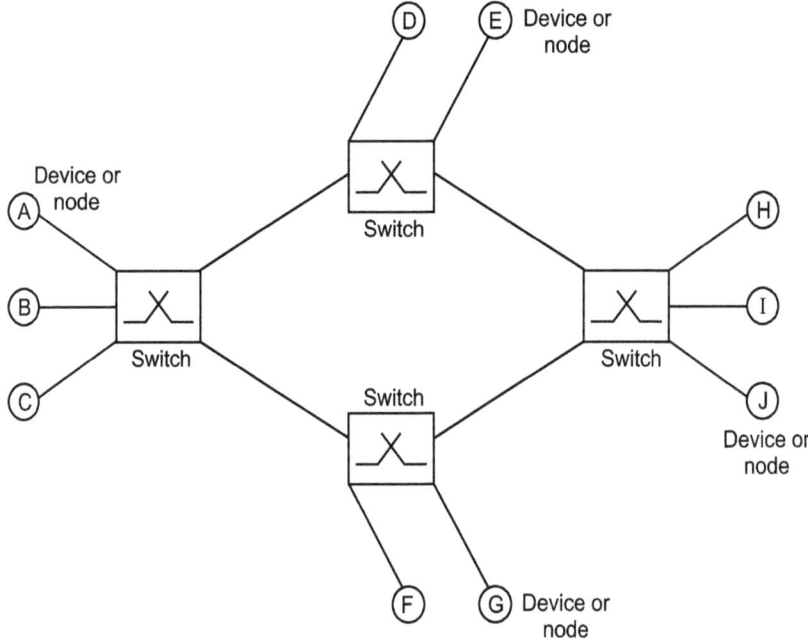

Fig. 2.42: Typical switch based network

6. Thus, different devices/nodes can communicate with each other with the help of switches connected in the typical switch based network.
7. The switches work on the principle of switching system.

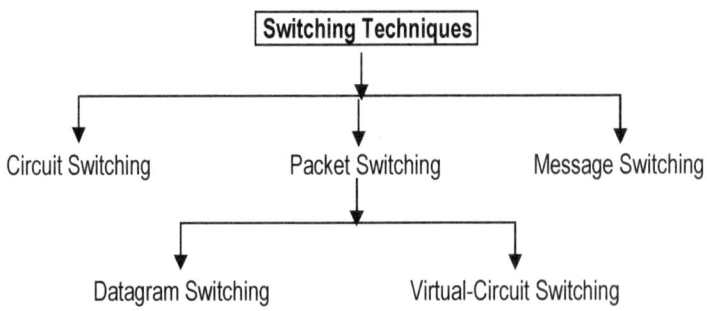

2.14 Circuit Switching Networks

1. In circuit switching networks, nodes or devices are connected to each other by physical links via switches.
2. Typical circuit switched network is as shown in Fig. 2.43.

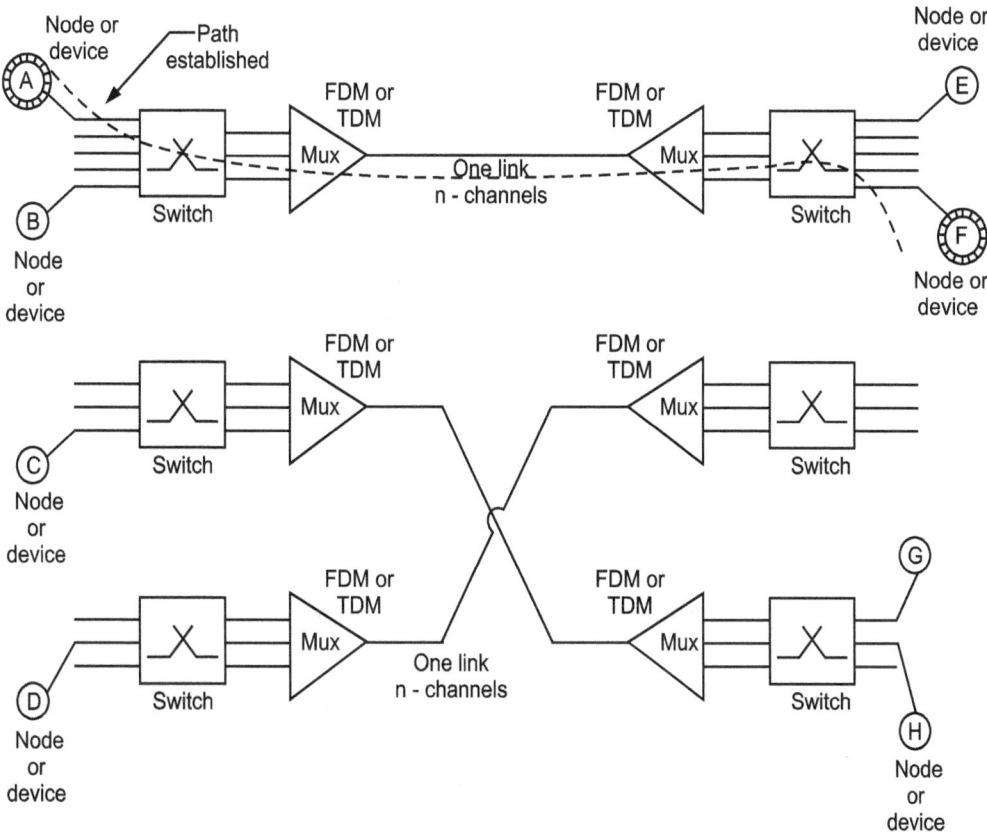

Fig. 2.43: Typical Circuit Switched Network and Communication between Two End Systems A and F

3. In this diagram, the multiplexer (MUX) symbol is explicitly shown and it is implicitly included in the switch fabric itself.
4. The end system can be a computer node or a device like a telephone set.
5. In Fig. 2.43, the communication between the two end systems A and F is highlighted.

6. In circuit switched network, the communication between node 'A' and node 'F' is done through 3 phases as follows:
- **Set-up phase (also known as connection establishment).**
- **Data transfer phase.**
- **Teardown phase (also known as connection release).**

7. **In set-up phase a dedicated circuit** (i.e. combination of channels in links) needs to be established. For this node 'A' sends set-up request through a switch fabric including a multiplexer, to node 'F'. Then node 'F' receives this request and sends acknowledgement to node 'A' through the same dedicated path. Thus, only after receiving this acknowledgement from node 'F', we can say that the connection is established or set-up phase is completed. In this circuit switched network, the end systems use addresses in TDM network whereas they use telephone numbers in FDM network.

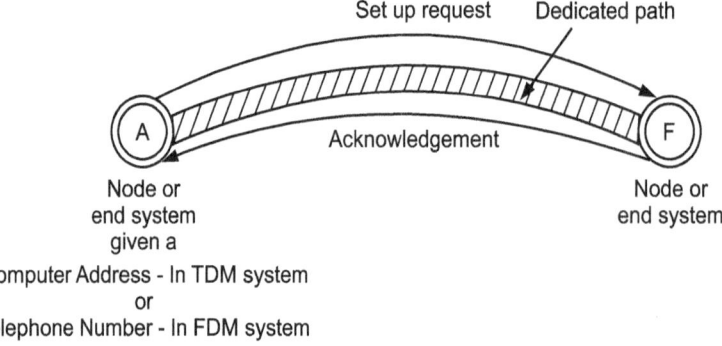

Fig. 2.44: Typical set-up phase between end systems A and F

8. **In data transfer phase**, the end systems 'A' and 'F' can transfer data (or communication between two end systems is done).

9. **In teardown phase (or connection release process)**, either the 'A' system or 'F' system can stop the communication and release the common resources like dedicated link and switch etc.

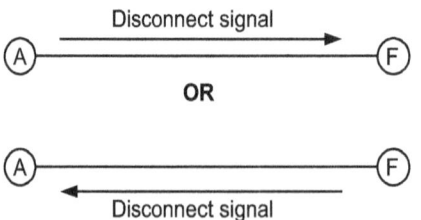

Fig. 2.45: Teardown phase (or connection release process)

10. **The circuit switched network is less efficient as compared to others** because network resources (switch and link) are allocated to 'A' and 'F' node and cannot be used by others or other connections are deprived.
11. The total delay in communication between 'A' and 'F' end systems is given as:

$$\text{Total delay} = \text{Connection establishment delay} + \text{Data transfer delay} + \text{Connection release delay}$$

12. Data transfer delay is also given as:

$$\text{Data transfer delay} = \text{Propagation time delay} + \text{Data transfer time delay}$$

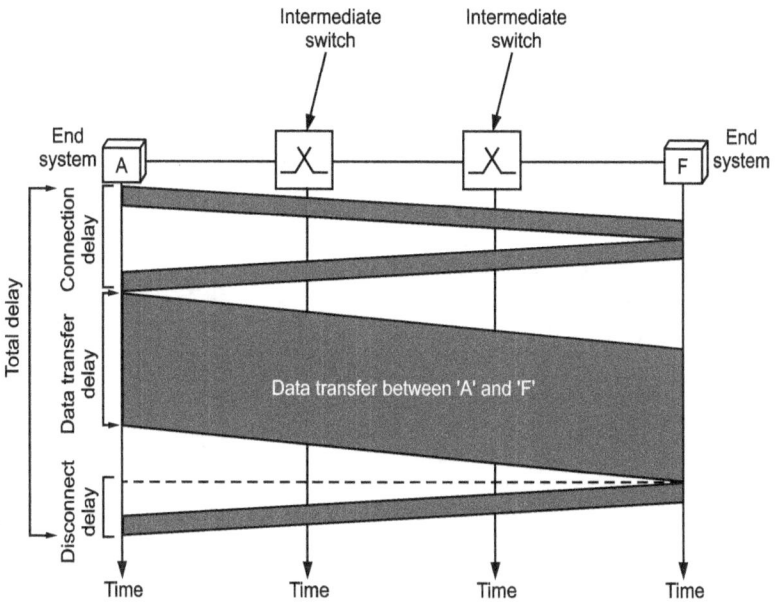

Fig. 2.46: Typical delays in circuit switched network
(Here between two end systems like 'A' and 'F')

13. Thus, typical example or application of a circuit switched network in a telephone communication is as shown in Fig. 2.47.
14. There is a common misunderstanding that circuit switching is used only for connecting voice circuits (analog or digital). The concept of a dedicated path persisting between two communicating parties or nodes can be extended to signal a content other than voice. Its advantage is that it provides for non-stop transfer without requiring packets and without most of the overhead traffic usually needed, making maximal and optimal use of available bandwidth for that communication. The disadvantage of inflexibility tends to reserve it for specialized applications, particularly with the overwhelming proliferation of Internet-related technology.

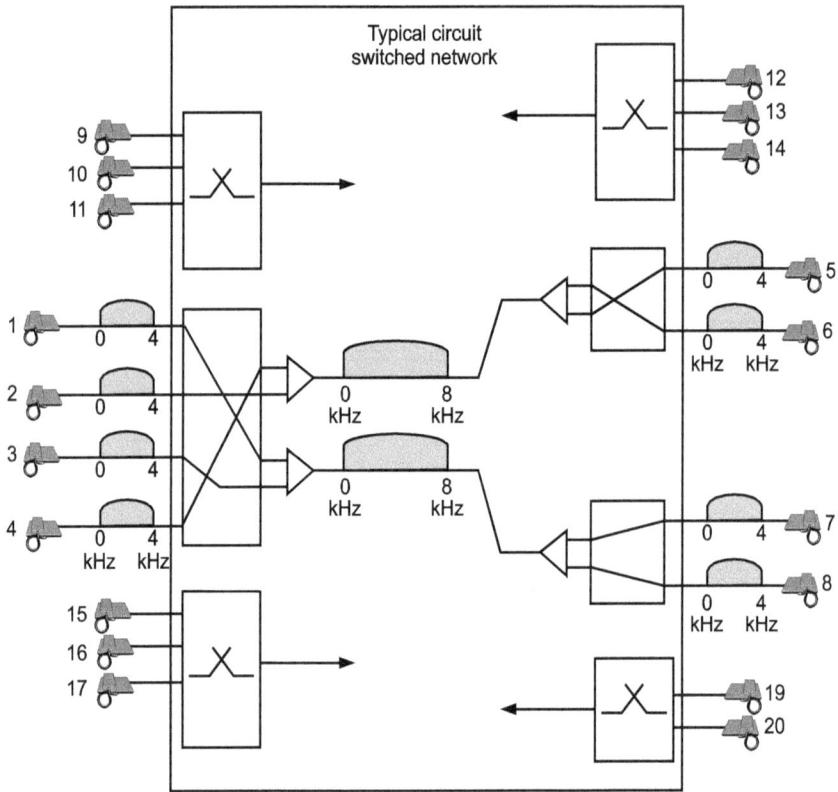

Fig. 2.47: Typical circuit switched network example

15. For call set-up and control (and other administrative purposes), it is possible to use a separate dedicated signaling channel from the end node to the network. **ISDN** is one such service that uses a separate signaling channel while **Plain Old Telephone Service (POTS)** does not.
16. The method of establishing the connection and monitoring its progress and termination through the network may also utilize a separate control channel as in the case of links between telephone exchanges which use SS7 packet-switched signaling protocol to communicate the call set-up and control information and use TDM to transport the actual circuit data. **Signaling System Number** 7 (SS7) is a set of telephony signaling protocols which are used to set-up most of the world's public switched telephone network telephone calls. The main purpose is to set-up and tear down telephone calls.
17. Early telephone exchange is a suitable example of circuit switching. The subscriber would ask the operator to connect to another subscriber, whether on the same exchange or via an inter-exchange link and another operator. In any case, the end result was a physical electrical connection between the two subscribers telephones for the

duration of the call. The copper wire used for the connection could not be used to carry other calls at the same time, even if the subscribers were in fact not talking and the line was silent.

18. Thus, generally, resources are frequency intervals in a **Frequency Division Multiplexing (FDM)** scheme or more recently time slots in a **Time Division Multiplexing (TDM)** scheme.
    - The set of resources allocated for a connection is called a **circuit.**
    - A path is a sequence of links located between nodes called *switches*.
    - The path taken by data between its source and destination is determined by the circuit on which it is flowing and does not change during the lifetime of the connection.
    - The circuit is *terminated* when the connection is closed.

19. In circuit switching, resources remain allocated during the full length of a communication, after a circuit is established and until the circuit is terminated and then the allocated resources are freed.
    - Resources remain allocated even if no data is flowing on a circuit, hereby wasting link capacity when a circuit does not carry as much traffic as the allocation permits.
    - This is a major issue since frequencies (in FDM) or time slots (in TDM) are available in infinite quantity on each link and establishing a circuit consumes one of these frequencies or slots on each link of the circuit.
    - As a result, establishing circuits for communication that carry less traffic than allocation permits can lead to resource exhaustion and network saturation, preventing further connections from being established.
    - If no circuit can be established between a sender and a receiver because of a lack of resources, the connection is *blocked*.

20. A second characteristic of circuit switching is the time cost involved when establishing a connection.
    - In a communication network, circuit-switched or not, nodes need to lookup in a *forwarding table* to determine on which link to send incoming data, and to actually send data from the input link to the output link.
    - Performing a lookup in a forwarding table and sending the data on an incoming link is called *forwarding*.
    - Building the forwarding tables is called *routing*. In circuit switching, routing must be performed for each communication, at circuit establishment time.
    - During circuit establishment, the set of switches and links on the path between the sender and the receiver is determined and messages are exchanged on all the links between the two end hosts of the communication in order to make the resource allocation and build the routing tables.
    - In circuit switching, forwarding tables are hardwired or implemented using fast hardware, making data forwarding at each switch almost instantaneous.

- Therefore, circuit switching is well suited for long-lasting connections where the initial circuit establishment time cost is balanced by the low forwarding time cost.
21. The circuit identifier (a range of frequencies in FDM or a time slot position in a TDM frame) is changed by each switch at forwarding time so that switches do not need to have a complete knowledge of all circuits established in the network but rather only local knowledge of available identifiers at a link.
    - Using local identifiers instead of global identifiers for circuits also enables networks to handle a larger number of circuits.
22. *Traffic Engineering* (TE) consists in optimizing resource utilization in a network by choosing appropriate paths followed by flow of data, according to static or dynamic constraints.
    - A main goal of traffic engineering is to balance the load in the network, i.e., to avoid congestion on links on a network while other links are under-utilized.
    - To achieve such goals, traffic engineering methods can vary from offline capacity planning algorithms to automatic, dynamic changes.
    - Since circuit switching allocates a fixed path for each flow, circuits can be established according to traffic engineering algorithms.
23. On the other hand, circuit switching networks are not reactive when a network topology change occurs.
    - For instance, on a link failure, all circuits on a failed link are cut and communication is interrupted.
    - Special mechanisms that handle such topological changes have to be devised. Traffic engineering can alleviate the consequences of a link failure by pre-planning failure recovery.
    - A back-up circuit can be established at the same time or after the primary circuit used for a communication is set-up, and traffic can be rerouted from the failed circuit to the back-up circuit if a link of the primary circuit fails.
    - Circuit switching networks are intrinsically sensitive to link failures and rerouting must be performed by additional traffic engineering mechanisms.

Examples of Circuit Switched Networks
- Public Switched Telephone Network (PSTN).
- ISDN B-channel.
- Circuit Switched Data (CSD) and High-Speed Circuit-Switched Data (HSCSD) service in cellular systems such as GSM.
- Datakit [It supports file transfers, remote login, remote printing, and remote command execution. At the physical layer, it can operate over multiple media, from slow speed EIA-232 to 500 Mbit fiber optic links (called FIBERKIT)].
- X.21 (Used in the German DATEX-L and Scandinavian DATEX circuit switched data network).

2.15 Message Switching

1. Sometimes there is no need for a circuit to be established all the way from the source to the destination.
2. Consider a connection between the users (A and D) in the figure below (i.e. A and D) is represented by a series of links (AB, BC, and CD).

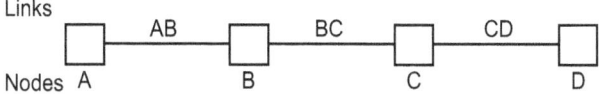

Fig. 2.48: A connection between two systems A and D formed from 3 links

3. For instance, when a telex (or email) message is sent from A to D, it first passes over a local connection (AB).
4. It is then passed at some later time to C (via link BC), and from there to the destination (via link CD).
5. At each message switch, the received message is stored, and a connection is subsequently made to deliver the message to the neighbouring message switch.
6. **Message switching is also known as store-and-forward switching since the messages are stored at intermediate nodes en route to their destinations.**

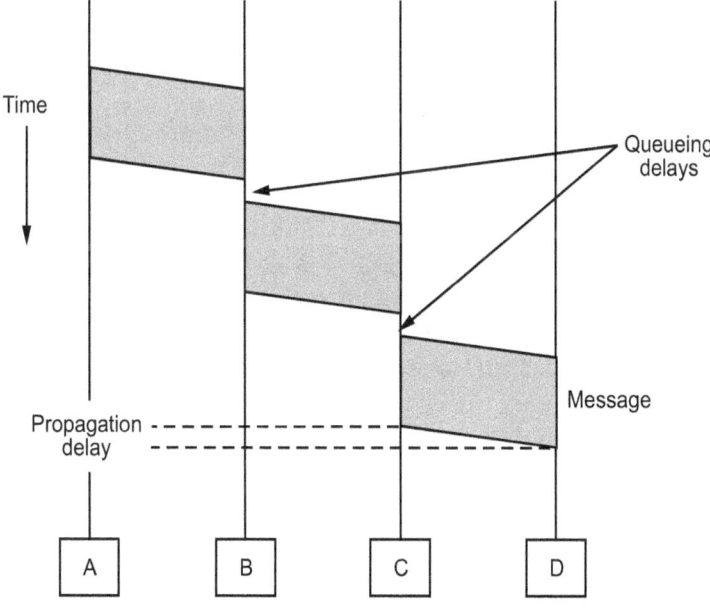

Fig. 2.49: The use of message switching to communicate between A and D

7. The figure illustrates message switching; transmission of only one message is illustrated for simplicity.
8. As the figure indicates, a complete message is sent from node A to node B when the link interconnecting them becomes available.
9. Since the message may be competing with other messages for access to facilities, a queuing delay may be incurred while waiting for the link to become available.
10. The message is stored at B until the next link becomes available, with another queuing delay before it can be forwarded.
11. It repeats this process until it reaches its destination.
12. **Circuit setup delays are replaced by queuing delays.**
13. Considerable extra delay may result from storage at individual nodes.
14. A delay for putting the message on the communications link (message length in bits divided by link speed in bps) is also incurred at each node en route.
15. Message lengths are slightly longer than they are in circuit switching, after establishment of the circuit, since header information must be included with each message; the header includes information identifying the destination as well as other types of information.
16. Most message switched networks do not use dedicated point-to-point links and therefore a call must be set-up using a circuit switched network.
17. The figure below illustrates the use of message switching over a circuit switched network, in this case using one intermediate message switch.

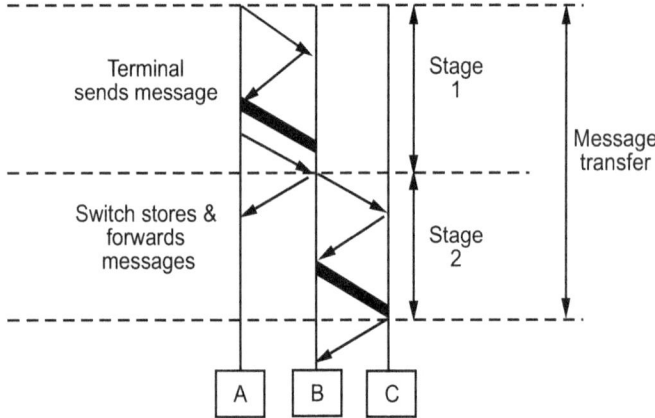

Fig. 2.50: Message Switching illustration

18. **Message switching using circuit switched connections between message switches.**
19. Although message switching is still used for electronic mail and telex transmission, it has largely **been replaced by packet switching** (in fact, most electronic mail is carried using message switching with the links between message switches provided by packet or circuit-switched networks).

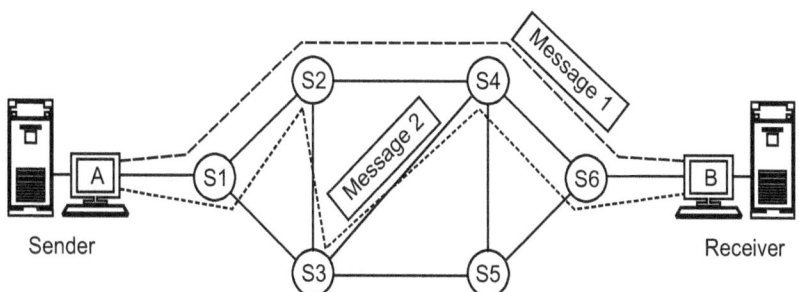

Fig. 2.51: Typical example of message switching network (Message switching forwards the complete message, one switch at a time)

20. Message switching transfers the complete message from one switch to the next, where the message is stored before being forwarded again.
21. Because each message is stored before being sent on to the next switch, this type of network frequently is called a *store and forward network*.
22. The message switches often are general-purpose computers and must be equipped with sufficient storage (usually hard drives, or RAM) to enable them to store messages until forwarding is possible.
23. Message switching is commonly used in email because some delay is permissible in the delivery of email.
24. Message switching uses relatively low-cost devices to forward messages and can function well with relatively slow communication channels.
25. Other applications for message switching include group applications such as workflow, calendaring, and groupware.
26. **Message switching offers the following advantages :**
    - Data channels are shared among communicating devices, improving the efficiency of available bandwidth.
    - Message switches can store messages until a channel becomes available, reducing sensitivity to network congestion.
    - Message priorities can be used to manage network traffic.
    - Broadcast addressing uses network bandwidth more efficiently by delivering messages to multiple destinations.
27. **The Main disadvantage of message switching** is that message switching is not suited for real-time applications, including data communication, video, and audio.

2.16 Packet Switching

1. Packet switching is similar to message switching using short messages.

2. Any message exceeding a network-defined maximum length is broken up into shorter units, known as packets, for transmission; the packets, each with an associated header, are then transmitted individually through the network.
3. The fundamental difference in packet communication is that the data is formed into packets with a pre-defined header format, and well-known "idle" patterns which are used to occupy the link when there is no data to be communicated.
4. Packet network equipment discards the "idle" patterns between packets and processes the entire packet as one piece of data.
5. The equipment examines the packet header information and then either removes the header (in an end system) or forwards the packet to another system.
6. If the out-going link is not available, then the packet is placed in a queue until the link becomes free.
7. A packet network is formed by links, which connect packet network equipment.

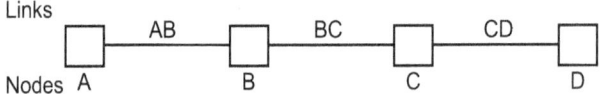

Fig. 2.52: Communication between A and D using circuits which are shared using packet switching

EXERCISE

1. Classify the different transmission media.
2. Write short notes on:
    (a) UTP   (b) STP cable   (c) Coaxial cable
3. What are the Cat3, Cat4, Cat5, Cat 5e cables?
4. Explain Cat6 and Cat7 wires in detail?
5. What is differentiate between thin Ethernet cable and thick ethernet cables?
6. Explain the typical fiber optic communication system.
7. Draw and explain electromagnetic spectrum.
8. Explain the concept and type of microwave communication
9. Write short note on:
    (a) Infrared transmission (b) Terrestrial and satellite microwave transmission
10. Explain elementary protocols: Stop and wait, Sliding window, Slip.
11. Explain Bridges.
12. Differentiate circuit switching, message switching, packet switching network.
13. Write short note on:
    (a) Packet switching network (b) Message switching (c) Circuit switching.

***

Unit III

NETWORK LAYER AND TRANSPORT LAYER

3.1 Introduction to Network Layer

Communication network or subnet consists of switching devices and transmission media as shown in Fig. 3.1.

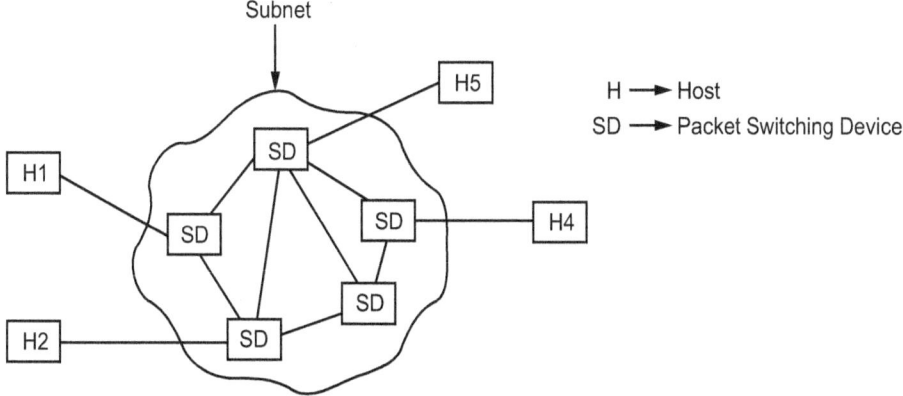

Fig. 3.1: Communication Network

Voice networks use circuit switching. In circuit switching, resources allocated to users who are communicating, are assigned to them only. These resources cannot be shared.

Computer networks use a different approach called Packet Switching, where there is no assignment of resources to fixed users but they can be shared.

Network layer deals with the operation of subnet i.e. transfer of information through the network of networks (Internetwork).

The functions of network layer include finding a path for packet in the network (routing), controlling congestion in the network, identifying the terminal attached in the network using hierarchical addressing as we have to deal with large scale networks.

3.1.1 Circuit Switching and Packet Switching

When there is a dedicated communication path between two stations, it is called circuit switched communication. In this case resources within the network are dedicated to a particular call.

Packet switching communication transmit information in short packets which contain some control information. The control information is used to route the packet through the network and deliver it to the particular destination.

Circuit Switching:

It involves three stages:
  (1) **Circuit establishment:** Before the signal is transmitted, source to destination circuit is established. This can be done using techniques like FDM, TDM, etc.
  (2) **Data transfer:** Once circuit is established between two stations, data is transferred which may be analog or digital.
  (3) **Circuit release:** One of the two stations may initiate termination of the circuit so that the dedicated resources are deallocated.

Circuit Switching was developed to handle voice traffic but is also used to transmit data.

A public telecommunication network is a circuit switching network.

Circuit switching networks have some shortcomings for data traffic.
  (1) Most of the time the line remains idle. Hence, for bursty traffic (data) circuit switching is inefficient.
  (2) The data transmission is at a constant rate hence the two stations must transmit and receive data at the same rate. This limits the utility of network in interconnecting variety of host computers and work stations.

Circuit switching network is shown along with a switch in Fig. 3.2.

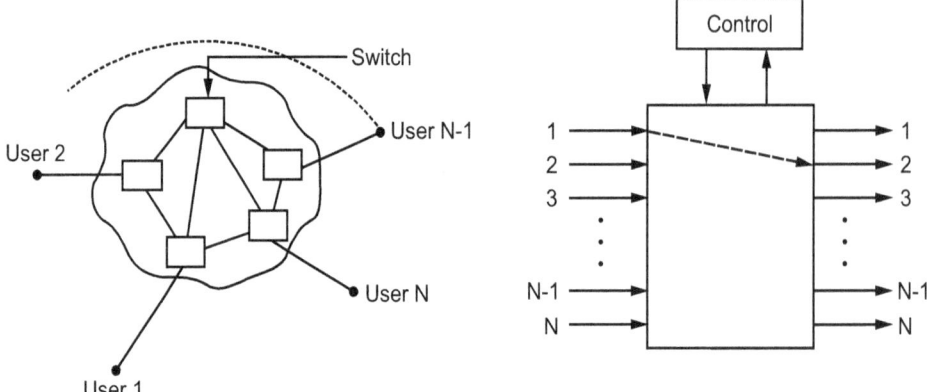

Fig. 3.2: Circuit Switching Network and Switch

There are following types of circuit switching techniques.
  (1) **Space division switching:** They provide a separate physical connection between inputs and outputs.
  (2) **Time division switching:** In this technique, slot within a frame corresponds to a single connection.

Packet Switching:

When a source has some message to be transmitted, it is divided into short packets. Each packet consists of control information called as packet header and the data. A packet switching network is shown in Fig. 3.3.

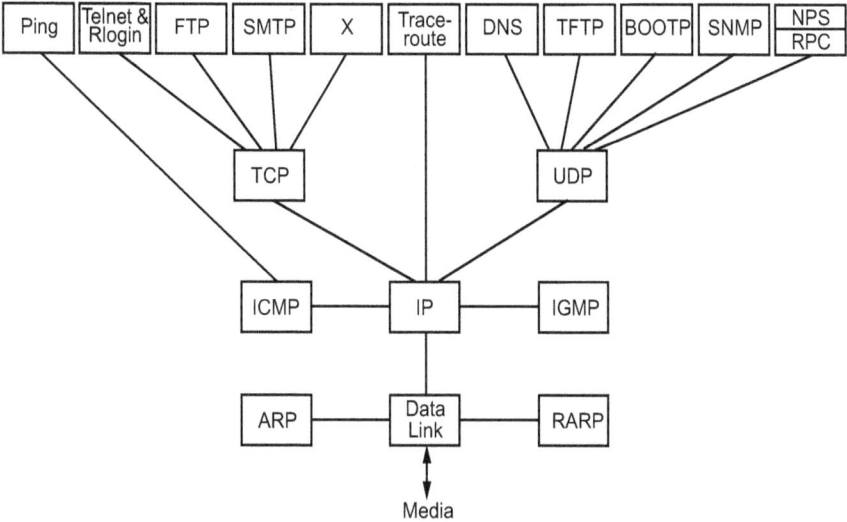

Fig. 3.3: Packet Switching Network

Consider that station A wants to transmit packet to station B. The packet has control information in it. The control information indicates the destination address (B). The packet is sent to appropriate node (switch/router) where it is stored and forwarded to next appropriate node so as to reach the destination B.

The advantages of packet switching over circuit switching are –

(i) Higher line efficiency as node-to-node link can be dynamically shared by many packets over time.

(ii) Data rate conversion can be done. Hence, two stations having different data rate can exchange packets.

(iii) In case of heavy traffic, packets are still accepted but at the cost of delivery delay. Circuit switching refuses to accept connections in such cases.

(iv) Priorities can be used i.e. higher priority packet is delivered faster.

Two different techniques of packet switching are in use:

(i) Datagram.

(ii) Virtual Circuit

In datagram approach, each packet is delivered separately. The path to destination is selected based on routing information contained in packet and information from neighbouring nodes. In virtual circuit approach, a predetermined route is used to deliver packets from a source to destination.

3.1.2 Network Layer Design Issues

- The main function of a network layer is to transfer information among users that are attached to the network or internetwork.
- The network layer provides services to transport layer that operates end to end across network as shown in Fig. 3.4.

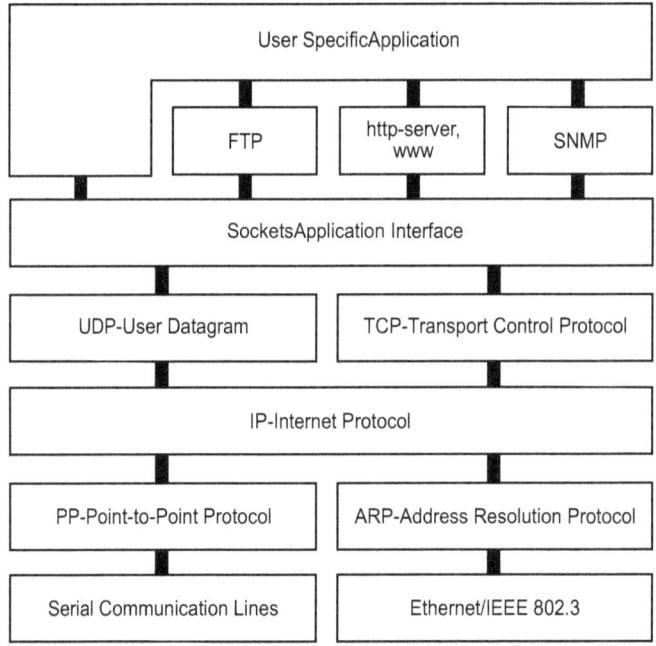

Fig. 3.4: Services provided by network layer to transport layer

- Following are the main goals that are taken into account while designing a network layer services.
    (i) Subnet technology should not affect the services provided by network layer.
    (ii) Transport layer should be shielded from the subnet's number, type and topology.
    (iii) The network addresses made available to the transport layer should use uniform numbering plan.
    The manner in which network layer can provides services to transport layer is irrelevant.
- The services provided by network layer can be connection-oriented or connectionless.
- Connectionless service is very simple. Transport layer requests network layer to send a packet or network layer indicates transport layer that a packet has arrived. The entire responsibility of error control, sequencing and flow control is with transport layer.

- Connection oriented service provided by network layer requires setting up of connection to its peer on receiving side. The connection is given a number which lasts till the connection is not released. While setting up connections, the two entities can negotiate quality and cost of service etc. Communication is duplex and packets are delivered in sequence. Flow control is also implemented.
- Thus, connectionless service is best effort service (like postal service) which puts the complexity in the host. Connection oriented service is reliable service (like telephone system) which puts the complexity in the subnet.
- Network layer can offer any of the following four types of services –
    (i) Best effort connectionless service.
    (ii) Low delay connectionless service.
    (iii) Connection-oriented reliable stream service.
    (iv) Connection oriented transfer of packets with delay and bandwidth guarantee.
- Internet has connectionless service by network layer whereas ATM networks have a connection oriented service.

3.1.3 Virtual Circuits and Datagram

Network layer offers two types of services as seen in previous section viz. connection oriented and connectionless service. There are two ways in which subnet is organised for offering those services.

In case of connection oriented services, the internal operation of network has packets going through a **virtual circuit** along a path from source to destination. Once the virtual circuit is set up between source and destination, packets are simply forwarded through it.

In case of connectionless service, the internal operation of network has packets transferred within the network as datagram. Here no routes are worked in advance and each packet is routed independently i.e. successive packets may take up different routes.

The packets in a virtual circuit follow the same route through the subnet. Each router has information about where to forward the pocket. For this each router maintains a table having one entry of virtual circuit passing through it. The packet travelling through the subnet has a virtual circuit number in the header. With this information router knows on which line it arrived and on which line it should be forwarded. The virtual circuit numbers are selected when a network connection is set up. Virtual circuits can be initiated by any host in the network. When the connection is terminated the virtual circuits are released.

In case of datagrams, the routers do not have table for each open virtual circuits. They maintain a table of outgoing line to be selected for each destination routers. Each datagram contains the full destination address. When a packet arrives at router, the router looks up the outgoing line to use and sends the packet. Routers need not worry about transport layer connections. There is also no need to establish and release of network.

Comparison of Virtual Circuits and Datagram Networks:

Circuit Switching	Virtual Circuit	Datagram
1. Circuit set up required before transmission starts.	1. It requires the circuit to be setup before transmission begins.	1. They do not require the circuit to be set up between source and destination before transmission begins.
2. No routers, only switches required.	2. Each virtual circuit requires large table space in the routers i.e. subet holds the state information.	2. Small table space is required as subnet does not hold state information.
3. All information goes through same route which is selected at the start of transmission.	3. All the packets follow the same route which is selected at the time of setting up virtual circuit.	3. Each packet is routed independently.
4. Failure in subnet can cause problem.	4. All virtual circuits that passed through the failed router need to be terminated. Thus, router failure causes problems in the network.	4. In case router fails, the packets can be diverted to some other router.
5. No congestion control required.	5. Congestion control is easier if enough buffers are allocated in advance for each virtual circuit.	5. Congestion control is difficult as one does not have control over the route followed by a packet.
6. Continuous transmission of data	6. Packet transmission (Bursty).	6. Packet transmission (Bursty).
7. Fast enough for interactive applications.	7. Fast enough for interactive applications.	7. Fast enough for interactive applications.
8. Fixed bandwidth.	8. Dynamic use of bandwidth.	8. Dynamic use of bandwidth.
9. Overhead bits are not there.	9. Overhead bits in each packet.	9. Overhead bits in each packet.
10. Messages are not stored.	10. Packets are stored and forwarded.	10. Packets stored and forwarded.
11. Heavy traffic causes new call setup block but no delay for current calls.	11. Heavy traffic delays the packet delivery. Does not block new calls.	11. Heavy traffic delays packet delivery. Does not block new calls.

3.1.4 Routing Algorithms

- Routing is a major function of network layer. It is concerned with finding feasible and optimum paths for packets from each source to each destination.
- The algorithms that choose the routes and data structures they use are major area of network layer design.
- For a pair of source and destinations there may be number of routes for transferring packets. The best one is decided on what you want to optimize
  e.g. number of hops, delay, cost, etc.
- Routing algorithm should have the following properties:
  (i) Accurate and rapid delivery of packets.
  (ii) Simplicity.
  (iii) Robustness or adaptability to changes in network topology resulting from node or link failures.
  (iv) Adaptability to varying source-destination traffic loads.
  (v) Ability to route packets away from temporarily congested links.
  (vi) Ability to avoid routing loops which make the packets go through the loops.
  (vii) Fairness and optimality i.e. they should be fair to all the packets and must transmit them with optimum value depending on the objective function (delay, cost, etc.). But these two requirements are contradictory.

3.1.4.1 Classification of Routing Algorithms

There are several ways in which we can classify routing algorithm.

(a) Based on responsiveness:

　(i) **Static Routing:** Paths are decided based on network topology, link capacities, etc. Computations are performed offline by a dedicated host and then loaded into the routing table.

They remain fixed for relatively long time.

Problems with static routing are performance hampers in case of increase in network size or change of traffic load. They are also not capable of reacting rapidly to network failures.

　(ii) **Dynamic Routing:** It is adaptive routing. Paths are computed based on information gathered from neighbouring nodes online. The routing tables keep on changing whenever there is change in network topology.

The disadvantage of dynamic routing is complexity added in the node.

(b) Based on Topology:

　(i) **Centralized Routing:** A network control center computes all paths and then uploads this information to the nodes in network.

(ii) **Distributed Routing:** Nodes exchange information among themselves and do their computation. Distributed routing algorithms scale better than centralized algorithms but may produce inconsistent results.

3.1.4.2 Routing Tables

Routing algorithms determines the set of paths which is stored in the routing tables.

Routing tables indicate how to forward packets at each node.

In case of virtual-circuit packet switching network, the routing tables have incoming and outgoing Virtual Circuit Indicator (VCI) pair.

In case of datagram packet switching network, routing tables have number of next node where packet is to be forwarded for a particular destination.

Let us consider a virtual-circuit packet switching network shown in Fig. 3.5 (a).

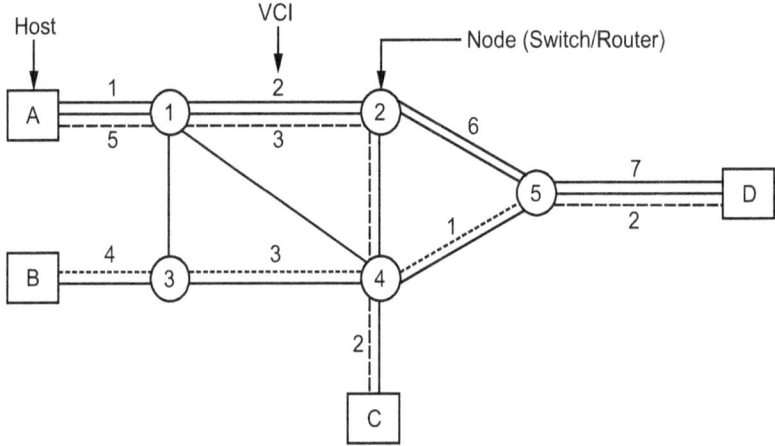

Fig. 3.5 (a): Virtual-Circuit Packet/Switching Network

It shows virtual circuits with the help of various types of lines. These circuits are bidirectional and given number which is same for both directions between two nodes.

There are two circuits between node 1 and node 2.

A packet coming from Host A and VCI 1 will be transferred to Node 2 on VCI 2. It will finally reach Host D.

A packet coming from Host A on VCI 5 will be transferred to Node 2 on VCI 3, it will finally reach Host C.

See that the virtual circuit values are local rather than global. This allows us to set up more virtual circuits. In the packet that is transferred from one node to another there is header field containing virtual circuit number, based on which it is forwarded to next node. This field if 2 bytes long, will allow us to set up 64 K virtual circuits.

The routing table of virtual circuit in Fig. 3.5 (a) is shown in Fig. 3.5 (b).

Node 1

Incoming		Outgoing	
Node	VCI	Node	VCI
A	1	1	2
A	5	1	3
2	3	A	5
2	2	A	1

Node 2

Incoming		Outgoing	
Node	VCI	Node	VCI
2	2	5	6
2	3	4	4
5	6	1	2
4	4	1	3

Node 5

Incoming		Outgoing	
Node	VCI	Node	VCI
2	6	D	7
4	1	D	2
D	7	2	6
D	2	4	1

Incoming		Outgoing	
Node	VCI	Node	VCI
B	4	4	3
4	3	B	4

Incoming		Outgoing	
Node	VCI	Node	VCI
3	3	5	1
2	4	C	2
5	1	3	3
C	2	2	4

Fig. 3.5 (b): Routing table for network in Fig. 3.5 (a)

It consists of incoming and outgoing virtual circuit number e.g. a packet coming from A to node 1 on VCI 1 is to be forwarded to node 2 on VCI 2. Hence, the entry in table at node 1 consists of Incoming node A and VCI 1 and Outgoing node 2 and VCI 2.

The datagram packet switching network is shown in Fig. 3.6 (a).

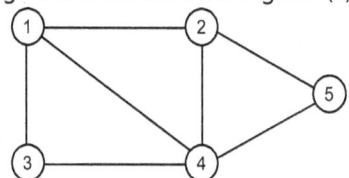

Fig. 3.6 (a): Datagram Packet Switching Network

There is no circuit set up before transmission begins. Routing table for the network is shown in Fig. 3.6 (b). The table is designed based on minimum-hop routing objective.

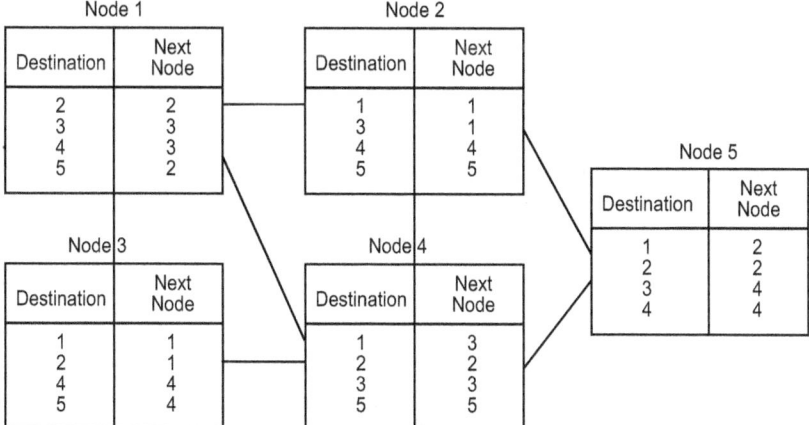

Fig. 3.6 (b): Routing table for datagram network in Fig. 3.6 (a)

Suppose that a packet is to be transmitted from Node 1 to Node 5, then at Node 1, the table indicates that if destination is Node 5 the packet is to be handed over to Node 2. At node 2, the table suggests, the packet is to be handed over to Node 5.

3.1.4.3 Optimality Principle

It is a generalised statement about optimum routes without regard to network topology or traffic:

Statement: If router J is on optimal path from router I to router K, then optimal path from J to K also falls on the same route.

Let R_1 be part of route between I and J.

Let R_2 be the remaining part of route. If route better than R_2 existed from J to K, it could be concatenated with R_1 to improve route from I to K. But we have route R_1R_2 already optimal. Hence, there cannot be other route between J to K other than R_2 which is optimal.

Sink Tree:

A set of optimal routes from all sources to a given destination form a tree whose root is the given destination, is called sink tree. Sink tree is not necessarily unique. Routing algorithms find and use sink trees for all routers.

Fig. 3.6 (c) and (d) show the network and its sink tree.

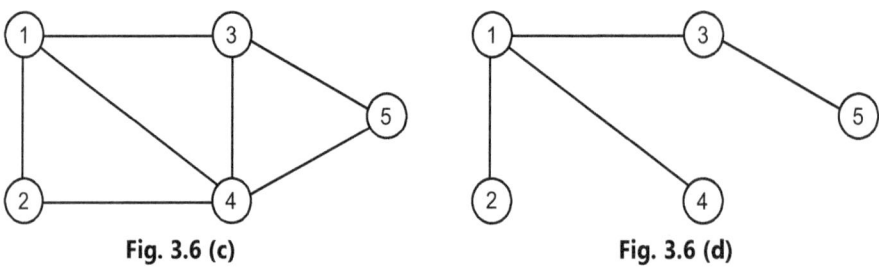

Fig. 3.6 (c) Fig. 3.6 (d)

3.1.5 Shortest-Path Routing

- It is widely used technique and has many variants of it.
- The shortest path algorithm determines shortest path based on some lost criterion.
- To find the shortest path, the subnet is represented in the form of graph consisting of nodes representing routers and edges representing set of links as shown in Fig. 3.7.

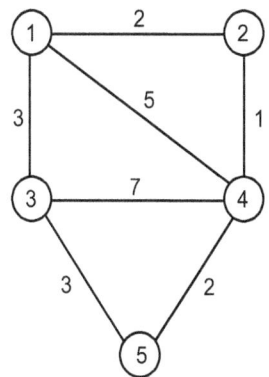

Fig. 3.7: A network represented as graph

- Associated with each link there is a value that represents cost or metric of that link.
- The metric or cost can be any one of the following:
  (1) Number of hops.
  (2) Geographic distance.
  (3) Link capacity.
  (4) Packet delay.
  (5) Congestion.
  (6) Bandwidth.
  (7) Communication cost.
  (8) Average traffic.
- e.g. if number of hops from a source to destination is minimum then that will be shortest path or if the packet goes through a highest capacity link then that will be the optimum path. For this, we have to assign higher cost to lower capacity links.
- Thus, labels on the arcs will be a function of any one of the parameters mentioned above.
- The algorithm then would compute shortest path measured according to any one of the criteria or even group criteria.
- There are two main algorithms that can be used to compute shortest paths.
  (i) Dijkstra's algorithm.
  (ii) Bellman-Ford algorithm.

3.1.5.1 Dijkstra's Algorithm

- It finds a shortest path from a source node to all other nodes in the network.
- It requires that the link costs to be positive.

- The algorithm is iterative and finds closest nodes progressively.
- In the first iteration closest node from source node is found which has minimum cost. This node is neighbour of source node.
- In the second iteration next closest node is found based on information gathered in earlier iteration. This node will be neighbour of source node or node found in earlier iteration.
- This process is repeated till all nodes are included.

Implementation:
- A set of nodes is maintained whose shortest path is determined. Let this set be S. Initially, it will contain only source node.
- At each iteration the next closest node is determined excluding the nodes already in S and is added to S.

  Let d_j be the current estimate of the minimum cost (or distance) from node j to destination.

  Let c_{ij} be the link cost between node i to the node j.

  e.g. in Fig. 3.8 (a), $c_{12} = 4$, $c_{14} = 3$, etc.

- Algorithm:

  (1) Initialization
  $$S = \{s\}$$
  $$d_j = c_{sj} \text{ for all } j \neq s$$
  $$d_s = 0$$

  (2) Find node $i \notin S$ such that
  $$d_i\underset{j \notin S}{} = \min \{d_j\}$$

  Add i to S

  If S contains all nodes stop.

  (3) Update minimum costs of nodes $j \notin S$
  $$d_j = \min \{d_j, d_i + c_{ij}\}$$

  (4) Repeat steps 2 and 3.

  Let us consider an example. Let us find shortest path in the network shown in Fig. 3.8 (a). The steps are as follows.

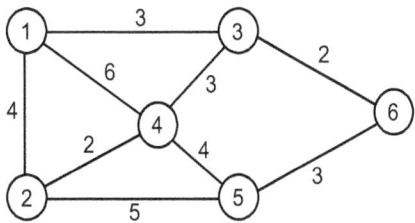

Fig. 3.8 (a): Network showing costs

Let node 1 be the source node.
(1) S = {1}.
(2) $d_2 = 4$, $d_3 = 3$, $d_4 = 6$, $d_5 = \infty$, $d_6 = \infty$.
(Note that d_5 and d_6 are ∞ because they do not have direct path from node 1).

(3) $$d_i = \min_{j \infty S} d_j$$
$$= d_3 = 3$$

(4) Node 3 is added to S.

∴ S = {1, 3}

Now,

$$d_2 = \min(d_2, d_3 + c_{32})$$
$$= \min(4, 3 + \infty)$$
$$= 4$$

$$d_4 = \min(d_4, d_3 + c_{34})$$
$$= \min(5, 3 + 3)$$
$$= 5$$

$$d_5 = \min(d_5, d_5 + c_{35})$$
$$= \min(\infty, \infty)$$
$$= \infty$$

$$d_6 = \min(d_6, d_3 + c_{36})$$
$$= \min(\infty, 3 + 2)$$
$$= 5$$

In the next iteration, we select minimum of d_2, d_4, d_5, d_6 which is $d_2 = 4$ and proceed on the same line as above.

Following table shows all the iterations.

Iteration Number	S	d_2	d_3	d_4	d_5	d_6
Initialize	{1}	4	(3)	6	∞	∞
1	{1, 3}	(4)	–	6	∞	5
2	{1, 3, 2}	–	–	6	9	(5)
3	{1, 3, 2, 6}	–	–	(6)	8	–
4	{1, 3, 2, 6, 4}	–	–	–	(8)	–
5	{1, 3, 2, 6, 4, 5}	–	–	–	–	–

Hence, shortest paths from node 1 are as below and depicted in Fig. 3.8 (b).

Source to Destination Path	Cost
1 – 3	3
1 – 2	4
1 – 3 – 6	5
1 – 4 or 1 – 3 – 4	6
1 – 3 – 6 – 5	8

The routing table at node 1 will have the following entries (Assuming datagram network).

Destination	Next Node	Cost
2	3	4
3	2	3
4	4 or 3	6
5	3	8
6	3	5

Fig. 3.8 (b)

3.1.5.2 Bellman-Ford Algorithm (Distance Vector Routing)

- It is also called Ford-Fulkerson algorithm.
- It is based on optimality principle.
- The estimate of distance to a fixed destination is made.
- We find minimum cost from a node i to destination node as,

$$d_i = \min\{c_{ij} + d_j\} \text{ For all } j \neq i$$

- Initially, the distances d_i's are assumed to be ∞ and destination distance (d_d) will be 0.
- The procedure is repeated till no more updates occur in the iteration.
- Algorithm:
    (1) Initialize

$$d_i = \infty \text{ for all } i \neq d$$
$$d_d = 0 \quad \text{(d is destination node)}$$

(2) Find minimum distance to destination through the neighbours for all $i \neq d$.
$$d_i = \min_j (c_{ij} + d_j) \text{ for all } s \neq i$$

(3) Repeat step 2 until no more changes occur in the iteration.

- Consider the network shown in Fig. 3.8 (c).

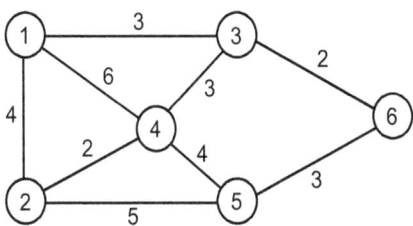

Fig. 3.8 (c): Shortest path for node 1 to other nodes

Let the destination node be 6.

1. Let us maintain a pair (n, d_i) where n is next node along current shortest path and d_i is current minimum cost from node i to destination.
2. Initially, $d_1 = d_2 = d_3 = d_4 = d_5 = \infty$ and $d_6 = 0$.

Iteration 1:

$$d_1 = \min\{c_{12} + d_2, c_{13} + d_3, c_{14} + d_4, c_{15} + d_5, c_{16} + d_6\}$$
$$= \min(\infty, \infty, \infty, \infty, \infty)$$
$$= \infty$$

$$d_2 = \min\{c_{21} + d_1, c_{23} + d_3, c_{24} + d_4, c_{25} + d_5, c_{26} + d_6\}$$
$$= \min(\infty, \infty, \infty, \infty, \infty)$$
$$= \infty$$

$$d_3 = \min\{c_{31} + d_1, c_{32} + d_2, c_{34} + d_4, c_{35} + d_5, c_{36} + d_6$$
$$= \min\{\infty, \infty, \infty, \infty, 2 + 0\}$$
$$= 2 \text{ [Next node 6]}$$

$$d_4 = \min\{c_{41} + d_1, c_{42} + d_2, c_{43} + d_3, c_{45} + d_5, c_{46} + d_6$$
$$= \min\{\infty, \infty, 3 + 2, \infty, \infty\}$$
$$= 5 \text{ [Next node 3]}$$

$$d_5 = \min\{c_{51} + d_1, c_{52} + d_2, c_{53} + d_3, c_{54} + d_4, c_{56} + d_6\}$$
$$= \min\{\infty, \infty, \infty, 4 + 5, 3 + 0\}$$
$$= 3 \text{ [Next node 6]}$$

Repeating on the same line the iterations are shown in the following table.

Iteration Number	Node 1	Node 2	Node 3	Node 4	Node 5
Initialize	(−1, ∞)	(−1, ∞)	(−1, ∞)	(−1, ∞)	(−1, ∞)
1	(−1, ∞)	(−1, ∞)	(6, 2)	(3, 5)	(6, 3)
2	(3, 5)	(4, 7)	(6, 2)	(3, 5)	(6, 3)
3	(3, 5)	(4, 7)	(6, 2)	(3, 5)	(6, 3)

The shortest path is shown in Fig. 3.8 (d).

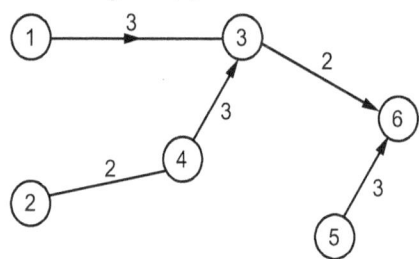

Fig. 3.8 (d): Shortest path to destination 6

- The Bellman Ford algorithm computes cost of a node to each destination independently. These costs are periodically broadcast to its neighbours.
- Since the cost vectors (Distance Vectors) are exchanged among neighbours it is also called **distance vector routing.**
- Whenever there is a failure of link in the network. The Bellman ford algorithm can recompute the minimum cost of exchanging the updated information with neighbours. But then this recomputation requires the convergence to be achieved which makes this algorithm slower.
- Consider Fig. 3.9 where there is failure in link from Node 3 to Node 6.

∴

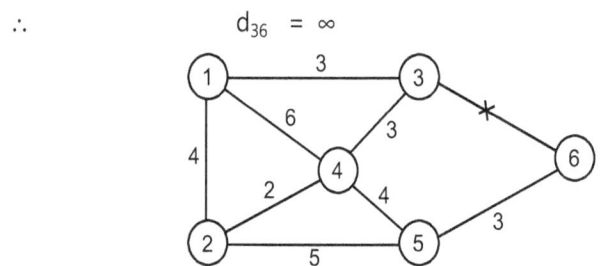

Fig. 3.9: Recomputing cost following break

As a result of which Node 3 recomputes the minimum cost to Node 6 through its neighbours Nodes 1 and 4.

Following equations are used to update the costs.

$$d_{ii} = 0$$
$$d_{ij} = \min\{c_{ik} + d_{kj}\} \text{ for all } k \neq i$$

where, d_{ij} is minimum cost from node i to destination j.

Initially, in our case $d_{16} = 5$, $d_{26} = 7$, $d_{36} = \infty$, $d_{46} = 5$, $d_{56} = 3$ and $d_{66} = 0$.

Thus,

$$d_{36} = \min\{c_{31} + d_{16}, c_{32} + d_{26}, c_{34} + d_{46}, c_{35} + d_{56}, c_{36} + d_{66}\}$$
$$= \min\{3 + 5, \infty, 3 + 5, \infty, \infty\}$$
$$= 1 \text{ or } 4 \text{ [Next Node 1/4]}$$

For next iteration $d_{36} = 8$ which is sent to Node 1 and Node 4.

Node 1 and Node 4 recompute their minimum costs as below parallely.

$$d_{16} = \min\{c_{12} + d_{26}, c_{13} + d_{36}, c_{14} + d_{46}, c_{15} + d_{16}, c_{16} + d_{66}\}$$
$$= \min\{4 + 7, 3 + 8, 6 + 5, \infty, \infty\}$$
$$= 11 \text{ [Next Node 3]}$$

$$d_{46} = \min\{c_{41} + d_{16}, c_{42} + d_{26}, c_{43} + d_{36}, c_{45} + d_{56}, c_{46}, d_{66}\}$$
$$= \min\{6 + 5, 2 + 7, 3 + 8, 4 + 3, \infty\}$$
$$= 7 \text{ [Next Node 5]}$$

This information is broadcast to neighbours of 1 and 4 i.e. Node 1 transmits it to Node 2, 3, and 4 and Node 4 transmits it to nodes 1, 2, 3 and 5. Then they update again. Following table shows updated values at each iteration.

Update	Node 1	Node 2	Node 3	Node 4	Node 5
Before Break	(3, 5)	(4, 7)	(6, 2)	(3, 5)	(6, 3)
1	(3, 5)	(4, 7)	**(4, 8)**	(3, 5)	(6, 3)
2	**(3, 11)**	(4, 7)	(4, 8)	**(5, 7)**	(6, 3)
3	(3, 11)	(5, 8)	(4, 10)	(5, 7)	(6, 3)
4	(2, 12)	(4, 9)	(4, 10)	(5, 7)	(6, 3)
5	(2, 12)	(4, 9)	(4, 10)	(5, 7)	(6, 3)

Reaction to link failure:

(Count-to-infinitely problem)

Bellman-Ford algorithm may react very slowly to a link failure. For this consider the network as shown in Fig. 3.10.

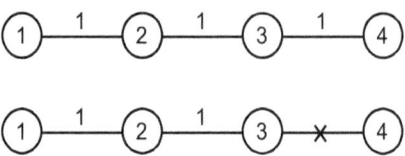

Fig. 3.10: Link-failure leading to count-to-infinity

With Node 4 as destination the distances from each node are $d_1 = 3$, $d_2 = 2$ and $d_3 = 1$. If now link (3, 4) breaks, the recomputation of minimum cost of each node will lead to infinite cost making the destination unreachable. This problem is called count-to-infinity problem.

Update	Node 1	Node 2	Node 3
Before Break	(2, 3)	(3, 2)	(4, 1)
After Break	(2, 3)	(3, 2)	(2, 3)
1	(2, 3)	(3, 4)	(2, 3)
2	(2, 5)	(3, 4)	(2, 5)
3	(2, 5)	(3, 6)	(2, 5)
:	:	:	:
:	:	:	:

During the computation if (3, 4) is restored the algorithm will converge quickly. To avoid count-to-infinity problme, some changes to algorithm are required. Two methods widely implemented for this are:

    (i)   Split Horizon.

    (ii)   Split Horizon with poisoned reverse.

In Split Horizon Method, the minimum cost to a given destination is not sent to neighbour if neighbour is the next node along the shortest path e.g. if node A has best route to node C via. node B then A should not send corresponding minimum cost to B.

Split Horizon with Poisoned reverse method allows a node to send the minimum costs to all its neighbours, but the minimum cost to a given destination is set to infinity if the neighbour is next node along shortest path.

3.1.6 Link State Routing

The distance vector routing discussed in earlier section, takes long time to converge. Secondly, the metric used was queue length which could not take bandwidth into account while selecting a path. Initially, all lines were 65 kbps but later on lines with upgraded bandwidth started coming like 230 kbps, 1.544 Mbps, etc. Hence, not taking bandwidth into account was major problem. Hence, distance vector routing which was used in ARPANET was replaced by link state routing.

The link state routing involves –
    (i)   Discover neighbours and learn their network addresses.
    (ii)   Measure delay or cost of each neighbour.
    (iii) Construct a packet consisting of recently learned information.
    (iv) Send the packet to all routers.
    (v)   Compute shortest path to every other router.

Learning about neighbours:
A special hello packet is sent on each outgoing line from a router. The router on the other end replies telling who it is. When two or more routers are connected to a LAN, then the LAN itself is treated as one node (artificial).

Measuring Line Cost:
Routing algorithms require each router to know delay to each of its neighbours. This delay is measured by sending special ECHO packet so that other side immediately replies. The round trip delay can be measured.

Building Link State Packets:
When the information required for exchange is collected, the router builds a packet containing all the data. The packet has senders identity, sequence number and age and a lot of neighbours. The delay to each neighbour is also given.

Fig. 3.11 shows the link state packets for a subnet. The link state packets are built at regular intervals or whenever there is change of activity in the subnet (e.g. a line or neighbour goes down).

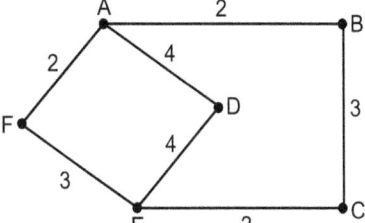

Fig. 3.11: Subnet and its link state packets

Distributing the Link State Packets:
Whenever, link state packets are distributed the routers which get them, change their routes. The basic distribution algorithm, has following steps:
(1) The link state packets are flooded, each packet consists of a sequence number which is incremented for each new packet.
(2) When a new link state packet comes in, it is checked against the list of packets already arrived, if it is new it is forwarded on all lines except the one that it arrived on. If the packet is duplicate, it is discarded.
(3) If the packet with sequence number lower than the highest one arrives, it is rejected.

The problems with above algorithm are –
(1) If sequence number is reset, there will be problem, A 32 bit sequence number is used, which is quiet long.
(2) If a router crashes, there will be no track of sequence number.
(3) If a sequence number is corrupted, some packets will be rejected.

The solution to all those problems is to have another field called age of each packet. This field is decremented once per second. When the age becomes zero, information from that router is discarded.

Computing New Router:
When a router accumulates all the link state packets, the subnet graph can be created. Dijkstra's algorithm can be implemented locally to construct shortest part to all possible destinations. The results of this algorithm are installed in the routing table.
The link state algorithm is used in the following protocols.
(1) OSPF   (2) IS – IS

3.1.7 Flooding
It is a static algorithm.
In this technique, every incoming packet is sent out on every outgoing line except the one from where it arrived.
If each packet switch performs this flooding process the packet will eventually reach the destination provided at least one path exists between source and destination.
This technique is useful when there is no routing information available (say during system startup).
It is also useful when the packets are to be sent to all nodes in the network. (Broadcast). The disadvantage of this technique is that it can cause congestion in the network as multiple copies of packets are created. Flooding can be controlled to avoid excessive number of packets in the network.

(i) We can use a time-To-Live (TTL) field in each packet which is initialized to some value and keeps on decrementing after every hop. If TTL value of a packet becomes zero it is discarded.

(ii) Each node will add an identifier in the header of the packet. If the packet arrives at the node second time it can be discarded by looking at the identifier.

(iii) Each node will have an entry of source address and sequence number of packet in its own memory. If that packet arrives again it is discarded.

A variation of flooding is selective flood in which the packet arriving is not sent on all outgoing lines, but only selected lines based on some criteria.

3.1.8 Flow Based Routing

Shortest path routing algorithm and flooding take into account only topology. If there is a shortest path between source and destination and there is huge amount of traffic on the path then there will be problem. Flow based routing is a static algorithm that uses both topology and the traffic (load) for routing.

If average traffic between each pair of node is relatively stable and predictable, it is possible to analyze the flows mathematically to optimize the routing.

The basic idea behind the analysis is that, for given line, if capacity and average flow are known, we can compute the mean packet delay. From mean delays on all the lines, we can calculate flow weighted average to get the mean packet delay for whole subnet. The routing problem is to find routing algorithm that produces minimum average delay for the subnet.

3.1.9 Hierarchical Routing

When the network is of large sized the routing tables are also large. This requires higher router memory. Time required to scan these tables will also be more.

The size of the routing table can be reduced if the hierarchical approach is used for assignment of addresses. In this technique, the routers are divided into regions. Each router in a region knows how to route the packets within its own region, but doesn't know anything about other regions.

A two level hierarchy can be used for large networks. The hosts that are near to each other will have address that have common prefixes. By examining this prefixes the router knows where to forward the packet. For example, if there are four sites having four hosts each without hierarchical routing, each router need to maintain sixteen entries. If hierarchical routing is used i.e. same prefixes for all hosts at a site then there will be only four entries as shown in Fig. 3.12.

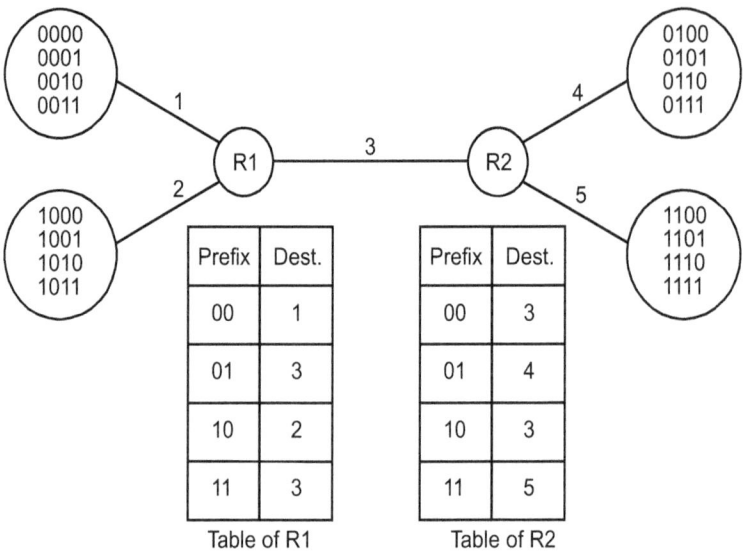

Fig. 3.12: Hierarchical Routing

3.1.10 Congestion Control

Congestion is a fundamental problem in packet-switched networks which usually occurs when the number of transmitted packets exceeds the capacity of the network. In other words, when the traffic load is greater than the amount of packets the network can handle, we say that the network is congested. *Congestion control* comprises all the widely used mechanisms that try to detect, prevent and handle in general, network congestion.

3.1.10.1 Factors that Cause Congestion

Once we have defined the terms *congestion* and *congestion control*, it is time to discuss some more technical issues and specifically about the factors that cause congestion.

To begin with, in order to reach their destination, packets pass through several switches and routers where they are stored in buffers (queues) until they are able to be processed and sent to the next host within the network. Network buffers have limited capacity in terms of storage and processing of arriving packets, which implies that if the traffic increases dramatically, the available queues will fill rapidly and therefore many packets will be dropped. This phenomenon affects significantly the performance of the network causing long delays and packet loss. A typical buffer overflow that leads to congestion is depicted in the following Fig. 3.13.

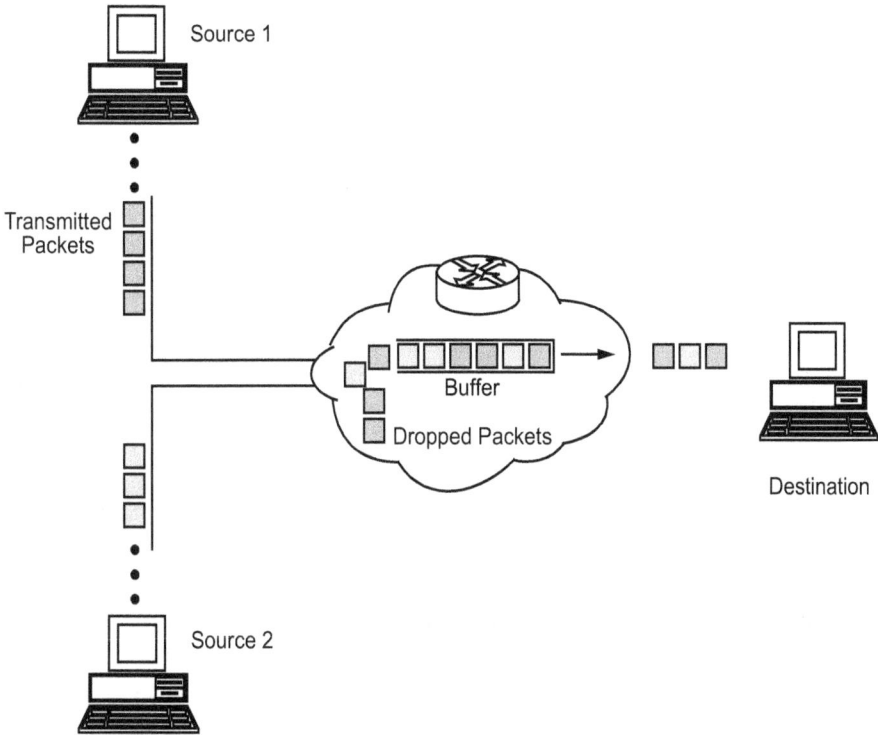

Fig. 3.13: A Typical Buffer Overflow that Leads to Congestion

Relying on the above figure we also have to consider how the transport layer or more explicitly the TCP protocol deals with the dropped packets. To be exact, in case that some packets fail to arrive to their destination because of congestion (or for any other reason), the source hosts will not receive any acknowledgement (ACK) and therefore they will be forced to retransmit the lost packets causing even more drops and extra congestion. This phenomenon is most commonly known as congestion feedback. Also, one of the main causes of network congestion is bursty traffic, whereby the data rate changes suddenly and frequently leading to high overload and wastage of the available bandwidth.

Apart from the above issues, routers' CPUs play their own important role, implying that insufficient processing resources can increase the duration of the entire network procedures, making the network more susceptible to congestion. Also, another issue that can be related to congestion is the balance in the available bandwidth of the incoming and outgoing traffic links, which means that either low-bandwidth lines or large variation between the connections can lead to congestion as well. Although some profound solutions to the above issues could be to increase or adjust appropriately the available resources in terms of processing units, memory, bandwidth and so on, congestion seems to be a more complicated problem. Such mechanisms can only provide a partial solution, implying that potential bottlenecks or congestion in general will shift to other points within the network that will need to be addressed too.

3.1.10.2 Difference between Flow Control and Congestion Control

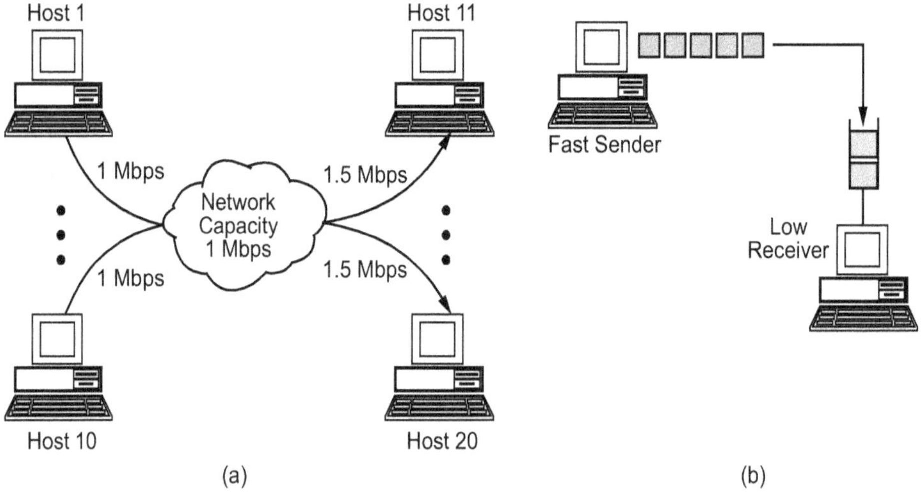

Fig. 3.14: Difference between Flow and Congestion Control

Trying to offer a better understanding of the discussing issues we need to distinguish the difference between congestion and flow control, due to these two terms can be easily confused. As we mentioned previously, congestion control ensures that the traffic load will not exceed the capacity of the available network recourses, implying that the network will be able to carry the offered traffic without problems (e.g. overflow, drops etc.). Another key feature is that congestion concerns all the involved network components such as hosts, routers, switches, links etc. and therefore could be considered as a broad networking issue. On the other hand, flow control is applied to a point-to-point connection between a sender and a receiver, ensuring that a fast sender will be able to transmit the appropriate amount of data that the receiver can accept. In case that a receiver accepts from a fast sender more packets that it can process, flow control is necessary to adjust the data transmission rate among the two hosts (e.g. by notifying the sender to transmit more slowly). As a result, we can lead to the argument that while congestion control techniques try to protect the network against overload, flow control focus on a specific network link among two hosts.

3.1.10.3 How congestion affects network performance?

There is no doubt that congestion affects the performance of the network in several ways. For example, in an overloaded network buffers or queues growing dramatically and even more packets start to being discarded increasingly. Obviously, if the network continues to remain congested, all the incoming packets will be dropped sharply, leading to a situation that is widely known as *congestion collapse*.

Two factors that are very important in terms of network performance are *delay* and *throughput*. Firstly, as the name implies, delay is the time needed for a packet to reach its destination, while throughput indicates the number of total packets that can be passed through the network in a specific time. Network congestion tends to affect both the factors in different ways. High traffic load increases the length of the queues and similarly long queues increase the delay of the transmitted packets. On the other hand, when routers start dropping packets, throughput declines sharply. As a result, delay and throughput are two important parameters that offer important information regarding the network congestion. Below we can see how traffic load affects delay and throughput.

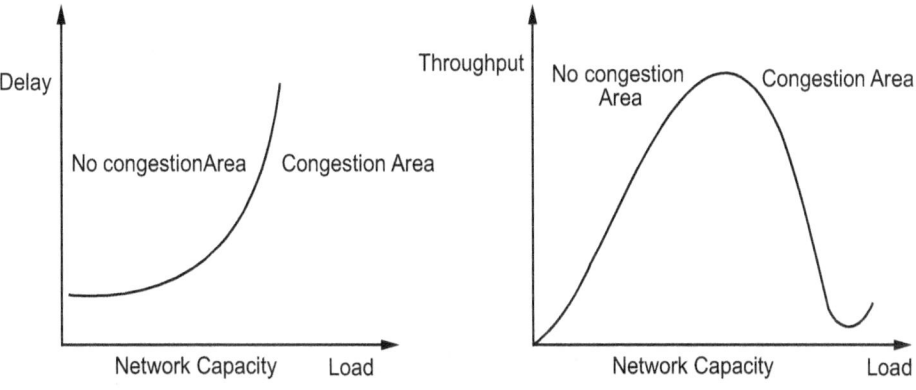

Fig. 3.15: Delay and Throughput parameters versus load

3.1.11 Congestion Control Techniques

In order to discuss about congestion control techniques we need to classify the available solutions from the control perspective. More specifically, congestion control techniques are divided into two main categories which are *open loop* and *closed loop*. Open loop techniques try to prevent congestion from occurring, deciding about the appropriate traffic, the discarding packets, as well as providing scheduled solutions for various network states. Also, the performed actions can be managed by either the source or the destination within the network. A significant issue about open loop techniques is that they do not provide feedback, implying that most of the actions that aim to prevent congestion neglect in some way the current state of the network. On the other hand, closed loop mechanisms deal with congestion after it happens or at the early stages, using feedback methods. More specifically, closed loop techniques monitor the network in order to detect congestion and perform the appropriate adjustments according to the problem. Closed loop algorithms can either use *explicit* or *implicit* feedback in order to pass important information about congestion to the appropriate points within the network. In *explicit feedback*, packets are sent from congestion points to the sources in order to inform them about the problem. An explicit feedback can be either *persistent* if it's available anytime or *responsive* if it becomes available at certain conditions. In *implicit feedback*, sources identify a possible congestion state, by taking into account various network parameters (e.g. the delay in the received acknowledgements) and adapt their behavior accordingly to alleviate congestion (e.g. by slowing down their transmission rate). A common classification of congestion control techniques is depicted in the Fig. 3.16.

Classification of Congestion Control Techniques

```
                    Congestion Control
                        Techniques
                   ┌────────┴────────┐
                Open Loop        Closed Loop
               ┌────┴────┐      ┌────┴────┐
           Act at     Act at   Implicit   Explicit
         the source  the       Feedback   Feedback
                     destination            ┌────┴────┐
                                        Persistent  Responsive
```

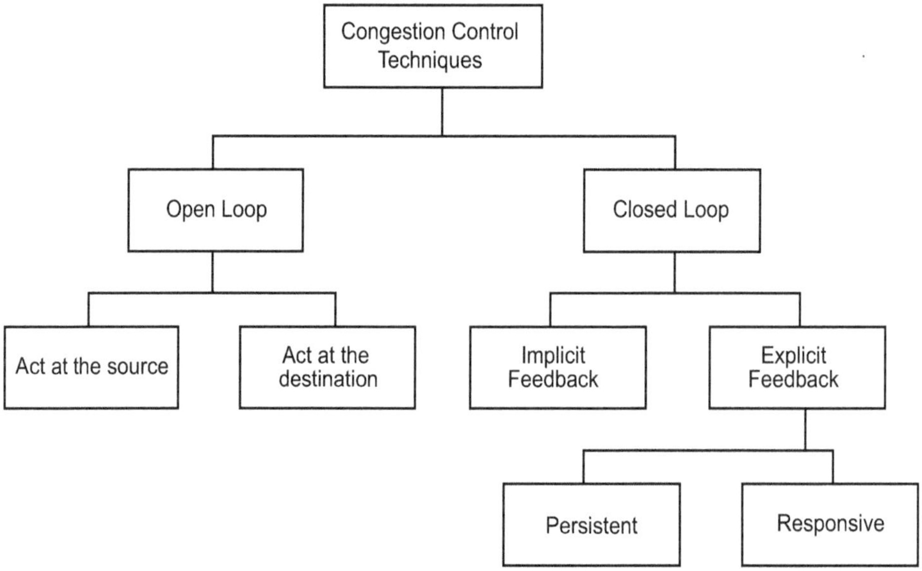

Fig. 3.16: A Common Taxonomy of Congestion Control Techniques

3.1.11.1 Open-Loop Congestion Control Techniques

Having classified the categories of the available congestion control techniques it is time to examine the main features and capabilities of the provided solutions. As we have mentioned in the previous paragraphs the main goal of open loop techniques is to prevent congestion from happening, providing efficient and well-designed scheduled mechanisms.

To begin with, open loop systems take into account several prevention policies that can be adjusted accordingly in order to identify and tackle congestion in advance. These policies are specified at transport, network and data link layers as we can see in Table 3.1.

Table 3.1: Policies that affect congestion

Transport	• Retransmission policy • Out-of-order caching policy • Acknowledgement policy • Flow control policy • Timeout determination
Network	• Virtual circuit versus datagram • Packet queuing and service policy • Packet discard policy • Routing algorithm • Packet lifetime management
Data link	• Retransmission policy • Out-of-order caching policy • Flow control policy

Below we examine some of the available open-loop congestion control policies highlighting the key points of each approach.

Retransmission Policy:

The retransmission policy determines the time interval in which the sender can retransmit an unacknowledged segment. If the sender's timer expires quickly then it will be forced to retransmit the packets more frequently causing extra load. Obviously, a well defined retransmission policy that will adjust efficiently the sender's timer and retransmission states can reduce the redundant packets and prevent congestion.

Acknowledgment Policy:

The acknowledgement packets that are sent from the receiver in order to confirm the receipt of each packet, may also affect congestion. If the receiver sends immediately the appropriate acknowledgments to the sender, then these packets can increase dramatically the traffic load. In this case, a balanced control of the transmitted acknowledgments is essential to reduce the sender's data rate and prevent congestion.

Packet Discard Policy:

Packet discard policy is of crucial importance as well, providing efficient strategies against congestion. More specifically, a good discarding policy must reject packets to enter in queues when the buffer load tends to increases rapidly, without degrading excessively the quality of the data transmission. On the other hand, a bad discard policy may drop packets improperly deteriorating congestion and network performance in general.

Packet Lifetime Management:

Apart from the above policies we also have to consider the lifetime of each packet, namely the time during packets remain active before being discarded. A long lifetime implies that more packets will be accumulated increasing the processing demands and the load as well, while a short time can prevent many packets to reach their destination causing further retransmissions.

3.1.11.2 Traffic Shaping

As we have mentioned in the previous section, bursty traffic affects network congestion to great extent. Trying to deal with this kind of problem, traffic shaping techniques are necessary to regulate the rate of the transmitted data accordingly, before they pass through the network. For example as we can see in Fig. 3.17 a bursty traffic in the input can be converted to a fixed-rate traffic in the output, applying the appropriate traffic shaping techniques.

Although traffic shaping is used to improve quality of service, the provided mechanisms can prevent congestion as well, following the open loop approach.

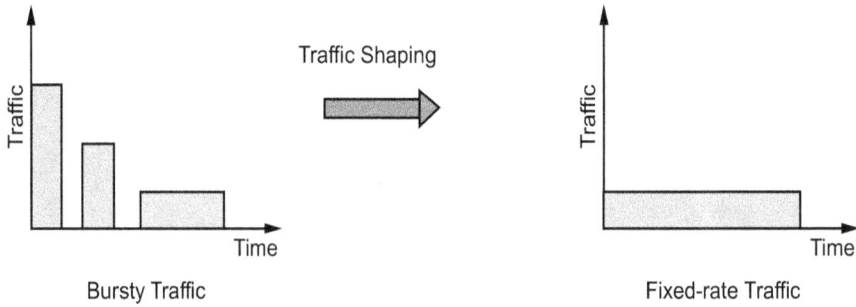

Fig. 3.17: The main Concept of Traffic Shaping

Two common traffic shaping algorithms that we are going to describe into the following paragraphs are leaky bucket and token bucket.

Leaky Bucket:

The main concept of the leaky bucket algorithm is that, the output data flow remains constant despite the variant input traffic, such as the water flow in a bucket with a small hole at the bottom. In case the bucket contains water (or packets) then the output flow follows a constant rate, while if the bucket is full any additional load will be lost because of spillover. In a similar way if the bucket is empty the output will be zero.

From network perspective, leaky bucket consists of a finite queue (bucket) where all the incoming packets are stored in case there is space in the queue, otherwise the packets are discarded. In order to regulate the output flow, leaky bucket transmits one packet from the queue in a fixed time (e.g. at every clock tick). In Fig. 3.17 (a), we can notice the main rationale of leaky bucket algorithm, for both the approaches (e.g. leaky bucket with water (a) and with packets (b)).

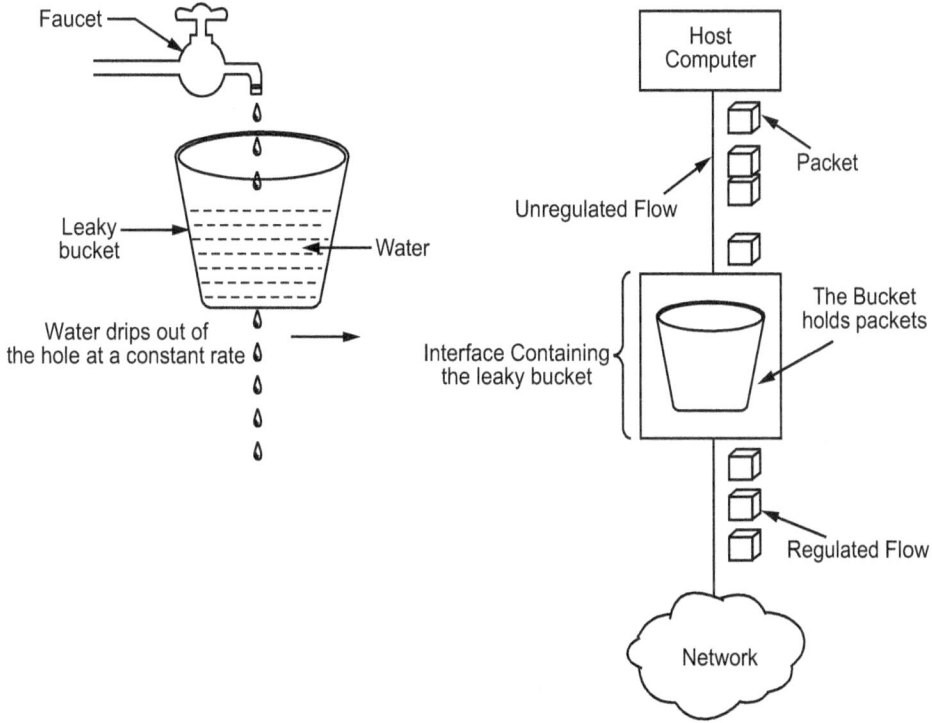

Fig. 3.17 (a): The Leaky Bucket Traffic Shaping Algorithm

While leaky bucket eliminates completely bursty traffic by regulating the incoming data flow its main drawback is that it drops packets if the bucket is full. Also, it doesn't take into account the idle process of the sender which means that if the host doesn't transmit data for some time the bucket becomes empty without permitting the transmission of any packet.

There are many variations of the leaky bucket algorithm. When the packets are of the same length and when the packets are of variable length different algorithm are used.

(1) When packets are of fixed length:

The counter is used to record contents of leaky bucket.

When a packet arrives, the counter is incrimented by some value n, in case this value does not exceed the queue length of bucket.

If the content exceeds the limit, the counter remains unchanged and packet is discarded or said to be non-conforming.

As long as the bucket is not empty, it will drain at a continuous rate of one unit per packet time.

Fig. 3.17 (b) shows the leaky bucket algorithm.

When first packet arrives, contents of bucket X is set to zero and the last conforming time (LCT) is made equal to arrival time of the packet (t_a).

Whenever a new packet arrives an auxiliary variable X' is calculated as
X' = X − (t_a − LCT). This will give the contents of bucket when the packet arrives. t_a − LCT is the time during which the leaky bucket has given out that many packets.

If X' > 0 and X' < L. The contents of bucket are updated to X = X' + n.

If X' > 0 and X' > L, the contents are not updated and packet is discarded.

If X' < 0, then X' is made 0 i.e. auxiliary variable is ensured to be non-negative.

Fig. 3.17 (c) shows an example of leaky bucket.

(2) When packets are of different length:

In this case a fixed number of bytes are allowed per tick instead of one packet. The counter value is incremented in bytes. The size of bucket is also set in bytes. The algorithm works the same way as described above.

If a leaky bucket has output rate of 2 MB/sec and capacity of bucket is 1 MB. Then a source producing data at a rate 25 MB/sec and connected to above leaky bucket will result into output rate 2 MB/sec for 500 m/sec. as shown in Fig. 3.17 (a).

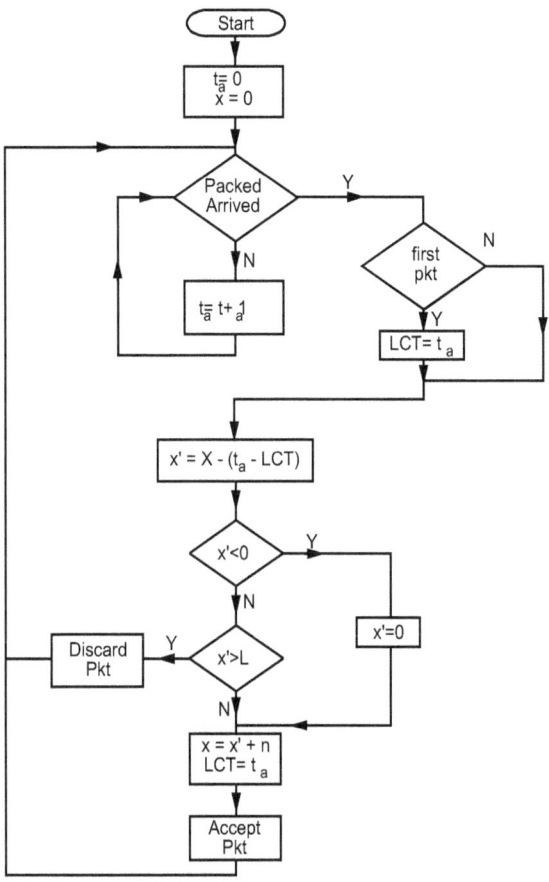

Fig. 3.17 (b): Leaky Bucket Algorithm

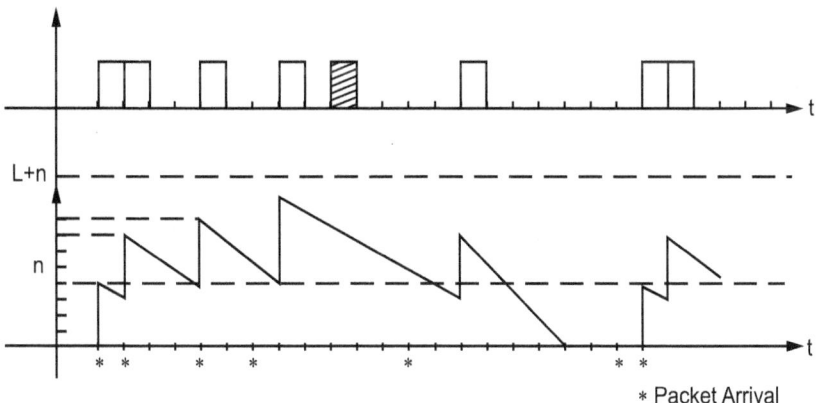

Fig. 3.17 (c): Leaky Bucket Example

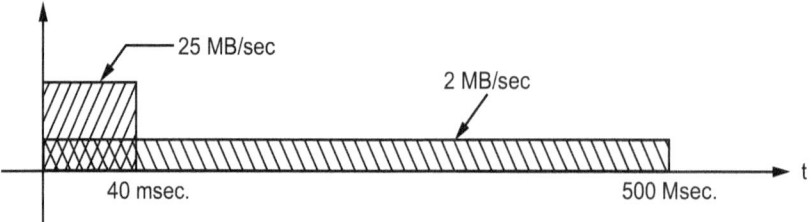

Fig. 3.17 (d): Leaky Bucket Example

Token Bucket:

A more flexible traffic shaping algorithm that allows a specific amount of bursty traffic in the output, is the token bucket.

According to this algorithm the bucket holds tokens that are generated at each tick of the clock (e.g. every Δt sec at a clock rate).

The number of the available tokens determines how many packets can be transmitted, while for any packet that is sent, one token is destroyed.

For the sake of simplicity it is more useful to assume that each token is one byte as well as packets can be transmitted only if the available tokens are able to cover at least the length of the packets in bytes.

For example as we can see in the Fig. 3.18 (a), the bucket contains four tokens and five packets are sent from the host.

Relying on this algorithm four of the input packets will be transmitted consuming all the available tokens (in bytes), while the one left will be waiting for new tokens to be generated.

We can realize that the host can use all the available tokens at once sending bursty data equal to the amount of tokens.

Although token bucket offers a flexible control of the transmitted data, one of its main constraints is that it cannot ensure smooth output traffic on a constant basis.

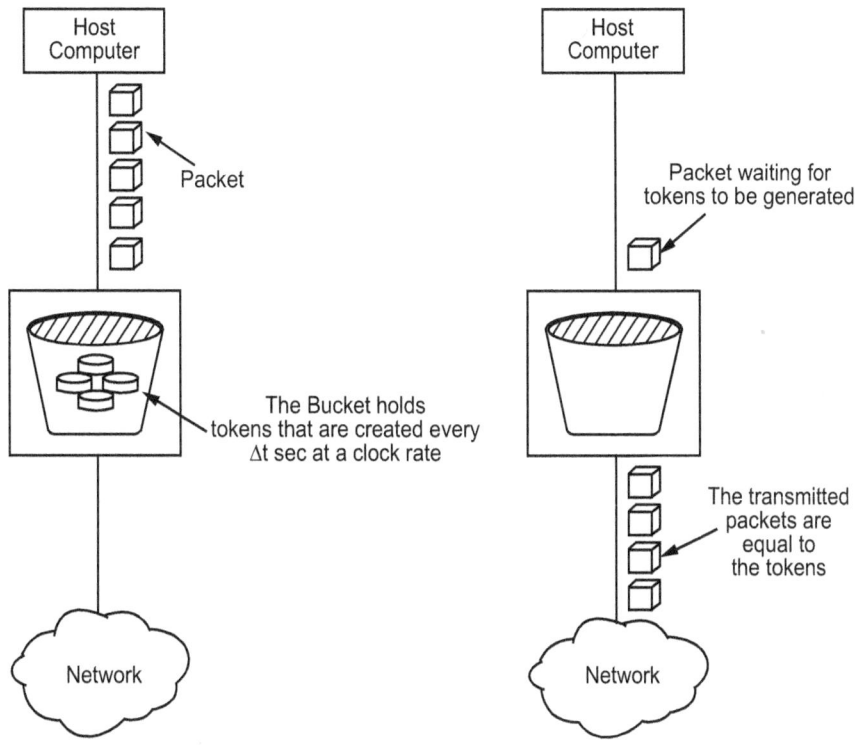

Fig. 3.18 (a): The Token Bucket Traffic Shaping Algorithm

Token bucket allows bursts of regulated maximum length. Let us consider an example. Let the capacity of token bucket be 500 kB. Let the token arrival rate be 2MB/sec. If a burst of 25 MB/40 msec. = 1 MB arrives then length of maximum burst is calculated using formula.

$$MS = C + \rho S$$

where,

    S — Burst length in sec.
    ρ — Token arrival rate bytes/sec
    C — Token bucket capacity bytes
    M — Maximum output rate bytes/ec.

$$\therefore S = \frac{C}{M - \rho}$$

$$= \frac{500 \times 10^3}{25 \times 10^6 - 2 \times 10^6}$$

$$= 21.74 \text{ ms}$$

It means a burst of 1 Mb arrives then it can be drained out at a rate of 25 MB/sec. for 21.74 ms and then 2 MB/s for about 228 ms i.e. till it has to cut back to entire burst is drained out as shown in Fig. 3.18 (b).

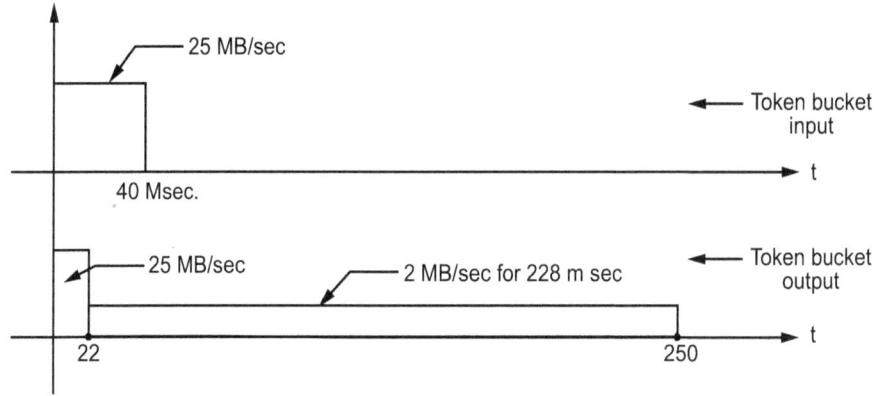

Fig. 3.18 (b)

The problem with token bucket is that it allows large bursts again even though the maximum burst length is controlled by careful selection of ρ and M.

One way to get smoother traffic is to put a leaky bucket after the token bucket. The rate of leaky bucket should be higher than token buckets ρ but lower than what network can allow.

3.1.11.3 Closed Loop Congestion Control Techniques

In contrast to the above open loop control techniques that aim to prevent congestion from happening, closed loop methods deal with congestion after it occurs. The basic idea behind closed loop techniques is to monitor the network trying to detect a possible congestion as well as to recover the congested network using the appropriate feedback mechanisms. Below we describe some of the available closed loop techniques, discussing about the main features of each approach.

Warning bit:

According to this closed loop method, when the router detects a possible congestion within the network, it enters in a warning state, by setting a warning bit in the packet's header, in order to warn the source about the congestion. Upon the receipt of ACK packet the source checks the warning bit and adjusts its transmission rate accordingly. When the router returns to a normal state it stops sending packets with a warning bit, implying that the sender can increase its transmission rate until it receives the next warning. Fig. 3.19 depicts the main operation of warning bit congestion control technique.

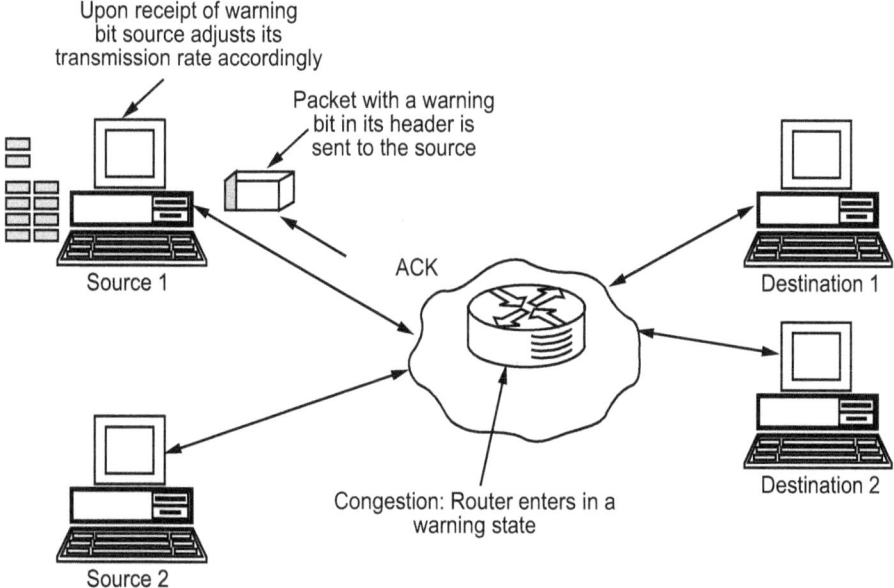

Fig. 3.19: The Warning Bit Congestion Control Technique

Choke packets:

This technique is a more straightforward way to make the source slow down its transmission rate in case of congestion. More specifically relying on this method, when a router detects a congested destination node, it sends a choke packet to the source to inform it about congestion as well as indicating to reduce its data rate by a specific percentage. Upon receipt of the choke packet the source must ignore the next choke packets that come from the same destination node for a fixed period of time. After the end of this period, the source starts waiting for other choke packets in a new time interval. If the source receives a choke packet during this new period it must reduces its transmission rate further because the congestion is still present. On the other hand if none choke packet arrives within the fixed time interval the source can start sending faster implying that congestion has been alleviated.

Fig. 3.20 (a) shows chocke packets affecting source flow.

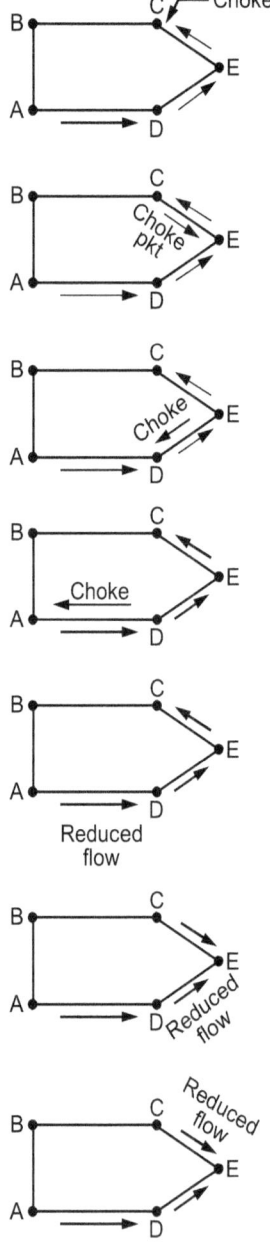

Fig. 3.20 (a)

Hop by Hop Choke Packet:

Considering that choke packets need to travel over the network and more specifically from a remote destination to the appropriate source, it can take enough time for the hosts to respond, if the distance is too long or generally the subnets of each host are far among them. An alternative approach that tries to address this problem is to use choke packets at each hop between the destination and the source. Relying on this method each node that receives a choke packet will be forced to reduce its transmission rate before the packet arrives at the source. This hop by hop control provides an efficient usage of the connection link alleviating congestion more quickly.

The hop by hop choke packet are shown in Fig. 3.20 (b) of the choke packet.
At each hop, the flow is reduced.

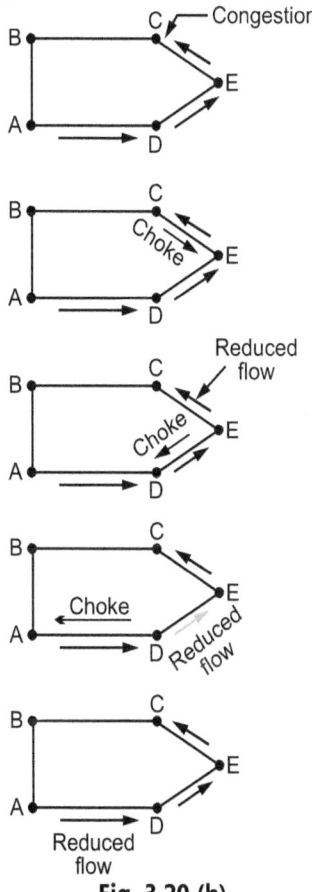

Fig. 3.20 (b)

Admission Control:

A common congestion control technique that is widely used in virtual-circuit subnets is admission control. The main idea of this method is to decide about the traffic before it enters into the network, if it can be accepted or rejected depending on the congestion state.

More specifically, in case of network congestion no more virtual circuits are being set up, implying that new traffic requests are rejected until the network has been recovered successfully. A more generous approach would be to form new virtual circuits that will avoid the congested areas allowing the traffic to pass through these connection paths. For example in the following scenario the connection links among host 1 and host 2 contain two congested routers that must be avoided (Fig. 3.21 (a)), by sending the traffic through a new virtual circuit between the two hosts (Fig. 3.21 (b)).

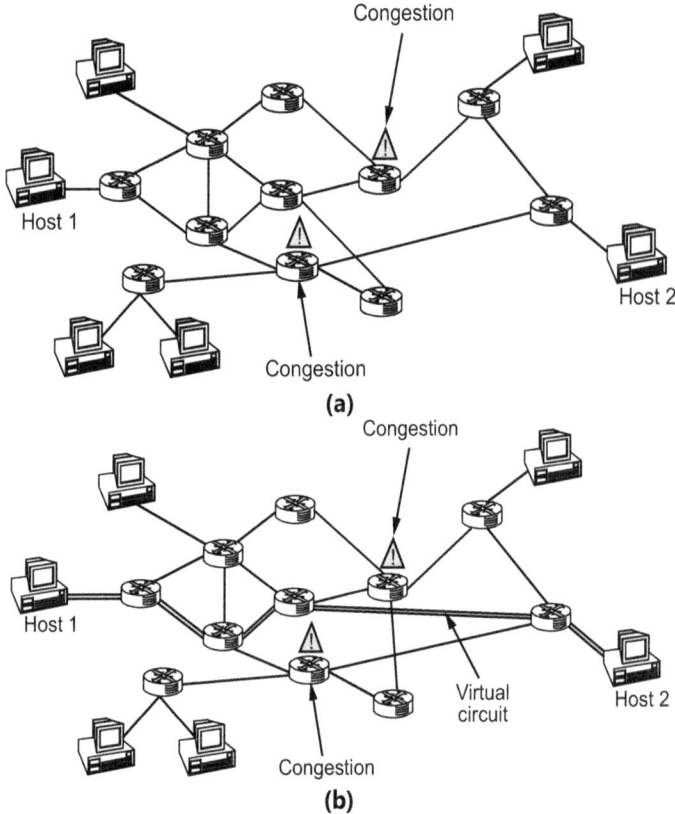

Fig. 3.21: Admission Control in Virtual Circuits

Random Early Detection (RED):
RED is one of the most widely deployed congestion avoidance algorithms which monitors the average queue size in order to discard incoming packets when the queue starts being overloaded.

More specifically, for every packet that arrives at the router, RED calculates the average queue length which is compared with a minimum (min_{Th}) and a maximum threshold (max_{Th}).

If the average queue length is greater than the maximum threshold then each arriving packet is dropped (or marked), implying that the line is congested.

In case the average queue length is between the two thresholds then RED drops (or marks) each packet with a probability, proportional to the average queue size. This implies that as the queue grows then the dropping probability for each packet increases too.

When the probability reaches its maximum limit it indicates that the queue is full and therefore all the incoming packets are discarded. Obviously, a dropped packet will prevent the transmission of the necessary acknowledgement, forcing the source to transmit more slowly by reducing its window size.

In case the average queue size is smaller than the minimum threshold then the incoming packet can be inserted in the queue normally.

Some of the major advantages of RED are that it provides more fairness than traditional TCP techniques such as tail drop, as well as addresses the significant problem of global synchronization (occurs when sources reduce their transmission window at the same time).

Fig. 3.22 describes clearly the main operation of the random early detection (RED) algorithm.

Random Early Detection (RED)

A_{vg} = Average Queue Length
Max Thres = Maximum Queue Length Threshold
MinThres = Minimum Queue Length Threshold

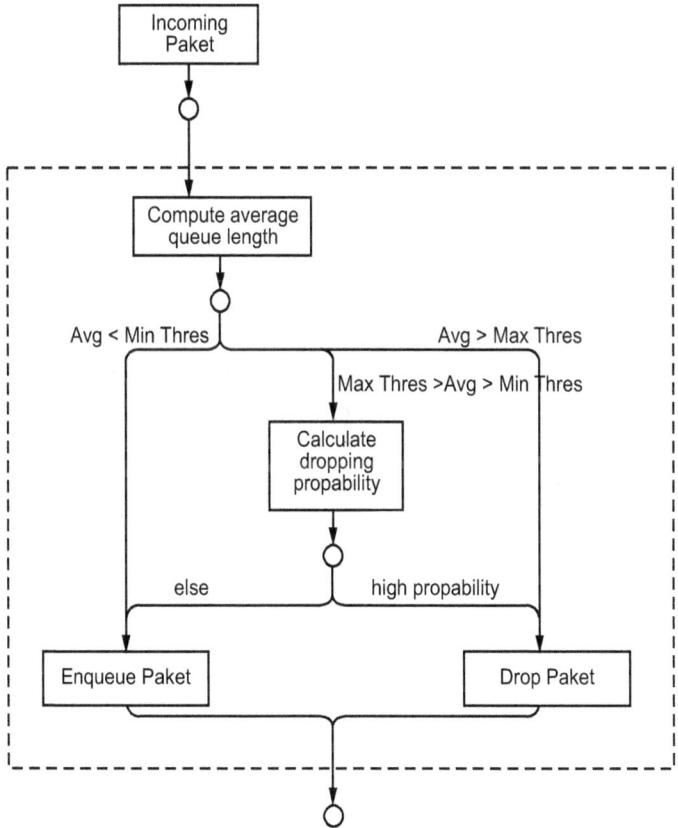

Fig. 3.22: The RED Congestion Avoidance Algorithm

Jitter Control:

In case of applications like audio and video transmission, the packets delivered can vary in time i.e. some packets may take 20 msec and some 25 msec. It does not matter as long as transit time is constant. But then this will result into bad quality of sound.

In such case, one has to arrive at an agreement that 99% packets should be delivered with a predecided delay.

The expected transit time for each form is computed in order to decide the Jitter. When a packet arrives at router, the router checks whether packet is behind or ahead of its schedule. The information regarding this timing is updated at each hop. If the packet is ahead of schedule it is delayed. And if it is behind schedule the router tries to forward it quickly. Thus, the amount of jitter can be reduced.

Congestion Control For Multicasting:

All the above methods of congestion control deal with transmission from single source to destination. In case where multiple sources transmit to multiple destination. The method for management of congestion is different.

The example of this type of transmission is several closed circuit television stations transmitting audio and video to a group of receivers. Each receiver can view any station. This can be used in video conferencing.

In such multicast scenario, we can use Resource Reservation Protocol (RSVP). This protocol uses spanning trees. Each group is assigned to group address. Whenever a sender wants to send information to a group the packets contain groups address. A multicast routing algorithm is used to build spanning tree including all group members.
(The routing algorithm is not part of RSVP). Some extra information is also multicast to the group periodically so that the routers maintain certain data structure in their memories.

3.2 The Transport Layer
3.2.1 Introduction
In the OSI 7-layer Reference Model, the *transport layer* is the lowest layer that operates on an end-to-end basis between two or more communicating hosts.

This layer lies at the boundary between these hosts and an internetwork of routers, bridges, and communication links that moves information between hosts.

A good transport layer service (or simply, *transport service*) allows applications to use a standard set of primitives and run on a variety of networks without worrying about different network interfaces and reliabilities.

Essentially, the transport layer isolates applications from the technology, design, and behavior of the network.

3.2.2 Transport Service
To illustrate the role that the transport layer plays in a familiar application, the remainder of Section examines the role of TCP.

The Web is an example of a client/server application. A human interacts with a Web browser (client) running on a "local" machine. The Web browser communicates with a server on some "remote" machine. The Web uses an application layer protocol called the Hypertext Transfer Protocol (HTTP). HTTP is a simple request/response protocol
In the simplest case, the client sends a request containing the filename of the desired Web page ("GET/research.html") to a server "www.google.com", and the server sends back a response consisting of the contents of that file.

This communication takes place over a complex inter-network of computers that is constantly changing in terms of both technology and topology.

A connection between two particular hosts may involve such diverse technologies as Ethernet, Token Ring, X.25, ATM, PPP, SONET, just to name a few.

However, a programmer writing a Web client or server does not want to be concerned with the details of *how* communication takes place between client and server. The programmer simply wants to send and receive messages in a way that does not change as the underlying network changes. This is the function of the transport layer: to provide an abstraction of inter-process communication that is independent of the underlying network.

HTTP uses TCP as the transport layer. The programmer writing code for an HTTP client or server would access TCP's service through function calls that comprise that transport layer's *Application* Program Interface (API). At a minimum, a transport layer API provides functions to send and receive messages; for example, the Berkeley Sockets API provides functions called write()and read().Because TCP is connection-oriented, the Berkeley Sockets API also provides a connect() function for setting up a connection between the local and remote processes. It also provides a close() function for closing a connection. Note that while TCP is connection-oriented, not all transport services establish a connection before data is sent. There can be connectionless services and protocols are discussed in next Sections.

Throughout this discussion, we use a simplified communication model (Fig. 3.23) that employs some OSI terminology.

1. At the top layer, a *user sender* (e.g., a Web client) has some messages to communicate to the *user receiver* (e.g., a Web server). These so called *application entities* use the service of the transport layer.
2. Communication between *peer* entities consists of an exchange of *Protocol Data Units* (PDUs).
3. Application peers communicate using Application PDUs (APDUs), while transport peers communicate using Transport PDUs (TPDUs), etc.
4. In our Web example, the first APDU is the request "GET /research.html" sent from the client (application entity) to the server (its peer application entity).
5. The Web server will respond with an APDU containing the entire text of the file "research.html". Many transport and application protocols are *bidirectional*; that is, both sides can send and receive data simultaneously. However, it is frequently useful to focus on one direction while remaining aware that the other direction is also operational.
7. As Fig. 3.23 shows, each application entity can assume both the role of sender and receiver; for the APDU "GET /research.html", the client is the user sender and the server is the user receiver (as shown by more prominent labels).
8. When the APDU containing the contents of the file "research.html" is sent, user sender and user receiver reverse roles (as indicated by the dotted line boxes, and the lighter italicized labels).

The term *transport entity* refers to hardware and/or software within transport layer.

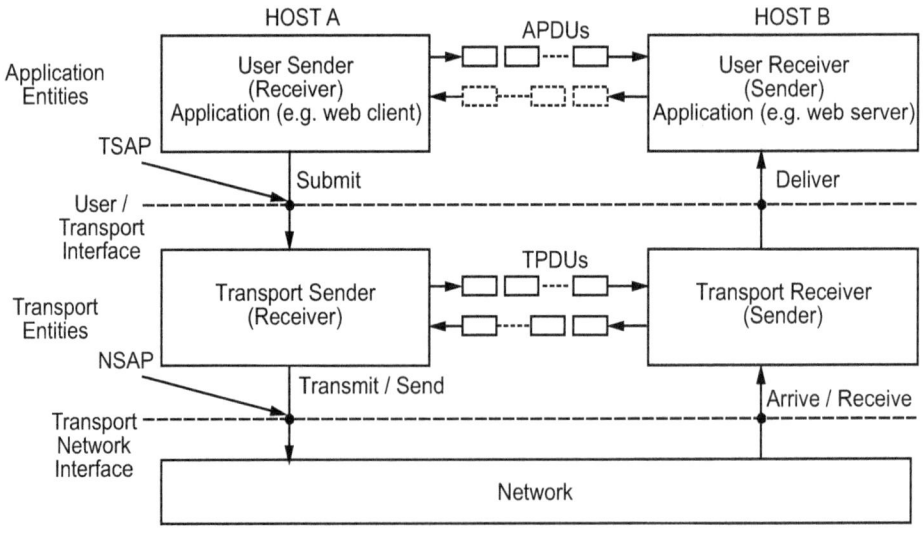

Fig. 3.23: Transport service

Fig. 3.24 shows what happens to the request APDU "`GET /research.html`" as it passes through the various layers on its way from the Web client to the Web server.

1. When the user sender submits the request APDU to the transport sender, that APDU becomes a TSDU.
2. The transport sender adds its own header information to the TSDU, to construct a TPDU that it can send to the transport receiver.
3. TPDUs exchanged by the transport entities are *encapsulated* (i.e., contained) in NPDUs which are exchanged between the network entities, as illustrated in Fig. 3.24.
4. The network layer routes NPDUs between the local and remote network entities over intermediate links.
5. When an NPDU arrives, the network layer entity processes the NPDU header and passes the payload of the NPDU to a transport layer entity.
6. The transport entity either passes the payload of the TPDU to the transport user if it is user data, or processes the payload itself if it is a control TPDU.

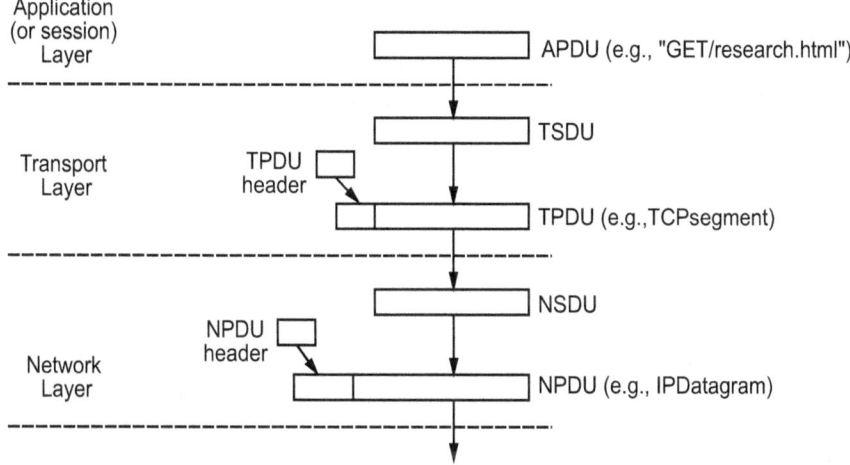

Fig. 3.24: Relationship between Service Data Units (SDUs) and Protocol Data Units (PDUs)

Terminology commonly used in the Internet protocol suite to identify PDUs at various layers. TCP's PDUs are called *segments*, while IP's NPDUs are called *datagrams*.

However, the Internet community's terminology can be confusing. For example, the term *packet* is often used informally to refer to both IP Datagrams (NPDUs) and TCP segments (TPDUs). The term *datagram* can refer either to IP's NPDUs, or to the TPDUs of the User Datagram Protocol. To avoid such confusion, we make use of some OSI terms to understand transport layer operation.

3.2.2.1 Quality-of-service

A transport layer that provides *Quality of Service* (QoS) that allows a user to specify the quality of transmission service desired. The protocol then presumably optimizes network resources to provide the requested QoS.

Since the underlying network places limits on the service that can be provided by the transport protocol, a user sender should recognize two facts:
  (1) Depending on the underlying network's capabilities, a transport protocol will have varying degrees of success in providing the requested QoS,
  (2) There is a trade-off among QoS parameters such as reliability, delay, throughput, and cost of service. Transport QoS is a broad and complicated issue.

No universally accepted list of parameters exists, and how the transport layer should behave for a desired QoS under different circumstances is unclear. The ISO Transport Service [ITU-T 1995c] defines a number of possible performance QoS parameters that are negotiated during connection establishment.

User senders can specify (sustained) target, acceptable, and minimum values for various service parameters. The transport protocol examines these parameters, and determines whether it can provide the required service; this depends in part on the available network service.

ISO specifies eleven QoS parameters:
  1. *Connection Establishment Delay* is the maximum acceptable time between a transport connection being requested and its confirmation being received by the user sender.
  2. *Connection Establishment Failure* is the probability a connection cannot be established within the maximum connection establishment delay time due to network or internal problems.
  3. *Throughput* is the number of bytes of user sender data transferred per unit time over some time interval.
  4. *Transit Delay* is the elapsed time between a message being submitted by a user sender and being delivered to the user receiver.
  5. *Residual Error Rate* is the ratio of incorrect, lost, and duplicate TSDUs to the total number of TSDUs that were sent.
  6. *Transfer Failure Probability* is the ratio of total transfer failures to total transfer samples observed during a performance measurement.
  7. *Connection Release Delay* is the maximum acceptable time between a transport user initiating release of a connection and the actual release at the peer transport service user.

8. *Connection Release Failure Probability* is the fraction of connection release attempts that did not complete within the agreed upon connection release delay interval.
9. *Protection* is used by the user sender to specify interest in having the transport protocol provide protection against unauthorized third parties reading or modifying the transmitted data.
10. *Priority* allows a user sender to specify the relative importance of transport connections. In case of congestion or the need to recover resources, lower-priority connections are degraded or terminated before the higher-priority ones.
11. *Resilience* is the probability that the transport protocol itself will spontaneously terminate a connection due to internal or network problems.

A transport layer that provides *No- Quality-of-Service* (No-QoS) does not allow a user sender to specify desired quality of transmission service.

3.2.3 Transport Service Primitives

- In order to access transport service application programs (transport users) use the transport service primitives.
- Each transport service has a separate access primitives.
- The connection oriented transport service provides reliability on top of unreliable network. It hides the imperfections of the network service.
- There can be unreliable connectionless service provided by transport layer.
- The transport service is used by many programs and is convenient and easy to use.

Table 3.2 lists the transport service primitives.

Table 3.2: Transport Service Primitives

Primitives	TPDU sent	Meaning
LISTEN	(None)	Block until some process tries to connect.
CONNECT	CONNECTION REQUEST	Actively attempt to establish a connection.
SEND	DATA	Send Information.
RECEIVE	(None)	Block Until TDPU arrives.
DISCONNECT	DISCONNECTION REQUEST	This side wants to release the connection.

- The LISTEN primitive is executed on server which blocks itself until a client calls up.
- When a client wants to connect to server it executes CONNECT primitives. This is done by the transport entity, by sending a packet to the server.
- When the REQUEST TPDU arrives, the transport entity checks whether the server is in LISTEN mode (interested in handling request). If so the server is unblocked and it

sends accepted TPDU back to the client. When this TPDU arrives at the client it is unblocked and CONNECTION is established.
- SEND AND RECEIVE primitives are used to exchange data. For this the receiver has to be in blocking receive state. When the TPDU arrives the receiver is unblocked. TPDU is processed and replay by sent back.
- Whenever CONNECTION is not required it is released by using DISCONNECT primitives which sends DISCONNECT TPDU to the remote transport entity.

Fig. 3.25 shows the state diagram for these primitives.

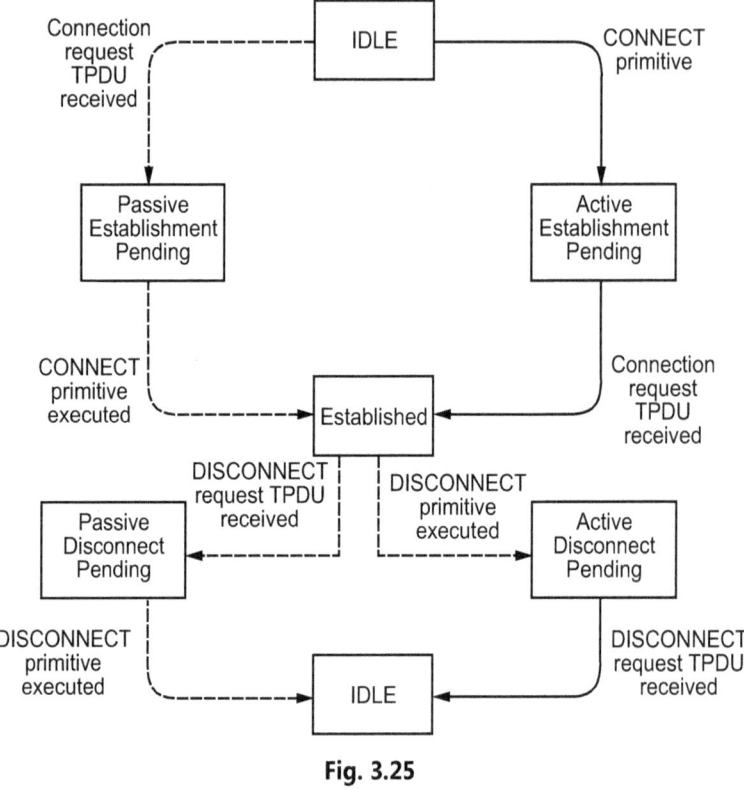

Fig. 3.25

Whenever an event occurs there will be transition and each TPDU is separately acknowledged.

Berkeley Sockets:

Application Programming Interface (API) allows application programs (e.g. FTP, Telnet, Web Browsers) to access certain resources through a predefined interface.

Berkeleys sockets are such predefined interface. This is available on UNIX. Its counterpart on windows is Winsock.

A typical socket interface is shown in Fig. 3.26.

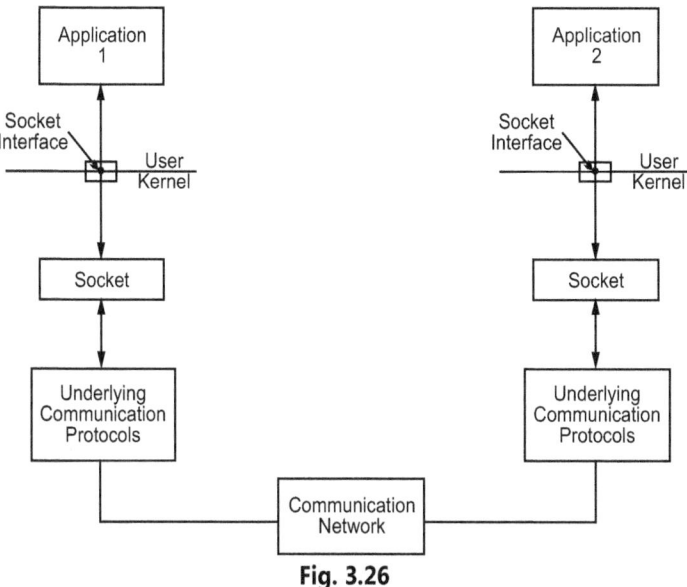

Fig. 3.26

One of the applications will be server and the other will be a client. Socket interface can provide connection oriented or connection less services.

Fig. 3.27 shows a sequence of socket calls for connection oriented mode.

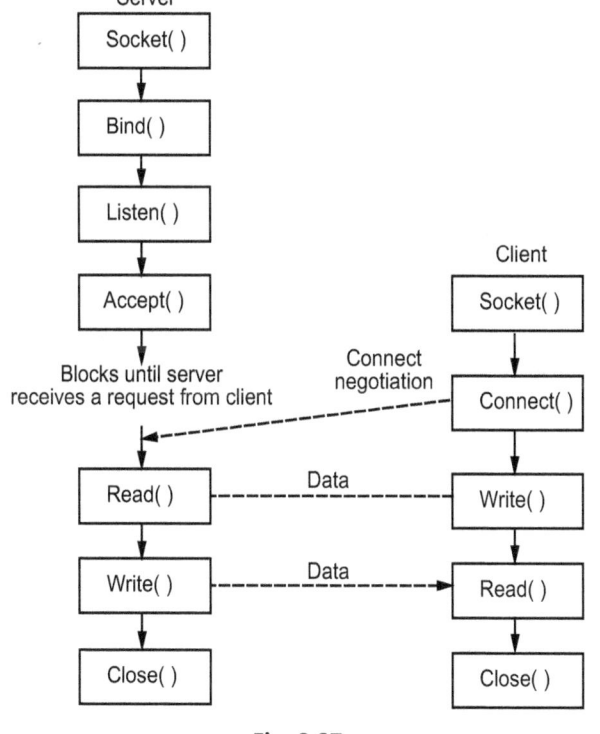

Fig. 3.27

(a) Server Side:
1. A TCP socket is created with **socket calls.**
2. The **bind call** binds a port number of server with the socket (say Port 80).
3. The **listen call** makes he socket listen to incoming connections from client.
4. The **accept call** makes the server process to sleep until a connection request comes from and client.

(b) Client Side:
1. A socket is created on client side with a **socket call**.
2. **Connect call** tries to establish a connection to the server with specified destination socket address.
3. When connection is established the server wakes up due to accept call and returns IP address, source port number, destination IP address and destination port number which is description of the connection established.

The client and server can now exchange information.

Read and write procedures are used to transfer data.

These procedures use socket descriptor, buffer to store data and length of buffer.

The close procedure is used to terminate the socket.

Fig. 3.28 shows the sequence of socket calls for connectionless mode. Here no connection is established prior to data transfer.

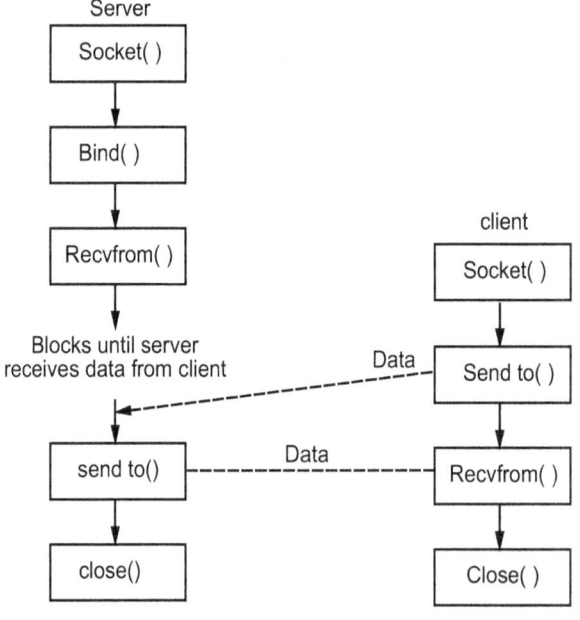

Fig. 3.28

Receive from procedure is used to receive both message and address of sender.

Send to and **send message** allow a client or server to send a message if socket is unconnected. The caller should specify a destination.

A detailed program on socket interface is given in Chapter 6.

3.2.4 Elements of Transport Protocol

Transport protocols implement transport services such as –
- (i) Addressing.
- (ii) Flow control.
- (iii) Error control
- (iv) Sequencing.
- (v) Establishing and releasing connection.
- (vi) Multiplexing.

Some of the services are similar to the services provided by data link layer. But then there is difference in the situations under which these two layers provide their services.

The data link layer has an underlying physical connection which provides the services, whereas transport layer has entire subnet under it. This has the following implications.

- (i) In DLL explicit addressing of destination is not required as each outgoing line specifies a particular device (switch/router). But in case of transport layer explicit addressing of destination is required as subnet is complex.
- (ii) Establishing connection in DLL is easy whereas in transport layer, it is complex.
- (iii) In DLL, the frame transmitted may be lost or transmitted. But transport layer packet can cause problem because of storing capacity of subnet. Hence, special protocols are required to handle this problem.
- (iv) Flow control and buffering is required at both layers. But in DLL we have to manage only one connection whereas in transport layer number of dynamically varying connections will complicate the problem of buffering and flow control.

3.2.4.1 Addressing

When an application entity (source) wants to connect to a destination application entity, an address is required. It is the transport address through which entities listen for connection requests. In case of internet, it is (IP address, local port) pair that defines transport address. IP address which is unique, identifies a particular host in the network and port number specifies the port through which the application entity is accessed on the host. Thus, there can be number of ports through which number of connections can be established. The port through which the service is accessed is called Service Access Point (SAP) and since it is transport service accessed by an application entity. Let us call it as TSAP. Similarly, network services are accessed through NSAP's (e.g. IP address).

Consider an example of Host 1 application entity trying to access Host 2 application entity as shown in Fig. 3.29.

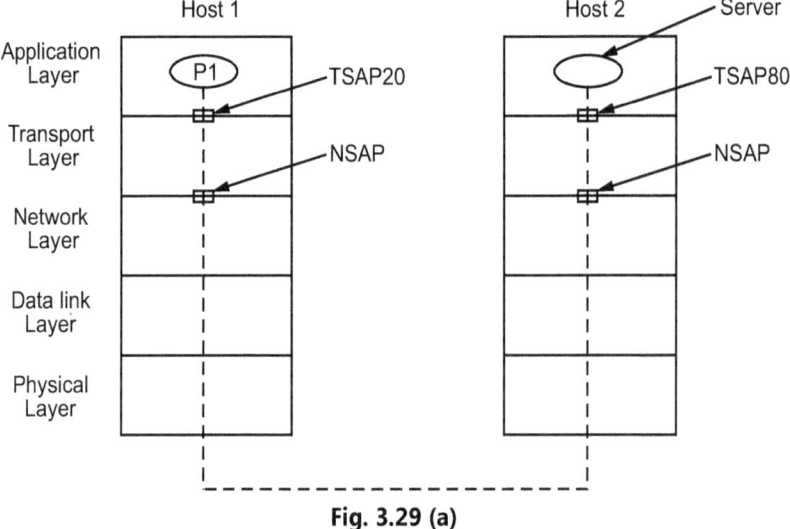

Fig. 3.29 (a)

The connection is established between the two entities through the TSAPs and NSAPs as shown in Fig. 3.29 (a). Host 1 entity is communicating through TSAP 20 to Host 2 entity through TSAP 80.

There can be more than one TSAP's as shown in Figure.

In Fig. 3.29 (b), there are two hosts. Host 1 and Host 2 trying to access services provided by Host 2 server.

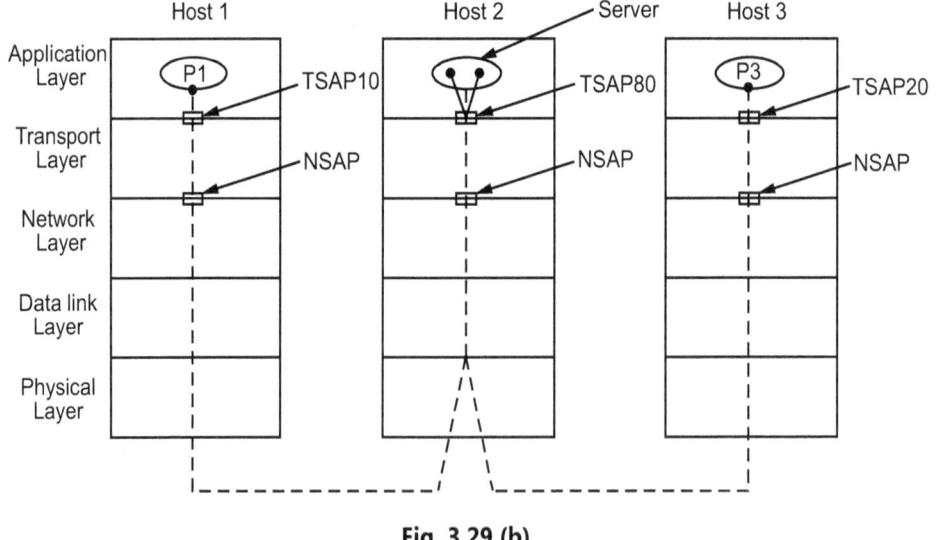

Fig. 3.29 (b)

Following points are to be noted:

(i) Hosts initiating connection know the TSAP of the peer entity before hand. Same ports are used for years by the server entities and hence are known e.g. port 80 is used by HTTP. Those servers not heavily used will not have devoted port, instead they will offer their services through a special process server that acts as proxy server for them. When connection is requested by some client to these server it is established through a set of ports at process server and then handed over to the requested server.

(ii) There might be some services which are to be created as they are needed and hence not related to process server. In such situation, the new service can register itself at a central place called name server giving service name and address. The client which wants to establish connection is first directed to this name server from where it gets the TSAP address.

3.2.4.2 Connection Establishment

- Establishing connection is not an easy as it looks to be. It is not just sending CONNECTION Request and getting back CONNECTION Accepted. It is because we may lose these packets in the network or these can be delay due to congestion in the network.
- The lost or delayed packets can result into problems in connection establishment.
- The delayed packets will result in retransmission of packets for another connection establishment whereas earlier packets also reach the destination.
- Hence, there are delayed duplicates. Following are few methods to solve this problem (but none of them are satisfactory).

1. Use connection identifier for each connection. Hence, whenever a new connection request comes it is checked whether it belongs to previously released connection. This requires some History to be maintained regarding connections and if machine crashes, it may lose this information making it difficult to identify old/new connection request.

2. The delayed packets can be killed in the network after some time. For this we need to maintain.

    (i) Hop counter which is decremented after each hop. Packet discarded when counter reaches 0.

    (ii) Timestamp which is decremented after every second. Packet discarded when count reaches specified value.

    (iii) Having subnet design which prevents looping of packets in network.

(iii) We can use clock based approach, where each host will maintain a clock of its own which never goes down even if Host crashes. The clock time can be used as initial sequence number for each connection. But then this will land into problem.

A service as well as protocol be classified as Connection Oriented (CO) or Connectionless (CL). The distinction depends on the establishment and maintenance of state information, a record of characteristics and events related to the communication between the transport sender and receiver. Perhaps the most important piece of state information is the sequence number that identifies a TPDU. Consistent viewpoints of the sequence numbers used by transport sender and transport receiver are required for reliable data transfer. Choosing an initial value for the sequence number can be hazardous, particularly when two transport entities close and immediately reopen a connection.

A transport protocol is CO (e.g., TCP) if state information is maintained between transport entities.

Typically, a CO protocol has three phases:

Connection establishment

Data transfer

Connection termination.

In the connection establishment phase, state information is initialized either explicitly by exchanging control TPDUs, or implicitly with the arrival of first data TPDU. During a connection's lifetime (i.e., data transfer phase), state information is updated to reflect the reception of data and control PDUs (e.g., ACKs). When both transport entities agree to terminate the connection, they discard the state information.

Note the distinction between a CO service and a CO protocol. A CO service entails a three phase operation to establish a logical connection between transport *users*. A CO protocol entails a three phase operation to maintain state information between transport *entities*.

If no state information is maintained at the transport sender and receiver, the protocol is CL. A CL protocol is based on individually self-contained units of communication often called *datagrams*; that are exchanged independently without reference to each other or to any shared state information. Each datagram contains all of the information that the receiving transport entity needs to interpret it.

Three modes of connection establishment are shown in Fig. 3.30 and Fig. 3.31.

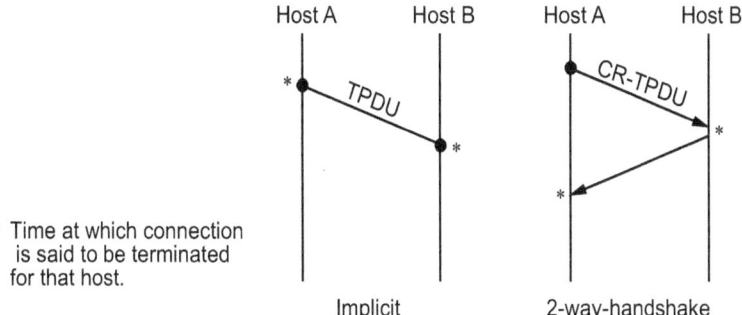

Fig. 3.30: Modes of connection establishment

* Time at which connection is said to be established for that host.

1. Protocols for short-lived connections have been designed using a timer-based connection establishment and termination mechanism.
2. For longer connections and when avoiding false connections is important, 2-way or 3-way *handshake* mechanisms are needed.
3. A handshake involves the explicit exchange of control TPDUs.
4. In *implicit* connect, the connection is open as soon as the first TPDU is sent or received. The transport sender starts transmitting data without any explicit connection verification by the transport receiver. Further data TPDUs can be sent without receiving an ACK from the transport receiver. Implicit connections can provide reliable service only if the protocol definition guarantees that delayed TPDUs from any previously closed connection cannot cause a false open.
5. In *2-way-handshake* connect, a *CR-TPDU* (Connection Request) and a *CC-TPDU* (Connection Confirm) are exchanged to establish connection. The transport sender may transmit data in the CR-TPDU, but sending additional data is prohibited until the CC-TPDU is received. During this handshake, QoS parameters such as buffer size, burst size, burst rate, etc., can be negotiated. When the underlying network service provides a small degree of loss, a 2-way handshake mechanism may be good enough to establish new connections without significant risk of false connections.
6. In *3-way-handshake* connect (e.g., TCP), the transport sender sends a *CR-TPDU* to the transport receiver, which responds with a *CC-TPDU*. The procedure is completed with an *ACK-CCTPDU* (ACK for Connection Confirm).

Normally, no user data is carried on these connection establishment TPDUs.

If the underlying network service provides an unacceptable degree of loss, a 3-way-handshake is needed to prevent false connections that might result from delayed TPDUs. as shown in Fig. 3.31.

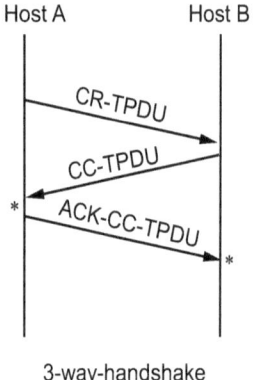

3-way-handshake

Fig. 3.31: Modes of connection establishment

Since TCP is designed specifically for use over an unreliable network service, it uses a 3-way handshake.

3.2.4.3 Connection Termination

Four modes of connection termination are shown in Fig. 3.32.

1. With *implicit* disconnect, when a transport entity does not hear from its peer for a certain time period, the entity terminates the connection. Typically, implicit disconnection is used with implicit connection establishment.
2. In *abortive* disconnect, when a transport entity must close the connection abnormally due to an error condition, it simply sends an *abort-TPDU* and terminates the connection. The entity does not wait for a response. Thus TPDUs in transit in either direction may be lost.
3. In *2-way-handshake* disconnect, a transport entity sends a *DR-TPDU* (Disconnect Request) to its peer and receives a *DC-TPDU* (Disconnect Confirm) in return. If a connection is unidirectional, the transport sender usually initiates connection termination, and before discarding its state information verifies the reception of all TPDUs by the transport receiver. In a bidirectional connection, a 2-way-handshake can only verify reception of TPDUs in one direction. TPDUs in transit in the reverse direction may be lost.
4. Finally, in 4(3)-way-handshake disconnect (e.g., TCP), two 2-way-handshakes are used, one for each direction of data flow.

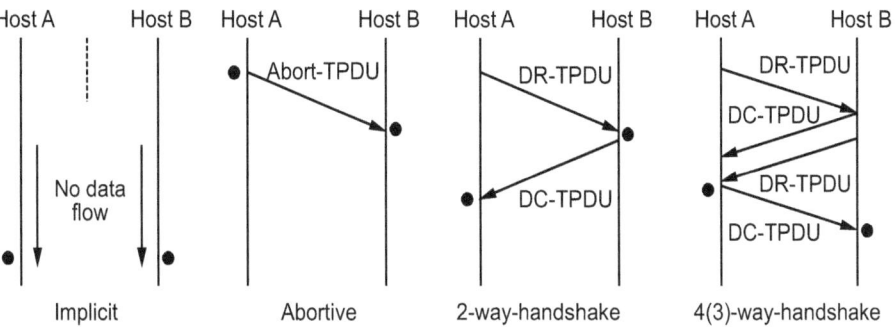

● Pdnt in time at which connection is said to be terminated for that host.

Fig. 3.32: Four Modes of Connection Termination

The transport entity that closes its sending flow, sends a DR-TPDU to its peer entity (in TCP the FIN flag is set in its last TPDU). This disconnect request is then acknowledged by the transport receiver as soon as all preceding TPDUs have been received. The connection is terminated when data flows in both directions are closed. The number of control TPDUs exchanged can be reduced to three if the first DC-TPDU also functions as a DR-TPDU for the reverse direction. Connections may be terminated either gracefully or ungracefully. In an ungraceful termination, some data in transit may be lost. In a graceful close, no data in transit is lost since a connection is closed only after all data have arrived at their destination. For bidirectional connections, only a 4(3)-way-handshake can guarantee graceful close.

3.2.4.4 Flow/Congestion Control and Buffering

The terms flow control and congestion *control* create confusion, since different authors approach these subjects from different perspectives. In this section we try to make a useful distinction between the terms while recognizing that overlap exists. First, we define transport layer *flow control* as any scheme by which the transport sender limits the rate at which data is sent over the network.

The goals of flow control may include one or both of the following:
(1) Preventing a transport sender from sending data for which there is no available buffer space at the transport receiver, or
(2) Preventing too much traffic in the underlying network. Flow control for (2) also is called congestion control, or congestion *avoidance*.

Congestion is essentially a network layer problem. However, congestion often is addressed by transport layer flow control (also known as end-point flow control). Techniques used to implement both goals are often tightly integrated, as is the case in TCP. Regardless of which goal is being pursued, the flow of data is being controlled. Therefore, some authors use "flow control" to refer to protocol features that address both goals, thus blurring the distinction between flow and congestion control.

In this section, we use *flow control* as the overall term for such techniques, but emphasize that –
(1) flow control is only one example of many possible congestion control techniques,
(2) congestion control is only one of the two motivations for flow control.

General Flow Control Techniques:
As seen earlier, Transport layer flow control is more complex than network or data-link layer flow control. This is because storage and forwarding at intermediate routers causes highly variable delays that are generally longer than actual transmission time. Transport layer flow control usually is provided in tandem with error control, by using sequence numbers and windowing techniques.

If there are n connections and a 4-bit sequence is used for Go-back-N protocol, $n \times 2^4$ buffers will be required [Sender + Receiver].

In case of datagrams service the TPDUs are buffered by sender, until they are acknowledged by the receiver. Hence, receiver will allocate buffers dynamically i.e. dedicated buffers are not maintained for each connections. If buffers are not available at receiver, it will discard the TPDU.

For reliable network service, receiver will have buffer space and transmitter need not maintain copies of TPDU's. However, if receiver cannot guarantee that every incoming TPDU is accepted then, sender has to retain the copy of it.

The buffer size selected depends on whether TDPU's are of same size or variable size. A pool of identical size buffers can be used if TPDU's are of same size with one TPDU per buffer.

If there is wide variation in TPDU size, fixed size buffers will create problems. If buffer size is less than TPDU size more number of buffers will be required to store one TPDU. If buffer size is more than TPDU size, there will be wastage of memory. Hence, variable memory size buffers can be used. One large circular buffer can also be used per connection.

Two techniques may be used, either alone or together, to avoid network congestion and overflowing receiver buffers. These are:
(1) Window flow control
(2) Rate control.

In window (or sliding-window) flow control, the transport sender continues sending new data as long as there remains space in the sending window. In general, this window may be fixed or variable in size.
1. In fixed size window control, ACKs from the transport receiver are used to advance the transport sender's window.
2. In variable size window control, also called a *credit scheme*, ACKs are decoupled from flow control.

A TPDU may be acknowledged without granting the transport sender additional credit to send new TPDUs, and additional credit can be given without acknowledging a TPDU. The transport receiver adopts a policy concerning the amount of data it permits the transport sender to transmit, and *advertises* the size of this window in TPDUs that flow from receiver to sender.

Early experience with TCP showed a problem, known as the *Silly Window Syndrome*, that can afflict protocols using the credit scheme. The silly window syndrome can start either because the transport receiver advertises a very small window, or the transport sender sends a very small TPDU. This can degenerate into a vicious cycle where the average TPDU size ends up being much smaller than the optimal case, and throughput suffers as a result. TCP includes mechanisms in both the transport sender and transport receiver to avoid the conditions that lead to this problem. Credit schemes may be described as conservative or aggressive (optimistic).

The conservative approach, as used in TCP, only allows new TPDUs up to the transport receiver's available buffer space. This approach has the disadvantage that it may limit a transport connection's throughput in long delay or large bandwidth-product situations. The aggressive approach attempts to increase throughput by allowing a transport receiver to optimistically grant credit for space it does not have. A disadvantage of the aggressive approach is its potential for buffer overflow at the transport receiver (hence, wasted bandwidth) unless the credit-granting mechanism is carefully timed

Rate control uses timers at the transport sender to limit data transmission.
A transport sender can be assigned
(1) A *burst size* and *interval* (or *burst rate*), or
(2) An interpacket delay time.

In (1), a transport sender transmits a burst of TPDUs at its maximum rate, then waits for the specified burst interval before transmitting the next burst. This is often modeled as a *tokenbucket* scheme.

In (2), a transport sender transmits data as long as it has credit available, but artificially causes between each TPDU according to the interpacket delay. This is often modeled as a *leaky-bucket* scheme. Case (2) improves performance because spreading TPDU transmissions helps avoid network congestion and receiver overflow.

3.2.4.5 Multiplexing/Demultiplexing

Multiplexing, as shown in Fig. 3.33, supports several transport layer connections using a single network layer association.

Multiplexing maps several user/transport interface points (what ISO calls TSAPs) onto a single transport/network interface point (NSAP).

An association is a virtual circuit in the case of a CO network. In the case of a CL network, an association is a pair of network addresses (source and destination).

When the underlying network is CL, multiplexing/demultiplexing as provided by TCP's port numbers is necessary to serve multiple transport users.

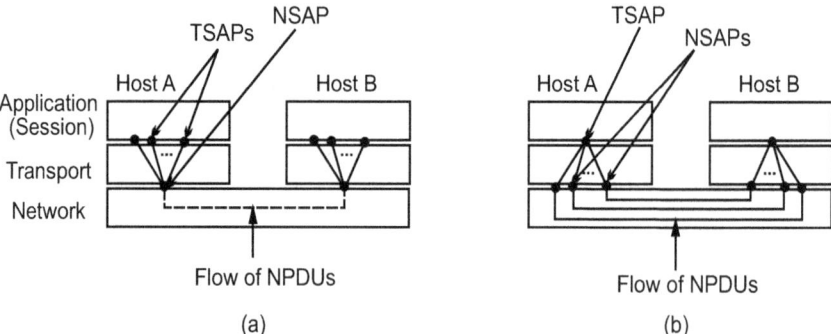

Fig. 3.33 (a): Multiplexing/demultiplexing (b) Splitting/recombining

Multiplexing uses network layer resources more efficiently by reducing the network layer's context-state information. Additionally, it can provide primitive stream synchronization. For example, video and audio streams of a movie can be multiplexed to maintain "lip sync," in which case the multiplexed streams are handled as a single stream in a single, uniform manner. This method works only if all streams require the same network layer QoS.

Multiplexing's advantages come at the expense of having to *demultiplex* TPDUs at the transport receiver and to ensure fair sharing of resources among the multiplexed connections.

Demultiplexing requires a look-up operation to identify the intended receiver and possibly extra process switching and data copying.

3.2.4.6 Crash Recovery

In case of crashes of hosts or routers, how to recover from it is an important issue of transport layer.

(i) Router Crash:

- In case of datagram service, there is no problem of crashes as it knows how to handle it inherently.
- In case of virtual circuits a new connection can be established and information regarding TPDU's received can be obtained when crash occured.

(ii) Host Crash:

- Recovery from host crash is difficult to handle.
- Suppose we are using stop-and-wait protocol and a client is transmitting data to a server and server crashes in between. Suppose server receives data and does not send acknowledgement because of crash. If server goes up again immediately the client which has timed out will send same TPDU received already by server. Also, server has no way to identify whether it is new or duplicate TPDU.
- An enough status information regarding the ongoing connection has to be maintained by the transmitting and receiving entities in order to recover from the crash, occurring in the entities, which are working in layer below them. i.e. Transport layer can recover from crashes in network layer provided that each end-to-end connection keeps track of where it is.

3.2.5 The Internet Transport Protocols (TCP and UDP)

Internet has two main protocols in transport layer viz. TCP and UDP. TCP provides multiplexing, demultiplexing, and error detection (but not recovery) in exactly the same manner as UDP. TCP and UDP differ in many ways.

The most fundamental difference is that UDP is **connectionless,** while TCP is **connection-oriented**. UDP is connectionless because it sends data without establishing a connection. TCP is connection-oriented because before one application process can begin to send data to another, the two processes must first "handshake" with each other, that is, they must send some preliminary segments to each other to establish the parameters for data transfer.

3.2.5.1 Connection-Oriented Transport: TCP
The TCP Connection:

As part of the TCP connection establishment, both sides of the connection will initialize many TCP "state variables" associated with the TCP connection.

The TCP "connection" is not an end-to-end TDM or FDM circuit as in a circuit-switched network. Nor is it a virtual circuit, as the connection state resides entirely in the two end systems.

Since the TCP protocol runs only in the end systems and not in the intermediate network elements (routers and bridges), the intermediate network elements do not maintain TCP connection state. In fact, the intermediate network elements see datagrams, not connections. A TCP connection provides for **full duplex** data transfer. That is, application-level data can be transferred in both directions between two hosts - if there is a TCP connection between process A on one host and process B on another host, then application-level data can flow from A to B at the same time as application-level data flows from B to A.

TCP connection is also always **point-to-point**, i.e., between a single sender and a single receiver. So called "multicasting" the transfer of data from one sender to many receivers in a single send operation is not possible with TCP. With TCP, two hosts are company and three are a crowd.

Let us now take a look at how a TCP connection is established.(Though we have discussed this in earlier section let us have relook at it).
1. Suppose a process running in one host wants to initiate a connection with another process in another host. Recall that the host that is initiating the connection is called the **client host,** while the other host is called the **server host**.
2. The client application process first informs the client TCP that it wants to establish a connection to a process in the server. A Java client program does this by issuing the command:
Socket clientSocket= new Socket("hostname","port number");
3. The TCP in the client then proceeds to establish a TCP connection with the TCP in the server. For this the client first sends a special TCP segment; the server responds with a second special TCP segment; and finally the client responds again with a third special segment. The first two segments contain no "payload," i.e., no application-layer data; the third of these segments may
carry a payload. Because three segments are sent between the two hosts, this connection establishment procedure is often referred to as a **three-way-handshake**.

Once a TCP connection is established, the two application processes can send data to each other; because TCP is full-duplex they can send data at the same time. Let us consider the sending of data from the client process to the server process.

1. The client process passes a stream of data through the socket (the door of the process).
2. Once the data passes through the door, the data is now in the hands of TCP running in the client.
3. As shown in Fig. 3.34, TCP directs this data to the connection's **send buffer**, which is one of the buffers that is set aside during the initial three-way handshake. From time to time, TCP will "grab" chunks of data from the send buffer.

The maximum amount of data that can be grabbed and placed in a segment is limited by the **Maximum Segment Size (MSS).** The MSS depends on the TCP implementation (determined by the operating system) and can often be configured; common values are 1,500 bytes, 536 bytes and 512 bytes. (These segment sizes are often chosen in order to avoid IP fragmentation) Note that the MSS is the maximum amount of application-level data in the segment, not the maximum size of the TCP segment including headers.

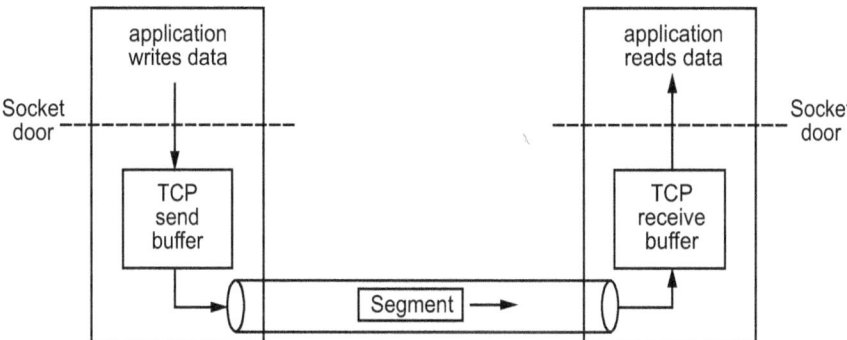

Fig. 3.34: TCP send and receive buffers

TCP encapsulates each chunk of client data with TCP header, thereby forming **TCP segments**. The segments are passed down to the network layer, where they are separately encapsulated within network-layer IP datagrams. The IP datagrams are then sent into the network. When TCP receives a segment at the other end, the segment's data is placed in the TCP connection's **receive buffer.** The application reads the stream of data from this buffer. Each side of the connection has its own send buffer and its own receive buffer. The send and receive buffers for data flowing in one direction are shown in Fig. 3.34.

We see from this discussion that a TCP connection consists of buffers, variables and a socket connection to a process in one host, and another set of buffers, variables and a socket connection to a process in another host. As mentioned earlier, no buffers or variables are allocated to the connection in the network elements (routers, bridges and repeaters) between the hosts.

TCP Segment Structure:

Having taken a brief look at the TCP connection, let's examine the TCP segment structure.

The TCP segment consists of header fields and a data field. The data field contains a chunk of application data.

As mentioned above, the MSS limits the maximum size of a segment's data field.

When TCP sends a large file, such as an encoded image as part of a Web page, it typically breaks the file into chunks of size MSS (except for the last chunk, which will often be less than the MSS).

Interactive applications, however, often transmit data chunks that are smaller than the MSS; for example, with remote login applications like Telnet, the data field in the TCP segment is often only one byte.

Because the TCP header is typically 20 bytes (12 bytes more than the UDP header), segments sent by Telnet may only be 21 bytes in length.

Fig. 3.34 shows the structure of the TCP segment. The header includes **source and destination port numbers**, that are used for multiplexing/demultiplexing data from/to upper layer applications. Also as with UDP, the header includes a **checksum field**. A TCP segment header also contains the following fields.

- The 32-bit **sequence number field**, and the 32-bit **acknowledgment number field** are used by the TCP sender and receiver in implementing a reliable data transfer service, as discussed below.

- The 16-bit **window size** field is used for the purposes of flow control. We will see shortly that it is used to indicate the number of bytes that a receiver is willing to accept.

- The 4-bit **length field** specifies the length of the TCP header in 32-bit words. The TCP header can be of variable length due to the TCP options field, discussed below. (Typically, the options field is empty, so that the length of the typical TCP header is 20 bytes.)

- The optional and variable length **options field** is used when a sender and receiver negotiate the maximum segment size (MSS) or as a window scaling factor for use in high-speed networks. A timestamping option is also defined

- The **flag field** contains 6 bits. The **ACK bit** is used to indicate that the value carried in the acknowledgment field is valid. The **RST, SYN** and **FIN** bits are used for connection setup and teardown. When the **PSH** bit is set, this is an indication that the receiver should pass the data to the upper layer immediately. Finally, the **URG** bit is used to indicate there is data in this segment that the sending-side upper layer entity has marked as "urgent". The location of the last byte of this urgent data is indicated by the 16-bit urgent data pointer. TCP must inform the receiving-side upper layer entity when urgent data exists and pass it a pointer to the end of the urgent data. (In practice, the PSH, URG and pointer to urgent data are not used. However, we mention these fields for completeness).

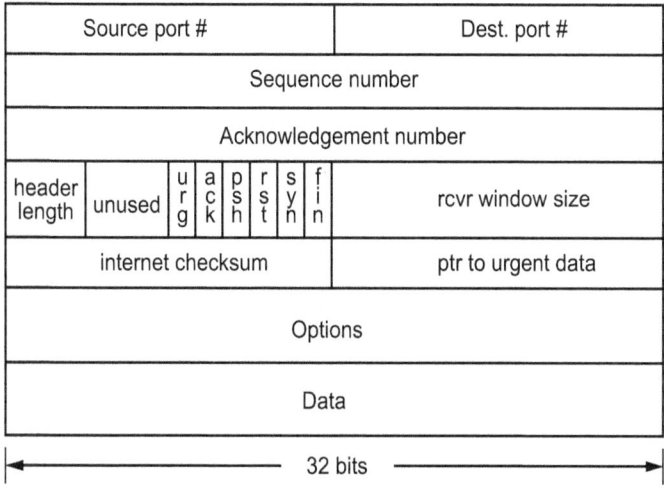

Fig. 3.35: TCP segment structure

Sequence Numbers and Acknowledgment Numbers:

Two of the most important fields in the TCP segment header are the sequence number field and the acknowledgment number field. These fields are a critical part of TCP's reliable data transfer service. But before discussing how these fields are used to provide reliable data transfer, let us first explain what exactly TCP puts in these fields. TCP views data as an unstructured, but ordered, stream of bytes. TCP's use of sequence numbers reflects this view in that, sequence numbers are over the stream of transmitted bytes and *not* over the series of transmitted segments.

The **sequence number for a segment** is the byte-stream number of the first byte in the segment. Let's look at an example. Suppose that a process in host A wants to send a stream of data to a process in host B over a TCP connection. The TCP in host A will implicitly number each byte in the data stream. Suppose that the data stream consists of a file consisting of 500,000 bytes, that the MSS is 1,000 bytes, and that the first byte of the data stream is numbered zero. As shown in Fig. 3.36, TCP constructs 500 segments out of the data stream. The first segment gets assigned sequence number 0, the second segment gets assigned sequence number 1000, the third segment gets assigned sequence number 2000, and so on. Each sequence number is inserted in the sequence number field in the header of the appropriate TCP segment.

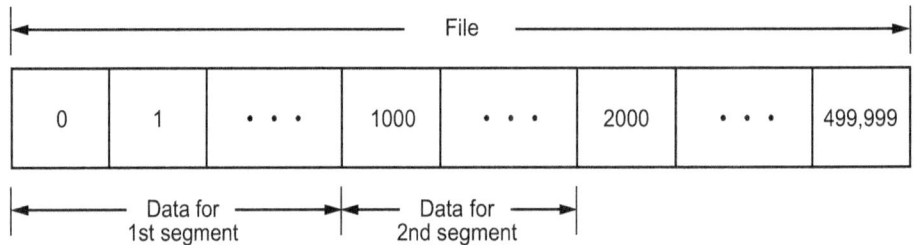

Fig. 3.36: Dividing File Data into TCP Segments

Now let us consider acknowledgment numbers. These are a little trickier than sequence numbers. Recall that TCP is full duplex, so that host A may be receiving data from host B while it sends data to host B (as part of the same TCP connection). Each of the segments that arrive from host B have a sequence number for the data flowing from B to A. *The acknowledgment number that host A puts in its segment is sequence number of the next byte host A is expecting from host B.* It is good to look at a few examples to understand what is going on here. Suppose that host A has received all bytes numbered 0 through 535 from B and suppose that it is about to send a segment to host B. In other words, host A is waiting for byte 536 and all the subsequent bytes in host B's data stream. So host A puts 536 in the acknowledgment number field of the segment it sends to B.

As another example, suppose that host A has received one segment from host B containing bytes 0 through 535 and another segment containing bytes 900 through 1,000. For some reason host A has not yet received bytes 536 through 899. In this example, host A is still waiting for byte 536 (and beyond) in order to recreate B's data stream. Thus, A's next segment to B will contain 536 in the acknowledgment number field. Because TCP only acknowledges bytes up to the first missing byte in the stream, TCP is said to provide **cumulative acknowledgements**.

This last example also brings up an important but subtle issue. Host A received the third segment (bytes 900 through 1,000) before receiving the second segment (bytes 536 through 899). Thus, the third segment arrived out of order. The subtle issue is: What does a host do when it receives out of order segments in a TCP connection ? Interestingly, the TCP RFCs do not impose any rules here, and leave the decision up to the people programming a TCP implementation. There are basically two choices: either *(i)* the receiver immediately discards out-of-order bytes; or *(ii)* the receiver keeps the out-of-order bytes and waits for the missing bytes to fill in the gaps. Clearly, the latter choice is more efficient in terms of network bandwidth, whereas the former choice significantly simplifies the TCP code. Throughout the remainder of this introductory discussion of TCP, we focus on the former implementation, that is, we assume that the TCP receiver discards out-of-order segments.

Fig. 3.36, we assumed that the initial sequence number was zero. In truth, both sides of a TCP connection randomly choose an initial sequence number. This is done to minimize the possibility a segment that is still present in the network from an earlier, already-terminated connection between two hosts is mistaken for a valid segment in a later connection between these same two hosts (who also happen to be using the same port numbers as the old connection)

Reliable Data Transfer:

Recall that the Internet's network layer service (IP service) is unreliable. IP does not guarantee datagram delivery, does not guarantee in-order delivery of datagrams, and does not guarantee the integrity of the data in the datagrams. With IP service, datagrams can overflow router buffers and never reach their destination, datagrams can arrive out of order, and bits in the datagram can get corrupted (flipped from 0 to 1 and vice versa). Because transport-layer segments are carried across the network by IP datagrams, transport-layer segments can also suffer from these problems as well.

TCP creates a **reliable data transfer** service on top of IP's unreliable best-effort service. Many popular application protocols including FTP, SMTP, HTTP and Telnet use TCP rather than UDP primarily because TCP provides reliable data transfer service. TCP's reliable data transfer service ensures that the data stream that a process reads out of its TCP receive buffer is uncorrupted, without gaps, without duplication, and in sequence, i.e., the byte stream is exactly the same byte stream that was sent by the end system on the other side of the connection. In this subsection we provide an informal overview of how TCP provides reliable data transfer.

Retransmissions:

Retransmission of lost and corrupted data is crucial for providing reliable data transfer. TCP provides reliable data transfer by using positive acknowledgments and timers. TCP acknowledges data that has been received correctly, and retransmits segments when segments or their corresponding acknowledgements are thought to be lost or corrupted.

TCP also uses **pipelining,** allowing the sender to have multiple transmitted but yet-to-be-acknowledged segments outstanding at any given time. We saw in the previous section that pipelining can greatly improve the throughput of a TCP connection when the ratio of the segment size to round trip delay is small. The specific number of outstanding unacknowledged segments that a sender can have is determined by TCP's flow control and congestion control mechanisms. For the time being, we must simply be aware that the sender can have multiple transmitted, but unacknowledged, segments at any given time.

A Few Interesting Scenarios:

We end this discussion by looking at a few simple scenarios. Fig. 3.37 depicts the scenario where host A sends one segment to host B. Suppose that this segment has sequence number 92 and contains 8 bytes of data. After sending this segment, host A waits for a segment from B with acknowledgment number 100.

Although the segment from A is received at B, the acknowledgment from B to A gets lost. In this case, the timer expires, and host A retransmits the same segment. Of course, when host B receives the retransmission, it will observe that the bytes in the segment are duplicate bytes it has already deposited in its receive buffer. Thus TCP in host B will discard the bytes in the retransmitted segment.

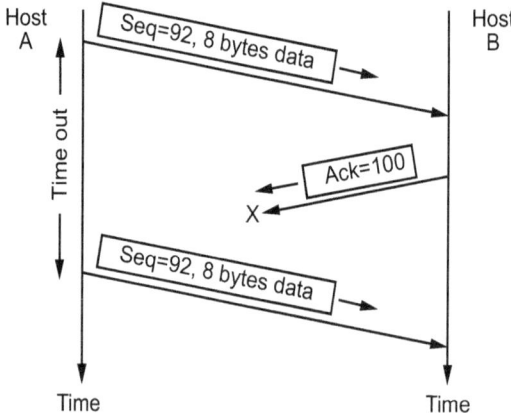

Fig. 3.37: Retransmission due to a lost Acknowledgment

In a second scenario, host A sends two segments back to back. The first segment has sequence number 92 and 8 bytes of data, and the second segment has sequence number 100 and 20 bytes of data. Suppose that both segments arrive intact at B, and B sends two separate acknowledgements for each of these segments. The first of these acknowledgements has acknowledgment number 100; the second has acknowledgment number 120. Suppose now that neither of the acknowledgements arrive at host A before the timeout of the first segment.

When the timer expires, host A resends the first segment with sequence number 92. Now, you may ask, does A also resend second segment ? According to the rules described above, host A resends the segment only if the timer expires before the arrival of an acknowledgment with an acknowledgment number of 120 or greater. Thus, as shown in Fig. 3.38, if the second acknowledgment does not get lost and arrives before the timeout of the second segment, A does not resend the second segment.

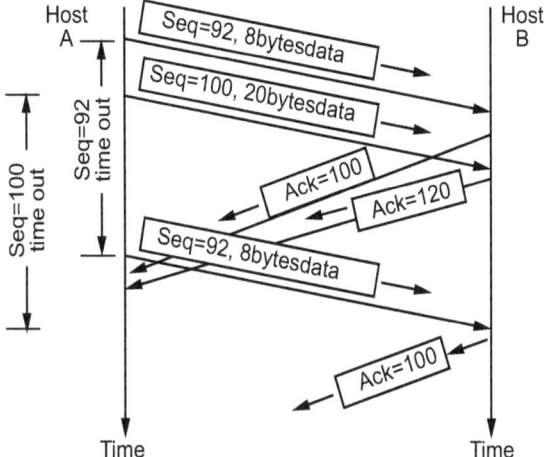

Fig. 3.38: Segment is not retransmitted because its acknowledgment arrives before the timeout

In a third and final scenario, suppose host A sends the two segments, exactly as in the second example. The acknowledgment of the first segment is lost in the network, but just before the timeout of the *first segment*, host A receives an acknowledgment with acknowledgment number 120. Host A therefore knows that host B has received *everything* up through byte 119; so host A does not resend either of the two segments. This scenario is illustrated in the Fig. 3.39.

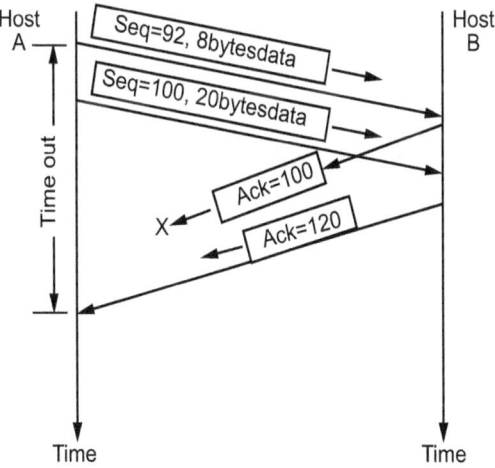

Fig. 3.39: A cumulative acknowledgment avoids retransmission of first segment

Recall that in the previous section we said that TCP is a Go-Back-N style protocol. This is because acknowledgements are cumulative and correctly-received but out-of-order segments are not individually ACKed by the receiver. But the reader should keep in mind that although the reliable-data-transfer component of TCP resembles Go-Back-N, it is by no means a pure implementation of Go-Back-N. To see that there are some striking differences between TCP and Go-Back-N, consider what happens when the sender sends a sequence of segments $1, 2,..., N$, and all of the segments arrive in order without error at the receiver. Further suppose that the acknowledgment for packet $n < N$ gets lost, but the remaining $N-1$ acknowledgments arrive at the sender before their respective timeouts. In this example, Go-Back-N would retransmit not only packet n, but also all the subsequent packets $n+1$, $n+2,...,N$. TCP, on the other hand, would retransmit at most one segment, namely, segment n. Moreover, TCP would not even retransmit segment n if the acknowledgement for segment $n+1$ arrives before the timeout for segment n.

Flow Control:

Recall that the hosts on each side of a TCP connection each set aside a receive buffer for the connection. When the TCP connection receives bytes that are correct and in sequence, it places the data in the receive buffer. The associated application process will read data from this buffer, but not necessarily at the instant the data arrives. Indeed, the receiving application may be busy with some other task and may not even attempt to read the data until long after it has arrived. If the application is relatively slow at reading the data, the sender can very easily overflow the connection's receive buffer by sending too much data too quickly. TCP thus provides a **flow control service** to its applications by eliminating the possibility of the sender overflowing the receiver's buffer. Flow control is thus a speed matching service - matching the rate at which the sender is sending to the rate at which the receiving application is reading. As noted earlier, a TCP sender can also be throttled due to congestion within the IP network; this form of sender control is referred to as **congestion control,** a topic we will explore in detail in Sections 3.6 and 3.7. While the actions taken by flow and congestion control are similar (the throttling of the sender), they are obviously taken for very different reasons. Unfortunately, many authors use the term interchangeably, and the servant reader would be careful to distinguish between the two cases. Let's now discuss how TCP provides its flow control service.

TCP provides flow control by having the sender maintain a variable called the receive window. Informally, the receive window is used to give the sender an idea about how much free buffer space is available at the receiver. In a full-duplex connection, the sender at each side of the connection maintains a distinct receive window. The receive window is dynamic, i.e., it changes throughout a connection's lifetime. Let's investigate the receive window in the context of a file transfer. Suppose that host A is sending a large file to host B over a TCP connection. Host B allocates a receive buffer to this connection; denote its size by RcvBuffer.

From time to time, the application process in host B reads from the buffer. Define the following variables.

LastByteRead = The number of the last byte in the data stream read from the buffer by the application process in B.

LastByteRcvd = The number of the last byte in the data stream that has arrived from the network and has been placed in the receive buffer at B.

Because TCP is not permitted to overflow the allocated buffer, we must have:

LastByteRcvd - LastByteRead <= RcvBuffer

The receive window, denoted RcvWindow, is set to the amount of spare room in the buffer:

RcvWindow = RcvBuffer - [LastByteRcvd - LastByteRead]

Because the spare room changes with time, RcvWindow is dynamic. The variable RcvWindow is illustrated in Fig. 3.40.

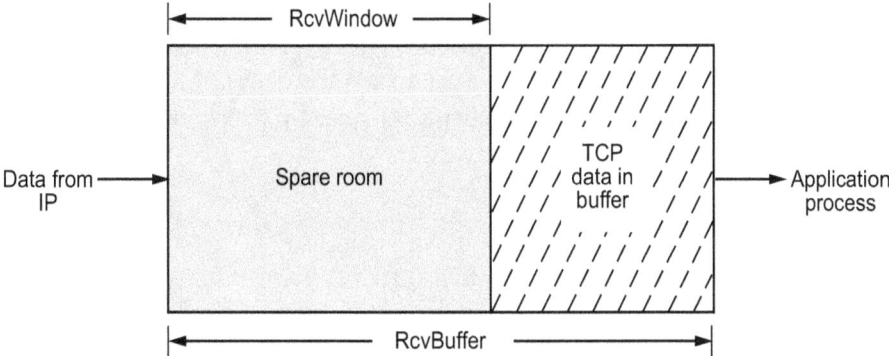

Fig. 3.40: The receive window (RcvWindow) and the receive buffer (RcvBuffer)

How does the connection use the variable RcvWindow to provide the flow control service? Host B informs host A of how much spare room it has in the connection buffer by placing its current value of RcvWindow in the window field of every segment it sends to A. Initially host B sets RcvWindow = RcvBuffer. Note that to pull this off, host B must keep track of several connection-specific variables.

Host A in turn keeps track of two variables, LastByteSent and LastByteAcked, which have obvious meanings. Note that the difference between these two variables, LastByteSent - LastByteAcked, is the amount of unacknowledged data that A has sent into the connection. By keeping the amount of unacknowledged data less than the value of RcvWindow, host A is assured that it is not overflowing the receive buffer at host B. Thus host A makes sure throughout the connection's life that

LastByteSent - LastByteAcked <= RcvWindow

There is one minor technical problem with this scheme. To see this, suppose host B's receive buffer becomes full so that RcvWindow = 0. After advertising RcvWindow = 0 to host A, also suppose that B has nothing to send to A. As the application process at B empties the buffer, TCP does not send new segments with new RcvWindows to host A -- TCP will only send a segment to host A if it has data to send or if it has an acknowledgment to send. Therefore host A is never informed that some space has opened up in host B's receive buffer: host A is blocked and can transmit no more data. To solve this problem, the TCP specification requires host A to continue to send segments with one data byte when B's receive window is zero. These segments will be acknowledged by the receiver. Eventually the buffer will begin to empty and the acknowledgements will contain non-zero RcvWindow.

Having described TCP's flow control service, we briefly mention here that UDP does not provide flow control. To understand the issue here, consider sending a series of UDP segments from a process on host A to a process on host B. For a typical UDP implementation, UDP will append the segments (more precisely, the data in the segments) in a finite-size queue that "precedes" the corresponding socket (i.e., the door to the process). The process reads one entire segment at a time from the queue. If the process does not read the segments fast enough from the queue, the queue will overflow and segments will get lost.

Round Trip Time and Timeout:

Recall that when a host sends a segment into a TCP connection, it starts a timer. If the timer expires before the host receives an acknowledgment for the data in the segment, the host retransmits the segment. The time from when the timer is started until when it expires is called the **timeout** of the timer. A natural question is, how large should timeout be? Clearly, the timeout should be larger than the connection's round-trip time, i.e., the time from when a segment is sent until it is acknowledged. Otherwise, unnecessary retransmissions would be sent. But the timeout should not be much larger than the round-trip time; otherwise, when a segment is lost, TCP would not quickly retransmit the segment, thereby introducing significant data transfer delays into the application. Before discussing the timeout interval in more detail, let us take a closer look at the round-trip time (RTT).

TCP Connection Management:

In this subsection we take a closer look at how a TCP connection is established and torn down. Although this particular topic may not seem particularly exciting, it is important because TCP connection establishment can significantly add to perceived delays (for example, when surfing the Web). Let's now take a look at how a TCP connection is established. Suppose a process running in one host wants to initiate a connection with another process in another host. The host that is initiating the connection is called the **client host** whereas the other host is called the **server host**. The client application process first informs the client TCP that it wants to establish a connection to a process in the server. A Java client program does this by issuing the command:

>   Socket client Socket=new Socket("hostname", "port number");

The TCP in the client then proceeds to establish a TCP connection with the TCP in the server in the following manner:

- **Step 1.** The client-side TCP first sends a special TCP segment to the server-side TCP. This special segment contains no application-layer data. It does, however, have one of the flag bits in the segment's header (see Figure 3.3-2), the so-called SYN bit, set to 1. For this reason, this special segment is referred to as a **SYN segment**. In addition, the client chooses an initial sequence number (*client_isn*) and puts this number in the sequence number field of the initial TCP SYN segment. This segment is encapsulated within an IP datagram and sent into the Internet.
- **Step 2.** Once the IP datagram containing the TCP SYN segment arrives at the server host (assuming it does arrive!), the server extracts the TCP SYN segment from the datagram, allocates the TCP buffers and variables to the connection, and sends a connection-granted segment to client TCP. This connection-granted segment also contains no application-layer data. However, it does contain three important pieces of information in the segment header. First, the SYN bit is set to 1. Second, the acknowledgment field of the TCP segment header is set to *isn+1*. Finally, the server chooses its own initial sequence number (*server_isn*) and puts this value in the sequence number field of the TCP segment header. This connection granted segment is saying, in effect, "I received your SYN packet to start a connection with your initial sequence number, *client_isn*. I agree to establish this connection. My own initial sequence number is *server_isn*." The conenction-granted segment is sometimes referred to as a **SYNACK** segment.
- **Step 3.** Upon receiving the connection-granted segment, the client also allocates buffers and variables to the connection. The client host then sends the server yet another segment; this last segment acknowledges the server's connection-granted segment (the client does so by putting the value *server_isn+1* in the acknowledgment field of the TCP segment header). The SYN bit is set to 0, since the connection is established.

Once the following three steps have been completed, the client and server hosts can send segments containing data to each other. In each of these future segments, the SYN bit will be set to zero. Note that in order to establish the connection, three packets are sent between the two hosts, as illustrated in Figure 3.41. For this reason, this connection establishment procedure is often referred to as a **three-way handshake**. Several aspects of the TCP three-way handshake (Why are initial sequence numbers needed ? Why is a three-way handshake, as opposed to a two-way handshake, needed ?) are explored in the homework problems.

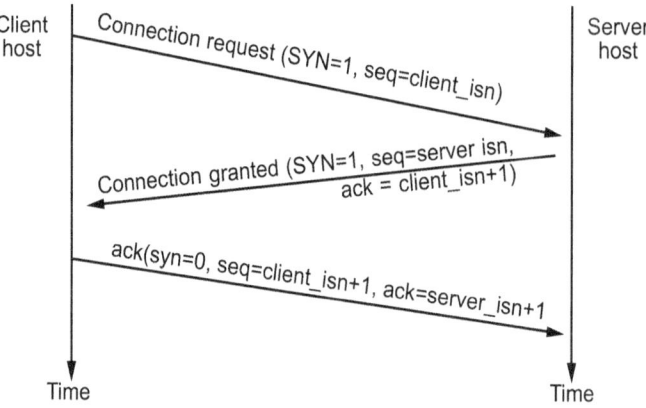

Fig. 3.41: TCP three-way handshake: segment exchange

All good things must come to an end, and the same is true with a TCP connection. Either of the two processes participating in a TCP connection can end the connection. When a connection ends, the "resources" (i.e., the buffers and variables) in the hosts are de-allocated. As an example, suppose the client decides to close the connection. The client application process issues a close command. This causes the client TCP to send a special TCP segment to the server process. This special segment has a flag bit in the segment's header, the so-called FIN bit (see Fig. 3.41), set to 1. When the server receives this segment, it sends the client an acknowledgment segment in return. The server then sends its own shut-down segment, which has the FIN bit set to 1. Finally, the client acknowledges the server's shut-down segment. At this point, all the resources in the two hosts are now de-allocated.

During the life of a TCP connection, the TCP protocol running in each host makes transitions through various **TCP states**. Fig. 3.42 illustrates a typical sequence of TCP states that are visited by the *client* TCP. The client TCP begins in the closed state. The application on the client side initiates a new TCP connection (by creating a Socket object in our Java examples). This causes TCP in the client to send a SYN segment to TCP in the server. After having sent the SYN segment, the client TCP enters the SYN_SENT sent. While in the SYN_STATE the client TCP waits for a segment from the server TCP that includes an acknowledgment for the client's previous segment as well as the SYN bit set to 1. Once having received such a segment, the client TCP enters the ESTABLISHED state. While in the ESTABLISHED state, the TCP client can send and receive TCP segments containing payload (i.e., application-generated) data.

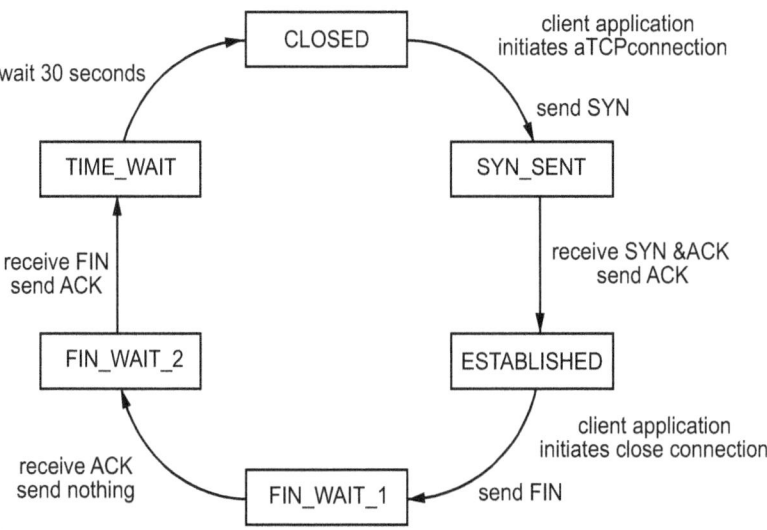

Fig. 3.42: A typical sequence of TCP states visited by a client TCP

Suppose that the client application decides it wants to close the connection. This causes the client TCP to send a TCP segment with the FIN bit set to 1 and to enter the FIN_WAIT_1 state. While in the FIN_WAIT state, the client TCP waits for a TCP segment from the server with an acknowledgment.

When it receives this segment, the client TCP enters the FIN_WAIT_2 state. While in the FIN_WAIT_2 state, the client waits for another segment from the server with the FIN bit set to 1; after receiving this segment, the client TCP acknowledges the server's segment and enters the TIME_WAIT state. The TIME_WAIT state lets the TCP client resend the final acknowledgment in the case the ACK is lost.

The time spent in the TIME-WAIT state is implementation dependent, but typical values are 30 seconds, 1 minute and 2 minutes. After the wait, the connection formally closes and all resources on the client side (including port numbers) are released.

Fig. 3.43 illustrates the series of states typically visited by the server-side TCP; the transitions are self-explanatory. In these two state transition diagrams, we have only shown how a TCP connection is *normally* established and shut down. We are not going to describe what happens in certain pathological scenarios, for example, when both sides of a connection want to shut down at the same time.

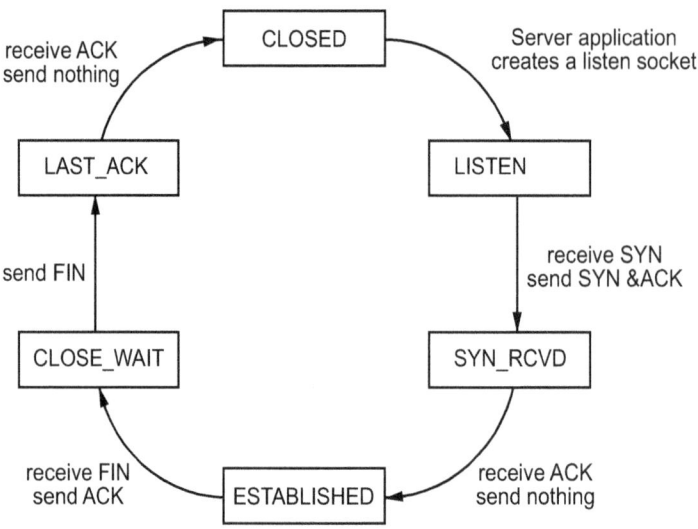

Fig. 3.43: A typical sequence of TCP states visited by a server-side TCP

3.2.5.2 Connectionless Transport: UDP

The Internet makes two transport protocols available to its applications, UDP and TCP. In this section we take a close look at UDP.

UDP, does just about as little as a transport protocol can. Aside from the multiplexing/demultiplexing function and some light error checking, it adds nothing to IP. In fact, if the application developer chooses UDP instead of TCP, then the application is talking almost directly with IP.

1. UDP takes messages from application process, attaches source and destination port number fields for the multiplexing/demultiplexing service, adds two other fields of minor importance, and passes the resulting "segment" to the network layer.
2. The network layer encapsulates the segment into an IP datagram and then makes a best-effort attempt to deliver the segment to the receiving host.
3. If the segment arrives at the receiving host, UDP uses the port numbers and the IP source and destination addresses to deliver the data in the segment to the correct application process.

Note that with UDP there is no handshaking between sending and receiving transport-layer entities before sending a segment. For this reason, UDP is said to be *connectionless*.
DNS is an example of an application-layer protocol that uses UDP. When the DNS application, in a host wants to make a query, it constructs a DNS query message and passes the message to a UDP socket. Without performing any handshaking, UDP adds a header fields to the message and passes the resulting segment to the network layer. The network

layer encapsulates the UDP segment into a datagram and sends the datagram to a name server. The DNS application at the querying host then waits for a reply to its query. If it doesn't receive a reply (possibly because UDP lost the query or the reply), it either tries sending the query to another nameserver, or it informs the invoking application that it can't get a reply. We mention that the DNS specification permits DNS to run over TCP instead of UDP; in practice, however, DNS almost always runs over UDP.

Now you might be wondering why an application developer would ever choose to build an application over UDP rather than over TCP. Isn't TCP always preferable to UDP since TCP provides a reliable data transfer service and UDP does not? The answer is no, as many applications are better suited for UDP for the following reasons:

- **No connection establishment.** As we shall discuss in Section 3.5, TCP uses a three-way handshake before it starts to transfer data. UDP just blasts away without any formal preliminaries. Thus UDP does not introduce any delay to establish a connection. This is probably the principle reason why DNS runs over UDP rather than TCP -- DNS would be much slower if it ran over TCP. HTTP uses TCP rather than UDP, since reliability is critical for Web pages with text. The TCP connection establishment delay in HTTP is an important contributor to the "world wide wait".

- **No connection state.** TCP maintains connection state in the end systems. This connection state includes receive and send buffers, congestion control parameters, and sequence and acknowledgment number parameters. We will see in Section 3.5 that this state information is needed to implement TCP's reliable data transfer service and to provide congestion control. UDP, on the other hand, does not maintain connection state and does not track any of these parameters. For this reason, a server devoted to a particular application can typically support many more active clients when the application runs over UDP rather than TCP.

- **Small segment header overhead.** The TCP segment has 20 bytes of header overhead in every segment, whereas UDP only has 8 bytes of overhead.

- **Unregulated send rate.** TCP has a congestion control mechanism that throttles the sender when one or more links between sender and receiver becomes excessively congested. This throttling can have a severe impact on real-time applications, which can tolerate some packet loss but require a minimum send rate. On the other hand, the speed at which UDP sends data is only constrained by the rate at which the application generates data, the capabilities of the source (CPU, clock rate, etc.) and the access bandwidth to the Internet. We should keep in mind, however, that the receiving host does not necessarily receive all the data - when the network is congested, a significant fraction of the UDP-transmitted data could be lost due to router buffer overflow. Thus, the receive rate is limited by network congestion even if the sending rate is not constrained.

Table 3.3 lists popular Internet applications and the transport protocols that they use. As we expect, e-mail, remote terminal access, the Web and file transfer run over TCP -- these applications need the reliable data transfer service of TCP. Nevertheless, many important applications run over UDP rather TCP. UDP is used for RIP routing table updates, because the updates are sent periodically, so that lost updates are replaced by more up-to-date updates. UDP is used to carry network management data. UDP is preferred to TCP in this case, since network management must often run when the network is in a stressed state - precisely when reliable, congestion-controlled data transfer is difficult to achieve. Also, as we mentioned earlier, DNS runs over UDP, thereby avoiding TCP's connection establishment delays

Table 3.3: Popular Internet applications and their underlying transport protocols

Application	Application-layer protocol	Underlying Transport Protocol
Electronic mail	SMTP	TCP
Remote terminal access	Telnet	TCP
Web	HTTP	TCP
File transfer	FTP	TCP
Remote file server	NFS	typically UDP
Streaming multimedia	proprietary	typically UDP
Internet telephony	proprietary	typically UDP
Network Management	SNMP	typically UDP
Routing Protocol	RIP	typically UDP
Name Translation	DNS	typically UDP

As shown in Table 3.3, UDP is also commonly used today with multimedia applications, such as Internet phone, real-time video conferencing, and streaming of stored audio and video. We shall take a close look at these applications in Chapter 6. We just mention now that all of these applications can tolerate a small fraction of packet loss, so that reliable data transfer is not absolutely critical for the success of the application. Furthermore, interactive real-time applications, such as Internet phone and video conferencing, react very poorly to TCP's congestion control. For these reasons, developers of multimedia applications often choose to run the applications over UDP instead of TCP. Finally, because TCP cannot be employed with multicast, multicast applications run over UDP.

Although commonly done today, running multimedia applications over UDP is controversial to say the least. As we mentioned above, UDP lacks any form of congestion control. But congestion control is needed to prevent the network from entering a congested state in which very little useful work is done. If everyone were to start streaming high bit-rate video without using any congestion control, there would be so much packet overflow at routers that no one would see anything. Thus, the lack of congestion control in UDP is a potentially serious problem.

Before discussing the UDP segment structure, we mention that it is possible for an application to have reliable data transfer when using UDP. This can be done if reliability is built into the application itself (e.g., by adding acknowledgement and retransmission mechanisms, such as those we shall study in the next section). But this a non-trivial task that would keep an application developer busy debugging for a long time. Nevertheless, building reliability directly into the application allows the application to "have its cake and eat it too" -- that is, application processes can communicate reliably without being constrained by the transmission rate constraints imposed by TCP's congestion control mechanism. Application-level reliability also allows an application to tailor its own application-specific form of error control. An interactive real-time may occasionally choose to retransmit a lost message, provided that round trip network delays are small enough to avoid adding significant playout delays.

Many of today's proprietary streaming applications do just this -- they run over UDP, but they have built acknowledgements and retransmissions into the application in order reduce packet loss.

UDP Segment Structure:
The UDP segment structure, shown in Fig. 3.44.

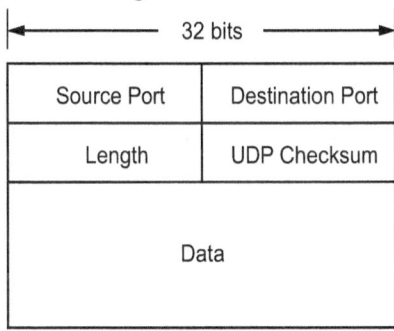

Fig. 3.44: UDP segment structure

1. The application data occupies the data field of the UDP datagram. For example, for DNS, the data field contains either a query message or a response message. For a streaming audio application, audio samples fill the data field.
2. The UDP header has only four fields, each consisting of four bytes. As discussed in the previous section, the port numbers allow the destination host to pass the application data to the correct process running on that host (i.e., perform the demultiplexing function).

3. The checksum is used by the receiving host to check if errors have been introduced into the segment during the course of its transmission from source to destination

UDP Checksum:

The UDP checksum provides for error detection. UDP at the sender side performs the one's complement of the sum of all the 16-bit words in the segment. This result is put in the checksum field of the UDP segment. (In truth, the checksum is also calculated over a few of the fields in the IP header in addition to the UDP segment. But we ignore this detail in order to see the forest through the trees.) When the segment arrives (if it arrives !) at the receiving host, all 16-bit words are added together, including the checksum. If this sum equals 1111111111111111, then the segment has no detected errors. If one of the bits is a zero, then we know that errors have been introduced into the segment.

Here we give a simple example of the checksum calculation. You can find details about efficient implementation of the calculation in the. As an example, suppose that we have the following three 16-bit words:

    0110011001100110
    0101010101010101
    0000111100001111

The sum of first of these 16-bit words is:

    0110011001100110
    0101010101010101

    1011101110111011

Adding the third word to the above sum gives –

    1011101110111011
    0000111100001111

    1100101011001010

The 1's complement is obtained by converting all the 0s to 1s and converting all the 1s to 0s. Thus the 1's complement of the sum 1100101011001010 is 0011010100110101, which becomes the checksum. At the receiver, all four 16-bit words are added, including the checksum. If no errors are introduced into the segment, then clearly the sum at the receiver will be 1111111111111111. If one of the bits is a zero, then we know that errors have been introduced into the segment. In section 5.1, we'll see that the Internet checksum is not foolproof -- even if the sum equals 1111111111111111, it is still possible that there are undetected errors in the segment. For this reason, a number of protocols use more sophisticated error detection techniques than simple checksumming.

You may wonder why UDP provides a checksum in the first place, as many link-layer protocols (including the popular Ethernet protocol) also provide error checking? The reason is that there is no guarantee that all the links between source and destination provide error checking -- one of the links may use a protocol that does not provide error checking. Because IP is supposed to run over just about any layer-2 protocol, it is useful for the transport layer to provide error checking as a safety measure. Although UDP provides error checking, it does not do anything to recover from an error. Some implementations of UDP simply discard the damaged segment; others pass the damaged segment to the application with a warning.

SOLVED EXAMPLES

Example 3.1:
The byte counting variant of leaky bucket algorithm is used in a particular system. The rule is that one 1024 byte packet, two 512 packets etc. may be sent on each tick. What are restrictions of this system?
Solution:
The restriction is that we cannot send a packet greater than 1024 bytes.

Example 3.2:
A computer on a 6 Mbps network is regulated by a token bucket. The token bucket is filled at a rate 1 Mbps. It is initially filled to capacity 8 Mbit. How long can the computer transmit at full rate of 6 Mbps ?
Solution:
The time taken by the token bucket to transmit at full rate is,

$$S = \frac{C}{M - \rho}$$

where,   C – Capacity
M – Maximum rate of transmission
ρ – Rate of arrival of tokens.

$$S = \frac{8}{6 - 1}$$
$$= 1.6 \text{ sec.}$$

Example 3.3:
Token bucket system is used for traffic stopping. A new token is put every 5 μsec into the bucket. What is maximum sustainable net data rate?
Solution:
   Given: Frame length = 100 bytes and 10 bytes header.
   Token arrival rate is 5 μsec.

Hence, $\frac{1}{5 \times 10^6}$ = 200000 frames can be sent every second.

Since each frame is 100 bytes and 10 bytes header, there will be 90 bytes data = 720 bits.

Hence, net data rate will be,

$$720 \times 200000 = 144 \times 10^6$$
$$= 144 \text{ Mbps}$$

EXERCISE

1. I.Pv$_6$ uses 16 bytes addreses. If a block of 1 million addresses is allocated every piseconds how long will the address last ? Angle of universe = 10^{10} years.
2. Produce a sketch showing the field that make up the UDP (User Datagram Protocol) and explain the functions of each field in brief.
3. What are the services provided by the network layer to the transport layer?
4. With suitable example, explain the working of virtual circuit and diagram packet switching protocol?
5. What are the transparent services primitives?
6. List the routing algorithm used in communication networks. What is the optimality principle? Explain in short shortest path routing algorithm.
7. What is the task of transport layer? List the services provided to upper layers by transport layer. Explain how Q.S. is improved by transport layer.
8. What is the main difference between TCP and UDP?
9. Compare circuit switching message switching and packet switching.
10. List the goals of the network layer. Define routing, flooding.
11. What is dynamic routing ? Discuss distance vector routing.
12. What are the general principles of congestion control? What are the congestion prevention policies?
13. List the typical transport layer quality of services parameters. Define each.
14. Identify the OSI layers under which the following network components operate.

    (i) Router, (ii) Repeater, (iii) Bridge, (iv) Gateway.
15. Can a connection oriented message transfer service to be provided across and connectionless packet network? Explain.
16. Can a connectionless datagram transfer service be provided across connection oriented network?
17. What different does it makes to the network layer if the underlying data link layer provider connection oriented services versus a connectionless service?
18. Explain distance vector routing and hierarchical routing.

Unit IV

APPLICATION LAYER

4.1 Introduction

1. In TCP/IP Application Layer, Presentation Layer and Sessional Layer are combined to form the Application Layer only.
2. The application layer interacts with software applications that implement a communicating component.
3. Such application programs are outside of the scope of the OSI model, but they translate an end user's typing into a Layer 7 request.
4. Application layer functions typically include the following:
    - **Identifying communication partners** - The application layer identifies and determines the availability of communication partners for an application with data to transmit.
    - **Determining resource availability** - The application layer must determine whether sufficient network resources for the requested communication are available.
    - **Synchronizing communication** - Communication between applications requires co-operation that is managed by the application layer.
5. Also it provides a variety of encoding and encryption functions that are applied to the application layer data.
6. **Common data *encryption schemes*** - The use of standard data encryption schemes allows data encrypted at the source device to be properly unencrypted at the destination.
7. Figure shows how a packet of information flows through the seven layers as it travels from one computer to another on the network.
8. The data begins its journey when an end-user application sends data to another network computer.
9. The data enters the network through an Application layer interface.
10. The data then works its way down through the protocol stack.
11. Along the way, the protocol at each layer manipulates the data by adding header information, converting the data into different formats, combining packets to form larger packets, and so on.
12. When the data reaches the Physical layer protocol, it is actually placed on the network media (in other words, the cable) and sent to the receiving computer.

13. When the receiving computer receives the data, the data works its way up through the protocol stack.

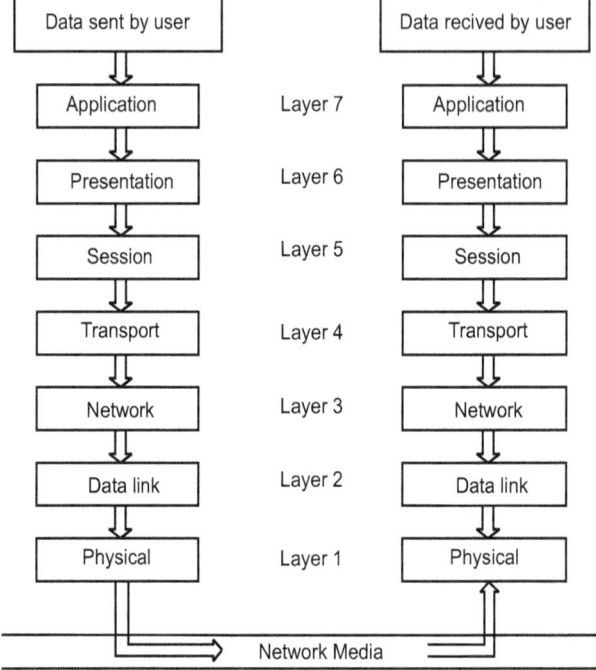

Fig. 4.1: How data travels through the seven layers (Application Layer to Application Layer)

14. Then, the protocol at each layer reverses the processing that was done by the corresponding layer on the sending computer.
15. Headers are removed, data is converted back to its original format, packets that were split into smaller packets are recombined into larger messages, and so on.
16. When the packet reaches the Application layer protocol, it is delivered to an application that can process the data.
17. In this Layer we will mainly Discuss the Network Security, DNS system, Electronic Mail, WWW, Socket Programming and Video on Demand Concept.

4.2 Introduction to Network Security

1. During this time when the Internet provides essential communication between tens of millions of people and is being increasingly used as a tool for commerce, security becomes a tremendously important issue to deal with.
2. There are many aspects to security and many applications, ranging from secure commerce and payments to private communications and protecting passwords.
3. One essential aspect for secure communications is that of cryptography, which is the focus of this chapter.

4. But it is important to note that while cryptography is *necessary* for secure communications, it is not by itself sufficient.
5. The reader is advised, then, that the topics covered in this chapter only describe the first of many steps necessary for better security in any number of situations.
6. This Study Network Security topic has two major purposes.
7. The first is to define some of the terms and concepts behind basic cryptographic methods, and to offer a way to compare the myriad cryptographic schemes in use today.
8. The second is to provide some real examples of cryptography in use today.

4.3 Who causes Network security problems?

Table 4.1: Some people causes security problems

Adversary	Goal
Student	To have fun snooping on people's e-mail.
Cracker	To test out someone's security system: steal data.
Sales rep	To claim to represent all of Europe, not just Andorra.
Businessman	To discover a competitor's strategic marketing plan.
Ex-employee	To get revenge for being fired.
Accountant	To embezzle money from a company.
Stockbroker	To deny a promise made to a customer by e-mail.
Con man	To steal credit card numbers for sale.
Spy	To learn an enemy's military or industrial secrets
Torrorist	To steam germ warfare secrets.

4.4 Cryptography

1. Cryptography is the study of secret (crypto) **writing** (graphy).
2. Concerned with developing algorithms which may be used to:
    - Conceal the context of some message from all except the sender and recipient (privacy or secrecy), and/or
    - Verify the correctness of a message to the recipient (**authentication**).
3. Form the basis of many technological solutions to computer and communications security problems.

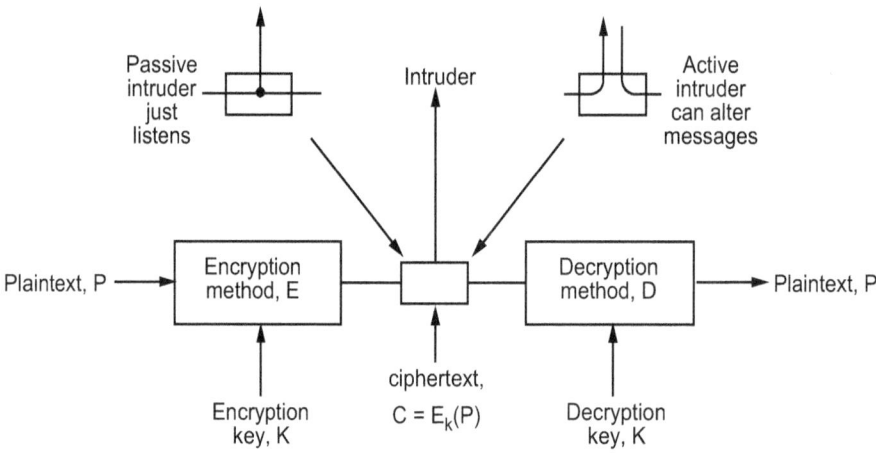

Fig. 4.2: The Basic Encryption Model

4. The messages to be encrypted, known as the **plaintext**, are transformed by a function that is parameterized by a **key**.
5. The output of the encryption process, known as the **ciphertext**, is then transmitted, often by messenger or radio.
6. We assume that the enemy, or **intruder**, hears and accurately copies down the complete ciphertext.
7. However, unlike the intended recipient, he does not know what the decryption key is and so cannot decrypt the cipher text easily.
8. Sometimes the intruder can not only listen to the communication channel (passive intruder) but can also record messages and play them back later, inject his own messages, or modify messages before they get to the receiver (active intruder).
9. The art of breaking ciphers, called **cryptanalysis**, and the art devising them (cryptography) is collectively known as **cryptology**.
10. **Encryption methods have historically been divided into two categories: substitution ciphers and transposition ciphers**. We will now deal with each of these briefly as background information for modern cryptography.

4.4.1 Monoalphabetic Substitution Cipher

1. The monoalphabetic substitution cipher involves replacing each letter of the alphabet with a different letter coming from a shifted set of letters.
2. For instance, the following is the perhaps the most simplest substitution cipher known as the Ceaser cipher:

a	b	c	d	e	f	g	h	i	j	k	l	m	n	o	p	q	r	s	t	u	v	w	x	y	z
D	E	F	G	H	I	J	K	L	M	N	O	P	Q	R	S	T	U	V	W	X	Y	Z	A	B	C

Shifted by 3 letters

Fig. 4.3

3. This algorithm would be: **CT = (PT + 3) mod 26** where CT is Cipher Text, PT is Plaintext.
4. So the following message on line 1 can be encrypted as line 2.
   Line 1: pick up supplies at location x.
   Line 2: SLFN XT VXTTOLHV DW ORFDWLRQ A
5. In order to easily break a monoalphabetic substitution cipher some knowledge of the language must be known, such as the relative frequency of letters.
6. For instance, the English language the most frequent letter used is 'e' and the second most frequent letter used is 't' and so on.
7. Another approach would be to look at **digrams**.
8. **Digrams** are 2 letter combinations such as 'th'.
9. So if one wanted to make this more difficult to crack then it is important to flatten out the relative frequency of letter substitutions by assigning letters to more than one.

4.4.2 Polyalphabetic Substitution Cipher

1. The polyalphabetic substitution cipher uses multiple monoalphabetic substitution ciphers of which a key determines which one to use. For instance,

   ```
   a b c d e f g h i j k l m n o p q r s t u v w x y z
   E F G H I J K L M N O P Q R S T U V W X Y Z A B C D
   F G H I J K L M N O P Q R S T U V W X Y Z A B C D E
   G H I J K L M N O P Q R S T U V W X Y Z A B C D E F
   H I J K L M N O P Q R S T U V W X Y Z A B C D E F G
   I J K L M N O P Q R S T U V W X Y Z A B C D E F G H
   J K L M N O P Q R S T U V W X Y Z A B C D E F G H I
   K L M N O P Q R S T U V W X Y Z A B C D E F G H I J
   ```

2. Line 1 would be the key, Line 2 would be the plain text and Line 3 is the cipher text below.
   Line 1: hikehikehikehikehike
   Line 2: meetmeatnooninlondon
   Line 3: TMOXTMKXUWYRPVVSULYR

3. So one would go down the first column to find the h's row.
4. The first letter of the plain text message is 'm' so then intersection of the 'm' column and the 'h' row produces the ciphered letter 'T'.
5. The next letter in the key is 'i' and 'e' in the plain text message.
6. Naturally enough the next ciphered letter is the intersection of the 'i' row and 'e' column with produces 'M'.
7. Probably the most popular polyalphabetic substitution cipher is the **Vigenere** cipher.
8. This technique flattens out the relative letter frequency.
9. However, this technique isn't too secure either because the length of the key can determine which monoalphabetic substitution cipher to use.
10. So the draw back to making this technique as tough as possible would be to make the key as long as the plaintext.
11. Gilbert Vernam an AT&T employee in 1918 introduced this concept.

4.4.3 Transposition Cipher

1. Transposition ciphers simply scramble the order of the letters in a plain text message.
2. For instance, the message: turnrightthenturnleftthengostraight could be transposed as

Plain Text	Cipher Text
turnrightthenturnleftthengostraight	Ttesuhftretrnntarthiiueggrnhhngttlo

3. The transposition cipher is fairly easy to crack.
4. One could play around with various column positions and utilize language frequencies such as digrams, etc.
5. However, to make this more difficult one could encrypt the message first and then transpose the letters.
6. Other Example of Transposition Cipher is given below
7. Transposition ciphers rearrange the letters of the plaintext without changing the letters themselves.
8. For example, a very simple transposition cipher is the *rail fence*, in which the plaintext is staggered between two rows and then read off to give the ciphertext.
9. In a two row rail fence the message MERCHANT TAYLORS' SCHOOL becomes:

M	R	H	N	T	Y	O	S	C	O	L
E	C	A	T	A	L	R	S	H	O	

Which is read out as: MRHNTYOSCOLECATALRSHO

10. The rail fence is the simplest example of a class of transposition ciphers called route ciphers.
11. These were quite popular in the early history of cryptography.
12. Generally, in route ciphers the elements of the plaintext (usually in this case single letters) are written on a pre-arranged route into a matrix agreed upon by the transmitter and receiver.
13. The example above has a two row by n-column matrix in which the plaintext is entered sequentially by columns, the encryption route is therefore to read the top row and then the lower.
14. Obviously, to even approach an acceptable level of security, the route would have to be much more complicated than the one in this example.
15. One form of transposition that has enjoyed widespread use relies on identifying the route by means of an easily remembered keyword.
16. This can be done in several ways.
17. One way, as in this example, is to define the order in which each column is written depending on the alphabetical position of each letter of the keyword relative to the other letters.
18. Using the keyword CIPHER, a matrix can be written out like the one below:

C	I	P	H	E	R
1	4	5	3	2	6
M	E	R	C	H	A
N	T	T	A	Y	L
O	R	S	S	C	H
O	O	L	Z	Z	Z

19. Unlike the previous example the plaintext has been written into the columns from left to right as normal, and the ciphertext will be formed by reading down the columns.
20. The order in which the columns are written to form the ciphertext is determined by the key.

This matrix therefore yields the ciphertext: MNOOHYCZCASZETRORTSLALHZ.

21. The first column is first because C is the earliest in the alphabet, followed by the second to last column because E is the next in the alphabet.
22. The security of this method of encryption can be significantly improved by re-encrypting the resulting cipher using another transposition.
23. Because the product of the two transpositions is also a transposition, the effect of multiple transpositions is to define a complex route through the matrix which would not by itself by easy to define with a simply remembered mnemonic.

24. When decrypting a route cipher, the receiver simply enters the ciphertext into the agreed-upon matrix according to the encryption route and then simply reads out the plaintext.
25. There are three types of transpositions are possible
    1. Columnar transposition
    2. Double transposition
    3. Disrupted transposition

Columnar Transposition:
1. All letters of the key word are written.
2. Numbers are assigned to these letters according to there position in the alphabet and the key word.
3. All letters of the alphabet are written line by line below these numbers:

W	I	L	L	I	A	M
7	2	4	5	3	1	6
A	B	C	D	E	F	G
H	I	J	K	L	M	N
O	P	Q	R	S	T	U
V	W	X	Y	Z		

4. The cipher alphabet is obtained by reading column by column in the order of the numbers.

Plain	A	B	C	D	E	F	G	H	I	J	K	L	M	N	O	P	Q	R	S	T	U	V	W	X	Y	Z
Cipher	F	M	T	B	I	P	W	E	L	S	Z	C	J	Q	X	D	K	R	Y	G	N	U	A	H	O	V

Double Transposition:
1. The procedure outlined above is applied twice. Using the result given above we obtain:

W	I	L	L	I	A	M
7	2	4	5	3	1	6
F	M	T	B	I	P	W
E	L	S	Z	C	J	Q
X	D	K	R	Y	G	N
U	A	H	O	V		

2. The cipher alphabet is obtained by reading column by column in the order of the numbers.

Plain	A	B	C	D	E	F	G	H	I	J	K	L	M	N	O	P	Q	R	S	T	U	V	W	X	Y	Z
Cipher	P	J	G	M	L	D	A	I	C	Y	V	T	S	K	H	B	Z	R	O	W	Q	N	F	E	X	U

3. In modern cryptography transposition cipher systems serve mainly as one of several methods used as a step in forming a product cipher.

4.4.4 Product Ciphers

1. In the days of manual cryptography i.e. without the aid of a computer product ciphers were a useful device for the cryptographer and double transposition ciphers on keyword-based matrices were, in fact, widely used.
2. There was also some use of a particular class of product ciphers called fractionation systems.
3. In a fractionation system a substitution is first made from symbols in the plaintext to multiple symbols (usually pairs, in which case the cipher is called a bilateral cipher) in the ciphertext, which is then super encrypted by a transposition.
4. One of the most famous field ciphers ever was a fractionation system - the ADFGVX cipher that was employed by the German Army during the First World War.
5. This system was so named because it used a 6 ∞ 6 matrix to substitution-encrypt the 26 letters of the alphabet and 10 digits into pairs of the symbols A, D, F, G, V and X.
6. The resulting bilateral cipher is only an intermediate cipher, it is then written into a rectangular matrix and transposed to produce the final cipher, which is the one, which would be transmitted.

	A	D	F	G	V	X
A	S	U	B	J	E	C
D	T	A	D	F	G	H
F	I	K	L	M	N	O
G	P	Q	R	V	W	X
V	Y	Z	0	1	2	3
X	4	5	6	7	8	9

7. Here is an example of enciphering the phrase "Merchant Taylors" with this cipher using the key word "Subject".

	A	D	F	G	V	X
A	S	U	B	J	E	C
D	T	A	D	F	G	H
F	I	K	L	M	N	O
G	P	Q	R	V	W	X
V	Y	Z	0	1	2	3
X	4	5	6	7	8	9

Plaintext: M E R C H A N T   T A Y L O R S
Ciphertext: FG AV GF AX DX DD FV DA   DA DD VA FF FX GF AA

8. This intermediate ciphertext can then be put in a transposition matrix based on a different key.

C	I	P	H	E	R
1	4	5	3	2	6
F	G	A	V	G	F
A	X	D	X	D	D
F	V	D	A	D	A
D	D	V	A	F	F
F	X	G	F	A	A

9. The final cipher is therefore: FAFDFGDDFAVXAAFGXVDXADDVGFDAFA.

4.4.5 Block Ciphers

1. Generally, ciphers transform pieces of plaintext of a fixed size into ciphertext.
2. In older, manual systems, these pieces were usually single letters or characters (or sometimes, as in the Playfair cipher, digraphs), since these were the largest units that could be easily encrypted or decrypted by hand.
3. Although systems which operated on sets of three characters and other, larger groups of numbers, were proposed and understood to potentially be more secure they were never implemented because of the extra difficulty in the manual encryption or decryption process.
4. In modern, single key cryptography however, the units of information can be much larger.
5. **A block cipher is a type of symmetric-key encryption algorithm that changes a fixed-length block of the plaintext into the same length of ciphertext.**

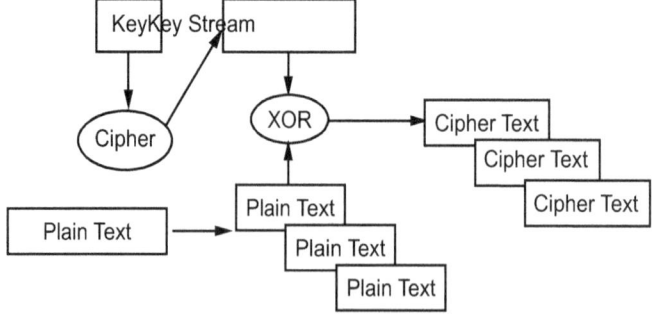

Fig. 4.4: Block Cipher Generation

6. The encryption works by means of a key.
7. Decryption is simply the reverse of the encryption process using the same secret key.
8. The fixed length is called the block size and for modern block ciphers is usually 64 bits.
9. As processors become more sophisticated, however, it is likely that this block size will increase to 128 bits.
10. Since different plaintext blocks are mapped to different ciphertext blocks, a block cipher effectively provides a permutation of the set of all possible messages.
11. The actual permutation produced during any particular operation is of course secret, and determined by the key.
12. An *iterated block cipher* encrypts a plaintext block using a process with several stages (rounds).
13. At each stage the same process (known as a *round function*) is applied to the data using a *subkey* (the set of subkeys usually being derived from a user provided key).
14. The number of rounds in an iterated block cipher depends on the desired security level of the encrypted ciphertext and the trade-off that must be made with performance; fairly obviously a iterated block cipher with a large number of rounds will require more processing time.
15. It is worth noting that in some cases the number of rounds required to provide an accurate level of security will be too large for the cipher to be practical.
16. An example of an iterated block cipher is a **Feistel cipher**. Feistel ciphers are a special class of iterated block ciphers.
17. In this type of cipher the ciphertext is calculated from the repeated application of the same *round function*.

4.4.6 Stream Ciphers

1. A *stream cipher* also breaks the plaintext into units, this time it is normally a single character.
2. It then encrypts the nth unit of the plaintext with the nth unit of the key stream.
3. Stream ciphers can be designed to be exceptionally fast, much faster than any block cipher.
4. While the encryption of any particular plaintext with a block cipher will result in the same ciphertext when the same key is used; with a stream cipher, the transformation of the smaller plaintext units will vary, depending on when they are encountered during the encryption process.

5. A stream cipher generates what is known as a *keystream* - a sequence of bits, which is used as a key.
6. The encryption process involves combining the keystream with the plaintext.
7. The keystream can be generated in two ways:
   - Independent of the plaintext and ciphertext (this yields what is known as a *synchronous* stream cipher).
   - Depending on the data and its encryption (in which case the stream cipher is said to be *self-synchronizing*).
8. The majority of stream cipher designs are for synchronous stream ciphers.
9. Interest in stream ciphers is currently attributed to the appealing properties of the *one-time pad*.
10. A one-time pad, which is sometimes called the Vernam cipher, uses a keystream which is the same length as the plaintext message and consists of a series of bits generated completely at random.
11. Theoretically this should produce ciphertext, which is the most secure possible, because since the keystream is random even a cryptanalyst with infinite computational resources can still only guess at the underlying plaintext.

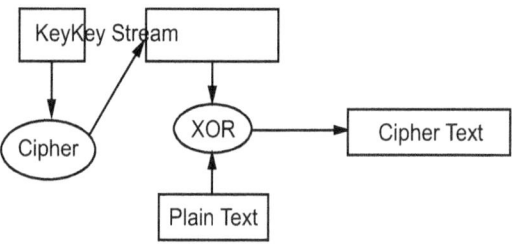

Fig. 4.5: Stream Chiper

12. While the one-time pad has occasionally seen use in wartime for ultra secret transmissions the fact that the key is as long as the message introduces severe practical problems and so, while theoretically perfectly secure, the one-time pad is generally impractical.
13. Stream ciphers were developed as an approximation to the one-time pad.
14. At this time there is no de facto standard for stream ciphers although the most widely used stream cipher is RC4, a stream cipher designed by Rivest for RSA Data Security Inc.
15. It is a variable key-size stream cipher with an algorithm based on the use of a random permutation.

16. Strangely, certain modes of operation of a block cipher transform it into a keystream generator and so, in this way, any block cipher can be used as a stream cipher.
17. Stream ciphers with a dedicated design and typically much faster, however.
18. One method for generating a keystream is a *Linear Feedback Shift Register* (LFSR).
19. This is a mechanism for generating a sequence of binary bits.
20. LFSRs are easy to implement and fast operating in both hardware and software however a single LFSR is not secure because over the years a mathematical framework has been developed which allows for the analysis of their output.
21. This problem can be solved by using a *shift register cascade*, a set of LFSRs connected together so that the behaviour of one of them depends on another.
22. The detailed operation of LFSRs and shift register cascades is beyond the scope of this book.

4.5 The Purpose of Cryptography

1. Cryptography is the science of writing in secret code and is an ancient art.
2. When an Egyptian scribe used non-standard hieroglyphs in an inscription.
3. Some experts argue that cryptography appeared spontaneously sometime after writing was invented, with applications ranging from diplomatic missives to war-time battle plans.
4. It is no surprise, then, that new forms of cryptography came soon after the widespread development of computer communications.
5. In data and telecommunications, cryptography is necessary when communicating over any untrusted medium, which includes just about *any* network, particularly the Internet.
6. Within the context of any application-to-application communication, there are some specific security requirements, including:
7. **Authentication:**
   - The process of proving one's identity. (The primary forms of host-to-host authentication on the Internet today are name-based or address-based, both of which are notoriously weak.)
   - A secure communication should ensure that the parties involved in the communication are who they claim to be.
   - In other words, we should be protected from malicious users who try to impersonate one of the parties in the secure conversation.
   - Again, this is relatively easy to do with some network sniffing tools.
   - However, modern encryption algorithms also protect against this kind of attacks.

8. **Authorization:**
    - Another important concept in computer security, although not generally considered a 'pillar' of secure communications, is the concept of *authorization*.
    - Simply put, authorization refers to mechanisms that decide when a user is *authorized* to perform a certain task.
    - Authorization is related to authentication because we generally need to make sure that a user is who he claims to be (authentication) before we can make a decision on whether he can (or cannot) perform a certain task (authorization).
    - For example, once we've ascertained that a user is a member of the Mathematics Department, we would then allow him to access all the MathServices. However, we might deny him access to other services that are not related to his department (BiologyService, ChemistryService, etc.).

9. **Authorization vs. Authentication**
    - It is very easy to confuse *authentication* and *authorization*, not so much because they are related (you generally need to perform authentication on a user to make authorization decisions on that user), but because they sound alike ! ("auth...ation").
    - This is somewhat aggravated by the fact that many people tend to shorten both words as "auth" (especially in programming code).
    - At this point, you might be saying to yourself: "That's pretty silly, they're different concepts... I'm not going to confuse them just because they sound alike !" Well, believe me, it happens, and quite a lot). When in doubt, remember that *authentication* refers to finding out it somebody's identify is *authentic* (if they really are who they claim to be) and that *authorization* refers to finding out is someone is *authorized* to perform a certain task.

10. **Privacy/confidentiality:**
    - Ensuring that no one can read the message except the intended receiver.
    - A secure conversation should be *private*.
    - In other words, only the sender and the receiver should be able to understand the conversation.
    - If someone eavesdrops on the communication, the eavesdropper should be unable to make any sense out of it.
    - This is generally achieved by encryption/decryption algorithms.
    - For example, imagine we want to transmit the message "INVOKE METHOD ADD", and we want to make sure that, if a third party intercepts that message (e.g. using a network sniffer), they won't be able to understand that message.
    - We could use a trivial encryption algorithm which simply changes each letter for the next one in the alphabet.
    - The encrypted message would be "JOWPLFANFUIPEABEE" (let's suppose 'A' comes after the whitespace character).

- Unless the third party knew the encryption algorithm we're using, the message would sound like complete gibberish.
- On the other hand, the receiving end would know the decryption algorithm beforehand (change each letter for the *previous* one in the alphabet) and would therefore be able to understand the message.
- Of course, this method is trivial, and encryption algorithms now-a-days are much more sophisticated.

11. **Integrity:**
    - Assuring the receiver that the received message has not been altered in any way from the original.
    - A secure communication should ensure the *integrity* of the transmitted message.
    - This means that the receiving end must be able to know *for sure* that the message he is receiving is exactly the one that the transmitting end sent him.
    - Take into account that a malicious user could intercept a communication with the intent of modifying its contents, not with the intent of eavesdropping.
    - 'Traditional' encryption algorithms don't protect against these kind of attacks.
    - For example, consider the simple algorithm we've just seen.
    - If a third party used a network sniffer to change the encrypted message to "JAMJAMJAMJAMJAMJA", the receiving end would apply the decryption algorithm and think the message is "I LI LI LI LI LI ".
    - Although the malicious third party might have no idea what the message contains, he is nonetheless able to modify it (this is relatively easy to do with certain network sniffing tools).
    - This confuses the receiving end, which would think there has been an error in the communication.
    - Public-key encryption algorithms *do* protect against this kind of attacks (the receiving end has a way of knowing if the message it received is, in fact, the one the transmitting end sent and, therefore, not modified).

12. ***Non-repudiation:***
    - A mechanism to prove that the sender really sent this message.
    - Cryptography, then, not only protects data from theft or alteration, but can also be used for user authentication.
    - There are, in general, three types of cryptographic schemes typically used to accomplish these goals: secret key (or symmetric) cryptography, public-key (or asymmetric) cryptography, and hash functions, each of which is described as follows.
    - In all cases, the initial unencrypted data is referred to as *plaintext*. It is encrypted into *ciphertext*, which will in turn (usually) be decrypted into usable plaintext.

In many of the descriptions below, two communicating parties will be referred to as Alice and Bob; this is the common nomenclature in the crypto field and literature to make it easier to identify the communicating parties. If there is a third or fourth party to the communication, they will be referred to as Carol and Dave. Mallory is a malicious party, Eve is an eavesdropper, and Trent is a trusted third party.

4.6 Types of Cryptographic Algorithms

1. There are several ways of classifying cryptographic algorithms.
2. For purposes of this chapter, they will be categorized based on the number of keys that are employed for encryption and decryption, and further defined by their application and use.
3. The three types of algorithms that will be discussed are:

    - **Secret Key Cryptography (SKC):** Uses a single key for both encryption and decryption.
    - **Public Key Cryptography (PKC):** Uses one key for encryption and another for decryption.
    - **Hash Functions:** Uses a mathematical transformation to irreversibly "encrypt" information.

plaintext ⟶ ciphertext ⟶ plaintext

(a) Secret key (symmetric) cryptography. SKC uses a single key for both encryption and decryption

plaintext ⟶ ciphertext ⟶ plaintext

(b) Public key (asymmetric) cryptography. PKC uses two keys, one for encryption and the other for decryption

plaintext ⟶ ciphertext (hash function)

(c) Hash function (one-way cryptography). Hash functions have no key since the plaintext is not recoverable from the ciphertext

Fig. 4.6: (a, b and c): Three types of cryptography: secret-key, public key, and hash function

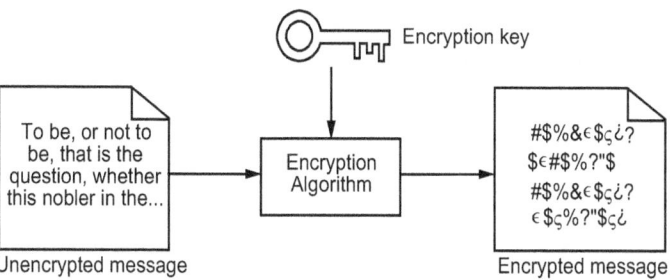

Fig. 4.7: Key-based encryption

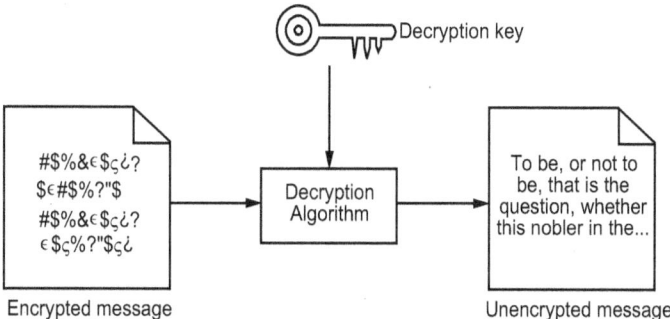

Fig. 4.8: Key-based decryption

4.6.1 Secret Key Cryptography

1. With secret key cryptography, a single key is used for both encryption and decryption. As shown in **Fig. 4.6 (a)**, the sender uses the key (or some set of rules) to encrypt the plaintext and sends the cipher text to the receiver.
2. The receiver applies the same key (or ruleset) to decrypt the message and recover the plaintext.
3. Because a single key is used for both functions, secret key cryptography is also called **symmetric encryption**.

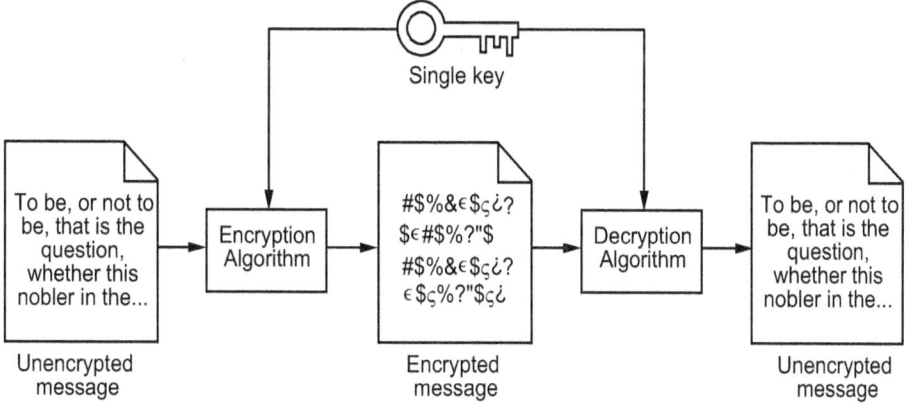

Fig. 4.9: Key-based symmetric algorithm

4. With this form of cryptography, it is obvious that the key must be known to both the sender and the receiver; that, in fact, is the secret.

5. The biggest difficulty with this approach, of course, is the **distribution of the key**.

6. **Secret key cryptography schemes are generally categorized as being either *stream ciphers* or *block ciphers*.**

7. Stream ciphers operate on a single bit (byte or computer word) at a time and implement some form of feedback mechanism so that the key is constantly changing.

8. A block cipher is so-called because the scheme encrypts one block of data at a time using the same key on each block.

9. In general, the same plaintext block will always encrypt to the same ciphertext when using the same key in a block cipher whereas the same plaintext will encrypt to different cipher text in a stream cipher.

10. Stream ciphers come in several flavors but two are worth mentioning here.

11. **Self-synchronizing stream ciphers** calculate each bit in the keystream as a function of the previous *n* bits in the keystream.

12. It is termed "self-synchronizing" because the decryption process can stay synchronized with the encryption process merely by knowing how far into the *n*-bit keystream it is.

13. One problem is error propagation; a garbled bit in transmission will result in *n* garbled bits at the receiving side.

14. **Synchronous stream ciphers** generate the keystream in a fashion independent of the message stream but by using the same keystream generation function at sender and receiver.

15. While stream ciphers do not propagate transmission errors, they are, by their nature, periodic so that the keystream will eventually repeat.

16. **Block ciphers can operate in one of several modes; the following four are the most important:**
    - **Electronic Codebook (ECB) mode** is the simplest, most obvious application: the secret key is used to encrypt the plaintext block to form a ciphertext block. Two identical plaintext blocks, then, will always generate the same ciphertext block. Although this is the most common mode of block ciphers, it is susceptible to a variety of brute-force attacks.
    - **Cipher Block Chaining (CBC) mode** adds a feedback mechanism to the encryption scheme. In CBC, the plaintext is exclusively-ORed (XORed) with the previous ciphertext block prior to encryption. In this mode, two identical blocks of plaintext never encrypt to the same ciphertext.

- **Cipher Feedback (CFB) mode** is a block cipher implementation as a self-synchronizing stream cipher. CFB mode allows data to be encrypted in units smaller than the block size, which might be useful in some applications such as encrypting interactive terminal input. If we were using 1-byte CFB mode, for example, each incoming character is placed into a shift register the same size as the block, encrypted, and the block transmitted. At the receiving side, the ciphertext is decrypted and the extra bits in the block (i.e., everything above and beyond the one byte) are discarded.
- **Output Feedback (OFB) mode** is a block cipher implementation conceptually similar to a synchronous stream cipher. OFB prevents the same plaintext block from generating the same ciphertext block by using an internal feedback mechanism that is independent of both the plaintext and ciphertext bitstreams.

17. **Secret key cryptography algorithms that are in use today include Data Encryption Standard (DES):**

    Two important variants that strengthen DES are:
    - **Triple-DES (3DES):** A variant of DES that employs up to three 56-bit keys and makes three encryption/decryption passes over the block;
    - **DESX:** A variant devised by Ron Rivest. By combining 64 additional key bits to the plaintext prior to encryption, effectively increases the key length to 120 bits.

18. **Advanced Encryption Standard (AES):**
    - AES uses an SKC scheme called **Rijndael**, a block cipher designed by Belgian cryptographers Joan Daemen and Vincent Rijmen.
    - The algorithm can use a variable block length and key length; the latest specification allowed any combination of keys lengths of 128, 192, or 256 bits and blocks of length 128, 192, or 256 bits.

19. **International Data Encryption Algorithm (IDEA):** Secret-key cryptosystem written by Xuejia Lai and James Massey, in 1992. A 64-bit SKC block cipher using a 128-bit key. Also available internationally.

20. **Rivest Ciphers (aka Ron's Code):** Named for Ron Rivest, a series of SKC algorithms.
    - *RC1:* Designed on paper but never implemented.
    - *RC2:* A 64-bit block cipher using variable-sized keys designed to replace DES. It's code has not been made public although many companies have licensed RC2 for use in their products.

- *RC3:* Found to be breakable during development.
- *RC4:* A stream cipher using variable-sized keys; it is widely used in commercial cryptography products, although it can only be exported using keys that are 40 bits or less in length.
- *RC5:* A block-cipher supporting a variety of block sizes, key sizes, and number of encryption passes over the data.
- *RC6:* An improvement over RC5, RC6 was one of the AES Round 2 algorithms.

21. **Blowfish:** A symmetric 64-bit block cipher invented by Bruce Schneier; optimized for 32-bit processors with large data caches, it is significantly faster than DES on a Pentium/PowerPC-class machine. Key lengths can vary from 32 to 448 bits in length. Blowfish, available freely and intended as a substitute for DES or IDEA, is in use in over 80 products.

22. **Twofish:** A 128-bit block cipher using 128-, 192-, or 256-bit keys. Designed to be highly secure and highly flexible, well suited for large microprocessors, 8-bit smart card microprocessors, and dedicated hardware. Designed by a team led by Bruce Schneier and was one of the Round 2 algorithms in the AES process.

23. **Camellia:** A secret-key, block-cipher crypto algorithm developed jointly by Nippon Telegraph and Telephone (NTT) Corp. and Mitsubishi Electric Corporation (MEC) in 2000. Camellia has some characteristics in common with AES: a 128-bit block size, support for 128-, 192-, and 256-bit key lengths, and suitability for both software and hardware implementations on common 32-bit processors as well as 8-bit processors (e.g., smart cards, cryptographic hardware, and embedded systems).

24. **MISTY1:** Developed at Mitsubishi Electric Corp., a block cipher using a 128-bit key and 64-bit blocks, and a variable number of rounds. Designed for hardware and software implementations, and is resistant to differential and linear cryptanalysis.

25. **Secure and Fast Encryption Routine (SAFER):** Secret-key crypto scheme designed for implementation in software.

26. **KASUMI:** A block cipher using a 128-bit key that is part of the Third-Generation Partnership Project (3GPP), formerly known as the Universal Mobile Telecommunications System (UMTS). KASUMI is the intended confidentiality and integrity algorithm for both message content and signaling data for emerging mobile communications systems.

27. **SEED:** A block cipher using 128-bit blocks and 128-bit keys. Developed by the Korea Information Security Agency (KISA) and adopted as a national standard encryption algorithm in South Korea.

28. **Skipjack:** SKC scheme proposed for Capstone. Although the details of the algorithm were never made public, Skipjack was a block cipher using an 80-bit key and 32 iteration cycles per 64-bit block.

4.6.2 Public-Key Cryptography

1. Public-key cryptography has been said to be the most significant new development in cryptography in the last 300-400 years.
2. Modern PKC was first described publicly by Stanford University professor Martin Hellman and graduate student Whitfield Diffie in 1976.
3. They described a two-key crypto system in which two parties could engage in a secure communication over a non-secure communications channel without having to share a secret key.
4. PKC depends upon the existence of so-called *one-way functions*, or mathematical functions that are easy to computer whereas their inverse function is relatively difficult to compute. Consider simple examples:
   - **Multiplication vs. factorization:** Suppose we have two numbers, 9 and 16, and that we want to calculate the product; it should take almost no time to calculate the product, 144. Suppose instead that we have a number, 144, and we need you tell me which pair of integers If multiplied together to obtain that number. One will eventually come up with the solution but whereas calculating the product took milliseconds, factoring will take longer because you first need to find the 8 pair of integer factors and then determine which one is the correct pair.
   - **Exponentiation vs. logarithms:** Suppose we want to take the number 3 to the 6th power; again, it is easy to calculate $3^6 = 729$. But if we have the number 729 and want one to calculate the two integers that can be used, x and y so that $\log_x 729 = y$, it will take you longer to find all possible solutions and select the pair that we used.
5. While the examples above are trivial, they do represent two of the functional pairs that are used with PKC; namely, the ease of multiplication and exponentiation versus the relative difficulty of factoring and calculating logarithms, respectively.
6. The mathematical "trick" in PKC is to find a **trap door** in the one-way function so that the inverse calculation becomes easy given knowledge of some item of information.
7. Public-key algorithms are *asymmetric* algorithms and, therefore, are based on the use of two different keys, instead of just one. In public-key cryptography, the two keys are called the *private key* and the *public key*
   - **Private key:** This key must be know *only* by its owner.
   - **Public key:** This key is known to everyone (it is *public*)
   - **Relation between both keys:** What one key encrypts, the other one decrypts, and vice versa. That means that if you encrypt something with my public key (which you would know, because it's public), we would need our private key to decrypt the message.

8. In a basic secure conversation using public-key cryptography, the sender encrypts the message using the receiver's *public* key.
9. Remember that this key is known to everyone.
10. The encrypted message is sent to the receiving end, who will decrypt the message with his *private* key.
11. Only the receiver can decrypt the message because no one else has the private key. Also, notice how the encryption algorithm is the same at both ends: what is encrypted with one key is decrypted with the other key using the same algorithm.

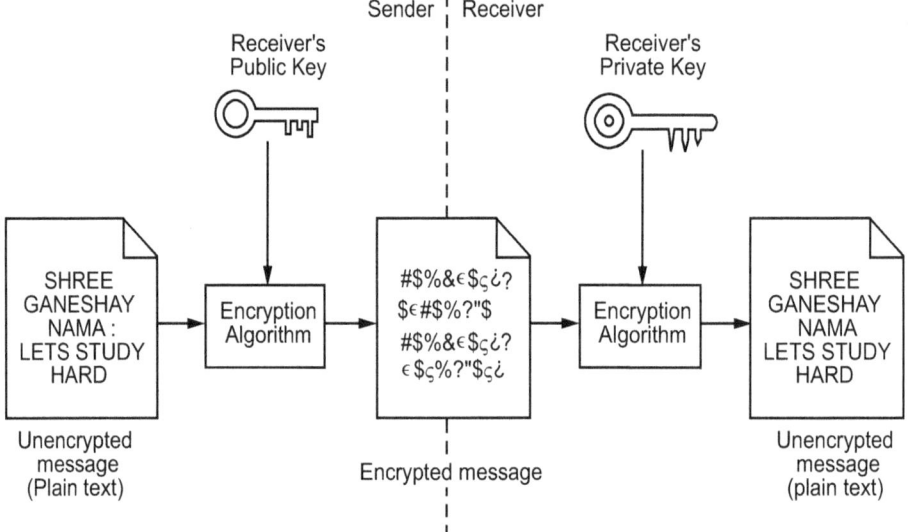

Fig. 4.10: Key-based asymmetric algorithm

12. Generic PKC employs two keys that are mathematically related although knowledge of one key does not allow someone to easily determine the other key.
13. One key is used to encrypt the plaintext and the other key is used to decrypt the ciphertext.
14. The important point here is that it **does not matter which key is applied first**, but that both keys are required for the process to work **(Fig. 4.6 (b))**.
15. **Because pair of keys are required, this approach is also called asymmetric cryptography.**
16. In PKC, one of the keys is designated the public key and may be advertised as widely as the owner wants.
17. The other key is designated the *private key* and is never revealed to another party.
18. It is straightforward to send messages under this scheme.
19. Suppose Alice wants to send Bob a message. Alice encrypts some information using Bob's public key; Bob decrypts the ciphertext using his private key. This

method could be also used to prove who sent a message; Alice, for example, could encrypt some plaintext with her private key; when Bob decrypts using Alice's public key, he knows that Alice sent the message and Alice cannot deny having sent the message (**non-repudiation**).
20. Public-key cryptography algorithms that are in use today for key exchange or digital signatures include:
21. **RSA:**
    - The first, and still most common, PKC implementation, named for the three mathematicians who developed it Ronald Rivest, Adi Shamir, and Leonard Adleman.
    - RSA today is used in hundreds of software products and can be used for key exchange, digital signatures, or encryption of small blocks of data.
    - RSA uses a variable size encryption block and a variable size key.
    - The key-pair is derived from a very large number, *n*, that is the product of two prime numbers chosen according to special rules; these primes may be 100 or more digits in length each, yielding an *n* with roughly twice as many digits as the prime factors.
    - The public key information includes *n* and a derivative of one of the factors of *n*; an attacker cannot determine the prime factors of *n* (and, therefore, the private key) from this information alone and that is what makes the RSA algorithm so secure.
22. **Diffie-Hellman:** After the RSA algorithm was published, Diffie and Hellman came up with their own algorithm. D-H is used for secret-key key exchange only, and not for authentication or digital signatures.
23. **Digital Signature Algorithm (DSA):** The algorithm specified as Digital Signature Standard (DSS), provides digital signature capability for the authentication of messages.
24. **ElGamal:** Designed by Taher Elgamal, a PKC system similar to Diffie-Hellman and used for key exchange.
25. **Elliptic Curve Cryptography (ECC):** A PKC algorithm based upon elliptic curves. ECC can offer levels of security with small keys comparable to RSA and other PKC methods. It was designed for devices with limited compute power and/or memory, such as smartcards and PDAs.
26. **Public-Key Cryptography Standards (PKCS):** A set of interoperable standards and guidelines for public-key cryptography, designed by RSA Data Security Inc. It is ranging from PKCS#1 to PKCS#15.
27. **Key Exchange Algorithm (KEA):** A variation on Diffie-Hellman; proposed as the key exchange method for Capstone.

28. **LUC:** A public-key cryptosystem designed by P. J. Smith and based on Lucas sequences. Can be used for encryption and signatures, using integer factoring.

29. **Pros And Cons Of Public-Key Systems:**
    - Public-key systems have a clear advantage over symmetric algorithms: there is no need to agree on a common key for both the sender and the receiver.
    - As seen in the previous example, if someone wants to receive an encrypted message, the sender only needs to know the receiver's public key (which the receiver will provide; publishing the *public* key in no way compromises the secure transmission).
    - As long as the receiver keeps the private key secret, no one but the receiver will be able to decrypt the messages encrypted with the corresponding public key.
    - This is due to the fact that, in public-key systems, it is relatively easy to compute the public key from the private key, but *very hard* to compute the private key from the public key (which is the one everyone knows).
    - In fact, some algorithms need several *months* (and even years) of constant computation to obtain the private key from the public key.

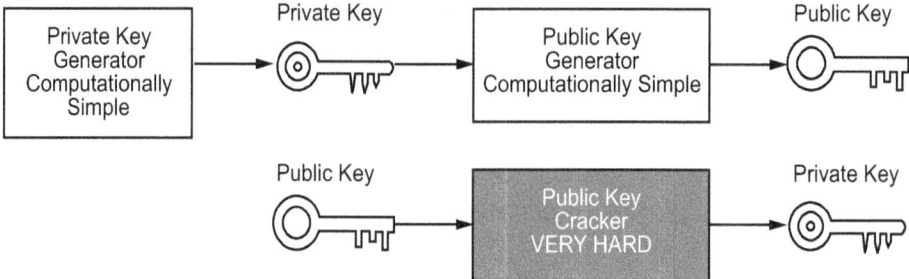

Fig. 4.11: Public key generation

1. Another important advantage is that, unlike symmetric algorithms, public-key systems can guarantee integrity and authentication, not only privacy.
2. The basic communication seen above only guarantees privacy.
3. Integrity and authentication fit into public-key systems.
4. **The main disadvantage of using public-key systems is that they are not as fast as symmetric algorithms.**

4.6.3 Hash Functions Cryptography

1. **Hash functions**, also called **message digests** and **one-way encryption**, are algorithms that, in some sense, use no key **(Fig. 4.6 (c))**.
2. Instead, a fixed-length hash value is computed based upon the plaintext that makes it impossible for either the contents or length of the plaintext to be recovered.
3. Hash algorithms are typically used to provide a *digital fingerprint* of a file's contents, often used to ensure that the file has not been altered by an intruder or virus.
4. Hash functions are also commonly employed by many operating systems to encrypt passwords. Hash functions, then, provide a measure of the integrity of a file.
5. Hash algorithms that are in common use today include:

    - **Message Digest (MD) algorithms:** A series of byte-oriented algorithms that produce a 128-bit hash value from an arbitrary-length message.
    - **MD2:** Designed for systems with limited memory, such as smart cards.
    - **MD4:** Developed by Rivest, similar to MD2 but designed specifically for fast processing in software.
    - **MD5:** Also developed by Rivest after potential weaknesses were reported in MD4; this scheme is similar to MD4 but is slower because more manipulation is made to the original data. MD5 has been implemented in a large number of products although several weaknesses in the algorithm are there.

6. **Secure Hash Algorithm (SHA):** Algorithm for Secure Hash Standard (SHS). SHA-1 produces a 160-bit hash value.
7. **RIPEMD:** A series of message digests that initially came from the RIPE (RACE Integrity Primitives Evaluation) project. It was designed optimized for 32-bit processors to replace the then-current 128-bit hash functions. Other versions include RIPEMD-256, RIPEMD-320, and RIPEMD-128.
8. **HAVAL (HAsh of VAriable Length):** Designed a hash algorithm with many levels of security. HAVAL can create hash values that are 128, 160, 192, 224, or 256 bits in length.
9. **Whirlpool:** A relatively new hash function, and Whirlpool operates on messages less than 2^{256} bits in length, and produces a message digest of 512 bits. The design of this hash function is very different than that of MD5 and SHA-1, making it immune to the same attacks as on those hashes.

4.6.3.1 Hash Functions

1. Is a type of one-way function these are fundamental for much of cryptography.
2. A one way function - is a function that is easy to calculate but hard to invert.
3. It is difficult to calculate the input to the function given its output.
4. The precise meanings of "easy" and "hard" can be specified mathematically.
5. With rare exceptions, almost the entire field of public key cryptography rests on the existence of one-way functions.
6. In this application, functions are characterized and evaluated in terms of their ability to withstand attack by an adversary.
7. More specifically, given a message x, if it is computationally infeasible to find a message y not equal to x such that H(x) = H(y) then H is said to be a weakly collision-free hash function.
8. A *strongly collision-free hash function* H is one for which it is computationally infeasible to find any two messages x and y such that H(x) = H(y).
9. The requirements for a good cryptographic hash function are stronger than those in many other applications (error correction and audio identification *not* included).
10. For this reason, cryptographic hash functions make good stock hash functions even functions whose cryptographic security is compromised, such as MD5 and SHA-1. The SHA-2 algorithm, however, has no known compromises"
11. Hash function also be referred to as a function with certain additional security properties to make it suitable for use as a primitive in various information security applications, such as authentication and message integrity.
12. It takes a long string (or message) of any length as input and produces a fixed length string as output, sometimes termed a message digest or a digital fingerprint.

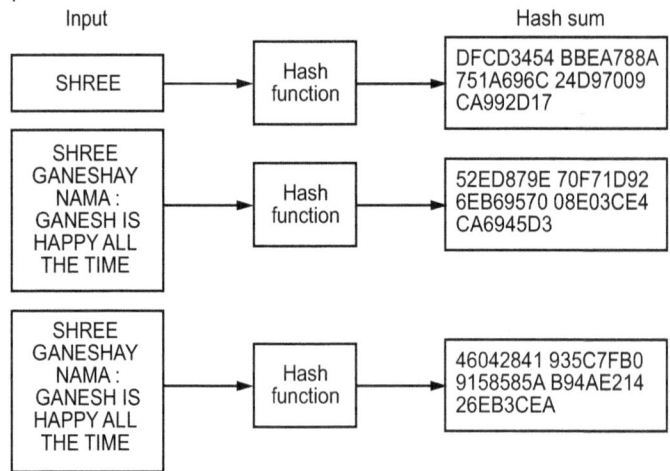

Fig. 4.12: Application of hash function in Cryptography

In various standards and applications, the two most-commonly used hash functions are MD5 and SHA-1.

4.6.3.2 Cryptographic Hash Function

1. The given Figure below illustrates the proper and intended used of public/private key cryptography for sending confidential messages.
2. In the illustration, a user, Bob, has a public/private key pair.
3. The public portion of that key pair is placed in the public domain (for example, in a Web server).
4. The private portion is guarded in a private domain, for example, on a digital key card or in a password-protected file.

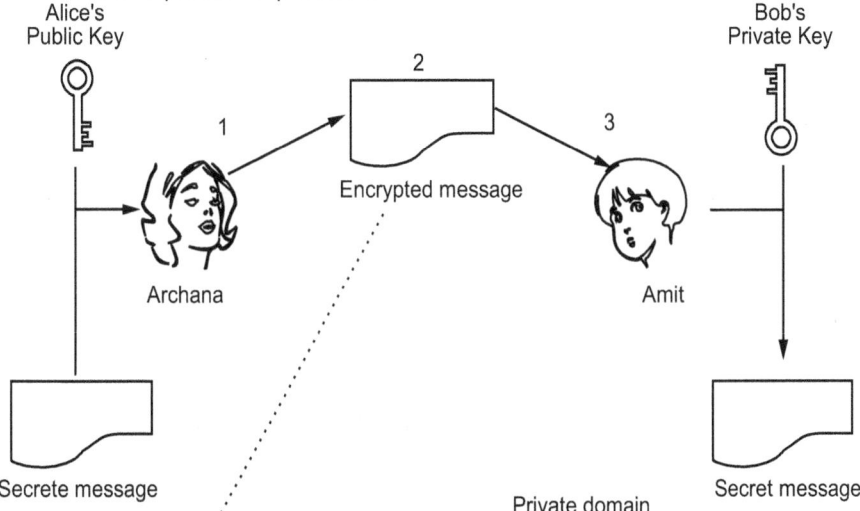

Fig. 4.13: Proper Use of Public Key Cryptography

For Alice to send a secret message to Bob, the following process needs to be followed:
1. Alice passes the secret message and Bob's public key to the appropriate encryption algorithm to construct the encrypted message.
2. Alice transmits the encrypted message (perhaps via e-mail) to Bob.
3. Bob decrypts the transmitted, encrypted message with his private key and the appropriate decryption algorithm.

Bob can be assured that Alice's encrypted secret message was not seen by anyone else since only his private key is capable of decrypting the message

4.6.3.3 Both Are Used Together

1. Secret key and public key systems are often used together, such as the AES secret key and the RSA public key.
2. **The secret key method provides the fastest decryption, and the public key method provides a convenient way to transmit the secret key.**
3. This is called a "digital envelope".
4. For example, the PGP e-mail encryption program uses one of several public key methods to send the secret key along with the message that has been encrypted with that secret key.

4.7 Why Three Encryption Techniques?

1. So, why are there so many different types of cryptographic schemes? Why can't we do everything we need with just one?
2. The answer is that each scheme is optimized for some specific applications.
3. Hash functions, for example, are well suited for ensuring data integrity because any change made to the contents of a message will result in the receiver calculating a different hash value than the one placed in the transmission by the sender.
4. Since it is highly unlikely that two different messages will yield the same hash value, data integrity is ensured to a high degree of confidence.
5. Secret key cryptography, on the other hand, is ideally suited to encrypting messages.
6. The sender can generate a session key on a per-message basis to encrypt the message; the receiver, of course, needs the same session key to decrypt the message.
7. Key exchange, of course, is a key application of public-key cryptography.
8. Asymmetric schemes can also be used for non-repudiation; if the receiver can obtain the session key encrypted with the sender's private key, then only this sender could have sent the message.
9. Public-key cryptography could, theoretically, also be used to encrypt messages although this is rarely done because secret-key cryptography operates about 1000 times faster than public-key cryptography.

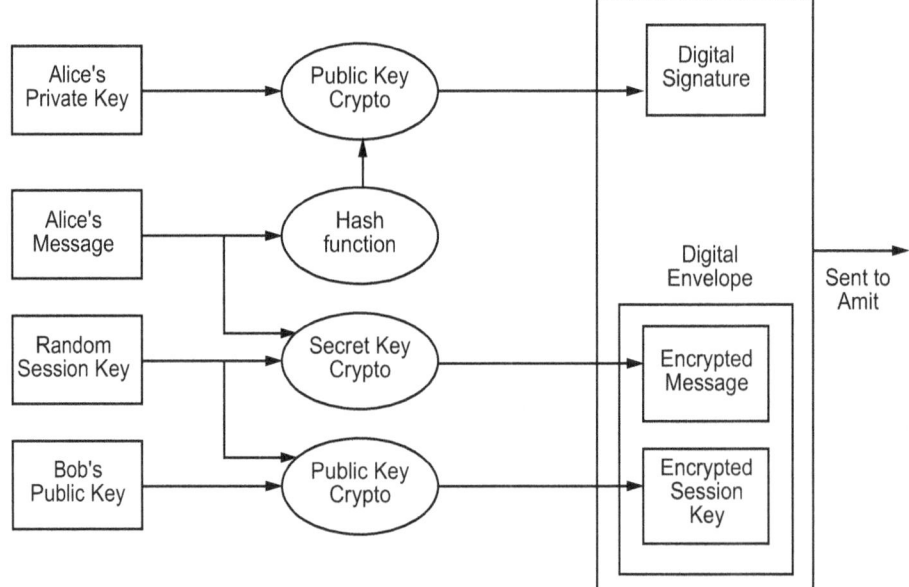

Fig. 4.14: Sample application of the three cryptographic techniques for secure communication

10. Figure puts all of this together and shows how a *hybrid cryptographic* scheme combines all of these functions to form a secure transmission comprising *digital signature* and *digital envelope*.
11. In this example, the sender of the message is Alice and the receiver is Bob.
12. A digital envelope comprises an encrypted message and an encrypted session key.
13. Alice uses secret key cryptography to encrypt her message using the *session key*, which she generates at random with each session.
14. Alice then encrypts the session key using Bob's public key.
15. The encrypted message and encrypted session key together form the digital envelope.
16. Upon receipt, Bob recovers the session secret key using his private key and then decrypts the encrypted message.
17. The digital signature is formed in two steps.
18. First, Alice computes the hash value of her message; next, she encrypts the hash value with her private key.
19. Upon receipt of the digital signature, Bob recovers the hash value calculated by Alice by decrypting the digital signature with Alice's public key.
20. Bob can then apply the hash function to Alice's original message, which he has already decrypted.
21. If the resultant hash value is not the same as the value supplied by Alice, then Bob knows that the message has been altered; if the hash values are the same, Bob should believe that the message he received is identical to the one that Alice sent.
22. This scheme also provides no repudiation since it proves that Alice sent the message; if the hash value recovered by Bob using Alice's public key proves that the message has not been altered, then only Alice could have created the digital signature.
23. Bob also has proof that he is the intended receiver; if he can correctly decrypt the message, then he must have correctly decrypted the session key meaning that his is the correct private key.

4.8 Secret Key and Private Key Algorithms

Here we will study Following Secret Key Algorithms
1. DES (Data encryption Standards)
2. AES (Advanced Encryption Standards)
3. Rijndael
4. IDEA (International Data Encryption Algorithm)
5. RC4

Here we will study Following Public Key Algorithms

1. RSA (Rivest-Shamir-Adleman)
2. DSA (Digital Signature Algorithm)

Here we will study Following Hash function Algorithms

1. MD (Message Digest)
2. MD5
3. SHA (Secure Hash Algorithm)

4.9 DES (Data encryption Standards)

Introduction:

1. The Data Encryption Standard (DES) was jointly developed in 1974 by IBM and the U.S. government to set a standard that everyone could use to securely communicate with each other.
2. It operates on blocks of 64 bits using a secret key that is 56 bits long.
3. The original proposal used a secret key that was 64 bits long.
4. It is widely believed that the removal of these 8 bits from the key was done to make it possible for agencies to secretly crack messages.

How DES Works:

1. Encryption of a block of the message takes place in 16 stages or rounds.
2. From the input key, sixteen 48 bit keys are generated, one for each round. In each round, eight so-called S-boxes are used.
3. These S-boxes are fixed in the specification of the standard.
4. Using the S-boxes, groups of six bits are mapped to groups of four bits.
5. The contents of these S-boxes has been determined by the Security Agency.
6. The S-boxes appear to be randomly filled, but this is not the case.
7. The block of the message is divided into two halves.
8. The right half is expanded from 32 to 48 bits using another fixed table.
9. The result is combined with the subkey for that round using the XOR operation.
10. Using the S-boxes the 48 resulting bits are then transformed again to 32 bits, which are subsequently permutated again using yet another fixed table.

11. This by now thoroughly shuffled right half is now combined with the left half using the XOR operation.
12. In the next round, this combination is used as the new left half.
13. The figure should hopefully make this process a bit more clear. In the figure, the left and right halves are denotes as L0 and R0, and in subsequent rounds as L1, R1, L2, R2 and so on. The function f is responsible for all the mappings described above.

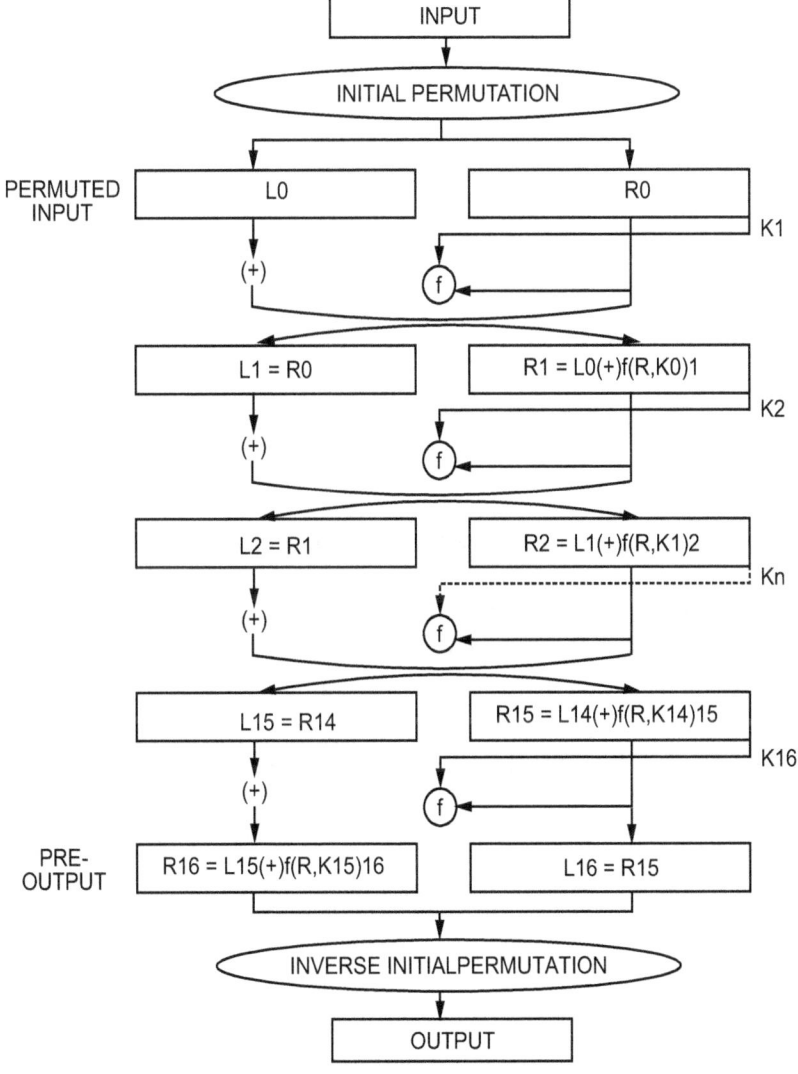

Fig. 4.15: DES Algorithm Implementation

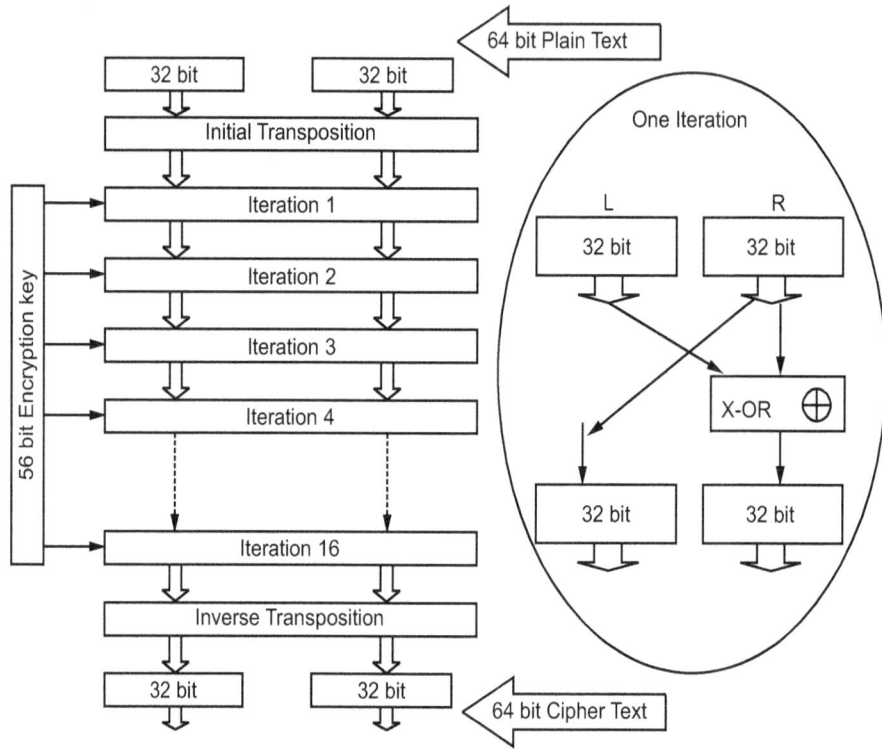

Fig. 4.16: Simplified Implementation of DES algorithm

Security of DES:
1. This secret key encryption algorithm uses a key that is 56 bits, or seven characters long.
2. At the time it was believed that trying out all 72,057,594,037,927,936 possible keys (a seven with 16 zeros) would be impossible because computers could not possibly ever become fast enough.

Triple-DES:
1. The Triple-DES variant was developed after it became clear that DES by itself was too easy to crack.
2. It uses three 56-bit DES keys, giving a total key length of 168 bits.
3. Encryption using Triple-DES is simply
   - Encryption using DES with the first 56-bit key
   - Decryption using DES with the second 56-bit key
   - Encryption using DES with the third 56-bit key
4. Because Triple-DES applies the DES algorithm three times (hence the name), Triple-DES takes three times as long as standard DES.
5. Decryption using Triple-DES is the same as the encryption, except it is executed in reverse.

DES Encryption Modes of Operation:

1. **ECB (Electronic Code Book).**
   - This is the regular DES algorithm.
   - Data is divided into 64-bit blocks and each block is encrypted one at a time.
   - Separate encryptions with different blocks are totally independent of each other.
   - This means that if data is transmitted over a network or phone line, transmission errors will only affect the block containing the error.
   - It also means, however, that the blocks can be rearranged, thus scrambling a file beyond recognition, and this action would go undetected.
   - ECB is the weakest of the various modes because no additional security measures are implemented besides the basic DES algorithm.
   - However, ECB is the fastest and easiest to implement, making it the most common mode of DES.

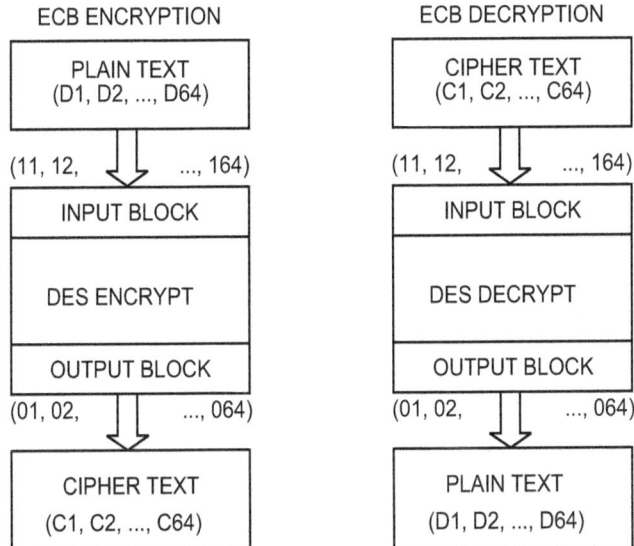

Fig. 4.17: Electronic Codebook (ECB) Mode

2. **CBC (Cipher Block Chaining).**
   - In this mode of operation, each block of ECB encrypted ciphertext is XORed with the next plaintext block to be encrypted, thus making all the blocks dependent on all the previous blocks.
   - This means that in order to find the plaintext of a particular block, you need to know the ciphertext, the key, and the ciphertext for the previous block.

- The first block to be encrypted has no previous ciphertext, so the plaintext is XORed with a 64-bit number called the Initialization Vector, or IV for short.
- So if data is transmitted over a network or phone line and there is a transmission error, the error will be carried forward to all subsequent blocks since each block is dependent upon the last.
- This mode of operation is more secure than ECB because the extra XOR step adds one more layer to the encryption process.

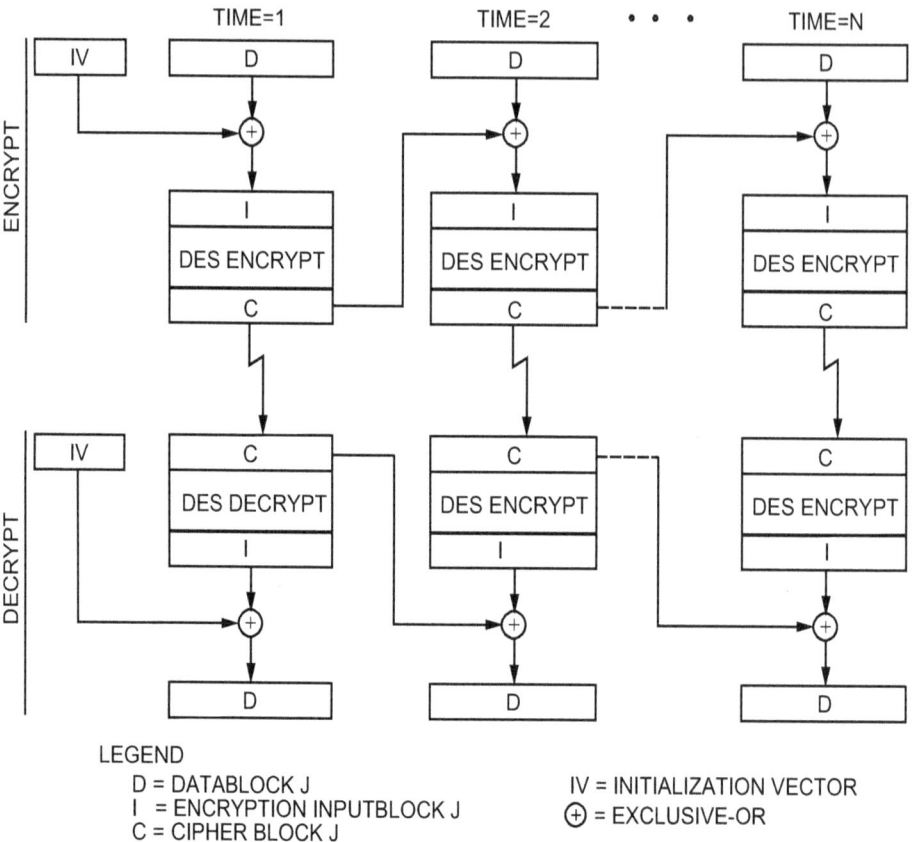

LEGEND
D = DATABLOCK J
I = ENCRYPTION INPUTBLOCK J
C = CIPHER BLOCK J
IV = INITIALIZATION VECTOR
⊕ = EXCLUSIVE-OR

Fig. 4.18: Cipher Block Chaining (CBC) Mode

3. **CFB (Cipher Feedback).**
   - In this mode, blocks of plaintext thatare less than 64 bits long can be encrypted.
   - Normally, special processing has to be used to handle files whose size is not a perfect multiple of 8 bytes, but this mode removes that necessity (Stealth handles this case by adding several dummy bytes to the end of a file before encrypting it).

- The plaintext itself is not actually passed through the DES algorithm, but merely XORed with an output block from it, in the following manner:
- A 64-bit block called the Shift Register is used as the input plaintext to DES.
- This is initially set to some arbitrary value, and encrypted with the DES algorithm.
- The ciphertext is then passed through an extra component called the M-box, which simply selects the left-most M bits of the ciphertext, where M is the number of bits in the block we wish to encrypt.
- This value is XORed with the real plaintext, and the output of that is the final ciphertext.
- Finally, the ciphertext is fed back into the Shift Register, and used as the plaintext seed for the next block to be encrypted.
- As with CBC mode, an error in one block affects all subsequent blocks during data transmission.
- This mode of operation is similar to CBC and is very secure, but it is slower than ECB due to the added complexity.

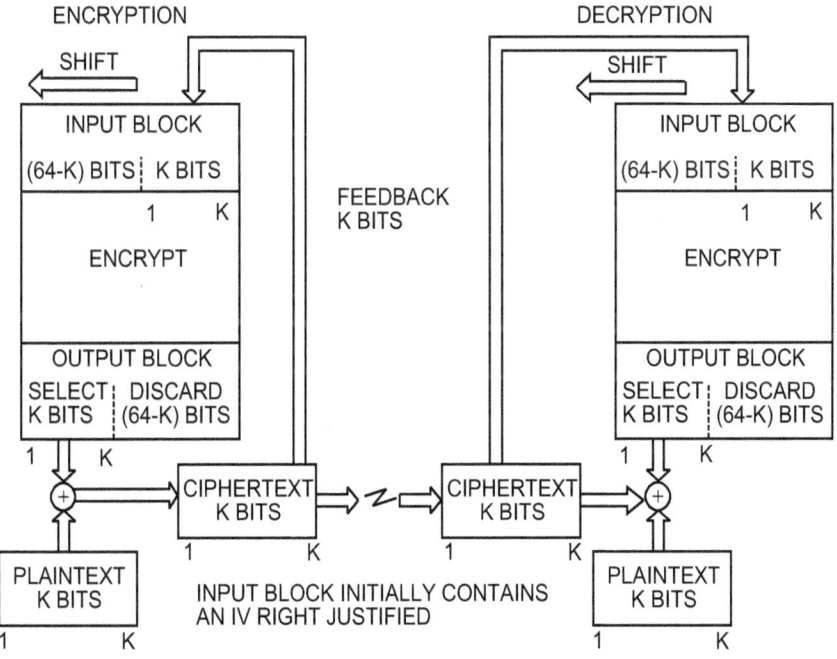

Fig. 4.19: k-bit Cipher Feedback (CFB) Mode

4. **OFB (Output Feedback).**
   - This is similar to CFB mode, except that the ciphertext output of DES is fed back into the Shift Register, rather than the actual final ciphertext.
   - The Shift Register is set to an arbitrary initial value, and passed through the DES algorithm.
   - The output from DES is passed through the M-box and then fed back into the Shift Register to prepare for the next block.
   - This value is then XORed with the real plaintext (which may be less than 64 bits in length, like CFB mode), and the result is the final ciphertext.
   - Note that unlike CFB and CBC, a transmission error in one block will not affect subsequent blocks because once the recipient has the initial Shift Register value, it will continue to generate new Shift Register plaintext inputs without any further data input.
   - However, this mode of operation is less secure than CFB mode because only the real ciphertext and DES ciphertext output is needed to find the plaintext of the most recent block. Knowledge of the key is not required.

4.10 AES (Advanced Encryption Standards)

Do we need AES?
1. AES is short form of Advanced Encryption Standard.
2. The effort to develop AES was started by NIST (National Institute for Standards and Technology), a US government organization.
3. The intention was to develop a viable successor to the well-known Data Encryption Standard (DES) which has now been in use worldwide.
4. The process of developing AES has been remarkably different from the one that led to the DES.
5. The process of developing DES was closed, and the design criteria for DES were classified.
6. Recently, NIST have announced that they have chosen Rijndael as the AES algorithm.
7. However, Rijndael consistently performs well in all environments: standard software platforms, limited space environments, and hardware implementations.

What's New in AES?
1. In this study, we focus on the higher level properties that AES has and what this will mean for practical use of the AES.
2. It was a goal of NIST that switching from DES to AES would not degrade performance of neither hardware nor software systems using encryption.
3. It would be unrealistic, however, to hope for improved performance. Indeed, the main reason to develop AES is to improve the security compared to DES.

4. This is the motivation for the main difference between AES and DES.
5. The block- and key sizes are different: DES has a block size of 64 bits, meaning that 64 bits (8 byte) can be encrypted in one run of the encryption algorithm, AES has a block size of 128 bits.
6. DES uses keys of 56 bits in its basic form whereas AES supports keys of at least 128 bits. In the following, we will look at the consequences this has for security.

Exhaustive Key Search:
1. Any practical cryptosystem can be broken by simply trying all possible keys: one must expect that in practice, the adversary trying to break the system will have some matching plain and cipher text available.
2. Then a candidate for the key can be tested by doing one encryption (or decryption) operation, and so the correct key will be found at the latest when all possible keys have been tried.
3. DES has 2^{56} possible keys, which is roughly 64 million billions.
4. Astronomic as this may sound, it is not large enough with today's technology.
5. In recent years, hardware has been built that will search through all DES keys in a few days, hours or minutes, depending on the investment one is willing to make.
6. It is worth noting that this remains the only realistic threat to DES.
7. In theoretical research, attacks have been proposed that can break DES using a number of encryptions that is much smaller than 2^{56}.
8. The catch, however, is that the adversary must trick the legal owner of the key to perform a very large number of the encryptions for him, the best such attack requires that the adversary knows 2^{43} matching pairs of ciphertext and plaintext blocks, that have all been processed by the owner of the key.
9. This corresponds to several Tbytes and in normal use, most DES keys would not be used for this much data, even in their entire lifetime.

Fig. 4.20: Key size does matter

10. So only exhaustive search remains a problem in real life.
11. The only viable answer to this is to use a longer key.
12. It is important to understand the effect of increasing the length: for instance, 112 bits of key is NOT only twice as good as 56 - it's MUCH better !
13. Every time we add one bit to the length of the key, we double the number of possibilities.
14. Just adding 20 bits to the length means we have a million times more possibilities for the key.
15. Indeed, exhaustive search over the 128 bits of AES keys is completely out of the question in any foreseeable future.
16. The problem with the rather short key length of DES has been recognized almost since DES was first proposed.
17. And in the absence of an encryption standard with longer keys, people have invented alternative ways of using DES that would make key search harder.
18. One obvious idea is to encrypt twice under two different DES keys.
19. Naively, one might assume that this would be as good as encrypting under one key with 112 bits.
20. At least this is the number of bits the adversary must find to break the system.
21. However, there is a way to break this that is much faster than trying all 112 bit possibilities, known as the meet-in-the-middle attack.
22. In fact the time the attacker must spend is little more than what he needs to break just a single DES key.
23. **This attack is the reason for the well-known practice of two-key triple encryption, where we encrypt using one key, encrypt using another key, and finally decrypt using the first key**.
24. This method foils meet-in-middle attacks, and seems to be as secure as a block cipher with 112 bits of key.
25. However, no one knows if there are unknown weaknesses here, and experts generally agree that it is much better to have a cipher that is "born" with a larger key length, than trying to artificially enlarge a smaller cipher.

Increasing the Block Length:
1. As mentioned, the block length tells you how large a chunk of data the algorithm can process in one run.
2. There can be many good practical reasons for wanting a larger block length than the 8 bytes of DES.
3. What is perhaps less well-known is that there is also a good security related reason.

4. This comes from the fact that we will of course want to encrypt much larger pieces of data than just one block.
5. For this, we use the so called modes of operation, of which the Cipher Block Chaining mode (CBC) is the most popular.
6. It is not necessary here to understand the technical details of CBC, it is enough to know that in order to use it, one splits the input data into input blocks for the encryption algorithm (8 byte blocks for DES), say we have N of these.
7. So we have to ask ourselves: how many (random) blocks of ciphertext can we make before there is a significant chance that two of them will be the same? It turns out that the answer is: roughly the square root of the number of possible blocks.
8. For DES we have 2^{64} different blocks, the square root is 2^{32}, which corresponds to 32 Gbyte of data.
9. So for DES the conclusion is that we must en-crypt well under this amount of data with any single key in order to maintain security.
10. Since 32 Gbyte is a large, but not completely unrealistic number, it is clear that we would rather be without this restriction.
11. Note also that two-key triple DES falls under the same restriction because it also has 8 byte blocks.

Key Length	Number of possible keys
2 bit	$2^2 = 4$
3 bit	$2^3 = 8$
DES: 56 bit	2^{56} = 64 million billions
AES: atleast 128 bit	2^{128} = incredibly huge number !

Fig. 4.21: Adding only one bit to the key length doubles the number of possibilities

12. For AES, the same calculation says that we can securely encrypt up to 2^{64} blocks with CBC, and this is a truly astronomic number.
13. In fact, the news is even better: in theoretical research, it has been proved that as long as one stays well below this limit of the square root of the number of blocks, then CBC mode is as secure as the underlying block cipher.
14. In other words, if anyone could find any information on the plaintext from the CBC ciphertext, this means that there was already something wrong with the blockcipher itself.
15. So if AES as such is well designed (as we have every reason to believe it is), then there is a guarantee that using it in CBC will give a way to encrypt also large amounts of data securely.

16. In conclusion: The main high-level changes from DES to AES are very well-motivated from a security point of view, even though DES was in fact a very well-designed cipher. Even systems using two-key triple DES today should seriously consider changing to AES at some point.

Development of AES:
The algorithm had to meet the following minimal acceptability requirements:
1. The algorithm must implement symmetric (secret) key cryptography.
2. The algorithm must be a block cipher.
3. The algorithm shall be capable of supporting *key-block combinations with sizes of 128-128, 192-128 and 256-128 bits.*

Following points are required to consider in network security:
- **Security** i.e. the effort required to crypt-analyze, in comparison to other submitted algorithms.
- **Licensing requirements:** AES shall be available on a world-wide, non-exclusive, royalty-free basis.
- **Computational efficiency:** Speed of the algorithm.
- **Memory requirements.**
- **Flexibility:** This includes a wide variety of platforms and applications the availability of key and block sizes other than the required ones (see above).
- **Hardware and software suitability:** It shall be possible to implement the algorithm in hardware as well as in software.
- **Simplicity:** The algorithm shall be judged according to relative simplicity of design.

Description of Cipher:
1. Strictly speaking, AES is not precisely Rijndael (although in practice they are used interchangeably) as Rijndael supports a larger range of block and key sizes.
2. AES has a fixed block size of 128 bits and a key size of 128, 192 or 256 bits, whereas Rijndael can be specified with key and block sizes in any multiple of 32 bits, with a minimum of 128 bits and a maximum of 256 bits.
3. The key is expanded using Rijndael's key schedule.
4. Most of AES calculations are done in a special finite field.
5. AES operates on a 4×4 array of bytes, termed the *state* (versions of Rijndael with a larger block size have additional columns in the state).
6. For encryption, each round of AES (except the last round) consists of four stages:
    - **AddRoundKey:** Each byte of the state is combined with the round key; each round key is derived from the cipher key using a key schedule.
    - **SubBytes:** A non-linear substitution step where each byte is replaced with another according to a lookup table.

- **ShiftRows:** a transposition step where each row of the state is shifted cyclically a certain number of steps.
- **MixColumns:** A mixing operation which operates on the columns of the state, combining the four bytes in each column using a linear transformation.

7. The final round replaces the MixColumns stage with another instance of AddRoundKey.

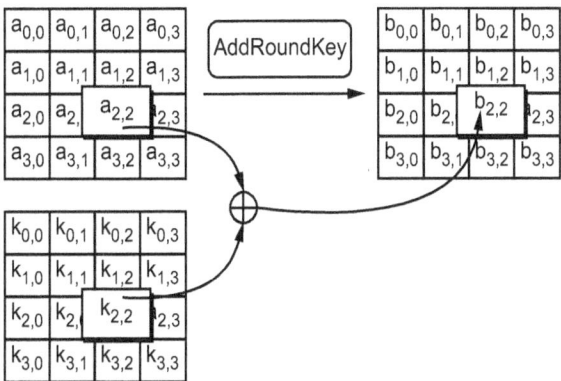

Fig. 4.22: In the AddRoundKey step, each byte of the state is combined with a byte of the round subkey using the XOR operation

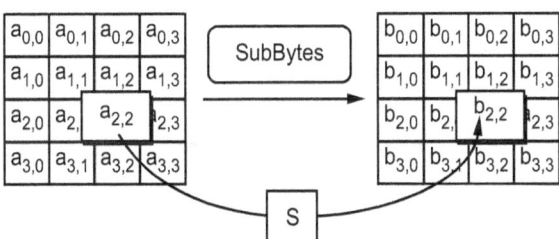

Fig. 4.23: In the SubBytes step, each byte in the state is replaced with its entry in a fixed 8-bit lookup table, S; $b_{ij} = S(a_{ij})$.

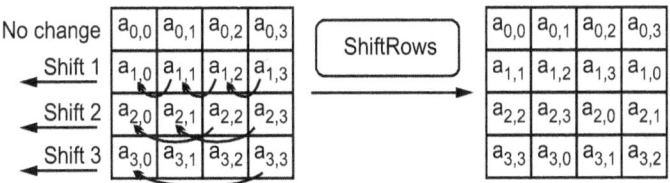

Fig. 4.24: In the ShiftRows step, bytes in each row of the state are shifted cyclically to the left. The number of places each byte is shifted differs for each row

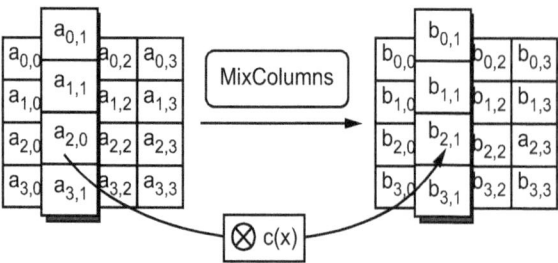

Fig. 4.25: In the MixColumns step, each column of the state is multiplied with a fixed polynomial c(x)

The AddroundKey Step:
1. In the AddRoundKey step, the subkey is combined with the state.
2. For each round, a subkey is derived from the main key using the key schedule;
3. Each subkey is the same size as the state.
4. The subkey is added by combining each byte of the state with the corresponding byte of the subkey using bitwise XOR.

The SubBytes Step:
1. In the SubBytes step, each byte in the array is updated using an 8-bit S-box.
2. This operation provides the non-linearity in the cipher.
3. The S-box used is derived from the inverse function over **GF(2^8)**, known to have good non-linearity properties.
4. To avoid attacks based on simple algebraic properties, the S-box is constructed by combining the inverse function with an invertible affine transformation.
5. The S-box is also chosen to avoid any fixed points (and so is a derangement), and also any opposite fixed points.
6. The S-box is more fully described in the article Rijndael S-box.

The ShiftRows Step:
1. The ShiftRows step operates on the rows of the state; it cyclically shifts the bytes in each row by a certain offset.
2. For AES, the first row is left unchanged.
3. Each byte of the second row is shifted one to the left.
4. Similarly, the third and fourth rows are shifted by offsets of two and three respectively.
5. In this way, each column of the output state of the ShiftRows step is composed of bytes from each column of the input state. (Rijndael variants with a larger block size have slightly different offsets).

The MixColumns Step:

1. In the MixColumns step, the four bytes of each column of the state are combined using an invertible linear transformation.
2. The MixColumns function takes four bytes as input and outputs four bytes, where each input byte affects all four output bytes.
3. Together with ShiftRows, MixColumns provides diffusion in the cipher.
4. Each column is treated as a polynomial over **GF(2^8)** and is then multiplied modulo $x^4 + 1$ with a fixed polynomial $c(x) = 3x^3 + x^2 + x + 2$.
5. The MixColumns step can also be viewed as a matrix multiply in Rijndael's finite field.
6. This process is described further in the article Rijndael mix columns.

Optimization of the Cipher:

1. On systems with 32-bit or larger words, it is possible to speed up execution of this cipher by converting the SubBytes, ShiftRows and MixColumns transformations into tables.
2. One then has four 256-entry 32-bit tables, which utilizes a total of four kilobytes (4096 bytes) of memory, a kilobyte for each table.
3. A round can now be done with 16 table lookups and 12, 32-bit exclusive-or operations, followed by four 32-bit exclusive-or operations in the AddRoundKey step.
4. If the resulting four kilobyte table size is too large for a given target platform, the table lookup operation can be performed with a single 256-entry 32-bit table by the use of circular rotates.

AES vs. Triple-DES

Description	Advanced Encryption Standard	Triple Data Encryption Standard
Timeline	Official standard since 2001	Standardized 1977
Type of algorithm	Symmetric block cipher	Symmetric feistel cipher
Key size (in bits)	128, 192, 256	112, 168
Speed	High	Low
Time to crack (assume a machine could try 255 keys per second - NIST)	149 trillion years	4.6 billion years
Resource consumption	Low	Medium

4.11 The Advanced Encryption Standard (Rijndael Algorithm)

Detailed Description of RIJNDAEL:
1. Since Rijndael is an iterated block cipher, the encryption or decryption of a block of data is accomplished by the iteration (a round) of a specific transformation (a round function).
2. As input, Rijndael accepts one-dimensional 8-bit byte arrays that create data blocks.
3. The plaintext is input and then mapped onto state bytes.
4. The cipher key is also a one-dimensional 8-bit byte array.
5. With an iterated block cipher, the different transformations operate in sequence on intermediate cipher results (states).
6. The design of Rijndael is based on easily understandable mathematical concepts including finite field mathematics and linear algebra for matrix manipulation.

Key and Block Size:
1. A prime feature of Rijndael is its ability to operate on varying sizes of keys and data blocks.
2. It provides extra flexibility in that both the key size and the block size may be 128, 192, or 256 bits.
3. Since Rijndael specifies three key sizes, this means that there are approximately 3.4×10^{38} possible 128-bit keys, 6.2×10^{57} possible 192-bit keys and 1.1×10^{77} possible 256-bit keys.
4. To compare, DES keys are only 56 bits long, which means there are approximately 7.2×10^{16} possible DES keys.
5. Therefore, there are on the order of 10^{21} times more AES 128-bit keys than DES 56-bit keys.

The Sub Key and the Key Schedule:
1. The sub keys are derived from the cipher key using the Rijndael key schedule.
2. The cipher key is expanded to create an expanded key and the sub key is created by deriving a 'round key' by round key.
3. The required round key length is equal to the data block length multiplied by the number of rounds plus 1. Therefore, the round keys are taken from the expanded key.

4. To maintain a secure system, the expanded key is always derived from the cipher key.
5. This method ensures that the expanded key is never directly specified, which would open Rijndael up to several cryptanalytic attacks against its key generation methods.
6. Recall that the security of this system depends entirely on the secrecy of the key, as the design of the algorithm itself is public and contains no secrecy.

Whole Byte Operations:
1. There are several mathematical preliminaries that define the addition and multiplication operations within a finite field and with matrices.
2. When performing finite mathematics, the bytes are treated as polynomials rather than numbers, which can allow different and occasionally allows for more simple implementations.

Encyphering with Rijndael:
1. The Rijndael cipher is an iterative block cipher.
2. It therefore consists of a sequence of transformations to encipher or decipher the data.
3. Rijndael encryption and decryption begin and end with a step to mix subkeys with the data block.
4. This extra step is done as a protection against cryptanalysis.
5. To encipher a block of data in Rijndael, you must first perform an Add Round Key step (XORing a subkey with the block) by itself, then the regular transformation rounds, and then a final round with the Mix Column step omitted.
6. The cipher itself is defined by the following steps:
   - An initial Round Key addition;
   - (**Nr–1**) Rounds;
   - A final round.
7. Where Nr is the number of rounds that must be performed.
8. Nr depends on the length of the data block (Nb) and the length of the key (Nk).
9. Not counting an extra round performed at the end of encipherment, the number of rounds in Rijndael is: 9 if both the block and the key are 128 bits long, 11 if either the block or the key is 192 bits long, and neither of them is longer than that, and 13 if either the block or the key is 256 bits long.

10. The round transformation is broken into layers.
11. These layers are the linear mixing layer, which provides high diffusion over multiple rounds.
12. The non-linear layer which are basically applications of the Rijndael S-box.
13. And the key addition layer which is simply an Exclusive OR of the round key and the intermediate state.
14. Each layer is designed to have its own well-defined function, which increases resistance to linear and differential cryptanalysis.
15. These layers are accomplished by four transformation steps.
16. **The Byte Sub step is a non-linear byte substitution.**
17. **The Shift Row transformation is a cyclic shift.**
18. **This is followed by the MixColumn step in which the columns of the State are considered as polynomials over a finite field and are modulo multiplied with a fixed polynomial.**
19. **Finally, the Add Round Key step is performed.**
20. The Byte Sub step is a non-linear byte substitution that operates on each of the 'state' bytes independently, where a state is an intermediate cipher result.
21. The operation of this step is accomplished with a substitution table (S-box).
22. ByteSub returns a word in which each byte from the incoming state are mapped by the S-box to corresponding bytes.
23. The Rijndael S-box is simple, invertible and composed of two transformations.
24. First, the multiplicative inverse of the data is taken in finite field space and then an affined transformation is applied.
25. Diffusion is defined as the minimum number of active S-boxes in a linear or differential characteristic.
26. Diffusion is important because within block cipher cryptanalysis, almost all the attacks have a complexity that depends on the number of active S-boxes.
27. The cryptanalytic complexity also is affected by the input/output correlation of the individual S-boxes.
28. Linear diffusion layer results in provable lower bounds on the number of active S-boxes.
29. They have provable lower bounds for the non-linear order, the difference to linear functions and the resistance to linear and differential cryptanalysis.

30. The Shift Row step ensures that the different bytes of each row do not only interact with the corresponding byte in other rows.
31. The rows of the State are cyclically shifted with different offsets.
32. Row 0 is not shifted, Row 1 is shifted over C1 bytes, row 2 over C2 bytes and row 3 over C3 bytes.
33. The shift offsets C1, C2 and C3 depend on the block length Nb.
34. The Mix Column step is where the different bytes interact with each other.
35. It causes every byte in a column to affect every other byte.
36. The state is viewed as polynomials and the transformation consists of matrix multiplication of the state with a multiplication polynomial over a finite field.
37. The mix column transformation step is the only place in Rijndael's round transformation that the columns are mixed.
38. This step works with the Shift Row step to ensure that all parts of the block impinge on each other.
39. The Add Round Key step generates a new round key for the following round of transformations.

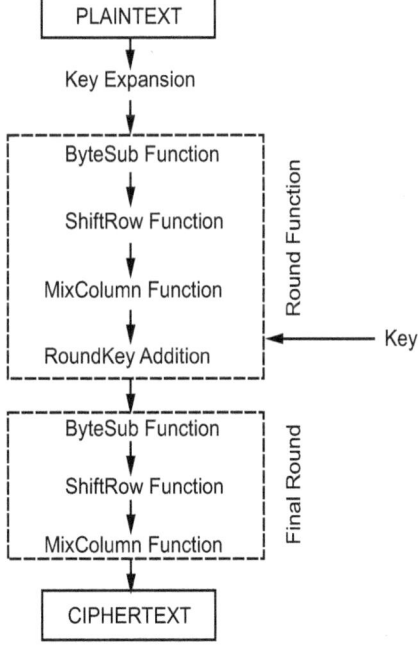

Fig. 4.26: Outline of One Round of Rijndael

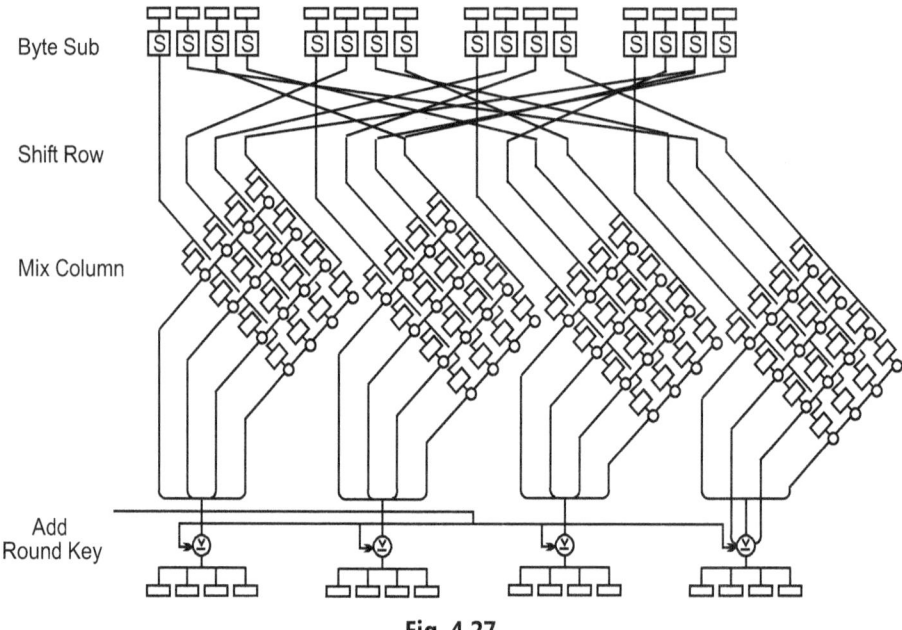

Fig. 4.27

Strengths of RIJNDAEL:

1. It is already specified Rijndael's advantages based on implementation aspects, simplicity of design, variable block length and extensions.
2. Rijndael's implementation is very flexible since it can be used with varying key sizes and block sizes.
3. It is also possible to change the sequence of some steps in Rijndael without affecting the cipher.
4. The cipher is has a simple and elegant structure.
5. It does not hide its structure by using complex components.
6. Instead, it benefits from the advantages gained by the use of simple components in a well-defined structure.
7. Rijndael's security is based on the interaction of the cipher's individual components.
8. Rijndael is described as having a 'rich algebraic structure', which allows the cipher's security to be easily assessed in a limited time frame.
9. This is an advantage over more complex designs that require extensive thinking, searching and 'bit tracing'.
10. Rijndael is consistently a very good performer in both hardware and software across a wide range of computing environments.

11. Its key setup time is excellent, and its key agility is good.
12. Rijndael's very low memory requirements make it very well suited for restricted-space environments.
13. There is additional security in that Rijndael's operations are among the easiest to defend against power and timing attacks.
14. The following scenario has been described to convey Rijndael's resistance to brute force attacks, "Assuming that one could build a machine that could recover a DES key in a second (i.e., try 255 keys per second), then it would take that machine approximately 149 thousand-billion (149 trillion) years to crack a 128-bit AES key.
15. To put that into perspective, the universe is believed to be less than 20 billion years old. It also provides good security against linear cryptanalysis, differential cryptanalysis and opportunistic attacks.

Weaknesses of RIJNDAEL:
1. Rijndael can be subject to standard techniques of differential and linear cryptanalysis.
2. It is also weak to an attack called the "Square attack" that is based on the way matrix multiplication works, and because all the coefficients of the Mix Column matrix have reciprocals.
3. However, in practical terms, this attack is not sufficient to compromise the security of the Rijndael algorithm.
4. Rijndael is also limited by its inverse cipher.
5. Though the encryption is suited for many applications and is quite fast, the inverse cipher takes more code and cycles is not as well suited for different implementations, such as a smart card.

Comparison of RIJNDAEL to other AESs and DESs:
1. Rijndael was chosen over four other algorithms; MARS, RC6, Serpent and Twofish.
2. Its performance was superior to all of the algorithms for the large majority of performance analyses.
3. Its encryption and decryption performance placed in the highest level for 64-bit (C and assembler), 8-bit (C and assembler), 32-bit smart card and for Digital Signal Processors.
4. Its performance placed it in the second level when implemented with 32-bit C or Java.
5. Its key scheduling performance placed in the first level for each platform.
6. Therefore, AES concluded that Rijndael placed in the highest level for overall performance.
7. The Rijndael cipher algorithm was not chosen over the other AES algorithms because it provided a higher level of security.

8. So far, none of the ciphers have fallen to a cryptanalytic attack, though many have been attempted.
9. Therefore, each cipher algorithm maintains a high level of security.
10. Rijndael was chosen because of the simplicity of its design.
11. The design uses simple components with easily proven and verified properties.
12. The simplicity of Rijndael's design and components provided an advantage over the other design candidates.

Comparison between Rijndael and DES:
1. Even though DES and the soon to be AES, are very different in structure, they have some similarities.
2. You can relate there fundamental parts based on the function they perform, The Add Round key step corresponds to the adding of the 8-bit to the block in DES before the f-function.
3. The Mix Column step is where the different bytes interact with each other, so it corresponds to the f-function output with the left half of the block in DES.
4. The Byte Sub step adds to the non-linearity Rijndael, and so is like the f-function too.
5. The Shift Row step ensures that the different bytes of each row do not interact with the corresponding bytes of the other rows, so it can be compared with the permutation P within DES.
6. The swapping of the half blocks in DES, is done in Rijndael by the Mix Column step as every byte in a column is altered by every other byte in the column.
7. The number of regular rounds in Rijndael is always an odd number, not counting the last round as there is no interaction between bytes.
8. Cryptanalysis attacks on DES become easier for variants of DES with an odd number of rounds.
9. Then if the Shift Row step in Rijndael corresponds to the swapping of the half block, this could possible be an important weakness in Rijndael.
10. Nevertheless no cryptanalysis results against Rijndael have shown this to be a problem.
11. Rijndael has three key sizes 128, 192, and 256 bits, which means there is at least $3.4*10^{38}$ possible keys and at most $1.1*10^{77}$ possible keys in comparsion DES is 56 bits long and has $7.2*10^{16}$ possible keys. Thus there is 10^{21} times more keys in the smallest Rijndael than DES keys.
12. In the late 1990s, "DES cracker" machine was built that could recover a DES key in a few hours.
13. Using a brute force attack, which checked each possible key. Assuming that one could build a machine that could recover a DES in a second that is 2^{55} keys per second, then it would take that machine approximately 149 thousand-billion years to crack a 128-bit Rijndael key.

14. The AES is being developed to replace DES, but the NIST believe that Triple DES will remain an approved algorithm for the foreseeable future. However DES is been phased out.

Rijndael was named the AES:
1. With the elimination of the remaining four algorithms, Rijndael was chosen as the AES.
2. Rijndael was submitted to NIST by Joan Daemen and Vincent Rijmen of Belgium.
3. It provided the best overall "software, hardware, and smart-card (called restricted space by NIST) implementations of the algorithms".
4. The results of the five different AES algorithms can be summarized as shown as follows.

Area/Algorithm	Rijndael	Mars	RC6	Serpent	Twofish
General Security	x x	x x x	x x	x x x	x x x
Implementation of Security	x x x	x	x	x x x	x x
Software Performance	x x x	x x	x x	x	x
Smart Card Performance	x x x	x	x	x x x	x x
Hardware Performance	x x x	x	x x	x x x	x x
Design Features	x x	x x	x	x	x x x

Fig. 4.28: Summary of AES algorithms

With this overall analysis, Rijndael was named the AES.

4.12 International Data Encryption Algorithm

IDEA is the name of a proven, secure, and universally applicable block encryption algorithm, which permits effective protection of transmitted and stored data against unauthorized access by third parties. The fundamental criteria for the development of IDEA were highest security requirements along with easy hardware and software implementation for fast execution.

Benefits:
The IDEA encryption algorithm
- Provides high level security not based on keeping the algorithm a secret, but rather upon ignorance of the secret key.
- Is fully specified and easily understood.
- Is available to everybody.

- Is suitable for use in a wide range of applications.
- Can be economically implemented in electronic components (VLSI Chip).
- Can be used efficiently.
- May be exported world wide.
- Is patent protected to prevent fraud and piracy.

Details:
1. The block cipher algorithm IDEA operates with 64-bit plaintext and ciphertext blocks and is controlled by a 128-bit key.
2. The fundamentals innovation in the design of this algorithm is the use of operations from three different algebraic groups.
3. The substitution boxes and the associated "table lookups" used in the block ciphers available to-date (amongst them DES) have been completely dispensed with.
4. The algorithm structure has been chosen such that, with the exception that different key sub-blocks are used, the encryption rounds) followed by an output transformation.
5. The structure of the first round is shown in detail.

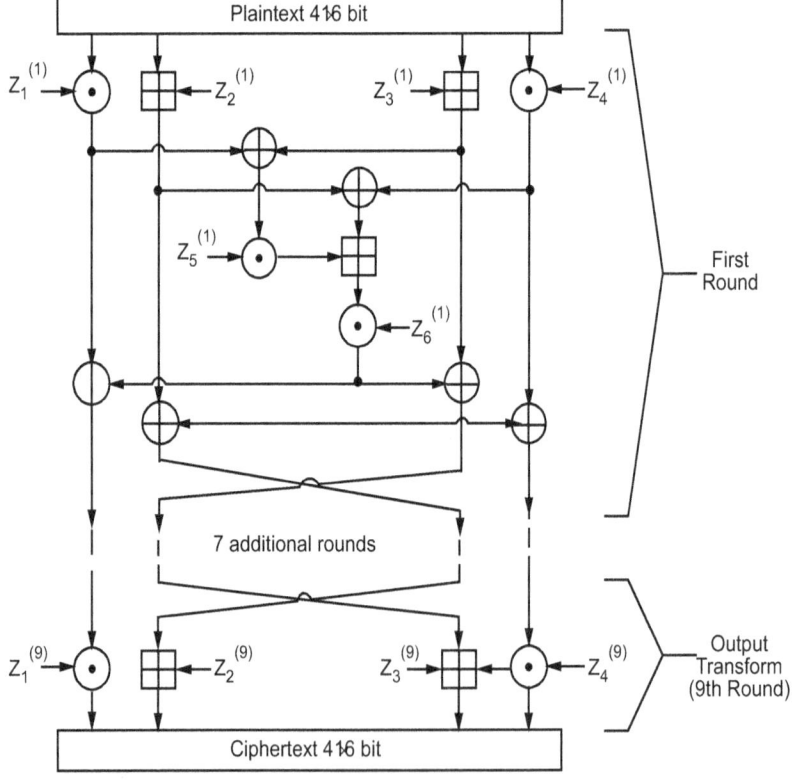

Fig. 4.29

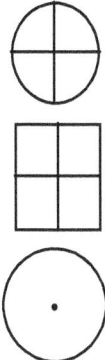

◯ = bit-by-bit exclusive OR of two 16-bit subblocks.

▦ = addition modulo 2^{16} of two 16-bit integers

⊙ = multiplication modulo $2^{16} + 1$ of two 16-bit integers, where subblocks of all zeros corresponds to 2^{16}

Fig. 4.30 Idea Structure

Table 4.2: Encryption of the key-blocks

Round 1	$Z_1^{(1)}$ $Z_2^{(1)}$ $Z_3^{(1)}$ $Z_4^{(1)}$ $Z_5^{(1)}$ $Z_6^{(1)}$
Round 2	$Z_1^{(2)}$ $Z_2^{(2)}$ $Z_3^{(2)}$ $Z_4^{(2)}$ $Z_5^{(2)}$ $Z_6^{(2)}$
Round 3	$Z_1^{(3)}$ $Z_2^{(3)}$ $Z_3^{(3)}$ $Z_4^{(3)}$ $Z_5^{(3)}$ $Z_6^{(3)}$
Round 4	$Z_1^{(4)}$ $Z_2^{(4)}$ $Z_3^{(4)}$ $Z_4^{(4)}$ $Z_5^{(4)}$ $Z_6^{(4)}$
Round 5	$Z_1^{(5)}$ $Z_2^{(5)}$ $Z_3^{(5)}$ $Z_4^{(5)}$ $Z_5^{(5)}$ $Z_6^{(5)}$
Round 6	$Z_1^{(6)}$ $Z_2^{(6)}$ $Z_3^{(6)}$ $Z_4^{(6)}$ $Z_5^{(6)}$ $Z_6^{(6)}$
Round 7	$Z_1^{(7)}$ $Z_2^{(7)}$ $Z_3^{(7)}$ $Z_4^{(7)}$ $Z_5^{(7)}$ $Z_6^{(7)}$
Round 8	$Z_1^{(8)}$ $Z_2^{(8)}$ $Z_3^{(8)}$ $Z_4^{(8)}$ $Z_5^{(8)}$ $Z_6^{(8)}$
Output Transform	$Z_1^{(9)}$ $Z_2^{(9)}$ $Z_3^{(9)}$ $Z_4^{(9)}$

Table 4.3: Decryption of the key sub-blocks

Round 1	$Z_1^{(9)-1}$ $-Z_2^{(9)}$ $-Z_3^{(9)}$ $Z_4^{(9)-1}$ $Z_5^{(8)}$ $Z_6^{(8)}$
Round 2	$Z_1^{(8)-1}$ $-Z_3^{(8)}$ $-Z_2^{(8)}$ $Z_4^{(8)-1}$ $Z_5^{(7)}$ $Z_6^{(7)}$
Round 3	$Z_1^{(7)-1}$ $-Z_3^{(7)}$ $-Z_2^{(7)}$ $Z_4^{(7)-1}$ $Z_5^{(6)}$ $Z_6^{(6)}$
Round 4	$Z_1^{(6)-1}$ $-Z_3^{(6)}$ $-Z_2^{(6)}$ $Z_4^{(6)-1}$ $Z_5^{(5)}$ $Z_6^{(4)}$
Round 5	$Z_1^{(5)-1}$ $-Z_3^{(5)}$ $-Z_2^{(5)}$ $Z_4^{(5)-1}$ $Z_5^{(4)}$ $Z_6^{(4)}$
Round 6	$Z_1^{(4)-1}$ $-Z_3^{(4)}$ $-Z_2^{(4)}$ $Z_4^{(4)-1}$ $Z_5^{(3)}$ $Z_6^{(3)}$
Round 7	$Z_1^{(3)-1}$ $-Z_3^{(3)}$ $-Z_2^{(3)}$ $Z_4^{(3)-1}$ $Z_5^{(2)}$ $Z_6^{(2)}$
Round 8	$Z_1^{(2)-1}$ $-Z_3^{(2)}$ $-Z_2^{(2)}$ $Z_4^{(2)-1}$ $Z_5^{(1)}$ $Z_6^{(1)}$
Output Transform	$Z_1^{(1)-1}$ $-Z_2^{(1)}$ $-Z_3^{(1)}$ $Z_4^{(1)-1}$

6. The 64-bit plaintext block is partitioned into four 16-bit sub-blocks, since all the algebraic operations used in the encryption process operate on 16-bit numbers.
7. Another process, which is described below, produces for each of the encryption rounds, zix 16-bit key sub-blocks from the 128-bit key.
8. Since a further four 16-bit key-sub-blocks are required for the subsequent output transformation, a total of 52 = (8 × 6 + 4) different 16-bit sub-blocks have to be generated from the 128-bit key.
9. Fig. 4.29 shows 10 of the 52 different 16-bit key sub-blocks designated as $Z_1^{(1)}$, ... $Z_4^{(8)}$.
10. In the first encryption round, the first four 16-bit key sub-blocks are combined with two of the 16-bit plaintext blocks using addition modulo 2^{16}, and with the other plaintext blocks using multiplication modulo $2^{16} + 1$.
11. The results are then processed further as shown in Fig. 4.29, whereby two more 16-bit key sub-blocks enter the calculation and the third algebraic group operator, the bit-by-bit exclusive, OR, is used.
12. At the end of the first encryption round for 16-bit value are produced which are used as input to the second encryption round in a partially changed order (See the crossovers in Fig. 4.29).
13. The process described above for round one is srepeated in each of the subsequent 7 encryption rounds using different 16-bit key sub-blocks for each combination.
14. During the subsequent output transformation, the four 16-bit values produced at the end of the 8th encryption round are combined with the last four of the 52 key sub-blocks using addition modulo 2^{16} and multiplication modulo $2^{16} + 1$ to form the resulting four 16-bit ciphertext blocks.
15. It should be noted that at no point in the encryption process is the same algebraic group operation used contiguously.
16. A special feature of the multiplication of two 16-bit sub-blocks modulo $2^{16} + 1$ is the fact that a 16-bit sub-block consisting of all 0 bits is not interpreted in its total value as 0 but rather as 2^{16}.

Determination of the key sub-blocks:

The key sub-blocks used for the encryption and the decryption in the individual rounds are shown in Table 4.2.

The 52 16-bit key sub-blocks which are generated from the 128-bit key are produced as follows:

- First, the 128-bit key is partitioned into eight 16-bit sub-blocks which are then directly used as the first eight key sub-blocks.

- The 128-bit key is then cyclically shifted to the left by 25 positions, after which the resulting 128-bit block is again partitioned into eight 16-bit sub-blocks to be directly used as the next eight sub-blocks.
- The cyclic shift procedure described above is repeated until all of the required 52 16-bit key sub-blocks have been generated.

Decryption:

The computational process used for decryption of the ciphertext is essentially the same as that used for encryption of the plaintext and hence the computational graph in Fig. 2.29 is also valid here. The only difference compared with encryption is that during decryption, different 16-bit key sub-blocks are generated.

More precisely, each of the 52 16-bit key sub-blocks used for decryption is the inverse of the key sub-blocks used during encryption in respect of the applied algebraic group operation. Additionally the key sub-blocks must be used in the reverse order during decryption in order to reverse the encryption process as shown in Table 4.3.

Applications:

The IDEA algorithm can easily be embedded in any encryption software.

Data encryption can be used to protect data transmission and storage.

Typical fields are:
- Audio and video data for pay-TV, video conferencing, distance learning, business-TV, and VoIP – Sensitive financial and commercial data.
- E-mail via public networks.
- Transmissions via modem, router or wireless, and mobile phone.
- Smart cards.

IDEA Security:

1. IDEA's key length is 128 bits over twice as long as the DES key.
2. Assuming that testing every possible key is the most efficient way to break the algorithm, it would require 2^{128} encryptions to recover the key.
3. DES only requires 2^{56} encryptions to break; a million chips capable of testing a million keys a second can break DES in 20 hours.
4. IDEA algorithm is much stronger. Design a chip that can test a billion keys per second, and throw a billion of them at the problem, and it will still take 10^{13} years to break IDEA.

5. An array of 10^{24} such chips can find the key in a day, but it questionable whether there are enough silicon atoms in the universe to build such a machine.
6. The algorithm is still too new for any definitive statements about its security.
7. The designers have done their best to make the algorithm immune to all known cryptanalytic attacks (including a new and powerful attack called "differential cryptanalysis").
8. While IDEA appears to be significantly more secure than DES, it isn't always easy to substitute one for the other in an existing application.
9. If your database and message templates are hardwired to accept a 64-bit key, it may be impossible to implement IDEA's 128-bit key.
10. For those applications, generate a 128-bit key by concatenating the 64-bit key with itself. Remember, however, that IDEA is weakened considerably by this modification.

Conclusions:
1. IDEA is a new algorithm that looks secure.
2. While it appears to be resistant to differential and related-key cryptanalysis, secure-looking algorithms have fallen to new forms of cryptanalysis time and time again.
3. Several academic and military groups currently cryptanalyzing IDEA.
4. None of them have succeeded yet, but who knows what they might come up with tomorrow.

4.13 RC4 Algorithm

RC4 Basics:
RC4 is a **stream cipher symmetric key algorithm**. A *cipher* is nothing but an encryption scheme. A *symmetric key algorithm* is an algorithm that uses the same key to encrypt and decrypt data.

Stream ciphers are an important class of encryption algorithms. They encrypt individual characters (usually binary digits) of a plaintext message one at a time, using an encryption transformation, which varies with time. They are also more appropriate, and in some cases mandatory (e.g., in some telecommunications applications), when buffering is limited or when characters must be individually processed as they are received. Because they have limited or no error propagation, stream ciphers may also be advantageous in situations where transmission errors are highly probable.

Now RC4 is a proprietary Encryption – Decryption algorithm of RSA Data Security. RC4 is used in many commercial software packages such as Lotus Notes and Oracle Secure SQL. It is also part of the Cellular network Specification.

How does RC4 Work?

RC4 uses a variable length key from 1 to 256 bytes to initialize a 256-byte state table. The state table is used for subsequent generation of pseudo-random bytes and then to generate a pseudo-random stream, which is XORed with the plaintext to give the cipher-text. Each element in the state table is swapped at least once. The RC4 key is often limited to 40 bits, because of export restrictions but it is sometimes used as a 128-bit key. It has the capability of using keys between 1 and 2048 bits.

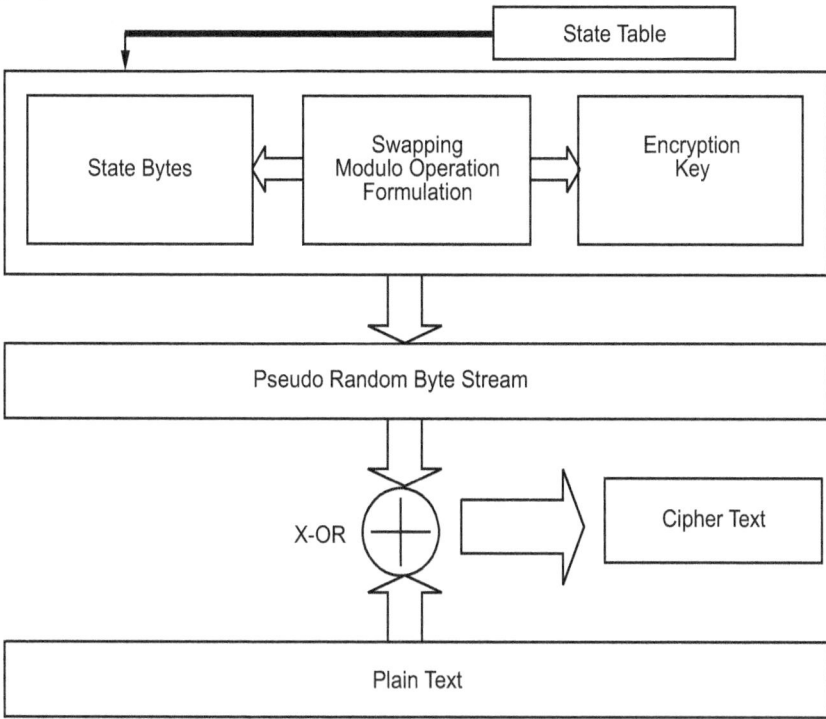

Fig. 4.31: Typical implementation of RC4 encryption algorithm

RC4 Algorithm Features:

1. Uses a variable length key from 1 to 256 bytes to initialize a 256-byte state table.
2. The state table is used for subsequent generation of pseudo-random bytes and then to generate a pseudo-random stream which is XORed with the plaintext to give the ciphertext.
3. Each element in the state table is swapped at least once.
4. The key is often limited to 40 bits, because of export restrictions but it is sometimes used as a 128 bit key.
5. It has the capability of using keys between 1 and 2048 bits.
6. RC4 is used in many commercial software packages such as Lotus Notes and Oracle Secure SQL.

7. The algorithm works in two phases, key setup and ciphering.
8. Key setup is the first and most difficult phase of this encryption algorithm.
9. During a N-bit key setup (N being your key length), the encryption key is used to generate an encrypting variable using two arrays, state and key, and N-number of mixing operations.
10. These mixing operations consist of swapping bytes, modulo operations, and other formulas.
11. A modulo operation is the process of yielding a remainder from division. For example, 11/4 is 2 remainder 3; therefore eleven mod four would be equal to three.
12. Once the encrypting variable is produced from the key setup, it enters the ciphering phase, where it is XORed with the plain text message to create an encrypted message.
13. XOR is the logical operation of comparing two binary bits. If the bits are different, the result is 1. If the bits are the same, the result is 0.
14. Once the receiver gets the encrypted message, he decrypts it by XORing the encrypted message with the same encrypting variable.

RC4 Algorithm Strengths:
1. The difficulty of knowing where any value is in the table.
2. The difficulty of knowing which location in the table is used to select each value in the sequence.
3. A particular RC4 Algorithm key can be used only once.
4. Encryption is about 10 times faster than DES.

RC4 Algorithm Weakness:
1. The algorithm is vulnerable to analytic attacks of the state table.
2. One in every 256 keys can be a weak key. These keys are identified by cryptanalysis that is able to find circumstances under which one of more generated bytes are strongly correlated with a few bytes of the key.
3. **WEAK KEYS:** These are keys identified by cryptanalysis that is able to find circumstances under which one or more generated bytes are strongly correlated with small subset of the key bytes. These keys can happen in one out of 256 keys generated.

4.14 RSA Algorithm

Introduction:
1. R.S.A. stands for Rivest, Shamir and Adleman - the three cryptographers who invented the first practical commercial public key cryptosystem.

2. Today it is used in web browsers, email programs, mobile phones, virtual private networks, secure shells, and many other places.
3. Exactly how much security it provides is debatable, but with sufficiently large keys you can be confident of foiling the vast majority of attackers.
4. RSA is an Internet encryption and authentication system that uses an algorithm developed in 1977 by Ron Rivest, Adi Shamir, and Leonard Adleman.
5. The RSA algorithm is the most commonly used encryption and authentication algorithm and is included as part of the Web browsers from Microsoft and Netscape.
6. It's also part of many other products.
7. The encryption system is owned by RSA Security.

Key Generation:
1. Generate two large prime numbers, p and q
2. Let $n = pq$
3. Let $m = (p-1)(q-1)$
4. Choose a small number e, coprime to m
5. Find d, such that $de \% m = 1$

Publish e and n as the public key. Keep d and n as the secret key.

Encryption:
$$C = P^e \% n$$

Decryption:
$$P = C^d \% n$$

x % y means the remainder of x divided by y.
The reasons why this algorithm works are discussed in the mathematics section.
Its security comes from the computational difficulty of factoring large numbers.
To be secure, very large numbers must be used for p and q, 100 decimal digits at the very least.

Example 4.1:

Key Generation:

(1) Generate two large prime numbers, p and q

To make the example easy to follow I am going to use small numbers, but this is not secure. To find random primes, we start at a random number and go up ascending odd numbers until we find a prime. Lets have:

$$p = 7$$
$$q = 19$$

(2) Let n = pq

$$n = 7 * 19$$
$$= 133$$

(3) Let m = (p − 1)(q − 1)

$$m = (7 - 1)(19 - 1)$$
$$= 6 * 18$$
$$= 108$$

(4) Choose a small number, e coprime to m

e coprime to m, means that the largest number that can exactly divide both e and m (their greatest common divisor, or gcd) is 1. Euclid's algorithm is used to find the gcd of two numbers, but the details are omitted here.

$$e = 2 => gcd(e, 108) = 2 \text{ (no)}$$
$$e = 3 => gcd(e, 108) = 3 \text{ (no)}$$
$$e = 4 => gcd(e, 108) = 4 \text{ (no)}$$
$$e = 5 => gcd(e, 108) = 1 \text{ (yes!)}$$

(5) Find d, such that de % m = 1

This is equivalent to finding d which satisfies de = 1 + nm where n is any integer. We can rewrite this as d = (1 + nm) / e. Now we work through values of n until an integer solution for e is found:

$$n = 0 => d = 1 / 5 \text{ (no)}$$
$$n = 1 => d = 109 / 5 \text{ (no)}$$
$$n = 2 => d = 217 / 5 \text{ (no)}$$
$$n = 3 => d = 325 / 5$$
$$= 65 \text{ (yes !)}$$

To do this with big numbers, a more sophisticated algorithm called extended Euclid must be used.

Public Key	Secret Key
n = 133	n = 133
e = 5	d = 65

Encryption:

The message must be a number less than the smaller of p and q. However, at this point we don't know p or q, so in practice a lower bound on p and q must be published. This can be somewhat below their true value and so isn't a major security concern. For this example, lets use the message "6".

$$C = P^e \% n$$
$$= 6^5 \% 133$$
$$= 7776 \% 133$$
$$= 62$$

Decryption:

This works very much like encryption, but involves a larger exponation, which is broken down into several steps.

$$P = C^d \% n$$
$$= 62^{65} \% 133$$
$$= 62 * 62^{64} \% 133$$
$$= 62 * (62^2)^{32} \% 133$$
$$= 62 * 3844^{32} \% 133$$
$$= 62 * (3844 \% 133)^{32} \% 133$$
$$= 62 * 120^{32} \% 133$$

We now repeat the sequence of operations that reduced 62^{65} to 120^{32} to reduce the exponent down to 1.

$$= 62 * 36^{16} \% 133$$
$$= 62 * 99^8 \% 133$$
$$= 62 * 92^4 \% 133$$
$$= 62 * 85^2 \% 133$$
$$= 62 * 43 \% 133$$
$$= 2666 \% 133$$
$$= 6$$

And that matches the plaintext we put in at the beginning, so the algorithm worked!

Practicalities:

1. The RSA algorithm itself only encrypts numbers.
2. What usually happens is that RSA is used to encrypt a key for a symmetric cipher, such as Rijndael, and then the message is encrypted using this key.
3. In interactive uses, the first step is called the 'key exchange' and after that, network traffic can flow in both directions using the same symmetric key.
4. Often this will be combined with authentication of client.
5. All computer data is ultimately just binary numbers, so you could just break this into suitable chunks and apply RSA to each chunk.
6. However, this puts you at some risk of being cryptanalysed, as plaintexts are often predicible to some extent.

7. For example, if an attacker knows you will say either 'attack by land' or 'attack by sea', they can try encrypting both messages with the public key, and compare these ciphertexts to the intercepted ciphertext.
8. You can mitigate this somewhat by including random junk in each encrypted chunk, but there are other attacks.
9. Another reason is that RSA is slow compared to symmetric ciphers.

Mathematics involved in RSA:
1. This page explains some of the maths concepts that RSA is based on, and then provides a complete proof that RSA works correctly.
2. However, there is no mathematical proof that RSA is secure, everyone takes that on trust !
3. This is fairly advanced material and not necessary to understand the use and applications of the algorithm.

Modular Arithmetic:

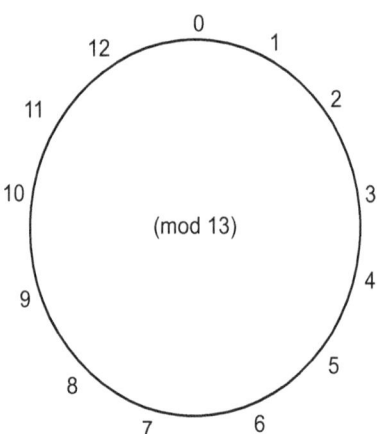

Fig. 4.32: Indication of RSA uses modular arithmetic

1. RSA uses modular arithmetic.
2. This is similar to conventional arithmetic, but only uses positive integers that are less than a chosen value, called the modulus.
3. Addition, subtraction and multiplication work like regular maths, but there is no division.
4. You can use any value for the modulus; the diagram uses 13, so counting goes 0, 1, 2, ..., 11, 12, 0, 1, 2 ... The notation used for expressions involving modular arithmetic is:

$$x \equiv y \pmod{m}$$

Which reads as "x is equivalent to y, modulo m".

5. What this means is that x and y leave the same remainder when divided by m. For example, 7 = 23 (mod 8) and 22 = 13 (mod 9). The following statement is a basic principle of modular arithmetic:

$$a + kp = a \pmod{p}$$

6. You can visualize this on the diagram - each time you add p you go round the circle, back to where you started. It doesn't matter where you start, how big the circle is, or how many times you do it, it's always true.

Primality and Coprimality:

1. A number is prime if the only numbers that exactly divide it are 1 and itself. e.g. 17 is prime, but 15 isn't, because it's divisible by 3 and 5.
2. A pair of numbers are coprime if the largest number that exactly divides both of them is 1. The numbers themselves don't have to be prime. e.g. 8 and 9 are coprime, but 8 and 10 are not, because they're both divisible by 2.
3. If you have a pair of distinct prime numbers, they will always be coprime to each other.

Chinese Remainder Theorem:
Theorem:

$$x = y \pmod{p}$$
$$x = y \pmod{q} \quad \text{with p and q coprime}$$

$$x = y \pmod{pq}$$

Proof:

$$x = y \pmod{p}$$
$$x = y + kp$$
$$x - y = kp$$

p divides (x – y)
by a similar route, q divides (x – y)
as p and q are coprime, pq divides (x – y)

$$x - y = l(pq)$$
$$x = y \pmod{pq}$$

Fermat/Euler Theorem:

This theorem is a surprising identity that relates the exponent to the modulus.

Theorem:

$$x^{p-1} = 1 \pmod{p}$$

if p is prime and $x \neq 0 \pmod{p}$

Proof:

Consider the set Q, of numbers 1, 2, ... p – 1
as p is prime, these numbers are coprime to p
0 is not coprime to p
Q includes all the numbers in (mod p) coprime to p
now consider the set U, obtained by multiplying each element of Q by x (mod p)
both x and each element of Q are coprime to p
each element of U is coprime to p
also, each element of U is distinct, which we prove by contradiction
start by assuming two elements are not distinct:
$xQ_i = xQ_j \pmod{p}$ with $i \neq j$
$Q_i = Q_j \pmod{p}$ as $x \neq 0$
but elements of Q are distinct, so this is a contradiction
elements of U are distinct
U uses all the numbers in (mod p) that are coprime to p, just like Q
U is a permutation of Q
$U_1 \cdot U_2 \ldots U_{p-1} = Q_1 \cdot Q_2 \ldots Q_{p-1} \pmod{p}$
$xQ_1 \cdot xQ_2 \ldots xQ_{p-1} = Q_1 \cdot Q_2 \ldots Q_{p-1} \pmod{p}$
and if we cancel $Q_1 \cdot Q_2 \ldots Q_{p-1}$
$x^{p-1} = 1 \pmod{p}$

RSA Correctness:

Here we prove that the combined process of encrypting and decrypting a message correctly results in the original message.

Theorem:

$$C = M^e \pmod{n}$$
$$M' = C^d \pmod{n}$$
$$M' = M \pmod{n}$$

where (d, e, n) is a valid RSA key, with n = pq
and 0 < M < minimum(p,q)

Proof:

First we combine the two exponentiations:
$$M' = M^{ed} \pmod{n}$$
d and e are generated so that de = k(p-1)(q-1) + 1
$$M' = M^{k(p-1)(q-1) + 1} \pmod{n}$$
$$M' = M \cdot M^{k(p-1)(q-1)} \pmod{n} *$$

consider X $= M^{k(p-1)(q-1)}$ (mod p)

$X = (M^{(p-1)})^{k(q-1)}$ (mod p)

the Fermat/Euler theorem tells us that $M^{(p-1)} = 1$ (mod p)

$X = 1^{k(q-1)}$ (mod p)

$X = 1$ (mod p)

by a similar route, $X = 1$ (mod q)

as p and q are distinct primes, we can combine these with the Chinese remainder theorem

$X = 1$ (mod pq)

$M^{k(p-1)(q-1)} = 1$ (mod n)

Finally, we substitute this back into the equation marked *

$M' = M.1$ (mod n)

$M' = M$ (mod n)

How the RSA System Works:

1. Briefly, the algorithm involves multiplying two large prime numbers (a prime number is a number divisible only by that number and 1) and through additional operations deriving a set of two numbers that constitutes the public key and another set that is the private key.
2. Once the keys have been developed, the original prime numbers are no longer important and can be discarded.
3. Both the public and the private keys are needed for encryption /decryption but only the owner of a private key ever needs to know it.
4. Using the RSA system, the private key never needs to be sent across the Internet.
5. The private key is used to decrypt text that has been encrypted with the public key.
6. Thus, if we send you a message, we can find out your public key (but not your private key) from a central administrator and encrypt a message to you using your public key.
7. When you receive it, you decrypt it with your private key.
8. In addition to encrypting messages (which ensures privacy), you can authenticate yourself to me (so we know that it is really you who sent the message) by using your private key to encrypt a digital certificate.
9. When we receive it, we can use your public key to decrypt it.
10. A table might help us remember this.

To do this	Use whose	Kind of key
Send an encrypted message	Use the receiver's	Public key
Send an encrypted signature	Use the sender's	Private key
Decrypt an encrypted message	Use the receiver's	Private key
Decrypt an encrypted signature (and authenticate the sender)	Use the sender's	Public key

11. RSA is much slower than DES (100 to 10000 times slower, depending on how much of the DES procedure is implemented in hardware rather than software).
12. This is its only major disadvantage compared to DES. This is not a huge problem though, as this is largely overcome with the Pretty Good Privacy system.
13. The security of RSA is second to none, which is why it is the accepted standard on the Internet, as well as in military and government codes.
14. As long as the prime numbers used are big enough, it takes too long to factor them by brute force, and there is no other known way.
15. The only known way to break RSA successfully is to attempt to guess certain parts of the message, and decode from there.
16. If a fragment can be solved, the rest follows fairly easily. This is generally prevented by the addition of some random data into the encrypted text.

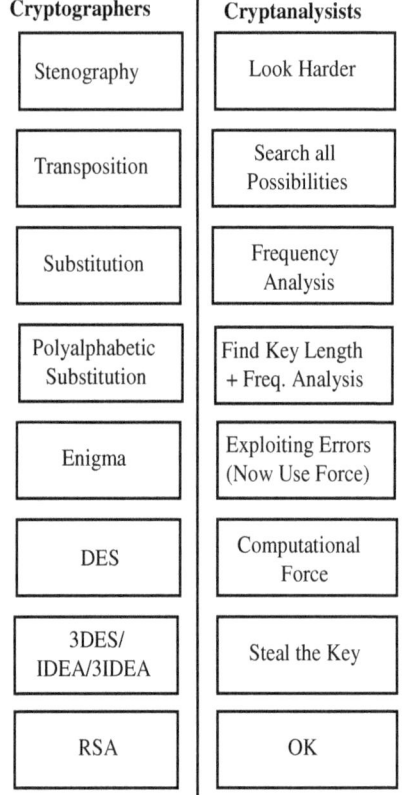

Fig. 4.33: Rough idea about the performances

Example 4.2:

A very simple example of RSA encryption.

This is an extremely simple example using numbers you can work out on a pocket calculator.

1. Select primes p = 11, q = 3.
2. n = pq = 11*3 = 33
   phi = (p − 1)(q − 1) = 10*2 = 20
3. Choose e=3
   Check gcd(e, p − 1) = gcd(3, 10) = 1 (i.e. 3 and 10 have no common factors except 1), and check gcd(e, q − 1) = gcd(3, 2) = 1
   therefore gcd(e, phi) = gcd(e, (p − 1)(q − 1)) = gcd(3, 20) = 1
4. Compute d such that ed ≡ 1 (mod phi)
   i.e. compute d = e^{-1} mod phi = 3^{-1} mod 20
   i.e. find a value for d such that phi divides (ed − 1)
   i.e. find d such that 20 divides 3d − 1.
   Simple testing (d = 1, 2, ...) gives d = 7
   Check: ed − 1 = 3.7 − 1 = 20, which is divisible by phi.
5. Public key = (n, e) = (33, 3)
   Private key = (n, d) = (33, 7).

This is actually the smallest possible value for the modulus n for which the RSA algorithm works.

Now say we want to encrypt the message m = 7,

$c = m^e$ mod n = 7^3 mod 33 = 343 mod 33 = 13.

Hence the ciphertext c = 13.

To check decryption we compute

$m' = c^d$ mod n = 13^7 mod 33 = 7.

Note that we don't have to calculate the full value of 13 to the power 7 here. We can make use of the fact that a = bc mod n = (b mod n).(c mod n) mod n so we can break down a potentially large number into its components and combine the results of easier, smaller calculations to calculate the final value.

One way of calculating m' is as follows:

$m' = 13^7$ mod 33 = $13^{(3+3+1)}$ mod 33 = $13^3.13^3.13$ mod 33

$= (13^3$ mod 33).$(13^3$ mod 33).(13 mod 33) mod 33
$= $ (2197 mod 33).(2197 mod 33).(13 mod 33) mod 33
$= $ 19.19.13 mod 33 = 4693 mod 33
$= $ 7

Now if we calculate the ciphertext c for all the possible values of m (0 to 32), we get

m 0 1 2 3 4 5 6 7 8 9 10 11 12 13 14 15 16
c 0 1 8 27 31 26 18 13 17 3 10 11 12 19 5 9 4

m 17 18 19 20 21 22 23 24 25 26 27 28 29 30 31 32
c 29 24 28 14 21 22 23 30 16 20 15 7 2 6 25 32

Note that all 33 values of m (0 to 32) map to a unique code c in the same range in a sort of random manner. In this case we have nine values of m that map to the same value of c - these are known as *unconcealed messages*. m = 0 and 1 will always do this for any N, no matter how large. But in practice, higher values shouldn't be a problem when we use large values for N.

If we wanted to use this system to keep secrets, we could let A=2, B=3, ..., Z=27. (We specifically avoid 0 and 1 here for the reason given above).

Thus the plaintext message "HELLOWORLD" would be represented by the set of integers m_1, m_2, ...

{9, 6, 13, 13, 16, 24, 16, 19, 13, 5}

Using our table above, we obtain ciphertext integers c_1, c_2, ...

{3, 18, 19, 19, 4, 30, 4, 28, 19, 26}

Note that this example is no more secure than using a simple Caesar substitution cipher, but it serves to illustrate a simple example of the mechanics of RSA encryption.

Remember that calculating m^e mod n is easy, but calculating the inverse c^{-e} mod n is very difficult, well, for large n's anyway. However, if we can factor n into its prime factors p and q, the solution becomes easy again, even for large n's. Obviously, if we can get hold of the secret exponent d, the solution is easy, too.

Example 4.3:
A slightly less simple example of the RSA algorithm

This time, to make life slightly less easy for those who can crack simple Caesar substitution codes, we will group the characters into blocks of three and compute a message representative integer for each block.

ATTACKxATxSEVEN = ATT ACK XAT XSE VEN

In the same way that a decimal number can be represented as the sum of powers of ten, e.g.

$$135 = 1 \times 10^2 + 3 \times 10^1 + 5,$$

We could represent our blocks of three characters in base 26 using A = 0, B = 1, C = 2, ..., Z = 25

$$ATT = 0 \times 26^2 + 19 \times 26^1 + 19 = 513$$
$$ACK = 0 \times 26^2 + 2 \times 26^1 + 10 = 62$$
$$XAT = 23 \times 26^2 + 0 \times 26^1 + 19 = 15567$$
$$XSE = 23 \times 26^2 + 18 \times 26^1 + 4 = 16020$$
$$VEN = 21 \times 26^2 + 4 \times 26^1 + 13 = 14313$$

For this example, to keep things simple, we'll not worry about numbers and punctuation characters, or what happens with groups AAA or AAB.

In this system of encoding, the maximum value of a group (ZZZ) would be $26^3 - 1 = 17575$, so we require a modulus n greater than this value.

1. We "generate" primes p = 137 and q = 131 (we cheat by looking for suitable primes around $\sqrt{n}$.
2. n = pq = 137.131 = 17947
   phi = (p-1)(q – 1) = 136.130 = 17680
3. Select e = 3
   check gcd(e, p – 1) = gcd(3, 136) = 1, OK and
   check gcd(e, q – 1) = gcd(3, 130) = 1, OK.
4. Compute d = e^{-1} mod phi = 3^{-1} mod 17680 = 11787.
5. Hence public key, (n, e) = (17947, 3) and private key (n, d) = (17947, 11787).

Question: Why couldn't we use e=17 here?
To encrypt the first integer that represents "ATT", we have
$$c = m^e \bmod n = 513^3 \bmod 17947 = 8363.$$
We can verify that our private key is valid by decrypting
$$m' = c^d \bmod n = 8363^{11787} \bmod 17947 = 513.$$
Overall, our plaintext is represented by the set of integers m
{513, 62, 15567, 16020, 14313}

We compute corresponding ciphertext integers c = m^e mod n, (which is still possible by using a calculator).
{8363, 5017, 11884, 9546, 13366}

You can compute the inverse of these ciphertext integers using **m = c^d mod n** to verify that the RSA algorithm still holds. However, this is now outside the realms of hand calculations unless you are very patient.

Note that this is still a very insecure example. Starting with the knowledge that the modulus 17947 is probably derived from two prime numbers close to its square root, a little testing of suitable candidates from a table of prime numbers would get you the answer pretty quickly. Or just work methodically through the table of prime numbers dividing n by each value until you get no remainder. You could also write a simple computer program to factor n that just divides by every odd number starting from 3 until it reaches a number greater than the square root of n.

Example 4.4:
A Real Example
- In practice, we don't have a series of small integers to encrypt like we had in the above examples, we just have one big one.
- Also, rather than trying to represent the plaintext as an integer directly, we generate a random *session key* and use that to encrypt the plaintext with a conventional, much faster symmetrical algorithm like Triple DES.

- We then use the much slower public key encryption algorithm to encrypt just the session key.
- The sender A then transmits a message to the recipient B in a format something like this:

  > Encrypted session key = xxxx
  >
  > Plaintext encrypted with session key = xxxxxxxxxxxxxxxxxx

- The recipient B would extract the encrypted session key and use his private key (n, d) to decrypt it.
- He would then use this session key with a conventional symmetrical decryption algorithm to decrypt the actual message.
- Typically the transmission would include in plaintext details of the encryption algorithms used, padding and encoding methods, initialization vectors and other details required by the recipient.
- The only secret required to be kept, as always, should be the keys.
- If Mallory intercepts the transmission, he can either try and crack the conventionally-encrypted plaintext directly, or he can try and decrypt the encrypted session key and then use that in turn.
- Obviously, this system is as strong as its weakest link.

Key length:
- The key length for a secure RSA transmission is typically 1024 bits.
- 512 bits is now no longer considered secure.
- For more security or if you are paranoid, use 2048 or even 4096 bits.
- With the faster computers available today, the time taken to encrypt and decrypt even with a 4096-bit modulus really isn't an issue anymore.
- In practice, it is still effectively impossible for you or we to crack a message encrypted with a 512-bit key.
- The longer your information is needed to be kept secure, the longer the key you should use.
- Keep up to date with the latest recommendations in the security journals.
- No one is going to criticize you for using a key that is too long provided your software still performs adequately.
- However, in our opinion, the biggest danger in using a key that is too large is the false sense of security it provides to the implementers and users.

- If we are encrypting the plaintext with a conventional symmetrical algorithm like DES, our session key is going to be 64 bits long.
- Triple DES will need 192 bits, and AES will need up to 256 bits.
- That gives us lots of security.
- Unlike our simple examples above where we had to deal with a series of integers, to encrypt a 256-bit key with a 1024-bit RSA modulus means we only need a single representative message integer.
- In fact, you need to pad the 256 bits to ensure that we have a large enough integer before we encrypt it with RSA.
- 1024 bits is 128 bytes long, so we have quite a handful of data to deal with.

Recommended Techniques:
- [PKCS1] describes the latest recommended techniques to encode the plaintext octets using RSA.
- Again, in our opinion, you and we will have perfectly adequate security using the older version encoding techniques.
- If you are encrypting state secrets or bank codes for millions of dollars you should be following the latest recommendations.
- ANSI standard X9.31 [AX931] recommends using strong primes and other restrictions on p and q to minimize the possibility of known techniques being used against the algorithm.
- It is probably better just to use a longer key length.
- [KALI93] describes in great detail everything you need to know about encrypting and encoding using RSA.

4.15 DSA Algorithm

Description:
1. One of the most common digital signature mechanisms, the Digital Signature Algorithm (DSA) is the basis of the Digital Signature Standard (DSS).
2. As with other digital signature algorithms, DSA lets one person with a secret key "sign" a document, so that others with a matching public key can verify it must have been signed only by the holder of the secret key.
3. Digital signatures depend on *hash functions*, which are one-way computations done on a message.

4. They are called "one-way" because there is no known way (without infeasible amounts of computation) to find a message with a given hash value.
5. In other words, a hash value can be determined for a given message, but it is not known to be possible to construct *any* message with a given hash value.
6. Hash functions are similar to the scrambling operations used in symmetric key encryption, except that there is no decryption key: the operation is irreversible.
7. The result has a fixed length, which is 160 bits in the case of the Secure Hash Algorithm (SHA) used by DSA.
8. In practice, digital signatures are used to sign the *hash values* of messages, not the messages themselves.
9. Thus it is possible to sign a message's hash value, without even knowing the content of the message.
10. This makes it possible to have *digital notaries*, who can verify a document existed (and was signed), without the notary knowing anything about what was in the document.
11. The private key in DSA is a number X. It is known only to the signer.
12. The public key in DSA consists of four numbers:

   - P is a prime number, between 512 and 1024 bits long
   - Q is a 160-bit prime factor of P-1.
   - $G = h^{(P-1)/Q}$, where H< P −1 and G mod Q> 1.
   - $Y = G^X$ mod P, which is a 160-bit number.

A signature on a document's hash value H consists of two numbers R and S:

- $R = (G^K \bmod P) \bmod Q$, where K is a randomly-chosen number <Q.
- $S = (K^{-1} (H + XR)) \bmod Q$

To verify the signature, a recipient must compute a value V from the known information:

- $W = S^{-1} \bmod Q$
- $U1 = HW \bmod Q$
- $U2 = RW \bmod Q$
- $V = ((G^{U1} Y^{U2}) \bmod P) \bmod Q$

If V = R, then document was signed by the person with the public key *(P, Q, G, Y)*.

The security of DSA is based on the computational infeasibility of finding a solution for the equation $S = (K^{-1} (H + XR)) \bmod Q$, when X is not known.

4.16 MD5 Algorithm

Executive Summary

1. This data describes the MD5 message-digest algorithm.
2. The algorithm takes as input a message of arbitrary length and produces as output a 128-bit "fingerprint" or "message digest" of the input.
3. It is conjectured that it is computationally infeasible to produce two messages having the same message digest, or to produce any message having a given prespecified target message digest.
4. The MD5 algorithm is intended for digital signature applications, where a large file must be "compressed" in a secure manner before being encrypted with a private (secret) key under a public-key cryptosystem such as RSA.
5. MD5 was designed by Ronald Rivest in 1991 to replace an earlier hash function, MD4.
6. MD5 is more secure than MD4.
7. However a number of weaknesses have been found in recent years.
8. The most recent discoveries in this area shows that a collision of MD5 can be found within one minute on a standard notebook PC, using a method called tunneling.
9. Despite its weaknesses, MD5 is widely used in digital signature processes. It's been implemented in many programming languages.
10. The MD5 algorithm is designed to be quite fast on 32-bit machines.
11. In addition, the MD5 algorithm does not require any large substitution tables; the algorithm can be coded quite compactly.
12. The MD5 algorithm is an extension of the MD4 message-digest algorithm.
13. MD5 is slightly slower than MD4, but is more "conservative" in design.
14. MD5 was designed because it was felt that MD4 was perhaps being adopted for use more quickly than justified by the existing critical review; because MD4 was designed to be exceptionally fast, it is "at the edge" in terms of risking successful cryptanalytic attack.
15. MD5 backs off a bit, giving up a little in speed for a much greater likelihood of ultimate security.
16. It incorporates some suggestions made by various reviewers, and contains additional optimizations.
17. The MD5 algorithm is being placed in the public domain for review and possible adoption as a standard.

Vulnerability:

1. Because MD5 makes only one pass over the data, if two prefixes with the same hash can be constructed, a common suffix can be added to both to make the collision more reasonable.
2. And because the current collision-finding techniques allow the preceding hash state to be specified arbitrarily, a collision can be found for any desired prefix for any given string of characters X, two colliding files can be determined which both begin with X.
3. All that is required to generate two colliding files is a template file, with a 128-byte block of data aligned on a 64-byte boundary, that can be changed freely by the collision-finding algorithm.

Applications:

1. MD5 digests have been widely used in the software world to provide some assurance that a downloaded file has not been altered.
2. A user can compare a published MD5 sum with the checksum of a downloaded file.
3. Unix based operating systems include MD5 sum utilities in their distribution packages, whereas Windows users use third-party applications like FastSum.
4. Now that it is easy to generate MD5 collisions, though, it is possible for the person who creates the file to create a second file with the same checksum, so this technique cannot protect against some forms of malicious tampering.
5. It is also often the case that the checksum cannot be trusted (for example, it was obtained over the same channel as the downloaded file), in which case MD5 can only provide error-checking functionality: it will recognize a corrupt or incomplete download, which becomes more likely when downloading larger files.
6. MD5 is widely used to store passwords.
7. A number of MD5 reverse lookup databases exist, which make it easy to decrypt password hashed with plain MD5.
8. To prevent such attacks you can add a salt to your passwords before hashing them.
9. Also, it is a good idea to apply the hashing function (MD5 in this case) more than once—see key strengthening.
10. It increases the time needed to encrypt a password and discourages dictionary attacks.

MD5 Algorithm Overview:

Below is a quick overview of the algorithm.

MD5 algorithm consists of 5 steps:

Step 1. Appending Padding Bits. The original message is "padded" (extended) so that its length (in bits) is congruent to 448, modulo 512. The padding rules are:
- The original message is always padded with one bit "1" first.
- Then zero or more bits "0" are padded to bring the length of the message up to 64 bits fewer than a multiple of 512.

Step 2. Appending Length. 64 bits are appended to the end of the padded message to indicate the length of the original message in bytes. The rules of appending length are:
- The length of the original message in bytes is converted to its binary format of 64 bits. If overflow happens, only the low-order 64 bits are used.
- Break the 64-bit length into 2 words (32 bits each).
- The low-order word is appended first and followed by the high-order word.

Step 3. Initializing MD Buffer. MD5 algorithm requires a 128-bit buffer with a specific initial value. The rules of initializing buffer are:
- The buffer is divided into 4 words (32 bits each), named as A, B, C, and D.
- Word A is initialized to: 0x67452301.
- Word B is initialized to: 0xEFCDAB89.
- Word C is initialized to: 0x98BADCFE.
- Word D is initialized to: 0x10325476.

Step 4. Processing Message in 512-bit Blocks. This is the main step of MD 5 algorithm, which loops through the padded and appended message in blocks of 512 bits each. For each input block, 4 rounds of operations are performed with 16 operations in each round.

Step 5. Output. The contents in buffer words A, B, C, D are returned in sequence with low-order byte first.

Algorithm:

1. MD5 processes a variable length message into a fixed-length output of 128 bits.
2. The input message is broken up into chunks of 512-bit blocks; the message is padded so that its length is divisible by 512.
3. The padding works as follows: first a single bit, 1, is appended to the end of the message.
4. This is followed by as many zeros as are required to bring the length of the message up to 64 bits fewer than a multiple of 512.
5. The remaining bits are filled up with a 64-bit integer representing the length of the original message.
6. The main MD5 algorithm operates on a 128-bit state, divided into four 32-bit words, denoted *A, B, C* and *D*.
7. These are initialized to certain fixed constants.

8. The main algorithm then operates on each 512-bit message block in turn, each block modifying the state.
9. The processing of a message block consists of four similar stages, termed *rounds*; each round is composed of 16 similar operations based on a non-linear function F, modular addition, and left rotation.
10. Figure illustrates one operation within a round. There are four possible functions F, a different one is used in each round:

$$F(X, Y, Z) = (X \wedge Y) \vee (\neg X \wedge Z)$$
$$G(X, Y, Z) = (X \wedge Z) \vee (Y \wedge \neg Z)$$
$$H(X, Y, Z) = X \oplus Y \oplus Z$$
$$I(X, Y, Z) = Y \oplus (X \vee \neg Z)$$

⊕, ∧, ∨, ¬ denote the XOR, AND, OR and NOT operations respectively.

$<<<_s$ denotes a left bit rotation by s places; s varies for each operation.

⊞ denotes addition modulo 2^{32}.

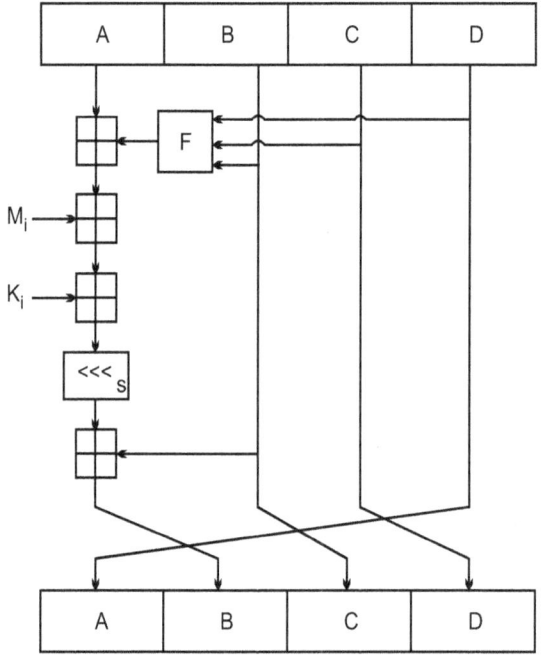

Fig. 4.34: One MD5 operation, MD5 consists of 64 of these operations, grouped in four rounds of 16 operations. F is a non-linear function; one function is used in each round. M_i denotes a 32-bit block of the message input, and K_i denotes a 32-bit constant, different for each operation

Md5 Hashes:

1. The 128-bit (16-byte) MD5 hashes (also termed *message digests*) are typically represented as a sequence of 32 hexadecimal digits.
2. The following demonstrates a 43-byte ASCII input and the corresponding MD5 hash:
   MD5("The quick brown fox jumps over the lazy dog")
   = 9e107d9d372bb6826bd81d3542a419d6
3. Even a small change in the message will (with overwhelming probability) result in a completely different hash, e.g. changing d to c:
   MD5("The quick brown fox jumps over the lazy cog")
   = 1055d3e698d289f2af8663725127bd4b
4. The hash of the zero-length string is:
   MD5("") = d41d8cd98f00b204e9800998ecf8427e

4.17 How do Digital Signatures Work?

1. A **digital signature** is basically a way to ensure that an electronic document (e-mail, spreadsheet, text file, etc.) is **authentic**.
2. Authentic means that you know who created the document and you know that it has not been altered in any way since that person created it.
3. Digital signatures rely on certain types of **encryption** to ensure authentication.
4. Encryption is the process of taking all the data that one computer is sending to another and encoding it into a form that only the other computer will be able to decode.
5. Authentication is the process of verifying that information is coming from a trusted source.
6. These two processes work hand in hand for digital signatures.

There are several ways to authenticate a person or information on a computer:
- **Password** - The use of a user name and password provide the most common form of authentication. You enter your name and password when prompted by the computer. It checks the pair against a secure file to confirm. If either the name or password does not match, then you are not allowed further access.
- **Checksum** - Probably one of the oldest methods of ensuring that data is correct, checksums also provide a form of authentication since an invalid checksum suggests that the data has been compromised in some fashion. A checksum is determined in one of two ways. Let's say the checksum of a packet is 1 byte long, which means it can have a maximum value of 255. If the sum of the other bytes in the packet is 255 or less, then the checksum contains that exact value. However, if the sum of the other bytes is more than 255, then the checksum is the remainder of the total value after it has been divided by 256. Look at this example:

Byte 1	Byte 2	Byte 3	Byte 4	Byte 5	Byte 6	Byte 7	Byte 8	Total	Checksum
212	232	54	135	244	15	179	80	1151	127

- 1151 divided by 256 equals 4.496 (round to 4) Multiply 4 ∞ 256, which equals 1024 1151 minus 1024 equals 127.

- **CRC (Cyclic Redundancy Check)** - CRCs are similar in concept to checksums but they use polynomial division to determine the value of the CRC, which is usually 16 or 32 bits in length. The good thing about CRC is that it is very accurate. If a single bit is incorrect, the CRC value will not match up. Both checksum and CRC are good for preventing random errors in transmission, but provide little protection from an intentional attack on your data. The encryption techniques below are much more secured.

- **Private key encryption** - Private key means that each computer has a secret key (code) that it can use to encrypt a packet of information before it is sent over the network to the other computer. Private key requires that you know which computers will talk to each other and install the key on each one. Private key encryption is essentially the same as a secret code that the two computers must each know in order to decode the information. The code would provide the key to decoding the message. Think of it like this. You create a coded message to send to a friend where each letter is substituted by the letter that is second from it. So "A" becomes "C" and "B" becomes "D". You have already told a trusted friend that the code is "Shift by 2". Your friend gets the message and decodes it. Anyone else who sees the message will only see nonsense.

- **Public key encryption** - Public key encryption uses a combination of a private key and a public key. The private key is known only to your computer while the public key is given by your computer to any computer that wants to communicate securely with it. To decode an encrypted message, a computer must use the public key provided by the originating computer and it's own private key.

The key is based on a **hash value**. This is a value that is computed from a base input number using a **hashing algorithm**. The important thing about a hash value is that it is nearly impossible to derive the original input number without knowing the data used to create the hash value. Here's a simple example:

Input number	Hashing algorithm	Hash value
10667	Input # x 143	1525381

You can see how hard it would be to determine that the value of 1525381 came from the multiplication of 10667 and 143. But if you knew that the multiplier was 143, then it would be very easy to calculate the value of 10667. Public key encryption is much more complex than this example but that is the basic idea. Public keys generally use complex algorithms and very large hash values for encrypting: 40-bit or even 128-bit numbers. A 128-bit number has a possible 2^{128} different combinations. That's as many combinations as there are water molecules in 2.7 million olympic size swimming pools. Even the tiniest water droplet you can image has billions and billions of water molecules in it !

- **Digital certificates** - To implement public key encryption on a large scale, such as a secure Web server might need, requires a different approach. This is where digital certificates come in. A digital certificate is essentially a bit of information that says the Web server is trusted by an independent source known as a Certificate Authority. The **Certificate Authority** acts as the middleman that both computers trust. It confirms that each computer is in fact who they say they are and then provides the public keys of each computer to the other.

The **Digital Signature Standard (DSS)** is based on a type of public key encryption method that uses the **Digital Signature Algorithm (DSA)**. DSS is the format for digital signatures that has been endorsed by the US government. The DSA algorithm consists of a private key that only the originator of the document (signer) knows and a public key.

4.18 What is a Digital Certificate?

1. Understanding digital certificates is central to understanding public key infrastructure systems.
2. A digital certificate, also known as a Digital ID, is the electronic equivalent of a passport or business license.
3. It is a credential, issued by a trusted authority those individuals or organisations can present electronically to prove their identity or their right to access information.
4. When a Certification Authority (CA) issues Digital IDs, it verifies that the owner is not claiming a false identity.
5. Just as when a government issues a passport, it is officially vouching for the identity of the holder, when a CA gives your business a digital certificate, it is putting its name behind your right to use your company name and Web address.

4.18.1 How Digital Certificates Work

1. In physical transactions, the challenges of identification, authentication, and privacy are solved with physical marks, such as seals or signatures.

2. In electronic transactions, the equivalent of a seal must be coded into the information itself.
3. By checking that the electronic "seal" is present and has not been broken, the recipient can confirm the identity of the message sender and ensure that the message content was not altered in transit.
4. To create an electronic equivalent of physical security, digital certificates use advanced cryptography.
5. Cryptographic systems have been used to protect valuable information for thousands of years.
6. Traditionally, cryptographic systems have attempted to ensure security using some variant of the secret key system.
7. Secret key systems require that both parties in a communication scheme have a copy of the same secret code or "key."
8. When two people wanted to share information, the sender would encrypt the information using his copy of the secret key.
9. The recipient could decrypt the message only by using her copy of the same key.
10. If somebody intercepted the message, that person could not decipher it without the key.
11. Despite their widespread use, secret key systems have several critical limitations.
12. First, simply transmitting the secret key poses risks, because the key can be intercepted in transit by unauthorized parties.
13. Second, if one of the sharing parties uses the key maliciously, that party can deny or repudiate, the transaction.
14. Alternatively, the malicious party can impersonate the sender, or can use the secret key to decrypt other sensitive information.
15. To prevent against this sort of attack, organisations must require users to have different secret keys for each party with whom they communicate.
16. If an organization has a hundred people, literally millions of different secret keys will need to be used to accommodate all possible combinations.
17. **Digital certificates employ the more advanced public key cryptography system, which does not involve the sharing of secret keys**.
18. **Rather than using the same key to both encrypt and decrypt data, a digital certificate uses a matched pair of keys that uniquely complement each other**.
19. **When a message is encrypted by one key, only the complementary key can decrypt it.**
20. In public key cryptography systems, when your key-pair is generated, you keep one key private.
21. This key is called the "private key," and nobody other than you, as the rightful owner, should ever have access to it.

22. However, the matching "public key," can be freely distributed as part of a digital certificate.
23. You can share your digital certificate with anyone, and can even publish your certificate in directories.
24. If someone wants to communicate with you privately, they use the public key in your digital certificate to encrypt information before sending it to you.
25. Only you can decrypt the information, because only you have your private key.

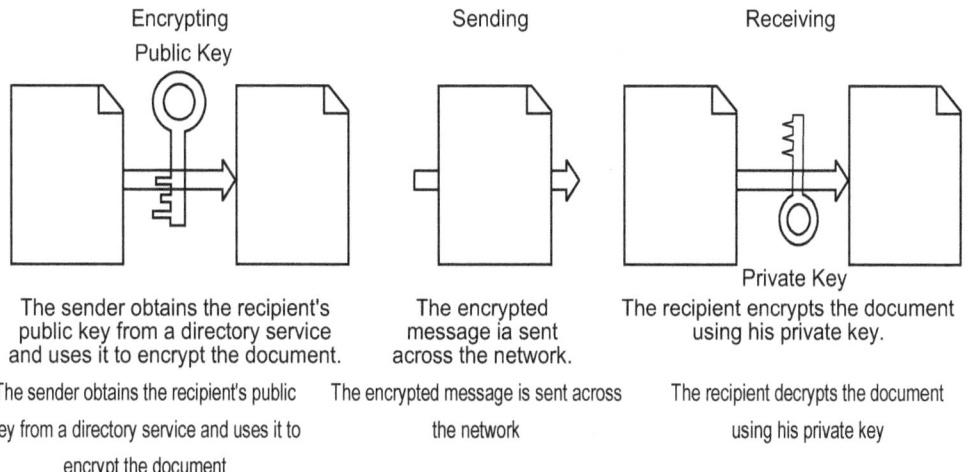

The sender obtains the recipient's public key from a directory service and uses it to encrypt the document

The encrypted message is sent across the network

The recipient decrypts the document using his private key

Fig. 4.35: Encrypting Information Using Digital Certificates

26. Conversely, you can use your key pair to digitally sign a message.
27. To sign a message, you simply encrypt the message with your private key.
28. The message can be decrypted using the public key contained within your certificate.
29. While many people have access to your certificate, only you could have signed the message, because only you have access to your private key.
30. **A digital certificate is a binary file**.
31. Your digital certificate contains your name and your identifying information along with your public key it tells correspondents that your public key belongs to you.
32. Digital certificates generally also contain a serial number, an expiration date, and information about the rights, uses, and privileges associated with the certificate.
33. Finally, the digital certificate contains information about the certificate authority (CA) who have issued the certificate.
34. All certificates are digitally signed using the private key of the Certificate Authority.
35. Generally, the Certification Authorities' own certificate (called a root certificate) is widely deployed in software packages, allowing people to seamlessly identify legitimate certificates issued by the certification authority.

36. If the CA maintains good security protection of their private key, it is virtually impossible for anyone to forge a digital certificate.

37. It is important to note that certificates are not only issued to individuals. Organisations, as well as entities such as servers and routers, can also be issued certificates.

38. Finally care to be taken are –

    - Before sending a secret message – ask to see the other party's certificate – to get their public key.

    - When signing a document – encrypt using your private key, and send encrypted document plus *your* certificate.

    - Before trusting a document, verify signature using the sender's certificate.

    - Before doing anything with a certificate, be sure you trust the Certificate Authority who issued it.

4.19 Intranet and Internet Security

4.19.1 Introduction

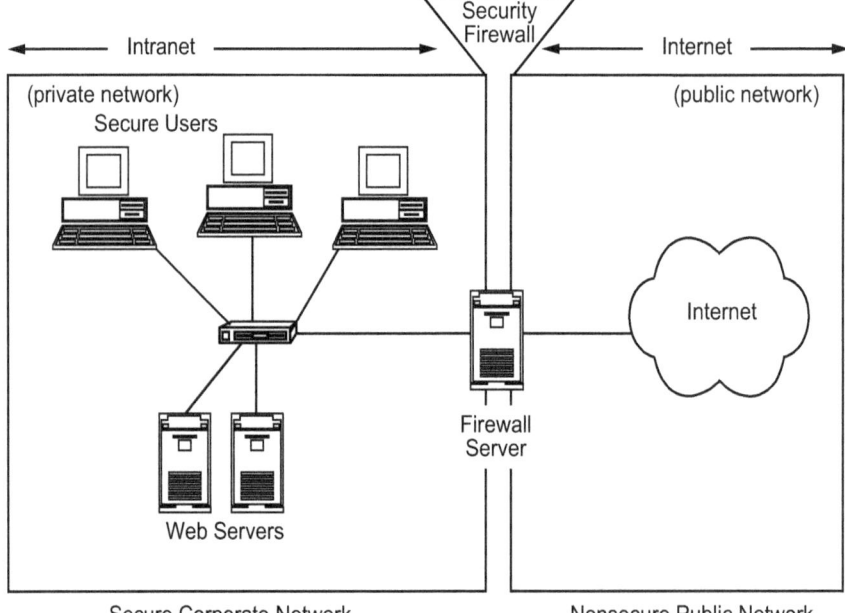

Fig. 4.36: Clearly indicated Intranet and Internet

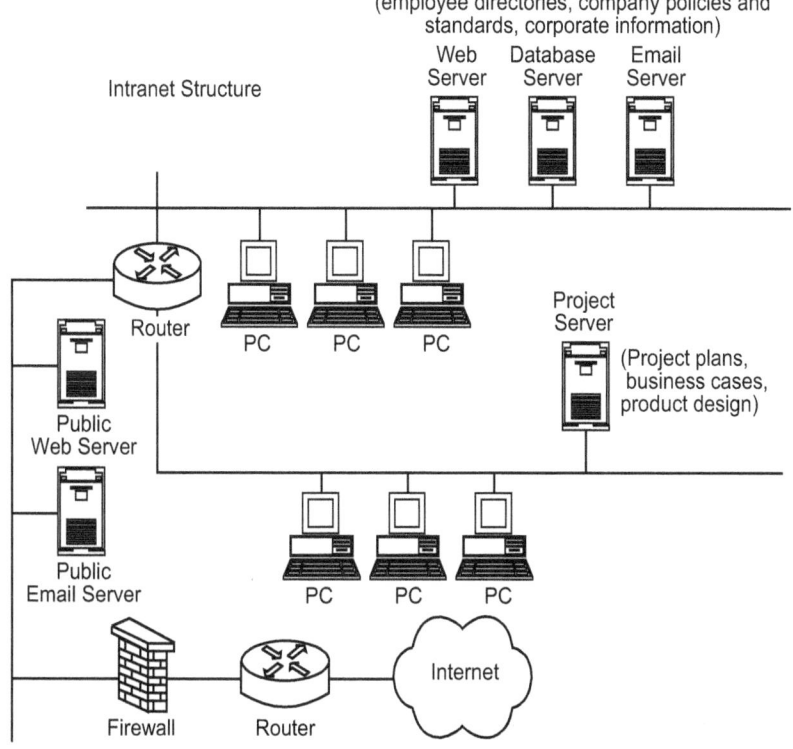

Fig. 4.37: Diagram of corporate Intranet

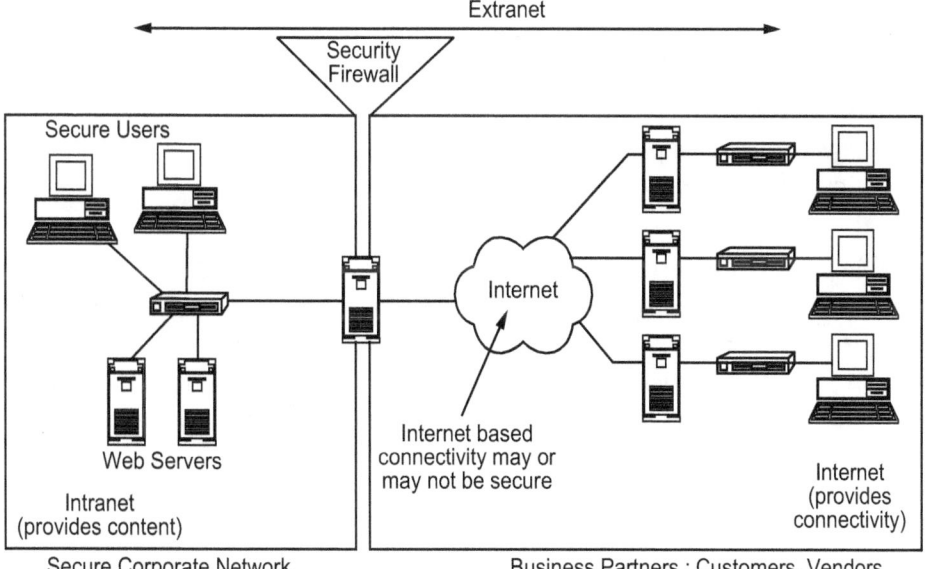

Fig. 4.38: Extranet is nothing but Extended Internet

What is an Intranet?
- An internal Website located on an existing Novell, Windows NT or other network.
- Based on TCP/IP protocols or can be proprietary protocol.
- Belongs to an organization and is accessible only by the organization's members, employees, or others with authorization.
- Not limited by physical location.
- Reside behind firewalls.
- May use public networks to transfer data.

Types of Intranets:
- Human Resources Intranet.
- Sales and Marketing Intranet.
- Information Systems Intranet.
- Executive or corporate Intranet.
- Customer Service Intranet.
- Finance Intranet.
- Educational Intranet.

What is an Extranet?
- **Extended Internet – Private business networks located outside of the corporate firewall**.
- Refers to an intranet that is partially accessible to authorized outsiders.
- A network that uses the Internet to link businesses with others that share the same common goals.

Extranet Applications:
- Private News Groups
- Common Business Materials
- Electronic Commerce
- Improved Customer Service

1. Over the last several years, organizations have embraced Intranets and Extranets enthusiastically.
2. A Local Area Network within an organization, which is designed to look like, and work in the same way as, the Internet. Intranets are essentially private networks, and are not accessible to the public.
3. This is not surprising. Intranets and Extranets offer clear cost savings and ease of installation compared with older leased line networks or WANS based on proprietary technology.
4. Furthermore, they enable highly productive and cost effective new ways of working.

5. Organizations can use Intranets and Extranets to distribute information more cost effectively and in a more timely manner.
6. They can use them to build a wide range of self-service applications that help reduce administrative costs.
7. And, they can use them to improve collaboration among employees across the organization and with business partners.
8. As Intranets and Extranets have become more widely deployed, new security challenges have emerged.
9. While many organizations have deployed firewalls and access control technology to improve security, these technologies leave many security issues un-addressed.
10. This chapter will give an overview of the main security risks of deploying Intranets and Extranets and will discuss the five fundamental goals of a security system: Privacy, Authentication, Content Integrity, Non-repudiation, and Ease-of-use.

4.19.2 The Growth of the Intranet and Extranet

Few technologies have been accepted as rapidly as Intranets within organizations, and many of these organizations are now extending their Intranets to reach key customers and/or business partners via. Extranets.

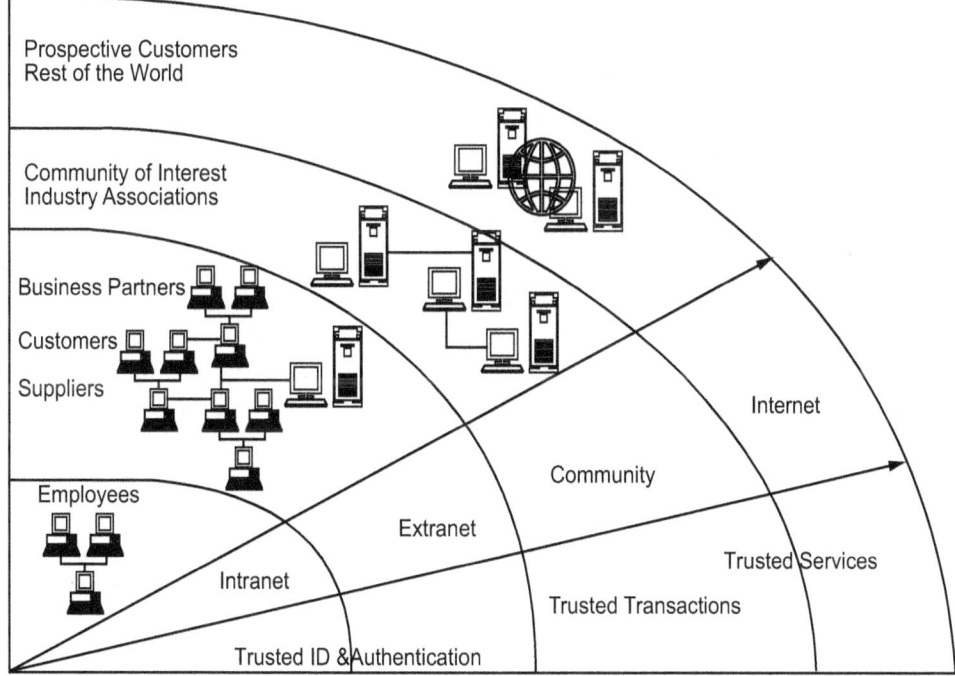

Fig. 4.39: The Expanding Network

4.19.3 Benefits of the Intranet and Extranet

1. The reasons for this growth are clear.
2. Compared with earlier wide area networks (WANs) based on proprietary technology or expensive leased lines, Intranets and Extranets are significantly easier and less expensive to set up and operate.
3. Intranets can offer organizations numerous operational efficiencies, and, as a result, they can generate staggering returns on investment.
4. Where WANs required expensive leased lines, Intranets and Extranets allow users to communicate over vast distances using inexpensive public Internet lines.
5. When organizations tried to link local area networks (LANs) over the WAN, diverse communications protocols (including IPX/SPX, NETBIOS, NETBUI, and DECnet) often limited applications' ability to talk to each other. (These are non-routable protocols which doesn't work beyond router which works before router only i.e. for LAN only).
6. By adhering to TCP/IP, the standard Internet protocol, Intranets and Extranets make it easy for different computer systems within or even outside an organization to speak to each other. (Because the TCP/IP is routable protocol which works in intranet LAN as well as it works beyond router i.e. Internet network).
7. Using the hypertext language and browser model of the World Wide Web, Intranets provide users with tools that are graphic and easy to operate.
8. Once up and running, Intranets and Extranets reduce costs and improve operations in many ways, including:
   - **Reducing costs of distributing information** - Intranets make it faster and easier to distribute policies, procedures, and company news to employees; Extranets make it easy and inexpensive to distribute online catalogs and price lists.
   - **Lowering administrative costs:** The interactive capabilities of the Intra/Extranet allow users to complete many tasks themselves that once required administrative assistance. For example, Intranets now allow employees access to personnel resources, while business-to-business customers can order their own supplies over the Extranet
   - **Improving collaboration:** Users become more productive by using the Intra/Extranet to form virtual, online teams. These virtual teams can collaborate without the expense of frequent travel or the delays of sending information via the postal service. Within an organization, the Intranet can flatten hierarchies, giving more employees access to the information they need to make strategic decisions. Extranets allow businesses to collaborate more closely with each other as well. For example, Extranets can be used to integrate the supply chain, replacing expensive and proprietary systems such as electronic data interchange.

9. The sum total of these benefits can mean a staggering boost to an organization's bottom line.
10. Industry Extranets show similar promise. For example, within the automotive and retail industries, many companies have established Extranet-based supply chain networks, allowing real-time inventory, order, and delivery information to be communicated between retailers, distributors, manufacturers, and suppliers.
11. This helps dramatically improve the ability of all organizations within the supply chain to match the supply of goods for the demand of goods, while simultaneously decreasing inventories.
12. This improves efficiency, inventory management, and, ultimately, profitability throughout the entire supply chain.

4.19.4 New Security Concerns

1. As the use of Intranets and Extranets has grown, so has the need for security.
2. The TCP/IP protocols and technology are inherently designed to be open. TCP/IP is a *connectionless* protocol; data is broken up into packets, which travel freely over the network, seeking the best possible route to reach their final destination.
3. Therefore, unless proper precautions are taken, data can readily be intercepted and/or altered-often without either the sending or the receiving party being aware of the security breach.
4. Because dedicated links between the parties in a communication usually are not established in advance, it is easy for one party to impersonate another party.

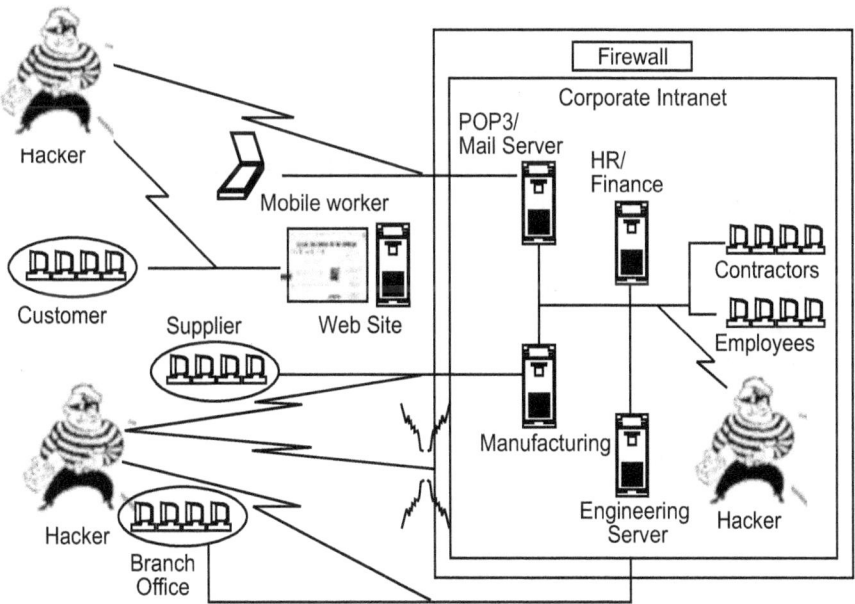

Fig. 4.40: Expanding Networks Increase Possible Points of Attack

5. **Fig. 4.40 illustrates the growth in network complexity has increased the potential points of attack both from outside and from within organisations.**
6. Fortunately, the methods of protecting against these attacks have also expanded.
7. **Two of the most common security precautions in use today are *firewalls* and *passwords*.**
8. Passwords are designed to prevent unauthorized individuals from directly gaining access to sensitive data stored on servers.
9. Firewalls, by contrast, are designed to provide a perimeter defense mechanism, preventing unauthorized individuals outside the organization from gaining access to sensitive data inside the organization.
10. According to a recent information, virtually 75% organisations have already deployed firewalls.
11. Despite their important role in network security and widespread adoption, firewalls provide only a partial solution.
12. As shown in Fig. 4.40, perimeter defenses can do little to prevent against attacks by insiders (e.g. disgruntled employees, contractors, or others).
13. Passwords are also largely ineffective against inside attacks.
14. Most passwords are notoriously easy to guess; where passwords are not guessed, they can often be discovered on sticky pads on employee's computers or intercepted as they pass, in the clear, over corporate networks.
15. Even when passwords are not guessed, or when more sophisticated access control methods are used, it is important to note that access control alone cannot ensure that information remains confidential.
16. While a good password system might prevent someone from directly entering a server to obtain confidential information, passwords do not protect data as it passes "over the wire" between the server and the client.
17. The same general problem applies to data that passes outside the firewall, between corporate servers and branch offices, customers, suppliers, and remote employees.
18. Any time that data is sent between your servers and organisations outside your firewall, the data can be intercepted using "sniffers." Hackers do not need to get "in" to your system, if you are sending data outside the perimeter.

4.19.5 Types of Security Risks Encountered on an Intranet and Extranet

Intranet and Extranet security breaches can take a variety of forms. For example,

- An unauthorized person, such as a contractor or visitor, might gain access to a company's computer system.

- An employee or supplier authorized to use the system for one purpose might use it for another. For example, an engineer might break into the HR database to obtain confidential salary information.
- Confidential information might be intercepted as it is being sent to an authorized user. For example, an intruder might attach a network-sniffing device to the network. While sniffers are normally used for network diagnostics, they can also be used to intercept data coming over the wire.
- Users may share documents between geographically separated offices over the Internet or Extranet, or telecommuters accessing the corporate Intranet from their home computer can expose sensitive data as it is sent over the wire.
- Electronic mail can be intercepted in transit.

These are not merely theoretical concerns. While computer hackers breaking into corporate computer systems over the Internet have received a great deal of press in recent years, in reality, corporate insiders-such as employees, former employees, contractors working onsite, and other suppliers-are far more likely to attack their own company's computer systems over an Intranet.

Such insider security breaches are likely to result in greater losses than attacks from the outside. Of the organisations that were able to quantify their losses, the most Computer Security organizations survey found that the most serious financial losses occurred through unauthorized access by insiders (see Fig. below). As organisations increasingly install Intranets and Extranets, therefore, it is becoming critical for them to secure these systems from inside attacks.

4.19.6 Goals of Intranet and Extranet Security Systems

Fortunately, there are a variety of techniques available to address these security holes within Extranets and Intranets. Before choosing a particular technology, however, it is important to understand the full range of issues that security systems should address:

- **Authentication** - Ensuring that entities sending messages, receiving messages, or accessing systems are who they say they are, and have the privilege to undertake such actions.
- **Privacy** - Enabling only the intended recipient to view an encrypted message
- **Content Integrity** - Guaranteeing that messages have not been altered by another party since they were sent.
- **Non-Repudiation** - Establishing the source of a message so that the sender cannot later claim that they did not send the message.
- **Ease of use** - Ensuring that security systems can be consistently and thoroughly implemented for a wide variety of applications without unduly restricting the ability of individuals or organisations to go about their daily business.

This last goal is frequently overlooked. Organisations must not only develop sound security measures, they must also find a way to ensure consistent compliance with them. If users find security measures cumbersome and time consuming to use, they are likely to find ways to circumvent them - thereby putting your Intranet and Extranet at risk. Organisations can ensure the consistent compliance to their security policy through:

- **Systematic application. The system should automatically enforce the security policy so that security** is maintained at all times.
- **Ease of end-user deployment.** The more transparent the system is, the easier it is for end-users to use-and the more likely they are to use it. Ideally, security polices should be built into the system, eliminating the need for users to read detailed manuals and follow elaborate procedures.
- **Wide acceptance across multiple applications.** The same security system should work for all applications a user is likely to employ. For example, you should be able to use the same security system whether you want to secure e-mail, e-commerce, server access via a browser, or remote communications over a virtual private network.

Making a More Robust Intranet:

The first order of business is to bring intranet servers up to the same level of readiness as our extranet servers. As the level of risk in the intranet approaches the level found in public networks, intranet servers require improved systems and methods to keep configurations in line with policies and to insure both the policies of our organization and the resulting configurations are valid for the evolving environment. All systems in the organization must be protected to the same, stringent degree. In order to accomplish this, the organization must first begin with a thorough risk assessment. This is accomplished as follows.

1. Identifying the threats facing the information.
2. Identifying the vulnerabilities in the systems containing the information, that could be exploited by each threat.
3. Estimating the probability of the threat exploiting the vulnerability (risk).
4. Estimating the value of restoring the information should an attack occur.
5. Using this value to determine the expenditure levels for the protection of the information and its systems.
6. Identifying areas where additional safeguards are needed.

Efforts to improve intranet security should then look to organization information security policy. Using management review and industry comparison techniques, organization information security policy should be periodically verified as complete and correct. This should include insuring that policies are current for the objectives of the organization and the operating environment. The misalignment of Information Security Policy to both industry best practice and organizational goals occurs over time both as the Information Security industry matures and as organizational goals evolve. An ongoing effort to maintain alignment is needed to insure success.

The following questions summarize the key points of Intranet Security Assurance:
1. How effective are your current information security policies? Regular policy review is key to ensuring effectiveness.
2. How effectively do your system configurations reflect your organization's policy? Aggressive security policy validation is another key element to ensuring program effectiveness.
3. Are your "shepherds" watching your "sheep"? Regular Intranet validation scans effectively test the readiness of your technical services team.
4. Are there "wolves" among your "sheep"? Proper education and training of employees ensure that accidental and intentional abuse of systems privileges are minimized.

4.19.7 Digital Certificates Meet Your Security Objectives

Given the ease and versatility of PKI, security technology based on Digital Certificates has been deployed widely over the past several years. These widely used security protocols include:

- **S/MIME:** The Secure, Multipurpose Internet Mail Extension protocol allows for sending signed and encrypted e-mail.
- **SSL:** The Secure Sockets Layer protocol allows for authenticated and encrypted communication between browsers and servers, or between different servers. This is a very important protocol.
- **IPSEC:** The IP Security Protocol allows authenticated and encrypted communication between routers, between firewalls, and between routers and firewalls.

The following table provides a summary of how these various protocols can be deployed in securing your Intranet or Extranet.

Table 4.4: Security Protocols for Various Types of Secure Communications

Connection	Privacy / Encryption	Authentication	Signing / Content Integrity (sometimes optional)
Internal / Remote employee to server	• SSL 2.0 or 3.0 (provided by Secure Server ID or Global Server ID)	• Server authenticated by Server ID • Client authenticated by passwords (phase 1) or by SSL 3.0 with Client IDs (preferred)	• Signed documents and controls (S/MIME, form signing). Signing Done using Client IDs
Customer to web server	• SSL 2.0 or 3.0 (provided by Secure Server ID or Global Server ID)	Same as above	Not usually needed
Remote employee using email	• SSL on POP3 or IMAP mail server • S/MIME Client IDs (phase 2) or VPN using IPSEC	• Server authenticated by Server ID passwords (not recommended) • S/MIME Client IDs	• S/MIME using Client IDs
	• SSL (phase 1) • VPNs using IPSEC	• Server authenticated by Server ID • Router/firewall authenticated by IPSEC ID • Clients authenticated by passwords or by SSL 3.0 with Client IDs	• Signed documents and controls (S/MIME, form signing)

4.19.8 Ultimate Remedies

1. Fortunately, a set of technologies have been developed over the past twenty years that are particular well suited to meeting these five security goals.

2. Broadly called **Public Key Infrastructure (PKI)**, this technology allows organisations using open networks, such as TCP/IP Intranets and Extranets, to replicate or even improve on the mechanisms used to ensure security in the physical world.

3. Envelopes and secure couriers are replaced with sophisticated methods of *data encryption*, which can ensure that messages are only read by their intended recipients.

4. Physical signatures and seals are replaced with **digital signatures** which, in addition to ensuring that messages came from a particular entity, can also ensure that message was not altered by as much as one bit during transit.

5. Identity documents, such as passports, employee ID cards, and business licenses, can be replaced with **digital certificates** (also known as Digital IDs).
6. Finally, the various mechanisms for centralized control, audit, and authorization, such as those provided by corporate governance structures, industry boards, or trusted third parties such as accountants, can be replicated in the digital world through the **infrastructure used to managed encryption, digital signatures, and Digital IDs.**

4.19.9 Conclusion

As your organisations moves to Intranet and Extranet solutions, you will need to be careful to ensure that your organization implements a robust security solution. Industry standards solutions based on Public Key Infrastructure can provide a framework for ensuring that the goals of privacy, authentication, content integrity, non-repudiation, and ease of use. To implement a proper PKI requires, however, that your Certificate Authority function is implemented with the highest quality technology, infrastructure, and practices.

4.20 Domain Name System

4.20.1 Introduction

Let's say you want a domain name - for the purpose of this explanation, we'll use *adomain.com*.

Let's break down what a domain name is first. And to do that, we'll need to break down and define what a URL is.

URL is an acronym for Uniform Resource Locator, which in layman's terms, means an internet address.

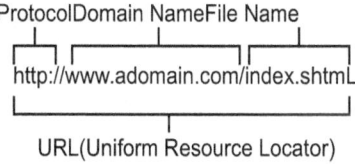

Fig. 4.41: URL (Uniform Resource Locator)

In the above diagram, we see that a URL is made up of 3 things:

Protocol:

This is the communication method with which one computer speaks to another. Just as we're using the written English language in this website as our communication method for our visitors, the computer systems that make up the internet have their own "languages", known as protocols. For example, HTTP stands for HyperText Transfer Protocol, which is one of the methods used for computer communication on the world wide web. HTTP is used to transmit web pages or other files to the person requesting them.

Other widely used Internet protocols you may or may not be familiar with are:
- Usenet: used for newsgroups.
- FTP: File Transfer Protocol - used for uploading and download files.
- Telnet: used to allow you to directly connect to a defined, specific computer.
- E-mail: uses POP, or **P**ost **O**ffice **P**rotocol, to receive mail; and uses SMTP, or **S**tandard **M**ail **T**ransport **P**rotocol to send mail.

You have accessed this page-using HTTP. If you tried to access it with one of these other protocols, it wouldn't have worked properly, or would have simply failed. Looking at the above diagram, you may be surprised to learn that you already knew what a domain name is, but didn't know the term. Basically, a domain name is a unique phrase that makes up every WWW and email address... a "mailing address" on the Internet where the "address" is a word or phrase that points to a particular site.

Domain Name:
A domain name consists of two parts: the name and the extension. The name is the part that you rack your brain with, trying to come up with a name that is both easy to remember and available. The extension is more correctly referred to as the **top-level domain**, or TLD. The name is referred to as the **second-level domain**. It's possible to have many levels in a domain name. For example, it would be quite common to refer to our example domain name as www.adomain.com. In that example, the *www* could be called a **third-level domain**. Or, we could get creative, and define something like *files.adomain.com*, or *secure.adomain.com*, or even something like –
i.love.my.beautiful.website.at.adomain.com.

There are a several top-level domains available to the general public:
- .com - generally for commercial purposes.
- .net - typically used for internet service providers.
- .org - generally used for non-profit organizations.
- (country extension) - these will be used more frequently, if not exclusively for new domains in the near future. Why? Because we're running out of useful names. There are a few more domain extensions available, but only to applicable institutions. You would need to provide proof of eligibility to use these domain extensions:
- .edu - used only for accredited educational institutions.
- .gov - used only for United States government departments.
- .mil - used only for the United States military.

File Name:
A particular page or file that a domain's web site offers for viewing.

4.20.2 Basic Domain Name System

- When you use the Web or send an e-mail message, you use a **domain name** to do it. For example, the URL "http://www.pict.com" contains the domain name **pict.com**. So does the e-mail address "iknow@pict.com."
- Human-readable names like "pict.com" are easy for people to remember, but they don't do machines any good.
- All of the machines use names called **IP addresses** to refer to one another.
- For example, the machine that humans refer to as "www.pict.com" has the IP address **256.153.105.155.**
- Every time you use a domain name, you use the Internet's domain name servers (DNS) to translate the human-readable domain name into the machine-readable IP address.
- During a day of browsing and e-mailing, you might access the domain name servers hundreds of times !
- Domain name servers translate domain names to IP addresses. That sounds like a simple task, and it would be except for five things:

1. There are billions of IP addresses currently in use, and most machines have a human-readable name as well.
2. There are many billions of DNS requests made every day. A single person can easily make a hundred or more DNS requests a day, and there are hundreds of millions of people and machines using the Internet daily.
3. Domain names and IP addresses change daily.
4. New domain names get created daily.
5. Millions of people do the work to change and add domain names and IP addresses every day.

The DNS system is a database, and no other database on the planet gets this many requests. No other database on the planet has millions of people changing it every day, either. That is what makes the DNS system so unique !

4.20.3 How DNS is Organized

1. The Domain Name System is implemented as a hierarchical and distributed database containing various types of data including host names and domain names.
2. The names in a DNS database form a hierarchical tree structure called the *domain name space*.
3. At the top of the DNS hierarchy are 13 root name servers, which contain name server information for all of the generic top-level domains such as .com and .org as well as country-specific DNS addresses such as .uk or .nz.
4. The name servers for each of these top-level domains contains name server information for domains within that top-level domain.

5. So the name server for .com will contain information about microsoft.com but will not contain information about microline.co.uk.
6. Your name server will have to contact the server that contains the information for .co.uk.
7. The hierarchy goes from the least specific top-level domain to the most specific hostname.

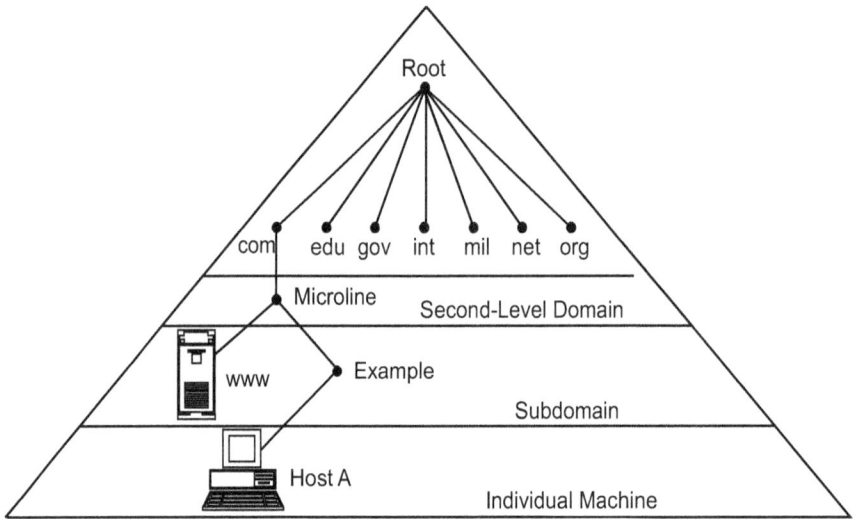

Fig. 4.42: DNS Hierarchy

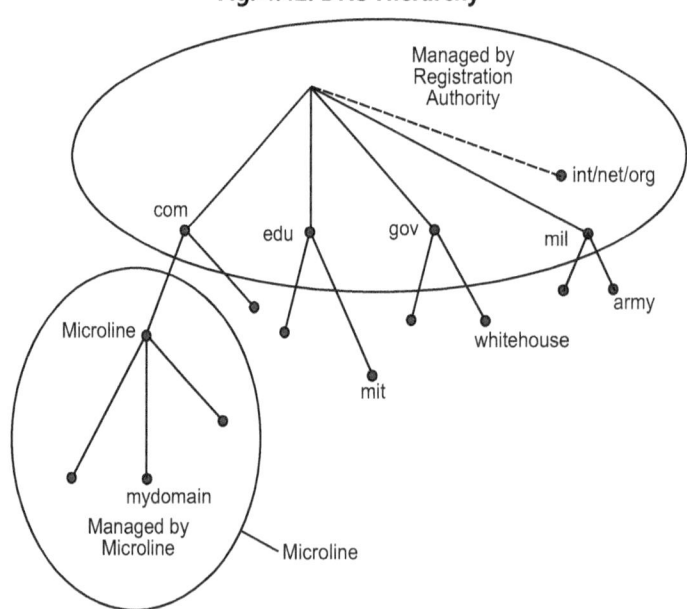

Fig. 4.43: Example of a DNS tree with a host called *mydomain* within the *microline.com.* domain

8. All DNS records actually end with the period character (.) which represents the root of the DNS hierarchy, but it's rarely printed and is usually just assumed.
9. A domain name that includes the trailing period character is said to be a Fully Qualified Domain Name (FQDN). However, domain names where the period character is implicit are also commonly referred to as FQDNs.
10. Domain names consist of individual labels separated by dots. For example: *mydomain.microline.com*
11. A Fully Qualified Domain Name (FQDN) uniquely identifies the host's position within the DNS hierarchical tree by specifying a list of names separated by dots on the path from the referenced host to the root.
12. The following figure shows an example of a DNS tree with a host called *mydomain* within the *microline.com.* domain. The FQDN for the host would be *mydomain.microline.com.*

4.20.4 DNS and Internet

1. The Internet Domain Name System is managed by a Name Registration Authority on the Internet, responsible for maintaining top-level domains that are assigned by organization and by country.
2. These domain names follow the International Standard 3166. Existing abbreviations, reserved for use by organizations, as well as two-letter and three-letter abbreviations used for countries, are shown in the following table.

DNS Domain Name	Type of Organization
com	Commercial organizations
edu	Educational institutions
org	Non-profit organizations
net	Networks (the backbone of the Internet)
gov	Non-military government organizations
mil	Military government organizations
num	Phone numbers
arpa	Reverse DNS
xx	Two-letter country code

3. **Here are a few additional details that you need to remember about DNS names:**

   - DNS names are not case-sensitive. When you use a domain name, you can use capitalization to make the name easier to read, but DNS ignores the difference between capital and lowercase letters.
   - The name of each DNS node can be up to 63 characters long (not including the dot) and can include letters, numbers, and hyphens. No other special characters are allowed.

- A *subdomain* is a domain that's beneath an existing domain. For example, in www.pict.com the com domain is actually a subdomain of the root domain. Likewise, PICT is a subdomain of the com domain.
- DNS is a hierarchical naming system that's similar to the hierarchical folder system used by Unix. When you construct a complete DNS name, you start at the bottom of the tree and work your way up to the root. In Windows paths are the opposite: They start at the root and work their way down. For example, in the path \Windows\System32\dns, dns is the lowest node.
- The DNS tree can be up to 127 levels deep. However, in practice, the DNS tree is pretty shallow. Most DNS names have just three levels (not counting the root), and although you'll sometimes see names with four or five levels, you'll rarely see more levels than that.
- Although the DNS tree is shallow, it's very broad. In other words, each of the top-level domains has a huge number of second-level domains immediately beneath it.

4.20.5 Top-Level Domains

- A *top-level domain* is a domain that appears immediately beneath the root domain.
- Top-level domains come in two categories: generic domains and geographic domains.
- These categories are described in the following sections. (Actually, a third type of top-level domain exists; it's used for reverse lookups. we describe it later in this chapter, in the section, "Reverse Lookup Zones.")

4.20.5.1 Generic Domains

Generic domains are the popular top-level domains that you see most often on the Internet. Originally, seven top-level organizational domains existed.

Table 4.5 given summarizes the original seven generic top-level domains.

Table 4.5

Domain	Description
com	Commercial organisations
edu	Educational institutions
gov	U.S. Government institutions
int	International treaty organisations
mil	U.S. Military institutions
net	Network providers
org	Non-commercial organisations

Table 4.6: The New Seven Top-Level Domains

Domain	Description
aero	Aerospace industry
biz	Business
coop	Co-operatives
info	Informational sites
museum	Museums
name	Individual users
pro	Professional organisations

4.20.5.2 Geographic Domains

- An additional set of top-level domains corresponds to international country designations.
- Organizations outside of the United States often use these top-level domains to avoid the congestion of the generic domains.
- Next Table lists those geographic top-level domains that had more than 200 registered subdomains at the time of this writing.
- In all, about 150 geographic top-level domains exist. The exact number varies from time to time as political circumstances change.

Table 4.7: Geographic Top-Level Domains with more than 2000 Sub-domains

Domain	Description	Domain	Description
ac	Ascension Island	fr	France
ae	Arab Emirates	gr	Greece
ag	And Barbuda	hr	Croatia
am	Armenia	hu	Hungary
an	Netherlands Antilles	ie	Ireland
as	American Samoa	is	Iceland
at	Austria	it	Italy
be	Belgium	jp	Japan
bg	Bulgaria	kz	Kazakhstan
bm	Bermuda	la	Laos
br	Brazil	li	Liechtenstein
by	Belarus	lk	Sri Lanka
bz	Belize	lt	Lithuania
ca	Canada	lu	Luxembourg
cc	Cocos Islands	lv	Latvia
ch	Switzerland	ma	Morocco
cl	Chile	md	Moldova

Domain	Description	Domain	Description
cn	China	nl	Netherlands
cx	Christmas Island	no	Norway
cz	Czech Republic	nu	Niue
de	Germany	pl	Poland
dk	Denmark	pt	Portugal
ee	Estonia	ro	Romania
es	Spain	ru	Russian Federation
fi	Finland	se	Sweden
fm	Micronesia	si	Slovenia
fo	Faroe Islands	sk	Slovakia

4.20.6 The Hosts File

1. The hosts file listed, line by line, Internet domain names and their associated IP addresses.

2. The master host file was compiled and stored on the machines at the Network Information Center (NIC) and was downloaded by on a regular basis by everyone accessing the Internet.

3. Obviously this hosts file quickly grew much to large to be manageable.

4. As the Internet grows, new domain names are added by the minute, and it is impossible for every computer on the Internet to keep downloading this file.

5. The solution of course was the DNS server system. Unlike the hosts file, DNS servers don't rely on a single large mapping file.

6. Instead DNS servers only contain information about the domain names they are directly responsible for and some limited reference data on how to find other domain names.

7. Understanding the Hosts file is important for two reasons:
   - The Hosts file is not dead. For small networks, a Hosts file may still be the easiest way to provide name resolution for the network's computers. In addition, a Hosts file can coexist with DNS. The Hosts file is always checked before DNS is used, so you can even use a Hosts file to override DNS if you want.
   - The Hosts file is the precursor to DNS. DNS was devised to circumvent the limitations of the Hosts file. Appreciate the benefits of DNS when you understand how the Hosts file works.

8. The Hosts file is a simple text file that contains lines that match IP addresses with host names.

9. You can edit the Hosts file with any text editor, including Notepad or by using the MS-DOS EDIT command.
10. The exact location of the Hosts file depends on the client operating system.

4.20.7 Understanding DNS Servers and Zones

1. A *DNS server* is a computer that runs DNS server software, helps to maintain the DNS database, and responds to DNS name resolution requests from other computers.
2. The key to understanding how DNS servers work is to realize that the DNS database — that is, the list of all the domains, subdomains, and host mappings — is a massively distributed database. No single DNS server contains the entire DNS database. Instead, authority over different parts of the database is delegated to different servers throughout the Internet.
3. For example, suppose that we set up a DNS server to handle name resolutions for our PICT.com domain. Then, when someone requests the IP address of E&TC.PICT.com, our DNS server can provide the answer.
4. However, our DNS server wouldn't be responsible for the rest of the Internet.
5. Instead, if someone asks my DNS server for the IP address of some other computer, such as sun.Lacme.com, our DNS server will have to pass the request on to another DNS server that knows the answer.

Zones:

1. To simplify the management of the DNS database, the entire DNS namespace is divided into *zones*, and the responsibility for each zone is delegated to a particular DNS server.
2. In many cases, zones correspond directly to domains.
3. For example, if we set up a domain named pict.com, we can also set up a DNS zone called pict.com that will be responsible for the entire pict.com domain.
4. However, the subdomains that make up a domain can be parceled out to separate zones, as shown in Figure. Here, a domain named Pict.com has been divided into two zones. One zone, us.Pict.com, is responsible for the entire us.Pict.com subdomain. The other zone, Pict.com, is responsible for the entire Pict.com domain except for the us.Pict.com subdomain.
5. Why would you do that? The main reason is to delegate authority for the zone to separate servers. For example, Figure suggests that part of the Pict.com domain is administered in the United States, and part of it is administered in France. The two zones in the figure allow one server to be completely responsible for the U.S. portion of the domain, while the other server handles the rest of the domain.

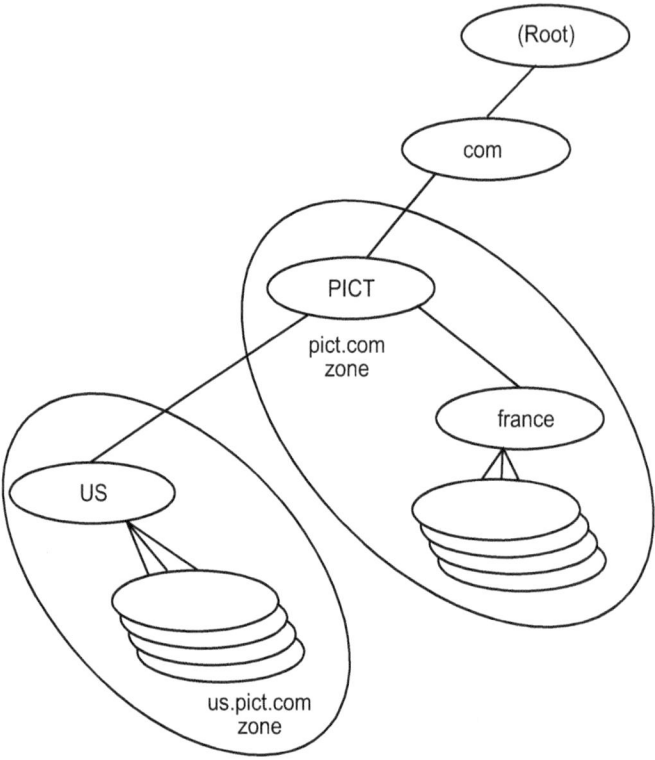

Fig. 4.44: DNS Zone

6. DNS data is divided into manageable sets of data called zones.
7. Zones contain name and IP address information about one or more parts of a DNS domain. A server that contains all of the information for a zone is the authoritative server for the domain. Sometimes it may make sense to delegate the authority for answering DNS queries for a particular subdomain to another DNS server.
8. In this case, the DNS server for the domain can be configured to refer the subdomain queries to the appropriate server.
9. For backup and redundancy, zone data is often stored on servers other than the authoritative DNS server.
10. These other servers are called secondary servers, which load zone data from the authoritative server.
11. Configuring secondary servers allows you to balance the demand on servers and also provides a backup in case the primary server goes down.
12. Secondary servers obtain zone data by doing zone transfers from the authoritative server. When a secondary server is initialized, it loads a complete copy of the zone data from the primary server.
13. The secondary server also reloads zone data from the primary server or from other secondaries for that domain when zone data changes.

DNS Zone Types:

The following are the two basic types of zones:

- A *primary zone* is the master copy of a zone. The data for a primary zone is stored in the local database of the DNS server that hosts the primary zone. Only one DNS server can host a particular primary zone. Any updates to the zone must be made to the primary zone.
- A *secondary zone* is a read-only copy of a zone. When a server hosts a secondary zone, the server doesn't store a local copy of the zone data. Instead, it obtains its copy of the zone from the zone's primary server by using a process called *zone transfer*. Secondary servers must periodically check primary servers to see whether their secondary zone data is still current. If not, a zone transfer is initiated to update the secondary zone.

Primary Zone:

Loads zone data directly from a file on a host. A primary zone may contain a subzone, or child zone. It may also contain resource records such as host, alias (CNAME), address (A), or reverse mapping pointer (PTR) records.

Note: Primary zones are sometimes referred to as "master zones" in other BIND documentation.

Subzone:

A subzone defines a zone within the primary zone. Subzones allow you to organize zone data into manageable pieces.

Child zone:

A child zone defines a subzone and delegates responsibility for the subzone data to one or more name servers.

Alias (CNAME):

An alias defines an alternate name for a primary domain name.

Host:

A host object maps A and PTR records to a host. Additional resource records may be associated with a host.

Secondary Zone:

Loads zone data from a zone's primary server or another secondary server.
A secondary server maintains a complete copy of the zone for which it is a secondary.

Note: Secondary zones are sometimes referred to as "slave zones" in other documentation.

Stub Zone:

A stub zone is similar to a secondary zone, but it only transfers the name server (NS) records for that zone.

Forward Zone:

A forward zone directs all queries for that particular zone to other servers.

4.20.8 Three Main Components of DNS

1. Resolver
2. Name server
3. Database of resource records (RRs)

4.20.8.1 Resolver
- When a DNS client needs to resolve a DNS name to an IP address, it uses a library routine called a *resolver* to handle the query.
- The resolver takes care of sending the query message over the network to the DNS server, receiving and interpreting the response, and informing the client of the results of the query.
- The resolver program or library is located on each host and provides a means of translating a users request for, say, www.thing.com into one or more queries to DNS servers using UDP (or TCP) protocols.
- While BIND is the best known of the DNS servers and much of this guide documents BIND features, it is by no means the only solution or for that matter the only Open Source solution.

4.20.8.2 Name Server

There are three types of name servers:
1. The primary master builds its database from files that were preconfigured on its hosts, called zone or database files. The name server reads these files and builds a database for the zone it is authoritative for.
2. Secondary masters can provide information to resolvers just like the primary masters, but they get their information from the primary. Any updates to the database are provided by the primary.
3. Caching name server - It gets all its answers to queries from other name servers and saves (caches) the answers. It is a non-authoritative server.

The caching only name server generates no zone transfer traffic. A DNS Server that can communicate outside of the private network to resolve a DNS name query is referred to as **forwarder**.

The Name Server program typically does three things:
- It will read a configuration file which defines the zones for which it is responsible.
- Depending on the Name Servers functionality the configuration file may describe various behaviours e.g. to cache or not. Some DNS servers are very specialized and do not provide this level of control.
- Respond to questions (queries) from local or remote hosts.

Primary Vs. Secondary Servers:
- **Primary**
    - Data loaded from a file.
    - One primary server per zone.
- **Secondary**
    - Data transferred from a primary server.
    - Data may be stored in a file.
    - Checks every refresh period with the primary, looking for changes.
    - Might have many secondaries per zone

Also the difference between a secondary server and a caching server is that a caching server only queries for the specific records it needs and will discard those records when their TTL expires. A secondary server will download the zone files of the zones for which it is authoritative. A secondary server will download the entire zone rather than just the specific records a user requests, and it will keep the zone file information until it has been unable to reach the primary server for some long period of time (often a week or more). These time intervals are configured in the Start Of Authority section of the zone file on the primary server.

Almost all primary and secondary DNS servers also provide a caching service for queries about records for which they are not authoritative.

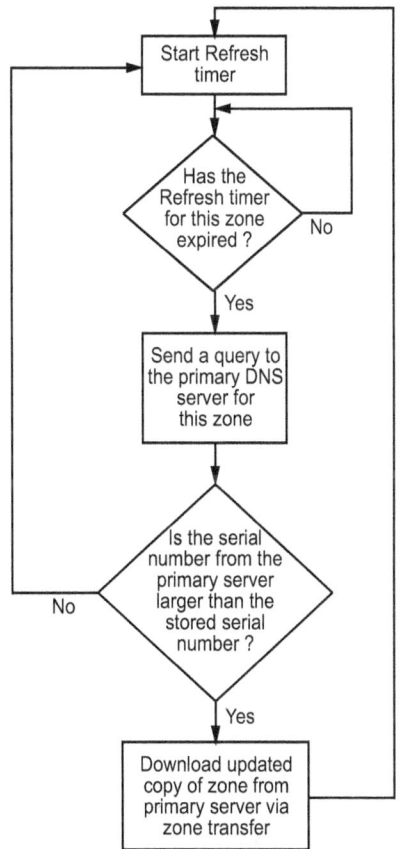

Fig. 4.45: Primary/Secondary Servers

4.20.9 Understanding DNS Queries

1. When a DNS client needs to resolve a DNS name to an IP address, it uses a library routine called a *resolver* to handle the query.
2. The resolver takes care of sending the query message over the network to the DNS server, receiving and interpreting the response, and informing the client of the results of the query.
3. A DNS client can make two basic types of queries: recursive and iterative.
4. The following list describes the difference between these two query types.

(The following discussion assumes that the client is asking the server for the IP address of a host name, which is the most common type of DNS query. You find out about other types of queries later; they, too, can be either recursive or iterative).

- **Recursive queries:** When a client issues a *recursive DNS query*, the server must reply with either the IP address of the requested host name or an error message indicating that the host name doesn't exist. If the server doesn't have the information, it asks another DNS server for the IP address. When the first server finally gets the IP address, it sends it back to the client. If the server determines that the information doesn't exist, it returns an error message.

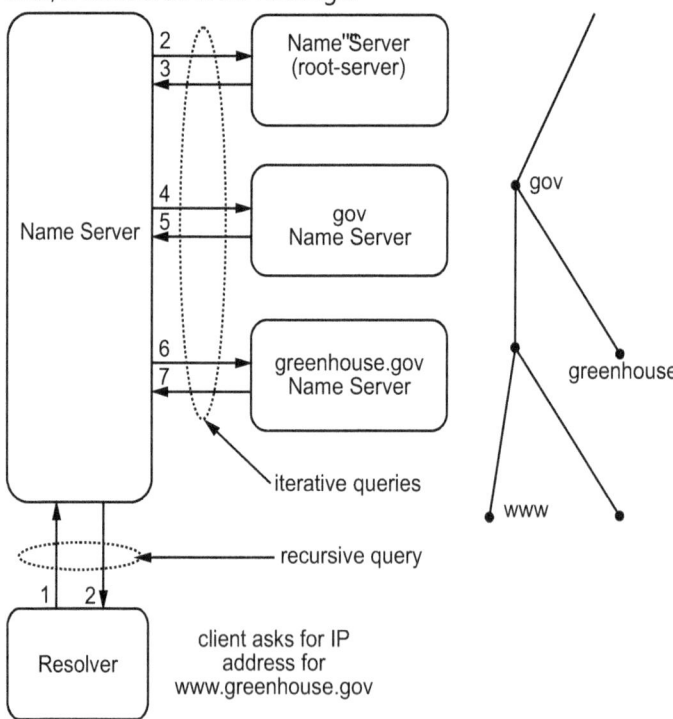

Fig. 4.46: The figure shows an example of both types of queries

- **Iterative queries:** When a server receives an iterative query, it returns the IP address of the requested host name if it knows the address. If the server doesn't know the

address, it returns a *referral,* which is simply the address of a DNS server that should know. The client can then issue an iterative query to the server to which it was referred.
- **An Inverse query** - Where the user wants to know the domain name given a resource record. An Inverse query maps a resource record to a domain. An example Inverse query would be 'what is the domain name for this MX record'. Inverse query support is optional and it is permitted for the DNS server to return a response **Not Implemented**. Inverse queries are NOT used to find a host name given an IP address. This process is called Reverse Mapping (Look-up) uses recursive and Iterative (non-recursive) queries with the special domain name IN-ADDR.ARPA.

Normally, DNS clients issue recursive queries to DNS servers. If the server knows the answer to the query, it replies directly to the client. If not, the server issues an iterative query to a DNS server that it thinks should know the answer. If the original server gets an answer from the second server, it returns the answer to the client. If the original server gets a referral to a third server, the original server issues an iterative query to the third server. The original server keeps issuing iterative queries until it either gets the answer or an error occurs. It then returns the answer or the error to the client.

In the provided example the following queries are used to determine IP address for www.greenhouse.gov:
- Recursive query for www.greenhouse.gov (A RR)
- Iterative query for www.greenhouse.gov (A RR)
- Referral to the gov name server (NS RRs, for gov); for simplicity iterative A queries by the DNS server (on the left) to resolve the IP addresses of the Host names of the name servers returned by other DNS servers have been omitted.
- Iterative query for www.greenhouse.gov (A RR)
- Referral to the greenhouse.gov name server (NS RR, for greenhouse.gov)
- Iterative query for www.greenhouse.gov (A RR)
- Answer from greenhouse.gov server (www.greenhouse.gov's IP address)
- Answer from local DNS server to Resolver (www.greenhouse.gov's IP address)
  In the provided example the following queries are used to determine IP address for www.greenhouse.gov:
- Recursive query for www.greenhouse.gov (A RR)
- Iterative query for www.greenhouse.gov (A RR)
- Referral to the gov name server (NS RRs, for gov); for simplicity iterative A queries by the DNS server (on the left) to resolve the IP addresses of the Host names of the name servers returned by other DNS servers have been omitted.
- Iterative query for www.greenhouse.gov (A RR)
- Referral to the greenhouse.gov name server (NS RR, for greenhouse.gov)
- Iterative query for www.greenhouse.gov (A RR)

- Answer from greenhouse.gov server (www.greenhouse.gov's IP address)
- Answer from local DNS server to Resolver (www.greenhouse.gov's IP address)

4.20.10 Zone Files and Resource Records

1. Each DNS zone is defined by a *zone file* (also known as a *DNS database* or a *master file*).
2. For Windows DNS servers, the name of the zone file is *domain*.zone.
3. For example, the zone file for the pict.com zone is named pict.com.zone.
4. For BIND DNS servers, the zone files are named db.*domain*.
5. Thus, the zone file for the pict.com domain would be db.pict.com. The format of the zone file contents is the same for both systems, however.
6. A zone file consists of one or more *resource records*.
7. Creating and updating the resource records that compose the zone files is one of the primary tasks of a DNS administrator.
8. The Windows DNS server provides a friendly graphical interface to the resource records.
9. However, you should still be familiar with the details of how to construct resource records.
10. Resource records are written as simple text lines, with the following fields:

Owner TTL Class Type RDATA, These fields must be separated from each other by one or more spaces. The following list describes the five resource record fields:

- **Owner:** The name of the DNS domain or the host that the record applies to. This is usually specified as a fully qualified domain name (with a trailing dot) or as a simple host name (without a trailing dot), which is then interpreted in the context of the current domain. You can also specify a single @ symbol as the owner name. In that case, the current domain is used.
- **TTL:** Also known as *time to live;* the number of seconds that the record should be retained in a server's cache before it's invalidated. If you omit the TTL value for a resource record, a default TTL is obtained from the SOA record. (For your reference, Table lists commonly used TTL values).
- **Class:** Defines the protocol to which the record applies. You should always specify IN, for the Internet protocol. If you omit the class field, the last class field that you specified explicitly is used. As a result, you'll sometimes see zone files that specify IN only on the first resource record (which must be an SOA record) and then allow it to default to IN on all subsequent records.
- **Type:** The resource record type. The most commonly used resource types are summarized in Table and are described separately later in this section. Like the Class field, you can also omit the Type field and allow it to default to the last specified value.
- **RDATA:** Resource record data that is specific to each record type.

Table 4.8: Different Records

Description	Class	TTL	Type	Data
Start of Authority	Internet (IN)	Default TTL is 60 minutes	SOA	Owner Name, Primary Name Server DNS Name, Serial Number, Refresh Interval, Retry Interval, Expire Time, Minimum TTL
Host	Internet (IN)	Zone (SOA) TTL	A	Owner Name (Host DNS Name), Host IP Address
Name Server	Internet (IN)	Zone (SOA) TTL	NS	Owner Name, Name Server DNS Name
Mail Exchanger	Internet (IN)	Zone (SOA) TTL	MX	Owner Name, Mail Exchange Server DNS Name, Preference Number
Canonical Name (an alias)	Internet (IN)	Zone (SOA) TTL	CNAME	Owner Name (Alias Name), Host DNS Name

Most resource records fit on one line. If a record requires more than one line, you must enclose the data that spans multiple lines in parentheses. You can include comments to clarify the details of a zone file. A comment begins with a semicolon and continues to the end of the line. If a line begins with a semicolon, the entire line is a comment. You can also add a comment to the end of a resource record.

4.20.11 Types of Records

Address Records (A)

Address, or "A" records, map the name of a machine to its numeric IP address. In clearer terms, this record states the hostname and IP address of a certain machine. To "resolve" a hostname means to find its matching IP address. This is the record that A NAME server would send another name server to answer a resolution query. The record below is an example of how an A record should look:

    eric.pict.com. IN A 36.36.1.6

The first column contains the machine's hostname. The second column lists what class the record is. For most basic DNS work, all you will need is the IN designation, which stands for InterNet. The next column denotes the type of record the entry actually is, and the last column is the IP address itself.

It is possible to map more than one IP address to a given hostname. This often happens for people who run a firewall and have two ethernet cards in one machine. All you must do is add a second A record, with every column the same save for the IP address.

It is also possible to map more than one host name to one IP address. This is not recommended, however, since DNS has a special record for allowing machines to have aliases, called a canonical name, or CNAME record.

Canonical Name Records (*CNAME*):

"CNAME" records simply allow a machine to be known by more than one hostname. There must always be an A record for the machine before aliases can be added. The host name of a machine that is stated in an A record is called the canonical, or official name of the machine. Other records should point to the canonical name. Here is an example of a CNAME:

> **www.pict.com. IN CNAME eric.pict.com.**

You can see the similarities to the previous record. Records always read from left to right, with the subject to be queried about on the left and the answer to the query on the right. A machine can have an unlimited number of CNAME aliases. A new record must be entered for each alias.

Mail Exchange Records (*MX*):

"MX" records are far more important than they sound. They allow all mail for a domain to be routed to one host. This is exceedingly useful it abates the load on your internal hosts since they do not have to route incoming mail, and it allows your mail to be sent to any address in your domain even if that particular address does not have a computer associated with it. For example, we have a mail server running on the fictitious machine eric.pict.com. For convenience sake, however, we want our email address to be "user@pict.com" rather than "user@eric.pict.com". This is accomplished by the record shown below:

> **pict.com. IN MX 10 eric.pict.com.**

The column on the far left signifies the address that you want to use as an Internet email address. The next two entries have been explained thoroughly in previous records. The next column, the number "10", is different from the normal DNS record format. It is a signifier of priority. Often larger systems will have backup mail servers, perhaps more than one. Obviously, you will only want the backups receiving mail if something goes wrong with the primary mail server. You can indicate this with your MX records. A lower number in an MX record means a higher priority, and mail will be sent to the server with the lowest number (the lowest possible being 0). If something happens so that this server becomes unreachable, the computer delivering the mail will attempt every other server listed in the DNS tables, in order of priority.

Obviously, you can have as many MX records as you would like. It is also a good idea to include an MX record even if you are having mail sent directly to a machine with an A record. Some sendmail programs only look for MX records.

It is also possible to include wildcards in MX records. If you have a domain where your users each have their own machine running mail clients on them, mail could be sent directly to each machine. Rather than clutter your DNS entry, you can add an MX record like this one:
    *.pict.com. IN MX 10 eric.pict.com.

This would make any mail set to any individual workstation in the pict.com domain go through the server eric.pict.com.
One should use caution with wildcards; specific records will be given precedence over ones containing wildcards.

Pointer Records (*PTR*):
Although there are different ways to set up PTR records, we will be explaining only the most frequently used method, called "in-addr.arpa".

In-addr.arpa PTR records are the exact inverse of A records. They allow your machine to be recognized by its IP address. Resolving a machine in this fashion is called a "reverse lookup". It is becoming more and more common that a machine will do a reverse lookup on your machine before allowing you to access a service (such as a World Wide Web page). Reverse lookups are a good security measure, verifying that your machine is exactly who it claims to be. In-addr.arpa records look as such:
    6.1.36.36.in-addr.arpa. IN PTR eric.pict.com.

As you can see from the example for the A record in the beginning of this document, the record simply has the IP address in reverse for the host name in the last column.

A note for those who run their own name servers: although Internet is capable of pulling zones from your name server, we cannot pull the inverse zones (these in-addr.arpa records) unless you have been assigned a full class C network. If you would like us to put PTR records in our name servers for you, you will have to fill out the online web form on the support.allegianceinternet.com page.

Name Server Records (NS):

NS records are imperative to functioning DNS entries. They are very simple; they merely state the authoritative name servers for the given domain. There must be at least two NS records in every DNS entry. NS records look like this:

    pict.com. IN NS draven.pict.com.

There also must be an A record in your DNS for each machine you enter as A NAME server in your domain.

If Internet is doing primary and secondary names service, we will set up these records for you automatically, with "nse.algx.net" and "nsf.algx.net" as your two authoritative name servers.

SOA records:

Every zone must begin with a *start of authority* (SOA) record, which names the zone and provides default information for the zone. It lists the fields that appear in the RDATA section of an SOA record. Note that these fields are positional, so you should include a value for all of them and list them in the order specified. Because the SOA record has so many RDATA fields, you'll probably need to use parentheses to continue the SOA record onto multiple lines.

The SOA record controls how fast updated zones propagate from the master to the slave servers, and how long resource records (RRs) are cached in caching servers before they are flushed. Both of these affect your ability to effectuate "instant" changes in the zones you maintain.

The SOA defines global parameters for the zone (domain). There is only one SOA record allowed in a zone file.

Field	Description
name	The 'root name' of the zone. Most commonly written as @ or Origin Value.
ttl	Standard TTL values apply (range 0 to 2147483647). The data contained in the SOA record applies TTL values to the slave DNS - see below. For more information about TTL values.
class	Defines the class of record and normally takes the value IN = Internet. It may also take the value HS = Hesiod and CH = Chaos both historic MIT protocols.
name-server	A name server that will respond authoritatively for the domain and called the Primary Master in the context of dynamic DNS. If DDNS is not used this may be any suitable name server either in the zone file or in an external or foreign zone. This is most commonly written as a Fully-qualified Domain Name (FQDN and ends with a dot). If the record points to an EXTERNAL server (not defined in this zone) it MUST end with a '.' (dot) e.g. ns1.example.net. If the name server is defined in this domain (in this zone file) it can be written as ns1 (without the dot) which will be expanded to include the $ORIGIN. In the jargon this field is called MNAME field which is why we called it name-server.

Field	Description
email-addr	Email address of the person responsible for this zone. In the jargon this is called the RNAME field which is why we called it email. A suitable admin but more commonly the technical contact for the domain. By convention it is suggested that the reserved mailbox hostmaster be used for this purpose but any sensible and stable email address will work. NOTE: Format is mailbox-name.domain.com e.g. hostmaster.example.com (not the more normal @ sign since it has other uses in the zone file) but mail is sent to hostmaster@example.com. Most commonly ending with a '.' (dot) but if the email address is in this domain you can just use hostmaster (see also example below).
sn = serial number	Unsigned 32 bit value in range 1 to 4294967295 with a maximum increment of 2147483647. In BIND implementations this is defined to be a 10 digit field. This value MUST change when any resource record in the zone file is updated. The convention is to use a date based value to simplify this task - the most popular being yyyymmddss where yyyy = year, mm = month and dd = day ss = a sequence number in case you update it more than once in the day ! Using this date format means that the value 2005021002 means the last update was on the 10th February 2005 and it was the third update that day. The date format is just a convention not a requirement so BIND will provide no validation of the field. It is easy to make mistakes and get serial numbers out of sequence.
refresh	Signed 32 bit time value in seconds. Indicates the time when the slave will try to refresh the zone from the master.
retry	Signed 32 bit value in seconds. It defines the time between retries if the slave (secondary) fails to contact the master when refresh (above) has expired. Typical values would be 180 (3 minutes) to 900 (15 minutes) or higher.
expiry	Signed 32 bit value in seconds. Indicates when the zone data is no longer authoritative. Applies to Slaves or Secondaries servers only. BIND9 slaves stop responding to queries for the zone when this time has expired and no contact has been made with the master. Thus when the ref values expires the slave will attempt to read the SOA record for the zone - and request a zone transfer AXFR/IXFR if the sn has changed. If contact is made the expiry and refresh values are reset and tyhe cycle starts again. If the slave fails to contact the master it will retry every retry period but continue to supply authoritative data for the zone until the expiry value is reached at which point it will stop answering queries for the domain.
min = minimum	Signed 32 bit value in seconds. RFC 2308 (implemented by BIND 9) redefined this value to be the negative caching time - the time a NAME ERROR = NXDOMAIN record is cached. The maximum value allowed by BIND 9 for this parameter is 3 hours (10800 seconds). This value was (in BIND 4 and 8) used by any RR from the zone that did not specify an explicit TTL i.e. the zone default TTL. You may find older documentation or zone file configurations which reflect the old usage (there are still a lot of BIND 4 sites operational).

Note two things about the SOA fields:
- The e-mail address of the person responsible for the zone is given in DNS format; not in normal e-mail format. Thus, you separate the user from the mail domain with a dot rather than an @ symbol. For example, entc@pict.com would be listed as entc.pict.com.
- The serial number should be incremented every time you change the zone file. If you edit the file using the graphic interface provided by Windows DNS, the serial number is incremented automatically. However, if you edit the zone file using a simple text editor, you have to manually increment the serial number.

4.20.12 Distributing the Database: Zone Files and Delegation

1. A DNS database can be partitioned into multiple *zones*.
2. A zone is a portion of the DNS database that contains the resource records with the owner names that belong to the contiguous portion of the DNS namespace.
3. Zone files are maintained on DNS servers. A single DNS server can be configured to host zero, one or multiple zones.
4. Each zone is anchored at a specific domain name referred to as the zone's *rootdomain*.
5. A zone contains information about all names that end with the zone's root domain name.
6. A DNS server is considered authoritative for a name if it loads the zone containing that name.
7. The first record in any zone file is a Start of Authority (SOA) RR. The SOA RR identifies a primary DNS name server for the zone as the best source of information for the data within that zone and as an entity processing the updates for the zone.
8. Names within a zone can also be delegated to other zone(s). Delegation is a process of assigning responsibility for a portion of a DNS namespace to a separate entity.
9. This separate entity could be another organization, department or workgroup within your company. In technical terms, delegating means assigning authority over portions of your DNS namespace to other zones.
10. Such delegation is represented by the NS record that specifies the delegated zone and the DNS name of the server authoritative for that zone.
11. Delegating across multiple zones was part of the original design goal of DNS. Following are the main reasons for the delegation of a DNS namespace:
    - A need to delegate management of a DNS domain to a number of organizations or departments within an organization.
    - A need to distribute the load of maintaining one large DNS database among multiple name servers to improve the name resolution performance as well as create a DNS fault tolerant environment.

- A need to allow for host's organizational affiliation by including them in appropriate domains.
12. The NS RRs facilitate delegation by identifying DNS servers for each zone. They appear in all forward and reverse look-up zones.
13. Whenever a DNS server needs to cross a delegation, it will refer to the NS RRs for DNS servers in the target zone.
14. In the figure below, the management of the *microline.com.* domain is delegated across two zones, *microline.com.* and *mydomain.microline.com.*

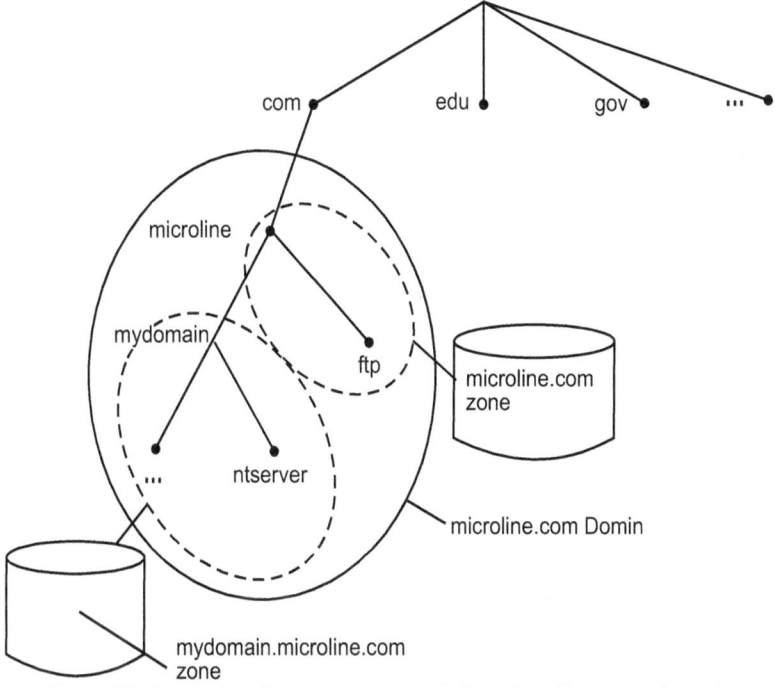

Fig. 4.47: Example of management of the microline.com domain

4.20.13 Replicating the DNS Database

1. There could be multiple zones representing the same portion of the namespace. Among these zones there are two types:
   - Primary
   - Secondary
2. *Primary* is a zone to which all updates for the records that belong to that zone are made.
3. A *secondary zone* is represented by a read-only copy of the primary zone. The changes made to the primary zone file are then replicated to the secondary zone file.
4. As mentioned above, a name server can host multiple zones.

5. A server can therefore be primary for one zone (it has the master copy of the zone file) and secondary for another zone (it gets a read-only copy of the zone file).
6. The process of replicating a zone file to multiple name servers is *called zone transfer*.
7. Zone transfer is achieved by copying the zone file information from the master server to the secondary server.
8. A *master server* is the source of the zone information.
9. The master server can be primary or secondary.
10. If the master is primary, then the zone transfer comes directly from the source. If the master server is secondary, the file received from the master server by means of a zone transfer is a copy of the read-only zone file.
11. The zone transfer is initiated in one of the following ways:
    - The master server sends a *notification* to the secondary server(s) of a change in the zone.
    - When the secondary server's DNS service starts or the secondary server's *refresh interval* has expired (by default it is set to 15 minutes in the SOA RR), it will query the primary server for the changes.
12. There are two types of zone file replication. The first, full zone transfer (AXFR), replicates the entire zone file. The second, incremental zone transfer (IXFR), replicates only the changed records of the zone.

4.20.14 Reverse Lookup Zones

1. A reverse lookup zone is not required for DNS services to function; however, you will want to create a reverse lookup zone to allow reverse lookup queries to function.
2. Without a reverse lookup zone, troubleshooting tools such as NSLOOKUP that can resolve host names from IP addresses cannot work.
3. Whereas forward lookup zones allow computers to resolve host names to IP addresses, reverse lookup zones allow computers to resolve IP addresses to host names.
4. As with forward lookup zones, you have the option of creating AD integrated, standard primary, or standard secondary zones.
5. Unlike naming a forward lookup zone, you name a reverse lookup zone by its IP address.
6. You can either type your network ID into the first field and watch the reverse lookup zone name automatically be created for you, or you can choose to type in the reverse lookup zone name into the second field following RFC conventions.
7. The information text between the network ID and reverse lookup zone name fields describes how to name a reverse lookup zone.
8. As with forward lookup zones, if you are creating an AD integrated zone, you are done after supplying the zone name.

9. With standard primary and standard secondary zones, you have to also supply the zone filename, which defaults to adding a .dns extension onto the end of your zone name.
10. With a standard secondary zone, you have to list the IP addresses of the primary DNS servers with which the secondary zone should communicate.
11. With your zones configured and DNS services functioning, let's look at the entries, known as *resource records*, you'll find within the server.

4.20.15 How DNS System Works (Simply and Practically)

1. The Client types in a web address or clicks on a link. Some **www.other.somedomain.com** address.
2. His PC's TCP/IP stack sends a DNS query to the first DNS server listed in his configuration, the **ORGANIZATION'S** DNS server.
3. The **ORGANIZATION'S** DNS server looks in its cache to see if it has the IP address (this is likely for names like www.Yahoo.com or www.Microsoft.com).
4. If it has the address in its cache, it sends it back to the requesting Client. All done !
5. If not, it sends the query to **A.Root-Servers.Net, or other Root DNS server** if that one is not available. (This depends on the order of records in the DNS server's cache file)
6. The **Root DNS server** looks into its records for the zone "com".
7. It finds the record for the destination zone.
8. It sends the NS records for that destination zone back to the requesting DNS server, i.e. your **ORGANIZATION'S** DNS server.
9. The **ORGANIZATION'S** DNS server now has the **address** of the **DNS server** for the destination domain it has a query pending for.
10. The **ORGANIZATION'S** DNS server sends its query, for **"www.somedomain.com"**, to that destination DNS server.
11. The DNS server for the destination domain "**somedomain.com**" says, "Hey, that's me ! I'm authoritative for that domain. I've got that record for **'www.other.somedomain.com'** !" (In the case of the secondary, it says, "Well I'm not authoritative, but I know the address because I have it in my zone files. Here it is.") This also counts for situations where the name is **www.long.name.other.somedomain.com.**
12. The somedomain.com DNS server sends back the IP address of the **www.other.somedomain.com** to your **ORGANIZATION'S** DNS server.
13. Your **ORGANIZATION'S** DNS server now caches that IP address it just got back since it is logical to assume that it may need it again.
14. Your **ORGANIZATION'S** DNS server then sends the IP address back to the Client PC. All done !

4.21 Electronic Mail

4.21.1 Introduction

We provide here, some background information about email and how it works, and a simple step-by-step diagram showing how an email message is sent and received.

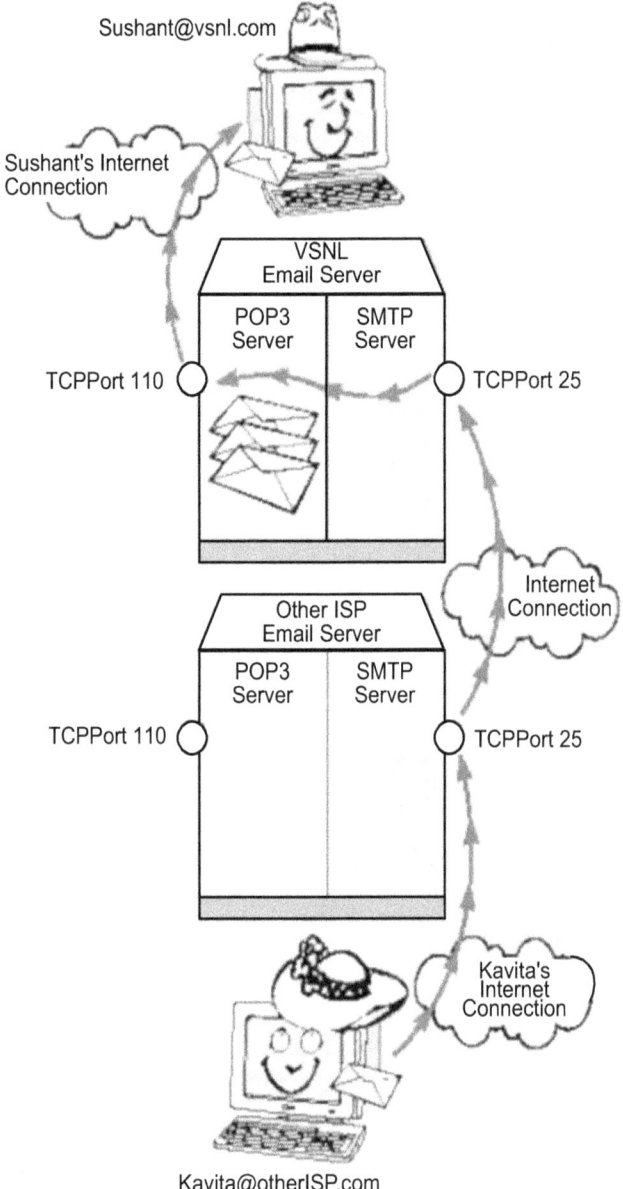

Fig. 4.48

What is an email client?
An email client is an email program such as Outlook Express, for sending, receiving and organizing your email messages.

What is an email server?
Email servers are used to process, store and send, and receive email messages. There are different types of email servers, such as POP 3, SMTP and IMAP servers. The most popular email servers are POP 3 (incoming mail servers for your incoming mail) and SMTP (outgoing mail servers for your outgoing mail).

What is SMTP or outgoing mail server?
When you send an email from your email program, if you have an Internet connection with VSNL, the email first arrives at VSNL's SMTP (outgoing mail server), then VSNL's SMTP server will check for the validity of both source and destination email addresses. Then it will send your email to the proper destination. You use your Internet conection's email server when you send mail.

What is POP3 or incoming mail server?
When someone sends you an email message, it arrives at VSNL's POP3 server and it waits for you to check your email. When you check your email, your email program accesses VSNL's POP3 servers and downloads your waiting messages from VSNL's POP3 server to your computer.

What is Web Mail?
Sending and receiving email messages using a web browser is referred to as "Web Mail." Using Web Mail is ideal when traveling or using another person's computer or an outside computer, such as at the library or at a trade show. You can access VSNL's Web Mail as long as you have a browser and an Internet connection. You can always use VSNL's Web Mail in conjunction with your usual email program, such as Outlook Express.

What is the difference between Web Mail and Client Email (such as Outlook Express)?
Client email, such as Outlook Express will ordinarily download and save your messages to your computer, and then it deletes your email messages from VSNL's servers. VSNL's Web Mail will not download and save your messages to your computer; it will leave your messages on our servers, unless you manually delete them.

How does email travel when I receive or send an email message?
When Kavita sends Sushant an email message, the following is a simplified step-by-step of how it travels:
1. Kavita opens her email program (Outlook Express), uses her email account, Kavita@otherisp.com, and writes an email message to Sushant@VSNL.com. Her

Outlook Express sends the message through TCP port 25 of Kavita's Internet connection, then to the other ISP's SMTP server (still on TCP port 25).
2. The other ISP's SMTP server finds the destination's SMTP server (in this case, VSNL) and sends the message out to VSNL's SMTP server (through TCP port 25 of her Internet connection).
3. VSNL's SMTP server sends the message to VSNL's POP3 server where the message waits for Sushant to pick it up.

4.21.2 How to use Electronic Mail

Introduction:
1. Email stresses content over form as it is basically limited to plain text.
2. When there is no letterhead or fancy stationary, it's really **the words** that count.
3. Some people seem to think that their capitalization, spelling, punctuation, and grammer doesn't matter because "it's just email", but when all that is there are is the words, these things really *do* matter.

How Email Works:
You compose a message in an email program, and send it to a **mail server** (a host computer providing mail service) using a protocol called SMTP (Simple Mail Transfer Protocol).
1. The mail server uses SMTP to send the email on to the appropriate mail server for the recipient.
2. The receiving mail server places the email message in the incoming message queue, or **inbox** belonging to the recipient.
3. The recipient retrieves their mail using one of several protocols and finds your message in their inbox or new mail folder.
4. They select and read your message.

Reading your mail:
Unless you intend to have your machine hooked up 24 hours a day and run your own mail server, their four valid options as to how to retrieve and read your email:

On the server:
Using a terminal or telnet connection, we can use programs that run on the server to read our mail directly from the incoming mail queue where the server places it. These are generally character-based programs with few bells or whistles, although *Pine (Program for internet news and Email)* is pretty nice. They allow you to manage your mail on the server and sort your mail into folders that remain on the server.

- **Advantages:**
    - read your email from any Internet-capable computer anywhere, anytime.
    - keep email you save on the server.
- **Disadvantages:**
    - character-based interface only; no bells & whistles, no drag and drop, etc.
    - attachments are extracted to the server and must be attached from the server.

Using POP mail (Post Office Protocol):

POPmail clients are programs that run on your local personal computer or workstation and download the contents of your incoming mail queue from the server onto your computer. Most are graphical programs with user-friendly interfaces. All mail is retained in folders on your own computer. Outgoing mail is written on your own computer and sent to the SMTP server; any attachments are sent from your own computer locally.

- **Advantages:**
    - Graphical interface.
    - Manage email on your own PC.
    - Attachments easy to manage.
- **Disadvantages:**
    - Cannot read your email anywhere other than at your own computer.
    - Long downloads when mailbox is full or with large attachments (not a problem on networks but can be serious over a modem).
    - Risk of virus infection from executable attachments.

Using IMAP (Internet Mail Access Protocol):

An IMAP client is very similar to a POPmail client (in fact sometimes they are the same program). IMAP allows you to download only the headers from your email; the messages are then downloaded only as you read them. You can read a message without downloading the attachments. If you delete a message, it is deleted on the server. You have the option of sorting your messages into folders on the server; you can also choose to store them on your own computer. Outgoing mail is written on your own computer and sent to the SMTP server; any attachments are sent from your own computer locally.

- **Advantages:**
    - Read your email from any Internet-capable computer anywhere, anytime.
    - Keep email you save on the server.
    - Graphical interface.
    - Attachments easy to manage.

- **Disadvantages:**
    - Must have a properly configured graphical client installed on the computer you will use to read your mail.

Using the World Wide Web:
Various Web-based email interfaces allow you to receive and send mail using your Web browser. A great many of these are offered as free services by Web portals as an incentive to come to their site. Some of the companies offering these services include Yahoo!, AltaVista, Netscape, Hotmail, Lycos, and more; that will let you read your email directly from your own account here on campus via the Web.

- **Advantages:**
    - Read your email from any Web browser, anywhere, anytime.
    - Keep email you save on the server.
- **Disadvantages:**
    - Services tend to be slow, sometimes painfully so.

Internet Domain Names and Email Addresses:
A. An example of a computer on campus offering electronic mail services is **itwebmaster.mit.edu**
   1. **itwebmaster** *is the name of the computer*
   2. **mit** *is the name of the institution*
   3. *The* **edu** *suffix indicates that this is an educational institution*
      (a) **mit.edu** is the "domain name" for all **mit** computers. A domain name is the "surname" of all Internet computers serving a particular school, company or organization.
      (b) Other suffixes in the United States domain names include –
         1. **.com** businesses
         2. **.org** non-profit organizations
         3. **.gov** government agencies
         4. **.mil** military agencies
         5. **.net** companies or organizations that run large networks
         6. **.int** International organizations
      (c) Other countries may use these same suffixes but their domain name will always end in a two-letter suffix indicating their country. Some example country suffixes include:
         1. **.au** Australia
         2. **.ch** Switzerland
         3. **.fi** Finland
         4. **.fr** France
         5. **.id** Indonesia

6. **.in** India
7. **.sg** Singapore
8. **.uk** United Kingdom

4. Each of these computers also has a distinctive numerical address, or **IP number**, which is four sets of one to three digit numerals separated by periods (or "dots" in Net-speak). The names are an easy-to-remember alias for the IP number.

B. Your email address is your username followed by the "at" sign, followed by the full name of the computer where your mail account is

1. Consequently your e-mail address on itwebmaster would be:

   username@itwebmaster.mit.edu
2. All e-mail addresses on the Internet look like this. The @, of course, means at

President of India can have e-mail address like:

president@india.gov

When spoken this would be:
president at India dot gov

Email Format:

E-mail messages follow a specific format.

- Date: (automatically inserted by the system)
- From: (who sent the message)
- To: (who the message is to)
- Cc: (copy/copies to these addressees, also)
- Bcc: (copy/copies to these addressees without their name/address appearing anywhere on the message)
- Attach: (attachments to the message)
- Subj: (the subject of the message)
- Body of the the message...
- "Sig" (signature)

1. When you compose a message you will not see the **Date:** line (it's automatically inserted by the system).
2. When you compose a message you will not see the **From:** line (it's from you...).
3. The complete email address of the recipient must be in the **To:** line (unless they are on the same computer you are on...then you can just type their user name).

4. You may want to send yourself a copy of your first message in the **Cc:** line, just to check it out.
5. **Attachments** allow you to attach text of even programs or graphics to your e-mail; we won't use any now.
6. The **Subject** line is important as it appears in the index of your inbox so you can get some idea of what the topic of ecah message is.
7. The body of the message (and the subject) can contain both upper and lower case letters.
8. The **"Sig"** is an e-mail signature designed to identify the sender more fully, and can contain business or academic titles, business or school, phone numbers, and more.

4.21.3 Email Software

Eudora is currently one of the most widely used Internet email programs. A special version called Eudora Light is free for academic use. WWW browsers, such as Netscape, now process email also. Good email programs include most of the following capabilities:

- An **address book** for the user to maintain a personal list of email addresses.
- Email **address groups:** allows you to automatically send messages to all members of a particular group of people by defining a list of addresses.
- Create mail folders or **sub-mailboxes:** allows you to organize your messages into categories. Advanced email packages have automatic filtering options, which can look at message components such as the subject line or sender and automatically place your incoming mail into the appropriate folders.
- Automatically **quote** from the original message when replying.
- Easily **forward** a message to someone else.
- **Signature:** automatically append a user-defined message to the bottom of all outgoing mail (usually information such as your name, organization name, address, fax no., etc.).
- **Attach files:** send files along with an email message.
- Compose and read email **off-line:** your incoming mail can be saved on your hard drive. You can then disconnect from your service provider and read it at your leisure without worrying about connect-time fees. Likewise you can compose a message in the email program while you are offline, and just connect long enough to actually transmit it.

4.21.4 Servers, Filters, and Clients

1. Incoming email addressed to accounts on the UOP (University of PUNE) central email system is received by the email server and placed in the appropriate inbox.
2. Using a method called IMAP (Internet Message Access Protocol), a person can view the messages in their inbox and file them in folders on the server, delete unwanted messages, and reply or forward the message to others.

3. POP services, which immediately upload all your messages to your local computer, are also available. Because people at the UOP read their email frequently and from various locations throughout the day, the IMAP protocol is particularly appropriate here.
4. Both incoming and outgoing email messages are checked by virus and spam filtering programs.
5. If a virus is found in a message, the message is cleaned and a notification is sent to the sender. Messages with very high spam scores (99% or more) are discarded.
6. Outgoing email goes from your email program to an SMTP (Simple Message Transfer Protocol) server, which sends the email toward its destination on the Internet.

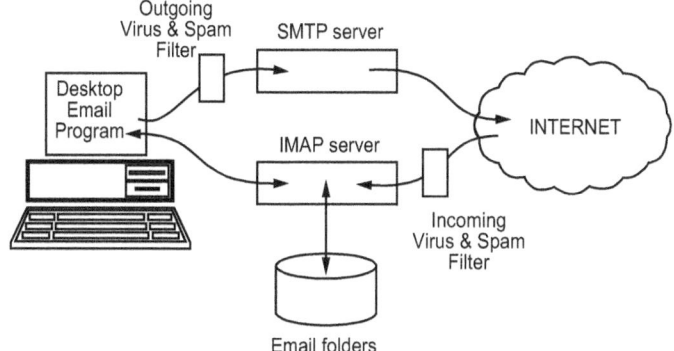

Fig. 4.49: Central email Server

7. **Desktop Email Program:** When you use Outlook Express, Mozilla Mail, PC-Pine, or other desktop email programs, your program is communicating directly with the email servers.

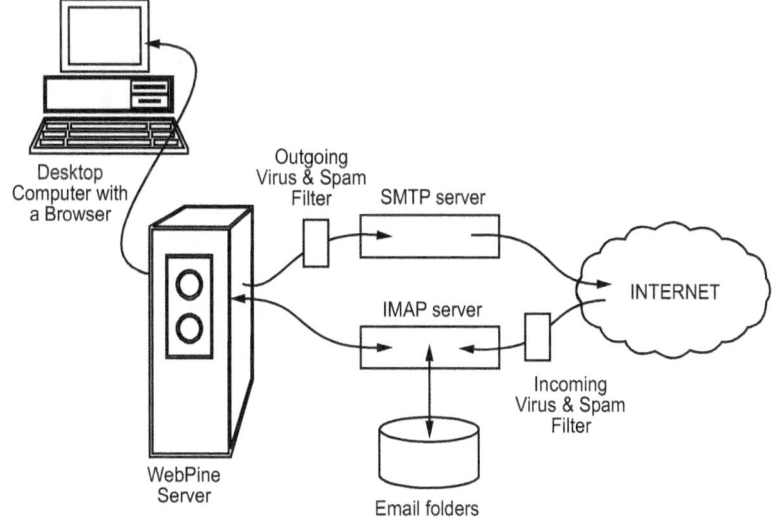

Fig. 4.50: Desktop to Internet email Path

8. **WebPine:** With WebPine, your browser is interacting with the WebPine Server, which in turn is communicating with the email servers.

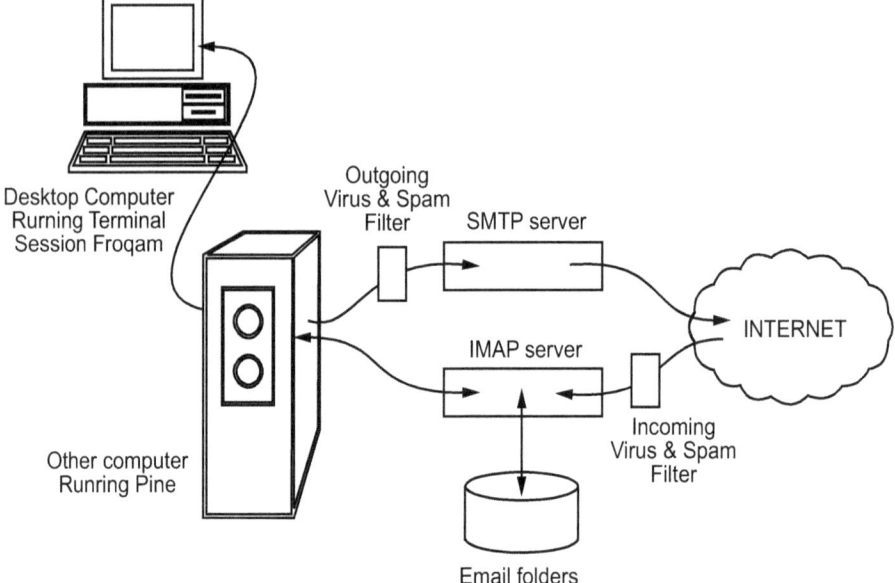

Fig. 4.51: Using PINE the program at remote terminal can be executed

9. **Pine:** When you use email on Unix computers you are using the Pine email program. Many other Unix computers on campus also run Pine. Usually, you connect to such computers using a terminal session program.

4.21.5 How UNIX Email Works

In general, each UNIX computer has two kinds of programs that handle mail:
- A *user agent* is a mail program that humans use. It collects the mail messages you send and shows messages you receive. The user agent is an interface to the second kind of program: the transfer agent.
- A *transfer agent* is a "system" program that you usually don't run directly.
  It accepts messages from the user agent and routes them to their destinations.
  A transfer agent usually also delivers mail into each user's *system mailbox*, a file where the user agent can get the new messages that other people send you.
- There are lots of user agent programs and there are several common transfer agents. The Figure How a mail message gets from A to B is a diagram that shows what happens when you send a message.
- Your user agent collects the message and gives it to your computer's transfer agent. Your transfer agent either delivers the message if you're sending it to someone on your computer or sends the message across a network to another computer's transfer agent.

- Then the person you sent the message to runs a user agent to bring in the message from the system mailbox, read it (view graphics, hear sounds, and so on) - and maybe also print the message, reply to it, delete it, etc.

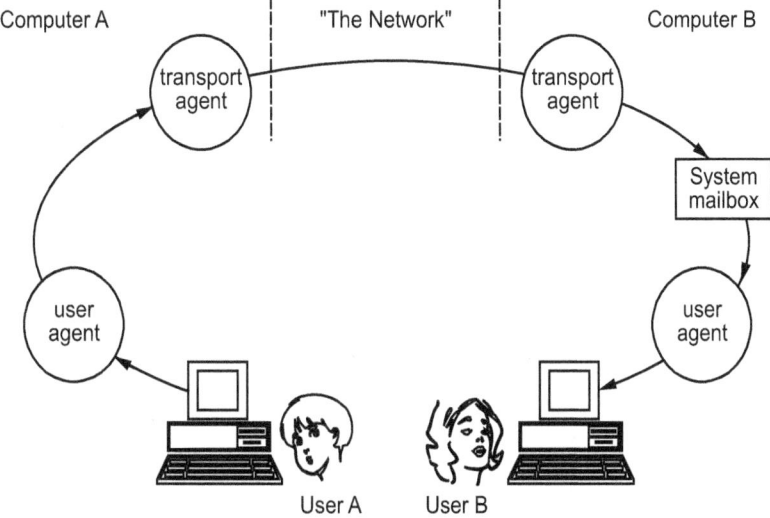

Fig. 4.52: How a mail message gets from A to B

Email Transfer Agents:
- Mail transfer agents (MTAs) are complicated programs.
- They have to understand all kinds of nasty details about message addressing, networks, error handling, and other functions.
- Some typical MTAs are *sendmail* and MMDF.

Email User Agents:
- If you send and receive only a few email messages, you probably don't need to learn much.
- Almost any user agent will do (and there are a lot of them). MH and *xmh* are fine for beginners: there are just a few basic concepts and commands to learn.
- But when you start to do more with email, you'll want a user agent that saves you time, lets you organize messages the way you want to, and helps you find messages you've stored.
- You'll probably want to automate routine work. You might even customize your email setup so it works exactly the way you'd like it to. This is where advanced, flexible systems like MH stand out.

Monolithic Mail Agents:

Most user mail agents are monolithic: you're in the mail program until you quit out of it. To start the program, you type its name, like *mail*, at a shell prompt. (The shell prompt is shown as a percent sign (%) here; your prompt may be a dollar sign ($) or something else.) Then that program takes over it reads and executes all the commands you type until you use its *quit* command.

4.21.6 Mobile Email - How It Works

Mobile phones may support different kinds of data connections such as the following:
- Circuit Switched Data (CSD)
- High Speed Circuit Switched Data (HSCSD)
- General Packet Radio Service (GPRS)
- Enhanced data rates for GSM evolution (EDGE)
- Wideband code division multiple access (W-CDMA)
- Wireless local area network (WLAN)

1. Typically, an access point for the data connection must be configured to connect to a data service such as an email provider. The necessary access point settings can be sent over-the-air (OTA) to your device by your network operator.
2. You will also need to define your email settings including your email address, your outgoing and incoming mail servers, your mailbox type, and other preferences.
3. This information can usually be found in the account settings in your desktop email client such as Microsoft Outlook, Outlook Express, and Eudora.
4. Your mailbox type defines the protocol for receiving emails, which can be POP3 or IMAP4.
5. You can also choose just to get the email headers (sender and subject line) first, and then decide which messages you'll download, saving you both time and connection charges.
6. After you have defined settings for a new mailbox, the name given to that mailbox will appear in the main view of the phone.
7. The only time you need to connect is when you are sending a message or collecting new messages you have received.
8. You can compose and read your messages offline.

4.21.7 Privacy Problems regarding e-mail

E-mail privacy, without some security precautions, can be compromised because
- e-mail messages are generally not encrypted;
- e-mail messages have to go through intermediate computers before reaching their destination, meaning it is relatively easy for others to intercept and read messages;

- many Internet Service Providers (ISP) store copies of your e-mail messages on their mail servers before they are delivered. The backups of these can remain up to several months on their server, even if you delete them in your mailbox.

There are cryptography applications that can serve as a remedy to the above, such as Virtual Private Networks, message encryption using PGP or the GNU Privacy Guard, encrypted communications with the e-mail servers using:

- Transport Layer Security
- Secure Sockets Layer
- Tor

4.22 World Wide Web (WWW) and Internet

What is the Internet?

1. The Internet is a network of networks, linking computers to computers sharing the TCP/IP protocols.
2. Each runs software to provide or "serve" information and/or to access and view information.
3. The Internet is the transport vehicle for the information stored in files or documents on another computer.
4. It can be compared to an international communications utility servicing computers.
5. It is sometimes compared to a giant international plumbing system.
6. The Internet itself does not contain information.
7. It is a slight misstatement to say a "document was found *on* the Internet." It would be more correct to say it was found *through* or *using* the Internet.
8. What it was found in (or on) is one of the computers linked to the Internet.

Computers on the Internet may use one or all of the following Internet services:

- Electronic mail (e-mail). Permits you to send and receive mail.
- Telnet or remote login. Permits your computer to log onto another computer and use it as if you were there.
- FTP or File Transfer Protocol. Allows your computer to rapidly retrieve complex files intact from a remote computer and view or save them on your computer.
- Gopher. An early, text-only method for accessing Internet documents. Gopher has been almost entirely subsumed in the World Wide Web, but you may still find gopher documents linked to in web pages.
- The World Wide Web (WWW or "the Web"). The largest, fastest growing activity on the Internet.

What is the World Wide Web and what makes it work?

1. The **World Wide Web** ("**WWW**" or simply the "**Web**") is a global, read-write information space.
2. Text documents, images, multimedia and many other items of information, referred to as *resources*, are identified by short, unique, global identifiers called Uniform Resource Identifiers (URIs) so that each can be found, accessed and cross-referenced in the simplest possible way.
3. **The World Wide Web is the combination of four basic ideas:**
   - Hypertext, that is the ability, in a computer environment, to move from one part of a document to another or from one document to another through internal connections among these documents (called "hyperlinks");
   - Resource Identifiers, that is the ability, on a computer network, to locate a particular resource (computer file, document or other resource) on the network through a unique identifier;
   - The Client-server model of computing, in which client software or a client computer makes requests of server software or a server computer that provides the client with resources or services, such as data or files; and
   - Markup language, in which characters or codes embedded in text indicate structure, semantic meaning or advice on presentation.
4. On the World Wide Web, a client program called a web browser retrieves information resources, such as web pages and other computer files, from web servers using their URLs and displays them, typically on a computer monitor.
5. One can then follow hyperlinks in each page to other resources on the **World Wide Web** whose location is provided by these hyperlinks.
6. It is also possible, for example by filling in and submitting web forms, to post information back to a server to interact with it.
7. The act of following hyperlinks is often called "*browsing*" or "*surfing*" the Web.
8. Web pages are often arranged in collections of related material called "websites."
9. Although the English word *world wide* is normally written as one word (without a space or hyphen), the proper name **World Wide Web** and abbreviation **WWW** are now well-established even in formal English.
10. The earliest references to the Web called it the WorldWideWeb (an example of computer programmers' fondness for intercaps) or the *World Wide Web* (with a hyphen, this version of the name is the closest to normal English usage).
11. Ironically, the abbreviation "WWW" is somewhat impractical as it contains three times as many syllables as the full term "World Wide Web", and thus takes longer to say; however it is easier to type.

How the Web Works:
1. When a viewer wants to access a web page or other resource on the World Wide Web, s/he normally begins either by typing the URL of the page into his or her web browser, or by following a hypertext link to that page or resource.
2. The first step, behind the scenes, is for the server-name part of the URL to be resolved into an IP address by the global, distributed Internet database known as the Domain name system or DNS.
3. The next step is for an HTTP request to be sent to the web server at that IP address, for the page required.
4. In the case of a typical web page, the HTML text, graphics and any other files that form a part of the page will be requested and returned to the client (the web browser) in quick succession.
5. The web browser's job is then to render the page as described by the HTML, and other files received, incorporating the images, links and other resources as necessary.
6. This produces the on-screen 'page' that the viewer sees.
7. Most web pages will themselves contain hyperlinks to other relevant and informative pages and perhaps to downloads, source documents, definitions and other web resources.

Final Summary:
1. The WWW incorporates all of the Internet services above and much more.
2. You can retrieve documents, view images, animation, and video, listen to sound files, speak and hear voice, and view programs that run on practically any software in the world, providing your computer has the hardware and software to do these things.
3. When you log onto the Internet using Netscape or Microsoft's Internet Explorer or some other browser, you are viewing documents on the World Wide Web.
4. The current foundation on which the WWW function is the programming language called HTML.
5. It is HTML and other programming imbedded within HTML that make possible Hypertext.
6. Hypertext is the ability to have web pages containing links, which are areas in a page or buttons or graphics on which you can click your mouse button to retrieve another document into your computer.
7. This "click-ability" using Hypertext links is the feature which is unique and revolutionary about the Web.

8. How do hypertext links work? Every document or file or site or movie or sound file or anything you find on the Web has a unique URL (uniform resource locator) that identifies what computer the thing is on, where it is within that computer, and its specific file name.
9. Every Hypertext link on every web page in the world contains one of the URLs.
10. When you click on a link of any kind on a Web page, you send a request to retrieve the unique document on some computer in the world that is uniquely identified by that URL.
11. **URLs are like addresses of web pages**.
12. A whole cluster of internationally accepted standards (such as TCP/IP and HTML) make possible this global information retrieval phenomenon that transcends all political and language boundaries.

What is a Browser? What is Netscape and Internet Explorer?

1. A browser is a computer program that resides on your computer enabling you to use the computer to view WWW documents and access the Internet taking advantage of text formatting, hypertext links, images, sounds, motion, and other features.
2. Netscape and Internet Explorer are currently the leading "graphical browsers" in the world (meaning they facilitate the viewing of graphics such as images and video and more).
3. There are other browsers (e.g., Macweb, Opera).
4. Most offer many of the same features and can be successfully used to retrieve documents and activate many kinds of programs.
5. Browsers all rely on "plug-ins" to handle the fancier files you find on the Web.
6. Plug-ins are sub-programs stored within a browser or elsewhere in your computer especially to support special types of files you may click on.
7. If you click on a link, and your computer does not currently have the plug-in needed for the file you clicked on, you are usually prompted with an opportunity to get the plug-in.
8. Most plug-ins are free, and easy and safe to install on your computer; follow the instructions you are given.
9. The main way in which browsers differ is in the convenience features they offer for navigating and managing the Web and all the URLs you may want to keep track of.
10. Netscape and Internet Explorer both offer the ability to e-mail documents, download them to diskette, print them, and keep track of where you've been and sites you want to "bookmark."

4.23 Writing Web Pages in HTML

This document is a generic introduction to HTML, the language used for World Wide Web documents ("WWW pages"). Some familiarity with WWW as a user (reader of documents) is assumed, but with regard to HTML no previous knowledge is assumed.

Contents

- Introduction
- Get ready...
- The requisites you need
- A closer look at our example and HTML notation
- Typing text - living with character code problems
- Organizing the contents: sections, headings, paragraphs, lists
- Emphasis and other classification
- Adding link
- Adding images
- Miscellaneous
- Check it !
- What next
- Summary

Introduction

- This document is *generic* in the sense of being independent of the particular version of HTML in use.
- It is *not exhaustive* with respect to any HTML specification.
- It aims at presenting the most *basic and recommendable* HTML constructs.
- This document aims at being *as easy as possible, but not easier*. (But if you feel that you don't learn from this, don't give up; try some other introduction to HTML which might be better suited for you.)
- We have tried to avoid assuming any particular prior knowledge about HTML and Web authoring.

Get ready...

- When you wish to put text, images, or other pieces or sets of data (collectively called *documents* here) onto the World Wide Web, the normal way is to write an HTML file.

- There are other ways, which can be taken in special cases, but HTML (HyperText Markup Language) is the "native" language of Web documents.
- An HTML file is a text file, and it can be read by human beings, not only by computers.
- It contains special *markup*, however, so you will have to learn how to read such notation. The following is a simple HTML file:

```
<!DOCTYPE HTML PUBLIC "-//W3C//DTD HTML 3.2//EN">
<TITLE>Demonstration</TITLE>
<H1>Demo</H1>
<P>
For demonstration purposes only.
Please do not regard this as an example of a
<EM>useful</EM> Web page!
</P>
<P>
This document was written by –
<A HREF="personal.html">Amit Dixit</A>.
</P>
```

- We'll discuss the contents of the file later.
- But it wasn't that bad, was it? At least it is something that pretty normal people have learned to read and write.
- The first line probably looks confusing, however, and it is obligatory and really has a meaning.
- Fortunately you can, for most purposes, just copy it into your documents and otherwise ignore it.
- If you think that the HTML file looks lawful, you may feel tempted to listen to people who offer you "Web editors", which would hide the dirty HTML behind the scenes where it belongs.
- Look out! It won't be any easier to learn to use a "Web editor" than to learn HTML (and use whatever text editor you are used to or can learn in a few minutes).
- Moreover, Web editors (such as FrontPage) often produce HTML files, which work only in some particular environment, since they don't obey HTML standards.
- Some Web editors *might* sometimes be useful e.g. for specifying tables (an advanced topic which will not be discussed here), since they might save the user from some routine work.
- But in order to be able to use a Web editor in a useful way - saving your time and work instead of wasting them - you have to know HTML so well that you *could* write it yourself !

- When a user (you or someone else) accesses something which is commonly called a "Web page", the actual process behind the scenes is developed the following manner:
    1. The user asks his *Web browser* (such as Netscape, Internet Explorer, Lynx, or Amaya) to show a document. This involves specifying the *Web address*, also known as *URL* (Uniform Resource Locator), either by just typing it or by following a *link* in another Web document.
    2. The browser looks at the address. One part of the address specifies a *Web server* on which the document resides. The browser sends a request to the server, specifying a file name (which is another part of the Web address).
       A Web server is a computer which hosts Web documents and makes them available upon request.
    3. The server locates the requested HTML file on its disk and sends it (well, a copy of it, to be exact) to the browser.
    4. The browser interprets the contents of the HTML file and formats it for display on the user's screen.
- Perhaps you didn't quite follow? Well, the essential thing - from your point of view as a future author of Web documents - is that **a Web document is formatted for display every time it is fetched and presented to a user**.
- Even if the same user asked for the same document again after ten seconds, he might see it differently.
- He might, for example, have narrowed the window of his Web browser, which in general means that at least the division into lines is different. (The document itself might have been changed by its author, too !)
- Let's presume that a user asks for a document with the simple contents of our trivial example.
- Different browsers will display it differently. For example, the text might be black on white, or something else - surprisingly many browsers use grey background by default.
- Due to the presence of the funny looking EM (for emphasis) tags around the word "useful", that word might be displayed in *italics* or underlined or in red or even blinking.
- You cannot, as an author, know what it really looks on the user's screen; such features can even be configurable by users themselves.
- The only thing which you can reasonably assume as an author about the EM tags is that they cause text to be presented in *some* manner, which makes them look more prominent than normal text in your document.

- Generally speaking, HTML elements specify *logical relationships* rather than any particular physical representation.
- The division of text into *lines* in the HTML file has *no* effect on what the document looks like on the user's screen.
- (There is an exception to this, called PRE element, but we'll come to that later.)
- Thus, a Web browser essentially throws all newline indicators away, taking the text as long piece of text, and inserts newlines as suitable, i.e. splits the text into lines as appropriate under the particular circumstances.
- Now you probably (and hopefully) say that this may screw things up badly.
- Indeed. This is one reason why HTML has special tags for indicating things like *paragraph division*.
- The tags <P> and </P> say that the text between them forms one paragraph, and a browser is expected to format it as such and *somehow* indicate the division into paragraphs to the reader.
- Typically, there is some extra vertical space between paragraphs. (You cannot know how much, and you shouldn't even ask, as an author.) But alternatively a Web browser could, for example, be in fact a speech synthesizer, which probably uses pauses for the same purpose.
- The lesson is that you must think somewhat more *abstractly* than you are accustomed to, especially if you have used text processing or layout programs.
- Think in terms *what* you wish to express (e.g. emphasis or paragraph division), not *how* it should be expressed.

The Requisites you Need:
1. Anyone who can read and write can learn HTML. However, you probably want to learn HTML in order to create Web documents.
2. You may hear different opinions about this, but the truth is that you only need
   - Some knowledge about the HTML language.
   - A text editor.
   - Access to a Web server.
3. You can use *any* text editor, provided only that it can save files in "text only" format (sometimes called "ASCII format" or "plain text format").
4. For instance, on Windows systems you can use NotePad; on Unix systems, you can use vi or Emacs.
5. You can also use text processing systems like WordPerfect or MS-Word, but this causes extra problems (e.g. you have to select the format to be "text only" instead of the default internal format) and doesn't bring real benefits.

6. But the essential thing is that *you can use your favorite text editor.* (If you don't know any editor, you should find out what is the *simplest* editor in your system and learn to use it.)
7. *Access to a Web server* may sound like a complicated technical thing.
8. However, here it only means that you can store files onto the disk of a computer acting as a Web server.
9. You really have to find *local information* about the details, since they vary a lot.
10. You need adequate permission to store files and you need related information about how to do that.
11. Typically that information should tell you some directory names (e.g. on Web servers running Unix, a user should create a directory named `public_html` into his home directory and use it for his personal Web pages) and recommended names for HTML document files (normally they should end with `.html` or `.htm`, depending on the system).
12. The Web server might be a computer to which you can log on and do all your Web authoring. Alternatively, you might have to create the documents elsewhere (e.g. on your PC) and transfer them onto a Web server (using e.g. the FTP program in a local area network or a modem connection).

A closer look at our example and HTML notation:

1. Let's have a closer look at our tiny example, reproduced here for your convenience:
   ```
   <!DOCTYPE HTML PUBLIC "-//W3C//DTD HTML 3.2//EN">
   <TITLE>Demonstration</TITLE>
   <H1>Demo</H1>
   <P>
   ```
For demonstration purposes only.
Please do not regard this as an example of a
   ```
   <EM>useful</EM> Web page!
   </P>
   <P>
   ```
This document was written by
   ```
   <A HREF="personal.html">Amit Dixit</A>.
   </P>
   ```
2. We already mentioned that the first line in a document is something you should put into the beginning of each HTML file without thinking about it too much.
3. But it has a purpose: It specifies that the file contains an HTML document, as opposite to other possible document formats, and it specifies the HTML version used (in our examples, version 3.2).
4. Usually Web browsers pay no attention to that line, but it is essential to so-called validators, which you should use to check your HTML code.

5. The next line begins with <TITLE> and ends with </TITLE>. As you may have guessed, these are the *start and end tags* for an HTML construct, the TITLE element. You can read the slash / in such contexts as *end of*....
6. The < and > characters are most appropriately called *angle brackets* in this context, but you should notice that in other contexts they are called and used as *less than* and *greater than* character. (The traditional character set used in computers, ASCII, is so small that language and software designers have to use one character for several purpose, which may of course cause confusion.)
7. Generally speaking, an HTML tag consists of
   - Opening angle bracket <
   - A slash /, if the tag is to be an end tag
   - Tag name, such as TITLE; there is a fixed (relatively small) set of allowed tag names, although this set is partly different in different versions of HTML
   - Optionally, one or more *attributes*, separated from the name and from each other with some white space; each tag has its own set (possibly empty set) of allowed attributes; the attributes are of the form name=value
   - Closing angle bracket >
8. Tag names can be written in upper case or in lower case or even in mixed case, just as you like. For instance, <Title> and <TITLE> are equivalent.
9. Normally start and end tags are paired. The two tags together with everything between them constitutes an *HTML element*. (There are some tags, such as <BR> for line break, which neither need nor allow an end tag, and such a tag is an HTML elements by itself.
10. In HTML 4.0, these tags are: AREA, BASE, BASEFONT, BR, COL, FRAME, HR, IMG, INPUT, ISINDEX, LINK, META, PARAM.) It depends on the element what is allowed as the contents of an element.
11. For example, the TITLE element allows plain text only, whereas many other elements allow other elements as well, e.g. elements can be *nested* - not arbitrarily, but according to specific rules.
12. The detailed rules for using TITLE are the following: Every HTML document must contain a TITLE element, and only one TITLE per document is allowed. The contents of the TITLE element is to be used, in a browser-dependent manner, as an informative title for the entire document.
13. It *does not appear as part of the document itself,* although a browser may display it in a special area of its window. You need a separate element if you wish to have a heading in the document itself (as you normally do). This may sound confusing, but there is wisdom behind it.
14. The title is information *about* the document and it can be used in several contexts outside the document when referring to it; typically, so-called hotlists (or lists of favourites, or whatever they are called in different browsers) contain titles of documents for easy reference.

15. Thus, there are good reasons for writing a descriptive title. Our tiny example doesn't even try, for obvious reasons, but the title of the document you are reading right now is HTML primer. Notice that this happens to be different from the main heading you see at the beginning of the document.
16. The next line specifies a *header*, using H1 tags, which stand for 1st level (most prominent) headers. As you may guess, there are also H2, H3 and H4 tags available for 2nd, 3rd and 4th level headers. (Actually, the repertoire contains H5 and H6, too, but there are several good reasons to avoid using them.) Typically 1st level headers are displayed very visibly, using a very large font if available.
17. Then we have two *paragraphs*, enclosed between start and end P tags. In the childhood of HTML, the <P> tag was regarded as paragraph separator, and several people still think that way. You can in fact omit the end P tags (</P>), but it is better to adopt the habit of thinking structurally.
18. The first of our paragraph contains one word within EM tags. This means that the word (or more generally, any text within EM start and end tags) is *emphasized*. It might, for example, be presented in italics or underlined or even in different color, according to browser features and user preferences. (If you are going to ask how to enforce **your** preferences in such issues, think twice.
19. The second paragraph contains, in addition to normal text, the strange-looking construct

    <A HREF="personal.html">Amit Dixit</A>
20. This may look strange, but you really have to learn how to read and write such things, because they belong to the core of HTML. The construct sets up a hypertext link (hyperlink), or *link* for short.
21. In this case, the text "Amit Dixit" will be presented to the user in a distinguished manner, e.g. underlined (the presentation depends on the browser), and by selecting this phrase (typically, by a mouse click) the user will be able to view the document to which the links points - here it happens to be a personal home page with relative address personal.html. We will discuss the details of setting up links later.

Typing text - living with Character Code Problems:
1. Since the characters < and > are used to designate HTML tags, they should not be entered as such, if they are to appear as data characters (e.g. in a mathematical expression like a < b).
2. For this purpose, so-called *escape sequences* are defined: < for < and > for >. This in turn makes the ampersand & a special character, and when it is to appear in the data, it shall be escaped as &. Thus, for example, to produce the notation R&D you should type R&D.

3. A bit clumsy, but such situations are pretty rare. But there are other character problems, which may appear more frequently.
4. You can safely use the so-called printable ASCII characters:

    ! " # $ % & ' ( ) * + , - . /

    0 1 2 3 4 5 6 7 8 9 : ; < = >?

    @ A B C D E F G H I J K L M N O

    P Q R S T U V W X Y Z [\ ] ^ _

    ` a b c d e f g h i j k l m n o

    p q r s t u v w x y z { | } ~

5. Provided that you represent & and < and > as explained above. All other characters, such as national letters ä and é, cause difficulties of some sort, partly because they have different internal representations in different computers.
6. Typing text is easy, but you should remember the following:
    - Line breaks in HTML do **not** imply line breaks in the visual appearance of the document; in fact, in HTML line breaks are generally equivalent to blanks.
    - Thus, you may use lines of any length you like, but for the ease of your work, use relatively short lines.
    - **Do not divide a word** into two lines.

Organizing the Contents: Sections, Headings, Paragraphs, Lists:

1. You should start with dividing your document into *major parts*, sections, according to its logical structure.
2. Then you may proceed with dividing sections into subsections and perhaps even subsections into subsubsections. (For further division into pieces, using just paragraphs or lists is usually preferable to having named subsubsections.)
3. Of course, very short documents do not need such divisions; you can just write a main heading and a few paragraphs.
4. Write descriptive *headings* for sections, subsections, and sub subsections.
5. Basically there are H1, H2, and H3 tags for headings of different levels. There is, however, a problem here: HTML does not provide a separate element for specifying a heading for the *entire* document. (Remember that the TITLE element is for another purpose.)
6. Therefore you have to *choose:*
    - Use H1 for both the overall document heading and top-level section headings, *or*

- Use H1 only for the overall document heading, using H2 for sections, H3 for subsections, and H4 for sub subsections.
7. In the first case you may consider using the attribute ALIGN=CENTER to make the overall heading centered, e.g.

   <H1 ALIGN=CENTER>Theory of Everything in a Nutshell</H1>
8. In the second alternative you may have problems with sub subsections, since browsers may display H4 headings in a non-distinctive way.
9. As regards to H5 and H6 headings, which are theoretically available, notice that popular browsers may display them as *smaller* than normal text ! Even more ridiculously, if possible, some people have started using those tags to *intentionally* get smaller text as if all browsers behaved so strangely.
10. If you have a section with, say, H2 heading and containing H3 headings, avoid inserting text between the H2 heading and the first H3 heading. Such "homeless" text can be acceptable if it only contains *very short* notes such as general orientation, some remarks about the section, or a motto. Long homeless texts confuse the reader who does not see your good intentions; therefore, use a subsection with a heading of the appropriate level and with text like *Introductory remarks*, *Generalities* or *Summary*.
11. When entering text into the structure, under the lowest-level headings, use the P tags to mark up *paragraph*. Generally, there should be more than one and at most seven (or so) paragraphs under one heading. Otherwise you should consider changing the structure.
12. Thus, the structure of your document should be something like the following (assuming you follow the second strategy of using H1 tags mentioned above):

<H1 ALIGN=CENTER>Document heading</H1>
<H2>First section</H2>
 <H3>First subsection of first section</H3>
  <P>Paragraph one. Ganesh Ganesh Ganesh...</P>
  <P>Paragraph two. Ganesh Ganesh Ganesh...</P>
 <H3>Second subsection of first section</H3>
  <P>A paragraph. Ganesh Ganesh Ganesh...</P>
  <P>Another paragraph. Ganesh Ganesh Ganesh...</P>
<H2>Second section</H2>
...

(The indentation is here just to show the structure. You don't need it in actual HTML files).
In addition to paragraphs, you may also use some special kind of blocks of text:

BLOCKQUOTE:

For quotations from external sources, such as a piece of text from a book. The use of these tags makes browsers present the text in a manner which distinguishes it from your normal flow of text (e.g. using italics or indentation or both). If the quotation contains several paragraphs, use P tags to show this.

ADDRESS:

For address information about the author. Might contain an E-mail address or a postal address. This too is presented in some distinctive manner suitable for such information.

PRE:

For preformatted text. This means that contrary to all normal rules of HTML, the text between <PRE> and </PRE> is presented as such with respect to the division into lines and use of blanks. This implies that a monospaced ("teletype") font is used, in contrast with proportional fonts normally used by graphic browsers. Suitable for presenting computer output and primitive "hand-formatted" tabular information.

If you have information, which is most suitably presented as a *list*, you can use –

- *Unordered* list where items appear in the order written but with e.g. bullets instead of ordinal numbers.
- *Ordered* list where items have numbers 1, 2, 3, ... generated by the Web browser
- *Definition* list which consists of term-definition pairs.

An *unordered list* is presented in HTML as follows:

1. Begin with the start tag <UL>
2. For each item of the list, type the list item start tag <LI> followed by the item itself; the list item end tag </LI> is optional and usually omitted.
3. End with the end tag </UL>

Example:

We sell:
```
<UL>
<LI> apples
<LI> oranges
<LI> bananas
</UL>
```

An *ordered list* is marked up in exactly the same way except for the start and end tags which are <OL> and </OL>.

A *definition list* is somewhat more complicated. The start and end tags are <DL> and </DL>. Within them, you will write items as follows:

<DT>term<DD>definition data for that term

Example:

Some hypertext concepts:

<DL>

<DT> anchor

<DD> one of two ends of a hyperlink

<DT> hyperlink

<DD> a relationship between two anchors, called

the <DFN>head</DFN> and the <DFN>tail</DFN>;

the link goes from the tail to the head

<DT> <DD>

</DL>

There are some practical problems with definition lists, and you might find more appropriate tools among the more advanced features of modern HTML, such as tables. Here we will only remark that a natural way of *avoiding overly large lists* is to use normal text paragraphs preceded by headings. That is, make each term a heading (of suitable level) and provide its definition as text under the heading.

Emphasis and other classification:
1. When writing text by hand or using a typewriter or a text-processing program, there are various means of emphasizing things, e.g. underlining, bolding, different colors, etc.
2. In HTML, you should use the EM tags or, for stronger emphasis, STRONG tags. Leave it to the various browsers how they physically present the emphasis.
3. For example:

Avoid emphasizing too much, since emphasis means separating some important things from the normal flow of text. If the entire flow of text is "emphasized", you are in fact not emphasizing anything !

4. There are various other ways of classifying pieces of text (typically, a word or phrase):

CITE:
Citation (title of a book or article or equivalent).

CODE:
Computer program code or equivalent.

SAMP:
Sample output from e.g. computer program.

KBD:
Text to be typed by a user; this is typically used when giving instructions about computer usage.

I:
Text to be presented in italics, e.g. scientific names of animal species.

SMALL:
Text to be presented in a font smaller than normal.

5. The classification tags are allowed to contain text and even other (nested) classification tags but not paragraph markers (P tags).
6. If you really need to emphasize several consecutive paragraphs, you have to put the emphasis tags into each paragraph separately.
   (e.g. <P><EM>paragraph text</EM></P>).

Adding Links:

1. Presumably you roughly know, as a Web user, what a link looks like: typically there are words which are designated in some particular, browser-dependent manner (using e.g. underlining or special colors), and if you *select* a link (typically by "clicking it" with the mouse if you use a graphical browser), your browser will display a new document - the *target* of the link - to you. (Please notice that not all use of the Web involves mouses and clicking, so you should not use stupid phrases like *Click here !* in your documents.)
2. Now, to *construct a link* as an HTML author, you just type the following:
   - The start tag <A HREF="URL">
     where URL is the target address (for the document to which the link shall point).
   - The text which you wish to appear in your document as the link text (underlined, colored, or in whatever special way each browser presents it)
   - The end tag </A>
3. The URL, or Web address, typically begins with http://. When looking at a document in a Web browser, you can normally see its URL somewhere in the browser window; it might be labelled URL or Netsite or Address or Location, for example. Copy it (using cut and paste, if possible) into your document.

4. Notice that URLs published in newspapers or other printed media very often contain types, and even URLs published in the Internet aren't always correct.
5. For this reason, and for checking the real contents as well, you should check the URL with your browser before constructing a link.
6. The tag name A comes from the word *anchor*. (Some metaphors in the Web world are really strange.)
7. That's all it takes to set up a link. Our simple example HTML file contains the following:

    <A HREF="personal.html">Amit Dixit</A>
8. Here the link points to the personal home page of the author (that's me, by the way).
9. This is a comfortable way to allow people find information about you without bothering those who don't like to see that information right now.
10. **Other typical uses of links include –**
    - Separating details from main discussion, by just mentioning a document detail with a short phrase and making that phrase a link.
    - Creating a file which acts as a *table of contents* by containing just a list of links.
    - Referring to a related document, such as a discussion of the same theme by someone else or a translation of the current document into another language.
11. More generally, links are a powerful tool for creating documents which allow each user to select what interests him. Unfortunately, there is no well-supported structured way of telling what kind of information the link points to, i.e. what the user is going to get by selecting the link, though there are some techniques for expressing the nature of a link.
12. In many cases you can rely on intuition, but you might need to consider formulating your sentences so that the context is a sufficient clue to the idea behind each link. As the last resort, add a parenthetic remark after the link, such as "(technical details)".
13. In addition to linking to a document as a whole, you can make a link point to a particular **location** in the same or another document. When a user selects such a link, the document will be displayed positioned to that location. (What this really means depends on the browser. It is not always obvious to the user exactly which location is pointed to).
14. To create such a link, use the same method as above but append the character # and a location name to the URL; for example, such a link above has been coded as follows:

    - - there are

    <a href="5.7.html#linknature">some techniques for expressing the nature of a link</a>.

15. This example links to location named linknature in the document 5.7.html. This only works if that document really contains such a location; in practice this means that it contains a structure of the form

    `<A NAME="rfc">some text</A>`

16. Thus, such a structure specifies that the beginning of some text is a location to which links can refer. In our example, the markup in the other document is

    `<H3><A name="linknature">Expressing the nature of a link</A></H3>`

17. Note the correct nesting of A elements and heading elements. Since A elements may contain text-level elements only, they need to appear *inside* heading elements.

18. You can, of course, refer to locations in *other people's documents* only if they have named locations that way. Using your Web browser (with a function named *View source* or *View HTML* or something like that) you can speak at people's HTML constructs to see if they contain named locations and what the names are.

19. In *your own documents* you can yourself decide where to put named locations. It might be a good idea to put them at the beginning of each major part, since this allows others to link to such parts when appropriate.

20. As a special case, when referring to a location *within the same document*, the URL can be omitted, using just the location specifier. Thus, if your document contains a preface with the heading
    `<H1><A NAME="preface">Preface</A></H1>`
    Then you could refer to it as follows:

As mentioned in the `<A HREF="#preface">preface</A>`, our discussion Ganesh Ganesh Ganesh...

Adding Images:
1. The ability to link to images and to embed images into documents is an essential feature of HTML. An image could be a photograph, or a drawing, or graphic presentation produced by a computer, for instance.
2. If you want to put images onto Web, the most difficult and time-consuming job is to create a file which contains a JPEG or GIF presentation of the image. You need not know what JPEG and GIF are, except that they are specific standardized formats of presenting graphic information in digital (i.e. computer readable) form; JPEG is more suitable for photographs, GIF for other graphics.
3. But you need to find programs, which can produce a JPEG or GIF presentation for your graphics. For example, you might find a scanner, which can read a paper or photograph and produce JPEG or GIF, or an interactive graphics program with which you can do some drawing on the screen and get it stored as JPEG or GIF.

4. But be prepared for some complications; for instance, you may have to use a scanner which can only produce some strange graphics format X, and then you have to find a conversion program which converts from X to GIF.
5. There is a large number of other graphics formats, too, and even formats for movies and sounds. However, JPEG and GIF are the most universally supported in Web browsers, so use them for images to be put onto the Web, unless there is a very good reason do otherwise.
6. Now let us assume that you have made your way through that. For definiteness, let's assume that you have a photo of yourself in JPEG format in a file named `ganeshphoto.jpg`, in the same directory where your HTML files are (on a Web server).
7. The rest, the HTML side of the issue, is quite easy:
   - To put a *link* to the photo into a Web document, use the A tags described above, specifying the file name as URL, e.g.
   - There is a <A HREF="ganeshphoto.jpg">photo of me</A> available.
   - To embed the photo into a Web document, use the IMG tag as follows:
   - <IMG SRC="ganeshphoto.jpg" ALT="a photo of me">
8. Notice that IMG is an element by itself; there is no end tag. You may wish to put an explanatory text under the image. It requires no special tags; just write the text.
9. The ALT attribute is displayed *instead of* the image, if a browser cannot display the image for some reason (such as text-only terminal !), or as a *description of* the image, when automatic loading of images has been disabled by the user.
10. This makes design of good ALT texts sometimes difficult, but normally you should aim at helping the latter group of users to decide whether to load the image or not. If the image is purely decorative, use ALT="".
11. For *several reasons*, it is usually better to link to images than to embed them, especially if images are large or there are lots of them.

Miscellaneous:
1. You can force a **line break** using the <BR> tag. It is an element by itself: no end tag is needed or allowed, so there can be no contents either.
2. It does not cause a paragraph break (e.g. empty line). The most typical use is in address information like the following:

   <ADDRESS>
   Amit Dixit
   Päivänsäteenkuja 4 as. 1
   FIN-02210 Espoo
   Finland
   </ADDRESS>

3. You can indicate **change of topic** using the <HR> tag. It is an element by itself, too. It typically causes a full-width horizontal rule to be drawn.
4. Authors often use <HR> after the document content proper, to separate that from final remarks about authorship, copyright, etc. You may also, for example, separate the major sections of your document from each other in such a manner.

Check it !
1. People make typing errors alot. In HTML, a simple type may have a serious effect on the entire document. For instance, if you forget the slash from the end tag </H1>, you would typically get *all the rest* of your document printed as a top-level heading !
2. Therefore, and for other good reasons as well, you should ask a suitable program to do some basic formal checking of your HTML file. Several **validation programs**, such as the WDG Validator, and miscellaneous checkers such the W3C Link Checker exist for a short list.
3. Passing such a check does not mean that your HTML file is sensible in every respect, but the checks do find a lot of errors.
4. Checking what the document *looks like* on your browser is a good thing to do. But remember that it only shows what it looks like to you under the particular circumstances.
5. Therefore, it is important to follow HTML specifications and to use validators, in order to try to make your document reasonably presented in any environment, on any browser, current and future.
6. If your document is important, consider the additional check of looking at in on different browsers and different screens and windows.

What next:
1. This document has described only a basic part of HTML.
2. There are lots of other tags, and even the tags described here may have additional options and features which do not belong to this fundamental introduction.
3. When you have read this document and exercised the basic features of HTML in practice, refer HTML 3.2.

Summary

Title and Headings	
<TITLE>	title associated with the document
<H1 ALIGN=CENTER>	top-level heading, centered
<H1>	top-level heading
<H2>	second-level heading
<H3>	third-level heading

Blocks of Text	
<P>	normal paragraph
<BLOCKQUOTE>	quotation from external source
<ADDRESS>	address info about author
<PRE>	preformatted tex
Lists	
<UL>	unordered list
<OL>	ordered list
<LI>	list item
<DL>	definition list
<DT>	term in definition list
<DD>	definition data for term
Classification of phrases (text markup)	
<EM>	emphasized text
<STRONG>	strongly emphasized text
<CITE>	citation (title of a book or article or equivalent)
<CODE>	computer program code or equivalent
<SAMP>	sample output from e.g. computer program
<KBD>	text to be typed by a user
<I>	text to be presented in italics
<SMALL>	text to be presented in a font smaller than normal
Hypertext links	
<A HREF="URL">text</A>	link to a document
<A HREF="URL#name">text</A>	link to a named location in a document
<A HREF="#name">text</A>	link to a named location within the same document
<A NAME="name">text</A>	names a target location for links
Other elements	
<IMG SRC="URL" ALT="text">	image to be embedded
 	forced line break
<HR>	change of topic (horizontal rule)

4.24 Introduction to Sockets and Socket Programming

Simple Introduction to Sockets:
1. A socket is a connection from a process to another process.
2. The two processes are typically on different machines, but they can also be on the same machine.
3. The most common use of a socket is to connect a client with a server, similar to placing a phone call to some phone service.
4. The client creates a socket (picks up the phone), then connects it to the server (dials the phone, waits for an answer).
5. Once the sockets are connected, communication is generally bi-directional, using some agreed-upon protocol.
6. You must have a protocol to know who is talking at any given time, and what it means.
7. For example, the Hyper Text Transfer Protocol (HTTP) defines how to get a Web page, including defining precisely each side's role in the conversation.
8. Simple Mail Transfer Protocol (SMTP) defines the transmission of email, and so on. When the connection is finished, both sides hang up.

Basic Concepts:
1. The basic building block for communication is the socket.
2. A socket is an endpoint of communication to which a name may be bound.
3. Each socket in use has a type and an associated process.
4. Sockets exist within communication domains.
5. A communication domain is an abstraction introduced to bundle common properties of threads communicating through sockets.
6. Sockets normally exchange data only with sockets in the same domain (it may be possible to cross domain boundaries, but only if some translation process is performed).
7. The Windows Sockets facilities support a single communication domain: the Internet domain, which is used by processes, which communicate using the Internet Protocol Suite. (Future versions of this specification may include additional domains.)
8. Sockets are typed according to the communication properties visible to a user.
9. Applications are presumed to communicate only between sockets of the same type, although there is nothing that prevents communication between sockets of different types should the underlying communication protocols support this.
10. Two types of sockets currently are available to a user. A stream socket provides for the bi-directional, reliable, sequenced, and unduplicated flow of data without record boundaries.
11. A datagram socket supports bi-directional flow of data, which is not promised to be sequenced, reliable, or unduplicated.

12. That is, a process receiving messages on a datagram socket may find messages duplicated, and, possibly, in an order different from the order in which it was sent.
13. An important characteristic of a datagram socket is that record boundaries in data are preserved.
14. Datagram sockets closely model the facilities found in many contemporary packet switched networks such as Ethernet.

What is a Socket?

1. Normally, a server runs on a specific computer and has a socket that is bound to a specific port number.
2. The server just waits, listening to the socket for a client to make a connection request.
3. On the client-side: The client knows the hostname of the machine on which the server is running and the port number to which the server is connected.
4. To make a connection request, the client tries to connect to the server on the server's machine and port.

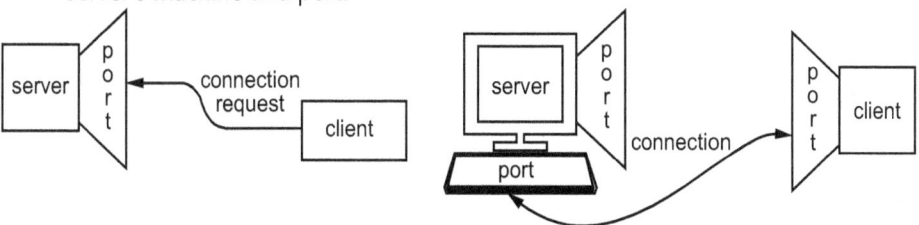

Fig. 4.53: Client server Socket communication

5. If everything goes well, the server accepts the connection.
6. Upon acceptance, the server gets a new socket bound to the same port.
7. It needs a new socket so that it can continue to listen to the original socket for connection requests while tending to the needs of the connected client.
8. On the client side, if the connection is accepted, a socket is successfully created and the client can use the socket to communicate with the server.
9. The client and server can now communicate by writing to or reading from their sockets.

Definition: A socket is one endpoint of a two-way communication link between two programs running on the network. A socket is bound to a port number so that the TCP layer can identify the application that data is destined to be sent.

Type of Sockets:

1. There are two widely used socket types, stream sockets (applications like telnet, http), and datagram sockets (applications like *streaming audio/video* real player).
2. Stream sockets treat communications as a continuous stream of characters, while datagram sockets have to read entire messages at once.

3. Each uses its own communications protocol. Stream sockets use TCP (Transmission Control Protocol), which is a reliable, stream oriented protocol, and datagram sockets use UDP (Unix Datagram Protocol), which is unreliable and message oriented.

There are several differences between a datagram socket and a stream socket.

1. Datagrams are unreliable, which means that if a packet of information gets lost somewhere in the Internet, the sender is not told (and of course the receiver does not know about the existence of the message). In contrast, with a stream socket, the underlying TCP protocol will detect that a message was lost because it was not acknowledged, and it will be retransmitted without the process at either end knowing about this.
2. Message boundaries are preserved in datagram sockets. If the sender sends a datagram of 100 bytes, the receiver must read all 100 bytes at once. This can be contrasted with a stream socket, where if the sender wrote a 100 byte message, the receiver could read it in two chunks of 50 bytes or 100 chunks of one byte.
3. The communication is done using special system calls sendto() and receivefrom() rather than the more generic read() and write().
4. There is a lot fewer overheads associated with a datagram socket because connections do not need to be established and broken down, and packets do not need to be acknowledged. This is why datagram sockets are often used when the service to be provided is short, such as a time-of-day service.

Socket Usages:

1. Network applications use sockets at some level, often using higher level protocols on top of sockets like File transfer apps (FTP), Web browsers (HTTP), Email (SMTP/POP3), etc. ...
2. Simplify and expedite application development process.
3. Most exploits client-server model.

Ports:

A socket provides an interface to send data to/from the network through a port
Each host has 65,536 ports
Some ports are *reserved for specific apps*
- 21: FTP
- 23: Telnet
- 80: HTTP
- 53: DNS
- 25: SMTP
- (About 2000 ports are reserved. Port no 0000 to 2000 are reserved for standard applications).

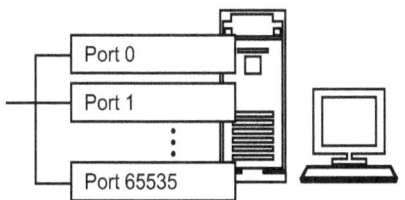

Fig. 4.54: Indicates Each host has 65,536 ports

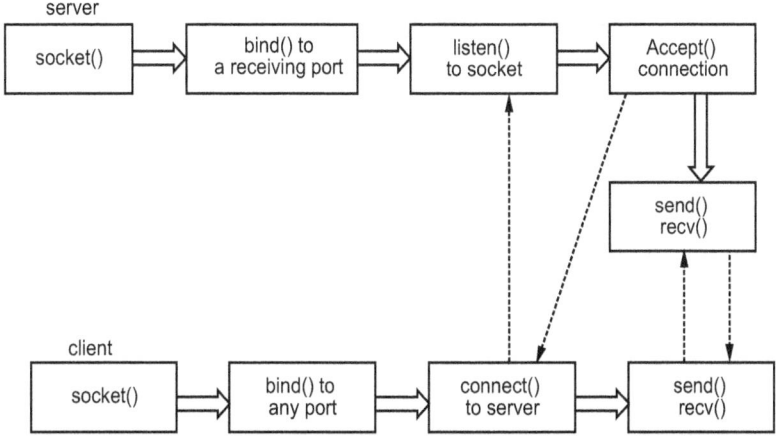

Fig. 4.55: Typical Client- Server Socket communication (TCP)

Fig. 4.56: Typical Client-Server Socket communication (UDP)

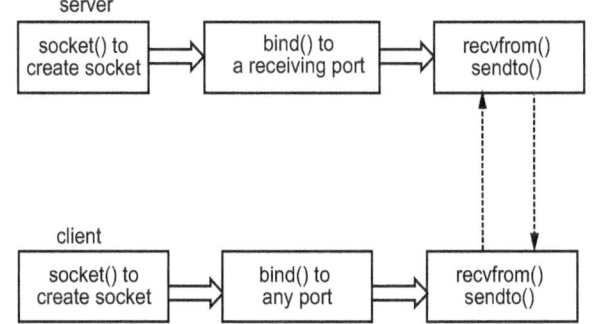

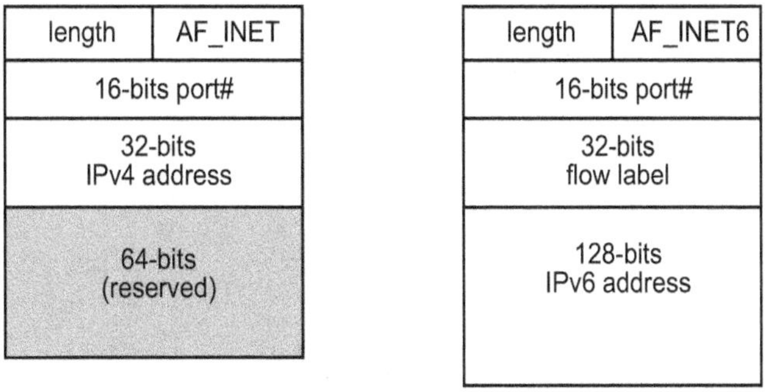

Fig. 4.57: Typical IPv4 vs IPv6 socket address structures

Connection Setup for (SOCK_STREAM):

1. There is no connection setup required for SOCK_DGRAM.
2. For example In Sock_Stream a connection occurs between two kinds of participants –
   - Passive: Waits for an active participant to request connection.
   - Active: Initiates connection request to passive side.
3. Once connection is established, passive and active participants are "similar" –
   - Both can send and receive data.
   - Either can terminate the connection.

Passive Participant
Step 1: Listen (for incoming requests)
Step 3: Accept (a request)
Step 4: Data transfer

Active Participant
Step 2: Request and establish connection
Step 4: Data transfer

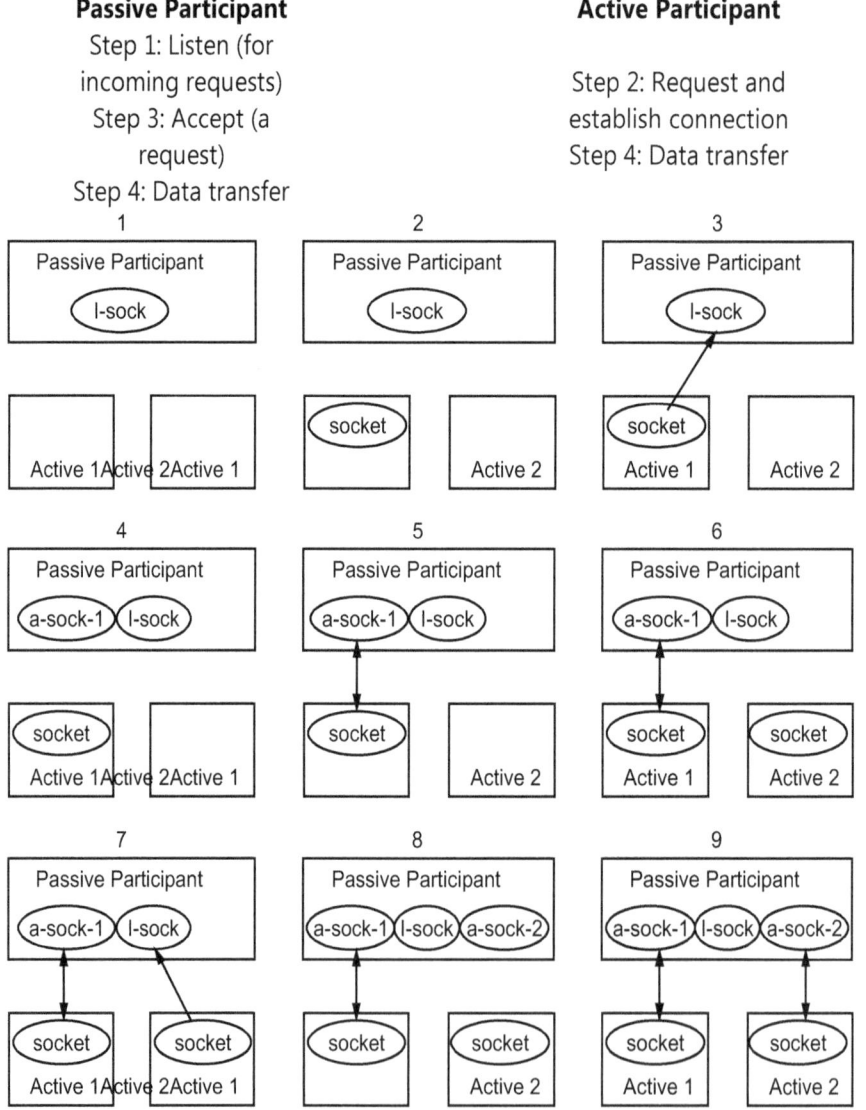

Fig. 4.58: Connection Setup flow

Blocking vs. Non-Blocking Sockets:

1. One of the first issues that you'll encounter when developing your Windows Sockets applications is the difference between blocking and non-blocking sockets.
2. Whenever you perform some operation on a socket, it may not be able to complete immediately and return control back to your program.
3. For example, a read on a socket cannot complete until some data has been sent by the remote host.
4. If there is no data waiting to be read, one of two things can happen: the function can wait until some data has been written on the socket, or it can return immediately with an error that indicates that there is no data to be read.
5. The first case is called a **blocking socket**.
6. In other words, the program is "blocked" until the request for data has been satisfied.
7. When the remote system does write some data on the socket, the read operation will complete and execution of the program will resume.
8. The second case is called a **non-blocking socket**, and requires that the application recognize the error condition and handle the situation appropriately.
9. Programs that use non-blocking sockets typically use one of two methods when sending and receiving data.
10. The first method, called polling, is when the program periodically attempts to read or write data from the socket (typically using a timer).
11. The second, and preferred method, is to use what is called *asynchronous notification*.
12. This means that the program is notified whenever a socket event takes place, and in turn can respond to that event.
13. For example, if the remote program writes some data to the socket, a "read event" is generated so that program knows it can read the data from the socket at that point.
14. For historical reasons, the default behaviour is for socket functions to "block" and not return until the operation has completed.
15. However, blocking sockets in Windows can introduce some special problems. For 16-bit applications, the blocking function will enter what is called a "message loop" where it continues to process messages sent to it by Windows and other applications.
16. Since messages are being processed, this means that the program can be re-entered at a different point with the blocked operation parked on the program's stack.
17. For example, consider a program that attempts to read some data from the socket when a button is pressed. Because no data has been written yet, it blocks and the program goes into a message loop.

18. The user then presses a different button, which causes code to be executed, which in turn attempts to read data from the socket, and so on.
19. Blocking socket functions can introduce a different type of problem in 32-bit applications because blocking functions will prevent the calling thread from processing any messages sent to it.
20. Since many applications are single-threaded, this can result in the application being unresponsive to user actions.
21. To resolve the general problems with blocking sockets, the Windows Sockets standard states that there may only be one outstanding blocked call per thread of execution.
22. This means that 16-bit applications that are re-entered (as in the example above) will encounter errors whenever they try to take some action while a blocking function is already in progress.
23. With 32-bit programs, the creation of *worker threads* to perform blocking socket operations is a common approach, although it introduces additional complexity into the application.
24. In summary, there are three general approaches that can be taken when building an application with the control in regard to blocking or non-blocking sockets:
    - Use a blocking (synchronous) socket. In this mode, the program will not resume execution until the socket operation has completed. Blocking sockets in 16-bit application will allow it to be re-entered at a different point, and 32-bit applications will stop responding to user actions. This can lead to complex interactions (and difficult debugging) if there are multiple active controls in use by the application.
    - Use a non-blocking (asynchronous) socket, which allows your application to respond to events. For example, when the remote system writes data to the socket, a Read event is generated for the control. Your application can respond by reading the data from the socket, and perhaps send some data back, depending on the context of the data received.
    - Use a combination of blocking and non-blocking socket operations. The ability to switch between blocking and non-blocking modes "on the fly" provides a powerful and convenient way to perform socket operations. Note that the warning regarding blocking sockets also applies here.

If you decide to use non-blocking sockets in your application, it's important to keep in mind that you must check the return value from every read and write operation, since it is possible that you may not be able to send or receive all of the specified data. Frequently, developers encounter problems when they write a program that assumes a given number of bytes can always be written to, or read from, the socket. In many cases, the program works as expected when developed and tested on a local area network, but fails unpredictably when the program is released to a user that has a slower network connection (such as a serial dial-up connection to the Internet). By always checking the return values of these operations, you insure that your program will work correctly, regardless of the speed or configuration of the network.

Introduction to Socket Programming:

Introduction to network functions in C

Contents:
- Introduction
- Creating a socket
- Binding a socket to a port
- Listening for connections
- Accepting a connection
- Closing connections
- Sending data to a connection
- Receiving data from a connection
- Setting socket options
- Handling more than one connection
- Converting a hostname into a network address
- Establishing an outgoing connection

Introduction:
In this tutorial, we will attempt to explain the use and syntax of some of the basic UNIX networking functions in C. Separate study is there to have Windows Sockets programming. With some versions of UNIX, the example programs will not link, complaining about things such as undefined symbols bind, accept, listen and socket. This topic assumes you know how to program in C.

Creating a socket:
The first thing to do is to create a socket which you can then manipulate in many ways. To create a socket, you can use the socket() function.
Includes:
    #include<sys/types.h>
    #include<sys/socket.h>
Syntax:
    int socket(int af, int type, int protocol);

C source:
```
int socket_desc;
socket_desc=socket(AF_INET,SOCK_STREAM,0);
if (socket_desc==-1)
 perror("Create socket");
```

socket() returns a socket descriptor which can be used in other network commands. This will create a socket, which uses DARPA Internet addresses, and the method of connection is a byte stream, which is similar to a pipe. An alternative to byte streams is a datagram but this tutorial does not cover them.

With servers, the first socket created is often known as a "master socket". Before the socket can send or receive data, it must be connected to another socket. If acting as a master socket, it must be bound to a port number so that clients can know where to "find" the socket and connect to it.

If successful, socket() returns a valid socket descriptor; otherwise it returns -1 and sets errno to indicate the error. perror() or strerror() can be used to turn the errno value into a human readable string.

Binding a socket to a port:
To set up a master socket, you need to bind the socket descriptor to a in many ways. To create a socket, you can use the socket() function as described above in Creating a socket.

Includes:
```
#include<sys/socket.h>
#include<netinet/in.h>
```

Syntax:
```
int bind(int s, struct sockaddr *addr, int addrlen);
```

C source:
```
struct sockaddr_in address;

/* type of socket created in socket() */
address.sin_family = AF_INET;
address.sin_addr.s_addr = INADDR_ANY;
/* 7000 is the port to use for connections */
address.sin_port = htons(7000);
/* bind the socket to the port specified above */
bind(socket_desc,(struct sockaddr *)&address,sizeof(address));
```

If successful, bind() returns 0; otherwise it returns -1 and sets errno to indicate the error.

The port specified in the source code above (port 7000) is where the server can be connected to. To test this, compile the program 'sockbind' from the source code directory and run it. While it is running, type:

telnet localhost 7000
and you should get
Trying...
for a few seconds and then
telnet: Unable to connect to remote host: Connection refused

as the server program finishes. This indicates the server was ok. If the connection is refused immediately, there is probably a problem with the server.

Listening for connections:
Before any connections can be accepted, the socket must be told to listen for connections and also the maximum number of pending connections using listen()

Includes:
 #include<sys/socket.h>

Syntax:
 int listen(int s, int backlog);

C source:
 listen(socket_desc,3);

The above line specifies that there can be up to 3 connections pending. If a connection request arrives when there are already 3 connections pending, the client receives a timeout error.

listen() applies only to unconnected sockets of type SOCK_STREAM. If the socket has not been bound to a local port before listen() is invoked, the system automatically binds a local port for the socket to listen on.

If successful, listen() returns 0; otherwise it returns -1 and sets errno to indicate the error.

Accepting a connection:
To actually tell the server to accept a connection, you have to use the function accept()

Includes:
 #include<sys/socket.h>

Syntax:
 int accept(int s, struct sockaddr *addr, int *addrlen);

C source:
 int addrlen;
 struct sockaddr_in address;

 addrlen = sizeof(struct sockaddr_in);
 new_socket = accept(socket_desc, (struct sockaddr *)&address, &addrlen);
 if (new_socket<0)
  perror("Accept connection");

Accept() is used with connection based sockets such as streams. The parameters are the socket descriptor of the master socket followed by a sockaddr_in structure and the size of the structure. If successful, accept() returns a positive integer which is the socket descriptor for the accepted socket. If an error occurs, -1 is returned and errno is set to indicate the cause.

There is some example source code in the directory, the program to compile is called 'accept' While it is running, type:

    telnet localhost 7000

    and you should get

    Trying...

    Connected to localhost.

    Escape character is '^]'.

and then 10 seconds later, it should close the connection. Once again, if the connection is refused immediately, there is probably a problem with the server.

Closing connections:

Probably one of the easiest things to do with a socket, is close it. This is done using close()

Includes:
    #include<unistd.h>

Syntax:
    int close(int sockdes);

C source:
    close(socket_desc);
    Close() closes the socket descriptor indicated by sockdes.

Upon successful completion, close() returns a value of 0; otherwise, it returns -1 and sets errno to indicate the error.

Sending data to a connection:

Accepting a connection would not be any use without the means to send or receive data. Send without receive could be used for an information server which always returns a fixed message.

Includes:
    #include<sys/socket.h>

Syntax:
    int send(int s, const void *msg, int len, int flags);
C source:
    char *message="This is a message to send\n\r";
    send(socket_desc,message,strlen(message),0);

The message should have \n\r instead of just \n or \r because otherwise the text which appears on some clients may seem strange. e.g the text with just a \n would appear as follows:
    This is a message
            and this is the second line
                    and the third.
Instead of:
    This is a message
    and this is the second line
    and the third.

send() is used to transmit a message to another socket and can be used only when the socket is in a connected state. The socket descriptor that specifies the socket on which the message will be sent is 's' in the syntax above. 'msg' points to the buffer containing the message and the length of the message is given by len, in bytes.

The supported values for flags are zero, or MSG_OOB (to send out-of-band data) - a write() call made to a socket behaves in exactly the same way as send() with flags set to zero.

Upon successful completion, send() returns the number of bytes sent. Otherwise, it returns -1 and sets errno to indicate a locally-detected error. The 'accept' program is modified to send a welcome message to the connection before it closes the socket.

Receiving data from a connection:
Accepting a connection would not be any use without the means to send or receive data. Receive only could be used as a data collection method.
Includes:
    #include<sys/socket.h>
Syntax:
    int recv(int s, void *msg, int len, int flags);
C source:
    int bufsize=1024;   /* a 1K buffer */
    char *buffer=malloc(bufsize);
    recv(socket_desc,buffer,bufsize,0);

The flags parameter can be set to MSG_PEEK, MSG_OOB, both, or zero. If it is set to MSG_PEEK, any data returned to the user still is treated as if it had not been read, i.e. the next recv() re-reads the same data. A read() call made to a socket behaves in exactly the same way as a recv() with flags set to zero. If successful, recv() returns the number of bytes received, otherwise, it returns -1 and sets errno to indicate the error. recv() returns 0 if the socket is blocking and the connection to the remote node failed.

Setting socket options:
To allow certain socket operations requires manipulation of socket options using setsockopt()

Includes:
   #include<sys/socket.h>

Syntax:
int setsockopt(int s, int level, int optname,
      const void *optval, int optlen);

C source:
   #define TRUE 1
   #define FALSE 0

   int socket_desc;   /* master socket returned by socket() */
   int opt=TRUE;   /* option is to be on/TRUE or off/FALSE */

   setsockopt(socket_desc,SOL_SOCKET,SO_REUSEADDR,
      (char *)&opt,sizeof(opt));

SOL_SOCKET specifies the option is a 'socket level' option, these are defined in <sys/socket.h>
The socket is identified by the socket descriptor s.
The option SO_REUSEADDR is only valid for AF_INET sockets.
There are two kinds of options: boolean and non-boolean. Boolean options are either set or not set and also can use optval and optlen to pass information. Non-boolean options always use optval and optlen to pass information.

Handling more than one connection:
To enable a socket to be read without waiting if there is no input, the socket must be set non-blocking using the following snippet of code.
      fcntl(mastersocket, F_SETFL, FNDELAY);
      or
      fcntl(mastersocket, F_SETFL, O_NONBLOCK);
If the above returns a non-zero result, the operation failed and errno should be set to an appropriate value.

Using select to monitor a number of sockets (or just one) is fairly straightforward and is shown in the code below. Please note this is incomplete code as the creation of the master socket is not included (see previous details).

```
fd_set readfds;

/* create a list of sockets to check for activity */
FD_ZERO(&readfds);

/* specify mastersocket - i.e. listen for new connections */
FD_SET(mastersocket, &readfds);

/* wait for connection, forever if have to */
new_conns=select(max_conns, readfds, NULL, NULL, NULL);

if ((new_conns<0)&&(errno!=EINTR))
{
 /* there was an error with select() */
}
if (FD_ISSET(mastersocket,&readfds))
{
 /* Open the new socket */
}
```

Of course, the above will only wait for activity on the master socket. What you need to do is run it inside a loop, which repeats until the server is shut down. Any newly created sockets will need to be monitored as well (unless the connections accepted are closed after outputting a message).

Converting a hostname into a network address:
Includes:
    #include<netdb.h>
Syntax:
    struct hostent *gethostbyname(const char *name);
C source:
    struct hostent *hent;
    hent = gethostbyname("www.foobar.net");
    A hostent structure:
    struct hostent
    {
      char *h_name;   /* official name of host */
      char **h_aliases; /* alias list */
      int h_addrtype; /* host address type */
      int h_length;   /* length of address */
      char **h_addr_list; /* list of addresses */
    }

Some of the network functions require a structure containing the network address and sometimes the port number to connect to or from. The easiest way to convert a hostname to a network address is to use the **gethostbyname() function**.

gethostbyname() returns a structure of type hostent - this structure contains the name of the host, an array of alternative names and also an array of network addresses (in network byte order).

Establishing an outgoing connection:
To establish a connection to another socket (similar to telnet), use the function connect().

```
#include<sys/types.h>
#include<sys/socket.h>

int connect(int sockfd, struct sockaddr *serv_addr, int addrlen);
```

Create the socket using socket(), convert the hostname to an IP address using gethostbyname() and then issue the connect() call passing the relevant structures containing the IP address and port to connect to.

```
struct hostent   *he;
struct sockaddr_in server;
int      sockfd;

/* resolve localhost to an IP (should be 127.0.0.1) */
if ((he=gethostbyname("localhost"))==NULL)
{
 puts("error resolving hostname..");
 exit(1);
}
/*
* copy the network address part of the structure to the
* sockaddr_in structure which is passed to connect()
*/
memcpy(&server.sin_addr, he->h_addr_list[0], he->h_length);
server.sin_family = AF_INET;
server.sin_port = htons(7000);

/* connect */
if (connect(sockfd, (struct sockaddr *)&server, sizeof(server))
{
 puts("error connecting..");
 exit(1);
}
```

Using **connect()** ... more to come when/if I get around to it.

4.25 Video on Demand

Introduction:

- **Video on Demand (VoD)** is an interactive multimedia system that works like cable Television, the difference being that the customer can select a movie from a large video database.

- Individual customers in an area are able to watch different programmes when they wish to, making the system a realization of the video rental shop brought into the home.

- As the underlying technologies are relatively new, Video on Demand still lacks a universal standardization.

- Nevertheless, many research institutes and commercial organizations have established de-facto standards and consequently, there are many operational VoD-related services available today.

- Some of the key areas of today's VoD-related applications are,
    1. Providing Video Films on Demand
    2. Local News and Weather Forecasting
    3. Games, Music and Leisure
    4. Education and Remote Learning Facilities
    5. Home Shopping and Other Consumer Services
    6. Banking

- The rest of this article explains the important issues and concerns behind the realization of *Video on Demand*.

- Different perspectives on technological, economical and social aspects are also emphasized.

Video on Demand: A Brief Look

The Setup requirement

The main components of a video on demand service are shown in Fig. 4.59. The **video server** to store and provide access to programmes, the **data delivery network** to interconnect the subscriber and the user-end **set-top box** to interface home TV equipment with the VoD services.

Formats used:

Prerecorded videos be digitally stored in a video server. These videos are then transmitted in a coded, compressed format. After the videos are ordered (either via interactive voice response or two-way remote control), they are decoded and decompressed by set-top converters in individual homes. In preliminary demonstrations, picture quality has been equal to standard VHS.

Functionality:

The customer can call on a range of services. While watching movies, performing operations such as video selection, pause, rewinding etc. can be selected as if it were a video player. These are processed by the *set-top-box* and sent to the local server. The local server processes the request if possible; otherwise it relays the request to a video archive server, much as a hierarchy system. Digital video/audio can be compressed and stored on hard disk and advertised for users on the network. Multiple archive servers can simultaneously be running over the network, depending on the bandwidth available.

Network:

Video-on-Demand currently runs over cabled networks, the most widespread being the standard telephone line. The difficulty in this, though, is the relatively low transmission speed of the telephone line. To overcome this shortfall, there are several viable networking standards, developed for multimedia transmission over the Internet as explained later. We will now examine the roles of the set-top-box, video server storage, Media compression standards and Transmission protocols. Following that, we shall see how these relate to VoD.

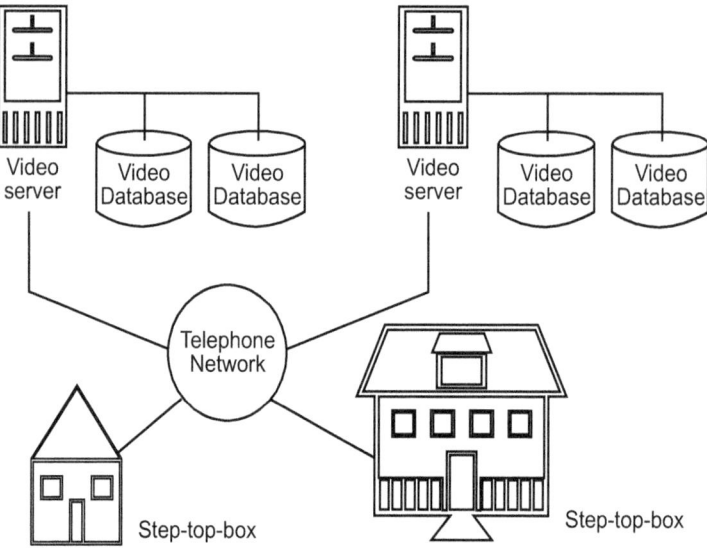

Fig. 4.59: System elements of typical Video on Demand

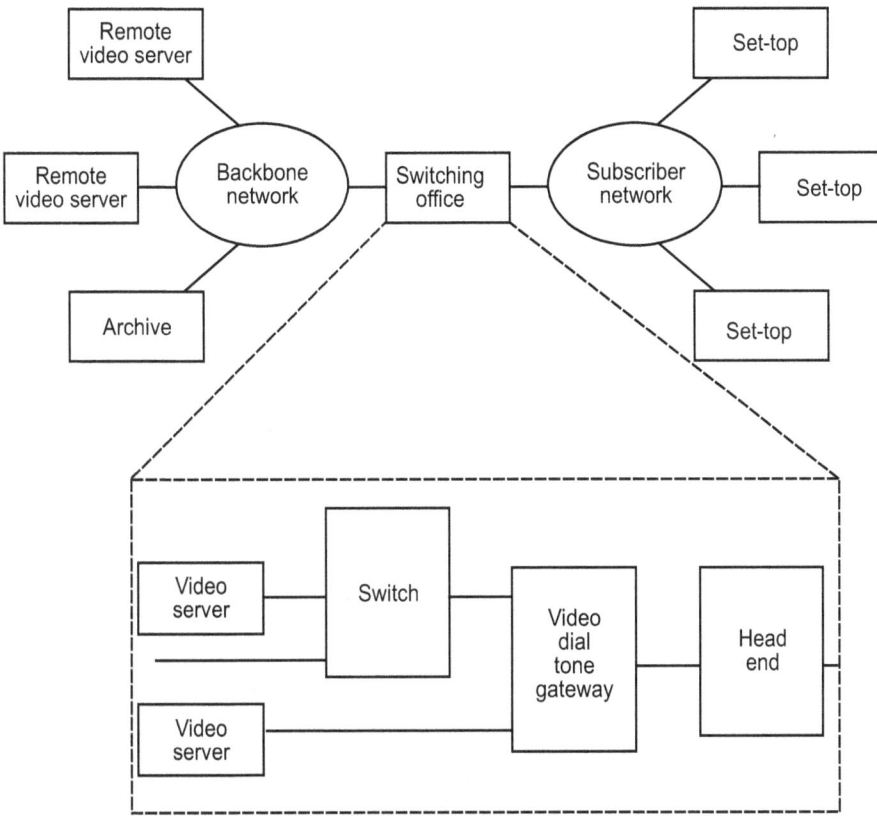

Fig. 4.60: System elements in block forms

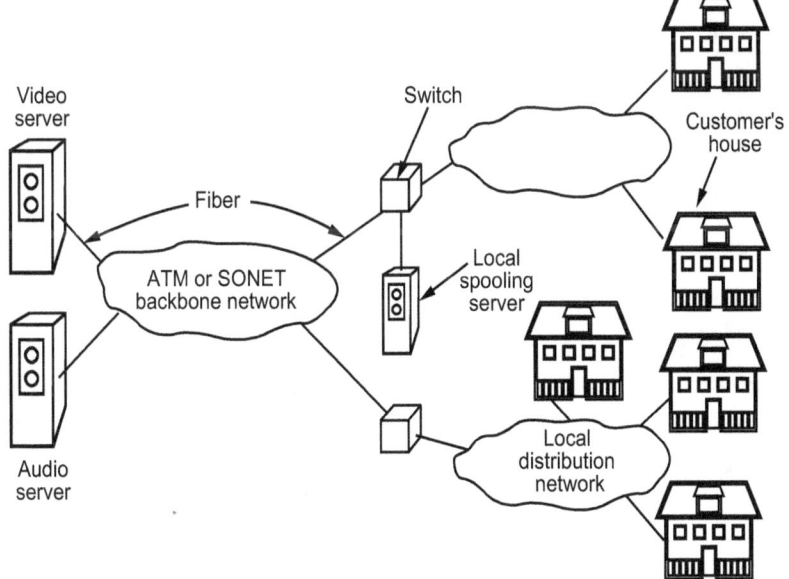

Fig. 4.61: Latest Video on Demand system

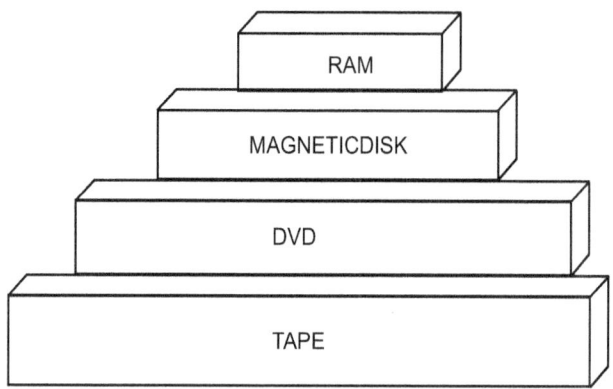

Fig. 4.62: A video server storage hierarchy

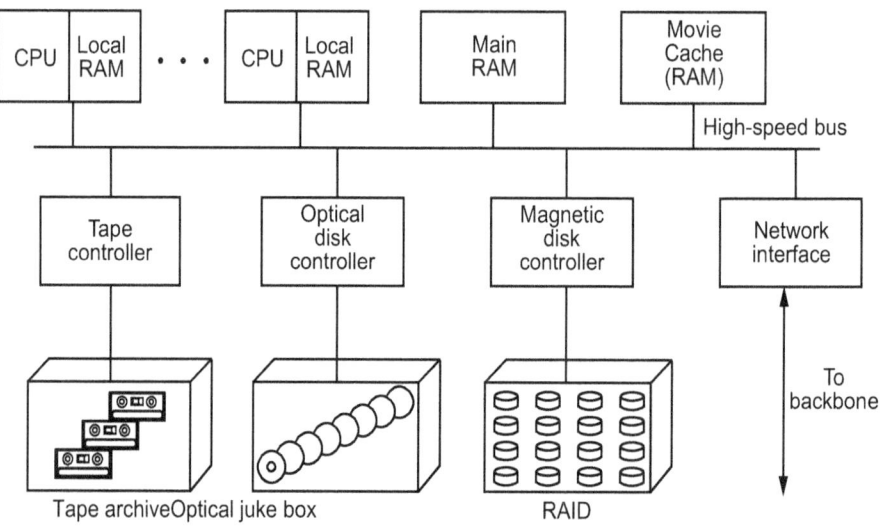

Fig. 4.63: The hardware architecture of a typical video server

Set-Top Box:

The Set-top box, interfaces the home TV into the video subscriber network, decompresses video and converts into a standard TV transmission format. A VoD set-top box will provide VCR-like functionality, allowing the user to rewind, fast-forward, pause, slow-motion play etc., by sending user commands upstream via the channel. To minimize the cost, it should contain a minimal amount of solid-state storage, only enough to compensate for network jitters, essentially to compete with its existing rivals: CATV & DSB (*Direct Satellite Broadcast*) services and VCRs. Consequently, the set-top box does not provide excessive buffering and gives hardware support to decompress video in real time.

Video Server:

Implementing a cost-effective and efficient video server is one of the most demanding engineering hurdles to be overcome. Such a server should have the following characteristics:

- Capacity to hold hundreds of Mbytes (or perhaps order of Terabytes) of digital information.
- Provide simultaneous access to several hundreds (or thousands) of subscribers on real-time, giving each one an appropriate bandwidth (usually in the order of 1.5-6 Mbps).
- Make economical use of resources by dynamically allocating programmes into different media such as Magnetic tape, optical W/R disks, hard disks, by considering the relative usage and level of interactivity supported.

Table 4.9: Cost comparison of currently available storage options

Storage	Cost/Mbyte	Sessions/Device
RAM	Costliest	Approx 200
Hard Disk	Costlier than R/W optical disk	Approx 5
R/W Optical	Costlier than Magnetic tape	Approx 2
Magnetic Tape	Cheapest	Approx. 1

As the table 1 indicates, solid-state storage as RAM is prohibitively expensive. On the other hand, cheap alternatives such as tapes limits the sessions per device and also impose difficulties in *virtual VCR* functioning.

There are several important considerations in designing a feasible video server:
- Hierarchical storage scheme
- Scalable Architecture
- Storage Subsystem
- Expanded Storage

1. Hierarchical storage scheme:

- Here, a hybrid of RAM, hard disk and a tertiary storage like optical R/W disks and Magnetic tape is used.
- An important concern here is to develop an efficient **medium allocating algorithm** to migrate programmes from one medium to another by considering the relative demand for programmes.

- As the figure shows, a set of intelligent storage subsystems, loosely coupled by a software controlled switching node is an ideal implementation to cater for variable demand/user conditions.

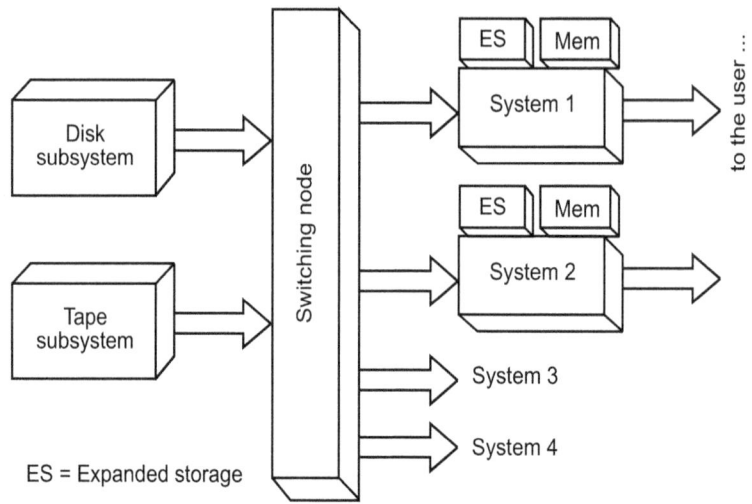

Fig. 4.64: A loosely coupled implementation of a Video storage system

2. Scalable Architecture:
The server system should be expandable both in terms of the number of titles held and the number of subscribers. This can be achieved by incorporating set of parallel data servers and a **name server** to store the location and access control information of the programmes, as shown in the figure. Thus any user request is served by first accessing the Name Server to locate the appropriate Data Server.

3. Storage Subsystem:
The storage subsystem consists of control units, disk/tape storage and access mechanism. There are several techniques to increase the performance by interleaving digital data of a programme on multiple disks:

- **Striping** involves interleaving portions of disk blocks on multiple disks. The aim here is to reduce the latency for block access by parallel reading of the complete block.

- **Declustering**, on the other hand, distributes blocks of files on several disks, thus allowing parallel block access from the same file and increasing the rate of the video stream.

- The overall performance can also be enhanced by **replicating** files among the servers by considering the demand for a programme, relative dispersion of subscribers and the access patterns (e.g. time/day of peak access, average number of simultaneous viewer).

SCSI interface is currently under consideration by *Hewlett-Packard* to be used in their video servers, allowing 8 devices in the bus giving 20 Mbps bandwidth.

4. Expanded Storage (ES) (i.e. solid-state memory) containing RAM modules would be the best for storing programmes with the highest demands, as in theory, ES has *infinite bandwidth*; and in practice the transfer rate is only limited by the system bus speed.

Audio/Video Standards:

The main multimedia protocols used on internet are the compressed digital video standards of Motion Picture Experts Group (**MPEG**), which is almost becoming the digital audiovisual *de-facto* and **Apple Quicktime** video. Digital video enables us to transmit higher rates of information in a given bandwidth

Transmission Protocols:

We shall next examine some common transmission protocols that are appropriate for multimedia transmission. Because the media is contained digitally, the protocol must support digital data transfer. As such, many of these are closely related and are likely to be compatible with Local Area Networks (LAN) and Wide Area Networks (WAN).

Following are the most practical transmission protocols recommended.

- ISDN
- ADSL
- ATM

ISDN (Integrated Services Digital Network):

ISDN is a set of communications standards allowing a single wire or optical fiber to carry voice, digital network services and video. ISDN is intended to replace POTS (Plain Old Telephone System) and differs in the telephone company central switches, software and other equipment. Its bandwidth standards range from 64 kps up to 2.0 Mbps.

An **ISDN-2 BRI** (Basic Rate Interface) line consists of two B-channels (Bearer) that provide 64 kbps transmission speed. The popular V.32 bis modem operates at 14.4 kbps or approximately one-tenth the speed of ISDN.

ADSL (Asymmetric Digital Subscriber Loop):

ADSL has the advantage that it runs over the current twisted pair copper (POTS) phone lines addressing the problem with changing to coax/fiber.

The technology for ADSL involves carving up the bandwidth of the medium into different layers to accommodate voice, data and control information. In this way, it supports up to 6 Mbps (simplex) or 576 Kbps (duplex), allowing a voice call (or fax), Video-on-Demand, Internet access and video conferencing over a common, single line.

This makes ADSL an important component in VoD. Companies researching on VoD are taking ADSL very seriously.

ATM (Asynchronous Transfer Mode):

It is a method for dynamic allocation of bandwidth using a fixed 53 byte packet (cell), known also as "fast packet". The cells use characteristics of both time-division-multiplexing of transmission media, and packet switching of data networks. A "virtual path" is set up through the involved switches when two endpoints wish to communicate. This provides a bit-rate independent protocol that can be implemented on several network types.

Characteristics of ATM:

1. Scalable technology; potential for extremely high speeds.
2. Cell switching, a compromise between delay-sensitive and conventional data transmissions.
3. Flexible implementation on many media (copper, coax, fiber).

The SONET (Synchronous Optical Net) operates at 155 Mbps. ATM speeds could operate up to 2.2 Gbps over a cell-switched network, being limited to the medium, since its scalable technology is not tied to any specific data rate. However, ATM requires wideband fiber/coax cables to exploit it's capacity. ATM is being implemented for national back-bone and long-distance carriers.

Table 4.10: Types of Communications Networks

Type	Copper Bitrate (Mbit/s)	Fiber Bitrate (Mbit/s)	Cable requirements
ISDN-2	0.128 (BRI)	0.128 (BRI)	Copper/Coax/Fiber
ISDN-30	2.00 (PRI)	2.00 (PRI)	Copper/Coax/Fiber
HDSL	0.800	2.00	Copper/Coax/Fiber
ADSL	1.536	-	Copper
ADSL 2	6.00	-	Copper
ATM	51.0	155 (in future 2500)	Copper/Coax/Fiber

Thus we can summarize like the types of network suitable for Video-on-Demand are ADSL and ATM. ISDN (the current highest being 2 Mbps) does not meet VoD bandwidth, but it is suitable for video conferencing. A major problem in implementing the transmission protocols is the limitation of bandwidth of the medium. Copper lines exist; fiber/coax lines are rare, yet. As it will be several years before fiber is laid to the home, protocols have to run over twisted copper or in the urban areas, co-axial cable.

ATM is ideal for its high bit rate. A shortfall for linking ATM all the way to the home is the enormous cost of the equipment and the sheer size (currently the size of a medium TV). This makes ATM an unfeasible solution for the time being.

ADSL is currently rather popular with the developing companies for the very reason that it can run over the Plain Old Telephone Service (POTS). ADSL meets bandwidth requirements for NTSC, broadcast and HDTV transmissions.

To date, trials are conducted fairly extensively on ADSL and ATM, with ATM forming the backbone from the video servers to the local exchange/curb, and ADSL linking that to the individual homes.

EXERCISE

1. What are the main functions/responsibilities of application layer?
2. Explain the 'cryptography' and basic encryption model.
3. Write short notes on:
   (a) Substitution cipher
   (b) Transposition cipher
   (c) Product cipher
   (d) Block cipher
   (e) Stream cipher
4. With example explain secret key cryptography.

5. With example explain public key cryptography.
6. Write short note on:
   (a) DES algorithm
   (b) AES algorithm
   (c) RSA algorithm
   (d) MD5 algorithm
   (e) Digital signatures
   (f) Digital certificates
7. Explain the security aspects of intranet and internet.
8. Write short notes on:
   (a) DNS system
   (b) E-mail system
   (c) WWW and internet
9. With example explain how to write web page in HTML.
10. Explain what is socket?
11. Write a short note on video on demand.

Unit V

TCP / IP PROTOCOL SUIT

5.1 Introduction to TCP/IP

1. TCP/IP is a suite of protocols, also known as the Internet Protocol Suite.
2. It should not be confused with the OSI reference model, although elements of TCP/IP exist in OSI.
3. The transmission control protocol and the Internet protocol are fundamental to the suite, hence the TCP/IP title.
4. TCP/IP is a set of protocols developed to allow co-operating computers to share resources across a network.
5. A community of researchers centered around the ARPAnet developed this TCP/IP.
6. The **internet protocol suite** is the set of communications protocols that implement the protocol stack on which the Internet and most commercial networks run.
7. The internet protocol suite like many protocol suites can be viewed as a set of layers, each layer solves a set of problems involving the transmission of data, and provides a well-defined service to the upper layer protocols based on using services from some lower layers.
8. Upper layers are logically closer to the user and deal with more abstract data, relying on lower layer protocols to translate data into forms that can eventually be physically transmitted.
9. The Transmission Control Protocol/Internet Protocol (TCP/IP) protocol suite is the engine for the Internet and networks worldwide.
10. Its simplicity and power has lead to its becoming the single network protocol of choice in the world today. In this chapter, we give an overview of the TCP/IP protocol suite.
11. The main design goal of TCP/IP was to build an interconnection of networks, referred to as an Internetwork, or Internet, that provided universal communication services over heterogeneous physical networks.
12. The clear benefit of such an internetwork is the enabling of communication between hosts on different networks, perhaps separated by a large geographical area.

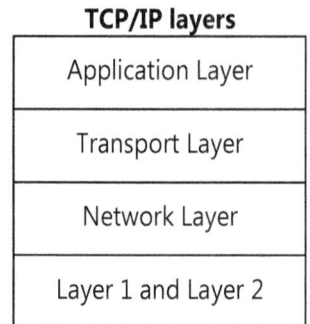

Fig. 5.1: Four Layer TCP/IP Model

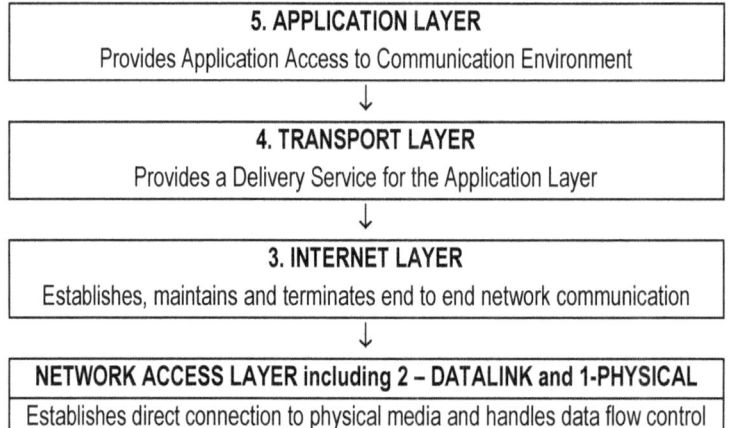

Fig. 5.2: Function of each layer of TCP/IP model

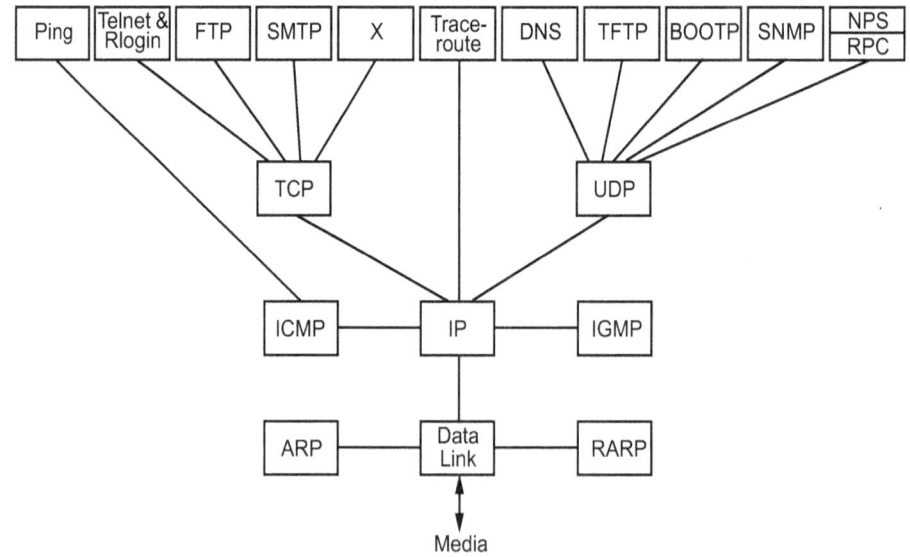

Fig. 5.3: Detail diagram of TCP/IP protocol Suit

13. There are exceptions to my categorizations that don't fit into the normal layering scheme, such as IGMP is normally part of the link layer, but we have tried to list these categorizations according to network functions and their relative importance to the operation of the network.
14. Also note that Ethernet, which is not really a protocol, but an IEEE standard along with PPP, SLIP, Token Ring, and ArcNet are not TCP/IP protocols but may support TCP/IP at the hardware or link layer, depending on the network topology.
15. The list below gives a brief description of each protocol
    - Ethernet - Provides for transport of information between physical locations on Ethernet cable. Data is passed in Ethernet packets
    - SLIP - Serial line IP (SLIP), a form of data encapsulation for serial lines.
    - PPP - Point to point protocol (PPP). A form of serial line data encapsulation that is an improvement over SLIP.
    - IP - Internet Protocol (IP). Except for ARP and RARP all protocols' data packets will be packaged into an IP data packet. Provides the mechanism to use software to address and manage data packets being sent to computers.
    - ICMP - Internet control message protocol (ICMP) provides management and error reporting to help manage the process of sending data between computers.
    - ARP - Address resolution protocol (ARP) enables the packaging of IP data into Ethernet packages. It is the system and messaging protocol that is used to find the Ethernet (hardware) address from a specific IP number. Without this protocol, the Ethernet package could not be generated from the IP package, because the Ethernet address could not be determined.
    - TCP - A reliable connection oriented protocol used to control the management of application level services between computers.
    - UDP - An unreliable connection less protocol used to control the management of application level services between computers.
    - DNS - Domain Name Service, allows the network to determine IP addresses from names and vice versa.
    - RARP - Reverse address resolution protocol (RARP) is used to allow a computer without a local permanent data storage media to determine its IP address from its Ethernet address.
    - BOOTP - Bootstrap protocol is used to assign an IP address to diskless computers and tell it what server and file to load, which will provide it with an operating system.

- DHCP - Dynamic host configuration protocol (DHCP) is a method of assigning and controlling the IP addresses of computers on a given network. It is a server based service that automatically assigns IP numbers when a computer boots. This way the IP address of a computer does not need to be assigned manually. This makes changing networks easier to manage. DHCP can perform all the functions of BOOTP.
- IGMP - Internet Group Management Protocol used to support multicasting.
- SNMP - Simple Network Management Protocol (SNMP). Used to manage all types of network elements based on various data sent and received.
- RIP - Routing Information Protocol (RIP), used to dynamically update router tables on WANs or the Internet.
- OSPF - Open Shortest Path First (OSPF) dynamic routing protocol.
- BGP - Border Gateway Protocol (BGP). A dynamic router protocol to communicate between routers on different systems.
- CIDR - Classless Interdomain Routing (CIDR).
- FTP - File Transfer Protocol (FTP). Allows file transfer between two computers with login required.
- TFTP - Trivial File Transfer Protocol (TFTP). Allows file transfer between two computers with no login required. It is limited, and is intended for diskless stations.
- SMTP - Simple Mail Transfer Protocol (SMTP).
- NFS - Network File System (NFS). A protocol that allows UNIX and Linux systems remotely mount each other's file systems.
- Telnet - A method of opening a user session on a remote host.
- Ping - A program that uses ICMP to send diagnostic messages to other computers to tell if they are reachable over the network.
- Rlogin - Remote login between UNIX hosts. This is outdated and is replaced by Telnet.

16. Each protocol ultimately has it's data packets wrapped in an Ethernet, SLIP, or PPP packet (at the link level) in order to be sent over the Ethernet cable.
17. Some protocol data packets are wrapped sequentially multiple times before being sent.
18. For example, FTP data is wrapped in a TCP packet, which is wrapped in a IP packet which is wrapped in a link packet (normally Ethernet).

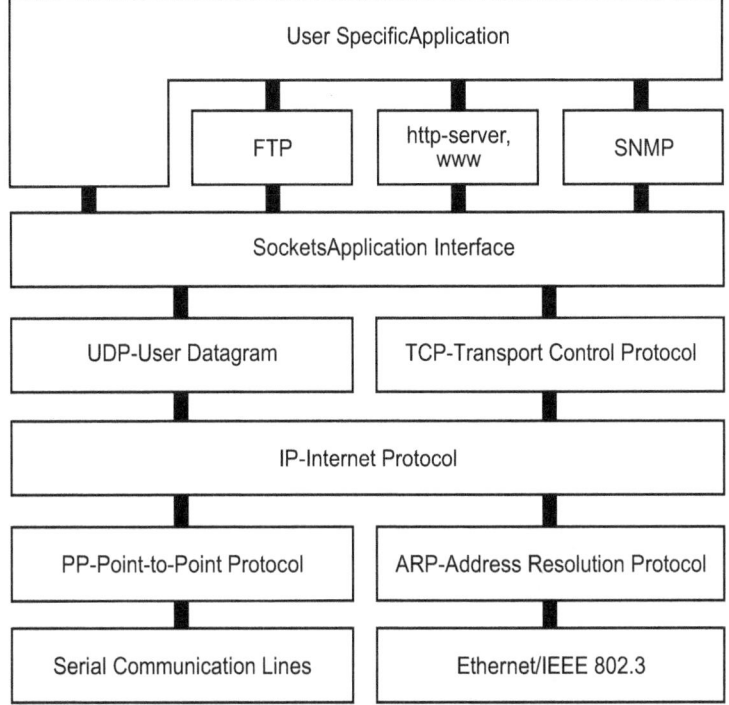

Fig. 5.4: Another example of TCP/IP protocol Suit

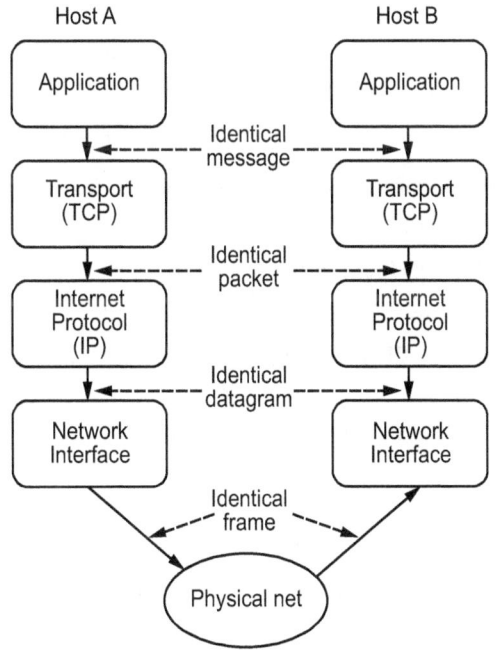

Fig. 5.5: Shows you how TCP/IP works

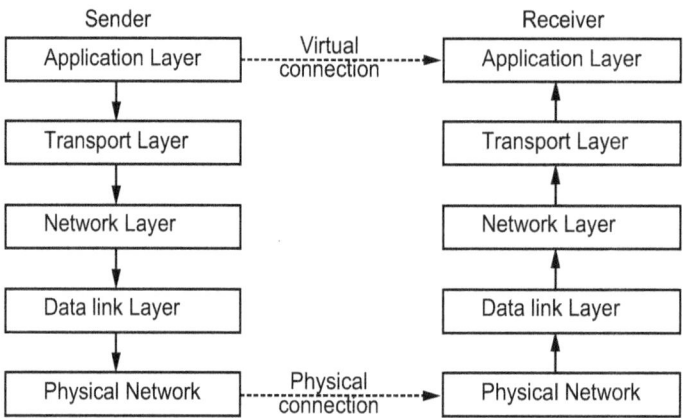

Fig. 5.6: Sender/receiver interaction in TCP/IP

19. An application program, transferring files using TCP/IP, performs the following,
    - the **application layer** passes the data to the transport layer of the source computer.
    - the **transport layer** divides the data into TCP segments adds a header with a sequence number to each TCP segment passes the TCP segments to the IP layer.
    - the **IP layer** creates a packet with a data portion containing the TCP segment adds a packet header containing the source and destination IP addresses determines the physical address of the destination computer passes the packet and destination physical address to the datalink layer.
    - the **datalink layer** transmits the IP packet in the data portion of a frame.
    - the **destination computers datalink layer** discards the datalink header and passes the IP packet to the IP layer.
    - the **destinations IP layer** checks the IP packet header and checksum if okay, it discards the IP header and passes the TCP segment to the TCP layer.
    - the **destinations TCP layer** computes a checksum for the TCP segment data and header if okay, sends acknowledge to the source computer discards the TCP header and passes the data to the application.

5.2 Layers in the Internet Protocol Suite Stack

1. The IP suite uses encapsulation to provide abstraction of protocols and services.
2. Generally a protocol at a higher level uses a protocol at a lower level to help accomplish its aims.

3. The internet protocol stack can be roughly fitted into the four fixed layers and are shown before.
4. TCP/IP is normally considered to be a 4-layer system, as shown in Fig. 5.7.

Application	Telnet, FTP, e-mail, etc.
Transport	TCP, UDP
Network	IP, ICMP, IGMP
Link	Device driver and interface card

Fig. 5.7: The four layers of the TCP/IP protocol suite

Application Layer:
1. This layer is broadly equivalent to the application, presentation and session layers of the OSI model.
2. It gives an application access to the communication environment.
3. Examples of protocols found at this layer are Telnet, FTP (File Transfer Protocol), SNMP (Simple Network Management Protocol), HTTP (Hyper Text Transfer Protocol) and SMTP (Simple Mail Transfer Protocol).
4. An application is a user process cooperating with another process usually on a different host (there is also a benefit to application communication within a single host).
5. The interface between the application and transport layers is defined by port numbers and sockets.

Transport Layer:
1. The transport layer is similar to the OSI transport model, but with elements of the OSI session layer functionality.
2. This layer provides an application layer delivery service.
3. The two protocols found at the transport layer are **TCP (Transmission Control Protocol) and UDP (User Datagram Protocol)**.
4. Either of these two protocols are used by the application layer process, the choice depends on the application's transmission reliability requirements.
5. Transport layer provides the end-to-end data transfer by delivering data from an application to its remote peer.
6. Multiple applications can be supported simultaneously.
7. The most-used transport layer protocol is the Transmission Control Protocol (TCP), which provides connection-oriented reliable data delivery, duplicate data suppression, congestion control, and flow control.
8. **TCP** is a **reliable, connection-oriented** protocol that provides error checking and flow control through a virtual link that it establishes and finally terminates.

9. This gives a reliable service, therefore TCP would be utilized by FTP and SNMP - file transfer and email delivery have to be accurate and error free.
10. **UDP** is an **unreliable, connectionless** protocol that provides data transport with lower network traffic overheads than TCP - UDP does not error check or offer any flow control, this is left to the application process.
11. SNMP uses UDP - SNMP is used to monitor network performance, so its operation must not contribute to congestion.

Network Layer or Internet Layer:
1. This layer is responsible for the routing and delivery of data across networks.
2. It allows communication across networks of the same and different types and carries out translations to deal with dissimilar data addressing schemes.
3. Internetwork layer, also called the *internet layer* or the *network layer*, provides the "virtual network" image of an internet (this layer shields the higher levels from the physical network architecture below it).
4. Internet Protocol (IP) is the most important protocol in this layer.
5. It is a connectionless protocol that doesn't assume reliability from lower layers.
6. IP does *not* provide reliability, flow control, or error recovery.
7. These functions must be provided at a higher level.
8. A message unit in an IP network is called an *IP* datagram.
9. This is the basic unit of information transmitted across TCP/IP networks.
10. Other internetwork layer protocols are IP, ICMP, IGMP, ARP and RARP.
11. With the advent of the concept of Internetworking, additional functionality was added to this layer, namely getting data from the source network to the destination network.
12. This generally involves routing the packet across a network of networks, known as an internet.
13. In the internet protocol suite, IP performs the basic task of getting packets of data from source to destination.
14. IP can carry data for a number of different upper layer protocols; these protocols are each identified by a unique protocol number.
15. ICMP and IGMP are protocols 1 and 2, respectively.
16. Some of the protocols carried by IP, such as ICMP (used to transmit diagnostic information about IP transmission) and IGMP (used to manage multicast data) are layered on top of IP but perform internetwork layer functions, illustrating an incompatibility between the internet and the IP stack and OSI model.
17. All routing protocols, such as BGP, OSPF, and RIP are also really part of the network layer, although they might seem to belong higher in the stack.

Layers 2 and 1 (Network Access Layers):

1. The combination of data link and physical layers deals with pure hardware (wires, satellite links, network interface cards, etc.) and access methods such as **CSMA/CD** (carrier sensed multiple access with collision detection).
2. Ethernet exists at the network access layer - its hardware operates at the physical layer and its medium access control method (CSMA/CD) operates at the datalink layer.
3. Network interface layer, also called the *link layer* or the *data-link layer*, is the interface to the actual network hardware.
4. This interface may or may not provide reliable delivery, and may be packet or stream oriented.
5. In fact, TCP/IP does not specify any protocol here, but can use almost any network interface available, which illustrates the flexibility of the IP layer.
6. The link layer is not really part of the internet protocol suite, but is the method used to pass packets from the network layer on two different hosts.
7. This process can be controlled both in the software device driver for the network card, as well as on firmware or specialist chipsets.
8. These will perform data link functions such as adding a packet header to prepare it for transmission, then actually transmit the frame over a physical medium.
9. The link layer can also be the layer where packets are intercepted to be sent over a virtual private network.
10. When this is done, the link layer data is considered the application data and proceeds back down the IP stack for actual transmission.
11. On the receiving end, the data goes up the IP stack twice (once for the VPN and the second time for routing).

The physical layer is made up of the actual physical network components (hubs, repeaters, network cable, fiber optic cable, coaxial cable, network cards, Host Bus Adapter cards and the associated network connectors: RJ-45, BNC, etc).

5.3 What Platforms Support TCP/IP?

1. *Most* platforms support TCP/IP. However, the quality of that support can vary.
2. Today, most mainstream operating systems have native TCP/IP support (that is, TCP/IP support that is built into the standard operating system distribution).
3. However, older operating systems on some platforms lack such native support.
4. Table describes TCP/IP support for various platforms.
5. If a platform has native TCP/IP support, it is labeled as such. If not, the name of a TCP/IP application is provided.

Table 5.1: Platforms and their support for TCP/IP

Platform	TCP/IP Support
UNIX	Native
DOS	Piper/IP By Ipswitch
Windows	TCPMAN by Trumpet Software
Windows 95	Native
Windows NT	Native
Macintosh	MacTCP or OpenTransport (Sys 7.5+)
OS/2	Native
AS/400 OS/400	Native

6. Platforms that do not natively support TCP/IP can still implement it through the use of proprietary or third-party TCP/IP programs.
7. In these instances, third-party products can offer varied functionality. Some offer very good support and others offer marginal support.
8. For example, some third-party products provide the user with only basic TCP/IP.
9. For most users, this is sufficient. (They simply want to connect to the Net, get their mail, and enjoy easy networking.) In contrast, certain third-party TCP/IP implementations are comprehensive. These may allow manipulation of compression, methods of transport, and other features common to the typical UNIX TCP/IP implementation.
10. Widespread third-party support for TCP/IP has been around for only a few years. Several years ago, for example, TCP/IP support for DOS boxes was very slim.

5.4 Features of TCP/IP

Below are a few of the common features of TCP/IP.

- **File Transfer**
The file transfer protocol (FTP and remote copy (RCP) applications let users transfer files between their computer systems.
- **Terminal Emulation**
Telnet and rlogin provide a method for establishing an interactive connection between computer systems.
- **Transparent distributed file access and sharing**
The Network File System (NFS) uses the IP protocol to extend the file system to support access to directories and disk on other computer systems.
- **Remote command execution**
Using the remote shell (rsh) and remote execution (rexec) programs, users can run programs on remote computers and see the results on their own computer. This lets users of slow computers take advantage of faster computers by running their programs on the faster remote computer.

- **Remote Printing**
  The UNIX command lpr provides remote printing services.

5.5 TCP/IP Encapsulation/Decapsulation of Application Data

1. Encapsulation/decapsulation of application data within a network stack" shows how each layer adds (or removes) header information to data travelling away from (or toward) the application layer.

2. The process of adding header information is termed "encapsulation"; removing header information is termed "decapsulation" or "unencapsulation".

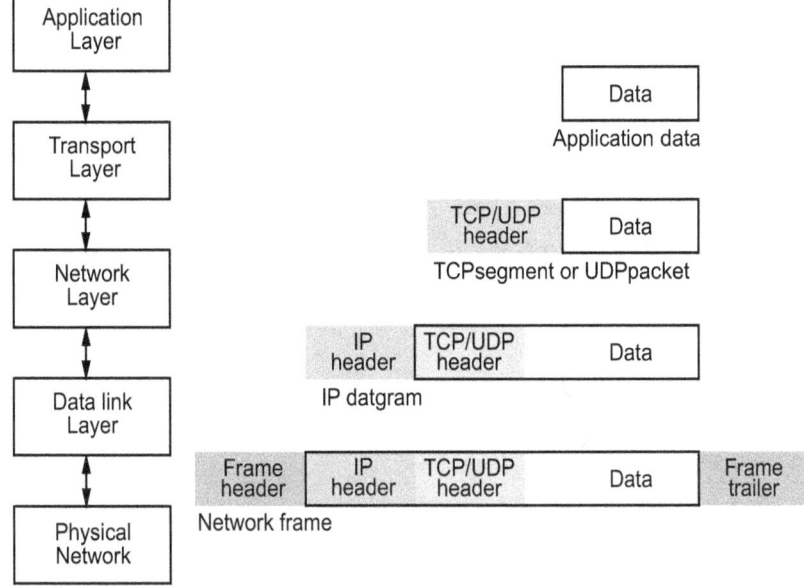

Fig. 5.8: Encapsulation/decapsulation of application data within a network stack

3. Networking application programs send messages or streams of data to one of the Internet transport Layer protocols, either the User Datagram Protocol (UDP) or the Transmission Control Protocol (TCP).

4. These protocols receive the data from the application, divide it into smaller pieces called TCP segments or UDP packets, add a destination address, and then pass the packets down to the next protocol layer, the network layer.

5. The network layer encloses the packet in an Internet Protocol (IP) datagram, adds the datagram header, decides where to send the datagram (either directly to the destination system or indirectly via a router or gateway), and passes the datagram down to the data link layer.

6. The data link layer accepts IP datagrams, encapsulates them within frames that are specific to the network hardware such as Ethernet, Token-Ring or Fiber Distributed Data Interface (FDDI), and transmits these over the network.

7. Frames received by a host are processed through the protocol layers in the reverse order.

8. Each layer strips off the corresponding header information, until the data ends up at the application layer.

9. Frames are received by the data link layer, which strips off the frame header and trailer, and sends the datagram up to the network layer.

10. The network layer strips off the IP header and sends the packet up to the transport layer. The transport layer strips off the TCP or UDP header and sends the data up to the application.

11. As hosts on a network can send and receive information simultaneously, data may be travelling both up and down the layers of the networking stack at the same time.

5.6 Data Flow in TCP/IP Stack in Different Scenarios

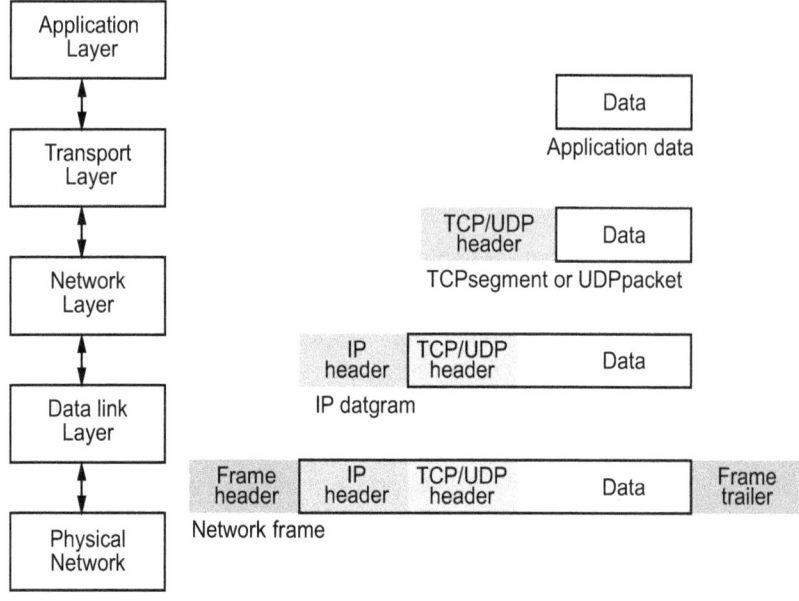

Fig. 5.9: Encapsulation/decapsulation of application using TCP OR UDP

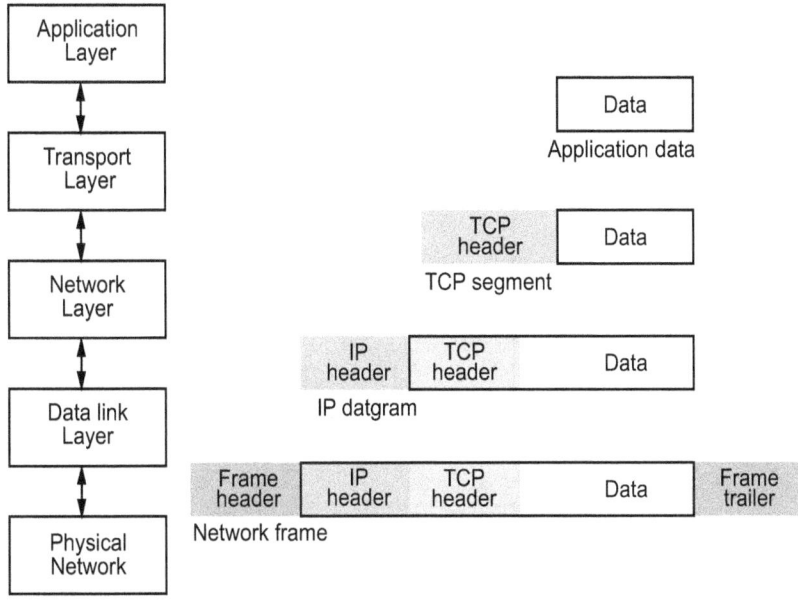

Fig. 5.10: Encapsulation/decapsulation of application using TCP

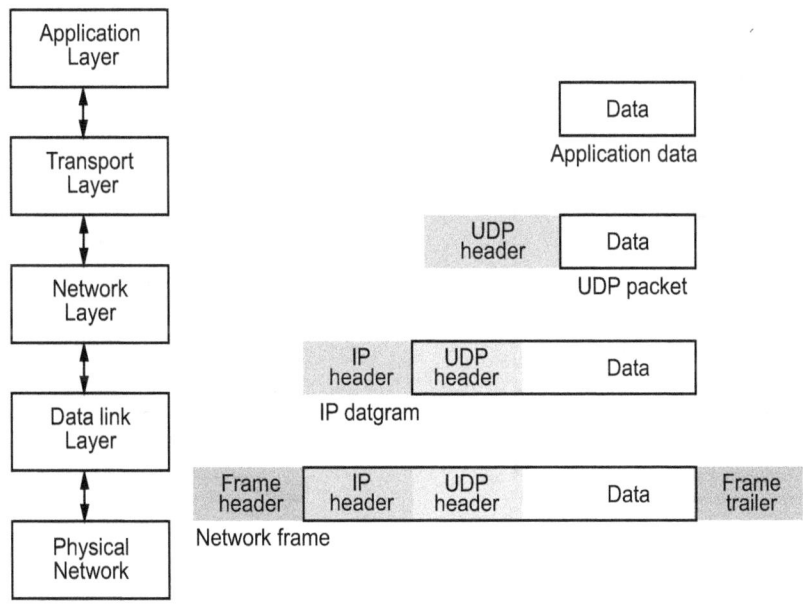

Fig. 5.11: Encapsulation/decapsulation of application using UDP

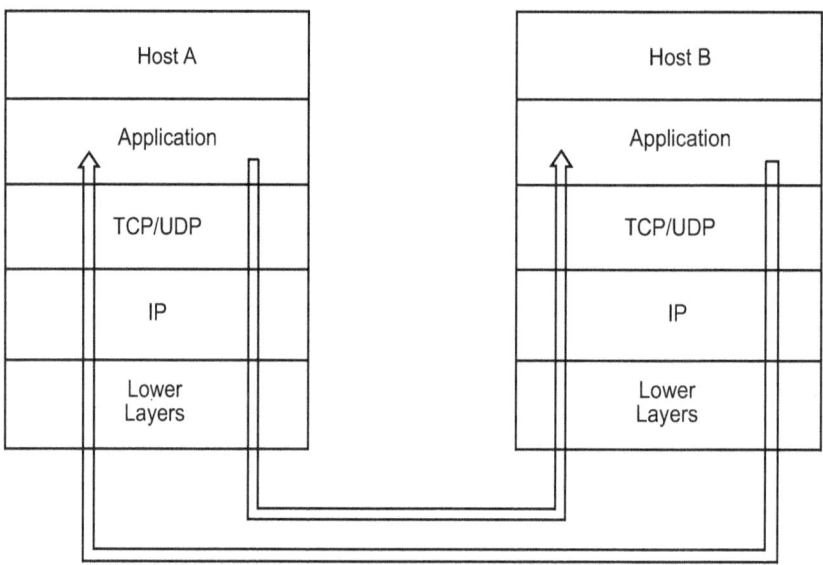

Fig. 5.12: The two types of Data TCP or UDP connection

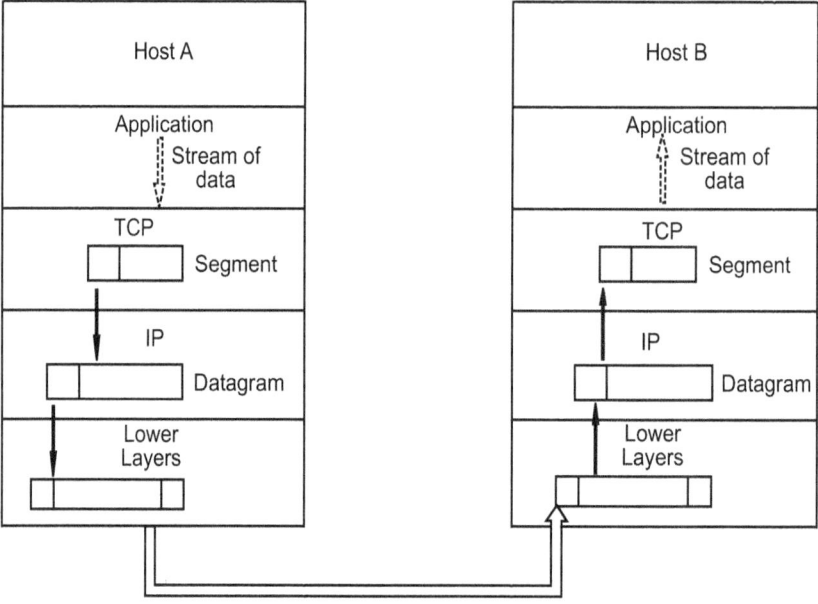

Fig. 5.13: TCP Data Architecture

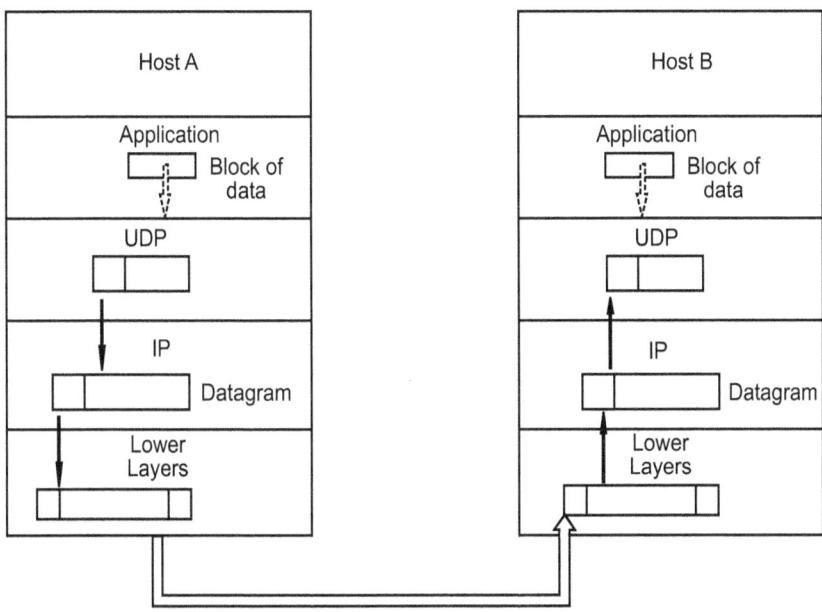

Fig. 5.14: UDP Data Architecture

5.6.1 TCP/IP Support for Different Networks in Different Scenarios

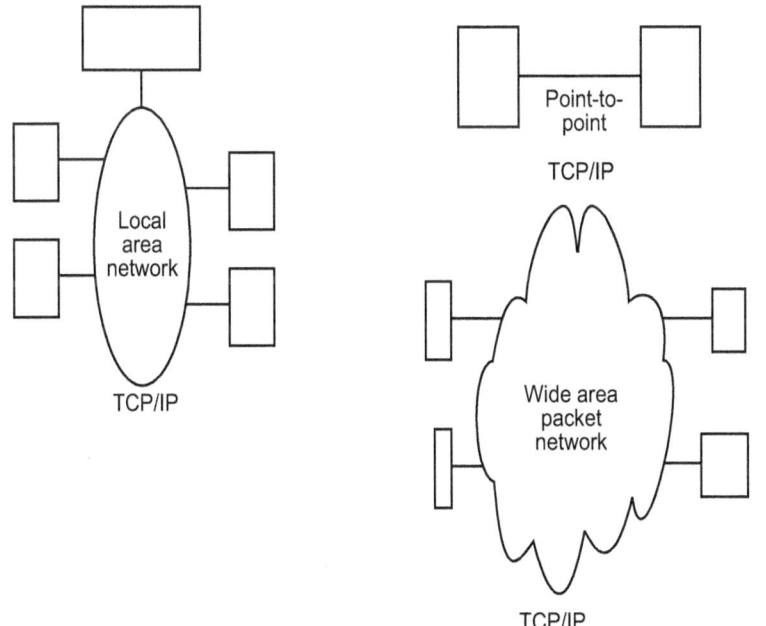

Fig. 5.15: TCP/IP on standalone, LANs, WANs and point to point networks

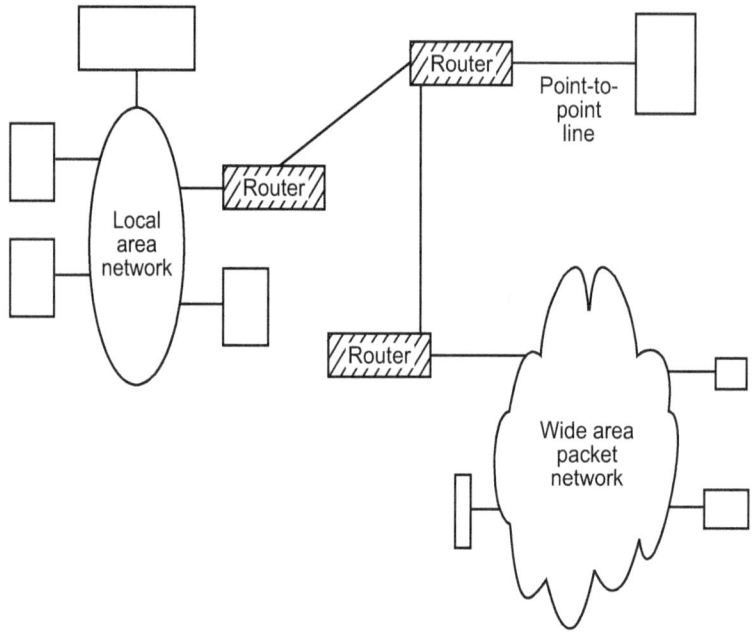

Fig. 5.16: TCP/IP connects, LAN, WAN and point to point networks

5.7 Addressing, Routing, and Multiplexing

To deliver data between two Internet hosts, it is necessary to move data across the network to the correct host, and within that host to the correct user or process.

TCP/IP uses three schemes to accomplish these tasks:

- *Addressing*: IP addresses deliver data to the correct host.
- *Routing*: Gateway deliver data to the correct network.
- *Multiplexing*: Protocol and port numbers deliver data to the correct software module within the host.

Each of these functions is necessary to send data between two co-operating applications across the Internet.

5.7.1 TCP/IP Network Works with Different Addresses

- In TCP/IP three different levels of addresses are used.
  - (a) Physical Address (Hardware Address or Link Address).
  - (b) Logical Address (IP Address).
  - (c) Port Address.

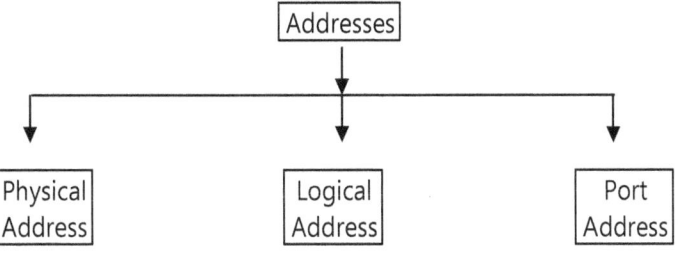

Fig. 5.17: Addresses in TCP/IP

- Physical address is basically a part of Data Link Layer.
- Logical address is a part of Network Layer.
- Port Address is a part of Transport Layer.

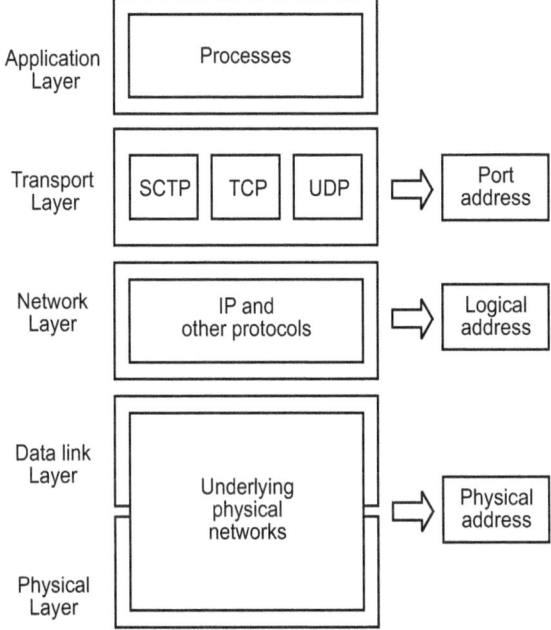

Fig. 5.18: Relationship of layers and addresses in TCP/IP

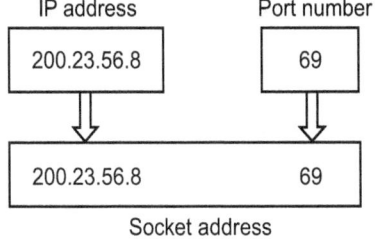

Fig. 5.19: Socket address

Addresses:

1. MAC addresses   2. IP addresses   3. Port addresses

- The reason, there is an address for the hardware card (Ethernet address, also called MAC address), and another assigned address for that same card (IP address), is to keep the parts of the network system that deal with the hardware and the software, independent of each other.
- Also there are hundreds of ports and services registered with the Internet Assigned Number Authority (IANA) in practice, less than one hundred are in common use. These are known as port addresses.
- Services have assigned ports so that a client can find the service easily on a remote host. For example, FTP servers listen at port 21, telnet servers listen at port 23, SMTP (Simple Mail Transport Protocol) servers listen at port 25, DNS servers listen at port 53 and WEB servers listen at port 80 (HTTP, the protocol used for accessing Web servers). Client applications, like a telnet program or mail order reader, use randomly assigned ports typically greater than 1023.

Typical MAC Addresses:

00000C	Cisco
00067C	Cisco
001111	Intel
00AA00	Intel
000011	Tektronix
00003D	AT&T
000048	Epson
0060B0	Hewlett-Packard
0000E1	Hitachi (laptop built-in)
000204	Novell NE3200
0004AC	IBM
002063	Wipro Infotech Ltd.
004043	Nokia Data Communications
004F49	Realtek
00809F	Alcatel Business Systems
0050BA	D-Link
0080C8	D-Link

MAC addresses uniquely identify each node in a network at the Media Access Control Layer, the part of Data Link Layer, the one that directly interfaces with the media, such as the actual wires in a twisted-pair Ethernet. In modern Ethernets the MAC address consists of six bytes (or 48 bits) which are usually displayed in hexadecimal e.g.

00 - 0A - CC - 77 - FO - 7D

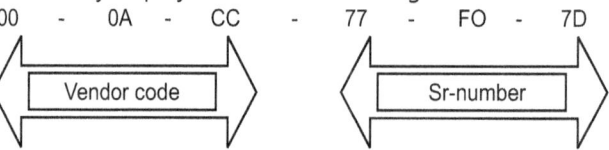

IP Host Address:

1. The *Internetwork Protocol* identifies hosts with a 32-bit number called *IP address* or *a host address*.
2. To avoid confusion with MAC addresses, which are machine or station addresses, the term IP address will be used to designate this kind of address. IP addresses are written as four dot-separated decimal numbers between 0-255.
3. IP addresses must be unique among all connected machines (are any hosts that you can get over a network or connected set of networks, including your local area network, remote offices joined by the company's wide-area network, or even the entire Internet community).
4. The *Internet Protocol* moves data between the hosts in the form of datagrams. Each datagram is delivered to the address contained in the destination address of the datagrams header.
5. The *Destination Address* is a standard 32-bit IP address that contains sufficient information to uniquely identify a network and a specific host on that network.
6. If your network is connected to the Internet, you have to get a range of IP addresses assigned to your machines through a central network administration authority. The IP address uniqueness requirement differs from the MAC addresses.
7. IP addresses are unique only on connected networks, but machine MAC addresses are unique in the world, independent of any connectivity. Part of the reason for the difference in the uniqueness requirement is that IP addresses are 32-bits, while MAC addresses are 48-bits, so mapping every possible MAC address into an IP address requires some overlap.
8. Of course, not every machine on a Ethernet is running IP protocols, so the many-to-one mapping isn't as bad as the numbers might indicate. There are a variety of reasons why the IP address is only 32 bits, while the MAC address is 48 bits, most of which are historical.
9. Since the network and data link layer use different addressing schemes, some system is needed to convert or map the IP addresses to the MAC addresses. Transport-layer services and user processes use IP addresses to identify hosts, but packets that go out on the network need MAC addresses.
10. The *Address Resolution Protocol (ARP)* is used to convert the 32-bit IP address of a host into its 48-bit MAC address. When a hosts wants to map an IP address to a MAC address, it broadcasts an ARP request on the network, asking for the host using the IP address to respond.
11. The host that sees its own IP address in the request returns its MAC address to the sender. With a MAC address, the sending host can transmit a packet on the Ethernet and know that the receiving host will recognize it.

Network Addressing and IP Address Classes:

IP addresses are broken into 4 octets (IPv4) separated by dots called dotted decimal notation. An octet is a byte consisting of 8 bits. The IPv4 addresses are in the following form:

192.168.10.1

There are two parts of an IP address:
- Network ID
- Host ID

The various classes of networks specify additional or fewer octets to designate the network ID versus the host ID.

Class	1st Octet	2nd Octet	3rd Octet	4th Octet
A	Net ID		Host ID	
B	Net ID			Host ID
C	Net ID			Host ID

Class A-E Networks:

The addressing scheme for class A through E networks is shown below.

Note: We use the 'x' character here to denote don't care situations which includes all possible numbers at the location. It is many times used to denote networks.

Network Type	Address Range	Normal Netmask	Comments
Class A	001.x.x.x to 126.x.x.x	255.0.0.0	For very large networks
Class B	128.1.x.x to 191.254.x.x	255.255.0.0	For medium size networks
Class C	192.0.1.x to 223.255.254.x	255.255.255.0	For small networks
Class D	224.x.x.x to 239.255.255.255		Used to support multicasting
Class E	240.x.x.x to 247.255.255.255		Reserved for future use

Class A Addressing:

- first byte specifies the network portion.
- remaining bytes specify the host portion.
- the highest order bit of the network byte is always 0.
- network values of 0 and 127 are reserved.
- there are 126 class A networks.
- there are more than 16 million host values for each class A network.

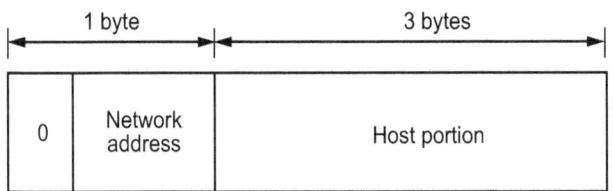

Fig. 5.19 (a)

Class B Addressing:
- the first two bytes specify the network portion.
- the last two bytes specify the host portion.
- the highest order bits 6 and 7 of the network portion are 10.
- there are more than 16 thousand class B networks.
- there are 65 thousand nodes in each class B network.

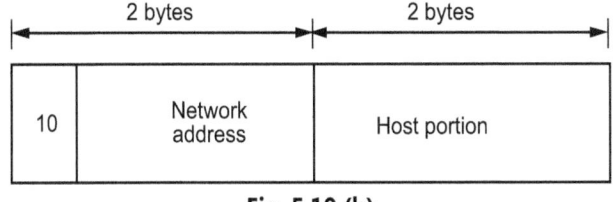

Fig. 5.19 (b)

Class C Addressing:
- the first three bytes specify the network portion.
- the last byte specifies the host portion.
- the highest order bits 5, 6 and 7 of the network portion are 110.
- there are more than 2 million class C networks.
- there are 254 nodes in each class C network.

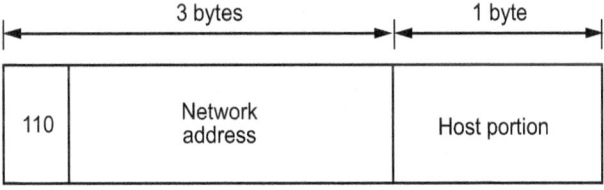

Fig. 5.20

Class 'D' Addressing:
- Class D address defines a group-ID and used for multicasting.
- Internet authorities have designated some multicast addresses to specific groups.

Table 5.2: Category Addresses

Address	Group
224.0.0.0	Reserved
2240.0.1	ALL SYSTEMS on this SUBNET
224.0.0.2	ALL ROUTERS on this SUBNET
224.0.0.4	DVMRP ROUTERS
224.0.0.5	OFPFIGP ALL ROUTERS
224.0.0.6	OSPFIGP Designated ROUTERS
224.0.0.7	ST Routers
224.0.0.8	ST Hosts
224.0.0.9	RIP2 Routers
224.0.0.10	IGRP Routers
224.0.0.11	Mobile Agents

- Category addresses are multicast addresses used for some special use as mentioned in Table 5.2.
- Some multicast addresses are used for conferencing and teleconferencing.

Table 5.3: Addresses for conferencing

Address	Group
224.0.1.7	AUDIONEWS
224.0.1.10	IETF-1-LOW-AUDIO
224.0.1.11	IETF-1-AUDIO
224.0.1.12	IETF-1-VIDEO
224.0.1.13	IETF-2-LOW-AUDIO
224.0.1.14	IETF-2-AUDIO
224.0.1.15	IETF-2-VIDEO
224.0.1.16	MUSIC-SERVICE
224.0.1.17	SEANET-TELEMETRY
224.0.1.18	SEANET-IMAGE

- Broadcast addresses are used for Broadcast communication.
- The Internet allows broadcasting only at the local level.
- No broadcasting is allowed at the global level, that means a system (host or router) cannot send a message to all hosts and routers in the Internet.

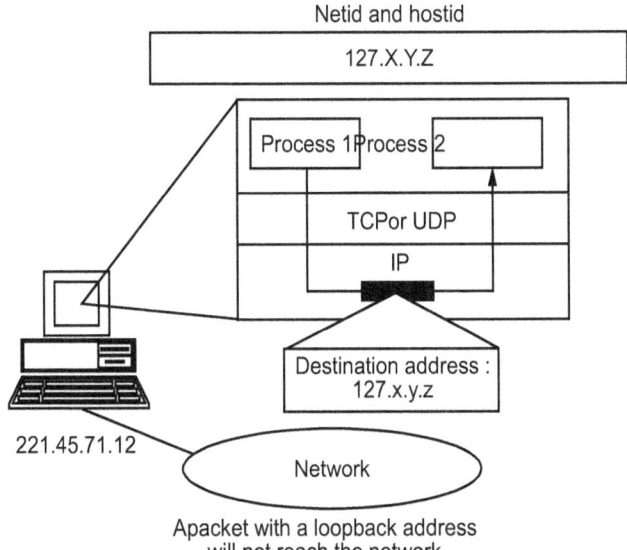

Fig. 5.21: Example of loopback address

- If IP address with the first byte equal to 127 is used for the loopback address.
- This address is used to test the IP software on the same machine.
- For example, **Ping 127.0.0.0** can send packet with a loopback address as a destination address to see if the IP software is capable of receiving and processing a packet.
- Also on the some machine client programs can test server program is running properly and vice-versa.

Private Address Space:
The Internet Assigned Numbers Authority (IANA) has reserved the following three blocks of the IP address space for private Internets:
- 10.0.0.0 - 10.255.255.255 -----A
- 172.16.0.0 - 172.31.255.255 -----B
- 192.168.0.0 - 192.168.255.255 ------C

Subnet Masks:
1. Subnetting is the process of breaking down a main class A, B, or C network into subnets for routing purposes.
2. A subnet mask is the same basic thing as a netmask with the only real difference being that you are breaking a larger organizational network into smaller parts, and each smaller section will use a different set of address numbers.
3. This will allow network packets to be routed between subnetworks. When doing subnetting, the number of bits in the subnet mask determine the number of available subnets.

4. Two to the power of the number of bits minus two is the number of available subnets. When setting up subnets the following must be determined:
   - Number of segments
   - Hosts per segment
5. **Subnetting provides the following advantages:**
   - Network traffic isolation - There is less network traffic on each subnet.
   - Simplified Administration - Networks may be managed independently.
   - Improved security - Subnets can isolate internal networks so they are not visible from external networks.
6. A 14 bit subnet mask on a class B network only allows 2 node addresses for WAN links. A routing algorithm like OSPF must be used for this approach.
7. These protocols allow the variable length subnet masks (VLSM). RIP and IGRP don't support this. Subnet mask information must be transmitted on the update packets for dynamic routing protocols for this to work.
8. The router subnet mask is different than the WAN interface subnet mask.
9. One network ID is required by each of:
   - Subnet
   - WAN connection
10. One host ID is required by each of:
    - Each NIC on each host.
    - Each router interface.
11. Types of subnet masks:
    - Default - Fits into a Class A, B, or C network category.
    - Custom - Used to break a default network such as a Class A, B, or C network into subnets.

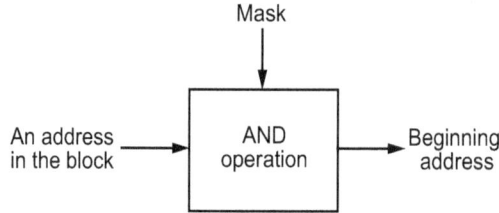

Fig. 5.22: Masking Concept

Fig. 5.23: AND Operation

Table 5.4: Default Masks

Class	Mask in Binary	Mask in dotted-decimal
A	11111111 00000000 00000000 00000000	255.0.0.0
B	11111111 11111111 00000000 00000000	255.255.0.0
C	11111111 111111111 11111111 00000000	255.255.255.0

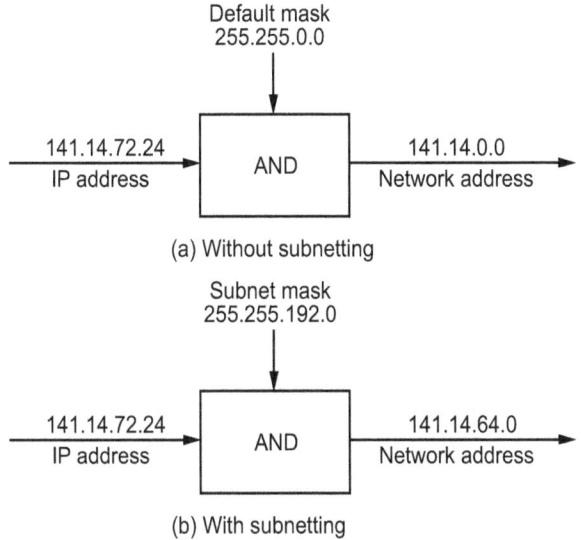

Fig. 5.24: Default mask and subnet mask

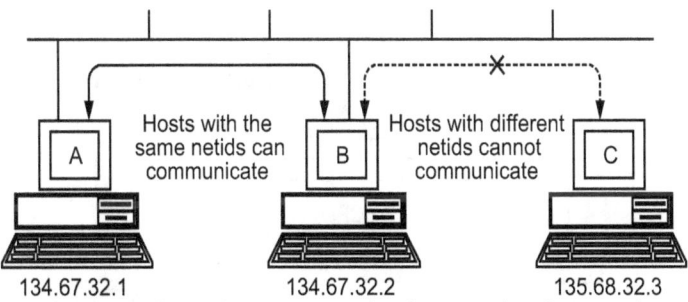

Fig. 5.25: Shows host communication on a local network

12. A subnet is defined by applying a bitmask, the subnetmask, to the IP address. If a bit is on the mask, that equivalent bit in the address is interpreted as a network bit.
13. If the bit in the mask is off, the bit belongs to the host part of the address. The subnet is only known locally.
14. To the rest of the Internet, the address is still interpreted as a standard IP address.

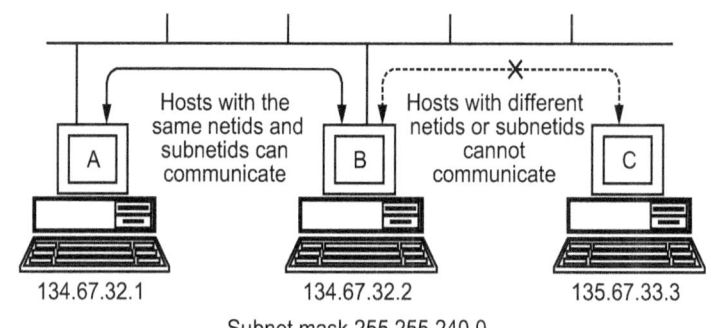

Fig. 5.26: Shows host communication with subnetting

5.7.2 DHCP

Introduction:
1. With the rapid growth of TCP/IP (Transmission Control Protocol/Internet Protocol, the common transmission protocol for communicating over the Internet) networks, tools are needed to automate administrative functions in managing large TCP/IP networks.
2. The Dynamic Host Configuration Protocol (DHCP) is a set of rules for dynamically allocating IP addresses and configuration options to workstations on a network. An IP (Internet Protocol) address is a 32-bit binary number written as four decimal numbers separated by periods that is used to uniquely identify a workstation on the Internet.
3. An Internet address (like 207.160.153.254 or 198.209.5.1) is analogous to a telephone number. While the telephone network directs calls to you by using your telephone number, the Internet network directs data to you by using your IP number.
4. This number can be statically (or manually) assigned by the administrator for a network workstation or assigned to it dynamically by a central server.

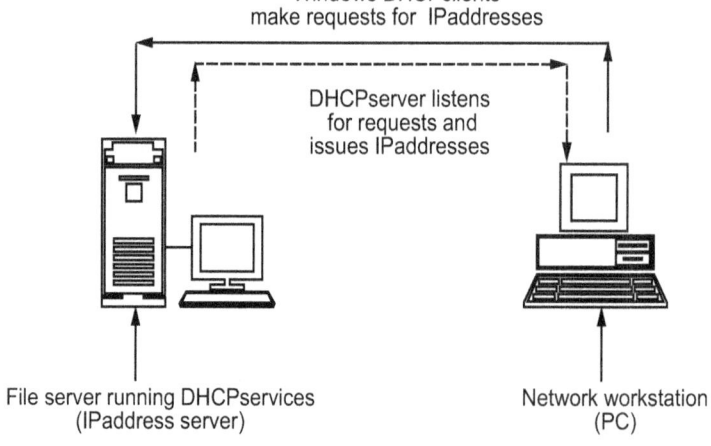

Fig. 5.27: DHCP Server and Client

How Does DHCP Work?
1. DHCP service runs on a central server that dynamically assigns an IP address to individual PCs or workstations.
2. This protocol delivers IP information on a local area network (LAN) or across several LANs.
3. DHCP reduces the work spent administering statically assigned IP addresses on a large network.
4. For example, the administrator does not have to visit each workstation on the network to configure it or manually make changes to its IP address if there is a network topology change.
5. Other network configuration parameters (such as gateway and DNS, Domain Name Services) can be passed along to a workstation with the IP. We will discuss a few of these important options.
6. The DHCP protocol provides a means of passing configuration parameters to requesting DHCP client workstation or hosts on a TCP/IP network. The term *host* refers to any IP device on a network such as a router, server or workstation.
7. The term *client* refers to a host requesting information from another host or server that provides this information. A *server* is a host that is running an application or service that provides information to requesting clients.
8. A DHCP server is a host on a network that runs a DHCP service. The DHCP service listens to network traffic waiting for DHCP broadcast requests. Once a request is heard, the server responds to the request with an IP address and additional (optional) configuration parameters.
9. When you set up the DHCP service you designate what IP address ranges you wish to distribute. You can also choose to pass Network Gateway information and DNS address (Domain Name Services) information.

DHCP Protocol Parameter Options:
1. Additional workstation configuration parameter options can be included in the DHCP protocol during the DHCP session.
2. These options are not a required part of the protocol but are extensions of the protocol that allow for optional configuration parameters.
3. Significant basic configuration information distributed in this protocol with the IP address might include:
    - IP address and mask of the workstation (required),
    - Gateway address for the workstation to reach the Internet,
    - DNS (Domain Name Services) server so the workstation can resolve Web addresses to IP address on the Internet.

4. Additional options not discussed here can include listing of other servers and services:
   - Log Servers
   - Time-Servers
   - Cookie Servers
   - Line Printers

Who Supports This Protocol?
1. Most Network Operating Systems (NOS) support DHCP, including Microsoft, Novell, IBM and UNIX platforms.
2. It is relatively easy to implement on any NOS, has been around for some time and is pretty stable.
3. There are three methods for DHCP to allocate IP addresses to workstations.
   - Manual allocation
   - Automatic allocation
   - Dynamic allocation
4. In the *manual allocation method*, the network administrator on the DHCP server manually configures the client's IP address in the server.
5. When the client workstation makes the request for an IP address, the server looks at the MAC address (Media Access Control address; manufacture's unique address of the network card) and assigns the client the manually set IP address.
6. In the *automatic allocation method*, the DHCP client workstation is assigned an IP address when it first contacts the DHCP server.
7. In this method the IP address is randomly assigned and is not set in the server. The IP address is permanently assigned to the DHCP client and is not reused by another DHCP client.
8. In the *dynamic allocation method*, the DHCP server assigns an IP address to a requesting client workstation on a temporary basis. The IP address is leased to the DHCP client for a specified duration of time.
9. When this lease expires, the IP address is revoked from the client and the client is required to surrender the address. If the DHCP client still needs an IP address to perform its functions, it can request another IP address.

Running DHCP Services Across Multiple Networks:
1. DHCP, by design, is not routable.
2. However most routers support a helper configuration option, or relay-agent that allows DHCP requests to be forwarded between connected or routed networks.

3. You can easily implement a single point of IP address management across expanded local and wide area networks where the DHCP server provides support for multiple IP address blocks.
4. Most network operating system developers are adding additional support for the ever changing IP addressing scheme.
5. Several have adopted support for the next release of the IP addressing scheme, IP Version 6 (an expanded IP address scheme changing the current 32-bit address to a 128-bit address).

Summary:
DHCP is a protocol designed to save time managing IPs on a large network. The DHCP service runs on a network server that allows centralized management of IP addresses to workstations on a network. Most Network Operating Systems (or network servers) support this feature and include it with their operating system.

5.7.3 IPv6 (IPng OR IP Next Generation)

1. IPv6 is short for "Internet Protocol Version 6". IPv6 is the "next generation" protocol designed by the IETF (The Internet Engineering Task Force) to replace the current version Internet Protocol, IP Version 4 ("IPv4").
2. Most of today's Internet uses IPv4, which is now nearly twenty years old.
3. IPv4 has been remarkably resilient in spite of its age, but it is beginning to have problems. Most importantly, there is a growing shortage of IPv4 addresses, which are needed by all new machines added to the Internet.
4. IPv6 fixes a number of problems in IPv4, such as the limited number of available IPv4 addresses. It also adds many improvements to IPv4 in areas such as routing and network auto configuration.
5. IPv6 is expected to gradually replace IPv4, with the two coexisting for a number of years during a transition period.

IPv6, and Key Features:
1. The IETF became aware of a global shortage of IPv4 addresses, and technical obstacles in deploying new protocols due to limitations imposed by IPv4.
2. An IPng (IP next generation) effort was started to solve these issues.
3. In a single sentence, *IPv6 is a re-engineering effort against IP technology*.
4. Key features are listed below:
    - **Larger IP address space.** IPv4 uses only 32 bits for IP address space, which allows only 4 billion nodes to be identified on the Internet. 4 billion may look like a large number; however, it is less than the human population on the earth ! IPv6 allows 128 bits for IP address space, allowing

340282366920938463463374607431768211456 (three hundred forty undecillion) nodes to be uniquely identified on the Internet. A larger address space allows true **end to end communication**, without short term workarounds against the IPv4 address shortage.

- **Deploy more recent technologies.** After IPv4 was specified 20 years ago, we saw many technical improvements in networking. IPv6 includes a number of those improvements in its base specification, allowing people to assume these features are available everywhere, anytime. "Recent technologies" include, but are not limited to, the following:
  - **Autoconfiguration.** With IPv4, DHCP exists but is optional. A novice user can get into trouble if they visit another site without a DHCP server. With IPv6, a "stateless host autoconfiguration" mechanism is mandatory. This is much simpler to use and manage than IPv4 DHCP.
  - **Security.** With IPv4, IPsec is optional and you need to ask the peer if it supports IPsec. With IPv6, IPsec support is mandatory. By mandating IPsec, we can assume that you can secure your IP communication whenever you talk to IPv6 devices.
  - **Friendly to traffic engineering technologies.** IPv6 was designed to allow better support for traffic engineering like diffserv or intserv (RSVP). We do not have a single standard for traffic engineering yet, so the IPv6 base specification reserves a 24-bit space in the header field for those technologies and is able to adapt to coming standards better than IPv4.
  - **Multicast.** Multicast is mandatory in IPv6, which was optional in IPv4. The IPv6 base specifications themselves extensively use multicast.
  - **Better support for ad-hoc networking.** Scoped addresses allow better support for ad-hoc networking. IPv6 supports any cast addresses, which can also contribute to service discoveries.
- **A cure to routing table growth.** The IPv4 backbone routing table size has been a big headache to ISPs and backbone operators. The IPv6 addressing specification restricts the number of backbone routing entries by advocating route aggregation.
- **Simplified header structures.** IPv6 has simpler packet header structures than IPv4. It will allow future vendors to implement hardware acceleration for IPv6 routers easier.
- **Allows flexible protocol extensions.** IPv6 allows more flexible protocol extensions than IPv4 does, by introducing a *protocol header chain*. Even though IPv6 allows flexible protocol extensions, IPv6 does not impose overhead to intermediate routers. It is achieved by splitting headers into two flavours: the headers intermediate routers need to examine, and the headers the end nodes will examine. This also eases hardware acceleration for IPv6 routers.

- **Smooth transition from IPv4.** There were number of transition considerations made during the IPv6 discussions. Also, there are large number of transition mechanisms available. You can pick the most suitable one for your site.
- **Follows the key design principles of IPv4.** IPv4 was a very successful design, as proven by the ultra large-scale global deployment. IPv6 is "new version of IP", and it follows many of the design features that made IPv4 very successful. This will also allow smooth transition from IPv4 to IPv6.

Differences Between IPv4 and IPv6:

Table 5.5 Highlights some of the key differences between IPv4 and IPv6.

Table 5.5: Differences between IPv4 and IPv6

IPv4	IPv6
Source and destination addresses are 32 bits (4 bytes) in length.	Source and destination addresses are 128 bits (16 bytes) in length. For more information, see "IPv6 Addressing."
IPsec support is optional.	IPsec support is required. For more information, see "IPv6 Header."
No identification of packet flow for QoS handling by routers is present within the IPv4 header.	Packet flow identification for QoS handling by routers is included in the IPv6 header using the Flow Label field. For more information, see "IPv6 Header."
Fragmentation is done by both routers and the sending host.	Fragmentation is not done by routers, only by the sending host. For more information, see "IPv6 Header."
Header includes a checksum.	Header does not include a checksum.
Header includes options.	All optional data is moved to IPv6 extension headers.
Address Resolution Protocol (ARP) uses broadcast ARP Request frames to resolve an IPv4 address to a link layer address.	ARP Request frames are replaced with multicast Neighbour Solicitation messages.
Internet Group Management Protocol (IGMP) is used to manage local subnet group membership.	IGMP is replaced with Multicast Listener Discovery (MLD) messages.
ICMP Router Discovery is used to determine the IPv4 address of the best default gateway and is optional.	ICMP Router Discovery is replaced with ICMPv6 Router Solicitation and Router Advertisement messages and is required.
Broadcast addresses are used to send traffic to all nodes on a subnet.	There are no IPv6 broadcast addresses. Instead, a link-local scope all-nodes multicast address is used.

IPv4	IPv6
Must be configured either manually or through DHCP.	Does not require manual configuration or DHCP.
Uses host address (A) resource records in the Domain Name System (DNS) to map host names to IPv4 addresses.	Uses host address (AAAA) resource records in the Domain Name System (DNS) to map host names to IPv6 addresses.
IPv4	IPv6
Uses pointer (PTR) resource records in the IN-ADDR.ARPA DNS domain to map IPv4 addresses to host names.	Uses pointer (PTR) resource records in the IP6.ARPA DNS domain to map IPv6 addresses to host names.
Must support a 576-byte packet size (possibly fragmented).	Must support a 1280-byte packet size (without fragmentation).

IPv6 Packets over LAN Media

A link layer frame containing an IPv6 packet consists of the following structure:
- Link Layer Header and Trailer – The encapsulation placed on the IPv6 packet at the link layer.
- IPv6 Header – The new IPv6 header. For more information, see "IPv6 Header."
- Payload – The payload of the IPv6 packet. For more information, see "IPv6 Header."

Fig. 5.28 shows the structure of a link layer frame containing an IPv6 packet.

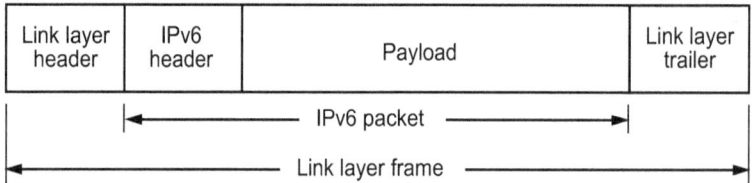

Fig. 5.28: IPv6 packets at the link layer

For typical LAN technologies such as Ethernet, Token Ring, and Fiber Distributed Data Interface (FDDI), IPv6 packets are encapsulated in one of two ways—with either the Ethernet II header or a Sub-Network Access Protocol (SNAP) header used by IEEE 802.3 (Ethernet), IEEE 802.5 (Token Ring), and FDDI.

The IPv6 Address Space:

1. The most obvious distinguishing feature of IPv6 is its use of much larger addresses.
2. The size of an address in IPv6 is 128 bits, which is four times the larger than an IPv4 address. A 32-bit address space allows for 2^{32} or 4,294,967,296 possible addresses.
3. A 128-bit address space allows for 2^{128} or
   340, 282, 366, 920, 938, 463, 463, 374, 607, 431, 768, 211, 456 (or $3.4 \infty 10^{38}$) possible addresses.

4. In the late 1970s when the IPv4 address space was designed, it was unimaginable that it could be exhausted. However, due to changes in technology and an allocation practice that did not anticipate the recent explosion of hosts on the Internet, the IPv4 address space was consumed to the point that by 1992 it was clear a replacement would be necessary.
5. With IPv6, it is even harder to conceive that the IPv6 address space will be consumed. To help put this number in perspective, a 128-bit address space provides 655, 570, 793, 348, 866, 943, 898, 599 (6.5 ∞ 10^{23}) addresses for every square meter of the Earth's surface.
6. It is important to remember that the decision to make the IPv6 address 128 bits in length was not so that every square meter of the Earth could have 6.5×10^{23} addresses.
7. Rather, the relatively large size of the IPv6 address is designed to be subdivided into hierarchical routing domains that reflect the topology of the modern-day Internet.
8. The use of 128 bits allows for multiple levels of hierarchy and flexibility in designing hierarchical addressing and routing that is currently lacking on the IPv4-based Internet.

IPv6 Address Syntax:

1. IPv4 addresses are represented in dotted-decimal format. This 32-bit address is divided along 8-bit boundaries. Each set of 8 bits is converted to its decimal equivalent and separated by periods.
2. For IPv6, the 128-bit address is divided along 16-bit boundaries, and each 16-bit block is converted to a 4-digit hexadecimal number and separated by colons. The resulting representation is called colon-hexadecimal.
3. The following is an IPv6 address in binary form:
   0010000111011010000000001101001100000000000000000010111100111011
   0000001010101010000000001111111111111111000101000100111000101101 0
   The 128-bit address is divided along 16-bit boundaries:
   0010000111011010 0000000011010011 0000000000000000 0010111100111011
   0000001010101010 0000000011111111 1111111000101000 1001110001011010
   Each 16-bit block is converted to hexadecimal and delimited with colons. The result is:
   21DA:00D3:0000:2F3B:02AA:00FF:FE28:9C5A
4. IPv6 representation can be further simplified by removing the leading zeros within each 16-bit block. However, each block must have at least a single digit. With leading zero suppression, the address representation becomes:
   21DA:D3:0:2F3B:2AA:FF:FE28:9C5A

IPv4 Addresses and IPv6 Equivalents:

Table 5.6 lists both IPv4 addresses and addressing concepts and their IPv6 equivalents.

Table 5.6: IPv4 Addressing Concepts and Their IPv6 Equivalents

IPv4 Address	IPv6 Address
Internet address classes	Not applicable in IPv6
Multicast addresses (224.0.0.0/4)	IPv6 multicast addresses (FF00::/8)
Broadcast addresses	Not applicable in IPv6
Unspecified address is 0.0.0.0	Unspecified address is::
Loopback address is 127.0.0.1	Loopback address is:: 1
Public IP addresses	Global unicast addresses
Private IP addresses (10.0.0.0/8, 172.16.0.0/12, and 192.168.0.0/16)	Site-local addresses (FEC0::/10)
Auto configured addresses (169.254.0.0/16)	Link-local addresses (FE80::/64)
Text representation: Dotted decimal notation	Text representation: Colon hexadecimal format with suppression of leading zeros and zero compression. IPv4-compatible addresses are expressed in dotted decimal notation.
Network bits representation: Subnet mask in dotted decimal notation or prefix length	Network bits representation: Prefix length notation only
DNS name resolution: IPv4 host address (A) resource record	DNS name resolution: IPv6 host address (AAAA) resource record
DNS reverse resolution: IN-ADDR.ARPA domain	DNS reverse resolution: IP6.ARPA domain

The IPv6 Packet:

5. The IPv6 packet is composed of two main parts: the header and the payload.

6. The header is in the first 40 octets of the packet and contains both source and destination addresses (128 bits each), as well as the version (4-bit IP version), traffic class (8 bits, Packet Priority), flow label (20 bits, QoS management), payload length (16 bits), next header (8 bits), and hop limit (8 bits, time to live).

7. The payload can be up to 64k in size in standard mode, or larger with a "jumbo payload" option.

8. The *protocol* field of IPv4 is replaced with a *Next Header* field. This field usually specifies the transport layer protocol used by a packet's payload.

9. In the presence of options, however, the Next Header field specifies the presence of an extra *options* header, which then follows the IPv6 header; the payload's protocol itself is specified in a field of the options header.

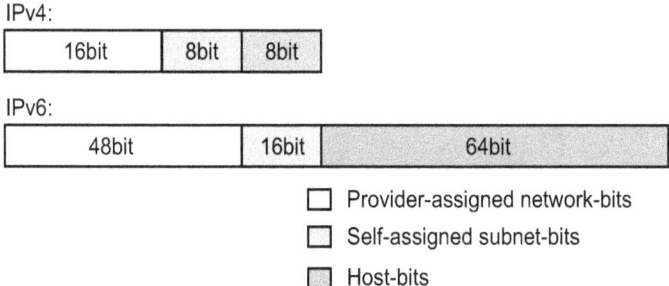

Fig. 5.29: IPv6 addresses have a similar structure to class B addresses

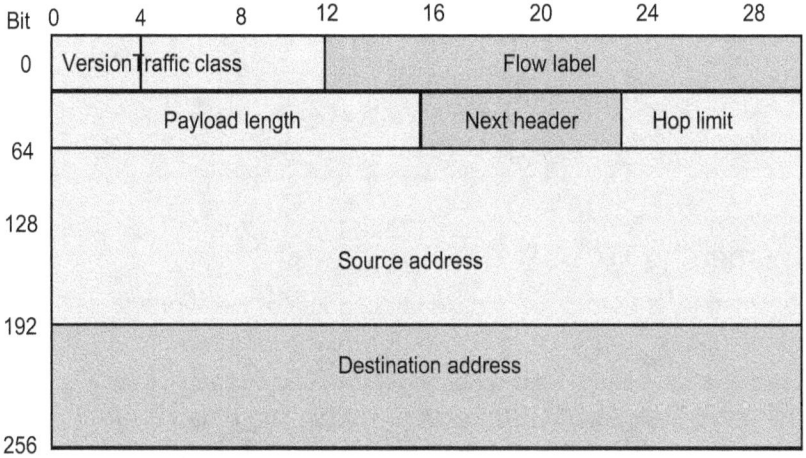

Fig. 5.30: The structure of an IPv6 packet header

Comparing the IPv4 and IPv6 Headers:

Table 5.7 shows the differences between the IPv4 and IPv6 header fields.

Table 5.7: IPv4 Header Fields and Corresponding IPv6 Equivalents

IPv4 Header Field	IPv6 Header Field
Version	Same field but with different version numbers.
Internet Header Length	Removed in IPv6. IPv6 does not include a Header Length field because the IPv6 header is always a fixed size of 40 bytes. Each extension header is either a fixed size or indicates its own size.
Type of Service	Replaced by the IPv6 Traffic Class field.

IPv4 Header Field	IPv6 Header Field
Total Length	Replaced by the IPv6 Payload Length field, which only indicates the size of the payload.
Identification Fragmentation Flags Fragment Offset	Removed in IPv6. Fragmentation information is not included in the IPv6 header. It is contained in a Fragment extension header.
Time to Live	Replaced by the IPv6 Hop Limit field.
Protocol	Replaced by the IPv6 Next Header field.
Header Checksum	Removed in IPv6. In IPv6, bit-level error detection for the entire IPv6 packet is performed by the link layer.
Source Address	The field is the same except that IPv6 addresses are 128 bits in length.
Destination Address	The field is the same except that IPv6 addresses are 128 bits in length.
Options	Removed in IPv6. IPv4 options are replaced by IPv6 extension headers.

5.7.4 Supernetting

1. Supernetting is used to help make up for some of the shortage if IP addresses for the internet.
2. It uses Classless Inter-Domain Routing (CIDR). If a business needs a specific number of IP addresses such as 1500, rather than allocating a class B set of addresses with the subnet mask of 255.255.0.0, a subnet mask of 255.255.248.0 may be allocated.
3. Therefore the equivalent of eight class C addresses have been allocated. With supernetting, the value of 2 is not subtracted from the possible number of subnets since the router knows that these are contiguous networks. 8 times 254 = 2032.
4. Supernetting, also known as Classless InterDomain Routing (CIDR), is another awesome subject. It exists thanks to the wide adoption of the Internet, which lead to the exhaustion of the available IP Addresses.
5. More specifically, supernetting was invented in 1993 with the purpose of extending the 32 bit IP address lifetime until the adoption of IPv6 was complete.
6. Putting it as simply as possible, supernets are used to combine multiple Class C networks into groups, which the router, in turn, treats as one big network.
7. It might not seem like a smart thing to do, but if you look at the picture on a larger scale you will notice some of the really awesome advantages this offers. The creation of Supernets is also known as *Address Aggregation*.

The Reason for Evolution:
Supernetting has become very popular and there are a lot of reasons why:
- Class B network address space has nearly been exhausted.
- A small percentage of class C network addresses have been assigned to networks.
- Routing tables in Internet routers have grown to a size beyond the ability of software and people to effectively manage.
- The 32-bit IP address space will eventually be exhausted.

How Supernets Work:
1. If you understand how Subnetting works, then you will surely understand Supernetting.
2. Supernets are the opposite of Subnets in that they combine multiple Class C networks into blocks rather than dividing them into segments.
3. When Subnetting, we borrow bits from the Host ID portion, which increases the number of bits used for the Network ID portion.
4. With Supernetting we do exactly the opposite, meaning we take the bits from the Network ID portion and give them to the Host ID portion, as illustrated in the picture below:

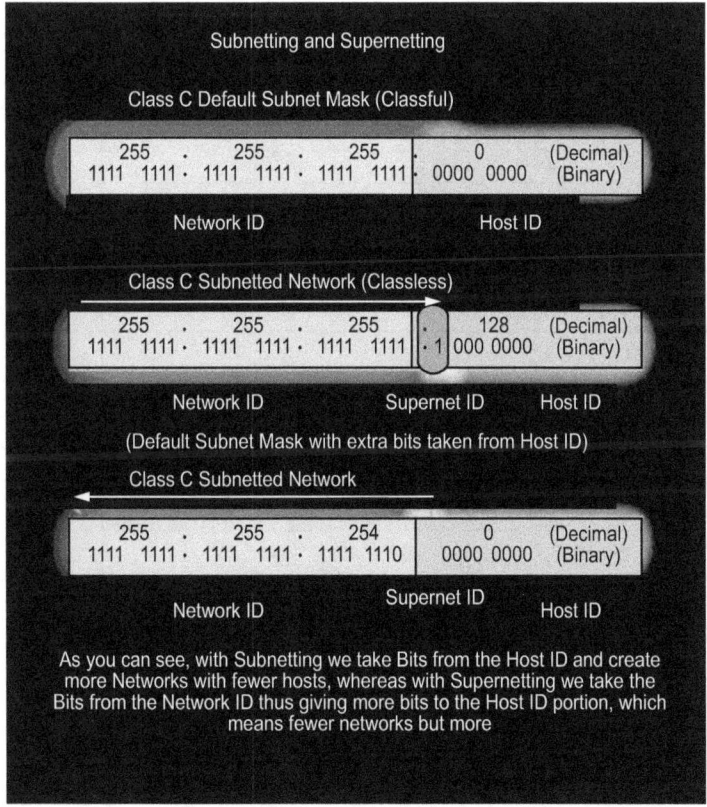

Fig. 5.31: Illustrating the Supernetting principle

The Supernetting/CIDR Chart:

1. Because subnet masks can get very confusing, the creators of this wonderful network technology also made available a few things to make life somewhat easier.
2. The following chart is really a summary of what we've seen so far. It gives you a good idea of the networks we can combine and the result we'd see.
3. **The Supernetting/CIDR chart.** There are four columns available in our chart:
   - The CIDR Block,
   - The Supernet Mask,
   - Number of Class C Networks and
   - The Number of Hosts column.

Class C Address			
CIDR Block	**Supernet Mask**	**Number of Class C Networks**	**Number of Hosts**
/14	255.252.0.0	1024	262144
/15	255.254.0.0	512	131072
/16	255.255.0.0	256	65536
/17	255.255.128.0	128	32768
/18	255.255.192.0	64	16384
/19	255.255.224.0	32	8192
/20	255.255.240.0	16	4096
/21	255.255.248.0	8	2048
/22	255.255.252.0	4	1024
/23	255.255.254.0	2	512
/24	255.255.255.0	1	254
/25	255.255.255.128	1/2	126
/26	255.255.255.192	1/4	62
/27	255.255.255.224	1/8	32
/28	255.255.255.240	1/16	16
/29	255.255.255.248	1/32	8
/30	255.255.255.252	1/64	4

We are going to explain the meaning of each column, although you probably already know most of them.

The CIDR Block:
1. The CIDR Block simply represents the number of bits used for the subnet mask. For example, /14 means 14 bits assigned to the subnet mask, it is a lot easier telling someone you have a 14 bit subnet mask rather than a subnet mask of 255.252.0.0:).
2. **Note:** In the above paragraph, we called the 14 bits as a subnet mask, when in fact it's a supernet mask, but because when you configure any network device, the field you will need to enter the value is usually named as the 'subnet mask', we decided to name it 'subnet mask' as well, in order to avoid confusion.
3. We'd like you to pay particular attention to the CIDR Block /24, and /25 to /30.
4. When we use a CIDR Block of 24 (24 bit subnet mask) we are not Supernetting !
5. This is a default subnet mask for a Class C network. With CIDR Blocks /25 to /30 we are actually Subnetting and not Supernetting !
6. Now you might wonder why we have them in the chart.
7. The fact is that those particular CIDR Blocks are valid, regardless of whether applying them to a network means we are Subnetting and not Supernetting. If you have dealt with any ISPs and IP Address assignments, chances are you would have been given your IP Addresses in CIDR format.
8. A good example is if you wanted a permanent connection to your ISP and only required 2 IP Addresses, one for your router and one for your Firewall, you would be assigned one /30 CIDR Block.
9. With such a subnet mask you will have 4 IP Addresses, from which 2 will be reserved (one for the Network address and one for the Broadcast address) and you're left with 2 that you can assign to your hosts (router and firewall).

The Supernet Mask:
1. Basically, this is your Subnet mask. When you configure the devices that will be attached to the specified network, this is the value you will enter as a Subnet mask.
2. It's also the decimal value the CIDR Block specifies. For example, a /24 CIDR block means a 24 bit Subnet mask, which in its turn translates to 255.255.255.0:) Simple stuff !

Number of Class C Networks:
1. This number shows us how many Class C Networks are combined by using a specific Supernet mask or, if you like, CIDR Block.
2. For example, the /24 CIDR Block, 255.255.255.0 Supernet mask is 1 Class C Network, whereas a /20 CIDR Block, 255.255.240.0 Supernet mask is 16 Class C networks.

Number of Hosts:
1. This value represents the number of hosts per Supernet. For example, when we use a /20 CIDR Block, which means a Subnet (or Supernet) mask of 255.255.240.0, we can have up to 4096 hosts. Pretty straightforward stuff.

2. There is one thing you must be careful of though ! The value 4096 does not represent the valid, usable IP Addresses.

3. If you wanted to find out how many of these IP Addresses you can actually use, in other words, assign to hosts, then you simply take 2 IP Addresses from that number (the first and last IP Address), so you're left with 4094 IP Addresses to play with:)

Why take 2 away ? You shouldn't be asking questions like that if you have read the IP and Subnetting sections but we'll tell you anyway:) One is reserved for the Network Address and one for the Broadcast Address of that network.

5.7.5 Routing

1. As networks grow in size, so does the traffic imposed on the wire, which in turn impacts the overall network performance, including responses.

2. To alleviate such a degradation, network specialist resort to breaking the network into multiple networks that are interconnected by specialized devices, including routers, bridges, and switches.

3. The routing approach calls on the implementation of various co-operative processes, in both routers and workstations, whose main concern is to allow for the intelligent delivery of data to its ultimate destination.

4. Data exchange can take place between any workstation, whether or not both belong to the same network.

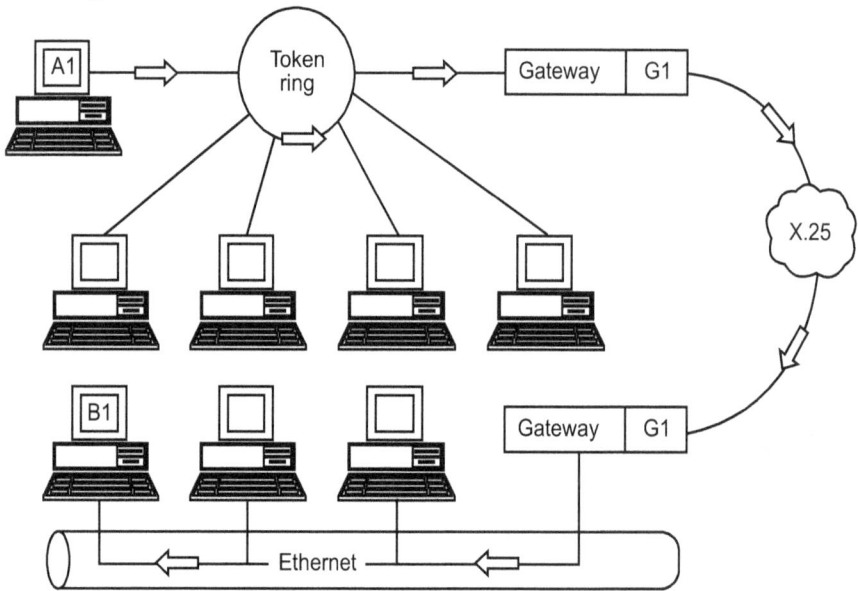

Fig. 5.32: Shows a view of routing

5. Fig. 5.32 emphasises that the underlying physical networks that a datagram travels through may be different and even incompatible.
6. Host A1 on the Token Ring network routes the datagram through gateway G1, to reach host B1 on the Ethernet.
7. Gateway G1 forwards the data through the X.25 network to gateway G2, for delivery to B1.
8. The datagram traverses three physical different networks, but eventually arrives intact at B1.
9. A good place to start when discussing routers is with a through discussion of the addresses, including MAC addresses, network addresses, and the complete addresses.

The Routing Table:
1. To perform its function reliably, the routing process is equipped with the capability to maintain a road map depicting the entire internetwork of which it is part.
2. This road map is commonly referred to as the routing table, and it includes routing information depicting every known network is, and how it can be reached.
3. The routing process builds and maintains the routing table by employing a route discovery process known as the *Routing Information Protocol (RIP)*.
4. Routers should be capable of selecting the shortest path connecting two networks. Routers discover the road map of the internetwork by dynamically exchanging routing information among themselves or by being statically configured by network installers, or both.
5. The dynamic exchange of routing information is handled by yet another process besides the routing process itself. In the case of TCP/IP, IP handles the routing process, whereas RIP handles the route discovery process.

Internet Routing Architecture:
1. When a hierarchical structure is used, routing information about all of the networks in the Internet is passed into the *core gateway* (a central delivery medium to carry long distance traffic).
2. The core gateway processes this information, and then exchange it among themselves using the *Gateway-to-Gateway Protocol (GGP)*.
3. The processed routing information is passed back out to the external gateways.

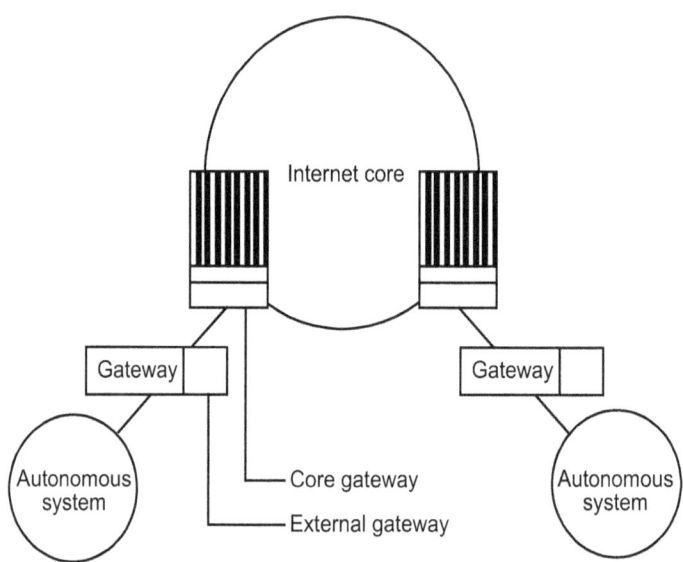

Fig. 5.33: Shows the Internet Routing Architecture

4. Outside of the Internet Core are groups of independent networks called *Autonomous Systems (AS)*, it is a collection of networks and gateways with its own internal mechanism for collection routing information and passing it to other network systems.

The Routing Table:
1. Gateways route data between networks, but all network devices, hosts as well as gateways, must make routing decisions.
2. For most hosts, the routing decisions are simple:
   - If the destination is on local network, the data is delivered to destination host.
   - If the destination is on the remote network, the data is forwarded to a local gateway.
3. Because routing is network oriented, IP makes routing decisions based on the network portion of the address. The IP module determines the network part of the destination's IP address by checking the high-order bits of the address to determine the address class.
4. The address class determines the portion of the address that IP uses to identify the network. If the destination network is the local network, the local subnet mask is applied to the destination address.
5. After determining the destination network, the IP module looks up the network in the *local routing table*. Packets are routed toward their destination as directed by the routing table.
6. The routing table may be built by the system administrator or by routing protocols, but the end result is the same, IP routing decisions are simple table look-ups.

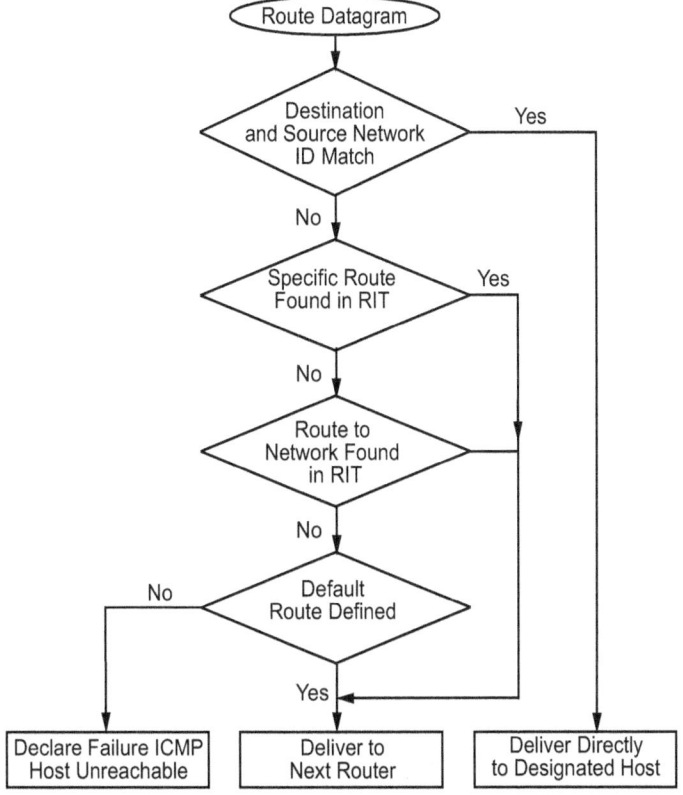

Fig. 5.34: Shows a flowchart depiction of the IP routing algorithm

7. You can display the routing table's contents with the **netstat -r** command.

The netstat command displays a routing table containing the following fields:

- *Destination*: The destination network or host.
- *Gateway*: The gateway to use to reach the specified destination.
- *Flags*: The flags describe certain characteristics of this route.

U: Indicates that the route is up and operational.

H: Indicates this is a route to a specific host.

G: Means the route uses a gateway.

D: Means that this route was adds because of an ICMP redirect.

- *Refcnt*: Shows the number of times the route has been referenced to establish a connection.
- *Use*: Shows the number of packets transmitted via this route.
- *Interface*: The name of the network interface used by this route.

8. All of the gateways that appear in a routing table are networks directly connected to the local system.

9. A routing table does not contain end-to-end routes. A rout only points to the next gateway, called *the next hop*, along the path to the destination network.

10. The host relies on the local gateway to deliver the data, and the gateways relies on the other gateways.

11. As a datagram moves from one gateway to another, it should eventually reach one that is directly connected to its destination network, It is this last gateway that finally delivers the data to the destination host.

Address Resolution:

1. The IP address and the routing table direct a datagram to a specific physical network, but when the data travels across a network, it must obey the physical layer protocol used by that network.

2. The physical networks that underlay the TCP/IP network do not understand IP addressing. Physical networks have their own addressing schemes.

3. And there are as many different addressing schemes as there are different types of physical networks.

4. One task of the network access protocols is to map IP addresses to physical network addresses.

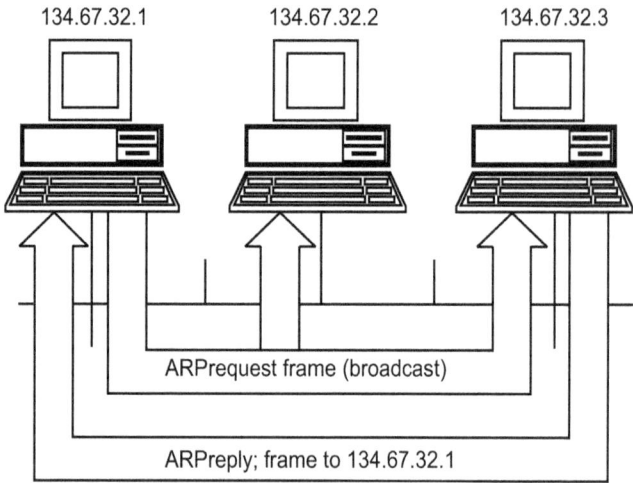

Fig. 5.35: Show the operation of ARP

5. The most common example of this network access layer function is the translation of IP addresses to Ethernet addresses.

6. The protocol that performs this function is *Address Resolution Protocol (ARP)*.

Hardware Type (16 bits)	
Protocol Type (16 bits)	
Protocol Address Length	Hardware Address Length
Operation Code (16 bits)	
Sender Hardware Address	
Sender IP Address	
Recipient Hardware Address	
Recipient IP Address	

Fig. 5.36: Shows the layout of an ARP request or ARP reply

7. In Fig. 5.36, when an ARP request is sent, all fields in the layout are used except the *Recipient Hardware Address* (which the request is trying to identify).
8. In an ARP reply, all the fields are used. The fields in the ARP request and reply can have several values.
9. The ARP software maintains a table of translations between IP addresses and Ethernet addresses.
10. This table is built dynamically. When ARP receives a request to translate an IP address, it checks for the address in its table.
11. If the address is found, it returns the Ethernet address in its table. If the address is not found in the table, ARP broadcast a packet to every host on the Ethernet.
12. The packet contains the IP address for which an Ethernet address is sought. If a receiving host identifies the IP address as its own, it responds by sending its Ethernet address back to the requesting host.
13. The response is then cached in the ARP table. The **arp-a** command display all the contents of the ARP table.

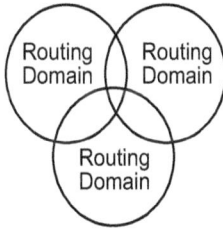

Fig. 5.37: Shows Routing Domains

RARP:
1. The *Reverse Address Resolution Protocol (RARP)*, is a variant of the address resolution protocol.
2. RARP also translates addresses, but in the opposite direction. It converts Ethernet addresses to IP addresses.

3. The RARP protocol really has nothing to do with routing data from one system to another.
4. RARP helps configure diskless systems by allowing diskless workstations to learn their IP address.
5. The diskless workstations uses the Ethernet broadcast facility to ask which IP address maps to its Ethernet address.
6. When a server on the network sees the request, it looks up the Ethernet address in the table. If it finds a match, the server replies with the workstation's IP address.
7. In Fig. 5.38, Shaded fields correspondent to the destination and source address of host A, (the sender) and Host B (the receiver).

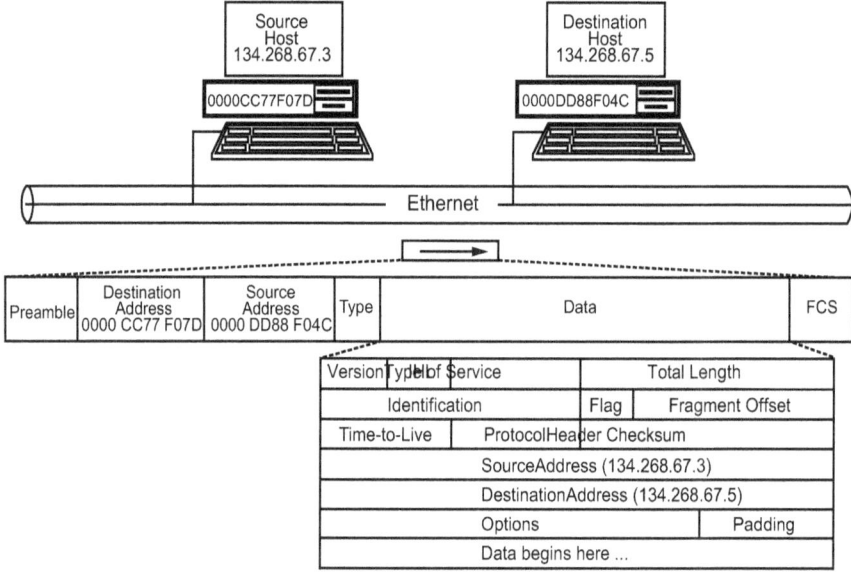

Fig. 5.38: Shows the interrelationship between IP and Ethernet MAC address as reflected in the Ethernet data frame

5.7.6 Multiplexing and Protocols/Ports/Sockets

1. Once data is routed through the network and delivered to a specific host, it must be delivered to the correct user or process.
2. As the data moves up or down the layers of TCP/IP, a mechanism is needed to deliver data to the correct protocols in each layer.
3. The system must be able to combine data from many applications into a few transport protocols, and from the transport protocols into the Internet Protocol. Combining many sources of data into a single data stream is called *multiplexing*.
4. Data arriving from the network must be demultiplexed, divided for delivery to multiple processes. To accomplish this, IP uses protocol numbers to identify transport protocols, and the transport protocols use port numbers to identify applications.

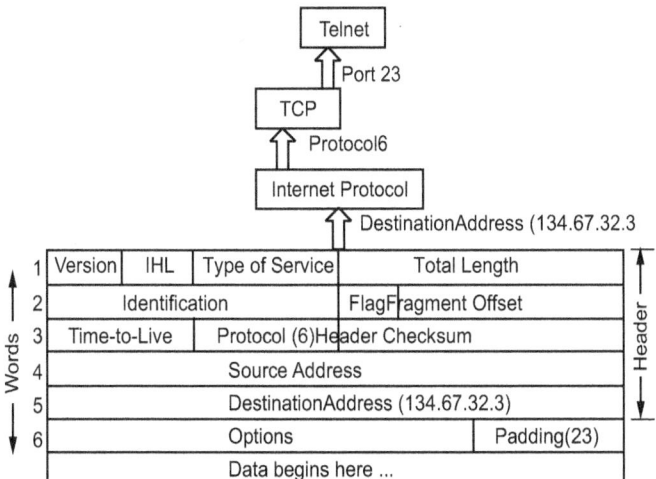

Fig. 5.39: Shows Protocol and Port Numbers

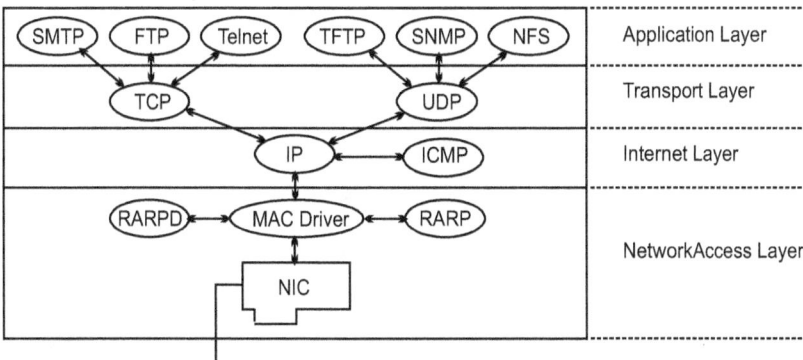

Fig. 5.40: Shows the protocol interdependency between Application level protocols and Transport level protocols

Protocol Numbers:
Is a single byte in the header of the datagram. The value identifies the protocol in the layer above IP to which the data should be passed.

Port Numbers:
1. A host may have many TCP and UDP connections at any time. Connections to a host are distinguished by a port number, which serves as a sort of mailbox number for incoming datagrams.
2. There may be many processes using TCP and UDP on a single machine, and the port numbers distinguish these processes for incoming packets.
3. When a user program opens a TCP or UDP socket, it gets connected to a port on the local host.
4. The application may specify the port, usually when trying to reach some service with a well-defined port number, or it may allow the operating system to fill in the port number with the next available free port number.

5. After IP passes incoming data to the transport protocol, the transport protocol passes data to the correct application process. Application processes are identified by port numbers, which are 16-bit values.

6. The source port number, which identifies the process that sent the data, and the destination port number, which identifies the process that is to receive the data are contained in the header of each TCP segment and UDP packet.

7. Port numbers are not unique between transport layer protocols, the numbers are only unique within a specific transport protocol. It is the combination of protocol and port numbers that uniquely identifies the specific process the data should be delivered to.

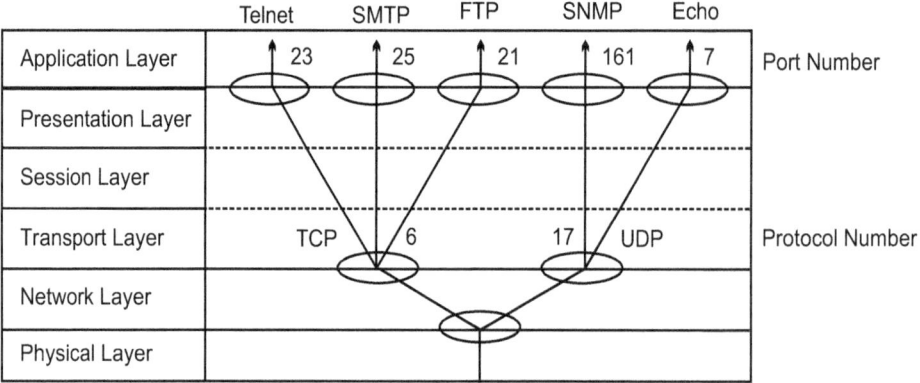

Fig. 5.41: Shows data packets multiplexed via TCP or UDP through port addresses and onto the targeted TCP/IP applications

In Fig. 5.41, if a data packet arrives specifying a transport protocol of 6, it is forwarded to the TCP implementation. If the packet specifies 17 as the required protocol, the IP layer would forward the packet to the programs implementing UDP.

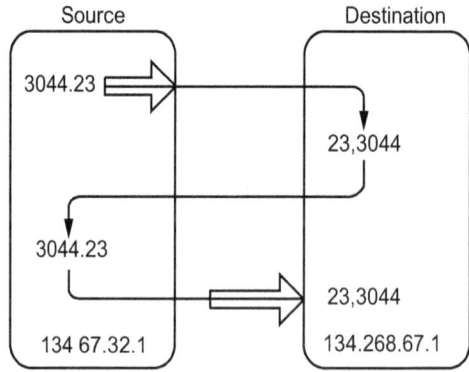

Fig. 5.42: Shows the exchange of port numbers during the TCP handshake·

In Fig. 5.42, the source host randomly generates a source port, in this example 3044. It sends out a segment with a source port of 3044 and a destination port of 23. The destination host receives the segment, and responds back using 23 as it source port and 3044 as its destination port.

Table 5.8: Well-known ports used by TCP

Port	Protocol	Description
7	Echo	Echoes a received datagram back to the sender.
9	Discard	Discards any datagram that is received.
11	Users	Active users.
13	Daytime	Returns the date and the time.
17	Quote	Returns a quote of the day.
19	Chargen	Returns a string of characters.
20	FTP. Data	File Transfer Protocol (data connection).
21	FTP. Control	File Transfer Protocol (control connection).
23	TELNET	Terminal Network.
25	SMTP	Simple Mail Transfer Protocol.
53	DNS	Domain Name Server.
67	BOOTP	Bootstrap Protocol.
79	Finger	Finger.
80	HTTP	Hypertext Transfer Protocol.
111	RPC	Remote Procedure Call.

Table 5.9: Well-known ports used with UDP

Port	Protocol	Description
7	Echo	Echoes a received datagram back to the sender.
9	Discard	Discards any datagram that is received.
11	Users	Active users.
13	Daytime	Returns the date and the time.
17	Quote	Returns a quote of the day.
19	Chargen	Returns a string of characters.
53	Nameserver	Domain Name Service
67	Bootps	Server port to download bootstrap information.
68	BOOTPE	Client port to download bootstrap information.
69	TFTP	Trivial File Transfer Protocol.
111	RPC	Remote Procedure Call
123	NTP	Network Time Protocol.
161	SNMP	Simple Network Management Protocol.
162	SNMP	Simple Network Management Protocol (trap).

Sockets:
1. Well-known ports are standardized port numbers that enables remote computers to know which port to connect to for a particular network service.
2. This simplifies the connection process because both the sender and the receiver know in advance that data bound for a specific process will use a specific port.
3. There is a second type of port number called *a dynamically allocated port*. As the name implies, this ports are not pre-assigned.
4. They are assigned to processes when needed. The system ensures that it does not assign the same port number to two processes, and that the number assigned are above the range of standard port numbers.
5. **The combination of an IP address and a port number is called *a socket*.**
6. A socket uniquely identifies a single network process within the entire Internet.
7. One pair of sockets, one socket for the receiving host and one for the sending host, define the connection for connection-oriented protocols such as TCP.

5.8 Operator Commands in the TCP/IP Environment

The TCP/IP suite does provide various commands and methods that can be used in problem determination exercises (which is handy, they are used frequently). Any user can employ these commands to check what the network is (or is not) doing. The most often used commands are given as follows.

- **The PING Command:** The PING command (it stands for **P**acket **I**nternet **G**roper) is used to send ICMP (Internet Control Message Protocol) packets from one host to another. Ping transmits packets using the ICMP ECHO_REQUEST command and expects an ICMP ECHO_REPLY.

Usage: ping IP address or Hostname

- **The TRACEROUTE Command:** The traceroute command is used to trace the route that a packet takes to reach its destination. This command works by using the time to live (TTL) filed in the IP packet. Note that the exact syntax of **tracert** is system dependent.

Usage: tracert IP or Hostname

- **The NETSTAT Command:** This command is used to query the network subsystem regarding certain types of information. Different types of information will be received depending on the switches used in conjunction with this command.

Usage: netstat [switch]

Switches:
- **-A** Shows the addresses of any associated protocol control blocks.
- **-a** Will show the status of all sockets. Sockets associated with network server processes are normally not shown.
- **-i** Shows the state of the network interfaces.

- **-m** Prints the network memory usage.
- **-n** Causes netstat to show actual addresses as opposed to hostnames or network names.
- **-r** Prints the routing table.
- **-s** Tells netstat to show the per protocol statistics.
- **-t** Replaces the queue length information with timer information.

• **The ARP Command:** The arp command will display internet to ethernet (IP to MAC) address translations which is normally handled by the ARP protocol. When the hostname is the only parameter, this command will display the correct ARP entry for that hostname.

Usage: ARP hostname

• **The FINGER Command:** By default, finger will list the login name, full name, terminal name, and write status (shown as a "*" before the terminal name if write permission is denied), idle time, login time, office location, and phone number (if known) for each current user connected to the network.

Usage: finger username@domain

5.8.1 TCP/IP and Security

1. The worldwide success of the Internet rapidly made TCP/IP the most used network protocol.
2. Despite its popularity, it lacks some important features especially regarding security.
3. In fact, TCP/IP can neither ensure the hosts you're communicating which are the ones you think nor prevent the data from being captured.
4. For example, passwords used in protocols like HTTP, POP3, or telnet are not usually encrypted.
5. The IPsec framework, ratified by the Internet Engineering Steering Group (IESG), allows defining a policy that specifies which packets you want to secure.
6. Those treated packets are simply encapsulated in IP datagrams by applying two kinds of layers:
   - **Authentication headers (AH):** Based on integrity checksum computed using data and a private key, it ensures the host you're communicating with is the one you suppose it to be. Data integrity is fully assured, but this method cannot prevent network listeners from getting sensitive information from your authenticated traffic.
   - **Encapsulating Security Payload (ESP):** Based on encryption algorithms, this method prevents other hosts from retrieving confidential information from your network. The ESP layer can provide the same features as AH. You should therefore use ESP both for authentication and encryption to fully secure your network.

7. This technology is absolutely independent of the protocols used behind it to implement AH and ESP entities.
8. Specifications exist for common algorithms such as MD5 or SHA1 for authentication and DES, 3DES, or Blowfish for encryption.
9. The IPsec policy defines which packets are secured.
10. It comprises a set of rules dependent on each implementation and generally based on criteria such as IP address, port, direction, or protocol. The rule can ask for communications to be secured or not in one or both directions.

5.9 TCP/IP Stack Link Layer

1. We see that the purpose of the link layer in the TCP/IP protocol suite is to send and receive,
   IP datagrams for the IP module,
2. ARP requests and replies for the ARP module, and
3. RARP requests and replies for the RARP module.
4. TCP/IP supports many different link layers, depending on the type of networking hardware being used: Ethernet, token ring, FDDI (Fiber Distributed Data Interface), RS-232 serial lines, and the like.

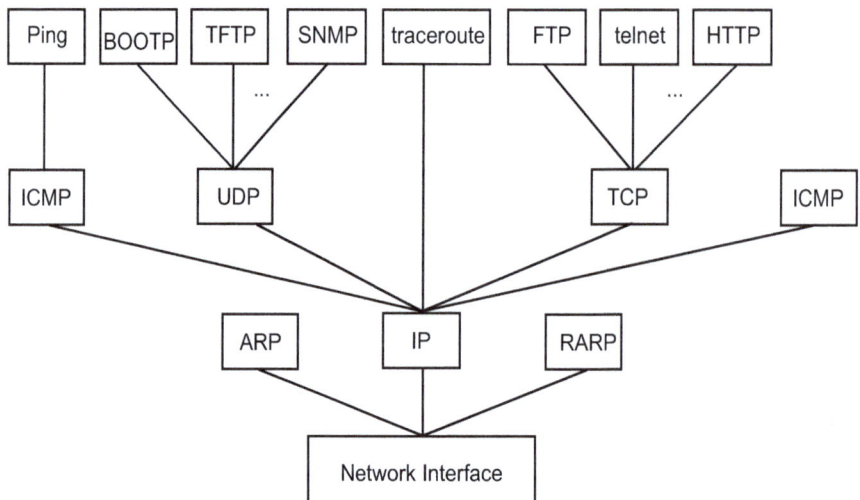

Fig. 5.43: The Interrelationship of The TCP/IP Protocols and Applications

6. Thus the lowest layer in the Internet protocol suite, the link layer.
7. The Network Interface layer (also called the Network Access layer) sends TCP/IP packets on the network medium and receives TCP/IP packets off the network medium.
8. TCP/IP was designed to be independent of the network access method, frame format, and medium.

9. Therefore, you can use TCP/IP to communicate across differing network types that use LAN technologies—such as Ethernet and 802.11 wireless LAN—and WAN technologies—such as Frame Relay and Asynchronous Transfer Mode (ATM).
10. The Internet layer assumes an unreliable Network Interface layer and that reliable communications through session establishment and the sequencing and acknowledgment of packets is the responsibility of either the Transport layer or the Application layer.
11. We have covered only a few of the common data-link technologies used with TCP/IP.
12. One reason for the success of TCP/IP is its ability to work on top of almost any data-link technology.

5.9.1 TCP/IP Link Layer (ARP and RARP Protocol)

1. In TCP/IP protocol stack ARP and RARP protocols are present.
2. ARP is address resolution protocol and RARP is Reserve ARP.
3. To understand the function of ARP and RARP take the examples Case I and Case II.
4. Case in indicates the operation of Ping command, for local destination host.
5. Case II indicates the operation of ping command for remote destination host.

Case I: Local destination host:

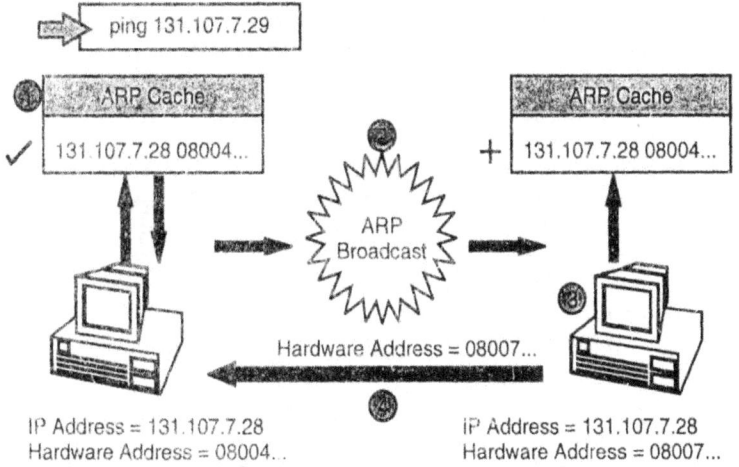

Fig. 5.44: Case I Local destination host

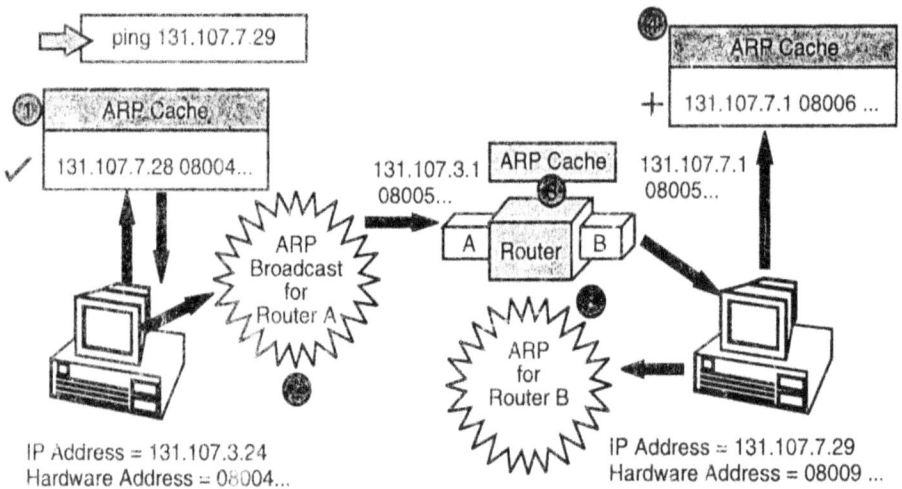

Fig. 5.45: Case II Remote destination host

6. Host must know the hardware address of other hosts to communicate on a network.
7. Address resolution is the process of mapping a host's IP address to its hardware address.
8. ARP is a part of TCP/IP internet (network) layer obtain hardware addresses of hosts located on the same physical network or TCP/IP hosts on broadcast-based networks.
9. ARP uses a local broadcast of the destination IP address to acquire the network address of the destination host or gateway.
10. ARP always checks the ARP cache for an IP address and hardware address mapping before initiating an ARP request broadcast.
11. Once ARP obtains the hardware address, both the IP address and network are stored as one entry in the ARP cache.
12. RARP is the process of mapping a hosts hardware address to its IP address.

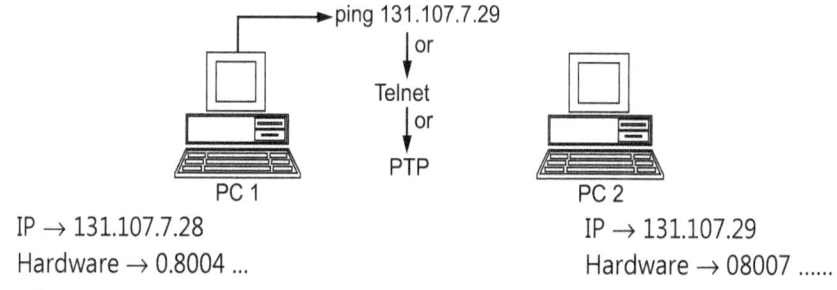

13. When you type Ping 131.107.7.29
    it checks its ARP cache first weather the
    Destination IP address
    Destination hardware address } is available in ARP cache ?

14. If it finds no mapping ARP builds a request with the question.
    (a) Who is this input address 131.107.7.29?
    (b) What is your hardware address ?
    (c) I am sending my source IP address and source hardware in ARP request
15. This ARP request is sent as broadcast so that all local hosts can receive and process it.
16. Each host on the local network receives and checks for a match to its own IP address. **If the host does not find match it ignores the request.**
17. The host which destination host determines that the IP address in the request matches its own IP address immediately it sends an ARP reply to the source host with its hardware address.
18. Thus, both host and destination update its ARP cache with the IP address/hardware address mapping of the source host.
19. Thus, communication is established when the source host receives the reply.
20. If the case II, Router comes into picture. At the Router, IP determines whether the destination IP address is local or remote.
21. If it is a local, the router obviously uses ARP to obtain its hardware, if it is remote, Router checks its routing table. For a specialised gateways and then uses ARP to obtain the gateways hardware address. Thus, packet is sent directly to the next destination host.

5.10 TCP/IP Internet/Network Layer

1. The Internet layer responsibilities include addressing, packaging, and routing functions.
2. The Internet layer is analogous to the Network layer of the OSI model.
3. The core protocols for the IPv4 Internet layer consist of the following:
   - The Internet Protocol (IP) is a routable protocol that addresses, routes, fragments, and reassembles packets.
   - The Internet Control Message Protocol (ICMP) reports errors and other information to help you diagnose unsuccessful packet delivery.
   - The Internet Group Management Protocol (IGMP) manages IP multicast groups.
4. The core protocols for the IPv6 Internet layer consist of the following:
   - IPv6 is a routable protocol that addresses and routes packets.
   - The Internet Control Message Protocol for IPv6 (ICMPv6) reports errors and other information to help you diagnose unsuccessful packet delivery.
   - The Neighbour Discovery (ND) protocol manages the interactions between neighbouring IPv6 nodes.
   - The Multicast Listener Discovery (MLD) protocol manages IPv6 multicast groups.

5.10.1 IP Routing Overview

1. IP routing is the process of forwarding a packet based on the destination IP address. Routing occurs at a sending TCP/IP host and at an IP router.
2. In each case, the IP layer at the sending host or router must decide where to forward the packet. For IPv4, routers are also commonly referred to as gateways.
3. To make these decisions, the IP layer consults a routing table stored in memory. Routing table entries are created by default when TCP/IP initializes, and entries can be added either manually or automatically.

Direct and Indirect Delivery:

1. Forwarded IP packets use at least one of two types of delivery based on whether the IP packet is forwarded to the final destination or whether it is forwarded to an IP router.
2. These two types of delivery are known as direct and indirect delivery.
   - Direct delivery occurs when the IP node (either the sending host or an IP router) forwards a packet to the final destination on a directly attached subnet. The IP node encapsulates the IP datagram in a frame for the Network Interface layer. For a LAN technology such as Ethernet or Institute of Electrical and Electronic Engineers (IEEE) 802.11, the IP node addresses the frame to the destination's media access control (MAC) address.
   - Indirect delivery occurs when the IP node (either the sending host or an IP router) forwards a packet to an intermediate node (an IP router) because the final destination is not on a directly attached subnet. For a LAN technology such as Ethernet or IEEE 802.11, the IP node addresses the frame to the IP router's MAC address.
3. End-to-end IP routing across an IP network combines direct and indirect deliveries.
4. In Fig. 5.46, when sending packets to Host B, Host A performs a direct delivery.
5. When sending packets to Host C, Host A performs an indirect delivery to Router 1, Router 1 performs an indirect delivery to Router 2, and then Router 2 performs a direct delivery to Host C.

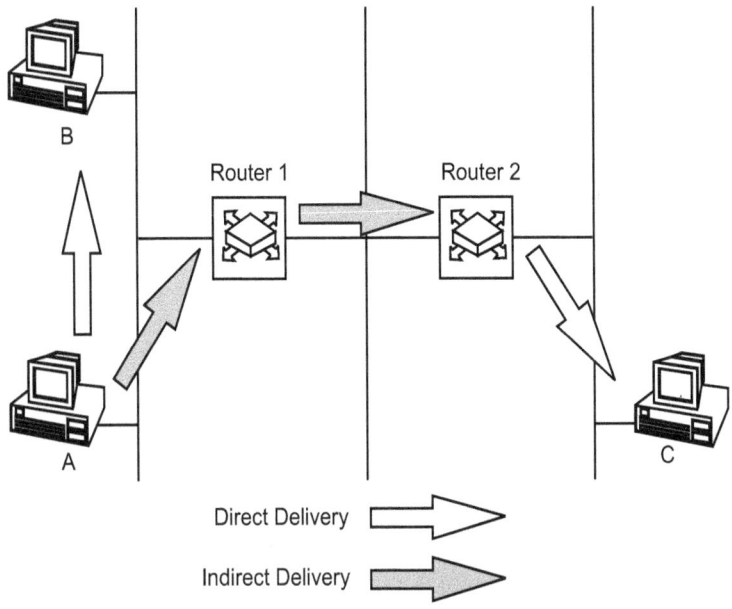

Fig. 5.46: Direct and indirect delivery

IP Routing Table:

1. A routing table is present on every IP node.
2. The routing table stores information about IP destinations and how packets can reach them (either directly or indirectly).
3. Because all IP nodes perform some form of IP routing, routing tables are not exclusive to IP routers.
4. Any node using the TCP/IP protocol has a routing table.
5. Each table contains a series of default entries according to the configuration of the node, and additional entries can be added manually, for example, by administrators that use TCP/IP tools, or automatically, when nodes listen for routing information messages sent by routers.
6. When IP forwards a packet, it uses the routing table to determine:
   - **The next-hop IP address:** For a direct delivery, the next-hop IP address is the destination address in the IP packet. For an indirect delivery, the next-hop IP address is the IP address of a router.
   - **The next-hop interface:** The interface identifies the physical or logical interface that forwards the packet.

Routing Table Entries:

1. A typical IP routing table entry includes the following fields:

- **Destination:**
  Either an IP address or an IP address prefix.
- **Prefix Length:**
  The prefix length corresponding to the address or range of addresses in the destination.
- **Next-Hop:**
  The IP address to which the packet is forwarded.
- **Interface:**
  The network interface that forwards the IP packet.
- **Metric**

2. A number that indicates the cost of the route so that IP can select the best route, among potentially multiple routes to the same destination.
3. The metric sometimes indicates the number of hops (the number of links to cross) in the path to the destination.
4. Routing table entries can store the following types of routes:
   - **Directly-attached subnet routes:**
     Routes for subnets to which the node is directly attached. For directly-attached subnet routes, the Next-Hop field can either be blank or contain the IP address of the interface on that subnet.
   - **Remote subnet routes:**
     Routes for subnets that are available across routers and are not directly attached to the node. For remote subnet routes, the Next-Hop field is the IP address of a neighbouring router.
   - **Host routes:**
     A route to a specific IP address. Host routes allow routing to occur on a per-IP address basis.
   - **Default route:**
     Used when a more specific subnet or host route is not present. The next-hop address of the default route is typically the default gateway or default router of the node.

Static and Dynamic Routing:

1. For IP packets to be efficiently routed between routers on the IP network, routers must either have explicit knowledge of remote subnet routes or be properly configured with a default route.
2. On large IP networks, one of the challenges that you face as a network administrator is how to maintain the routing tables on your IP routers so that IP traffic travels along the best path and is fault tolerant.

3. Routing table entries on IP routers are maintained in two ways:
   - **Manually:**
     Static IP routers have routing tables that do not change unless a network administrator manually changes them. Static routing requires manual maintenance of routing tables by network administrators. Static routers do not discover remote routes and are not fault tolerant. If a static router fails, neighbouring routers do not detect the fault and inform other routers.
   - **Automatically:**
     Dynamic IP routers have routing tables that change automatically when the routers exchange routing information. Dynamic routing uses routing protocols, such as Routing Information Protocol (RIP) and Open Shortest Path First (OSPF), to dynamically update routing tables. Dynamic routers discover remote routes and are fault tolerant. If a dynamic router fails, neighbouring routers detect the fault and propagate the changed routing information to the other routers on the network.

Dynamic Routing:

1. Dynamic routing is the automatic updating of routing table entries to reflect changes in network topology.
2. A router with dynamically configured routing tables is known as a dynamic router. Dynamic routers build and maintain their routing tables automatically by using a routing protocol, a series of periodic or on-demand messages that contain routing information.
3. Except for their initial configuration, typical dynamic routers require little ongoing maintenance and, therefore, can scale to larger networks.
4. The ability to scale and recover from network faults makes dynamic routing the better choice for medium, large, and very large networks.
5. Some widely used routing protocols for IPv4 are RIP, OSPF, and Border Gateway Protocol 4 (BGP-4).
6. Routing protocols are used between routers and represent additional network traffic overhead on the network. You should consider this additional traffic if you must plan WAN link usage.
7. When choosing a routing protocol, you should pay particular attention to its ability to sense and recover from network faults.
8. How quickly a routing protocol can recover depends on the type of fault, how it is sensed, and how routers propagate information through the network.
9. When all the routers on the network have the correct routing information in their routing tables, the network has converged. When convergence is achieved, the network is in a stable state, and all packets are routed along optimal paths.

10. When a link or router fails, the network must reconfigure itself to reflect the new topology by updating routing tables, possibly across the entire network. Until the network reconverges, it is in an unstable state.

11. The time it takes for the network to reconverge is known as the convergence time. The convergence time varies based on the routing protocol and the type of failure, such as a downed link or a downed router.

Routing Protocol Technologies:

1. Typical IP routing protocols are based the following technologies:

    - **Distance Vector:**

    Distance vector routing protocols propagate routing information in the form of an address prefix and its "distance" (hop count). Routers use these protocols to periodically advertise the routes in their routing tables. Typical distance vector-based routers do not synchronize or acknowledge the routing information they exchange. Distance vector-based routing protocols are easier to understand and configure, but they also consume more network bandwidth, take longer to converge, and do not scale to large or very large networks.

    - **Link State:**

    Routers using link state-based routing protocols exchange link state advertisements (LSAs) throughout the network to update routing tables. LSAs consist of address prefixes for the networks to which the router is attached and the assigned costs of those networks. LSAs are advertised upon startup and when a router detects changes in the network topology. Link state-based routers build a database of LSAs and use the database to calculate the optimal routes to add to the routing table. Link state-based routers synchronize and acknowledge the routing information they exchange.

    Link state-based routing protocols consume less network bandwidth, converge more quickly, and scale to large and very large networks. However, they can be more complex and difficult to configure.

    - **Path Vector:**

    Routers use path vector–based routing protocols to exchange sequences of autonomous system numbers that indicate the path for a route. An autonomous system is a portion of a network under the same administrative authority. Autonomous systems are assigned a unique autonomous system identifier. Path vector–based routers synchronize and acknowledge the routing information they exchange. Path vector–based routing protocols consume less network bandwidth, converge more quickly, and scale to networks the size of the Internet. However, they can also be complex and difficult to configure.

IPv4 Header Format:

1. IP packets are carried over link-layer technologies such as Ethernet (10 Mbps), Fast Ethernet (100 Mbps), Gigabit Ethernet (1000 Mbps), Frame Relay, and many others.
2. Each link-layer technology family has its own link-layer frame that carries IP packets.
3. As shown in Fig. 5.47, an IP packet is carried between the frame header and frame trailer of a link-layer frame. An IP packet has two fundamental components:

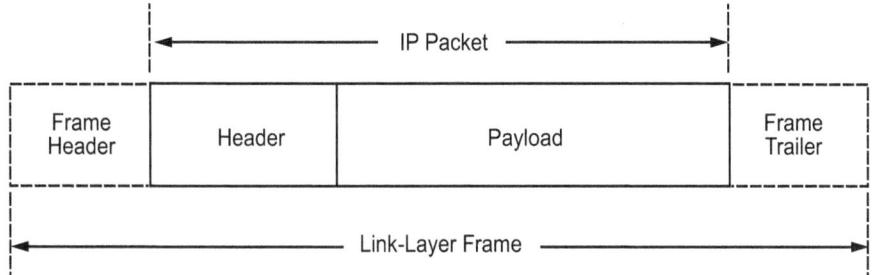

Fig. 5.47: IP Packet Carried by a Link-Layer Frame Contains a Header and a Payload

4. **IP header:** The IP header contains many fields that are used by routers to forward the packet from network to network to a final destination. Fields within the IP header identify the sender, receiver, and transport protocol and define many other parameters.
5. **Payload:** Represents the information (data) to be delivered to the receiver by the sender.
6. As shown in Fig. 5.48, the basic IPv4 header contains 12 fields. *Internet Protocol DARPA Internet Program Specification*, each field of the IPv4 header has a specific use.

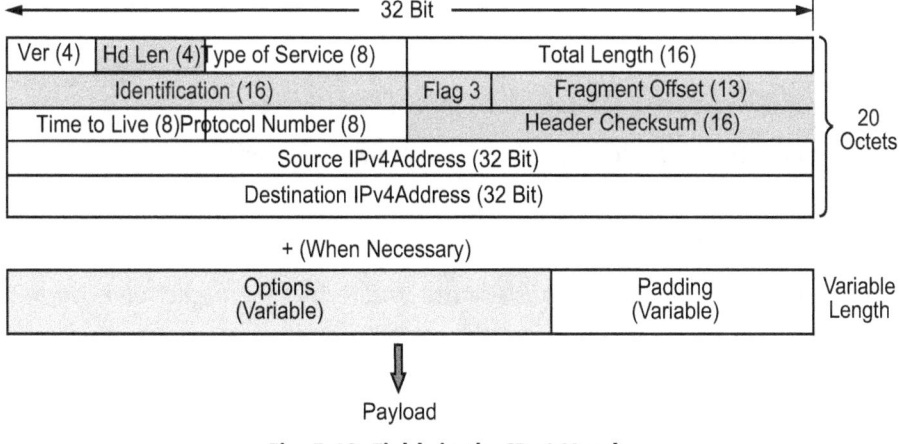

Fig. 5.48: Fields in the IPv4 Header

7. Following are the IPv4 header fields:

- **Version (4-bit):** The version of the IP (Internet Protocol) header. The current IP version used on the Internet is 4 (IPv4). This field contains the value 4.

- **Header Length (4-bit):** The length in octets of the header size up to the Payload field.

- **Type of Service (TOS) (8-bit):** Specifies the treatment of the datagram during its transmission through the routers. This field can also be interpreted as Differentiated Services Code Point (DSCP).

- **Total Length (16-bit):** The size of the IP packet in octets, including the header and the payload. This field is 16-bit, which means that the maximum size of an IPv4 packet is 65,535 octets.

- **Identification (16-bit), Flags (3-bit), and Fragment Offset (13-bit):** Fields related to packet fragmentation by routers when the MTU along a path is smaller than the sender's MTU. The MTU is the maximum size in octets of an IP packet that can be transmitted on a specific communication medium, such as Ethernet, Fast Ethernet, and so on. For Ethernet, the MTU is 1500 octets.

- **Time to Live (8-bit):** This field is decremented each time the packet passes through an intermediary router. When this field contains the value 0, the packet is destroyed, and an Internet Control Message Protocol for IPv4 (ICMPv4) Type 11 error message (Time Exceeded) is sent to the source node.

- **Protocol Number (8-bit):** Specifies the upper-layer protocol used in a packet's payload, such as Transport Control Protocol (TCP), User Datagram Protocol (UDP), Internet Control Message Protocol (ICMP), or any others. Protocols supported are defined by the Internet Assigned Numbers Authority (IANA).

- **Header Checksum (16-bit):** Represents the checksum of the IP header and is used for error checking. This field is verified and recomputed by each intermediary router along a path.

- **Source IPv4 Address (32-bit):** The sender's IPv4 address.

- **Destination IPv4 Address (32-bit):** The receiver's IPv4 address.

- **Options (variable):** This optional field might appear in an IPv4 packet. The Options field is variable in size and increases the length of the header when used.

- **Padding (variable):** Padding is used to ensure that the packet ends on a 32-bit boundary. It also increases the header's size.

- **Payload (variable):** The payload is not a field of the basic IPv4 header. Rather, it represents the data to be delivered to a destination address. The payload includes an upper-layer header.

5.10.2 ICMP Internet Control Message Protocol

1. ICMP is often considered part of the IP layer.
2. It communicates error messages and other conditions that require attention.
3. ICMP messages are usually acted on by either the IP layer or the higher layer protocol (TCP or UDP).
4. Some ICMP messages cause errors to be returned to user processes.
5. ICMP messages are transmitted within IP datagrams, as shown in Fig. 5.49.
6. Fig. 5.50, ICMP messages encapsulated within an IP datagram.

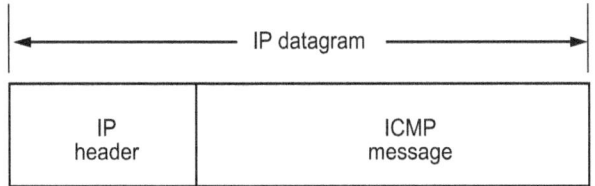

Fig. 5.49: Shows the format of an ICMP message

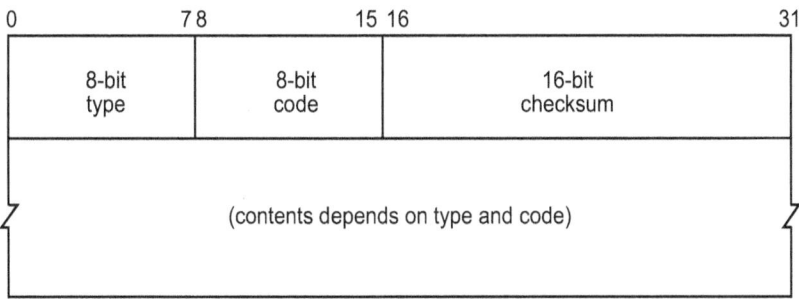

Fig. 5.50: ICMP message

7. The first 4 bytes have the same format for all messages, but the remainder differs from one message to the next. We'll show the exact format of each message when we describe it.
8. There are 15 different values for the *type* field, which identify the particular ICMP message.
9. Some types of ICMP messages then use different values of the *code* field to further specify the condition.

Ping uses ICMP Protocol:
Verifies connections to a remote computer or computers. This command is available only if the TCP/IP protocol has been installed. Various commands used to check the connectivity between two systems using Ping utility are given below.
ping [-t] [-a] [-n *count*] [-l *length*] [-f] [-i *ttl*] [-v *tos*] [-r *count*] [-s *count*] [[-j *computer-list*] | [-k *computer-list*]] [-w *timeout*] *destination-list*

Parameters:

-t: Pings the specified computer until interrupted.
-a: Resolves addresses to computer names.
-n *count*: Sends the number of ECHO packets specified by *count*. The default is 4.
-l *length*: Sends ECHO packets containing the amount of data specified by *length*. The default is 32 bytes; the maximum is 65,527.
-f: Sends a Do not Fragment flag in the packet. The packet will not be fragmented by gateways on the route.
-i *ttl*: Sets the Time To Live field to the value specified by *ttl*.
-v *tos*: Sets the Type Of Service field to the value specified by *tos*.
-r *count*: Records the route of the outgoing packet and the returning packet in the Record Route field. A minimum of 1 and a maximum of 9 computers can be specified by *count*.
-s *count*: Specifies the timestamp for the number of hops specified by *count*.
-j *computer-list*: Routes packets by way of the list of computers specified by *computer-list*. Consecutive computers can be separated by intermediate gateways (loose source routed). The maximum number allowed by IP is 9.
-k *computer-list*: Routes packets by way of the list of computers specified by *computer-list*. Consecutive computers cannot be separated by intermediate gateways (strict source routed). The maximum number allowed by IP is 9.
-w *timeout*: Specifies a time-out interval in milliseconds.
destination-list: Specifies the remote computers to ping.

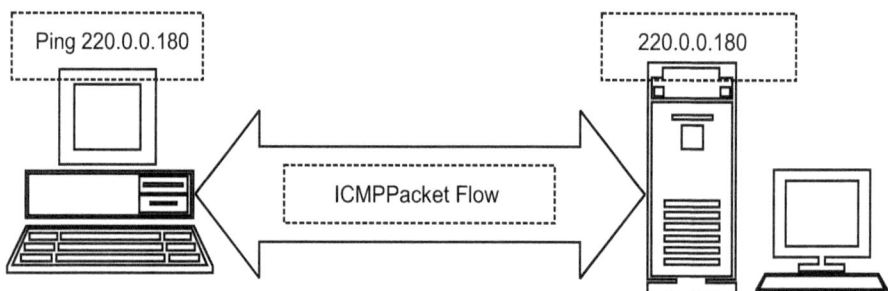

Fig. 5.51: Typical ICMP Packet Flow

If the IP address you specify is correct, you will see something like this:

C:\WINS5>pring 220.0.180

Pinging 220.0.0.180 with 32 bytes of data:

Reply from 220.0.0.180: bytes=32 time=3ms TTL=255
Reply from 220.0.0.180: bytes=32 time=1ms TTL=255
Reply from 220.0.0.180: bytes=32 time=2ms TTL=255
Reply from 220.0.0.180: bytes=32 time=2ms TTL=255

From this we can see that we have had a reply from the device (220.0.0.180). Which means that we can conclude that there isn't a problem. There are many PING parameters, and some implementations of PING perform differently to others. For example, on some systems if you use the PING command, it will constantly send packets of data to the specified device until you break out of the process.

5.10.3 IGMP Protocol

1. *Internet Protocol (IP) multicast* is a bandwidth-conserving technology that reduces traffic by simultaneously delivering a single stream of information to thousands of corporate recipients and homes.
2. Applications that take advantage of multicast include videoconferencing, corporate communications, distance learning, and distribution of software, stock quotes, Video over DSL, IP Video Conferencing, Streaming Media, news and others.
3. IP Multicast delivers source traffic to multiple receivers without adding any additional burden on the source or the receivers while using the least network bandwidth of any competing technology.
4. Multicast packets are replicated in the network by routers enabled with Protocol Independent Multicast (PIM) and other supporting multicast protocols resulting in the most efficient delivery of data to multiple receivers possible.
5. All alternatives require the source to send more than one copy of the data. Some even require the source to send an individual copy to each receiver.
6. If there are thousands of receivers, even low-bandwidth applications benefit from using IP Multicast.
7. High-bandwidth applications, such as MPEG video, may require a large portion of the available network bandwidth for a single stream.
8. In these applications, the only way to send to more than one receiver simultaneously is by using IP Multicast.

DEFINITIONS
Unicast:
1. Unicast traffic involves traffic going from one host to another.
2. A copy of every packet in the data stream goes to every host that requests it.
3. Unicast applications are very easy to implement as they use well established IP protocols, however they are extremely inefficient when many to many communication is required.
4. Since a copy of every packet in the data stream must be sent to every host requesting access to the data stream this type of transmission is inefficient in terms of both network and server resources and presents fairly obvious scalability issues.

5. See Fig. 5.52 for an example of unicast transmission.

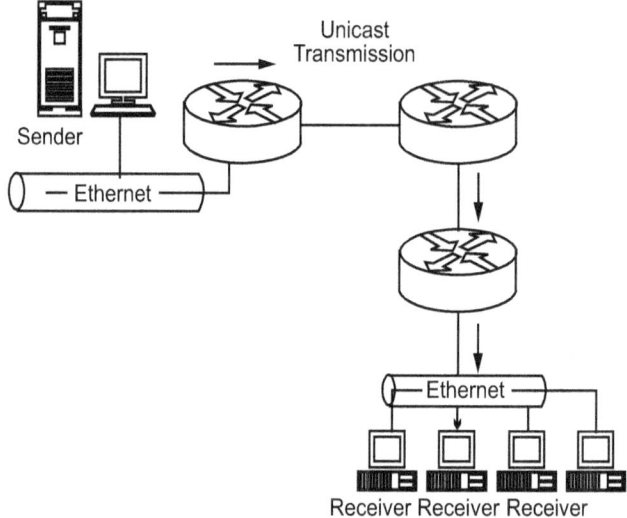

Fig. 5.52: A Unicast Transmission

Broadcast:
1. Broadcast applications allow one host, typically a server, to send to all receivers on a subnet.
2. The efficiency of a broadcast application increases with the number of hosts that need to receive the broadcast.
3. Most broadcasts, except subnet directed broadcasts, are non-routable and are thus contained to the local subnet, a significant restriction.
4. Another restriction or known issue is that all hosts on the broadcast subnet must process the broadcast packets, regardless of whether or not the user on those hosts is interested in the broadcast.
5. Thus, all hosts on that subnet will see increased CPU usage, which is not efficient for those hosts in the subnet who are not participating in the broadcast. See Fig. 5.53.

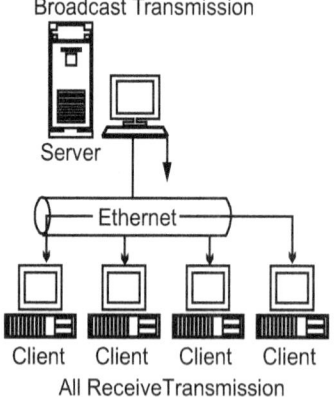

Fig. 5.53: A Broadcast Transmission

Multicast:
1. A hybrid of unicast and broadcast technologies, multicast allows servers to send single copies of data streams, which are then replicated and routed to hosts that signal that they want to receive the data stream.
2. Thus, instead of sending thousands of copies of a streaming sporting event, the server instead streams a single flow that is then directed by routers on the network to the hosts that have indicated that they want to receive the stream.
3. This eliminates the need to send redundant traffic over the network and also tends to eliminate CPU load on systems that are not using the multicast stream, yielding significant enhancements to efficiency for both server and network. See Fig. 5.54 for an example of multicasting.

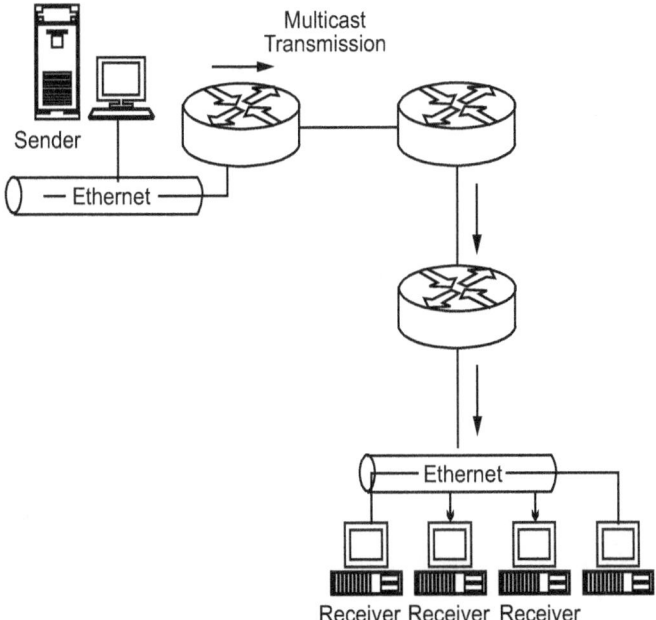

Fig. 5.54: A Multicast Transmission

Multicast Addressing:
1. Multicasts are delivered to a multicast group, which hosts can join should they want to access the data stream.
2. This is done by routing the data streams to a class D IP address in the address space 224.0.0.0 to 239.255.255.255.
3. In this space, which is reserved for multicast, there are a number of address ranges reserved for particular applications (see table below).
4. In general, IANA does not reserve multicast address ranges without good cause, an example of which would be stock feeds or some other mission critical stream.
5. Instead of static mappings, it is preferred to use dynamic mappings similar to DHCP for assigning streams to multicast IP addresses.

6. Although an in depth discussion of the various protocols used to achieve this is beyond the scope of this paper, SDR (Session Directory Protocol) was one of the first implemented but proved to have scalability issues.

Table 5.10: Multicast Addressing

Reserved Block Begin	Reserved Block End	Reserved Block Meaning	Reserved Block Use
224.0.0.0	224.0.0.255	Link local (not forwarded)	Subnet local communication (i.e. routing protocol discovery)
224.0.1.0	224.0.1.255	Non link local reserves	Network protocols or Network applications
232.0.0.0	232.255.255.255	Source Specific Multicast	Source Specific Multicast
233.0.0.0	233.0.0.0	GLOP addressing	Sources with AS's that want public multicast address
239.0.0.0	239.255.255.255	Administratively scoped	Used within a domain for private multicasting use

7. The layer 3 multicast group referenced above needs to be converted to a layer 2 MAC address to be used by end stations sending and receiving to the data stream.
8. This layer 2 multicast MAC address can be converted from the layer 3 IP address of the group.

IP Multicast Addresses:

Multicast addresses specify an arbitrary group of IP hosts that have joined the group and want to receive traffic sent to this group.

IP Class D Addresses:

- The *Internet Assigned Numbers Authority (IANA)* controls the assignment of IP multicast addresses.
- It has assigned the old Class D address space to be used for IP multicast.
- This means that all IP multicast group addresses will fall in the range of 224.0.0.0 to 239.255.255.255.

Note: This address range is only for the group address or destination address of IP multicast traffic. The source address for multicast datagrams is always the unicast source address.

Reserved Link Local Addresses:

- The IANA has reserved addresses in the 224.0.0.0 through 224.0.0.255 to be used by network protocols on a local network segment.
- Packets with these addresses should never be forwarded by a router; they remain local on a particular LAN segment.
- They are always transmitted with a time-to-live (TTL) of 1.
- Network protocols use these addresses for automatic router discovery and to communicate important routing information.
- For example, OSPF uses 224.0.0.5 and 224.0.0.6 to exchange link state information. Table 5.11 lists some of the well-known addresses.

Table 5.11: Link Local Addresses

Address	Usage
224.0.0.1	All systems on this subnet
224.0.0.2	All routers on this subnet
224.0.0.5	OSPF routers
224.0.0.6	OSPF designated routers
224.0.0.12	DHCP server/relay agent

Globally Scoped Address:
- The range of addresses from 224.0.1.0 through 238.255.255.255 are called globally scoped addresses.
- They can be used to multicast data between organizations and across the Internet.
- Some of these addresses have been reserved for use by multicast applications through IANA.
- For example, 224.0.1.1 has been reserved for Network Time Protocol (NTP).

Limited Scope Addresses:
- The range of addresses from 239.0.0.0 through 239.255.255.255 contains limited scope addresses or administratively scoped addresses.
- Routers are typically configured with filters to prevent multicast traffic in this address range from flowing outside an **autonomous system (AS)** or any user-defined domain.
- Within an autonomous system or domain, the limited scope address range can be further subdivided so those local multicast boundaries can be defined.
- This also allows for address reuse among these smaller domains.

Glop Addressing:
- It is proposed that the 233.0.0.0/8 address range be reserved for statically defined addresses by organizations that already have an AS number reserved.
- The AS number of the domain is embedded into the second and third octets of the 233.0.0.0/8 range.
- For example, the AS 62010 is written in hex as F23A.
- Separating out the two octets F2 and 3A, we get 242 and 58 in decimal.
- This would give us a subnet of 233.242.58.0 that would be globally reserved for AS 62010 to use.

Layer 2 Multicast Addresses:
- Normally, network interface cards (NICs) on a LAN segment will receive only packets destined for their burned-in MAC address or the broadcast MAC address.
- Some means had to be devised so that multiple hosts could receive the same packet and still be capable of differentiating among multicast groups.
- Fortunately, the IEEE LAN specifications made provisions for the transmission of broadcast and/or multicast packets.

- In the 802.3 standard, bit 0 of the first octet is used to indicate a broadcast and/or multicast frame.
- Fig. 5.55 shows the location of the broadcast/multicast bit in an Ethernet frame.

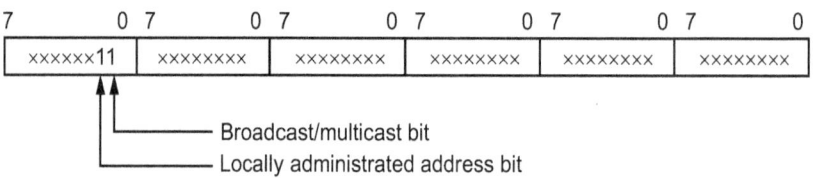

Fig. 5.55: IEEE 802.3 MAC Address Format

- This bit indicates that the frame is destined for an arbitrary group of hosts or all hosts on the network (in the case of the broadcast address, 0xFFFF.FFFF.FFFF).
- IP multicast makes use of this capability to transmit IP packets to a group of hosts on a LAN segment.

Ethernet MAC Address Mapping:

- The IANA owns a block of Ethernet MAC addresses that start with 01:00:5E in hexadecimal.
- Half of this block is allocated for multicast addresses.
- This creates the range of available Ethernet MAC addresses to be 0100.5e00.0000 through 0100.5e7f.ffff.
- This allocation allows for 23 bits in the Ethernet address to correspond to the IP multicast group address.
- The mapping places the lower 23 bits of the IP multicast group address into these available 23 bits in the Ethernet address (given in Fig. 5.56).

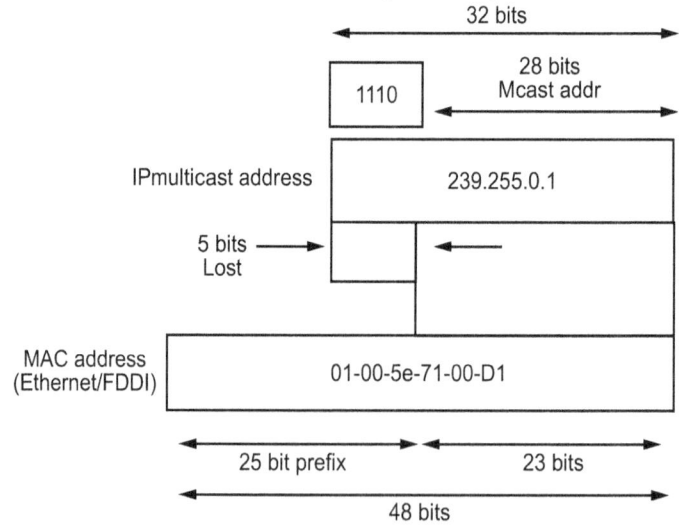

Fig. 5.56: Mapping of IP Multicast to Ethernet/FDDI MAC Address

- Because the upper 5 bits of the IP multicast address are dropped in this mapping, the resulting address is not unique.
- In fact, 32 different multicast group IDs all map to the same Ethernet address (see Fig. 5.57).

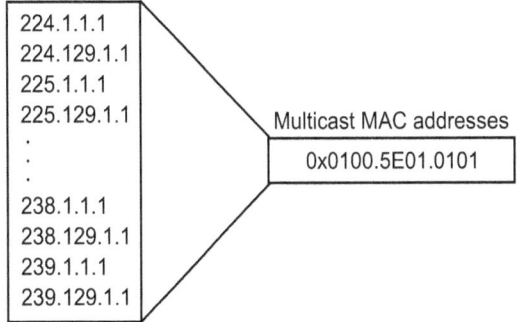

Fig. 5.57: MAC Address Ambiguities

Internet Group Management Protocol:
- IGMP is used to dynamically register individual hosts in a multicast group on a particular LAN.
- Hosts identify group memberships by sending IGMP messages to their local multicast router.
- Under IGMP, routers listen to IGMP messages and periodically send out queries to discover which groups are active or inactive on a particular subnet.

IGMP Version 1:
A diagram of the packet format is found in Fig. 5.58.

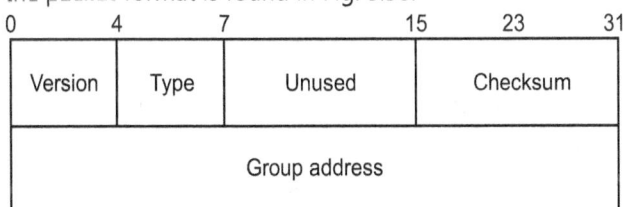

Fig. 5.58: IGMP Version 1 Packet Format

In Version 1, there are just two different types of IGMP messages:
- Membership query
- Membership report

Hosts send out IGMP membership reports corresponding to a particular multicast group to indicate that they are interested in joining that group. The router periodically sends out an IGMP membership query to verify that at least one host on the subnet is still interested in receiving traffic directed to that group. When there is no reply to three consecutive IGMP membership queries, the router times out the group and stops forwarding traffic directed toward that group.

IGMP Version 2:

A diagram of the packet format follows in Fig. 5.59.

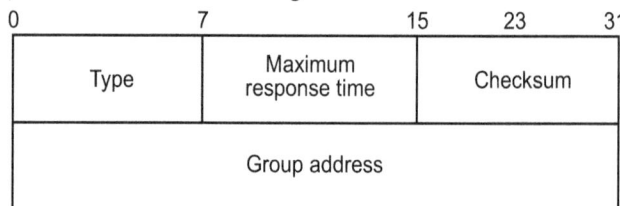

Fig. 5.59: IGMPv2 Message Format

In Version 2, there are four types of IGMP messages:
- Membership query
- Version 1 membership report
- Version 2 membership report
- Leave group

IGMP Version 2 works basically the same as Version 1. The main difference is that there is a leave group message. The hosts now can actively communicate to the local multicast router their intention to leave the group. The router then sends out a group-specific query and determines whether there are any remaining hosts interested in receiving the traffic. If there are no replies, the router times out the group and stops forwarding the traffic. This can greatly reduce the leave latency compared to IGMP Version 1. Unwanted and unnecessary traffic can be stopped much sooner.

Protocols:

Protocol	Function
Internet Group Membership Protocol (IGMP)	Discovers hosts that belong to multicast group
Protocol Independent Multicast Protocol (PIM)	Discovers other multicast routers that should receive multicast packets
Distance Vector Multicast Routing Protocol (DVMRP)	Routes multicast datagrams within autonomous systems
BGP Multicasting Protocol	Routes multicast datagrams between autonomous systems

1. **IGMP:** IP hosts use Internet Group Management Protocol (IGMP) to report their multicast group memberships to neighboring routers. Similarly, multicast routers system, use IGMP to discover which of their hosts belong to multicast groups.
2. **The IPv4** address scheme assigns Class D addresses for IP multicasting. IGMP is the protocol that uses these addresses, which can be in the range 224.0.0.0 to

239.255.255.255. This implementation of IGMP complies with IGMPv2. IGMPv2 routers support both IGMPv1 and IGMPv2 hosts.
3. **PIM:** Protocol Independent Multicast (PIM) is the protocol that allows multicast routers to identify other multicast routers that should receive packets. This implementation of PIM supports PIM dense mode (DM), PIM sparse mode (SM), and PIM sparse-dense mode (S-DM).
4. **DVMRP:** The router system supports Distance Vector Multicast Routing Protocol (DVRMP) on virtual routers to forward multicast datagrams through a network. DVMRP is an interior gateway protocol that supports operations within an autonomous system, but not between autonomous systems.
5. A **DVMRP** router sends prune messages to its neighbors if it discovers that:
    - The network to which a host is attached has no active members of the multicast group.
    - All neighbors, except the next-hop neighbor connected to the source, have pruned the source and the group.
6. When a neighbor receives a prune message from a DVMRP router, it removes that neighbor from its source group table, which provides information to the multicast forwarding table
7. If a host on a previously pruned branch wants to join a multicast group, it sends an IGMP message to its first-hop router.
8. The first-hop router then sends a graft message upstream.
9. **BGP Multicasting:** BGP multicasting is an extension of the BGP unicast routing protocol. Many of the functions available for BGP unicasting are also available for BGP multicasting. The BGP multiprotocol extensions specify that BGP can exchange information within different types of address families.
10. The address families available are unicast, multicast, and unicast VPN. When you enable BGP, the Router system employs unicast IPv4 addresses by default. To enable BGP multicasting, you must configure commands for the multicast address family.

IGMP DETAILS:
What about IGMP rules?
IGMP messages are used by routers to keep track of group memberships in their immediately connected subnetwork. The following rules apply:
1. Host sends an IGMP "report" for joining a group.
2. Host will never send a report when it wants to leave a group.
3. Multicast routers send IGMP queries to the all-hosts group periodically to see whether any group members exists on their subnetworks. If no response is received after a number of queries, the router assumes that there is not any group member on the network.

What about IGMP messages?
There is 2 types of IGMP messages:
- **Host membership query:** Multicast routers send Host Membership Query messages to discover which host groups have members on their attached local networks. Queries are addressed to the all-hosts group and carry an IP TTL of 1.
- **Host membership report:** Hosts respond to a Query by generating Host Membership Reports reporting each host group to which they belong on the network interface from which the Query was received. A Report is sent with an IP destination address equal to the host group address being reported, and with an IP TTL of 1.

In order to reduce the total number of Reports transmitted, two techniques are used:

When a host receives a Query, it doesn't send a report immediately but it starts a report delay timer for each group membership on the network interface of the incoming Query (randomly-chosen value between zero and D seconds). When a timer expires, a report is generated for the corresponding host group.	A Report is sent with an IP destination address equal to the host group address being reported, and with an IP TTL of 1. The other members of the same group on the same network can overhear the Report. Only one host send a report for the group and don't generate a Report when they hear one.

What about IGMP parameters ?
Report Delay: The maximum report delay, D, is 10 seconds.
The query interval: This is the interval at which IGMP Host Membership Queries are sent. The default value is 125 seconds.
The time-out interval: This is the longest interval that a group will remain in the local group database without receiving a Host Membership Report. The default value is 270 seconds.
The formula: 2*(query interval + 10) is used to calculate this time.

About Hosts and Process:
What are hosts specifications?
There are three levels of hosts:

Level 0: No support for IP multicasting.

Level 1: Support for sending but not receiving multicast IP datagrams.

Level 2: Full support for IP multicasting. Host belonging to this level are allowed to join and leave groups.

How to send multicast IP datagrams?
Multicast IP datagrams are sent using the same "Send IP" operation used to send unicast IP datagrams. An IP host group address, instead of an individual IP address, is specified as the destination by an upper-layer module.

The IP TTL of an outgoing multicast datagram must be specified, if such a capability doesn't exist. If the upper-layer protocol doesn't specify it, this one should default to 1 for all multicast IP datagrams.

For hosts attached to several networks, the service interface should provide a way for the upper-layer protocol to identify which network interface is used for the multicast transmission. Only one interface is used for the initial transmission. If the upper-layer protocol doesn't choose one, a default interface should be used.

- To support the sending of multicast IP datagrams and to allow multicast transmission, the IP module must recognize IP host group addresses when routing outgoing datagrams. Most IP implementations include the some logic.

> if IP-destination is on the same local network or IP-destination is a host group,
>
> send datagram locally to IP-destination
>
> else send datagram locally to GatewayTo(IP-destination)

How to receive multicast IP datagrams?

- Incoming multicast IP datagrams are received by upper-layer protocol modules using the same "Receive IP" operation as unicast datagrams. Before any datagrams destined to a group can be received, an upper-layer protocol must ask the IP module to join that group. Two new operations must be added:

JoinHostGroup (group-address, interface)	LeaveHostGroup (group-address, interface)
This host becomes a member of the host group identified by "group-address" on the given network interface.	This host gives up its membership in the host group identified by "group-address" on the given network interface.

The interface argument may be omitted on hosts that support only one interface.

To support the reception of multicast IP datagrams, the IP module must maintain a list of host group memberships associated with each network interface.

This list is updated in response to JoinHostGroup and LeaveHostGroup requests from upper-layer protocols. Each membership has an associated reference count or similar mechanism to handle these requests. Datagrams destined to groups to which the host doesn't belong to are discarded without any error report.

What about hosts states?

A host may be in one of three possible states:

States	When ?
Non-Member state	The host doesn't belong to the group on the interface. Initial state for all memberships on all network interfaces.

States		When ?
Delaying Member state		The host belongs to the group on the interface and has a report delay timer running for that membership.
Idle Member state		The host belongs to the group on the interface and haven't a report delay timer running for that membership.

There are five events that can cause IGMP state transitions:

Events	When ?	Who ?
"join group"	The host joins the group on the interface.	Non-Member state
"leave group"	The host leaves the group on the interface.	Delaying Member and Idle Member states
"query received"	The host receives a valid IGMP Host Membership Query message (to have at least 8 octets long, a correct IGMP checksum and an IP destination address of 224.0.0.1)	Ignored for memberships in the Non-Member or Delaying Member state
"report received"	The host receives a valid IGMP Host Membership Report message (to have at least 8 octets long, a correct IGMP checksum, and the same IP host group address in its IP destination field and its IGMP group address field).	Ignored for memberships in the Non-Member or Idle Member state
"timer expired"	The report delay timer for the group on the interface expires.	Delaying Member state

There are three possible actions that may be taken in response to the above events:

"send report"	for the group on the interface
"start timer"	for the group on the interface, using a random delay value between 0 and D
"stop timer"	for the group on the interface

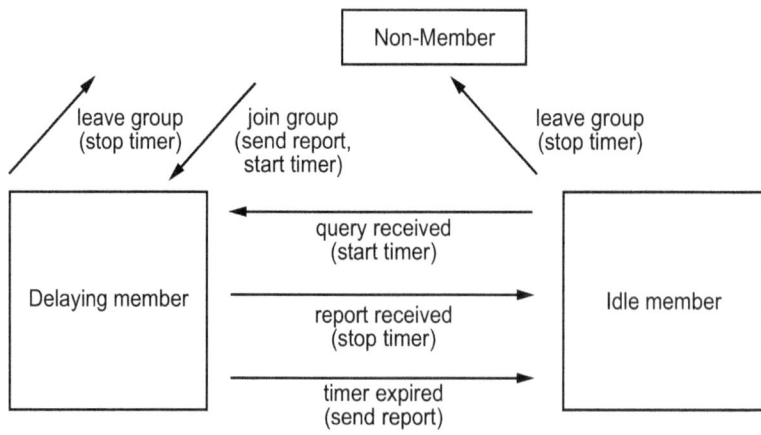

Fig. 5.60: All states and operations are shown in this figure

Multicast Forwarding:

1. In unicast routing, traffic is routed through the network along a single path from the source to the destination host.
2. A unicast router does not really care about the source address—it only cares about the destination address and how to forward the traffic towards that destination.
3. The router scans through its routing table and then forwards a single copy of the unicast packet out the correct interface in the direction of the destination.
4. In multicast routing, the source is sending traffic to an arbitrary group of hosts represented by a multicast group address.
5. The multicast router must determine which direction is upstream (toward the source) and which direction (or directions) is downstream.
6. If there are multiple downstream paths, the router replicates the packet and forwards the traffic down the appropriate downstream paths—which is not necessarily all paths.
7. This concept of forwarding multicast traffic away from the source, rather than to the receiver, is called *reverse path forwarding*.

Reverse Path Forwarding:

1. Reverse path forwarding (RPF) *is* a fundamental concept in multicast routing that enables routers to correctly forward multicast traffic down the distribution tree.
2. RPF makes use of the existing unicast routing table to determine the upstream and downstream neighbors.
3. A router forwards a multicast packet only if it is received on the upstream interface. This RPF check helps to guarantee that the distribution tree will be loop-free.

RPF Check:

When a multicast packet arrives at a router, the router performs an RPF check on the packet. If the RPF check is successful, the packet is forwarded. Otherwise, it is dropped.

For traffic flowing down a source tree, the RPF check procedure works as follows:

Step 1: Router looks up the source address in the unicast routing table to determine whether it has arrived on the interface that is on the reverse path back to the source.

Step 2: If packet has arrived on the interface leading back to the source, the RPF check is successful and the packet is forwarded.

Step 3: If the RPF check in Step 2 fails, the packet is dropped.

Fig. 5.61 shows an example of an unsuccessful RPF check.

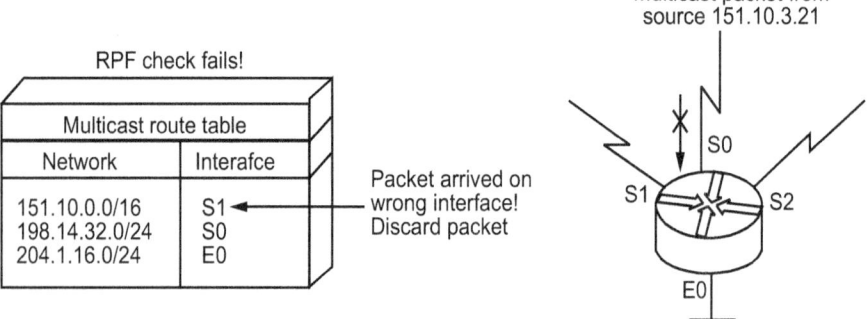

Fig. 5.61: RPF Check Fails

A multicast packet from source 151.10.3.21 is received on interface S0. A check of the unicast route table shows that the interface that this router would use to forward unicast data to 151.10.3.21 is S1. Because the packet has arrived on S0, the packet will be discarded.

Fig. 5.62 shows an example of a successful RPF check.

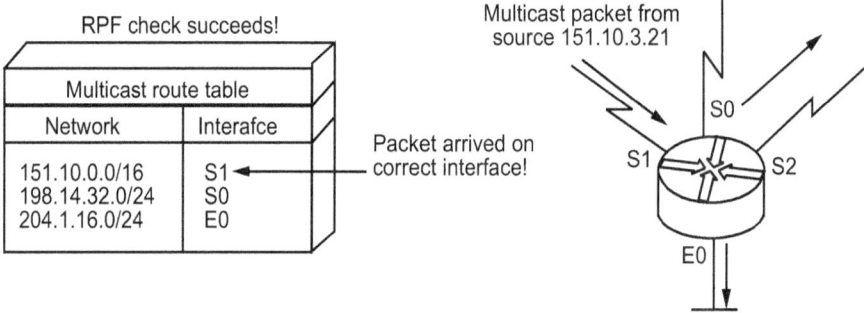

Fig. 5.62: RPF Check Succeeds

This time the multicast packet has arrived on S1. The router checks the unicast routing table and finds that S1 is the correct interface. The RPF check passes and the packet is forwarded.

5.11 Transport Layer

1. Transport layer's responsibilities include End-to-End message transfer capabilities independent of underlying network, along with error control, fragmentation and flow control.
2. End to end message transmission or connecting applications at the transport layer can be categorized as either:
   - connection-oriented e.g. TCP
   - connection-less e.g. UDP

3. Transport layer can be thought of as a literal transport mechanism e.g. a vehicle whose responsibility is to make sure that its contents (passengers/goods) reach its destination safe and sound.
4. The transport layer provides this service of connecting applications together through the use of ports.
5. Since IP provides only a best effort delivery, the transport layer is the first layer to address reliability.
6. For example, TCP is a connection-oriented protocol that addresses numerous reliability issues to provide a reliable byte stream:
   - data arrives in-order
   - data has minimal error-correctness
   - duplicate data is discarded
   - lost/discarded packets are resent
   - includes traffic congestion control
7. The dynamic routing protocols which technically fit at this layer in the TCP/IP Protocol Suite (since they run over IP) are generally considered to be part of the Network layer; an example is OSPF (IP protocol number 89).
8. The newer SCTP is also a "reliable", connection-oriented, transport mechanism. It is stream-oriented — not byte-oriented like TCP — and provides multiple streams multiplexed over a single connection.
9. It also provides multi-homing support, in which a connection end can be represented by multiple IP addresses (representing multiple physical interfaces), such that if one fails, the connection is not interrupted. It was developed initially for telephony applications (to transport SS7 over IP), but can also be used for other applications.
10. UDP is a connectionless datagram protocol. Like IP, it is a best effort or "unreliable" protocol.
11. The only reliability issue that it addresses is error-correctness of the data.
12. UDP is typically used for applications such as streaming media (audio and video, etc) where on-time arrival is more important than reliability, or for simple query/response applications like DNS lookups, where the overhead of setting up a reliable connection is disproportionately large.
13. Both TCP and UDP are used to carry a number of higher-level applications. The applications at any given network address are distinguished by their TCP or UDP port. By convention certain *well known ports* are associated with specific applications.
14. RTP is a datagram protocol that is designed for real-time data such as streaming audio and video. RTP is a session layer that uses the UDP packet format as a basis yet is said to sit within the transport layer of the Internet protocol stack.

5.11.1 Transmission Control Protocol (TCP)

1. The **Transmission Control Protocol (TCP)** is one of the core protocols of the Internet protocol suite.

2. Using TCP, applications on networked hosts can create *connections* to one another, over which they can exchange data or packets. The protocol guarantees reliable and in-order delivery of sender to receiver data. TCP also distinguishes data for multiple, concurrent applications (e.g. Web server and e-mail server) running on the same host.

3. TCP supports many of the Internet's most popular application protocols and resulting applications, including the World Wide Web, e-mail and Secure Shell.

4. In the Internet protocol suite, TCP is the intermediate layer between the Internet Protocol below it, and an application above it.

5. Applications often need reliable pipe-like connections to each other, whereas the Internet Protocol does not provide such streams, but rather only unreliable packets. TCP does the task of the transport layer in the simplified OSI model of computer networks.

6. Applications send streams of octets (8-bit bytes) to TCP for delivery through the network, and TCP divides the byte stream into appropriately sized segments (usually delineated by the maximum transmission unit (MTU) size of the data link layer of the network the computer is attached to).

7. TCP then passes the resulting packets to the Internet Protocol, for delivery through a network to the TCP module of the entity at the other end. TCP checks to make sure that no packets are lost by giving each packet a *sequence number*, which is also used to make sure that the data are delivered to the entity at the other end in the correct order.

8. The TCP module at the far end sends back an *acknowledgement* for packets which have been successfully received; a timer at the sending TCP will cause a *timeout* if an acknowledgement is not received within a reasonable round-trip time (or RTT), and the (presumably lost) data will then be *re-transmitted*.

9. The TCP checks that no bytes are damaged by using a checksum; one is computed at the sender for each block of data before it is sent, and checked at the receiver.

TCP header:

Let's take a closer look at a TCP header. A minimal header requires 20 octets, with the information shown in Table 5.12.

Table 5.12

Source port	16-bits	This is the number of the calling port.
Destination port	16-bits	This is the number of the called port.
Sequence number	32-bits	This number ensures that data is processed in the right sequence. The number represents the byte sequence number of the first octet of the enclosed data and will be incremented accordingly in subsequent segments.
Acknowledgement number	32-bits	This represents the next expected TCP octet.
Data offset	4-bits	This is the number of 32-bit words in the TCP header.
Reserved	6-bits	This is set to zero.
Flags	6-bits	These control the setup and termination of the connection, and data flow: URG: Urgent pointer field significant ACK: Acknowledgement field significant PHS: Push function RST: Reset connection SYN: Synchronize sequence numbers FIN: No more data from sender
Window	16-bits	This is the receive window size, indicating the number of octets the sender is willing to accept.
Checksum	16-bits	This is a checksum based on the IP address fields and the TCP header and length.
Urgent pointer	16-bits	This points to the first octet that follows the urgent data, allowing the receiver to know how much urgent data is coming.
Options	variable	Currently, only the maximum TCP segment size is defined.

The actual data stream follows the header. When used in conjunction with IP, an IP header that takes care of routing the information between the two hosts using their IP address information would prefix the TCP header. Fig. 5.63 shows how a TCP header will appear.

Source port							Destination port	
Sequence number									
Acknowledgement number									
Offset	Reserved	U	A	P	R	S	F	Window
Checksum									Urgent pointer
Options + Padding									
Data									

Fig. 5.63: TCP header diagram

TCP Connection Establishment:

The establishment of a TCP connection takes place with the usage of a 3 way handshaking protocol:

1. The initiator of the session sends a segment with the SYN flag set to the recipient.
2. Upon receipt of the segment, the recipient sends a SYN segment to the initiator with the ACK number set to the sequence number + 1, and sets new sequence number for its own end.
3. The initiator then sends an ACK of its own in response to the recipient's SYN, with the ACK number set to the recipeint's sequence number + 1.

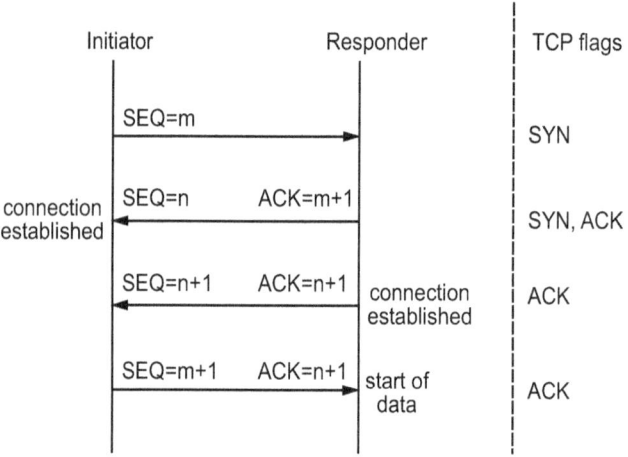

Fig. 5.64: TCP Connection Termination

TCP Connection Termination:

1. TCP is a full duplex protocol, i.e. data can be sent in both directions independently.
2. Therefore, to fully close the connection, it has to be terminated in both directions.
3. If one end of the connection sends segment with the FIN flag set, it means that that end has got no more data to send.
4. However, this end can still receive data from the other end until the other end has explicitly closed its end of the connection.
5. This is known as a half-close.
6. The full termination of a TCP connection takes place with the usage of a 4 way handshake:
   - The initiator of the close sends a FIN segment to the recipient.
   - The recipient sends an ACK of the FIN segment.
   - The recipient sends a FIN segment of its own to the initiator.
   - The initiator responds with an ACK to that FIN segment.

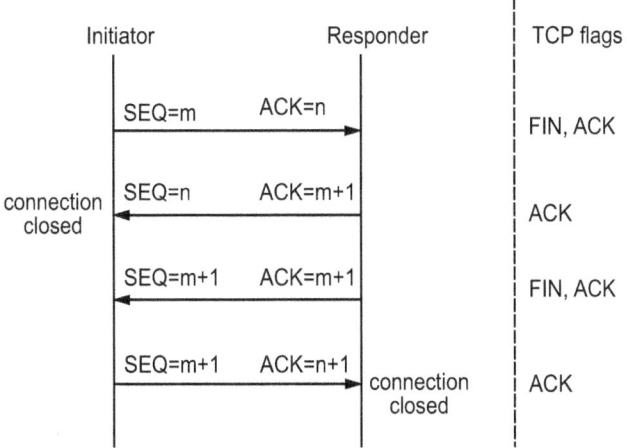

Fig. 5.65: TCP connection Termination

TCP Multiplexing Service:
1. Multiplexing services similar to those above are also provided by TCP.
2. Multiple processes within a host can simultaneously access the network via a single TCP entity.
3. Each process within a host which uses TCP services is identified with a *port*.
4. A port, when concatenated with an internet address, forms a *socket*, which is unique throughout the internet.
5. Service by TCP is provided by means of a logical connection between a pair of sockets.

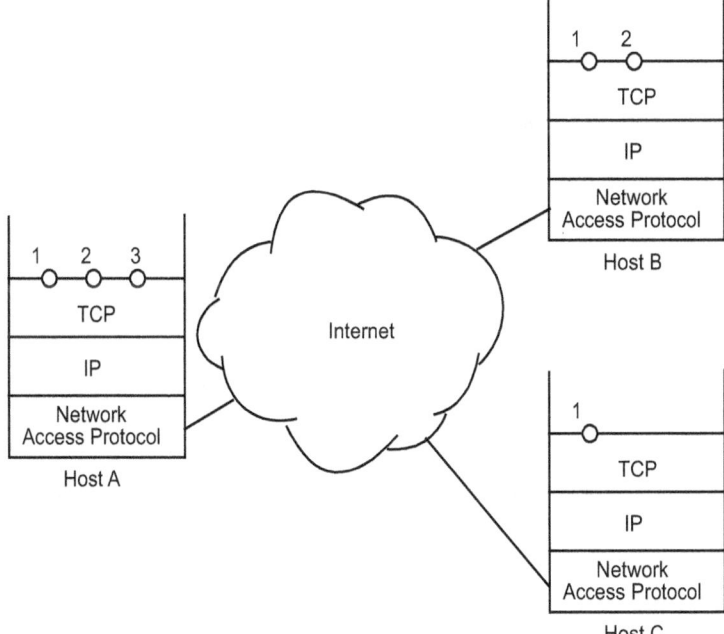

Fig. 5.66: TCP multiplexing is shown

6. As an example, the diagram above shows three hosts A, B and C connected over the internet.
7. The multiplexing service of TCP would enable a process X, say in host A to establish a connection to a process Y in host B.
8. This might involve use of port 2 in A and port 1 in B. At the same time a process P in B could establish a connection to a process Q in A using port 2 of B and port 1 of A.
9. Finally, a process M in A might establish a link to a process N in host C using ports 3 of A and 1 of C.
10. Thus multiple users or processes within a host can employ simultaneously the services of TCP to exchange data with remote processes.

5.11.2 UDP (User Datagram Protocol)

1. The User Datagram Protocol (UDP) is one of the core protocols of the Internet protocol suite.
2. Using UDP, programs on networked computers can send short messages known as *datagrams* to one another.
3. UDP does not provide the reliability and ordering guarantees that TCP does; datagrams may arrive out of order or go missing without notice.
4. However, as a result, UDP is faster and more efficient for many lightweight or time-sensitive purposes.
5. Also its stateless nature is useful for servers that answer small queries from huge numbers of clients.
6. Common network applications that use UDP include the Domain Name System (DNS), streaming media applications, Voice over IP, Trivial File Transfer Protocol (TFTP), and online games.

Ports:
1. UDP utilizes ports to allow application-to-application communication.
2. The port field is 16-bits so the valid range is 0 to 65,535.
3. Port 0 is reserved and shouldn't be used.
4. Ports 1 through 1023 are named "well-known" ports and on Unix-derived operating systems binding to one of these ports requires root access.
5. Ports 1024 through 49,151 are registered ports.
6. Ports 49,152 through 65,535 are ephemeral ports and are used as temporary ports primarily by clients when communicating to servers.

Packet Structure:
1. UDP is a minimal message-orientated transport layer protocol.

2. In the Internet protocol suite, UDP provides a very simple interface between a network layer below (e.g., IPv4) and an session layer or application layer above.
3. UDP provides no guarantees to the upper layer protocol for message delivery and a UDP sender retains no state on UDP messages once sent. (For this reason UDP is sometimes called the *Unreliable* Datagram Protocol).
4. UDP adds only application multiplexing and transactive, header and data checksumming also found in a TCP header on top of an IP datagram.
5. If any kind of reliability for the information transmited is needed, it must be implemented in upper layers.

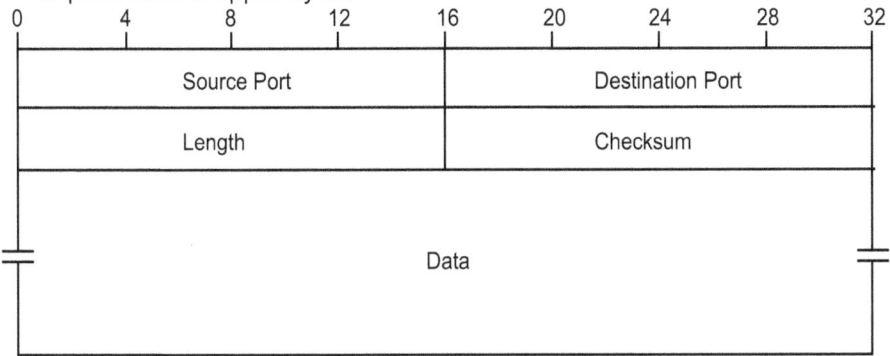

Fig. 5.67: Typical UDP Header format

6. The UDP header consists of only 4 fields of which two are optional (red background in table).

Source Port:
This field identifies the sending port when meaningful and should be assumed to be the port to reply to if needed. If not used then it should be zero.

Destination Port:
This field identifies the destination port and is required.

Length:
A 16-bit field that specifies the length of the entire datagram: header and data. The minimum length is 8 bytes since that's the length of the header.

Checksum:
- The 16-bit checksum field is used for error-checking of the header *and data*.
- Checksum is the 16-bit one's complement of the one's complement sum of a pseudo header of information from the IP header, the UDP header, and the data, padded with zero octets at the end (if necessary) to make a multiple of two octets.

- In other words, all 16-bit words are summed together using one's complement (with the checksum field set to zero).
- The sum is then one's complemented.
- This final value is then inserted as the checksum field. Algorithmically speaking, this is the same as for IPv4.
- The difference is in the data used to make the checksum. Included is a pseudo-header that mimics the IP header:

+	Bits 0-7	8-15	16-23	24-31
0	Source Address			
32	Destination Address			
64	Zeros	Protocol	UDP Length	
96	Source Port		Destination Port	
128	Length		Checksum	
160	Data			

Fig. 5.68: Typical IP Header

- The source and destination addresses are those in the IPv4 header.
- The UDP length field is the length of the UDP header and data.
- If the checksum is calculated to be zero (all 0's) or negative zero (all 1's) then the checksum sent should be negative zero since zero indicates an unused checksum.
- Lacking reliability, UDP applications must generally be willing to accept some loss, errors or duplication.
- Some applications such as TFTP may add rudimentary reliability mechanisms into the application layer as needed.
- Most often, UDP applications do not require reliability mechanisms and may even be hindered by them.
- Streaming media, real-time multiplayer games and voice over IP (VoIP) are examples of applications that often use UDP.
- If an application requires a high degree of reliability, a protocol such as the Transmission Control Protocol or erasure codes may be used instead.
- Lacking any congestion avoidance and control mechanisms, network-based mechanisms are required to minimize potential congestion collapse effects of uncontrolled, high rate UDP traffic loads.
- In other words, since UDP senders cannot detect congestion, network-based elements such as routers using packet queueing and dropping techniques will often be the only tool available to slow down excessive UDP traffic.
- While the total amount of UDP traffic found on a typical network is often on the order of only a few percent, numerous key applications use UDP, including the Domain Name System (DNS), the simple network management protocol (SNMP), the Dynamic Host Configuration Protocol (DHCP) and the Routing Information Protocol (RIP), to name just a few.

5.11.3 TCP Vs. UDP

1. TCP (Transmission Control Protocol) is the most commonly used protocol on the Internet.
2. The reason for this is because TCP offers error correction.
3. When the TCP protocol is used there is a "guaranteed delivery." This is due largely in part to a method called "flow control." Flow control determines when data needs to be re-sent, and stops the flow of data until previous packets are successfully transferred.
4. This works because if a packet of data is sent, a collision may occur.
5. When this happens, the client re-requests the packet from the server until the whole packet is complete and is identical to its original.
6. UDP (User Datagram Protocol) is anther commonly used protocol on the Internet.
7. However, UDP is never used to send important data such as webpages, database information, etc; UDP is commonly used for streaming audio and video.
8. Streaming media such as Windows Media audio files (.WMA), Real Player (.RM), and others use UDP because it offers speed !
9. The reason UDP is faster than TCP is because there is no form of flow control or error correction.
10. The data sent over the Internet is affected by collisions, and errors will be present.
11. Remember that UDP is only concerned with speed.
12. This is the main reason why streaming media is not high quality.

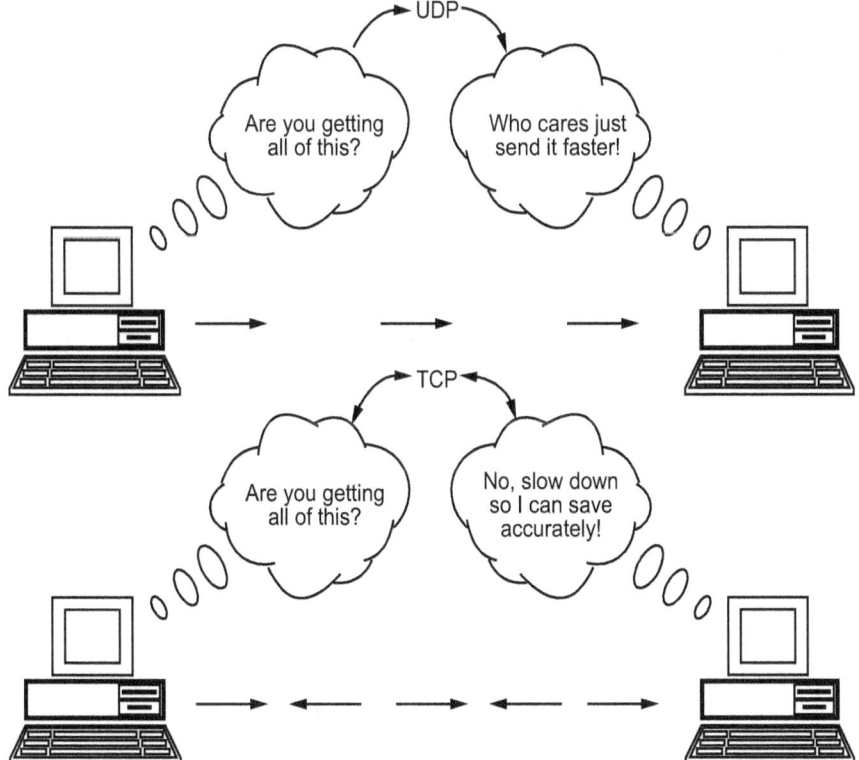

Fig. 5.69: Reliable TCP and Unreliable UDP

13. On the contrary, UDP has been implemented among some trojan horse viruses.
14. Hackers develop scripts and trojans to run over UDP in order to mask their activities.
15. UDP packets are also used in DoS (Denial of Service) attacks.

TCP	UDP
• Sets up an end-to-end connection (connection oriented).	• Does not set up an end-to-end connection (connectionless).
• Checks for errors (such as duplicate datagrams) If errors are found, packets are retransmitted.	• Does not check for errors (thought data maybe checksummed).
• Transmits to sender acknowledgement that the packet was received.	• Does not guarantee delivery.
• Is stream-oriented.	• Is packet-oriented.
• Has flow control.	• No flow control.
• duplex (bidirectional).	• duplex (bidirectional).
• All the above guarantees delivery (Because it does all the above and is very reliable, this option is not as fast as UDP).	• Offers a much faster packet transmission rate that TCP, but it is unreliable.
• Assigns datagram size dynamically for efficiency.	• Every datagram segment is the same size.

Finally the Frame formats for the IP, TCP and UDP is collectively shown in the following figure.

IP, TCP and UDP Header Formats:

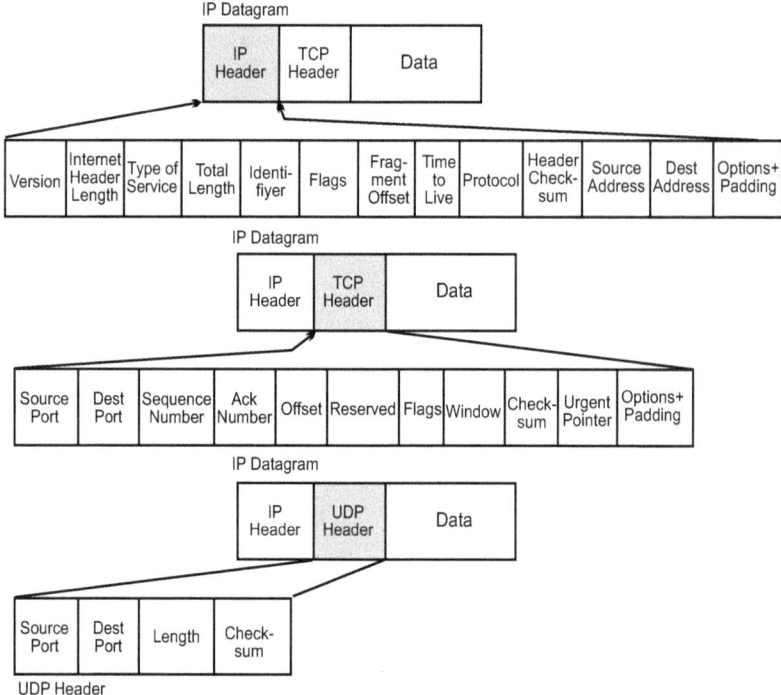

Fig. 5.70: Summarization of the IP, TCP and UDP Frame formats

5.12 Application Layer of the TCP/IP Protocol Stack

1. Application layer provides services for an application program to ensure that effective communication with another application program in a network is possible.
2. The Application layer is NOT the application itself that is doing the communication.
3. It is a service layer that provides these services:
   - Makes sure that the other party is identified and can be reached.
   - If appropriate, authenticates either the message sender or receiver or both.
   - Makes sure that necessary communication resources exist (for example, is there a modem in the sender's computer?)
   - Ensures agreement at both ends about error recovery procedures, data integrity, and privacy.
   - Determines protocol and data syntax rules at the application level.
4. It may be convenient to think of the Application layer as the high-level set-up services for the application program or an interactive user.
5. Defines protocols for node-to-node application communication and also controls user interface specifications.
6. Consists of a set of services that provide ubiquitous access to all types of networks. Applications utilize the services to communicate with other devices and remote applications.

Protocols and Applications:

Port	Protocol	Description
80	HTTP	HyperText Transfer Protocol (e.g. for web browsing).
23	Telnet	Terminal Emulation (Telephone network)
21	FTP	File transfers between computers (File Transfer Protocol)
25	SMTP	Used to send mail between mail servers (Simple Mail Transfer Protocol)
	X server	
	Traceroute	
53	DNS	Resolves FQDN to IP addresses (Domain Name Service)
69	TFTP	Have to know what you want and where it is on the server, no directory browsing, no user authentication (Trivial File Transfer Protocol)
67	BootP	Used by diskless workstations to receive boot file and other information via TFTP

161	SNMP	Collect and manipulates network information (Simple Network Management Protocol)
2049	NFS	Allows remote file systems to be mounted as local (Network File System)
135	RPC	
515	LPD	Used for print sharing of network printers with TCP/IP (Line Printer Daemon)
546-547	DHCP	Assigns IP addresses to hosts from a pool. Can send IP address, Subnet mask, Domain Name, Default Gateway, DNS IP, WINS info. (Dynamic Host Configuration Protocol). DHCP port 546 for client and 547 for server

5.12.1 HTTP (HyperText Transfer Protocol)

1. The HyperText Transfer Protocol, or *HTTP*, must be the most widely used Application layer protocol in the world today.
2. It forms the basis of what most people understand the Internet to be the World Wide Web. Its purpose is to provide a lightweight protocol for the retrieval of HyperText Markup Language (*HTML*) and other documents from Web sites throughout the Internet.
3. Each time you open a Web browser to surf the Internet, you are using *HTTP* over *TCP/IP*.
4. *HTTP* was first ratified in the early 1990's and has been through three main iterations:
   - **HTTP/0.9:** A simplistic first implementation of the protocol that only supported the option to get a Web page.
   - **HTTP/1.0:** This version added many supplemental data fields, known as *headers* to the specification. This allowed for other information passing between the client and server, alongside the request and consequent page.
   - **HTTP/1.1:** Implemented a number of improvements over and above the 1.0 specification. One of the main improvements of 1.1 over 1.0 was the implementation of techniques such as persistent *TCP* connections, pipelining, and cache control to improve performance within *HTTP*-based applications.
5. Most browsers these days offer support for both 1.0 and 1.1 implementations, with new browsers using 1.1 as a default but supporting the ability to fall back to earlier versions if required.
6. Definitions are clear to point out is that all implementations of the *HTTP* protocol should be backward compatible.

7. That is to say that a browser implementing the *HTTP*/1.1 specification should be capable of receiving a 1.0 response from a server.
8. Conversely, a 1.1 implementation on the server side should also be capable of responding to requests from a 1.0 browser.
9. It is well outside the bounds of this book to cover the *HTTP* protocols in huge detail, so let's concentrate on those elements most relevant to content switching.
10. Let's start at the beginning and see how a basic browser retrieves a Web page from a Web server.
11. The first important point to note is that a Web page is typically made up of many dozens of objects, ranging from the *HTML* base through to the images that are present on the page.
12. The *HTML* can be thought of as the template for the page overall, instructing the browser on the layout of the text, font sizes and colors, background color of the page, and which other images need to be retrieved to make up the page.

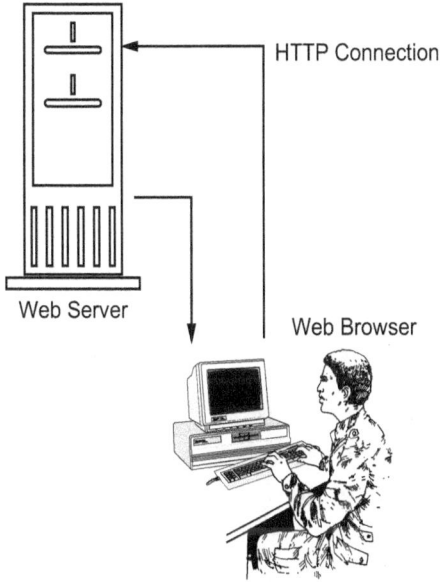

Fig. 5.71: Process is indicated in figure

13. Think of the process, taking place in the following order:
    - Client sends a request for the required page to the Web server.
    - The server analyzes the request and sends back an acknowledgment to the client along with the *HTML* code required to make the page.
    - The client will begin interpreting the *HTML* and building the page.
    - The client, in subsequent requests, will retrieve any embedded objects, such as images or other multimedia sources.

14. Once all elements of the page have been retrieved, the client browser will display the completed Web page.
15. The order and timing of the process described previously depends largely on which implementation of *HTTP* is used — 1.0 or 1.1 — although all browsers work in this way of request and response.
16. The main thing you need to know is that HTTP is a language spoken between your web browser (client software) and a web server (server software) so that they can communicate with each other and exchange files.
17. In its simplest form, we can think of HTTP as nothing more than a header, or shipping label, and the protocols for processing the data in this header.
18. The HTTP header is a protocol that tries to pass all the information an application on the client or server may need from the other end of the transaction.
19. An HTTP message can be broken into three parts.
    - the request/response line
    - the HTTP header
    - the body of the message
20. The body of the message is either the content being sent from the server to the client, or form data or an uploaded file being sent from the client to the server.
21. In other words, it is the thing we think of as being the document we sent or received. Not much more needs to be said about that here.

5.12.2 TELNET

1. Telnet is a terminal emulation application that enables a workstation to connect a host using TCP/IP link & interact with it as if it was directly connected terminal.
2. It is a client/server application.
3. The server runs on a host on which applications are running, and passes information between the applications and the Telnet clients.
4. The well-known port number for Telnet servers is TCP port 23.
5. Telnet clients must convert the user data between the form in which it is transmitted and the form in which it is displayed.
6. This is the difficult part of the application, the terminal emulation, and has little to do with the Telnet protocol itself.
7. Telnet protocol commands are principally used to allow the client and server to negotiate the display options, because Telnet clients and servers don't make assumptions about each other's capabilities.
8. TCP provides the reliability for Telnet, so neither the client nor the server need be concerned about re-sending data that is lost, nor about error checking.
9. This makes the Telnet protocol very simple. There is no special format for TCP segments that contain commands - they simply form part of the data stream.

10. Data is sent, usually as 7-bit ASCII, in TCP packets (which you may recall are called segments).
11. A byte value of 255, "interpret as command" (IAC), means that the bytes which follow are to be treated as Telnet commands and not user data.
12. This is immediately followed by a byte that identifies the command itself, and then a value.
13. Many commands are fixed length, so the byte after that, if not another IAC, would be treated as user data. To send the byte 255 as data, two consecutive bytes of value 255 are used.
14. Some commands, such as those that include text values, are variable length.
15. These are implemented using the sub-option begin (SB) and sub-option end (SE) command bytes.
16. These command bytes enclose the variable length data like parentheses.
17. The principal Telnet commands used to negotiate the display options when a client connects to a server are WILL (sender wants to enable this option), WONT (sender wants to disable this option), DO (sender wants the receiver to enable this option) and DONT (sender wants the receiver to disable this option).

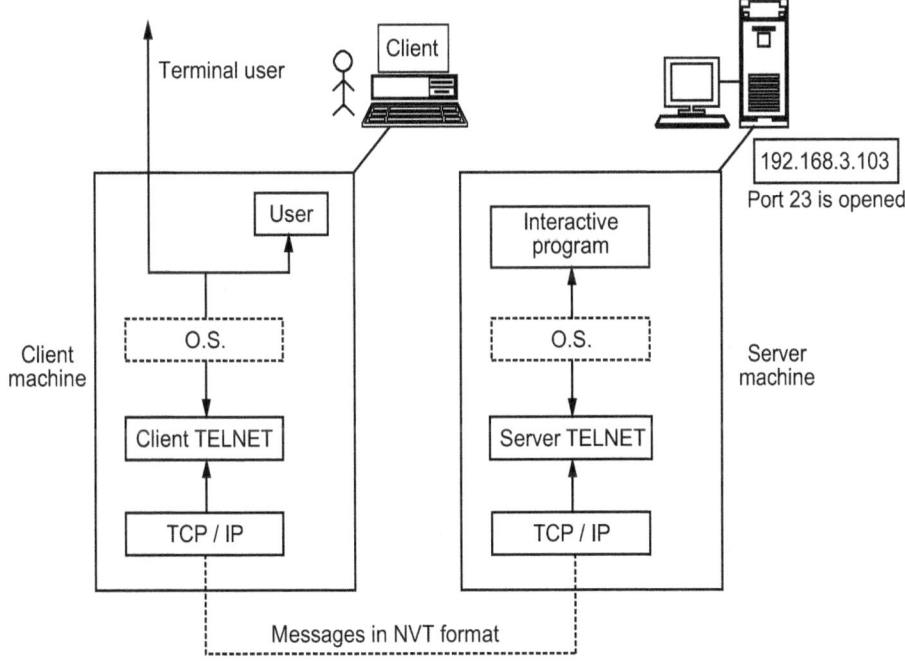

O.S. : Operating System
NVT : Network Virtual Terminal

Fig. 5.72: Typical Telnet Communication

18. To see how this works, consider an example.
19. On client command prompt just type c:> Telnet 192.168.3.103 then server will respond connection will be established and data will be transferred.
20. The telnet protocol gives you the ability to connect to a machine, by giving commands and instructions interactively to that machine, thus creating an interactive connection.
21. In such a case, the local system becomes transparent to the user, who gets the feeling that he is connected directly to the remote computer.
22. The commands typed by the user are transmitted directly to the remote machine and the response from the remote machine is displayed on the user's monitor screen. An interactive connection is also know as **remote login**.
23. In order to **remote login** the user's computer must have the ability to –
    - Establish a connection to another machine,
    - Emulate a terminal compatible with the remote machine,
    - Regulate the flow of data from the user's terminal to remote machine, and vice versa.

How application programs implement a TELNET client and server ?
1. The figure below describes the path of data in a **Telnet** remote terminal session as it travels from the user's keyboard to the remote operating system.
2. Adding a **Telnet** server to a timesharing system usually requires modifying the operating system.

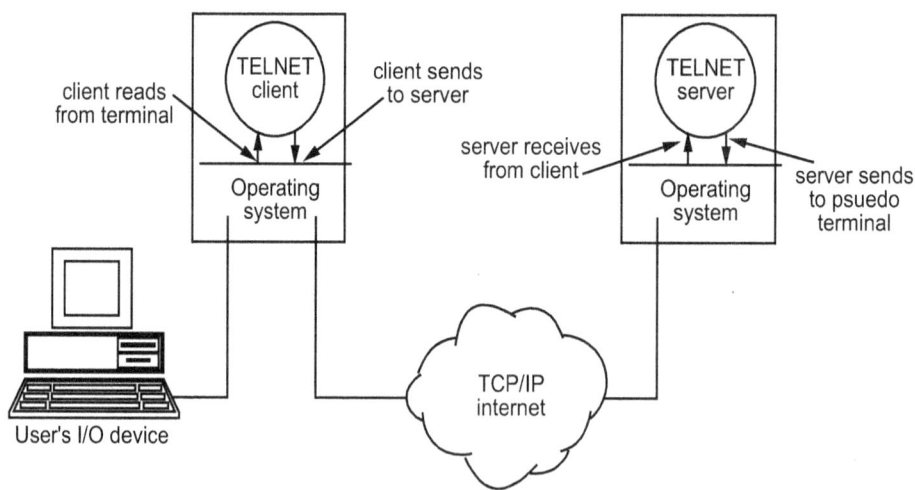

Fig. 5.73: Remote login using Telnet

Network Virtual Terminal

1. The **Network Virtual Terminal** is a device used by **Telnet** to enable a local computer to communicate with a remote machine.
2. To make **Telnet** interoperate between as many systems as possible, it must accommodate the details of heterogeneous computers and operating systems.
3. To accommodate heterogeneity, **Telnet** defines how data and command sequences are sent across the Internet.
4. The definition is known as the **Network Virtual Terminal (NVT)**.
5. The **NVT** defines how data and commands are sent across the Internet.
6. The **NVT** is a bi-directional character device that has a printer and a keyboard.
7. The printer responds to incoming data and the keyboard produces outgoing data which is sent over the **Telnet** connection.
8. The **NVT** is viewed as a half-duplex device.
9. The **Network Virtual Terminal** implements client-server architecture.
10. A **Telnet** client transfers characters between the user's terminal and a remote service.
11. On one side, it uses the local operating system functions when it interacts with the user's terminal.
12. On the other side, it uses a **TCP** connection when it communicates with the remote service.

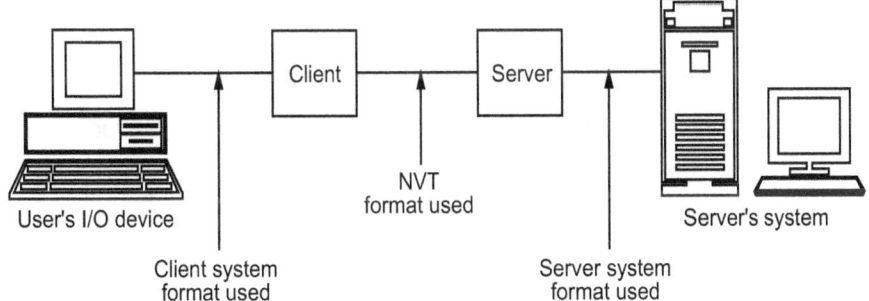

Fig. 5.74: Use of the Network Virtual Terminal (NVT) format by TELNET

13. The **Telnet** protocol defines the character set for the virtual terminal. Several of the keys correspond to conceptual operations instead of data values. For example, one key causes an **Interrupt** or **Abort**.
14. The definition of **NVT** format is fairly straightforward. All communication involves 8-bit bytes.

15. At startup, **NVT** uses the standard 7-bit **ASCII** representation for data and reserves bytes with the high order bit set for command sequences.
16. The ASCII character set includes 95 characters that have "printable" graphics (letters, digits and punctuation marks) as well as 33 "control" codes.
17. All printable characters are assigned the same meaning as in the standard ASCII character set.
18. The **NVT** standard defines interpretations for control characters as shown in the table below.

Table 5.13

ASCII Control Code	Decimal Value	Assigned Meaning
NUL	0	No operation (has no effect on output)
BEL	7	Sound audible/visible signal (no motion)
BS	8	Move left one character position
HT	9	Move right to the next horizontal tab stop
LF	10	Move down (vertically) to the next line
VT	11	Move down to the next vertical tab stop
FF	12	Move to the top of the next page
CR	13	Move to the left margin on the current line
other control	--	No operation (has no effect on output)

19. To provide a full-duplex connection between the user's terminal and a remote service, a **Telnet** client performs two tasks simultaneously:
    - The client must read characters that the user types on the keyboard and send them across a **TCP** connection to the remote service.
    - The client must read characters that arrive from the **TCP** connection and display them on the user's terminal screen.
20. Because the remote service can emit output at any time or the user can type at any time, a client cannot know which source of data will become available first.
21. Thus, it cannot block indefinitely waiting for input from one of the two sources without also checking for input from the other. In short, the client must transfer data in both directions concurrently.
22. The chief advantage of using a Network Virtual Terminal is that it permits clients from a variety of computers to connect to a service.

TELNET COMMANDS:

1. All **Telnet** commands consist of at least a two byte sequence: the "Interpret as Command" (IAC) escape character followed by the code for the command.
2. The commands dealing with option negotiation are three byte sequences, the third byte being the code for the option referenced.
3. This format was chosen so that as more comprehensive use of the "data space" is made -- by negotiations from the basic NVT, of course -- collisions of data bytes with reserved command values will be minimized, all such collisions requiring the inconvenience, and inefficiency, of "escaping" the data bytes into the stream.
4. With the current set-up, only the IAC need be doubled to be sent as data, and the other 255 codes may be passed transparently.
5. The following are the defined **Telnet** commands. Note that these codes and code sequences have the indicated meaning only when immediately preceded by an IAC.

NAME	CODE	MEANING
SE	240	End of subnegotiation parameters.
NOP	241	No operation
Data Mark	242	The data stream portion of a Synch. This should always be accompanied by a TCP Urgent notification
Break	243	NVT character BRK
Interrupt Process	244	The function IP
Abort output	245	The function AO
Are You There	246	The function AYT
Erase character	247	The function EC.
Erase Line	248	The function EL.
Go ahead	249	The GA signal
SB	250	Indicates that what follows is subnegotiation of the indicated option.
WILL (option code)	251	Indicates the desire to begin performing, or confirmation that you are now performing, the indicated option.
WON'T (option code)	252	Indicates the refusal to perform, or continue performing, the indicated option.
DO (option code)	253	Indicates the request that the other party perform, or confirmation that you are expecting the other party to perform, the indicated option.
DON'T (option code)	254	Indicates the demand that the other party stop performing, or confirmation that you are no longer expecting the other party to perform, the indicated option.
IAC	255	Data Byte 255

5.12.3 FTP (File Transfer Protocol)

1. File Transfer Protocol (FTP) powers one of the most fundamental Internet functions: the transfer of files between computers.
2. Today, Web developers use FTP protocols to upload/update their web sites and download other information.
3. A basic understanding about the FTP process and software programs is important for every Web developer.
4. FTP powers one of the fundamental Internet functions and is the prescribed method for the transfer of files between computers.
5. It is also the easiest and most secure way to exchange files over the Internet.
6. An FTP address looks a lot like an HTTP or web site address except it uses the prefix **ftp://** instead of **http://**.
7. The most common use of FTP is to download files.
8. FTP is vital to the MP3 music sharing, most online auctions and game enthusiasts.
9. The ability to transfer files quickly and reliably is essential for everyone creating and maintaining a web page.
10. The types of files that you can download includes:
    - Public domain and shareware software.
    - Documents on any topic imaginable.
    - Images from organizations in a variety of formats.
    - Sound and video files.

Terms to know:

Let's review some basic FTP terms.

1. **Anonymous FTP:** Transfers files from the public portion of an FTP server. "Anonymous" means that you don't have to have an account on the server. In most cases, use anonymous as your user name and your email address as your password.
2. **Archive:** An FTP site that contains a selection of files for download.
3. **Download:** Also called "**Get**". Copy a file from an FTP site to another computer. If you're merely downloading shared files an anonymous account is usually sufficient. However, if you're downloading Web pages for update, a password and user privileges is usually required.
4. **FTP site:** A Web site that stores files for download. You can access the sites with a Web browser by typing in the address. All FTP site addresses begin with **ftp://** (instead of http://).
5. **Upload:** Also called "**Put**". Place files on an FTP server. Upload privileges are usually password protected to keep unauthorized users from placing files that could contain viruses or other malicious code on the server.

FTP For The Web Developer:

1. When you purchase a web hosting account, the host assigns you a username and password for this purpose.
2. Depending your preference (and your Web host's capabilities), you may access an FTP connection directly using UNIX commands or use an interface.
3. Unless you're comfortable with UNIX commands, you probably use an FTP interface.
4. Your web host will generally provide specific instructions about how to access their FTP server, but it's important that you understand the basic process:
   - **Open your FTP program** and use your username and password to establish a connection with the server. You may also need to know the server's name.
   - **Find and open the directory** that you want to copy your page to.

Note: You may need to create a new directory or create a subdirectory in an existing directory.

   - **Choose the transfer mode:** This will be either *binary* or *ASCII*.

File Type	Usage	Description
ASCII	Text files	Use for all HTML files
Binary	Raw data (graphics, multimedia, executable files)	Use for all graphics and multimedia files

- **Upload your files** to the appropriate director on the server.
- **Disconnect** from the server. This is important ! You'd be surprised to know how many sites are disabled by careless webmasters who make changes by accident.
- **Test the pages** with a web browser to ensure that everything uploaded properly.

What Kind of FTP Program Do You Need?

1. If your Web page editor doesn't provide an FTP interface or if you code your pages by hand, you can choose from many FTP programs that don't require extensive UNIX knowledge. They provide a drag-and-drop interface familiar to Windows and Mac users.
2. FTP is platform independent: you can use it to upload files from a Mac to a UNIX server without any trouble.
3. There are three basic ways to use FTP - your choice depends on how you plan to use it.
   - **FTP using a Web browser.** This is most commonly used for anonymous FTP - like downloading software. Always run a current virus scan program on anything you download ! No extra software is required.
   - **FTP using an HTML editor.** Many Web page editors bundle this interface into their products. You don't need to install a separate FTP program.

- **FTP using a standalone program.** Use this if you're administering a complex site with programming or if you need to administer file permissions remotely. Very large, complex sites may require commercial FTP packages; otherwise, evaluate the freeware and shareware programs available for download.

PRACTICALLY USING THE "FTP"

1. FTP is a core protocol in the IP world to quickly transfer files between your hard drive and a remote server.
2. Typically a site on the Internet stores a number of files (they could be application executables, graphics, or audio clips, for example), and runs an FTP server application that waits for transfer requests.
3. To download a file to your own system, you run an FTP client application that connects to the FTP server, and request a file from a particular directory or folder.
4. Files can be uploaded to the FTP server, if appropriate access is granted. The following model may be diagrammed for an FTP service.

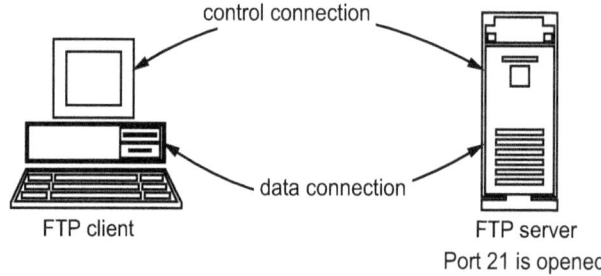

Fig. 5.75: FTP service (any FTP session between FTP server and FTP client uses two connections)

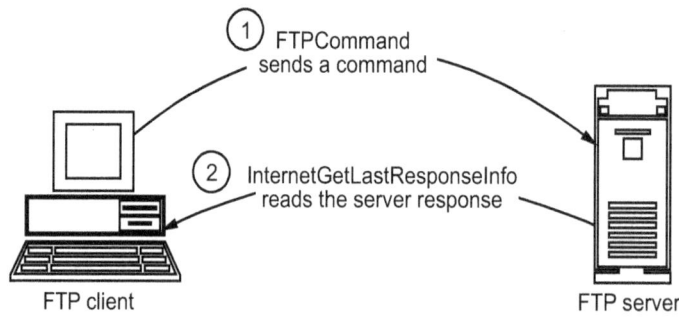

Fig. 5.76: FTP Command in control connection mode (This situation happens when we are maintaining the state of the FTP server and data connection is not involved)

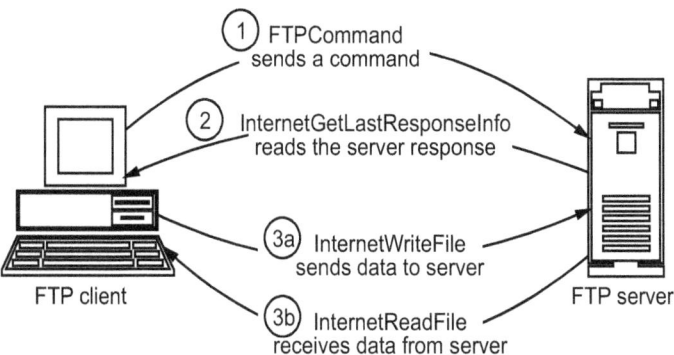

Fig. 5.77: FTP Command in data connection mode (FTP commands that sends or receives data files)

5. The File Transfer Protocol (FTP) is a user-level protocol for transferring files between host computers.
6. An FTP session involves two separate connections:

Control Connection:

- The server listens for client connections on port 21.
- The client opens a connection to the server port 21 on a client port above 1023.
- The client uses this connection to send commands to and receive replies from the server.

This connection lasts through the FTP session.

Data Connection:

- The data connection is used for transferring data between the client and server.
- A new data connection is opened for each FTP command.
- The way the data connection is created depends on the type of FTP session—active or passive.

Active FTP and Passive FTP:

1. In active FTP, the client actively opens a connection to the FTP server at port 21.
2. It uses a port number > 1023 as its port for the control connection.
3. The client then opens a new port (passive open) as its data port and sends this port number across to the server using the PORT command.

4. The server then opens a data connection (active open) to the data port specified in the PORT command of the client.
5. The server uses port 20 as its data connection port.
6. In passive FTP, the control connection is established the same as it is in active FTP.
7. In passive FTP, to establish a data connection the server opens an arbitrary data port >1023.
8. It uses the PASV command to send the data port number to the client.
9. The client connects to the port specified by the PASV command and uses a different port >1023 as its data port.

Basic FTP Commands:
FTP was originally developed to be used from the command-line prompt. A number of Windows-based software is now available, however, that eliminates the use of commands. If you use a program with a command-line prompt, however, the following FTP commands will be useful.
1. ftp - Begins the FTP session.
2. help - Gives you a list of FTP commands.
3. open - Opens an FTP session. Used as follows: open unb.ca This opens an FTP session with the site at the address: unb.ca
4. cd pub/win/games - Changes the directory to the games directory found under the win and pub subdirectories.
5. dir - List the contents of the current subdirectory.
6. cd up - Moves up one subdirectory.
7. cd down - Moves down one subdirectory.
8. binary - Changes the retrieval setting from text to binary format.
9. get - Retrieves a file. Used as follows: get doom.zip. Downloads the file doom.zip.
10. ascii - Changes the retrieval setting from binary to text format.
11. exit - Ends an FTP session.

5.12.4 SMTP (Simple Mail Transfer Protocol)
Introduction
1. Basically SMTP or Simple Mail Transfer Protocol is a way to transfer email reliably and efficiently.
2. SMTP is a relatively simple, text-based protocol, where one or more recipients of a message are specified (and in most cases verified to exist) and then the message text is transferred.
3. You can think of SMTP as the language that mail servers use to communicate among themselves.
4. Since this protocol started out as purely ASCII text-based, it did not deal well with binary files.
5. SMTP is used to send mail to the recipient's mailbox.

6. The recipient may use various methods to access the emails in his mailbox.
7. A couple of methods that are very popular are POP3 and IMAP.
8. These protocols allow a user to access his messages stored on a remote mail server.
9. We provide here, some background information about email and how it works, and a simple step-by-step diagram showing how an email message is sent and received.

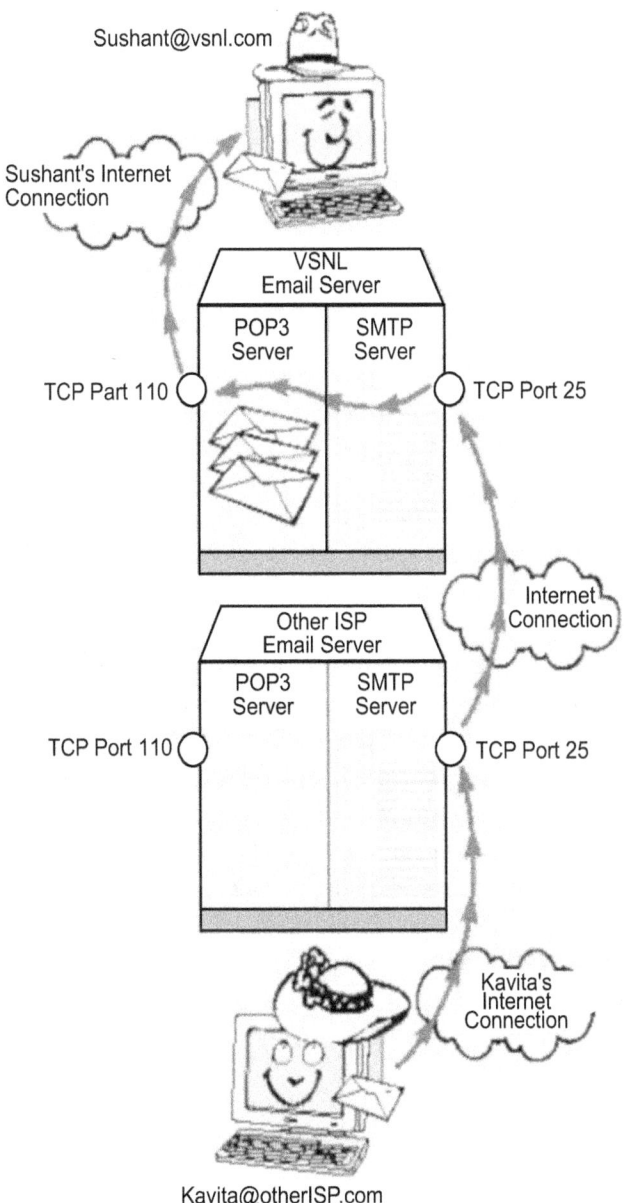

Fig. 5.78

What is an email client ?

An email client is an email program such as Outlook Express, for sending, receiving and organizing your email messages.

What is an email server ?

Email servers are used to process, store and send, and receive email messages. There are different types of email servers, such as POP 3, SMTP and IMAP servers. The most popular email servers are POP 3 (**incoming mail servers for your incoming mail) and SMTP (outgoing mail servers for your outgoing mail**).

What is SMTP or outgoing mail server?

When you send an email from your email program, if you have an Internet connection with VSNL, the email first arrives at VSNL's SMTP (outgoing mail server), then VSNL's SMTP server will check for the validity of both source and destination email addresses. Then it will send your email to the proper destination. You use your Internet connection's email server when you send mail.

What is POP3 or incoming mail server?

When someone sends you an email message, it arrives at VSNL's POP3 server and it waits for you to check your email. When you check your email, your email program accesses VSNL's POP3 servers and downloads your waiting messages from VSNL's POP3 server to your computer.

How does email travel when we receive or send an email message?

When Kavita sends Sushant an email message, the following is a simplified step-by-step of how it travels:

1. Kavita opens her email program (Outlook Express), uses her email account, Kavita@otherisp.com, and writes an email message to Sushant@VSNL.com. Her Outlook Express sends the message through TCP port 25 of Kavita's Internet connection, then to the other ISP's SMTP server (still on TCP port 25).
2. The other ISP's SMTP server finds the destination's SMTP server (in this case, VSNL) and sends the message out to VSNL's SMTP server (through TCP port 25 of her Internet connection).
3. VSNL's SMTP server sends the message to VSNL's POP3 server where the message waits for Sushant to pick it up.

SMTP Protocol:

1. SMTP transfers data from sender's mail servers to the recipient's mail servers.
2. The sender-SMTP first establishes a two-way transmission channel to a receiver-SMTP.

3. Then, receiver-SMTP may be either the ultimate destination or an intermediate.
4. Next SMTP commands are generated by the sender-SMTP and sent to the receiver-SMTP.
5. Lastly SMTP replies are sent from the receiver-SMTP to the sender-SMTP in response to the commands.
6. Once the transmission channel is established, the SMTP-sender sends a **MAIL** command indicating the sender of the mail.
7. If the SMTP-receiver can accept mail it responds with an OK reply.
8. The SMTP-sender then sends a **RCPT** command identifying a recipient of the mail.
9. If the SMTP-receiver can accept mail for that recipient it responds with an OK reply; if not, it responds with a reply rejecting that recipient (but not the whole mail transaction).
10. The SMTP-sender and SMTP-receiver may negotiate several recipients.
11. When the recipients have been negotiated the SMTP-sender sends the mail data, terminating with a special sequence.
12. If the SMTP-receiver successfully processes the mail data it responds with an OK reply.
13. The dialog is purposely lock-step, one-at-a-time.

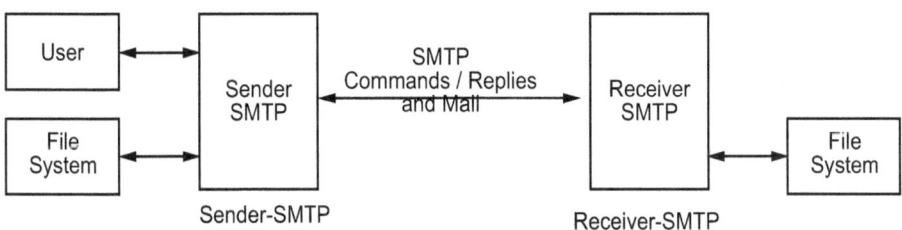

Fig. 5.79: SMTP communication model

14. Simple Message Transfer Protocol (SMTP) is a set of standards used for messaging applications.
15. It is the *de facto* standard for all mail transferred over the Internet.
16. An SMTP mail system operates at the application layer of the Open Systems Interconnect (OSI) stack, as shown in Fig. 5.79.
17. SMTP is a messaging protocol that runs only over TCP/IP networks and uses many of TCP/IP's features to discover routes by which to deliver mail.
18. In Fig. 5.1, a user on the host Amit.abc.com might use SMTP to send a message to a user on Sumit.xyz.com.

19. To send the message, the following conditions must be met:
    - The two hosts must be able to communicate over TCP/IP using port 25. (Any application or process using TCP for its transport is assigned a unique identification number called a TCP port.)
    - As long as the routers separating the two systems do not filter any of the IP ports, the two systems should also be able to ping each other.
    - Both hosts must be running an SMTP messaging program.
    - They do not need to run the same SMTP messaging program; any application that complies with the SMTP specifications can send messages to any other SMTP-compliant program.
    - For example, Amit.abc.com might be running Microsoft Exchange Server and Sumit.xyz.com might be a Unix system running Sendmail or a Windows NT system running Internet Shopper's Mail.
    - Also, users don't have to run the same mail clients on their desktops, user Mukesh could use the Microsoft Exchange client to communicate with Amit.abc.com and send mail to user Prajakta, who uses Eudora to access her mailbox on Sumit.xyz.com.

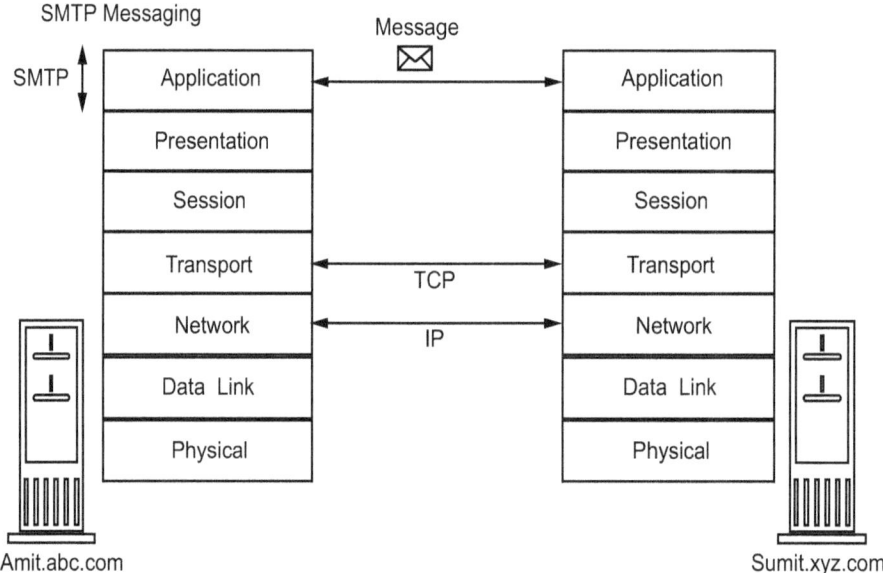

Fig. 5.80: Typical example of SMTP Messaging

SMTP Commands:

SMTP commands are ASCII messages sent between SMTP hosts. Possible commands are as follows:

Command	Description
DATA	Begins message composition.
EXPN <string>	Returns names on the specified mail list.
HELO <domain>	Returns identity of mail server.
HELP <command>	Returns information on the specified command.
MAIL FROM <host>	Initiates a mail session from host.
NOOP	Causes no action, except acknowledgement from server.
QUIT	Terminates the mail session.
RCPT TO <user>	Designates who receives mail.
RSET	Resets mail connection.
SAML FROM <host>	Sends mail to user terminal and mailbox.
SEND FROM <host>	Sends mail to user terminal.
SOML FROM <host>	Sends mail to user terminal or mailbox.
TURN	Switches role of receiver and sender.
VRFY <user>	Verifies the identity of a user.

SMTP Messages:

SMTP response messages consist of a response code followed by explanatory text, as follows:

Response Code	Explanatory Text
211	(Response to system status or help request).
214	(Response to help request).
220	Mail service ready.
221	Mail service closing connection.
250	Mail transfer completed.
251	User not local, forward to <path>.
354	Start mail message, end with <CRLF><CRLF>.
421	Mail service unavailable.
450	Mailbox unavailable.
451	Local error in processing command.
452	Insufficient system storage.
500	Unknown command.
501	Bad parameter.
502	Command not implemented.

Response Code	Explanatory Text
503	Bad command sequence.
504	Parameter not implemented.
550	Mailbox not found.
551	User not local, try <path>.
552	Storage allocation exceeded.
553	Mailbox name not allowed.
554	Mail transaction failed.

5.12.5 SNMP (Simple Network Management Protocol)

Overview:

- Administrator provides support for integration with SNMP (Simple Network Management Protocol).
- SNMP is the Internet standard protocol for managing nodes on an IP network.
- Administrator provides a gateway between the Administrator management service and SNMP applications.
- Events received from the management service are converted into SNMP management information.
- This section introduces SNMP and its key concepts.

SNMP:

- Simple Network Management Protocol (SNMP) is the Internet standard protocol for managing nodes on an IP network.
- SNMP can be used to manage and monitor all sorts of equipment (for example, network servers, routers, bridges, and hubs).
- You need to be familiar with some basic SNMP concepts to use Administrator's SNMP integration.

SNMP Managers and Agents:

- The two key components in internet management are managers and agents.
- An SNMP manager is a console that enables an administrator to perform network management tasks.

- An SNMP manager is sometimes also referred to as a Network Management Station (NMS).
- An SNMP agent is device-running software that understands SNMP and interfaces with the actual device being managed.
- A manager controls an agent by invoking operations on the agent.
- The SNMP manager-agent model is shown in Fig. 5.81.

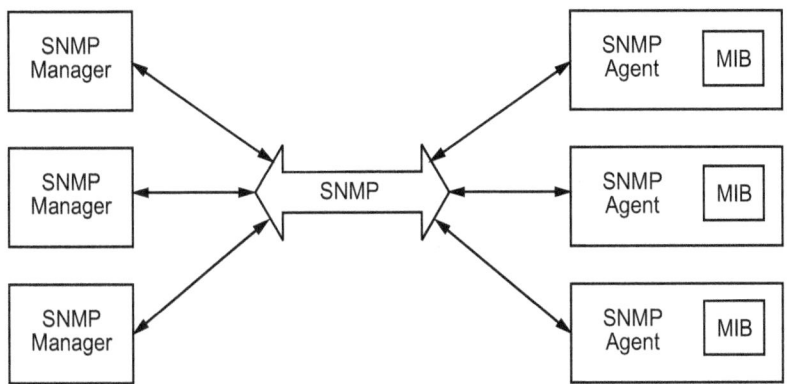

Fig. 5.81: The SNMP Manager-Agent Model

- The SNMP protocol specifies how data is transferred between a manager and an agent.
- It specifies the format and meaning of messages exchanged by the manager and agent.

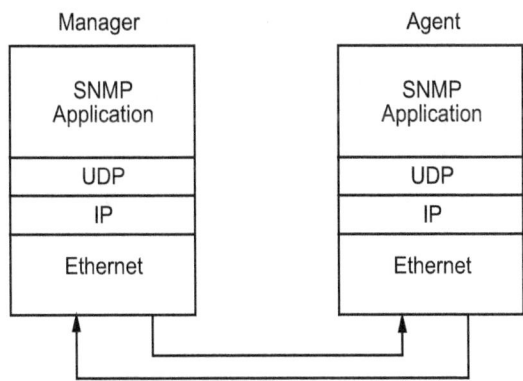

Fig. 5.82: SNMP Communication occurs between a manager and agent by means of UDP datagrams

- SNMP is an application layer protocol that sits above the TCP/IP stack.
- However, SNMP does not use TCP at all.
- It uses the UDP (datagram) protocol for communication, which provides no acknowledgment that a transmission was successful.
- This was done to minimize the software requirements in the "agent" which is the device being managed.
- The "manager" is the device requesting information from the agent and it is called a Network Management Station (NMS).
- The interaction between a manager and an agent is similar to the interaction between a master and a slave device.
- The manager can initiate a "poll" of the agent requesting information or directing an action.
- The agent, in turn, generates a response to the query from the manager.
- This is how a remote I/O protocol works.
- However, the manager can request that a "trap" be set by the agent.
- A trap is simply a report to be issued in the future which is triggered when a set of conditions are met, similar to an alarm.
- The trap is triggered upon an event and once it occurs, the agent immediately reports the occurrence without a poll from the manager.
- This is no different from having a remote I/O device report on a "change of state."
- The NMS that receives the trap can then take appropriate action such as notifying personnel of the event.
- In this situation, the NMS is acting as a server by gathering data from agents and providing information on the state of devices to clients.
- Let's consider a real-world example.
- We have a remote pumping station with a SCADA system attached to several devices.
- The SCADA system is powered from an uninterruptible power supply (UPS) that has an SNMP agent.
- An Ethernet fiber optic link is used for communication between the remote pumping station and the main control room.
- An Ethernet switch, located in the pump house, connects the UPS and the SCADA system to the Ethernet link.
- An SNMP manager application, running on a desktop workstation located in the main control room and functioning as a NMS, instructs the agent in the pump house UPS to set a trap that will be triggered if there's a loss of main power.

- If this condition occurs, the agent would send a trap message back to the NMS, which, in turn, pages the maintenance shop.
- This is a simple case in point of how SNMP can aid applications in our industry.

Management Information Base:

- Management Information Base (MIB) is the standard that specifies the data managed by a SNMP agent.
- MIB defines the data that a manager can request from an agent, and the actions permitted on this data.
- A MIB file is a database of objects that can be managed using SNMP.
- It has a hierarchical structure, similar to a DOS or UNIX directory tree.
- It contains both pre-defined values and values that can be customized.
- A MIB is the most basic element in network management.

SNMP Operations:

There are five primitive SNMP operations, sometimes referred to as Protocol Data Units (PDUs). These are the different kinds of messages that can be sent over an network using SNMP Version1:

- GetRequest
- GetNextRequest
- GetResponse
- SetRequest
- Trap

The additional commands for SNMPv2 and SNMPv3 are as follows:
- get bulk
- notification
- inform
- report

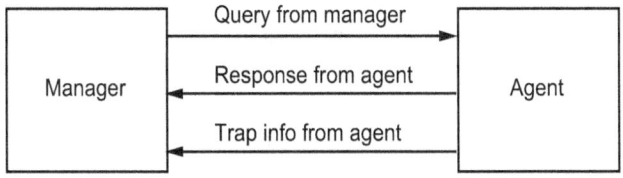

Fig. 5.83: A manager polls an agent in a similar fashion to a master/slave protocol

- A manager can issue GetRequest, GetNextRequest, and SetRequest messages to access single or multiple object variables.
- A managed agent can send a GetResponse message to complete the GetRequest, GetNextRequest, or SetRequest.
- An agent can also send an event notification, called a trap, to a manager in order to notify the occurrence of specific events (for example, a system exception, or when a managed server terminates unexpectedly).

SNMP Management Tools:
- There are several available software packages that can use SNMP to interact with any agent for which a valid MIB is available.
- These SNMP management tools are widely used in large organizations.
- These tools provide a common management console to manage all resources on an organization's network.

Administrator SNMP Agent:
- The MIB and the SNMP agent supplied with Administrator enable application to be integrated into your SNMP management consoles.
- To an SNMP management tool, the Administrator SNMP agent is no different from any other SNMP agent on the network.
- The Administrator MIB file specifies the data that can be obtained from the agent and the operations that are permitted on this data.

SNMP Message Format:

SNMP is a session protocol, which is encapsulated in UDP. The SNMP message format is shown below:

Version	Community	PDU
SNMP message format		

Fig. 5.84: SNMP Message format

Version:
SNMP version number. Both the manager and agent must use the same version of SNMP. Messages containing different version numbers are discarded without further processing.

Community:
Community name used for authenticating the manager before allowing access to the agent.

PDU:

There are five different PDU types: GetRequest, GetNextRequest, GetResponse, SetRequest, and Trap.

PDU Format:

The format for GetRequest, GetNext Request, GetResponse and SetRequest PDUs is shown here.

PDU type	Request ID	Error status	Error index	Object 1, value 1	Object 2, value 2	...

Fig. 5.85: SNMP PDU format

PDU Type:

Specifies the type of PDU:

0	GetRequest.
1	GetNextRequest.
2	GetResponse.
3	SetRequest.

Request ID:

Integer field, which correlates the manager's request to the agent's response.

Error Status:

Enumerated integer type that indicates normal operation or one of five error conditions. The possible values are:

0	noError: Proper manager/agent operation.
1	tooBig: Size of the required GetResponse PDU exceeds a local limitation
2	noSuchName: The requested object name does not match the names available in the relevant MIB View.
3	badValue: A SetRequest contains an inconsistent type, length and value for the variable.
4	readOnly
5	genErr: Other errors, which are not explicitly defined, have occurred.

Error Index:

Identifies the entry within the variable bindings list that caused the error.

Object/value:

Variable binding pair of a variable name with its value.

Trap PDU Format:

The format of the Trap PDU is shown below:

PDU type	Enterp	Agent addr	Gen trap	Spec trap	Time stamp	Obj 1, Val 1	Obj 1, Val 1	...

Fig. 5.86: SNMP trap PDU

PDU type:
Specifies the type of PDU (4=Trap).

Enterprise:
Identifies the management enterprise under whose registration authority the trap was defined.

Agent address:
IP address of the agent, used for further identification.

Generic trap type:
Field describing the event being reported. The following seven values are defined:

0	coldStart: Sending protocol entity has reinitialized, indicating that the agent's configuration or entity implementation may be altered.
1	warmStart: Sending protocol has reinitialized, but neither the agent's configuration nor the protocol entity implementation has been altered.
2	linkDown: A communication link has failed.
3	linkUp: A communication link has come up.
4	authenticationFailure: The agent has received an improperly authenticated SNMP message from the manager, i.e., community name was incorrect.
5	egpNeighborLoss: An EGP peer neighbor is down.
6	enterpriseSpecific: A non-generic trap has occurred which is further identified by the Specific Trap Type and Enterprise fields.

Specific trap type:

Used to identify a non-generic trap when the Generic Trap Type is enterprise Specific.

Timestamp:

Value of the sysUpTime object, representing the amount of time elapsed between the last (re-) initialization and the generation of that Trap.

Object/value:

Variable binding pair of a variable name with its value.

Conclusion:
- With more and more devices embracing Ethernet and Internet protocols, the addition of SNMP protocol support adds benefits to the device.
- Managed devices support the SNMP protocol and are called agents.
- Agents consist of a collection of managed objects that can be queried by a manager to determine the health of the network or the status of particular devices.
- By displaying this data in an easily understood format, operators and maintenance personnel, located at a central site, can monitor the performance of the entire network by observing selected devices and pinpointing potential problems before they occur.
- Although commercial and freeware network management software programs exist for this purpose, the trend is to use more web-based tools.
- SNMP is not restricted to just the management of switches and routers. Any industrial device can have SNMP support and could provide much aid in industrial applications.

5.12.6 X Window System

1. The *X Window System*, or just X, is a client-server application that lets multiple clients (applications) use the bit-mapped display managed by a server.
2. "The server is the software that manages a display, keyboard, and mouse.
3. The client is an application program that runs on either the same host as the server or on a different host.
4. In some instances the server is a dedicated piece of hardware (an X terminal) that communicates with clients on other hosts.
5. In another instance, a stand-alone workstation, the client and server are on the same host and communicate using interprocess communication on that host, without any network involvement at all.

6. Between these two extremes is a workstation that supports clients on the same host and clients on other hosts.

7. X requires a reliable, bi-directional stream protocol, such as TCP. (X was not designed for an unreliable protocol such as UDP.)

8. On a Unix system, when the X client and X server are on the same host, the Unix domain protocols are normally used instead of TCP, because there is less protocol processing than if TCP were used.

9. The Unix domain protocols are a form of interprocess communication that can be used between clients and servers on the same host.

10. Fig. 5.87 shows one possible scenario with three clients using one display.

11. One client is on the same host as the server, using the Unix domain protocols.

12. The other two clients are on different hosts, using TCP.

13. One client is normally a *window manager* that has authority for the layout of windows on the display.

14. The window manager allows us to move windows around the screen, or change their size, for example,

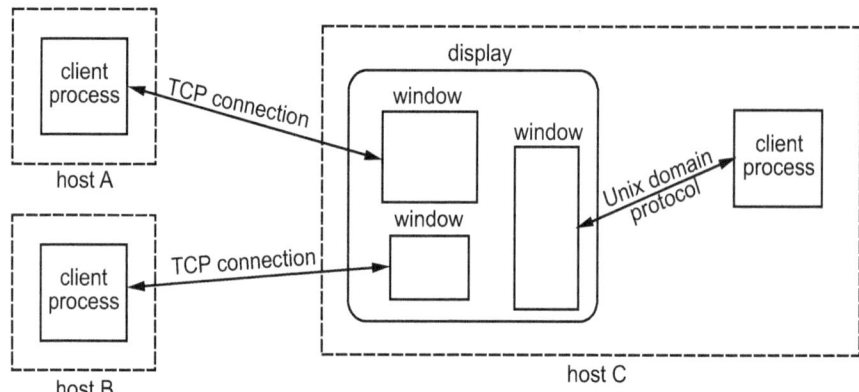

Fig. 5.87: Three 'X' client using one display

15. On first glance the terms *client* and *server* appear backward.
16. With applications such as Telnet and FTP we think of the client as the interactive user at the keyboard and display.
17. But with X, the keyboard and display belong to the server. Think of the server as the end providing the service.

18. The service provided by X is access to a window, keyboard, and mouse. With Telnet the service is logging in to the remote host. With FTP the service is the filesystem on the server.
19. The X server is normally started when the X terminal or workstation is bootstrapped.
20. The server creates a TCP end point and does a passive open on port 6000 + n, where n is the display number (normally 0).
21. It is the server's responsibility to multiplex all the clients.
22. From this point on the client sends requests to the server across the TCP connection (e.g., create a window), the server sends back replies, and the server also sends events to the client (mouse button pushed, keyboard key pressed, window exposed, window resized, etc.).
23. Fig. 5.88 emphasizing that the clients communicate with the X server process, which in turn manages the windows on the display.
24. Not shown here is that the X server also manages the keyboard and mouse.

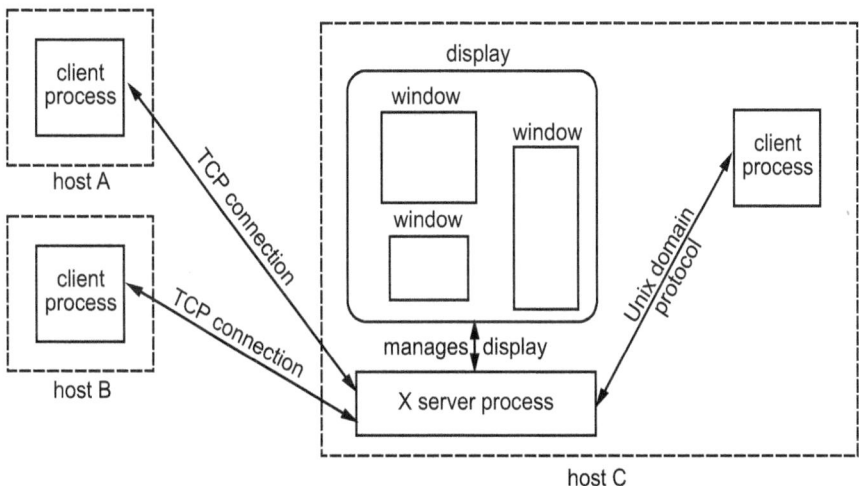

Fig. 5.88: Three clients using one display

25. This design, where a single server handles multiple clients, differs from the normal TCP concurrent server design.
26. The FTP and Telnet servers, for example, spawn a new process each time a new TCP connection request arrives, so each client communicates with a different server process.
27. With X, however, all clients, running on the same host or on a different host, communicate with a single server.

28. Lots of data can be exchanged across the TCP connection between an X client and its server.
29. The amount depends on the specific application design. For example, if we run the Xclock client, which displays the current time and date on the client in a window on the server, specifying an update of once a second, an X message is sent across the TCP connection from the client to the server once a second.

Summary:
- We have finished with a brief look at the X Window System, another heavy user of TCP/IP.
- We saw that the X server manages multiple windows on a display, and handles the communication between a client and its window.
- Each client has its own TCP connection to the server and a single server manages all the clients for a given display.

5.12.7 TraceRoute

1. Traceroute is a network debugging utility that attempts to *trace* the path a packet takes through the network - its *route*.
2. A key word here is "attempts" - by no means does traceroute work in all cases.
3. If you've been paying attention, you already know that the only facilities TCP/IP provide for tracing packet routes are IP packet options (record route and its variants) that are poorly specified, rarely implemented in a useful way, and often disabled for security reasons.
4. Traceroute does not depend on any of these facilities. Traceroute, to put it simply, is a hack.

How Traceroute Works:

1. Traceroute transmits packets with small TTL values.
2. Recall that the TTL (Time To Live) is an IP header field that is designed to prevent packets from running in loops.
3. Every router that handles a packet subtracts one from the packet's TTL.
4. If the TTL reaches zero, the packet has *expired* and is discarded.
5. Traceroute depends on the common router practice of sending an ICMP
6. By using small TTL values which quickly expire, traceroute causes routers along a packet's normal delivery path to generate these ICMP messages which identify the router.

7. A TTL value of one should produce a message from the first router; a TTL value of two generates a message from the second; etc.

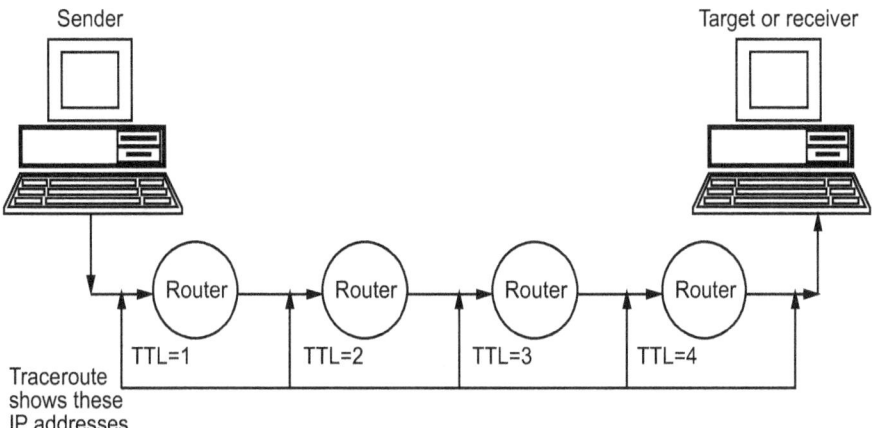

Fig. 5.89: Traceroute traces the path a packet takes through the network

8. In a typical traceroute session, a group of packets with TTL=1 are sent.
9. A single router should respond, using the IP address of the interface it transmits the ICMP Timeout messages on, which should be the same as the interface it received the original packets on.
10. The user is told this IP address, and DNS is used to convert this into a symbolic domain address.
11. Also, round trip times are reported for each packet in the group.
12. Traceroute reports any additional ICMP messages (such as destination unreachables) using a rather cryptic syntax - !N means network unreachable, !H means host unreachable, etc.
13. Once this first group of packets has been processed (this can take 10 seconds or no time at all), the second group (TTL=2) begins transmitting, and the whole process repeats.

Problems you might encounter:

Since TCP/IP was not designed to support traceroute, several kinds of problems might arise.

Changing paths:

Always remember - you are not tracing the path of one packet, but of many. Hopefully, all those packets will follow the same route, but this is by no means assured. What if a link fails during the traceroute ? Your packets may be rerouted, and traceroute's output becomes a confused combination of two separate routes.

No sending addresses:

You only see one IP address from each router - the address closest to you. To put it another way, traceroute can't tell you which interfaces routers are sending the packets on. It only shows the interfaces packets are being received on. The sending interfaces can often be deduced by matching each router with the next one in line - typically only one interface could be used between them.

Routing problems:

TCP/IP's sinister and ubiquitous *routing problems* may cause the router not to have a route back to the sender, or to have a route through some interface other than the one it received the packet on. In these cases, you will either receive no reply at all (no route), or a reply showing an IP address that *never* handled the original packet (it was handled by some other interface on the same router). In short, don't completely trust traceroute.

Buggy TCP/IP implementations:

Traceroute depends on a rather obscure feature that often doesn't work correctly. Some of the problems people have found: code that fails to decrement TTL, code that incorrectly forwards packets with zero TTL, code that does not generate ICMP Timeouts, and code that sends ICMPs with the same TTL as the original packet. This last problem, of course, results in our ICMP Timeouts being sent with zero TTL - guaranteed not to make it back to us.

Traceroute options:

Here's a list of common traceroute options:

    -m max-ttl

At some TTL value, traceroute expects to get a reply from the target host. Of course, if the host is unreachable for some reason, this may never happen, so *max-ttl* (default 30) sets a limit on how long traceroute keeps trying. If the target host is farther than 30 hops away, you'll need to increase this value.

-n

Numerical output only. Use this if you're having nameserver problems and traceroute hangs trying to do inverse DNS lookups.

-p port

Base UDP port. The packets traceroute sends are UDP packets targeted at strange port numbers that nothing will be listening on (we hope). The target host should therefore ignore the packets after generating port unreachable messages. *Port* is the UDP port number that traceroute uses on its first packet, and increments by one for each subsequent packet.

-q queries
How many packets should be sent for each TTL value. The default is 3, which is fine for finding out the route.

-w wait
Wait is the number of seconds packets have to generate replies before traceroute assumes they never will and moves on. The default is 3. Increase this if pings to the target host show round trip times longer than this.

Sample Traceroute Session:
- All of the sites along this path can be converted to symbolic names using inverse DNS lookups.
- Although the details don't all make sense, we can get the general picture.

access$ *traceroute terp.umd.edu*
traceroute to terp.umd.edu (128.8.10.90), 30 hops max, 40 byte packets
1 cisco (199.2.50.1)
3.08 ms 2.391 ms 2.653 ms
2 sl-stk-3-S17-128k.sprintlink.net (144.228.202.1)
232.955 ms 195.828 ms 309.079 ms
3 sl-stk-5-F0/0.sprintlink.net (144.228.40.5)
187.623 ms 24.72 ms 24.545 ms
4 icm-fix-w-H2/0-T3.icp.net (144.228.10.22)
28.927 ms 27.511 ms 34.684 ms
5 fix-west-cpe.SanFrancisco.mci.net (192.203.230.18)
124.641 ms 225.516 ms 192.667 ms
6 border3-hssi2-0.SanFrancisco.mci.net (204.70.34.9)
127.727 ms 29.322 ms 30.108 ms
7 core-fddi-0.SanFrancisco.mci.net (204.70.2.161)
227.059 ms 112.441 ms 29.868 ms
8 core-hssi-2.Denver.mci.net (204.70.1.37)
52.881 ms 53.632 ms 53.18 ms
9 core-hssi-3.Washington.mci.net (204.70.1.13)
93.393 ms 120.491 ms 92.691 ms
10 border1-fddi0-0.Washington.mci.net (204.70.2.2)
242.042 ms 94.312 ms 265.366 ms
11 suranet-cpe.Washington.mci.net (204.70.56.6)
193.482 ms 224.183 ms 93.427 ms
12 wtn8-wtn-cf.sura.net (128.167.7.8)
105.636 ms 92.919 ms 93.663 ms
13 sura9-wtn8-c3.sura.net (128.167.212.1)

```
        92.88 ms 92.708 ms 98.033 ms
    14 sura2-sura-ce.sura.net (128.167.1.2)
        105.182 ms 115.759 ms 130.195 ms
    15 umd-sura2-c1.sura.net (192.221.61.2)
        132.248 ms 145.699 ms 182.908 ms
    16 csc1hub-gw.umd.edu (128.8.1.224)
        168.827 ms 192.669 ms 191.198 ms
    17 terp.umd.edu (128.8.10.90)
        118.98 ms 156.011 ms 160.125 ms
    access$
```
- On a Windows system you can run it by typing the command **tracert** at a command prompt.
- Traceroute exploits the fact that traffic between two points will usually follow the same route at any given time, and that a router will notify the sender using an ICMP message whenever it receives an IP packet containing a time-to-live (TTL) field of one.
- Normally, the TTL field of an IP packet is set to the value 64.
- Traceroute starts by sending a UDP datagram to the destination you specify, setting the TTL field to 1.
- The first router that receives it discards it, and sends an ICMP "time-to-live equals 0" notification back. In the header of the ICMP message is the router's IP address, from which its name can be determined.
- Next, Traceroute sends the datagram with a TTL of 2. This gets as far as the second router before being discarded. Again, an ICMP message comes back.
- **This process is repeated with ever increasing TTLs until the datagram reaches the destination**.
- To create an error when the destination is reached, the UDP datagram is addressed to a non-existent port on the destination host.
- This causes the host to respond with an ICMP "destination port unreachable" message. Thus, Traceroute knows that the route has been completed.
- **Thus we can run traceroute on both LANs and WANs, and use it to examine IP source routing**.

5.12.8 Trivial File Transfer Protocol (TFTP)
- TFTP lives up to its name quite well.
- TFTP is the poor cousin of FTP in that it shares only a very small subset of the capabilities of FTP.
- It uses UDP, which, to use a similar metaphor, is TCP's poor relative.
- TFTP has no packet-monitoring capabilities and practically no error-handling capabilities.
- But then again, these limitations also reduce the process overhead.

- TFTP does not authenticate; it merely connects.
- As a built-in protection, TFTP can only move files that are publicly accessible.
- Security is of great concern when employing TFTP.
- As a result, TFTP is typically used for embedded applications and copying configuration files for router configuration and in situations where space is of concern, and where security is handled in another fashion.
- TFTP is also used in a network computer environment where each machine is booted from a remote server and where TFTP can be easily embedded in the ROMs (Read Only Memory) on network cards.
- The TFTP protocol is basically used for information transfer from a server to a client or vice versa.
- TFTP is intended to be used when bootstrapping diskless systems are used.
- This is also used by memory less devices like routers, switches, etc. to get their boot strap information from their servers.

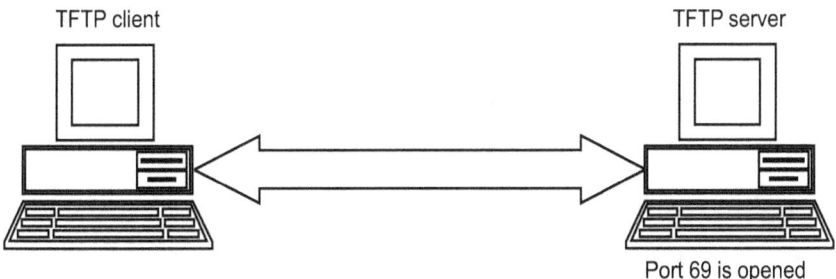

Fig. 5.90: Typical Communication between Client and TFTP Server

- TFTP protocol uses UDP for transferring files between server and the client and uses port "69" to transfer, by default.
- When TFTP is used, the file that is getting transferred is split up into packets each containing 512 bytes of data.
- The completion of the transfer is intimated to the receiver by sending a packet that has 0-511 bytes.
- The mode is one of the ASCII strings *netascii* or *octet*, in any combination of uppercase or lowercase, terminated by a byte of 0.
- "*netascii*" means the data are lines of ASCII text with each line terminated by the 2-character sequence of a carriage return followed by a linefeed (called CR/LF).
- Both ends must convert between this format and whatever the local host uses as a line delimiter. An "*octet*" transfer treats the data as 8-bit bytes with no interpretation.

- In order to load a file from a remote server, the client (the computer being booted) sends a standard TFTP read request to the server.
- The read request contains the name of the file to be transferred.
- Once the transfer has begun, the server sends data packets one at a time, and the client sends acknowledgment packets for each packet until the transfer is complete.
- Data packet is a packet that contains part or the entire file being transferred.
- An Acknowledgment packet (ACK) is sent for each data packet received, the server does not transmit the next Data packet until it has received an Acknowledgment packet for the previous Data packet that it sent.
- Thus it is a Stop-and-Wait Protocol.
- The normal end of a transmission is denoted by a data packet of length less than the maximum 512 bytes, when this occurs the transfer is complete.

Starting the TFTP Server:

- The TFTP server enables the client to upload or download files between the server and the client.
- The information transfer is done in TFTP through port "69".
- The various options with which the TFTP server can be started is specified in the file NmsProcessesBE.conf present in *<Web NMS Home>/conf* directory.

Process:

[TFTP_ROOT_DIRECTORY dir]

[PORT PortNo]

[RETRIES number]

[TIMEOUT time in ms]

[MAX_CLIENTS number]

[TFTP_LOGGER classname]

[PERMISSION_MODE mode]

The NmsTftpServer process starts the TFTP service that can be used to transfer files between nodes. It can be either started as one of the modules with Web NMS or as a standalone utility.

Arguments and Description:

Arguments	Description
TFTP_ROOT_DIRECTORY	This parameter is used to specify the root directory with respect to which the files should be transferred between machines. If this parameter is not given a value, a default value of "/" is taken.
PORT	This parameter is used to specify the port in which the TftpServer has to be started. By default, the TftpServer is started at port "**69**". Since, Linux systems do not allow the ordinary users to use the ports from 0 to 1023, the user has to log in as "root", in order to enable the TFTP service to be started at the default port.
RETRIES	This parameter is used to set the number of retries to be made for transferring files between the source and the destination. **Default Value: 0**
TIMEOUT	This parameter sets the timeout value for each retry of the TftpServer. This value should be specified in milliseconds. **Default Value: 5000**
MAX_CLIENTS	This parameter is used to set the maximum limit on the number of clients that can be connected to the TftpServer at a given time. **Default Value: 15**
TFTP_LOGGER	This parameter takes a class name as its input which implements TftpLogger interface. This is used to log the TFTP transaction messages.
PERMISSION_MODE	This parameter is used to selectively enable and disable read/write operations or both while performing TFTP put() operation, when the user is logged in as "root". The value can be READ_ONLY, WRITE_ONLY or BOTH. **Default Value: BOTH**

Dependencies:

- This process does not depend on any other process and can be started as a standalone application.
- If the user is not a "root" user, and if the PORT parameter is not specified with a value, error will be thrown in the log files.

Conclusion:

- TFTP is a simple protocol designed to fit into read-only memory and be used only during the bootstrap process of diskless systems.
- It uses only a few message formats and a stop-and-wait protocol.
- To allow multiple clients to bootstrap at the same time, a TFTP server needs to provide some form of concurrency.
- Because UDP does not provide a unique connection between a client and server (as does TCP), the TFTP server provides concurrency by creating a new UDP port for each client.
- This allows different client input datagrams to be demultiplexed by the server's UDP module, based on destination port numbers, instead of doing this in the server itself.
- The TFTP protocol provides no security features. Most implementations count on the system administrator of the TFTP server to restrict any client's access to the files necessary for bootstrapping only.

5.12.9 Bootstrap Protocol (BOOTP)

1. Before a device on a TCP/IP network can effectively communicate, it needs to know its IP address.
2. While a conventional network host can read this information from its internal disk, some devices have no storage, and so do not have this luxury.
3. They need help from another device on the network to provide them with an IP address and other information and/or software they need to become active IP hosts.
4. This problem of getting a new machine up and running is commonly called *bootstrapping*, and to provide this capability to IP hosts, the TCP/IP *Bootstrap Protocol (BOOTP)* was created.
5. In this section we provide a fairly detailed look at the TCP/IP Bootstrap Protocol.
6. We begin with an overview and history of the protocol and a look at the standards that define it.
7. We then discuss the general client/server nature of BOOTP and how addressing is done in communication between the client and the server.
8. We describe the operation of BOOTP step by step, and illustrate the format of BOOTP messages.
9. We conclude with a description of BOOTP vendor extensions, which are used to allow the information sent in BOOTP messages to be customized, and a discussion of BOOTP relay agents, which allow the protocol to operate even when the BOOTP server and client are on different networks.

10. BOOTP was the predecessor of the Dynamic Host Configuration Protocol. DHCP was built to be substantially compatible with BOOTP and so the two protocols have a fair degree of commonality.
11. To avoid duplication, certain information has been included only in the DHCP section, with links provided from the BOOTP topics where appropriate.
12. On the other hand, some of the historical background information behind features like vendor information extensions and relay agents, which were first developed for BOOTP and adopted by DHCP, is in this section and linked from the DHCP topics.
13. Why structure the sections this way? DHCP is far more popular than BOOTP today, so we wanted its description to be complete, but some features only really make sense if initially explained in the context of BOOTP's operation
14. The Internet Bootstrap Protocol (BOOTP) simplifies administration of your network by providing workstations and other peripherals such as network hubs and printers with the ability to obtain their TCP/IP network configuration information from a centralized database on a BOOTP server.
15. Configuration parameters that a client can obtain from the BOOTP server include its IP address, netmask, default router IP address, and DNS server IP address.
16. BOOTP is an Internet protocol that can provide network configuration information to diskless workstations, or other workstations if necessary, on a local network.
17. Diskless workstations need to obtain a boot image from a disk on the network because they do not have their own disks from which to obtain this information.
18. BOOTP is also used to initialize IP phones.
19. The boot image provides all the files required to start the operating system on the computer. BOOTP is also used to initialize IP phones.
20. BOOTP Enhanced what RARP (Reverse Address Resolution Protocol does. RARP obtains an IP address only. BOOTP obtains an IP address, a gateway address, and a name server address.
21. BOOTP is designed for LANs and bridged networks. It can be used across routed internetworks if the routers support BOOTP forwarding.
22. When a workstation boots, it broadcasts a BOOTP message on the network.
A BOOTP server receives this message, obtains the configuration information for the designated computer, and returns it to the computer.
23. The booting system does not have an IP address when it sends out a BOOTP message. Instead, the hardware address of the NIC (network interface card) is placed in the message and the BOOTP server returns its reply to this address.
24. Information returned by the BOOTP server to the booting computer includes its IP address, the IP address of the server, the host name of the server, and the IP address of a default router.

25. It also specifies the location of a boot image that the booting computer can obtain in order to complete its startup operation.
26. Note that administrators must manually configure the information on a BOOTP server. An IP address must be matched to the MAC (medium access control) addresses of computers on the network.
27. To minimize this configuration requirement, DHCP (Dynamic Host Configuration Protocol) was developed to automatically allocate IP addresses to clients.
28. Basically, BOOTP makes a request for IP Information while DHCP fulfills that request.

BOOTP Detailed Operation:

- Now that we have seen how BOOTP messaging works in general terms, let's take a closer look at the detailed operation of the protocol.
- This will let us more clearly see how clients and servers create and process messages, and also help make sense of some of the important fields in the BOOTP message field format.
- Understanding the basic operation of BOOTP will also be of use when we examine BOOTP relay agents, and even when we discuss DHCP.

BOOTP Bootstrapping Steps:

The following are the basic steps performed by the client and server in a regular BOOTP bootstrapping procedure (see Fig. 5.91).

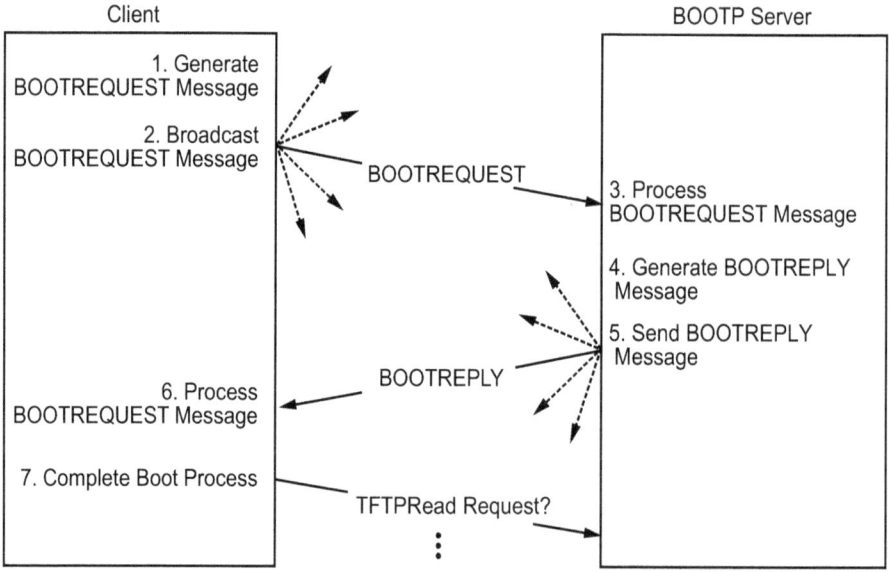

Fig. 5.91: Boot Protocol Operation

- The Boot Protocol uses a simple two-step message exchange consisting of a broadcast request and broadcast reply.
- After the client receives configuration information from the BOOTP server, it completes the bootstrapping process using a protocol such as TFTP.

1. Client Creates Request:
The client machine begins the procedure by creating a BOOTP request message. In creating this message, it fills in the following information:
- It sets the message type to the value 1, for a *BOOTREQUEST* message.
- If it knows its own IP address that it plans to keep using, it specifies it in the *CIAddr* field. Otherwise, it fills this field with zeroes. (See below for more on this.)
- It puts its own layer-two hardware address in the *CHAddr* field. This is used by the server to determine the right address and other parameters for the client.
- It generates a random transaction identifier, and puts this in the *XID* field.
- The client may specify a particular server that it wants to send it a reply and put that into the *SName* field. It may also specify the name of a particular type of boot file that it wants the server to provide in the *File* field.
- The client may specific vendor-specific information, if programmed to do so.

2. Client Sends Request:
The client broadcasts the *BOOTREQUEST* message by transmitting it to address 255.255.255.255. Alternately, if it already knows the address of a BOOTP server, it may send the request unicast.

3. Server Receives Request and Processes It:
A BOOTP server, listening on UDP port 67, receives the broadcasted request and processes it. If a name of a particular server was specified and this name is different than the name of this server, the server may discard the request. This is especially true if the server knows that the server the client asked for is also on the local network. If no particular server is specified, or this particular server was the one the client wanted, the server will reply.

4. Server Creates Reply:
The server creates a reply message by copying the request message and changing several fields:
- It changes the message type (*Op*) to the value 2, for a *BOOTREPLY* message.
- It takes the client's specified hardware address from the *CHAddr* field, and uses it in a table lookup to find the matching IP address for this host. It then places this value into the *YIAddr* ("your IP address") of the reply.
- It processes the *File* field and provides the filename type the client requested, or if the field was blank, the default filename.

- It puts its own IP address and name in the *SIAddr* and *SName* fields.
- It sets any vendor-specific values in the *Vend* field.

5. Server Sends Reply:

The server sends the reply, the method depending on the contents of the request:
- If the *B (Broadcast)* flag is set, this indicates that the client can't have the reply sent unicast, so the server will broadcast it.
- If the *CIAddr* field is non-zero, the server will send the reply unicast back to that *CIAddr*.
- If the *B* flag is zero and the *CIAddr* field is also zero, the server may either use an ARP entry or broadcast, as described.

6. Client Processes Reply:

The client receives the server's reply and processes it, storing the information and parameters provided. (See below for one important issue related to this processing.)

7. Client Completes Boot Process:

Once configured, the client proceeds to "phase two" of the bootstrapping process, by using a protocol such as TFTP to download its boot file containing operating system software, using the filename the server provided.

Bootstrap Protocol (BootP) and DHCP:

- The problem with using **Reverse Address Resolution Protocol (RARP)** for assigning IP addresses to clients is that it operates at the data link layer and is therefore limited to the local LAN.
- Bootp however uses IP/UDP (port 67 for the server destination port, and port 68 for the client source port) and can cross routers.
- If a client does not know its own IP address when it boots up then it can utilise a **Bootp** server to obtain its IP address.
- It will use a IP broadcast address of 255.255.255.255.
- This IP broadcast is transmitted in a link-layer broadcast of FFFF.FFFF.FFFF. If the client is on the same LAN as the Bootp server, then the Bootp server will respond to the broadcast, by using the MAC address of the client, and the IP address will be given to the client.

- If the Bootp server is on another LAN i.e. on the other side of a router then we are left with the situation whereby broadcasts are being sent by the client and the router is designed not to pass broadcasts. Consider the following scenario.

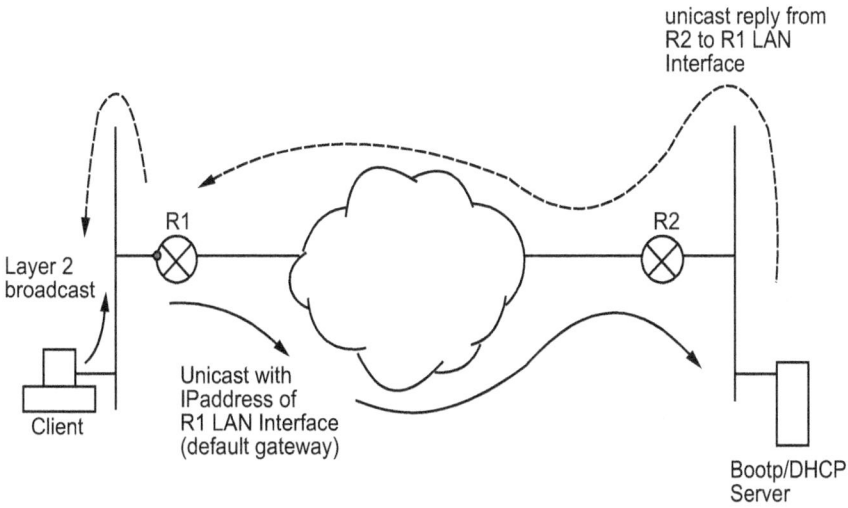

Fig. 5.92: BOOTP protocol and it's operation

1. The client requires an IP address and a default gateway address so it sends out an IP broadcast BOOTREQUEST.
2. No Bootp server exists locally so the router R1, which is configured to forward Bootp/DHCP requests, sends a unicast with the source IP address of it's LAN interface on which it received the initial broadcast. Note that this is different from TCP connections, which use the WAN IP address on the router, which owns the LAN interface from when the packet came. The unicast contains the IP address of the Bootp server which R1 knows since this is part of the Bootp forwarding configuration.
3. R2 forwards the unicast to the Bootp server.
4. The server examines the packet and checks for the client's hardware address in its database. If the MAC address has been entered then the server can map the client MAC address to the IP address configured in the database.
5. The server then looks to see if the client is requesting a configuration file (boot file).
6. The server replies with a unicast BOOTREPLY containing the client's IP address and details of the configuration file.
7. R1 recognizes the unicast reply and forwards the packet to the clients MAC address.

8. The client's TCP/IP stack then pings the IP address to check that it is not being used before taking it for itself.
9. The client then can use TFTP etc. to download the configuration file including information such as the default gateway to the LAN interface of R1.

Note that the TCP/IP stack needs to be in place on the client, since the client needs to be able to send an IP broadcast (not a layer 2 broadcast !).

Below is the frame format, which is used for both Bootp and DHCP:

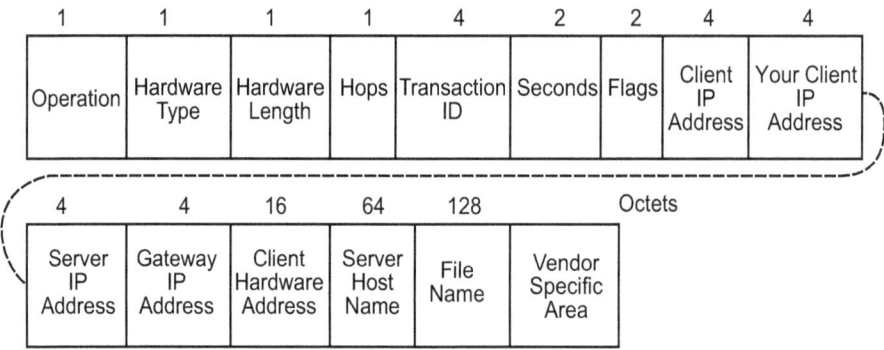

Fig. 5.93: Frame format, which is used for both Bootp and DHCP

- **Operation** - indicates a request **1** or a reply **2**.
- **Hardware Type** - Ethernet is **1**.
- **Hardware Length** - length of the address
- **Hops** - the client starts this off with **0** and then this increment by each Bootp server if the packet is passed on.
- **Transaction ID** - diskless nodes use this number to match responses with the requests.
- **Seconds** - this gives the elapsed time since the client started the boot process
- **Client IP Address** - if a client knows its IP address it puts it in here, otherwise it is a 0.
- **Your IP Address** - the server puts an IP address here if the Client IP address field is 0.
- **Server IP Address** - if the client knows this then the client can place the server address in here, otherwise the server does.
- **Server Host Name** - same as previously.
- **Gateway IP Address** - the client initially sets this to **0**. The router receiving the packet will put the IP address of the interface on which the packet was received (i.e. the LAN interface).

- **Client Hardware Address** - so that the servers/routers know where to send responses back to.
- **Server Host Name** - If the client puts a specific server name in here then it restricts itself to booting from that server alone. If no name is in here then the client can boot from any server that responds to a bootp request.
- **Boot File Name** - the client can request a specific boot filename.
- **Vendor Specific Area** - Up to 64 octets long for Bootp. This is called the **Options** field in a DHCP packet and is up to 312 octets long. In DHCP this field contains optional information that the server may wish to give the client e.g. **client identifier** and **server identifier**.

Conclusion:
- BOOTP uses UDP and is intended as an alternative to RARP for bootstrapping a diskless system to find its IP address.
- BOOTP can also return additional information, such as the IP address of a router, the client's subnet mask, and the IP address of a name server.
- Since BOOTP is used in the bootstrap process, a diskless system needs the following protocols implemented in read-only memory: BOOTP, TFTP, UDP, IP, and a device driver for the local network.
- The implementation of a BOOTP server is easier than an RARP server, since BOOTP requests and replies are in UDP datagrams, not special link-layer frames.
- A router can also serve as a proxy agent for a real BOOTP server, forwarding client requests to the real server on a different network.

5.12.10 NFS Overview, History, Versions and Standards

- Sun Microsystems was one of the early pioneers in the development of UNIX, and in TCP/IP networking. Early in the evolution of TCP/IP, certain tools were created to allow a user to access another machine over the network—after all, this is arguably the entire point of networking. Remote access protocols such as Telnet allowed a user to log in to another host computer and use resources there. The File Transfer Protocol (FTP) allowed someone to copy a file from a distant machine to their own and edit it.
- However, neither of these solutions really fit the bill of allowing a user to access a file on a remote machine in a way similar to how a local file is used. To fill this need, Sun created the *Network File System (NFS)*. NFS was specifically designed with the goal of eliminating the distinction between a local and a remote file. To a user, after

the appropriate setup is performed, a file on a remote computer can be used as if it were on a hard disk on the user's local machine. Sun also crafted NFS specifically to be vendor-independent, to ensure that both hardware made by Sun and that made by other companies could interoperate.

Overview of NFS Architecture and General Operation:

- NFS follows the classical TCP/IP client/server model of operation.
- A hard disk or a directory on a storage device of a particular computer can be set up by an administrator as a shared resource.
- This resource can then be accessed by client computers, which *mount* the shared drive or directory, causing it to appear like a local directory on the client machine.
- Some computers may act as only servers or only clients, while others may be both: sharing some of their own resources and accessing resources provided by others.
- NFS uses an architecture that includes three main components that define its operation.
- The External Data Representation (XDR) standard defines how data is represented in exchanges between clients and servers.
- The Remote Procedure Call (RPC) protocol is used as a method of calling procedures on remote machines.
- Then, a set of NFS procedures and operations works using RPC to carry out various requests. The separate Mount protocol is used to mount resources as mentioned above.
- One of the most important design goals of NFS was **performance**. Obviously, even if you set up a file on a distant machine as if it were local, the actual read and write operations have to travel across a network.
- Usually this takes more time than simply sending data within a computer, so the protocol itself needed to be as "lean and mean" as possible.
- This decision led to some interesting decisions, such as the use of the unreliable User Datagram Protocol (UDP) for transport in TCP/IP, instead of the reliable TCP like most file transfer protocols do.
- This in turn has interesting implications on how the protocol works as a whole.
- Another key design goal for NFS was **simplicity** (which of course is related to performance).
- NFS servers are said to be *stateless*, which means that the protocol is designed so that servers do not need to keep track of which files have been opened by which clients.

- This allows requests to be made independently of each other, and allows a server to gracefully deal with events such as crashes without the need for complex recovery procedures.
- The protocol is also designed so that if requests are lost or duplicated, file corruption will not occur.
- The *Network File System (NFS)* was created to allow client hosts to access files on remote servers as if they were local. It was designed primarily with the goals of performance, simplicity and cross-vendor compatibility.

NFS Versions and Standards:
- Since it was initially designed and marketed by Sun, NFS began as a de facto standard.
- The first widespread version of NFS was version 2, and this is still the most common version of the protocol.
- *NFS Version 3 Protocol Specification.* It is similar to version 2 but makes a few changes and adds some new capabilities.
- These include support for larger file transfers, better support for setting file attributes, and several new file access and manipulation procedures. NFS version 3 also provides support for larger files than version 2 did.
- *NFS version 4 Protocol.* Where version 3 of NFS contained only relatively small changes to version 2, NFSv4 is virtually a rewrite of NFS.

NFS Architecture and Main Components:
- Considered from the perspective of the TCP/IP protocol suite as a whole, the Network.
- File System (NFS) is a single protocol that resides at the application layer of the TCP/IP model.
- This TCP/IP layer encompasses the session, presentation and application layers of the OSI Reference Model.
- As discussed before in this scenario, We don't see much value in trying to differentiate between layers 5 through 7 most of the time.
- In some cases, however, these layers can be helpful in understanding the architecture of a protocol, and that's the case with NFS.
- The operation of NFS is defined in the form of three main components that can be viewed as logically residing at each of the three OSI model layers corresponding to the TCP/IP application layer (see Fig. 5.94). These components are:

1. **Remote Procedure Call (RPC):** RPC is a generic session layer service used to implement client/server internetworking functionality. It extends the notion of a program calling a local procedure on a particular host computer, to the calling of a procedure on a remote device across a network.
2. **External Data Representation (XDR):** XDR is a descriptive language that allows data types to be defined in a consistent manner. XDR conceptually resides at the presentation layer; its universal representations allow data to be exchanged using NFS between computers that may use very different internal methods of storing data.
3. **NFS Procedures and Operations:** The actual functionality of NFS is implemented in the form of procedures and operations that conceptually function at layer seven of the OSI model. These procedures specify particular tasks to be carried out on files over the network, using XDR to represent data and RPC to carry the commands across an internetwork.

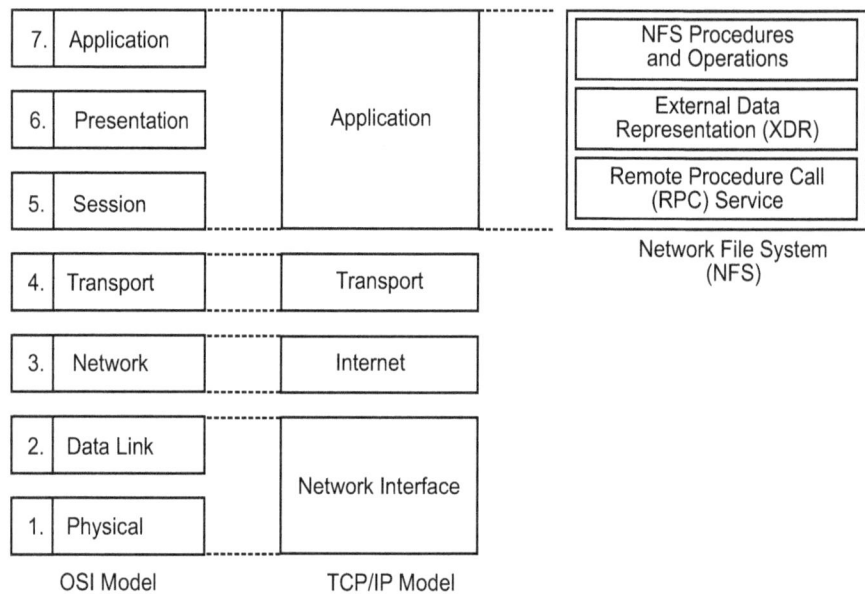

Fig. 5.94: NFS Architectural Components

- NFS resides architecturally at the TCP/IP application layer.
- Even though in the TCP/IP model no clear distinction is made generally between the functions of layers five through seven of the OSI Reference Model, NFS's three subprotocols correspond well to those three layers as shown.
- NFS resides architecturally at the application layer of the TCP/IP model.
- Its functions are implemented primarily through three distinct functional components that implement the functions of layers five through seven of the OSI reference model: the *Remote Procedure Call (RPC)*, which provide session-layer

services; the *External Data Representation (XDR)* standard, which manages data representation and conversion, and *NFS procedures and operations*, which allow application-layer tasks to be performed using the other two components.

Other Important NFS Functions:
Aside from these three components, the NFS protocol as a whole involves a number of other functions, some of which I think are worth specific mention:

- **Mount Protocol:** A specific decision was made by the creators of NFS to not have NFS deal with the particulars of file opening and closing. Instead, a separate protocol called the *Mount* protocol is used for this purpose. Accessing a file or other resource over the network involves first *mounting* it using this protocol. The Mount Protocol is architecturally distinct, but obviously closely related to NFS, and is even defined in an appendix of the NFS standard.
- **NFS File System Model:** NFS uses a particular model to implement the directory and file structure of the systems that use it. This model is closely based on the file system model of UNIX but is not specific to only that operating system. It is discussed in conjunction with the explanation of the Mount Protocol.
- **Security:** Versions 2 and 3 of NFS include only limited security provisions. They use UNIX style authentication to check permissions for various operations. NFS version 4 greatly increases the security options available for NFS implementations. This includes both the option of multiple authentication and encryption algorithms, and many changes made to the protocol as a whole to make it more "security minded".

Like other TCP/IP protocols, NFS is implemented in the form of client and server software that implements the functions above. The NFS standards, especially for versions 3 and 4, discuss numerous issues related to proper NFS client/server implementation, including interaction between servers and clients, file locking, permission issues, caching, retransmission policies, international support and more. Many of these issues require extensive discussion that is beyond the scope of this Guide.

NFS Client/Server Operation Using Remote Procedure Calls (RPCs):
1. Almost all applications deal with files and other resources.
2. When a software program on a particular computer wants to read a file, write a file or perform related tasks, it needs to use the correct software instructions for this purpose.
3. It would be inefficient to require each software program to contain a copy of these instructions, so instead, they are encoded as standardized software modules, sometimes called *procedures*.

4. To perform an action, a piece of software *calls* the procedure; the procedure temporarily takes over for the main program and performs a task such as reading or writing data.
5. The procedure then returns control of the program back to the software that called it, and optionally, returns data as well.
6. Since the key concept of NFS was to make remote file access look like local file access, it was designed around the use of a network-based version of the procedure calling method just described.
7. A software application that wants to do something with a file still makes a procedure call, but it makes the call to a procedure on a different computer instead of the local one.
8. A special set of routines is used to handle the transmission of the call across the network, in a way largely invisible to software performing the call.
9. This functionality could have been implemented directly in NFS, but instead Sun created a separate session-layer protocol component called the *Remote Procedure Call (RPC)* specification, which defines how this works.
10. RPC was originally created as a subcomponent of NFS, but is generic enough and useful enough that it has been used for other client/server applications in TCP/IP. For this reason, it is really considered in many respects a distinct protocol.
11. Because RPC is the actual process of communicating in NFS, NFS itself is different from many other TCP/IP protocols.
12. Its operation can't be described in terms of specific message exchanges and state diagrams the way a protocol like HTTP or DHCP or even TCP can, because RPC does all of that.
13. NFS is in fact defined in terms of a set of RPC server procedures and operations that an NFS server makes available to NFS clients.
14. These procedures and operations each allow a particular type of action to be taken on a file, such as reading from it, writing to it or deleting it

RPC Operation and Transport Protocol Usage:

1. When a client wants to perform some type of action on a file on a particular machine, it uses RPC to make a call to the NFS server on that machine.
2. The server accepts the request and performs the action required, then returns a result code and possibly data back to the client, depending on the request.
3. The result code indicates if the action was successful. If it was, the client can assume that whatever it asked to be done was completed.
4. For example, in the case of writing data, the client can assume the data has been successfully written to long-term storage.

5. NFS can operate over any transport mechanism that has a valid RPC implementation at the session layer. Of course in TCP/IP we have two transport protocols, UDP and TCP.
6. It's interesting to see that NFS has seen an evolution of sorts in its use of transport protocol.
7. The NFSv2 standard says that it operates "normally" using UDP, and this is still a common way that NFS information is carried.
8. NFS does not use a dedicated message format, like most other protocols do. Instead, clients and servers use the *Remote Procedure Call (RPC)* protocol to exchange file operation requests and data.

Summary:

- RPC is a way to build a client-server application so that it appears that the client just calls server procedures.
- All the networking details are hidden in the client and server stubs, which are generated for an application by the RPC package, and in the RPC library routines.
- RPC call and reply messages, and mentioned that XDR is used to encode the values, allowing RPC clients and servers to run on machines with different architectures.
- One of the most widely used RPC applications is Sun's NFS, a heterogeneous file access protocol that is widely implemented on hosts of all sizes.
- A client's access to an NFS server starts with the mount protocol, returning a file handle to the client.
- The client can then access files on the server's file system using that file handle.
- File names are looked up on the server one element at a time, returning a new file handle for each element.
- The end result is a file handle for the file being referenced, which is used in subsequent reads and writes.

EXERCISE

1. Draw and explain TCP/IP model.
2. Write short notes on:
   (a) TCP/IP link layer and its protocols
   (b) TCP/IP network layer and its protocols
   (c) TCP/IP Transport layer and its protocols
   (d) TCP/IP Application layer and its protocols.
3. List out the different platforms supported by TCP/IP,
4. What are the different features of TCP/IP?

5. Explain the different Encapsulation and Decapsulation of data.
6. Draw and explain data flow in TCP/IP stack in following scenarios with figures:
   (a) TCP
   (b) UDP
7. What are the different address, logical IP address and port address.
8. Compare physical address, logical IP address and port address.
9. Write short notes on:
   (a) MAC address
   (b) IP address
   (c) Port address
10. What is Multicast, Unicast and Broadcast operation?
11. What is subnet mask.
12. Explain subnetting and supernetting principles
13. Write short note in DHCP.
14. Compare IPV_4 Vs. IPV_6.
15. Write short note on:
    (a) IP
    (b) ICMP
    (c) IGMP
16. Draw and explain TCP header.
17. Draw and explain TCP header.
18. Explain TCP connection establishment and TCP connection termination process in detail.
19. Compare TCP Vs. UDP.
20. Write short notes on:
    (a) HTTP protocol
    (b) Telnet protocol
    (c) FTP
    (d) SMTP
21. How E-mail works?
22. How E-mail system works?
23. Write short notes on:
    (a) SNMP
    (b) Traceroute system
    (c) Window system
    (d) TFTP and BOOTP protocol
    (e) NFS and RPC
24. What are the different applications of TCP/IP?
25. What is the difference between routable and non-routable protocols?

Unit VI

DIGITAL NETWORK

6.1 Digital Transmission

In contrast, is concerned with the content of the signal. Digital signal can be propagated only a limited distance before attenuation endangers the integrity of the data. To achieve greater distances, repeaters are used. A repeater receives the digital signal, recovers the pattern of ones and zeros and retransmits a new signal. Thus, the attenuation is overcome.

The same technique may be used with an analog signal if the signal carries digital data. At appropriately spaced points, the transmission system has retransmission devices rather than amplifiers. The retransmission device recovers the digital data from the analog signal and generates a new, clean analog signal. Thus, noise is not cumulative.

The question naturally arises as to which is the preferred method of transmission. The answer being supplied by the telecommunications industry and customers is digital transmission, this despite an enormous investment in analog communications facilities. Both long-haul telecommunications facilities and intrabuilding services are being converted to digital transmission and, where possible digital signaling techniques.

6.1.1 Advantages of Digital Network

- **Cost:** The advent of very-large-scale-integration (VLSI) technology has caused a continuing drop in the cost and size of digital circuitry. Analog equipment has not shown a similar drop. Furthermore, maintenance costs for digital circuitry are a fraction of those for analog circuitry.

- **Data integrity:** With the use of digital repeaters rather than analog amplifiers, the effects of noise and other signal impairments are not cumulative. Thus, it is possible to transmit data longer distances and over lower-quality lines by digital means while maintaining the integrity of the data.

- **Capacity utilization:** It has become economical to build transmission links of very high bandwidth, including satellite channels and optical fiber. A high degree of multiplexing is needed to utilize such capacity effectively, and this is more easily and cheaply achieved with digital (time-division) rather than analog (frequency-division) techniques.

- **Security and privacy:** Encryption techniques can be readily applied to digital data and to analog data that have been digitized.

- **Integration:** By treating both analog and digital information digitally, all signals have the same form and can be treated similarly. Thus, economies of scale and convenience can be achieved by integrating voice, video, image, and digital data.

6.2 Signal Conversion

6.2.1 Analog and Digital Data Transmission

The terms analog and digital correspond, roughly, to continuous and discrete, respectively. These two terms are used frequently in data communications in at least three contexts: data, signaling, and transmission.

Very briefly, we define data as entities that, convey meaning. A useful distinction is that data have to do with the form of something; information data has to do with the content or interpretation of those data. Signals are electric or electromagnetic encoding of data. Signaling is the act of propagating the signal along some suitable medium. Finally, transmission is the communication of data by the propagation and processing of signals.

6.2.1.1 Analog and Digital Data

The concepts of analog and digital data are simple enough. Analog data take on continuous values on some interval. For example, voice and video are continuously varying patterns of intensity. Most data collected by sensors, such as temperature and pressure, are continuous valued. Digital data take on discrete values; examples are text and integers.

6.2.1.2 Analog and Digital Signaling

In a communications system, data are propagated from one point another by means of electric signals. An analog signal is a continuously varying electromagnetic wave that may be propagated over a variety of media, depending on frequency; examples are copper wire media, such as twisted pair and coaxial cable; fiber optic cable; and atmosphere or space propagation (wireless). A digital signal is a sequence of voltage pulses that may be transmitted over a copper wire medium; for example, a constant positive voltage level may represent binary 1 and a constant negative voltage level may represent binary 0.

The principal advantages of digital signaling are that it is generally cheaper than analog signaling and is less susceptible to noise interference. The principal disadvantage is that digital signals suffer more from attenuation than do analog signals. Figure 6.1 shows a sequence of voltage pulses, generated by a source using two voltage levels, and the received voltage some distance down a conducting medium. Because of the attenuation, or reduction, of signal strength at higher frequencies, the pulses become rounded and smaller. It should be clear that this attenuation can rather quickly lead to the loss of the information contained in the propagated signal.

Both analog and digital data can be represented, and hence propagated, by either analog or digital signals. This is illustrated in Figure 2.2. Generally, analog data are a function of time and occupy a limited frequency spectrum. Such data can be directly represented by an electromagnetic signal occupying the same spectrum. The best example of this is voice data. As sound waves, voice data have frequency components in the range 20 Hz to 20 kHz. However, most of the speech energy is in a much narrower range. The standard spectrum of voice signals is 300 to 3400 Hz, and this is quite adequate to propagate speech intelligibly and clearly. The telephone instrument does just that. For ail sound input in the range of 300 to 3400 Hz, an electromagnetic signal with the same frequency–amplitude pattern is produced. The process is performed in reverse to convert the electromagnetic energy back into sound.

Digital data can also be represented by analog signals by use of a modem (modulator-demodulator). The modem converts a series of binary (two-valued) voltage pulses into an analog signal by modulating a carrier frequency. The resulting signal occupies a certain spectrum of frequency centered about the carrier and may be propagated across a medium suitable for that carrier. The most common modems represent digital data in the voice spectrum and hence allow those data to be propagated over ordinary voice-grade telephone lines. At the other end of the line, a modem demodulates the signal to recover the original data.

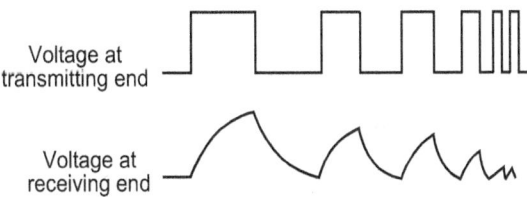

Fig. 6.1: Attenuation of digital signals

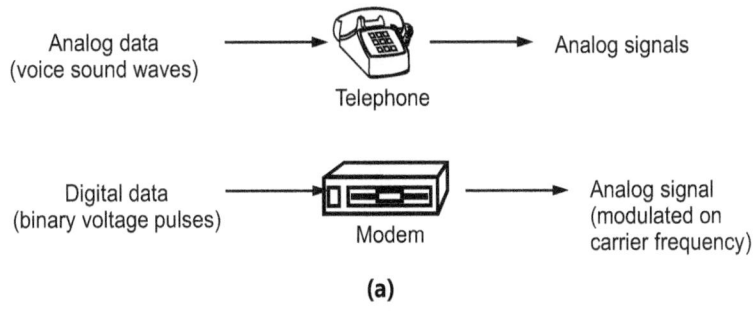

(a)

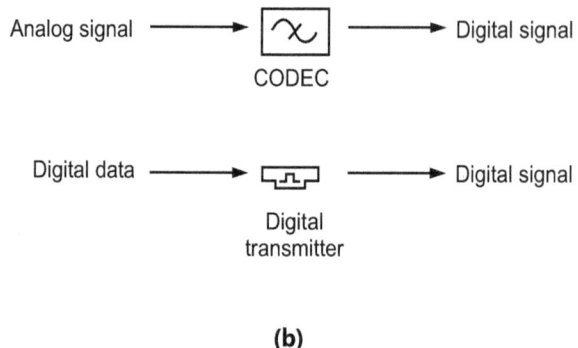

(b)

Fig. 6.2: Analog and digital signaling of analog and digital data

In an operation very similar to that performed by a modem, analog data can be represented by digital signals. The device that performs this function for voice data is a codec (coder-decoder). In essence, the codec takes an analog signal that directly represents the voice data and approximates that signal by a bit stream. At the other end of the line, the bit stream is used to reconstruct the analog data.

Finally, digital data can be represented directly, in binary form, by two voltage levels. To improve propagation characteristics, however, the binary data are often encoded into a more complex form of digital signal..

6.2.1.3 Analog and Digital Transmission

Analog and digital signals may be transmitted on suitable transmission media. The way these signals are treated is a function of the transmission system. Table summarizes the methods of data transmission. Analog transmission is a means of transmitting analog signals without regard to their content; the signals may represent analog data (e.g., voice) or digital data (e.g. data that pass through a modem). In either case, the analog signal will suffer attenuation that limits the length of the transmission link. To achieve longer distances, the analog transmission system includes amplifiers that boost the energy in the signal. Unfortunately, the amplifier also boosts the noise components. With amplifiers cascaded to achieve long distance, the signal becomes more and more distorted. For analog data, such. as voice, quite a bit of distortion can be tolerated and the data remain intelligible. However, for digital data transmitted as analog signals, cascaded amplifiers will introduce errors.

Table 6.1: Analog and Digital Transmission

(a) Data and Signals

	Analog signals	Digital signal
Analog data	Two alternatives: (1) signal occupies the same spectrum as, the analog data; (2) analog data are encoded to occupy a different portion of spectrum.	Analog data are encoded using a codec to produce a digital bit stream.
Digital data	Digital data are encoded using a modem to produce analog signal.	Two alternatives: (1) signal consists of a two voltage levels to represent the two binary values; (2) digital data are encoded to produce a digital signal with desired properties.

(b) Treatment of signals

	Analog transmission	Digital transmission
Analog data	Is propagated through amplifiers; same treatment whether signal is used to represent analog data or digital data.	Assumes that the analog signal represents digital data. Signal is propagated through repeaters; at each repeater, digital data are recovered from inbound signal and used to generate a new analog outbound signal.
Digital signal	Not used	Digital signal represents a stream of 1s and 0s, which may represent digital data or may be an encoding of analog data. Signal is propagated through repeaters; at each repeater, stream of 1s and 0s is recovered from inbound signal and used to generate a new digital outbound signal.

6.3 Digital Encoding of Analog Data

The evolution of public telecommunications networks to digital transmission requires that voice data be represented in digital form,. It is important to note that this does not necessarily imply that the voice data be transmitted using digital signals. Fig. 6.3 illustrates a common situation. Analog voice signals are digitized to produce a pattern of ones and' zeros. As a digital signal, this pattern of ones and zeros may be fed into a modem so that an analog signal may be transmitted. However, this new analog signal differs significantly from the original voice signal, in that it represents an encoding of a binary stream. In particular, retransmission devices rather than amplifiers are used to extend the length of a transmission link. Ultimately, of course, the new analog signal must be converted back to analog data that approximate the original voice input.

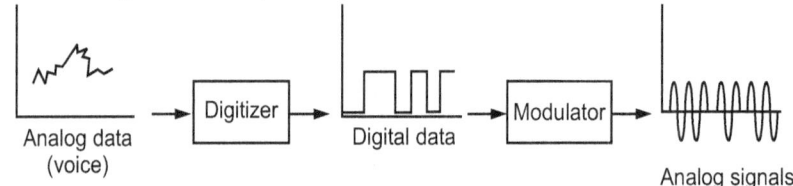

Fig. 6.3: Digitizing Analog Data

Pulse-Code Modulation

The best-known technique for voice digitization is pulse-code modulation (PCM). PCM is based on the sampling theorem, which states the following:

Statement of Sampling Theorem

If a -signal f(t) is sampled at regular intervals of time and at a rate higher than twice the highest significant signal frequency, then the samples contain all the information of the original signal. The function f(t) may be reconstructed from these samples by the use of a low-pass filter.

If voice data are limited to frequencies below 4000 Hz, a conservative procedure for intelligibility, then 8000 samples per second would be sufficient to characterize the voice signal completely. Note, however, that these are analog samples. To convert to digital, each of these analog samples must be assigned a binary code. Fig. 6.4 shows an example in which each sample is approximated by being "quantized" into one of 16 different levels. Each sample can then be represented by 4 bits. But because the quantized values are only approximations, it is impossible to recover the original signal exactly. By using an 8-bit sample, which allows 256 quantizing levels, the quantity of the recovered voice signal is comparable with that achieved via analog transmission. Klotz that this implies that a data rate of 8000 samples per second × 8 bits per sample = 64 kbps is needed for a single voice signal.

Typically, the PCM scheme is refined using a technique known as nonlinear! encoding, which means, in effect, that the 256 quantization levels are not equally; spaced. The problem with equal spacing is that the mean absolute error for each sample is the same, regardless of signal level. Consequently, lower-amplitude values are relatively more distorted. By using a greater number of quantizing steps for signals of low amplitude, and a smaller number of quantizing steps for signals of large amplitude, a marked reduction in overall signal distortion is achieved.

PCM can, of course, be used for other than voice signals. For example, a color TV signal has a useful bandwidth of 4.6 MHz, and reasonable quality can be achieved with 10-bit samples for a data rate of 92 Mbps.

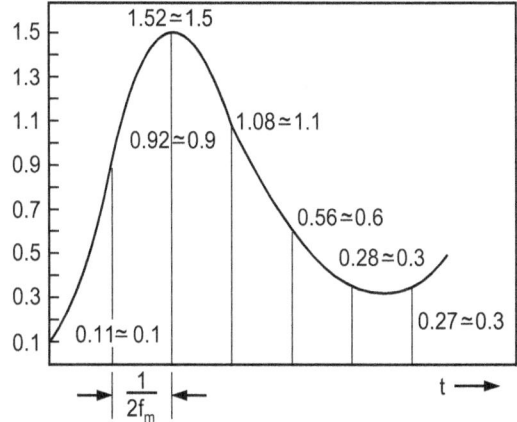

Digit	Binary equivalent	Pulse-code waveform
0	0000	
1	0001	
2	0010	
3	0011	
4	0100	
5	0101	
6	0110	
7	0111	
8	1000	
9	1001	
10	1010	
11	1011	
12	1100	
13	1101	
14	1110	
15	1111	

(b) Pulse code modulation
Fig. 6.4

Performance:

Good voice reproduction via. PCM can be achieved with 128 quantization levels, or 7-bit coding ($2^7 = 128$). A voice signal, conservatively, occupies a bandwidth of 4 kHz. Thus, according to the sampling theorem, samples should be taken at a rate of 8000 samples per second. This implies a data rate of 8000 × 7 = 56 kbps for the PCM-encoded digital data.

Consider what this means from the point of view of bandwidth requirement. An analog voice signal occupies 4 kHz. A 56-kbps digital signal will require on the order of at least 28 kHz. Even more severe differences are seen with higher-bandwidth signals. For example, a common PCM scheme for color television uses 10-bit codes, which works out to 92 Mbps for a 4.6-MHz bandwidth signal. However, techniques have been developed to provide more efficient codes. In the case of voice, a reasonable goal appears to be in. the neighborhood of 4 kbps. With video, advantage can be taken of the fact that from frame to frame, most picture elements will not change. Interframe coding techniques should allow the video requirement to be reduced to about 15 Mbps, and for slowly changing scenes, such as found in a video teleconference, down to 64 kbps or less.

6.4 Digital Carrier Systems

A wide area circuit-switched network will involve a number of interconnected nodes. A link between a pair of nodes, referred to as a trunk, uses multiplexing to carry the traffic on a number of channels, or circuits. This multiplexing may be in the form of frequency-division multiplexing (FDM) or synchronous time-division multiplexing (TDM). As wide area telecommunication networks evolve toward an integrated digital network, synchronous TDM techniques are becoming dominant.

The long-distance carrier system provided in the United States and throughout the world was designed to transmit voice signals over high-capacity transmission links, such as optical fiber, coaxial cable, and microwave. Part of the evolution of these telecommunications - networks to digital technology has been the adoption of synchronous TDM transmission structures. In the United States, AT&T developed a hierarchy of TDM structures of various capacities; this structure is used in Canada and Japan, as well as in the United States.

Table 6.2: North American and International TDM Carrier Standards

North American			International (ITU-T)		
Designation	Number of voice channels	Data Rate (Mbps)	Designation	Number of voice channels	Data Rate (Mbps)
DS-1	24	1.544	1	30	2.048
DS-1C	48	3.152	2	120	8.448
DS-2	96	6.312	3	480	34.368
DS-3	672	33.736	4	1920	139.264
DS-4	4032	274.176	5	7680	565.148

The basis of the North American TDM hierarchy is the DS-1 transmission format (Fig. 6.5) which multiplexes 24 channels. Each frame contains 8 bits per channel plus a framing bit for $24 \times 8 + 1 = 193$ bits. For voice transmission, the following rules apply: Each channel contains one word of digitized voice data. The original analog voice signal is digitized using pulse-code modulation (PCM) at a rate of 8000 samples per second. Therefore, each channel slot and hence each frame must repeat 8000 times per second. With a frame length of 193 bits, we have a data rate of 8000 × 193 = 1.544 Mbps. For five of every six frames, 8-bit PCM samples are used. For every sixth frame, each channel contains a 7-bit PCM word plus a signaling bit. The signaling bits form a stream for each voice channel that contains network control and routing information. For example, control signals are used to establish a connection or terminate a call.

The same DS-1 format is used to provide digital data service. For compatibility with voice, the same 1.544-Mbps data rate is used. In this case, 23 channels of data are provided. The twenty-fourth channel position is reserved for a special sync byte, which allows faster and more reliable refraining following a framing error. Within each channel, 7 bits per frame are used for data, with the eighth bit used to indicate whether the channel, for that frame, contains user data or system control data. With 7 bits per channel, and because each frame is repeated 8000 times per second, a data rate of 56 kbps can be provided per channel. Lower data rates are provided using a technique known as subrate multiplexing. For this technique, an additional bit is robbed from each channel to indicate which subrate multiplexing rate is being provided. This leaves a total capacity per channel of 6 × 8000 = 48 kbps. This capacity is used to multiplex five 9.6-kbps channels, ten 4.8-kbps channels, or twenty 2.4-kbps For example, if channel 2 is used to provide 9.6-kbps service, then up to five data subchannels share this channel. The data for each sub-channel appear as six bits in channel 2 every fifth frame.

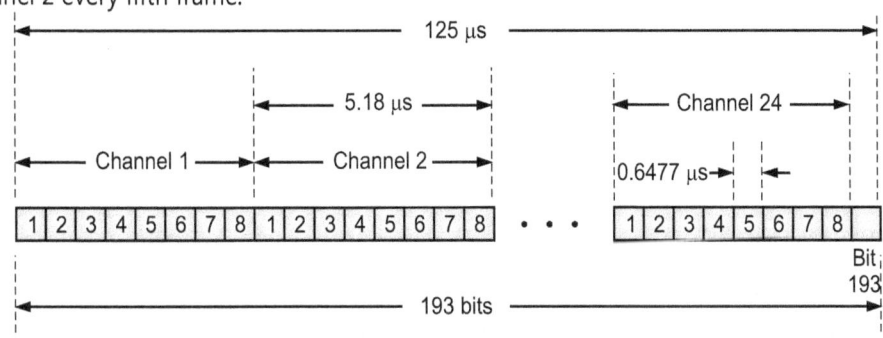

Fig. 6.5

Notes:
1. Bit 193 is a framing bit, used for synchronization.
2. Voice channels:
   - 8-bit PCM used on five of six frames.
   - 7-bit PCM used on every sixth frame; bit 8 of each channel is a signaling bit.
3. Data channels:
   - Channel 24 is used for signaling only in some schemes.
   - Bits 1-7 used for 56 kbps service
   - Bits 2-7 used for- 9.6, 4.8, and 2.4 kbps service.

Fig. 6.5: DS-1 Transmission Format

Finally, the DS-1 format can be used to carry a mixture of voice and data channels. In this case, all 24 channels are utilized; no sync byte is provided.

Above this basic data rate of 1.544 Mbps, higher-level multiplexing is achieved by interleaving bits from DS-1 inputs. For example, the DS-2 transmission system combines four DS-1 inputs into a 6.312-Mbps stream. Data from the four sources are interleaved 12 bits at a time. Note that $1.544 \times 4 = 6.176$ Mbps. The remaining capacity is used for framing and control bits.

Each higher level of the TDM hierarchy is formed by multiplexing signals from the next lower level or by combination of those signals plus input at the appropriate data rate from other sources. First, the DS-1 transmission rate is used to provide both a. voice and data service: The data service is known as the dataphone digital service (DDS)', The DDS provides digital transmission service between customer data devices at data rates of from 2.4 to 56 kbps. The service is available at customer premises over two twisted-pair lines.

Various standardized multiplexers are employed to create higher-capacity transmission facilities. The most commonly used ones are listed in Table 6.2. The designations DS-1, DS-1 C, and so on refer to the multiplexing scheme used for carrying information. AT&T and other carriers supply transmission facilities that support these various multiplexed signals, referred to as carrier systems. These are designated with a "T" label. Thus, the T1 carrier provides a data rate of 1.544 Mbps and is capable of supporting the DS-1 multiplex format and so on for higher data rates.

6.5 ISDN

6.5.1 Introduction

What is ISDN?

1. Integrated Services Digital Network (ISDN) is a state-of-the-art Public Switched Digital Network for provisioning of different services – voice, data and image transmission over the telephone line through the telephone network.
2. ISDN handles all types of information – voice, data, studio-quality sound, static and moving images.
3. They are all digitized, and transmitted at high speed.
4. ISDN can handle many devices and many telephone numbers on the same line.
5. Upto eight separate telephones, fax machines or computers can be linked to a single Basic Rate ISDN connection and have different phone numbers assigned to them.
6. A Basic Rate ISDN line can support upto two calls at the same time.
7. Any combination of voice, fax or PC connections can take place at the same time, through the same ISDN line.

8. From a digital ISDN telephone, you can place a call to an analogue telephone on the PSTN (Public Switched Telephone Network) and vice-versa.
9. Both networks are interconnected by the network carrier in a way similar to the connection between the mobile phone network and the analogue phone network.
10. For the user, it is completely transparent whether he is calling a GSM (Global System for Mobile) telephone, a conventional telephone or an ISDN digital telephone.
11. The single biggest disadvantage is likely to be your physical location. If you're not in an area that's reasonably close to a telephone company's central office (one with the required equipment already installed), ISDN may not be an option for you. If you live in a metro or near a city, ISDN is an ideal choice. But at other remote locations, ISDN is not available.

Availability:

ISDN service is available by and large in all major cities of India. Also ISDN has overseas connectivity with the following countries: Australia, Austria, Belgium, Canada, Denmark, France, Germany, Ireland, Israel, Italy, Japan, Malaysia, Netherlands, Norway, Philippines, Singapore, Switzerland, Thailand, U.A.E., UK, USA.

Services Provided by ISDN:

Due to the large amounts of information that ISDN lines can carry, ISDN applications are revolutionizing the way businesses communicate. ISDN is not restricted to public telephone networks alone; it may be transmitted via packet switched networks, telex, CATV (Community Antenna TV) networks, etc.

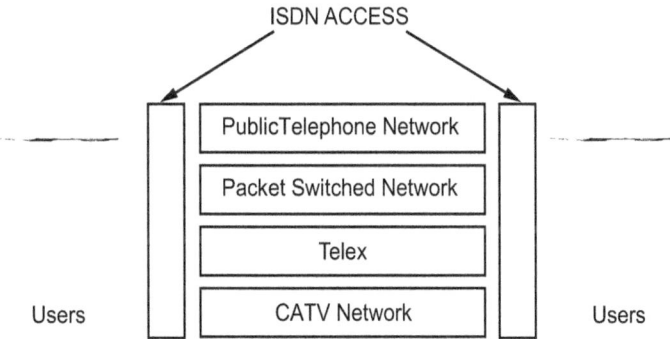

Fig. 6.6: Typical ISDN applications

There are two kinds of services provided by ISDN.

Network Services:
- Network services carry the interactions between the user and the network.
- For example: setting up calls and disconnecting them.

Bearer Services:
- Bearer services carry data between two users.
- For example: voice or fax information encoded as a bit stream.

The following services are offered on a dial-up basis between two ISDN subscribers:
(i) Desktop Video Conferencing on using three ISDN lines at 64/128 kbps.
(ii) High quality video conferencing by using three ISDN lines at 384 kbps.
(iii) Video telephony.
(iv) Teleconferencing, which facilitates the transmission of pictures, documents and drawings etc. apart from voice and images of the participants.
(v) High speed data transmission at 64/128 kbps.
(vi) High speed facsimile at 64/128 kbps with G4 Fax terminal.
(vii) Access to Internet with a higher bandwidth of 64/128 kbps giving significantly improved response time and quality of service.

Supplementary Services:
ISDN, being a Value Added Service, offers many supplementary features/services:
(i) Calling Line Identification Presentation
(ii) Advice of Charge
(iii) Line Hunting
(iv) Closed User Group
(v) User to User Signaling
(vi) Call Waiting
(vii) Call forwarding On No Reply, On Busy, Unconditional
(viii) Multiple Subscriber Number

Bearer Services:
- Circuit switched speech and audio.
- X.25 circuit and packed switched network.
- Frame Relay.
- Circuit switched data.

Teleservices:
- Facsimile – Telephony
- Telex
- Videotext

ISDN Standards:

ISDN is subject to standardization by the ITU-T (International Telecommunication Union-Telecommunication Standard Section) and ETSI (European Telecommunications Standards Institute), which issue recommendations and specifications covering ISDN equipment and interfaces. Standards also exist for types of service, protocols and ISDN numbering.

Operating System Software for ISDN:
- It is of course important to have an operating system, which will support ISDN hardware, allowing your software applications to communicate with and take full advantage of your ISDN terminal adapter.
- First of all, Point-to-Point Protocol (PPP) is the standard Internet access protocol, and it is required for a proper ISDN connection.
- Serial Line Internet Protocol (SLIP) is an older and less efficient protocol, but it is still fairly common.
- SLIP won't work with ISDN, so make sure you have a PPP account. Of course, if your ISP (Internet Service Provider) can provide you with ISDN connectivity, they should know this and it probably won't be an issue.

Different Kinds of ISDN Terminals:
The ISDN telephone line is terminated on a common box called the Network Termination (NT) at the subscriber's premises. The Network Termination unit along with accessories will be provided by the service provider like MTNL or can be procured by the subscriber. The terminal equipment has to be procured by the subscriber himself from the open market.

Types of ISDN Terminal:
(a) ISDN feature phone: This is a simplest type of ISDN phone which has an LCD display and some additional keys.
(b) Terminal adapter (TA).
(c) PC add-on ISDN card.
(d) Video phone.
(e) G4 fax.

Types of Non-ISDN Terminal:
- ISDN terminals such as DTE (Data Terminal Equipment) that predate the ISDN standards are referred to as Terminal Equipment type 2 (TE2).
- Ex. Terminal with physical interface as RS-232 and host computers with X.25 interface.
- This is the old analog telephone.
- Or old-style fax machine.
- Or modem.
- Or whatever we use to hook up to the analog phone line. It can also be other communications equipment that is handled by a TA (Terminal Adapter).

Benefits of ISDN for Network Operators:
1. Avoidance of separate networks for different services.
2. Economical use of the equipment of the digitalized telephone network, especially the copper pair of the subscriber line.
3. Reduction in costs due to simplified operation and maintenance procedures.

How is ISDN line superior to the phone line?

- The signal on the ISDN line – voice or data, is sent in digital mode.
- The signal level at subscriber's terminal equipment is independent of line length.
- An ISDN subscriber can establish two simultaneous independent calls, which could be voice, data, image or combination of any two, whereas only one call is possible on ordinary telephone lines.
- The call set-up time between two ISDN subscribers is extremely short.

6.5.2 ISDN for Voice, Data and Video

- It is the next-generation, digital telephone network that integrates circuit-switched voice and data services over a common access facility.
- There are two types of ISDN lines. Basic Rate ISDN (BRI) is designed for residential customers and small businesses.
- Primary Rate ISDN (PRI) is designed for larger businesses.

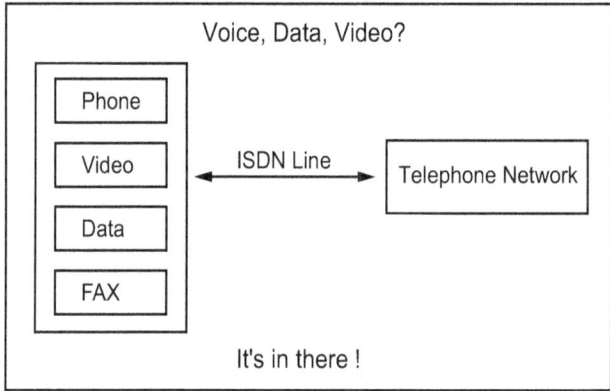

Fig. 6.7: Typical ISDN usage

- ISDN reduces the cost of network administration.
- ISDN simplifies wiring.
- ISDN combines separate voice and data networking requirements.
- ISDN is compatible with BRI/PRI, plus existing analog voice and switched 56 services.
- For residential customers, Basic Rate ISDN (BRI) costs about the equivalent of two phone lines.
- BRI customers can gain high speed Internet access (64 KBPS to 128 KBPS).
- BRI improves the quality of speech in telephone calls. BRI provides an ideal way to keep in touch through personal video conferencing.
- BRI offers improved modem connectivity to non-ISDN systems.

- For business customers, ISDN offers cost savings through the integration of voice and data services.
- PRI provides a great backup solution for leased data lines.
- PRI offers high-quality video conferencing capabilities. PRI costs about the same as standard "channelized T1" services.

6.5.3 Why Digital Communications?

- There are a number of reasons why it is advantageous to carry information, particularly computer data, in a digital format.
- For one, digital lines provide a far cleaner, error-free connection that can ensure reliable transmission worldwide.
- Secondly, digital lines allow equipment that processes data digitally, such as computers or networking routers, to be directly connected, and without the 4 kHz bandwidth limitations imposed by PSTN (voice) telephone lines.
- An ISDN line can carry data at nearly five times the fastest rate achievable using analog modems over PSTN lines.
- Further, while a PSTN line can carry only limited signaling information between the network and the end device (telephone or modem, for example), ISDN lines can carry detailed messages back and forth.
- This information can be used to define multiple incoming callers, to specify the type of incoming data, or to convey useful diagnostic information.
- With digital communications, it is finally possible to carry multiple service types (e.g., voice, computer data, Group 4 fax, motion video) simultaneously on the same network.
- ISDN offers the means to realize a universal in-box integrating voice, voice mail, e-mail, fax and video images from a single application.

6.5.4 ISDN Devices

ISDN Devices:

1. ISDN devices include terminals, terminal adapters (TAs), network-termination devices, line-termination equipment, and exchange-termination equipment.
2. ISDN terminals come in two types. Specialized ISDN terminals are referred to as terminal equipment type 1 (TE1).
3. Non-ISDN terminals, such as DTE, that predates the ISDN standards are referred to as terminal equipment type 2 (TE2).

4. TE1s connect to the ISDN network through a four-wire, twisted-pair digital link. TE2s connect to the ISDN network through a TA.
5. The ISDN TA can be either a standalone device or a board inside the TE2.
6. If the TE2 is implemented as a standalone device, it connects to the TA via a standard physical-layer interface. Examples include RS-232C, V.24, and V.35.
7. Beyond the TE1 and TE2 devices, the next connection point in the ISDN network is the network termination type 1 (NT1) or network termination type 2 (NT2) device.
8. These are network-termination devices that connect the four-wire subscriber wiring to the conventional two-wire local loop.
9. In most other parts of the world, the NT1 is a part of the network provided by the carrier.
10. The NT2 is a more complicated device that typically is found in digital private branch exchanges (PBXs) and that performs layer 2 and 3 protocol functions and concentration services.
11. An NT1/2 device also exists as a single device that combines the functions of an NT1 and an NT2.

ISDN specifies a number of reference points that define logical interfaces between functional groups; such as TAs and NT1s. ISDN reference points include the following:

- **R:** The reference point between non-ISDN equipment and a TA.
- **S:** The reference point between user terminals and the NT2.
- **T:** The reference point between NT1 and NT2 devices.
- **U:** The reference point between NT1 devices and line-termination equipment in the carrier network.
  - Figure 3.5 illustrates a sample ISDN configuration and shows three devices attached to an ISDN switch at the central office.
  - Two of these devices are ISDN-compatible, so they can be attached through an S reference point to NT2 devices.
  - The third device (a standard, non-ISDN telephone) attaches through the reference point to a TA.
  - Any of these devices also could attach to an NT1/2 device, which would replace both the NT1 and the NT2. In addition, although they are not shown, similar user stations are attached to the far-right ISDN switch.

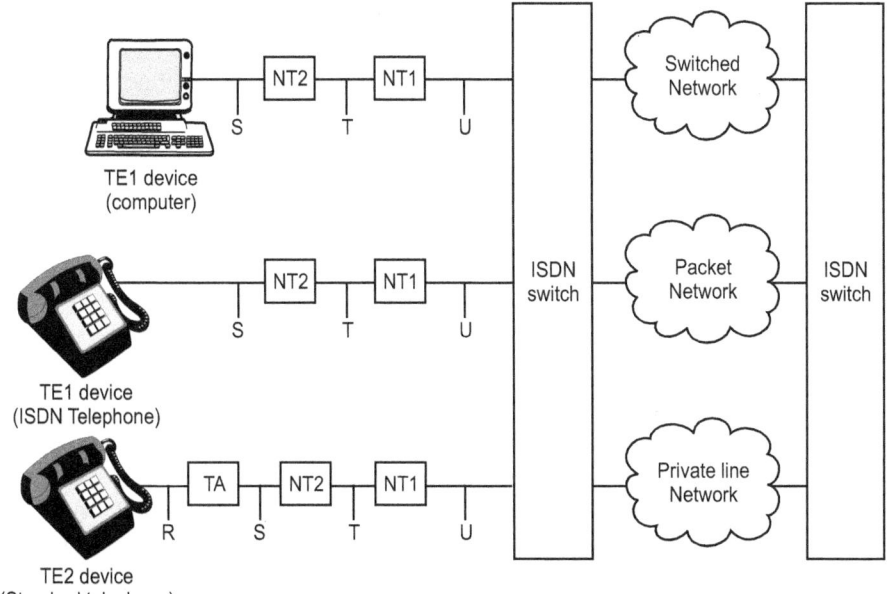

Fig. 6.8: Sample ISDN configuration illustrates relationships between devices and reference points

ISDN Services:

There are two types of services associated with ISDN:
- BRI (Basic Rate Interface) = 2B + 1D
- PRI (Primary Rate Interface) = 23B + 1D
- Hybrid Rate Interface = 1A + 1C

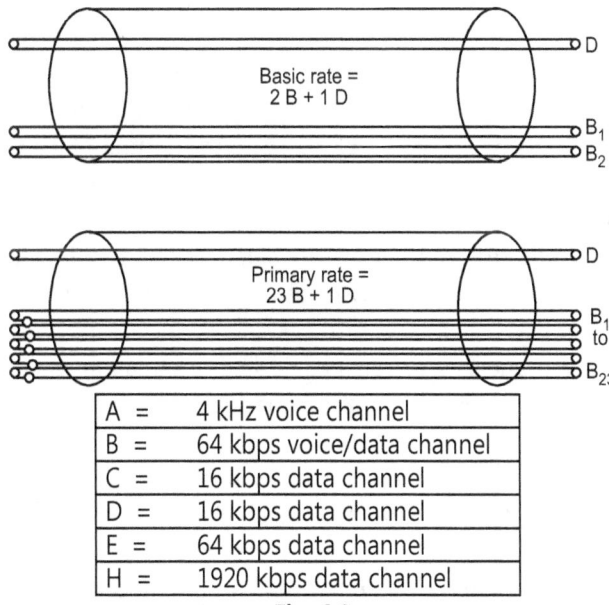

A =	4 kHz voice channel
B =	64 kbps voice/data channel
C =	16 kbps data channel
D =	16 kbps data channel
E =	64 kbps data channel
H =	1920 kbps data channel

Fig. 6.9

6.5.5 ISDN BRI Service

1. The ISDN Basic Rate Interface (BRI) service offers two B channels and one D channel (2B + D).
2. BRI B-channel service operates at 64 kbps and is meant to carry user data.
3. BRI D-channel service operates at 16 kbps and is meant to carry control and signaling information, although it can support user data transmission under certain circumstances.
4. The D channel signaling protocol comprises layers 1 through 3 of the OSI reference model.
5. BRI also provides for framing control and other overhead, bringing its total bit rate to 192 kbps.
6. The BRI physical layer specification is International Telecommunication Union-Telecommunication Standards Section (ITU-T) (formerly the Consultative Committee for International Telegraph and Telephone [CCITT]).

6.5.6 ISDN PRI Service

1. ISDN Primary Rate Interface (PRI) service offers 23 B channels and 1 D channel in North America and Japan, yielding a total bit rate of 1.544 Mbps (the PRI D channel runs at 64 kbps).
2. ISDN PRI in Europe, Australia, and other parts of the world provides 30 B channels plus one 64 kbps D channel and a total interface rate of 2.048 Mbps.
3. ISDN Primary Rate Service offers you the power to create a seamless communication system that speeds and smoothes the flow of information without the expense of dedicated lines, modems, and special cabling.
4. Primary Rate Service links your PBX to advanced central office systems to provide you with global, digital connectivity and the full functionality of ISDN service.
5. Primary Rate Service is the end-to-end digital network architecture that allows users around the world to transmit voice, data, video, and image – separately or simultaneously – over standard telephone lines or fiber optic circuits via standard interface.
6. A single ISDN channel is a fast and flexible information management tool, but Primary Rate Service is two dozen times more powerful - bundling 24 ISDN channels for delivery to your premises.
7. The Primary Rate Service configuration is known as 23B + D: 23B channels for transport of voice, data, video, and image at 64 kbps, plus a single D channel for call setup and control. The 23 B channels can be used as it is, or rearranged in a wide variety of ways to accommodate highly specific user needs.

Key Applications:
- LAN interconnection
- Video conferencing
- Virtual office
- Backbone LAN access
- Voice and data integration
- Image transfer
- Business continuation and disaster recovery
- PBX

User Benefits:
- Greater access
- Economy with bandwidth available on demand
- Borderless communications
- Exceptional flexibility
- Digital speed and accuracy
- Fast, reliable backup for lines and host computers

What does a B channel do?
- The B channel carries ISDN Bearer Services across the network and so carries the content of call (the voice, fax or data) between users.
- The B channel is a neutral conduit for bits and carries data at 64000 bits per second (56000 bits per second in some North American networks).
- The ISDN does not need to know what the bits represent. The job of the network is to accept a stream of bits supplied by one user at one end of the B channel and to deliver them to the other user at the opposite end of the channel.
- Within an interface, the B channels are numbered. In a Basic Rate Interface they are numbered 1 and 2; in a Primary Rate Interface, they are numbered 1 to 30 (or 23 in North America).
- When two users are connected, there is no relationship between the channel numbers used at each end.
- You might have one user's B channel number 17 connected with the other user's B channel number 2. The ISDN is responsible for managing this relationship.
- Notice that channel number 17 would only be possible on a PRI, while channel number 2 is possible on both a BRI and a PRI.

ISDN does not restrict the interconnection of B channels between the two kinds of interface.

What does the D channel do?

The D channel carries the ISDN Network Services between the user and the network. It maintains the user's relationship with the network.

This includes:
- The requests and responses used when you make or receive a call.
- Call progress messages.
- Messages informing you that the called party has closed the call.
- Error messages telling you why a call has not been established for you.

The D channel operates at 16000 bits per second in a BRI and at 64000 bits per second in a PRI.

B & D Channel Characteristics:

- An ISDN channel has two and only two ends. B channels terminate at a user. A B channel can therefore connect two and only two users.
- **B-channel** cannot be Y-shaped. B channels are therefore described as **end-to-end**.
- In the case of the D channel, one end is with the user. The other end is in the network.
- **D-channel is not end-to-end.**
- You cannot normally notice, how the D channels (the red lines) do not pass through the network.
- Notice also how each user has only one D channel and it is not connected in any way with the D channel of the other user.
- The B channel (the blue line) passes directly across the network.

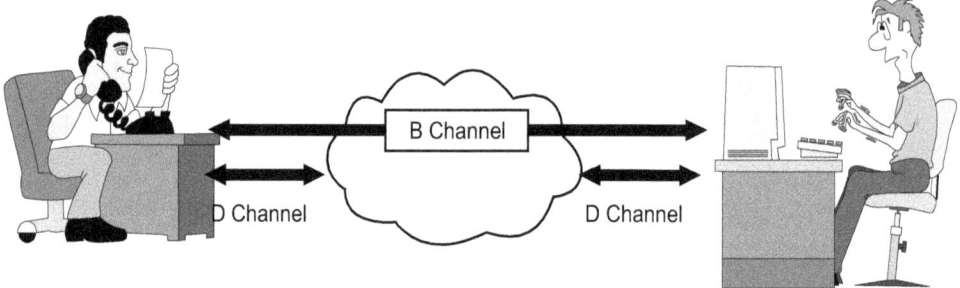

Fig. 6.10: D channel is not end-to-end

How B and D channels share the line: Basic Rate:

- The two B channels and the one D channel that make up a Basic Rate ISDN line are assembled together within the interface using a technique called **Time Division Multiplexing**.

B and D Channel Protocols:

- You must use a protocol to establish meaningful communication across a channel. It is important that both parties to the communication use the same protocol.

- This is particularly important for the D channel. Your signalling requests and responses must be understandable by the network. Even if your ISDN device and ISDN line are both functioning correctly, you might not be able to make successful calls if you're using a D channel protocol that is not the same as the network's.
- ISDN requires that you use a protocol defined by the ITU-T called **Q.931** for signalling in the D channel. However, there are several signalling protocols based on Q.931 in use round the world.
- You have a much greater choice of protocols for the B channel since the B channel is a neutral conduit for data of any type. You can use it to transmit any protocol you wish (e.g. SNA or PPP). However, if the network does not understand the protocol, it cannot give you any assistance if your call has to be delivered to a different type of network (e.g. PSTN), where data conversion is required.

B Channel Characteristics:
- It is important to remember that ISDN channels cannot be divided up into smaller units. Each is provided on an "all or nothing" basis.
- Two users communicating over a B channel have 64000 bits per second available to them. There is nothing they can do to reduce this bandwidth.
- What about the situation where the two users find that 64000 bits per second is not sufficient ? The only solution is to add another B channel. This gives them 128000 bits per second. They are **not** using a single B channel of 128000 bits per second. (Don't forget that the speed of a B channel is defined as 64 000 bits per second. Anything which operates at a different speed is not a B channel).
- This means that they will have two parallel calls between them and the phone bill will show two simultaneous calls.

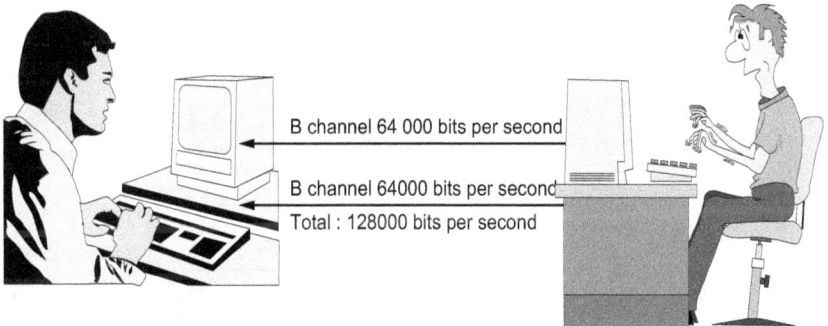

Fig. 6.11: Typical B channel characteristics

Using 2 B Channels:
- Imagine that you are a user communicating with someone else, using two parallel B channels.
- Does the ISDN network care whether these two B channels are connecting the same two users or if they are connecting one user with two others?
- The answer is no. The network treats these as two completely independent calls.

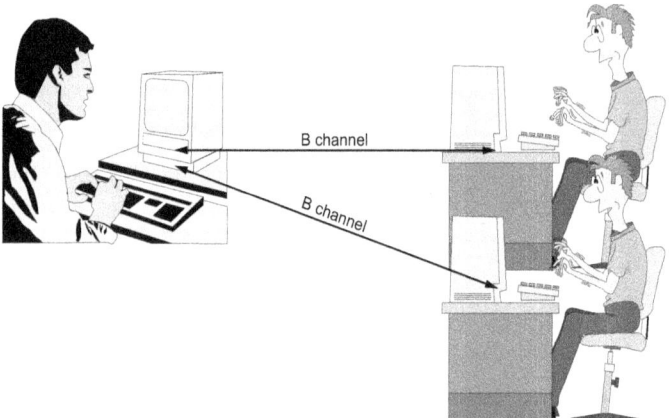

Fig. 6.12: Typical use of 2 B channels

- In the Fig. 6.13, the two users are connected using two B channels in parallel. The ISDN is able to route these B channels independently, because it takes no account of the fact that both the channels connect the same pair of users.
- The speed of the two B channels is identical.
- The time it takes for data to travel from one end of the channel to the other is, however, different.
- One user transmits two items of data simultaneously. One is sent in the B channel, which is routed via satellite; the other is sent in the B channel, which takes the direct route. Will both items of data arrive at the same time?

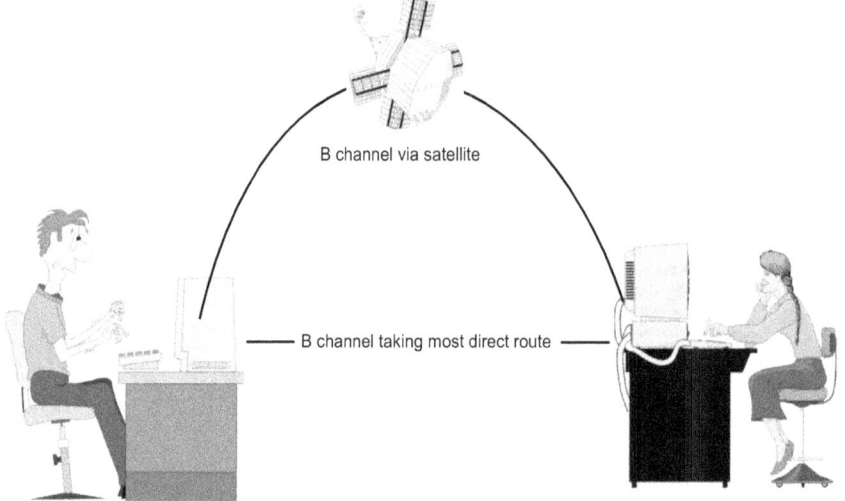

Fig. 6.13: The speed of the two B channels is not identical

- The item of data, which travels down the most direct path, will arrive first. That, which goes via satellite, will arrive later because it has further to travel.

- The ISDN makes no attempt to synchronise the data on the two B channels, possibly because it doesn't understand what the protocol in use. The two B channels are operating independently - the ISDN does not care that they are both connecting the same two users.

Thus regarding B and D channel we can summarize the following points:
- The D channel carries Network Services in the form of signalling. This is the way the user maintains his relationship with the network. Each user has one and only one D channel.
- The B channel carries Bearer Services, which are the communication between two users. A single B channel cannot connect more than two users together.
- B channels and D channels share time on the interface.
- B channels cannot be sub-divided to provide less bandwidth.
- More than one B channel can be used together to provide more bandwidth.

6.5.7 ISDN Operation

1. Each B channel can carry a separate telephone call and usually has its own telephone number, called a **Directory Number** (DN).
2. The two B channels can be combined (bonded) to form a single 128 kbps data channel.
3. The Fig. 6.14 illustrates a minimal ISDN setup connecting two computers.
4. The incoming twisted pair enters a box provided by the telephone company called the network terminator (NT1), which breaks the 144 kbps channel into the two B and single D sub-channels.
5. The B channels carry customer voice or data signals.
6. The D channel carries signals between your ISDN equipment and the phone company's central office.

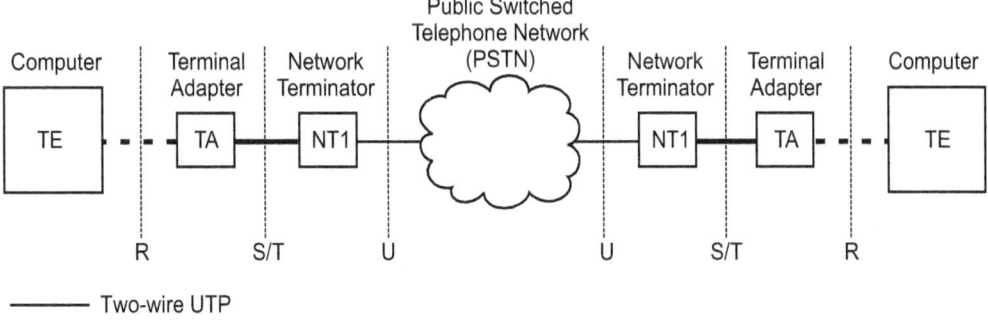

Fig. 6.14: Simple ISDN communication setup between two computers

7. A single four-wire cable carries the 2 B channels and the D channel to a **Terminal Adapter** (TA).

8. The function of this device is to connect any and all **Terminal Equipment** (TE) - computers, fax machines, Local Area Networks, or telephones - to one or both of the **B** channels.

9. In this example, the **TA** is shown as a separate unit, but it could be housed within the computer as an add-in card or integrated feature, or integrated with the **NT1** into a single box as a modem replacement or stand-alone TCP/IP router (network layer device).

10. Also shown are the external ISDN reference points - **R, S/T** and **U.** Each type of reference point represents a different type of interface.

11. The **U** reference point is the incoming unshielded twisted pair (UTP). The **S/T** reference point is a four-wire UTP cable.

12. A typical **TA** for data-only applications might simply emulate a pair of modems, translating standard modem setup and dialing commands into ISDN call-setup commands.

13. Computers are connected to this kind of TA with a normal RS-232 cable. The **TA** provides automatic rate adaptation to match whatever data rate your computer supports with ISDN's 64 kbps channel.

14. An example of a more sophisticated **TA** is the ISDN router, which connects to an ISDN line on one side and a Local Area Network on the other.

15. This type of device is able to support many different kinds of computer without special ISDN software, and contains all the intelligence necessary to move traffic over an ISDN link. Because ISDN is purely digital, the effects of noise are largely eliminated, and because the 64 kbps channel is essentially a pure "bit pipe" with no rate negotiation or handshaking involved, there are no modem speed or protocol differences to cause conflicts.

6.5.8 Analog Calls (NON-ISDN Terminals) and ISDN

Types of Non-ISDN Terminals

- ISDN terminals such as DTE, that predate the ISDN standards, are referred to as terminal equipment type 2 (TE2).
- Ex. Terminal with physical interface as RS-232 and host computers with X.25 interface.
- This is the old analog telephone.
- Or old-style fax machine.

- Or modem.
- Or whatever we use to hook up to the analog phone line. It can also be other communications equipment that is handled by a TA (Terminal Adapter).

1. The key characteristic of ISDN is that it is a digital network. However, many of the devices and networks, with which an ISDN user needs to communicate, are not digital, but analog. In order for these two types of device to communicate, the information which they are exchanging - must be converted from one form to the other.
2. In fact, except for data calls between computers across the ISDN network, almost all other types of calls - voice, fax, modems - will all involve some kind of conversion from digital to analog, or vice versa.
3. Much of this conversion takes place without the user's knowledge or intervention and is handled by the networks and devices involved. However, there are instances where an understanding of what is involved will assist in making successful connections and diagnosing problem areas.
4. You need to pay careful attention to the requirements of the ISDN device in use, particularly when sending and receiving faxes. This section provides the background to the various scenarios involved, and the practical implications for the different types of ISDN devices that are available.

6.5.8.1 Voice over ISDN – 1

- ISDN is a **Digital** network. Everything (including sounds such as voice and modem signals) is carried as a stream of bits.

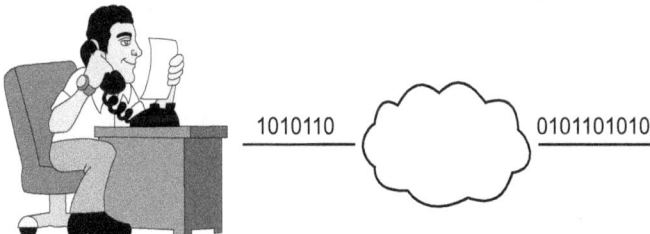

Fig. 6.15: Typical voice over ISDN is represented here

- This means that ISDN telephones need to be able to "digitize" and "un-digitize" sounds.
- This is performed by a device called a **CODEC** (Coder-Decoder), which is located inside the telephone.
- The CODEC translates the sounds into bits in one direction, and translates bits into sounds in the opposite direction.

6.5.8.2 Voice over ISDN – 2

- The analog signal originating in the microphone of the telephone handset is sampled and transformed into a stream of bits (64000 of them every second) that is placed on the B channel.

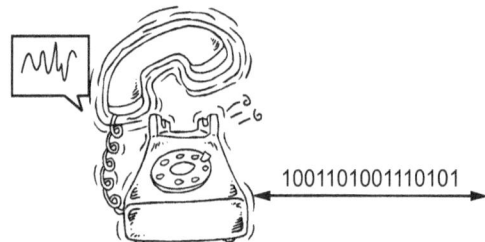

Fig. 6.16: Analog signal sent to the ear-piece of the handset

- Similarly, the incoming bit stream from the B channel is converted back into an analog signal and sent to the ear-piece of the handset.
- B channel is **full duplex**, which means that it can carry data in both directions at once.

6.5.8.3 Voice over ISDN – 3

- The ability to make voice calls from one ISDN telephone to another over a digital B channel is indeed useful. However, the majority of telephones, currently installed worldwide, are analogue devices which are not connected to an ISDN.
- Fortunately, you can make calls between the two networks. For this to work successfully, there has to be a conversion between the bit stream in the B channel and the analog signal required by the PSTN.

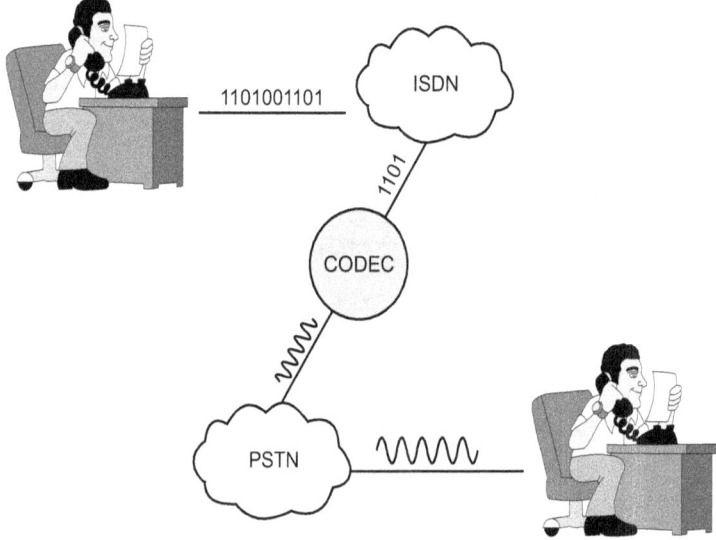

Fig. 6.17: Typical voice over ISDN and PSTN network

- CODECs are located at the boundaries of the digital and analog networks.
- Fortunately, you can make calls between the two networks.
- For this to work, the CODECs inside the network and the telephone **must** use the same rules when formatting the bit stream that represents the users' voices.
- Provided both devices are doing the same processing, then the information can be converted by applying the same rules in reverse.
- Given the presence of the CODEC in the network, and adherence to the correct protocols, any device that can be used on the PSTN, such as a modem or a fax machine, can also pass calls into the ISDN.

6.5.8.4 Analog Fax and Modem over ISDN (Scenario-1)
- Another important idea is introduced here; this is the Terminal Adapter.
- A Terminal Adapter (TA) is always necessary to connect non-ISDN devices (such as a serial port of a PC) to the ISDN. However, a TA can also contain a CODEC if it is intended to support analog phones, fax machines and modems.
- In Fig. 6.18, the modem at the top left can plug into the POTS ports on the TA. The TA will then convert sounds generated by the modem on its POTS port into a bit stream (and vice-versa). This bit stream is identical to that created by an ISDN telephone; that's to say it represents sounds.

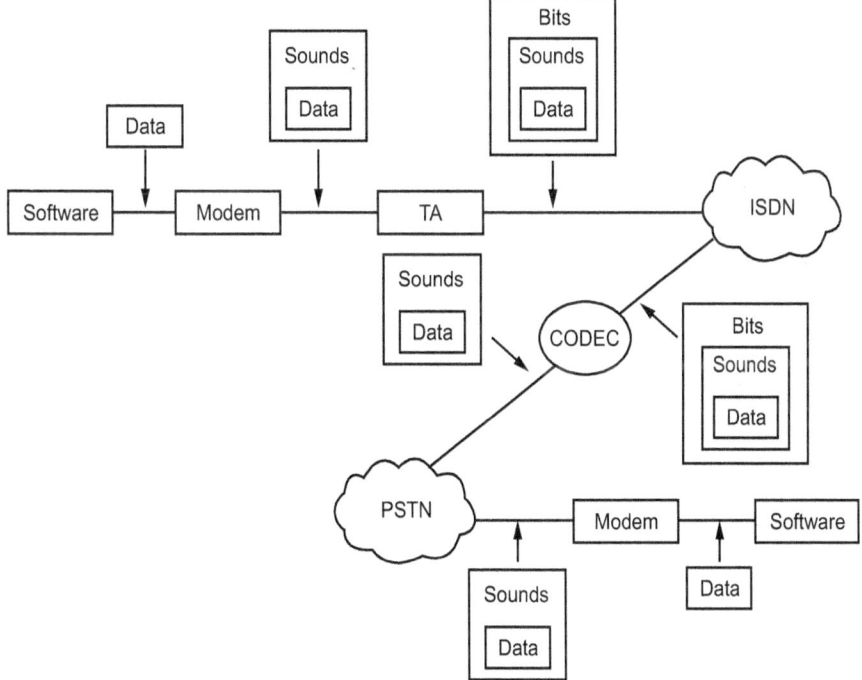

Fig. 6.18: Analog fax and modem over ISDN (scenario-1)

- Starting in the bottom right-hand corner, data leaves the PC as bits that are converted into sounds by the modem. We now have data encapsulated in sounds.
- These sounds cross the PSTN network until they are encapsulated inside a bit stream by the CODEC at the boundary between the ISDN and the PSTN. This bit stream is then passed from the ISDN network to the Terminal Adapter, which contains a CODEC that converts the bit stream back into sounds. These sounds are sent to the modem at the top left, which converts this back into the original data that entered the modem at the bottom left.
- The process runs in the opposite direction to send the data from the PC in the top left-hand corner to the PC in the bottom right-hand corner. This appears to be a lot of work: the data sent across the ISDN has been encapsulated twice.

6.5.8.5 Analogue Fax and Modem over ISDN (Scenario-2)
- The next step in evolving this configuration is to use an internal modem in the PC.
- Logically this is not different from the previous scenario.

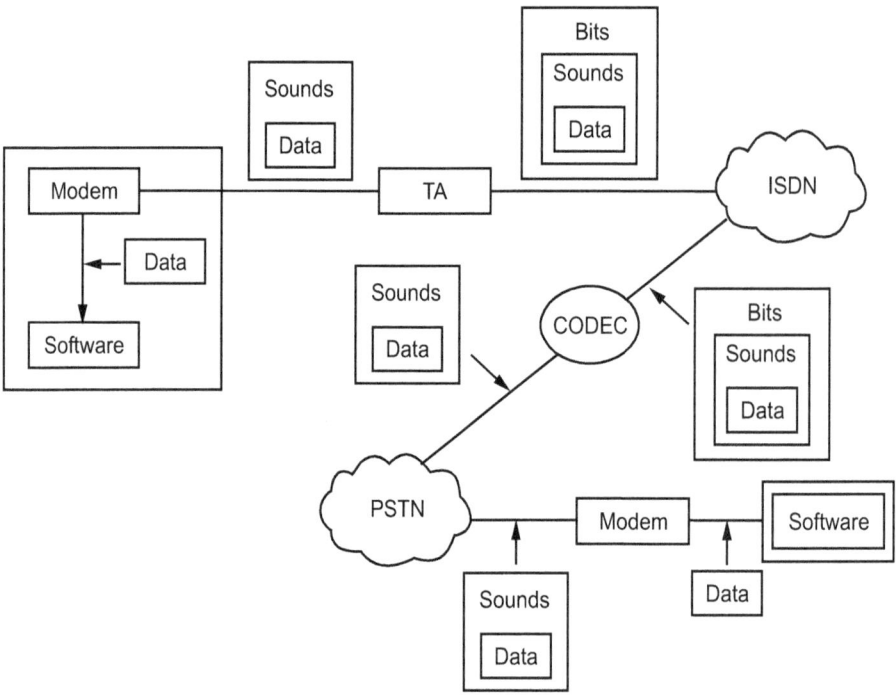

Fig. 6.19: Analog fax and Modem over ISDN (scenario-2)

6.5.8.6 Analog Fax and Modem over ISDN (Scenario-3)

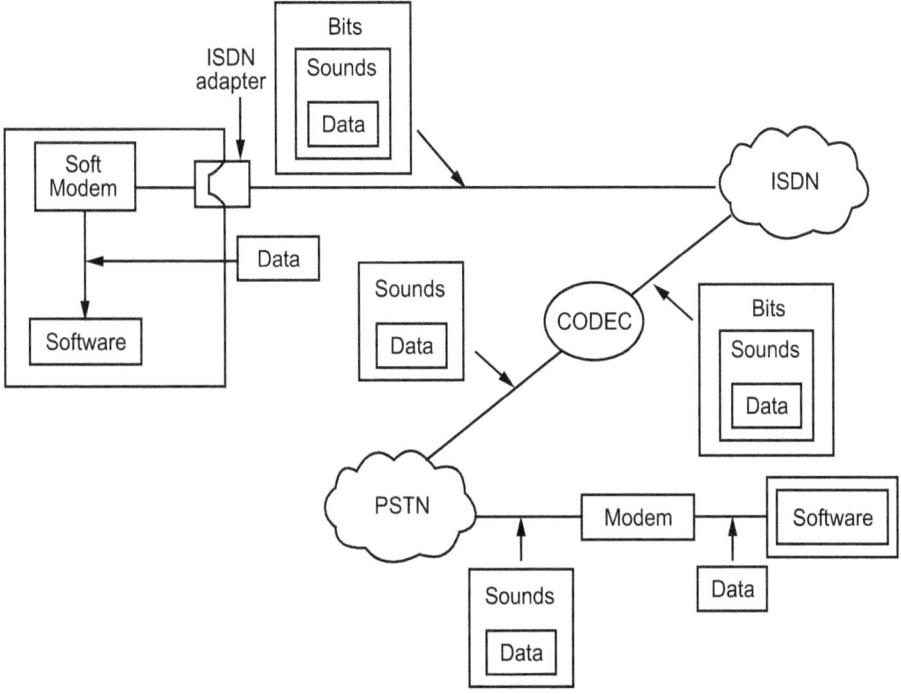

Fig. 6.20: Analog fax and modem over ISDN (scenario-3)

- We could replace the internal modem with an internal ISDN adapter and a driver, which appears to the application software to be a modem.
- In reality, this driver combines the functions of both the modem and the CODEC.
- This driver is known as a **soft modem**.
- A soft modem requires a lot of processing power, since it has to operate in real time.
- The PC is therefore likely to appear a bit sluggish while the connection is active.
- The advantage of this solution is that it can be used with an inexpensive passive ISDN adapter.

6.5.8.7 Analog Fax and Modem over ISDN (Scenario-4)
- The final step in evolving this scenario is to use an ISDN adapter which has a DSP (Digital Signal Processor).
- This takes the very heavy processing load due to the soft modem away from the PC.
- ISDN adapters with a DSP are generally more expensive than passive adapters.

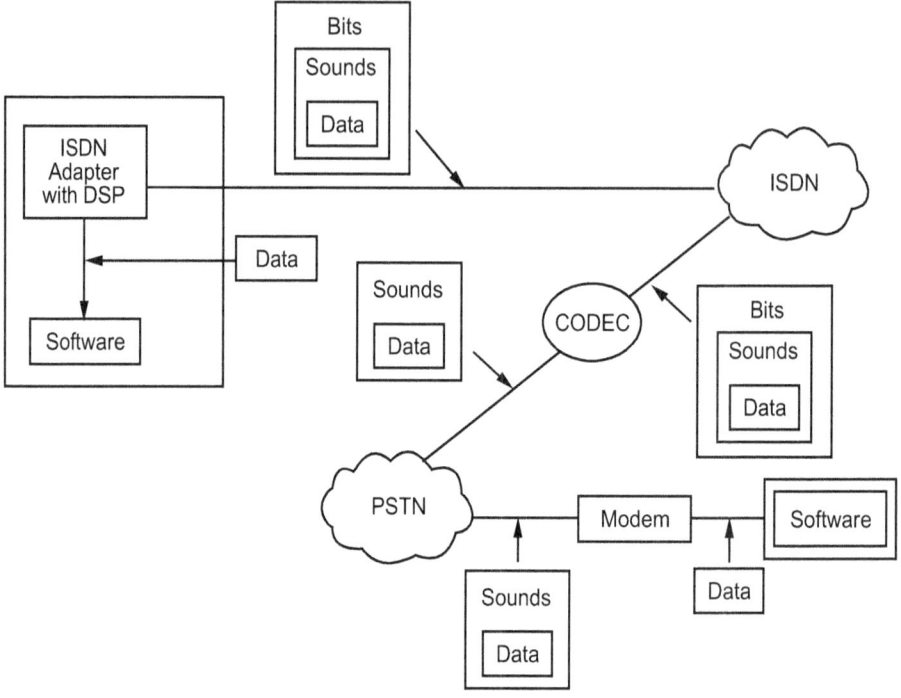

Fig. 6.21: Analog fax and modem over ISDN (Scenario-4)

6.5.8.8 Soft Fax and Soft Modem

- This means that an ISDN adapter with an on-board DSP can also communicate with any device that contains a modem.
- In Fig. 6.22, you can see that we have added a fax machine.

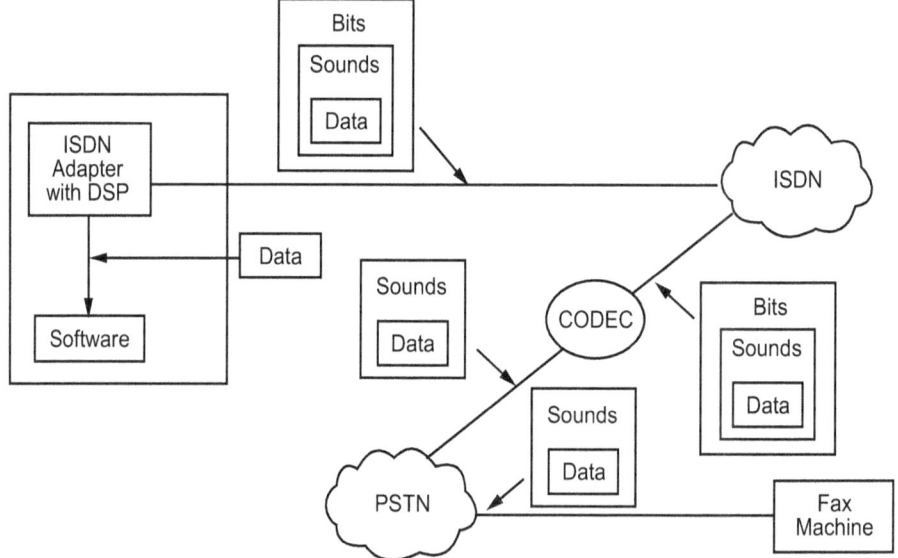

Fig. 6.22: Typical soft fax and soft modem concept implemented

- To perform the job of a modem and a CODEC at the same requires a large amount of processing power.
- DSPs are very powerful processors.
- Nevertheless, you need one DSP for each B channel for which you want to use this technique.
- There is, however, no reason why you couldn't use an ISDN adapter that has a single DSP and a soft modem driver to handle two modem calls at a time.

6.5.8.9 Analog Modems and ISDN

- So who will you call with your brand new ISDN connectivity? The obvious first answer is your Internet Service Provider (ISP).
- Many ISPs are recognizing the performance and reliability improvements of ISDN over modems and are rolling out ISDN services.
- The data applications of ISDN shown so far, all require that both parties in the connection have ISDN or packet data service.
- What if you need to connect with somebody that isn't ISDN capable ? The answer is that you use your analog modem and a TA that supports analog voice connections, or POTS.

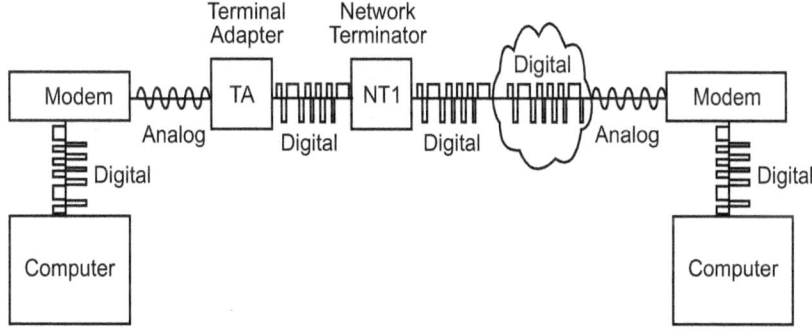

Fig. 6.23: Using analog modems in an ISDN environment

- This kind of TA accepts an ordinary voice or modem audio signal through a standard RJ11 modular jack and digitizes it for transport across the ISDN interface.
- It interprets the touch-tone dialing signals put out by your telephone set or modem and generates the required ISDN call-setup signals.

- If the number you are calling is not an ISDN POP, the telecommunication equipment at the remote end automatically translates the digitized audio back to analog audio, where the destination modem (or human being) hears what it is always heard before ISDN came along.
- In fact, some ISDN TAs include built-in analog modems (sometimes anomalously called "digital modems") just to provide compatibility with existing analog fax and data devices.
- So plan on keeping your modems around at least until the end of the decade; you will still need them occasionally. Fortunately, many TAs provide PSTN's ports without much additional cost, so this is a painless necessity.

Thus we can summarize this ISDN and communication of software, modem and fax machine as follows:
- In ISDN networks everything is carried as a stream of bits.
- Converting digital telephone signals into voice, and vice versa, is done by CODECs.
- Converting data into analog telephone signals, and vice versa, is done by modems.
- A CODEC is the device that allows telephony between an ISDN and the analog network.
- This same CODEC can be used to allow modem and fax calls to cross the same boundary.
- Modems and CODECs always work in pairs - they can be nested together but each must have a partner.
- A Terminal Adapter is an interface between the ISDN and any non-ISDN device, such as a computer or an analog phone.
- If analog devices need to be connected to the ISDN, then the Terminal Adapter will need to perform the function of a CODEC, and have analog (POTS) ports available for modems and fax machines to plug into.
- Internal ISDN adapters can use dedicated chips on the card, or software running on the PC, to implement the digital and analog conversions, thereby removing the requirement for any physical analog devices like fax machines and modems.
- There are three kinds of devices used in data communications with ISDN:
    1. Conventional Modems - These require Terminal Adapter to connect to the ISDN.
    2. ISDN Modems - These combine the functionality of CODEC and modem.
    3. Terminal Adapter - It allows analog devices to connect to the ISDN and contain a CODEC for this purpose.
    4. ISDN Adapters - These merely pass a stream of bits between a protocol driver and the ISDN.

6.5.9 ISDN Equipment and Interface Terminology

U-INTERFACE	U-interface is a 2-wire **digital telephone line** that runs from the telephone company's central office (CO) to an NT1 device. The customer is responsible for supplying all the equipments from the U-interface forward.
NT-1 Network Termination Type 1	The **NT1** acts as the boundary between the customer premise and the phone company's network. **NT1** is a Basic Rate **ISDN-only device** that converts a service provider's U-interface to a customer's S/T-interface. It can be stand-alone or integrated into a terminal adapter. The **NT1** interface combines the two B channels and the D channel into a single bit stream at the physical level and is also capable of supporting more than one device attached to an ISDN line, sometimes referred to as a multi-drop configuration.
S/T -INTERFACE	S/T-interface is a common way of referring to either an S- or T-interface. The S/T-interface breaks the signal into two paths- **one transmit, one receive**. In an ISDN PBX, the **NT1** connects using the **T**-interface, and the PBX connects using the S-interface. This intermediate track is called **NT2**.
TE1 Terminal Equipment Type 1	**TE1** (Terminal Equipment Type 1) is **ISDN-ready** equipment that can directly connect to the ISDN line (often using an **S/ T**-interface). Examples are ISDN phones, ISDN routers, ISDN computers, etc. They are manufactured from the outset to be completely ISDN compatible.
R-INTERFACE	R-interface is a **non-ISDN** interface such as an EIA-232 or a V.35 interface. **R**-interface provides a non-ISDN interface between equipment that is not ISDN compatible with the rest of the ISDN network.
TA Terminal Adapter	**TA** is a device that allows non-ISDN-ready equipment, such as PCs, to connect to an ISDN line.
TE2 Terminal Equipment Type 2	**TE2** is an equipment that **cannot directly connect** to an ISDN line. A common example of this device is a PC, or a non-ISDN-ready router. **TA** must be used to connect to the ISDN line. Examples of TE2 are RS-232 or [X.25] interface based devices, such as personal computers.
SPID Service Profile ID	The **SPID** is a number assigned to an ISDN line by the ISDN service provider that identifies certain characteristics of the line. Usually this number is the telephone number **PLUS** 0101 as an identifier.

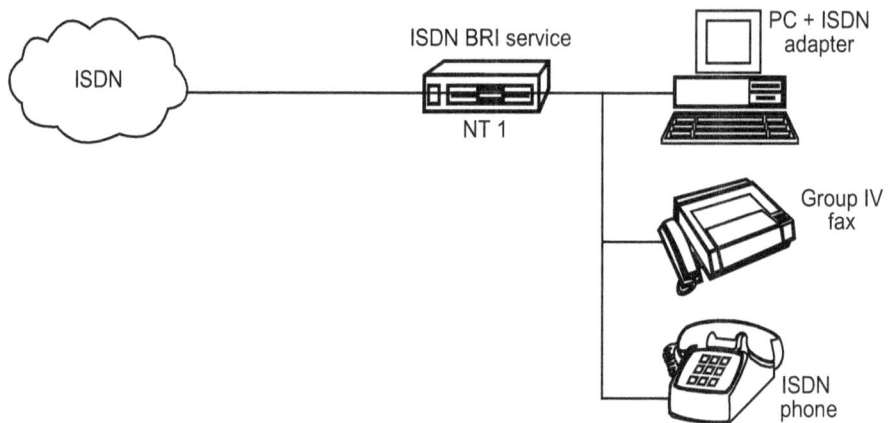

Fig. 6.24: Typical use of NT1 Interface

6.5.9.1 Interfaces

- Generally the **telephone company** provides its BRI customers with a **U-interface**.
- The U-interface is a two-wire (single pair) interface from the phone switch.
- It supports full-duplex data transfer over a single pair of wires, therefore only a single device can be connected to a U-interface.
- This device is called a **Network Termination-1 (NT-1)**.
- The NT-1 is a relatively simple device that converts the 2-wire U-interfaces into the 4-wire **S/T-interface**.
- The S/T-interface supports multiple devices (upto 7 devices can be placed on the S/T bus) because, while it is still a full-duplex interface, there is now a pair of wires for receiving data, and another for transmitting data.
- Today, many devices have NT-1s built into their design.
- Technically, ISDN devices must go through a **Network Termination-2 (NT-2)** device, which converts the T-interface into the S-interface (Note: The S and T-interfaces are electrically equivalent).
- Virtually all ISDN devices include an NT-2 in their design.
- The NT-2 communicates with terminal equipment, and handles the Layer 2 and 3 ISDN protocols.
- Devices most commonly expect either a U-interface connection (these have a built-in NT-1), or an S/T-interface connection.
- Devices, that connect to the S/T (or S) interface, include ISDN capable telephones and FAX machines, video teleconferencing equipment, bridge/ routers, and terminal adapters. All devices, that are designed for ISDN, are designated **Terminal Equipment 1 (TE1)**.

- All other communication devices that are *not* ISDN capable, but have a POTS telephone interface (also called the **R interface**), including ordinary analog telephones, FAX machines, and modems, are designated **Terminal Equipment 2 (TE2)**.
- A **Terminal Adapter (TA)** connects a TE2 to an ISDN S/T bus.
- Going one step in the opposite direction takes us inside the telephone switch.
- Remember that the U-interface connects the switch to the customer premises equipment.
- This local loop connection is called *Line Termination* (LT function).
- The connection to other switches within the phone network is called *Exchange Termination* (ET function).
- The LT function and the ET function communicate via. the **V-interface**.

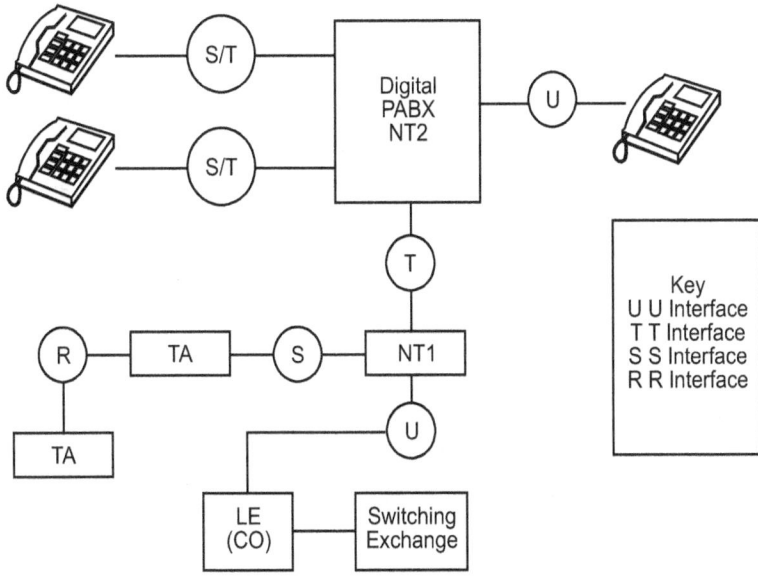

Fig. 6.25: An interface ('reference point') is said to exist between each piece of equipment on the ISDN

6.5.9.2 Examples

NETWORK INTERFACE	RJ-45 for ISDN Basic Rate U-interface (built-in NT1) 128 kbps
DTE INTERFACE	EIA-232 (DB-25) Modem pass through port (3000 only)
DTE DATA RATES	1.2 to 230.4 kbps asynchronous 2400 to 128 kbps synchronous (3010 only)

COMPRESSION	According to standards
PROTOCOLS	Multilink PPP, ITU-T V.120, Clear Channel, Async. BONDING etc.
DIALING SELECTIONS	AT commands, DTR assertion, V.25 bis.
DIAGNOSTICS AND TESTING	Network loopback Remote configuration
ANALOG PORTS	Two standard RJ-11 Each port rings upto three phones within 500 feet
CUSTOM CALLING FEATURES	• Stutter dial tone • Three- and six-way • Conferencing • Call forwarding • Reminder ring • Auto call back • Distinctive ring • Caller ID • Implicit transfer • Visual message waiting indication (Custom calling features must be provided by telephone company.)
ENVIRONMENT	Operating Temperature: 0° to 50°C, (32° to 122°F) Storage Temperature: –20° to 70°C, (–4° to 158°F) Relative Humidity: Upto 95%, non-condensing
PRODUCT INCLUDES	110 V wallmount power supply, CD ROM, one cable to connect ISDN line

6.5.10 ISDN Architectures

1. Basically, network architecture of ISDN is defined to follow an evolutionary path in telecommunication development and different application services.

2. The ISDN architectures play very important role in interfacing and operating the different switching networks and non-switching networks like:

    (a) Circuit switched networks.

    (b) Packet switched networks (Datagram and VC packet).

    (c) Non-switching networks.

    (d) Different signalling networks.

3. The ISDN architectures are simply categorized for better understanding.

ISDN Architectures
- Segregated Architecture
- Integrated Architecture
- ISDN Protocol Architecture
- ISDN Application Protocol Architecture
- ISDN and ISO Layered Architecture

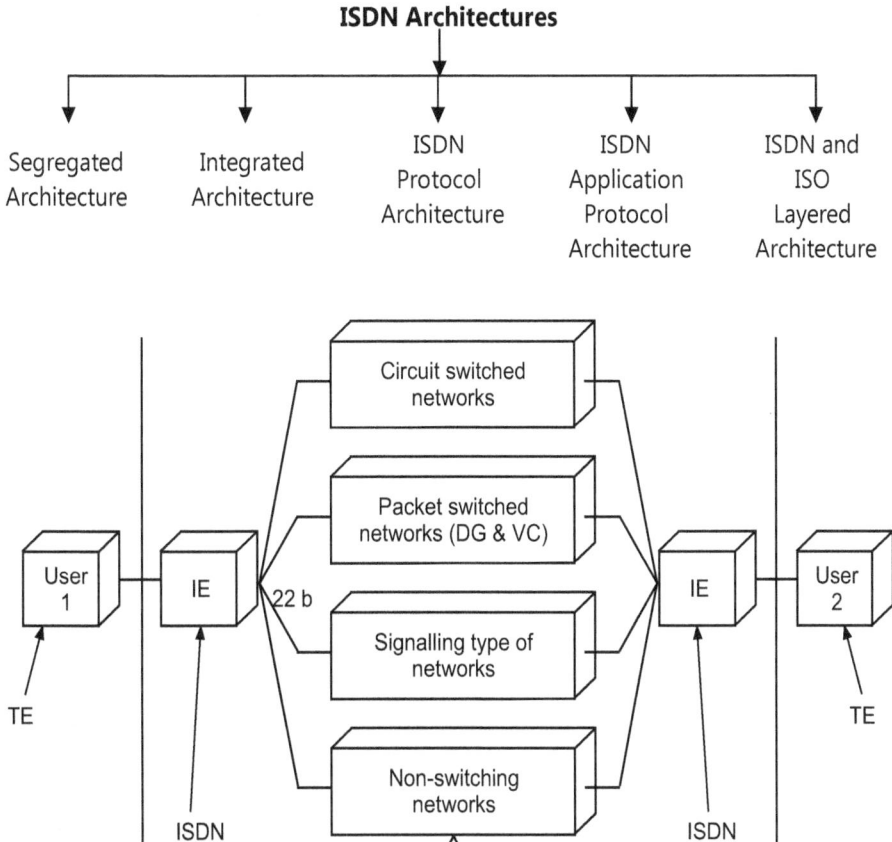

Fig. 6.26 (a): Typical segregated architecture of ISDN

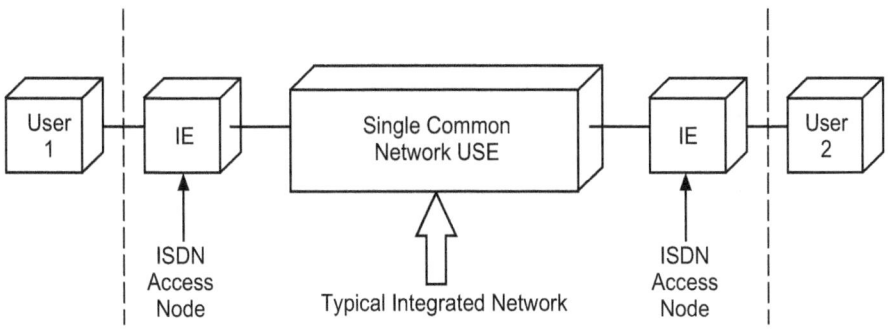

Fig. 6.26 (b): Typical integrated architecture of ISDN

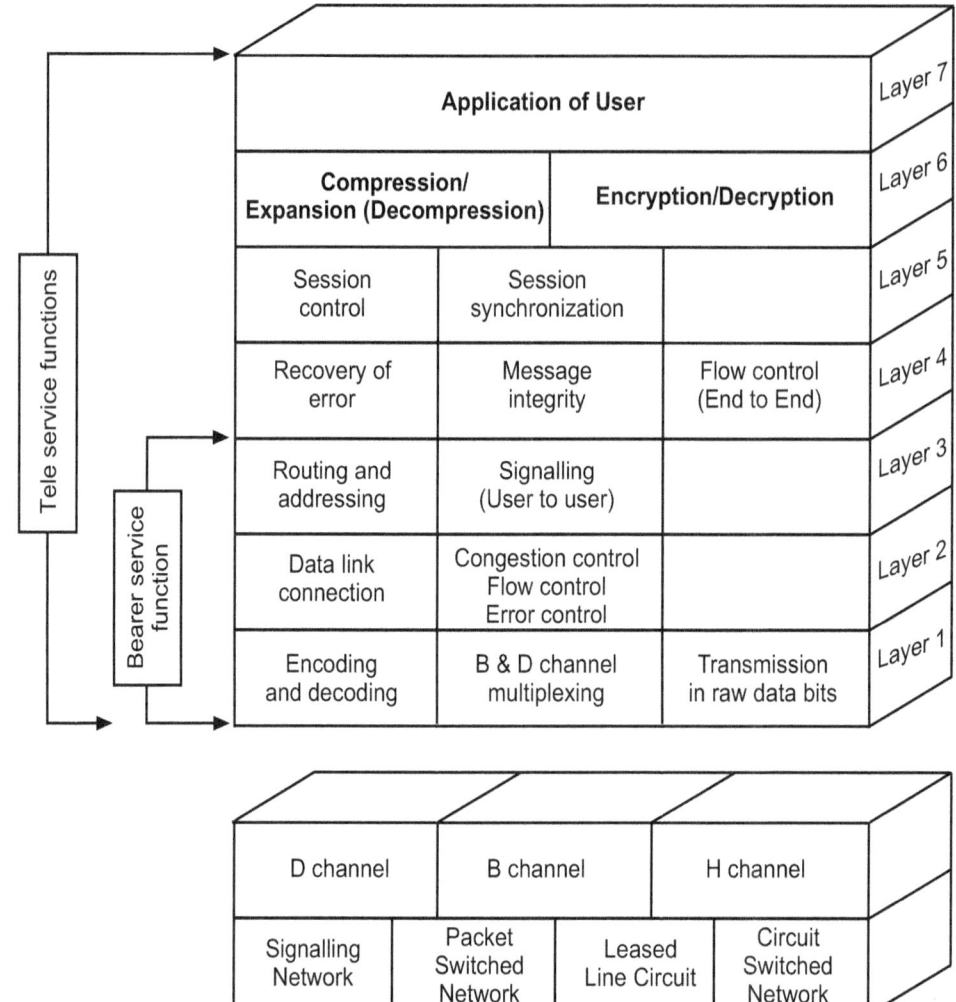

Fig. 6.26 (c): Typical ISDN protocol architecture

4. Thus, Layer 1, Layer 2 and Layer 3 of the ISDN protocol stack is very important.
5. Physical layer (Layer 1) tasks:
   - Encoding and decoding of digital signals.
   - Transmission of D, B and H channel data.
   - Multiplexing to form primary or basic rates of data.
   - Activation and deactivation of the physical circuits.
6. Datalink Layer (Layer 2) tasks:
   - Synchronization of trans-reception in data communication.
   - Establishment and clearing the datalinks.
   - Flow control at layer 2.
   - Error control at layer 2.
   - Congestion control at layer 2.

7. Network layer (Layer 3) tasks:
   - Routing and addressing in network.
   - Signalling (user to user).
   - Multiplexing at network layer level (at level 3).
   - Establishing and clearing network level connection.
   - Multiplexing in internetworking situation.
8. ISDN uses several protocols; which protocol each channel uses is crucial to understanding how ISDN works. ISDN stands for "Integrated Services Digital Networks" and it is a ITU-T (formerly CCITT) term for a relatively new telecommunications service package. ISDN is basically the telephone network turned all-digital end to end, using existing switches and wiring (for the most part) upgraded so that the basic "call" is a 64 kbps end-to-end channel.
9. It is offered by local telephone companies, but most readily in Australia, Western Europe, Japan and portions of the USA.
10. In France, ISDN is known as "RNIS".

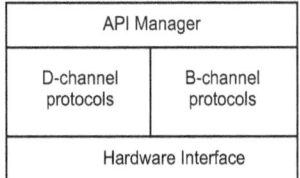

Fig. 6.26 (d): General ISDN protocol architecture with D and B channels

11. Different protocols used are as follows:
    IP: Internet protocol.
    DSSI (Digital Subscriber Signalling System No. 1).
    HDLC: High level datalink control protocol.
    PPP: Point to Point Protocol.

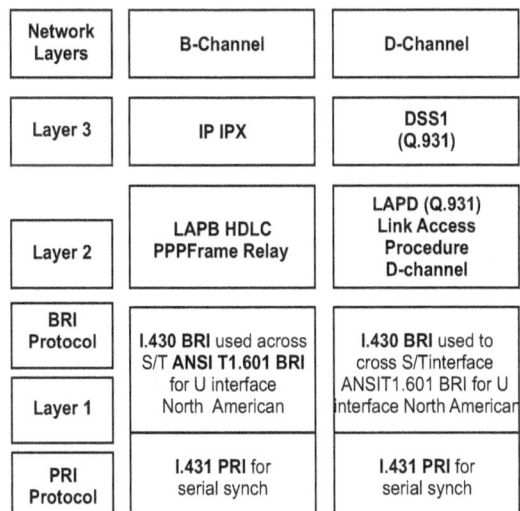

Fig. 6.26 (e): Detail ISDN protocol architecture which uses several protocols now-a-days

12. **ISDN Physical Interfaces – SERIAL INTERFACES used are:**
    - EIA/TIA 232.
    - EIA/TIA – 449.
    - EIA – 530.
    - X.21.

13. An understanding of the format of interfaces and channel type is critical to any analysis of ISDN because they provide the framework through which the protocols and applications flow.

14. ISDN defines a full network architecture as shown in Fig. 6.26 (e). This architecture separates access functions from actual network functions.

15. Thus, different protocols are compatible and fully supported for ISDN communication in today's Internet technology.

16. Numbering and addressing is also very important issue in the ISDN network system.

17. The component of the ISDN address which is used to identify the end point is known as the ISDN number and the component/Entity for identifying the specific instrument/equipment at the end point is called as the ISDN subaddress.

18. The numbering plan for ISDN network follows the following guidelines.
    - Enhanced telephone numbering plan defined by ITU standard is used in ISDN.
    - Numbering plan is independent of nature of the ISDN service (voice, video and data or fax).
    - Numbering plan is independent of routing.
    - ISDN numbers are basically a sequence of decimal digits. (No character or alphabets are allowed).
    - Number is designed in such a way that interworking between ISDNs requires only ISDN numbers and not any other addressing signals or additional digits.

19. Typical ISDN: Message format for user part is shown in Fig. 6.26 (f) which is simple and self explanatory.

20. Typical ISDN address structure is as shown in Fig. 6.26 (g) which is simple and self explanatory.

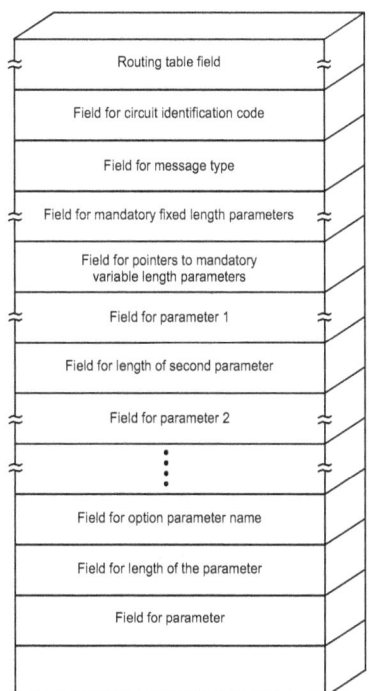

Fig. 6.26 (f): Typical message format for ISDN user part

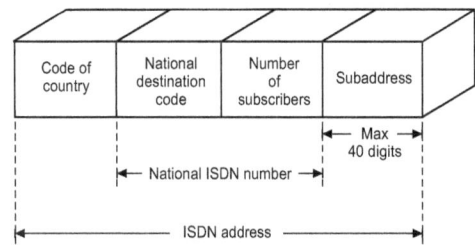

Fig. 6.26 (g): Typical structure of ISDN address

6.5.11 ISDN and OSI Architecture

From the point of view of the OSI architecture, an ISDN line has a stack of three protocols –

- Physical layer.
- Data link layer.
- Network layer (the ISDN protocol, properly).

Network layer (the ISDN protocol, properly) (Layer 3)
Data link layer (Layer 2)
Physical layer (Layer 1)

Fig. 6.27: ISDN line has a stack of three protocols

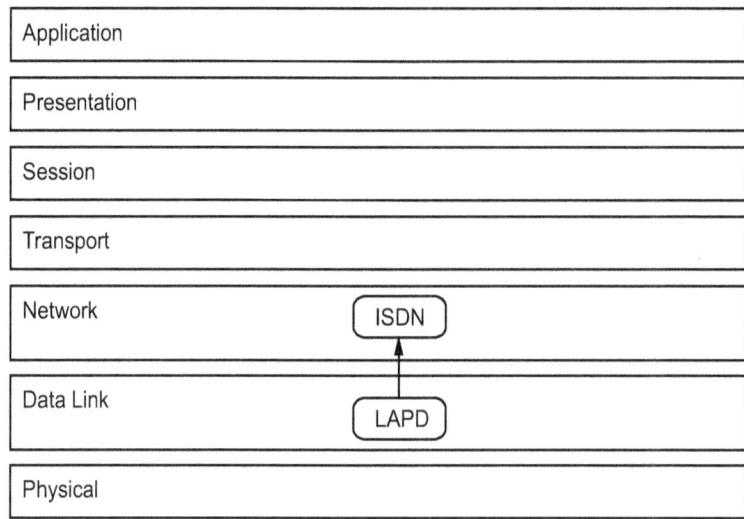

Fig. 6.28: The ISDN is illustrated here in relation to the OSI model

Layer 1 (Physical Layer):

1. ISDN physical layer (Layer 1) frame formats differ depending on whether the frame is outbound (from terminal to network) or inbound (from network to terminal).
2. Both physical layer interfaces are shown in Fig. 6.29.

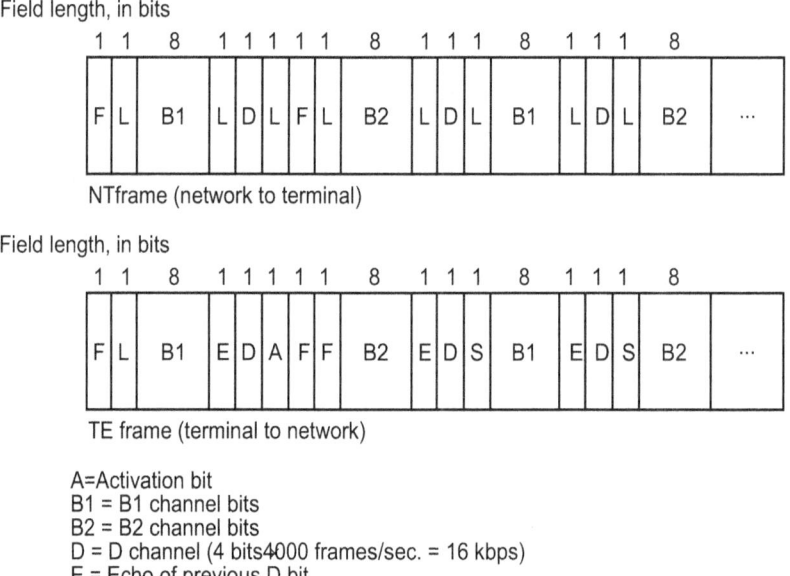

Fig. 6.29: ISDN physical layer frame formats

3. The frames are 48 bits long, of which 36 bits represent data. The bits of an ISDN physical layer frame are used as follows:
   - F – Provides synchronization.
   - L – Adjusts the average bit value.
   - E – Used for contention resolution when several terminals on a passive bus contend for a channel.
   - A – Activates devices.
   - S – Unassigned.
   - B1, B2, and D – Used for user data (B1 for B1 channel bits and B2 for B2 channel bits).
4. Multiple ISDN user devices can be physically attached to one circuit.
5. In this configuration, collisions can result if two terminals transmit simultaneously.
6. ISDN therefore provides features to determine link contention.
7. When an NT receives a D bit from the TE, it echoes back the bit in the next E bit position.
8. The TE expects the next E bit to be the same as its last transmitted D bit.
9. Terminals cannot transmit into the D channel unless they first detect a specific number of ones (indicating "no signal") corresponding to a pre-established priority.
10. If the TE detects a bit in the echo (E) channel that is different from its D bits, it must stop transmitting immediately.
11. This simple technique ensures that only one terminal can transmit its D message at one time.
12. After successful D message transmission, the terminal has its priority reduced by requiring it to detect more continuous ones before transmitting.
13. Terminals cannot raise their priority until all other devices on the same line have had an opportunity to send a D message.
14. Telephone connections have higher priority than all other services, and signaling information has a higher priority than non-signaling information.

Layer 2 (Data Link Layer):

1. Layer 2 of the ISDN signaling protocol is *Link Access Procedure, D channel*, also known as *LAPD*.
2. As LAPD's acronym indicates, it is used across the **D channel** to ensure that control and signaling information flows and has been received properly.

3. LAPD is similar to *High-Level Data Link Control* (HDLC) [HDLC supports a variety of link types and topologies. It can be used with point-to-point and multipoint links, bounded and unbounded media, half-duplex and full-duplex transmission facilities, and circuit-switched and packet-switched networks].
4. LAPD is similar to *Link Access Procedure, Balanced* (LAPB). [LAPB is best known for its presence in the X.25 (WAN service) protocol stack].
5. As the expansion of the LAPD acronym indicates, it is used across the D channel to ensure that control and signaling information flows and is received properly.
6. The LAPD frame format (see Fig. 6.30) uses *supervisory, information,* and *unnumbered* frames.

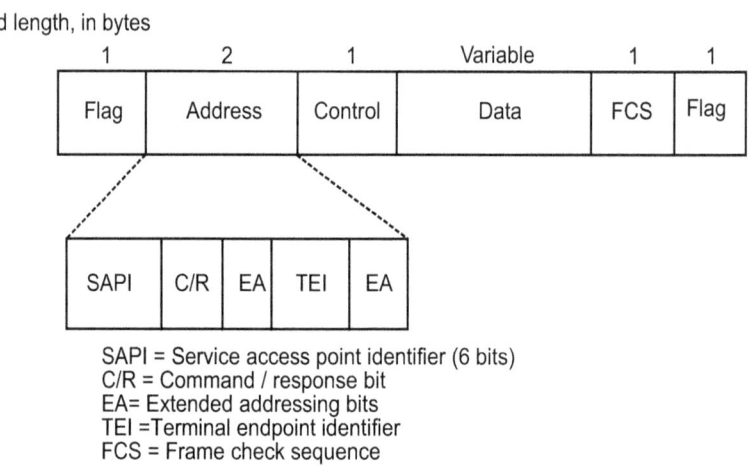

Fig. 6.30: LAPD frame format

7. The LAPD *address* field can be either one or two bytes long.
8. If the extended address bit of the first byte is set, the address is one byte; if it is not set, the address is two bytes.
9. The first address field byte contains the *service access point identifier* (SAPI), which identifies the portal at which LAPD services are provided to Layer 3.
10. The C/R bit indicates whether the frame contains a command or a response.
11. The *terminal end-point identifier* (TEI) field identifies either a single terminal or multiple terminals. A TEI of all ones indicates a broadcast.
12. **FCS:** The Frame Check Sequence (FCS) enables a high level of physical error control by allowing the integrity of the transmitted frame data to be checked. The sequence is first calculated by the transmitter using an algorithm based on the values of all the bits in the frame. The receiver then performs the same calculation on the received frame and compares its value to the CRC.

13. **Window size:** LAPD supports an extended window size (modulo 128) where the number of possible outstanding frames for acknowledgement is raised from 8 to 128. This extension is generally used for satellite transmissions where the acknowledgement delay is significantly greater than the frame transmission times. The type of the link initialization frame determines the modulo of the session and an "E" is added to the basic frame type name (e.g., SABM becomes SABME).

14. **Frame types:**

    The following are the Supervisory Frame Types in LAPD:

RR	Information frame acknowledgement and indication to receive more.
REJ	Request for retransmission of all frames after a given sequence number.
RNR	Indicates a state of temporary occupation of station (e.g., window full).

15. **The following are the Unnumbered Frame Types in LAPD:**

DISC	Request disconnection
UA	Acknowledgement frame
DM	Response to DISC indicating disconnected mode.
FRMR	Frame reject
SABM	Initiator for asynchronous balanced mode. No master/slave relationship
SABME	SABM in extended mode
UI	Unnumbered Information
XID	Exchange Information

Layer 3 (Network Layer):

1. Two Layer-3 specifications are used for ISDN signaling.

2. Together, these protocols support user-to-user, circuit-switched, and packet-switched connections.

3. A variety of call establishment, call termination, information, and miscellaneous messages are specified, including SETUP, CONNECT, RELEASE, USER INFORMATION, CANCEL, STATUS, and DISCONNECT.

4. Fig. 6.31 shows the typical stages of an ISDN circuit-switched call.

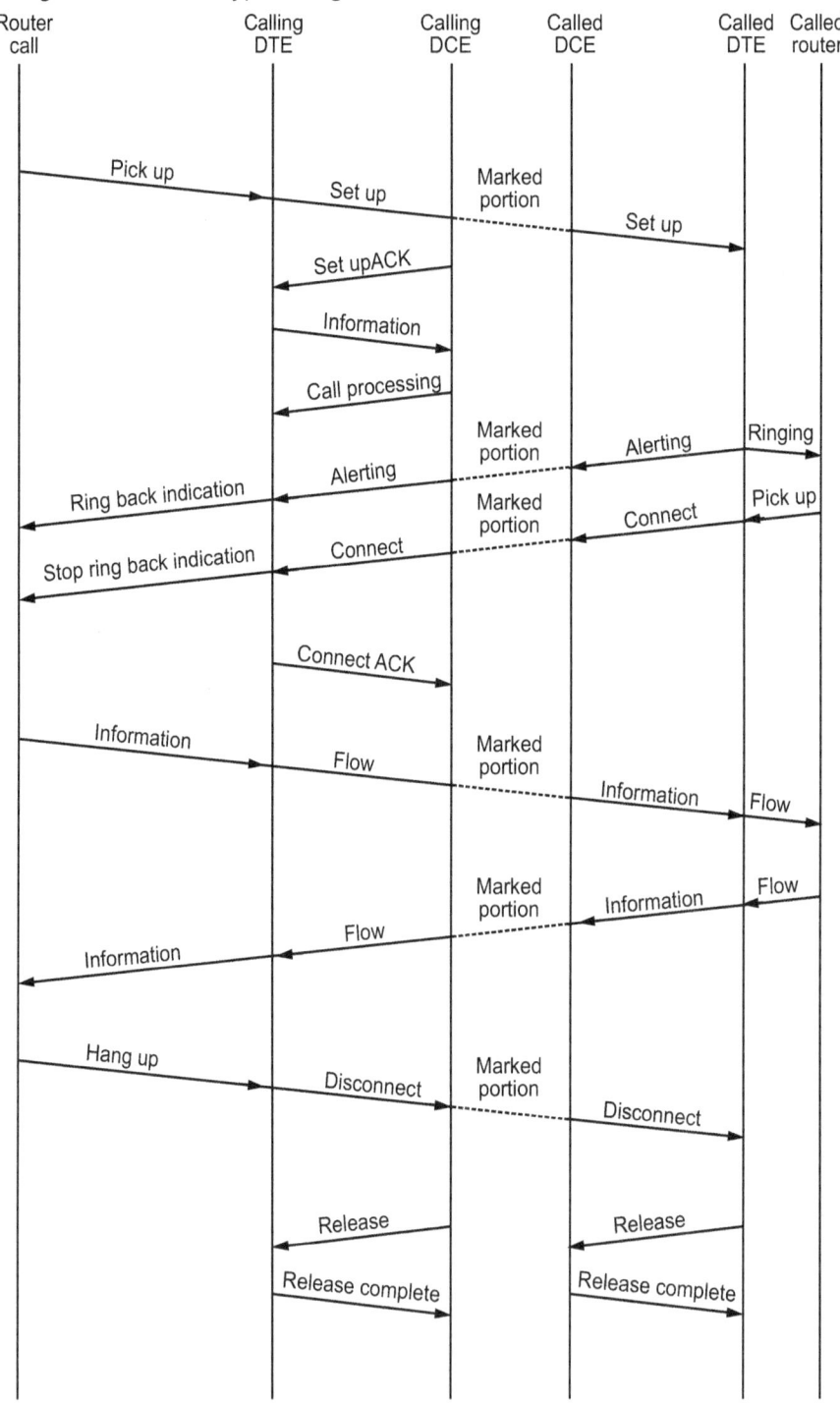

Fig. 6.31: ISDN circuit-switched call stages

6.6 Small Business Server (SBS)

Small Business Server offers direct ISDN support for ISDN adapters. This technology includes Dial-Up Networking via ISDN miniports, fax services, and modem sharing via ISDN modem emulation. The additional CAPI interface supports non-Microsoft and non-Eicon Technology ISDN applications.

Dial-Up Networking (RAS) can be used for dialing into a remote device. To support V.34+ clients, GSM clients, and ISDN with the same number, automatic protocol detection is available. RAS can also be used for dialing out to the Internet or to an Intranet. We recommend using the Proxy Server auto-dial functions.

Modem emulation can be used for fax communication over two B-channels simultaneously and supports all features from the Small Business Server embedded fax services. The DIVA ISDN adapter works as a fax group 3 device at up to 14.4 Kbps. ISDN modem emulation can support Small Business Server embedded modem sharing. Fax and modem sharing is based on different virtual modems and depends on the B-channel protocol.

6.7 Integrated Network

It is clear that there is never likely to be a single, monolithic, worldwide ISDN. In the near term, there will be a variety of non-ISDN public networks operating, with the need for the subscribers on these networks to connect to subscribers on ISDN networks. Even in the case of different national ISDNs, differences in services or the attributes of services may persist indefinitely. Accordingly, ITU-T has addressed the issue of the interworking of other networks with ISDN.

One issue related to interworking, that of interworking between numbering plans, was discussed in the preceding section. The interworking of numbering plans allows an ISDN subscriber to identify a non-ISDN subscriber for the purpose of establishing a connection and using some service. However, for successful communication to take place there must be agreement on, and the capability to provide, a common set of services and mechanisms. To provide compatibility between ISDN and existing network components and terminals, a set of interworking functions must be implemented. Typical functions include the following:

- Provide interworking of numbering plans.
- Match physical-layer characteristics at the point of interconnection between the two networks.
- Determine if network resources on the destination network side are adequate to meet the ISDN service demand.

- Map control signal messages such as services identification, channel identification, call status, and alerting between the ISDN's common-channel signaling protocol and the called network's signaling protocol, whether the latter is inchannel or common channel.
- Ensure service and connection compatibility.
- Provide transmission structure conversion, including information modulation technique and frame structure.
- Maintain synchronization (error control, flow control) across connections on different networks.
- Collect data required for proper billing.
- Coordinate operation and maintenance procedures to be able to isolate faults.

Thus, interworking may require the implementation of a set of interworking functions, either in ISDN or the network attached to ISDN. The approach identified by ITU-T for standardizing the interworking capability is to define additional reference e points associated with interworking and to standardize the interface at that reference point. This is a sound strategy that should minimize the impact both on ISDN and on other networks. The inclusion of these additional reference points is illustrated in Figure 6.32. As before, ISDN-compatible customer equipment attaches to ISDN via the S or T reference point. The following additional reference points are defined.

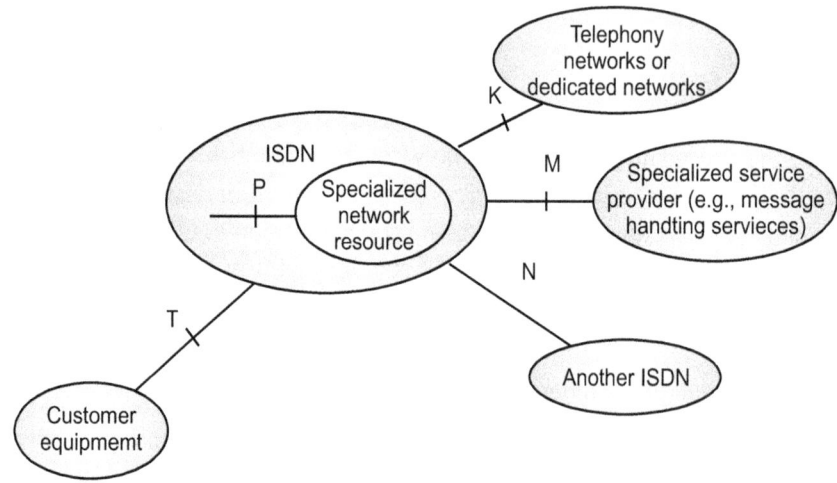

Fig. 6.32: Reference points associated with the interconnection of customer equipment and other networks to an ISDN

- **K:** Interface with an existing telephone network or other non-ISDN network requiring the internetworking functions are performed by ISDN.
- **M:** A specialized network, such as teletex or MHS. In this case, an adaption function may be needed, to be performed in the specialized network.
- **N:** Interface between two ISDNs. Some sort of protocol is needed, to determine the degree of service compatibility.
- **P:** There may be some specialized resource that is provided by the ISDN provider but that is clearly identifiable as a separate component or set of components.

In I.510, ITU-T identifies five other types of networks that support telecommunication services, that are also supported by an ISDN, and that are candidates, therefore, for with an ISDN:

- Another ISDN
- Public-switched telephone network (PSTN)
- Circuit-switched public data network (CSPDN)
- Packet-switched public data network (PSPDN)
- Telex

Table 6.3, from I.510, depicts the type of interworking functions that may be required for each interworking configuration. In this context, a connection is a network-oriented function relating to the establishment of an information transfer path through the network, while a communication is a user-oriented function relating to the end-to-end protocols needed for the exchange of information between subscribers.

Table 6.3: ISDN Support of Telecommunication Services in an Interworking Configuration (I.510)

Services supported by ISDN	ISDN interconnected with					
	ISDN	PSTN	CSPDN	PSPDN	TELEX	Other dedicated network
Telephony	O	N	-	-	-	N
Data transmission	(L)	N, L	N, (L)	N, (L)	-	N, (L)
Telex	O	-	-	-	N, L	N, L
Teletex	O	N, L	N, L	N, L	-	N, L, H
Facsmile	O,	N, L	N, L	N, L	-	N, L, H

O No interworking function foreseen
N Connection-dependent interworking needed
L Lower-layer communication-dependent interworking need d
H Higher-layer communication-dependent interworking needed
(X) X may be needed

ISDN-ISDN Interworking

The simplest case of interworking involves two ISDNs, if the two ISDNs provide identical bearers ices and teleservices, then no interworking capabilities are required. However, it may be the case that the two networks differ in the attribute values that they support for one or more services. In that case, interworking is needed. The internet would occur in two phases. In the control phase, a service negotiation takes place in order to reach a service agreement. A service agreement can be reached if the maximum common service that can be provided across the two networks equals or exceeds the minimum service that the caller will accept. If agreement is reached, then the connection is established, which involves splicing together connections from the two ISDN form a single connection from the user's point of view. User-to-user communication can then take place in the user phase.

It illustrates the call negotiation procedure used to reach service agreement. The following steps are involved:

1. A call from TEx to ISDN2 is routed to IWFL

2. IWF1 communicates with IWF2 and determines whether the requested service indicated by bearer capability of the calling user is supported by ISDN2, using a service list in IWF2. If the compatibility is satisfied, network inter-working between ISDN1 and ISDN2 begins.

3. If the service compatibility does not exist, IWF2 (or IWF1) negotiates with the calling user to change or abandon the service request.

4. With a changed service request, step 2 or 3 is repeated until service compatibility is satisfied or the effort abandoned.

5. When the connection between TEx and TEy is established, low-level compatibility (bearer) and high-level compatibility (teleservice) is examined on an end-to-end basis. The network does not participate in this procedure, but agreement between ISDNs concerning user-to-user information transfer method might be required.

Thus, it is first necessary to determine if the two ISDNs can support the required attributes of the caller's requested bearer service. Then the- end-to-end compatibility between the two users is determined.

ISDN-PSTN Interworking:

In many countries, digitization of the existing public switched telephone network (PSTN) has been ongoing for a number of years, including implementation of digital transmission and switching facilities and the introduction of common-channel signaling. The availability of digital subscriber loops has lagged behind the introduction of these other digital aspects. In any case, such networks exhibit some overlap with the capabilities of a full ISDN but lack some of the services that an ISDN will support. Thus, it will be necessary for some time to provide interworking between ISDN and PSTN facilities.

Table 6.4 (from I.530) identifies the key characteristics of an ISDN and a PSTN, indicating possible interworking functions to accommodate dissimilar characteristics. Some sort of negotiation procedure, similar to that depicted in Figure 6.33, will be needed to establish connections.

Table 6.4: Key ISDN and PSTN characteristics

	ISDN	PSTN	Interworking functions
Subscriber interface	Digital	Analog	a
User-network signaling	Out of band (1.441/1.451)	Mainly inband (e.g., DTMF)	b, e
User terminal equipment supported	Digital TE (ISDN NT, Tel or TE2 + TA)	Analog TE (e.g., dial pulse telephones, PBXs, modem-equipped DTEs)	c
Interexchange signaling	SS7 ISDN User Part (ISUP)	Inband (e.g., R1, R2, SS4, SS 5) or out of band (e.g., SS 6, SS7 TUP)	d, e
Transmission facilities	Digital	Analog/digital	a
Information transfer mode	Circuit/packet	Circuit	f
Information transfer capability	Speech, digital unrestricted, 3.1 kHz audio, video, etc.	3.1 kHz audio (voice/voiceband data)	f

a = Analog-to-digital and digital-to-analog conversion on transmission facilities.
b = Mapping between PSTN signals in the subscriber access and 1.451 messages for intra-exchange calls.
c = Support of communication between modem-equipped PSTN DTEs and ISDN terminals.
d = Conversion between the PSTN signaling system and Signaling System No. 7 ISDN user part.
e = Mapping between signals in the ISDN subscriber (I.441, 1.45I) access and PSTN inband interexchange signaling,(e.g., RI). I = Further study required.
f = Further study required.

The interworking between an ISDN and a PSTN is reasonably straightforward. The number plan of the telephone network is the same as that used for ISDN, so no conversion is required. The interworking function must include a mapping between the control signaling used in ISDN and that used in the telephone network. Finally, a conversion is needed between digital and analog forms of user information.

ISDN-CSPDN Interworking:

A circuit-switched public data ner. as e name implies, provides a digital transmission service using circuit switching. The interface for DTEs to this type of network is X.21. Like X.25., X.21 is actually a three-layer set of protocols that includes inband control signaling for setting up and terminating connections. In the case of X.21, the connections are actual rather than virtual circuits.

The interworking functions for this case have not been fully worked out; much has been left for further study. A mapping is required between the call control protocol X.21 and that used in ISDN. For addressing, ISDNs and CSPDNs utilize differing numbering plans (i.e., E.164 and X.121, respectively). A one-stage address translation, as described in the previous section, is specified.

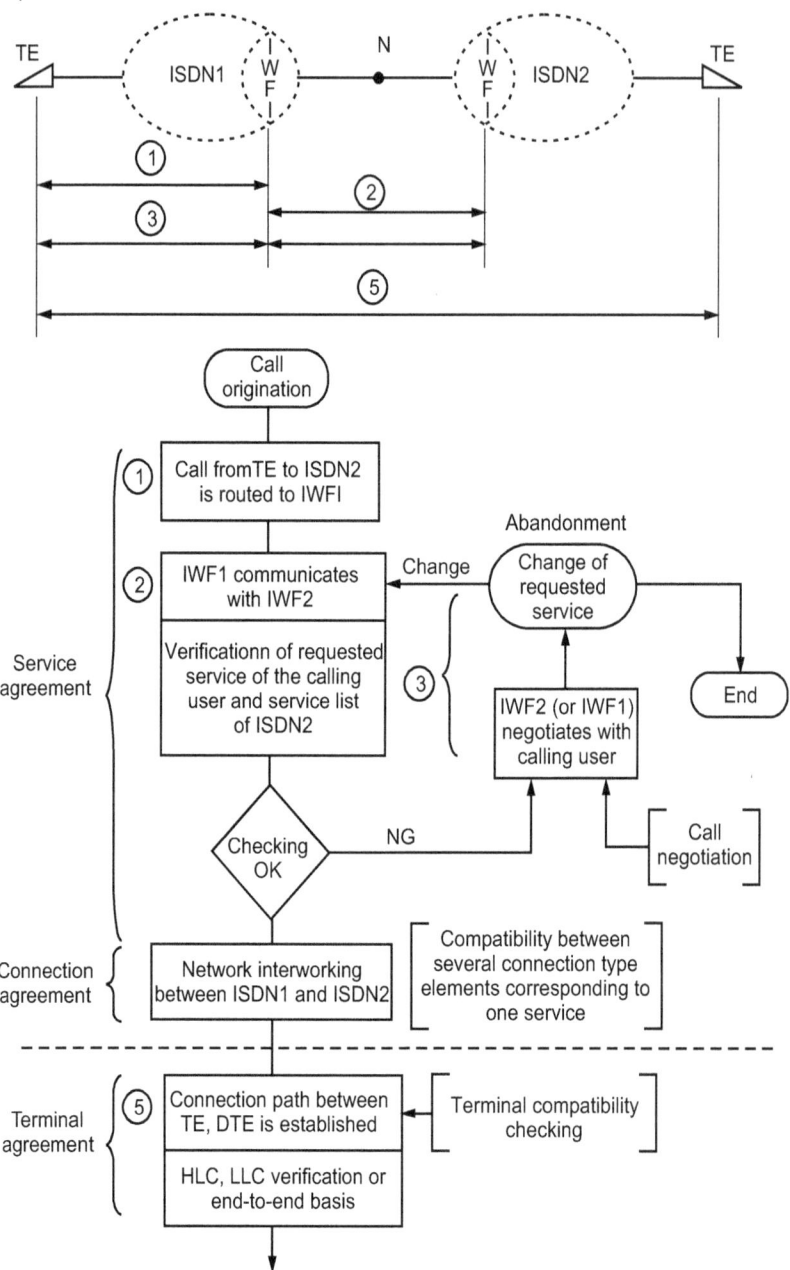

Fig. 6.33: Call negotiation procedure in ISDN-ISDN interworking

ISDN-PSPDN Interworking

CA packet-switched public data network provides a packet-switching service using an X.25 interface. There are two interworking cases:

- A circuit-mode bearer service is used on ISDN.
- A packet-mode bearer service is used on ISDN.

In the first case, interworking is achieved by means of a circuit-mode connection across ISDN from an ISDN subscriber to a packet handler in the PSPDN (see Figure 6.10). In the second c the-ISDN functions as a packet-switching network (Figure 6.13). For this case, is an established interworking protocol to be used between two public packet-switching networks: X.76 n essence, X.75 acts as a splicing mechanism to tie together two virtual circuits in the two networks in such a way that it appears as a single virtual circuit to the two end DTEs.

6.8 IEEE Standards

The IEEE 802 standards for LAN was adopted by ANSI in 1985 and also approved by ISO in 1987. The key LAN protocols are listed as follows:

\multicolumn{2}{c}{LAN - Local Area Network Protocols}	
Ethernet	Ethernet LAN protocols as defined in IEEE 802.3 suite
	Fast Ethernet: Ethernet LAN at data rate 100Mbps (IEEE 802.3u)
	Gigabit Ethernet: Ethernet at data rate 1000Mbps (IEEE 802.3z, 802.3ab)
	10 Gigabit Ethernet: Ethernet at data rate 10 Gbps (IEEE 802.3ae)
WLAN	Wireless LAN in IEEE 802.11, 802,11a, 802.11b, 802.11g and 802.11n
	IEEE 802.11i: WLAN Security Standards
	IEEE 802.1X: WLAN Authentication & Key Management
	IEEE 802.15: Bluetooth for Wireless Personal Area Network (WPAN)
VLAN	IEEE 802.1Q: Virtual LAN Bridging Switching Protocol
	GARP: Generic Attribute Registration Protocol (802.1P)
	GMRP: GARP Multicast Registration Protocol (802.1P)
	GVRP: GARP VLAN Registration Protocol (802.1P, 802.1Q)
Token Bus	IEEE 802.4: LAN Protocol
Token Ring	IEEE 802.5 LAN protocol
FDDI	Fiber Distributed Data Interface
Others	LLC: Logic Link Control (IEEE 802.2)
	SNAP: SubNetwork Access Protocol
	STP: Spanning Tree Protocol (IEEE 802.1D)
	IEEE 802.1p: LAN Layer 2 QoS/CoS Protocol

Ethernet protocols refer to the family of local-area network (LAN) covered by the IEEE 802.3. In the Ethernet standard, there are two modes of operation: half-duplex and full-duplex modes. In the half duplex mode, data are transmitted using the popular Carrier-Sense Multiple Access/Collision Detection (CSMA/CD) protocol on a shared medium. The main disadvantages of the half-duplex are the efficiency and distance limitation, in which the link distance is limited by the minimum MAC frame size. This restriction reduces the efficiency drastically for high-rate transmission. Therefore, the carrier extension technique is used to ensure the minimum frame size of 512 bytes in Gigabit Ethernet to achieve a reasonable link distance.

Four data rates are currently defined for operation over optical fiber and twisted-pair cables:
- 10 Mbps - 10Base-T Ethernet (IEEE 802.3)
- 100 Mbps - Fast Ethernet (IEEE 802.3u)
- 1000 Mbps - Gigabit Ethernet (IEEE 802.3z)
- 10-Gigabit - 10 Gbps Ethernet (IEEE 802.3ae).

The Ethernet system consists of three basic elements:
1. The physical medium used to carry Ethernet signals between computers,
2. A set of medium access control rules embedded in each Ethernet interface that allow multiple computers to fairly arbitrate access to the shared Ethernet channel, and
3. An Ethernet frame that consists of a standardized set of bits used to carry data over the system.

As with all IEEE 802 protocols, the ISO data link layer is divided into two IEEE 802 sublayers, the Media Access Control (MAC) sublayer and the MAC-client sublayer. The IEEE 802.3 physical layer corresponds to the ISO physical layer.

The MAC sub-layer has two primary responsibilities:
- Data encapsulation, including frame assembly before transmission, and frame parsing/error detection during and after reception.
- Media access control, including initiation of frame transmission and recovery from transmission failure.

The MAC-client sub-layer may be one of the following:
- Logical Link Control (LLC), which provides the interface between the Ethernet MAC and the upper layers in the protocol stack of the end station. The LLC sublayer is defined by IEEE 802.2 standards.
- Bridge entity, which provides LAN-to-LAN interfaces between LANs that use the same protocol (for example, Ethernet to Ethernet) and also between different protocols (for example, Ethernet to Token Ring). Bridge entities are defined by IEEE 802.1 standards.

Each Ethernet-equipped computer operates independently of all other stations on the network: there is no central controller. All stations attached to an Ethernet are connected to a shared signaling system, also called the medium. To send data a station first listens to the channel, and when the channel is idle the station transmits its data in the form of an Ethernet frame, or packet.

After each frame transmission, all stations on the network must contend equally for the next frame transmission opportunity. Access to the shared channel is determined by the Medium Access Control (MAC) mechanism embedded in the Ethernet interface located in each station. The medium access control mechanism is based on a system called Carrier Sense Multiple Access with Collision Detection (CSMA/CD).

As each Ethernet frame is sent onto the shared signal channel, all Ethernet interfaces look at the destination address. If the destination address of the frame matches with the interface address, the frame will be read entirely and be delivered to the networking software running on that computer. All other network interfaces will stop reading the frame when they discover that the destination address does not match their own address.

When it comes to how signals flow over the set of media segments that make up an Ethernet system, it helps to understand the topology of the system. The signal topology of the Ethernet is also known as the logical topology, to distinguish it from the actual physical layout of the media cables. The logical topology of an Ethernet provides a single channel (or bus) that carries Ethernet signals to all stations.

Multiple Ethernet segments can be linked together to form a larger Ethernet LAN using a signal amplifying and retiming device called a repeater. Through the use of repeaters, a given Ethernet system of multiple segments can grow as a "non-rooted branching tree". "Non-rooted" means that the resulting system of linked segments may grow in any direction, and does not have a specific root segment. Most importantly, segments must never be connected in a loop. Every segment in the system must have two ends, since the Ethernet system will not operate correctly in the presence of loop paths.

Even though the media segments may be physically connected in a star pattern, with multiple segments attached to a repeater, the logical topology is still that of a single Ethernet channel that carries signals to all stations.

6.9 Standard Ethernet
The standard Ethernet has a data rate of 10 Mbps.

6.9.1 MAC Layer
In standard Ethernet MAC layer performs two functions:
1. Controls the access.
2. Data received from network layer is used for preparation of frame to pass it to physical layer.

Frame Format

The Ethernet frame is shown below.

Number of bytes	7	1	2/6	2/6	2	46-1500bytes	4
Name of field	Pre	SFD	DA	SA	Length/Type	Data unit + pad	FCS

- **Preamble (PRE)** - 7 bytes. The PRE is an alternating pattern of ones and zeros that tells receiving stations that a frame is coming, and that provides a means to synchronize the frame-reception portions of receiving physical layers with the incoming bit stream.
- **Start-of-frame delimiter (SFD)** - 1 byte. The SFD is an alternating pattern of ones and zeros, ending with two consecutive 1-bits indicating that the next bit is the leftmost bit in the leftmost byte of the destination address.
- **Destination address (DA)** - 6 bytes. The DA field identifies which station(s) should receive the frame.
- **Source addresses (SA)** - 6 bytes. The SA field identifies the sending station.
- **Length/Type** - 2 bytes. This field indicates either the number of MAC-client data bytes that are contained in the data field of the frame, or the frame type ID if the frame is assembled using an optional format.
- **Data** - Is a sequence of n bytes ($46 \le n \le 1500$) of any value. (The total frame minimum is 64 bytes).
- **Frame check sequence (FCS)** - 4 bytes. This sequence contains a 32-bit Cyclic Redundancy Check (CRC) value, which is created by the sending MAC and is recalculated by the receiving MAC to check for damaged frames.

Frame Length:

The header and trailer consisting of source address (6 bytes), destination address (6 bytes), length or type (2 bytes) and CRC or FCS (4 bytes) has total 18 bytes. The minimum length of the frame is 512 bits or 64 bytes. Hence the payload (packet coming from upper layer) has to be 46 bytes long. If not some bits are to be padded. The maximum length of the frame without preamble and SFD is specified as 1518 byte (12,144 bits) with payload 1500 byte. This restricts one station from occupying shared medium for longer time.

Addressing:

The source and destination address is 6 byte long in case of Ethernet network. Each station in the network has network interface card which holds the address. His address has to be unique. It is specified in terms of hexadecimal notation as below.

30:10:04:C5:AA:BC

The address can be unicast, multicast or broadcast. If the address is unicast, the frame is meant for one station only. It is used for one to one transmission. The least significant bit of first byte in unicast address is always zero. If the address is multicast, the frame is meant for many station only. It is used for one to many transmission. The least significant bit of first byte in unicast address is always one. If the address is broadcast, the frame is meant for all station only. It is used for broadcast transmission. All the 48 bits in bits in broadcast address are 1's The addresses are sent out byte by byte from left to right. Each byte is sent out in reverse order i.e. least significant bit of the byte is sent out first and most significant bit in the end.

Access Method:
The access method used in standard Ethernet is CSMA/CD with 1-pesistent CSMA. The slot time is defined as round-trip time to send the frame from one end of the network to the other plus time required to send jamming sequence. This slot time in standard Ethernet is time require to send 512 bits. Since standard Ethernet has speed of 10Mbps, the slot time is 51.2 microsec. The maximum length of the network can be found from the slot time. If the propagation speed of the signal is (vp)2×10^8 m/s then the maximum length is given as below

$$L_{max} = Vp \times Slot\ time/2 = 2 \times 10^8 \times 51.2 \times 10^{-6} = 5120\ m$$

Considering the delay times in the repeaters and interfaces, and time required to send jamming signal this length will be not more than 2500 m.

6.9.2 Physical Layer
The standard Ethernet physical layer specifications include encoding and decoding of bits i.e. line codes and transmission media. The line codes used is split phase Manchester which is suitable for bit synchronization purpose. There are several physical layer implementations. Some of them are:
1. 10Base5: Bus, thick coaxial.
2. 10Base2: Bus thin coaxial.
3. 10Base7: Star UTP.
4. 10BaseF: Star, fibre.

10Base5: Thick Ethernet:
The first implementation is called 10Base5, thick Ethernet, or Thicknet. The nick name derives from the size of the cable, which is roughly the size of a garden hose and too stiff to bend with your hands. 10Base5 was the first Ethernet specification to use a bus topology with an external transceiver (transmitter/receiver) connected via to tap to a thick coaxial cable. Fig. 6.34 shows a schematic diagram of a 10Base5 implementation.

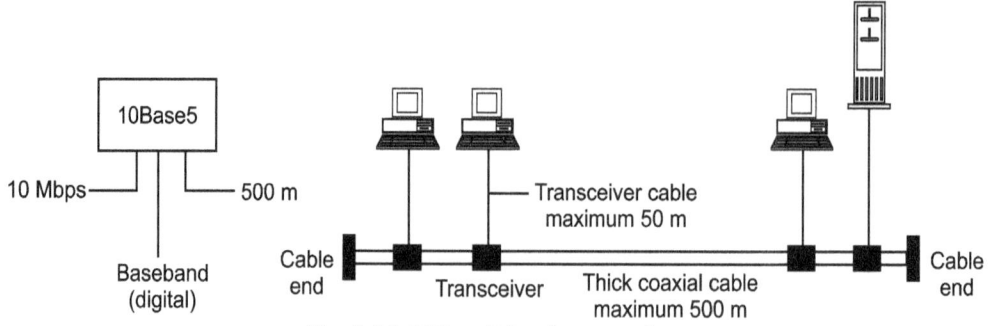

Fig. 6.34: 10Base5 implementation

The transceiver is responsible for transmitting, receiving and detecting collisions. The transceiver is connected to the station via a transceiver cable that provides separate path for sending and receiving. This means that collision can only happen in the coaxial cable. The maximum length of the coaxial cable must not exceed 500 m, otherwise, there is excessive degradation of the signal. If a length of more than 500 m is needed, upto five segments, each a maximum of 500 meter, can be connected using repeaters.

10Base2: Thin Ethernet:
The second implementation is called 10Base2, thin Ethernet, or Cheapernet, 10Base2 also uses a bus topology, but the cable is much thinner and more flexible. The cable can be bent to pass very close to the stations. In this case, the transceiver is normally part of the Network Interface Card (NIC), which is installed inside the station. Fig. 6.35 shows the schematic diagram of a 10Base2 implementation.

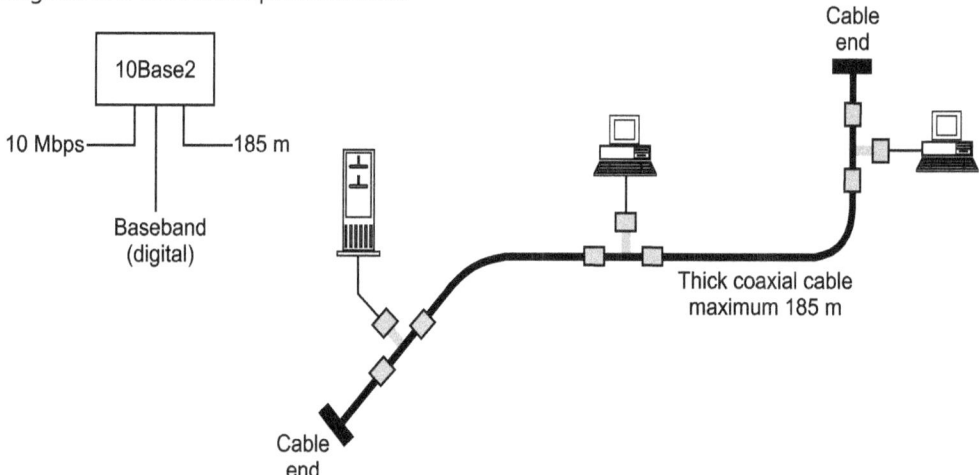

Fig. 6.35: 10Base2 implementation

Note that the collision here occurs in the thin coaxial cable. This implementation is more cost effective than 10Base5 because thin coaxial cable is less expensive than thick coaxial and the tee connections are much cheaper than taps. Installation is simpler because the thin coaxial cable is very flexible. However, the length of each segment cannot exceed 185 m (close to 200 m) due to the high level of attenuation in thin coaxial cable.

10Base-T: Twisted-Pair Ethernet:

The third implementation is called 10Base-T or twisted-pair Ethernet. 10Base-T uses a physical star topology. The stations are connected to a hub via two pairs of twisted cable, as shown in Fig. 6.36.

Note that two pairs of twisted cable create two paths (one for sending and one for receiving) between the station and the hub. Any collision here happens in the hub. Compared to 10Base5 or 10Base2, we can see that the hub actually replaces the coaxial cable as far as collision is concerned. The maximum length of the twisted cable here is defined as 100 m, to minimize the effect of attenuation in the twisted cable.

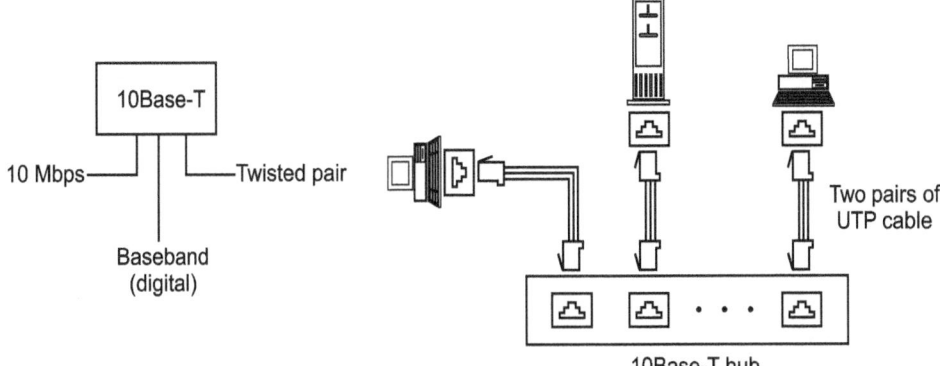

Fig. 6.36: 10Base-T implementation

10Base-F: Fiber Ethernet:

Although there are several types of optical fiber 10 Mbps Ethernet, the most common is called 10Base-F. 10Base-F uses a star topology to connect stations to a hub. The stations are connected to the hub using two fiber-optic cables, as shown in Fig. 6.37.

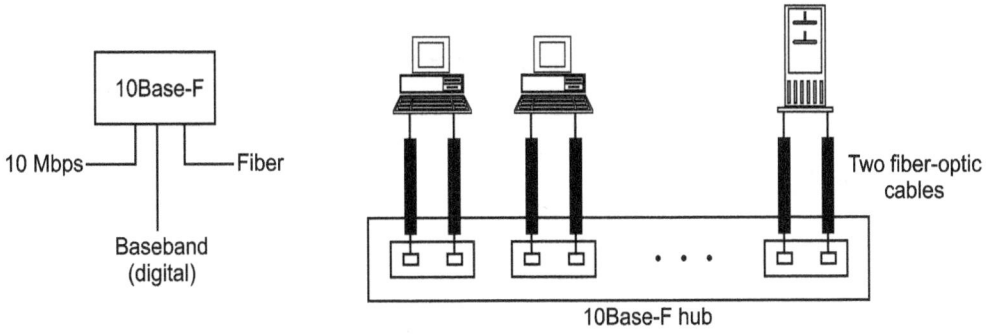

Fig. 6.37: 10Base-F implementation

Following table gives Comparison of Physical Layer Implementation of Ethernet.

Table 6.5: Summary of Standard Ethernet Implementations

Characteristics	10Base5	10Base2	10Base-T	10Base-F
Media used	Thick coaxial cable	Thin coaxial cable	2 UTP	2 Fiber
Max Length	< 500 m	< 185 m	< 100 m	< 2000 m
Line coding technique	Split phase Manchester	Split phase Manchester	Split phase Manchester	Split phase Manchester

6.10 Changes in the Standard

Before moving to the higher data rates i.e. from 10Mbps to 100 Mbps, many changes were done to 10 Mbps Ethernet. These changes made it possible to have compatibility between 10 Mbps and higher data rate LANs. They are:

1. Bridged Ethernet.
2. Switched Ethernet.
3. Full Duplex Ethernet

6.10.1 Bridged Ethernet

The bridged ethernet divides LAN by bridges because of which there is improvement in bandwidth and separation of collision domains.

If we have 10 Mbps LAN and 10 nodes are there, the bandwidth will be divided among these nodes depending on need. For example, if only one station wants to transmit entire bandwidth will be available to it. But if all of them want to transmit each one will have 1 Mbps bandwidth.

We can improve the bandwidth efficiency by using a bridge. If 10 nodes are divided into 2 groups of 5 each, each group will have an average bandwidth of 10/5 = 2 Mbps instead of 1 Mbps.

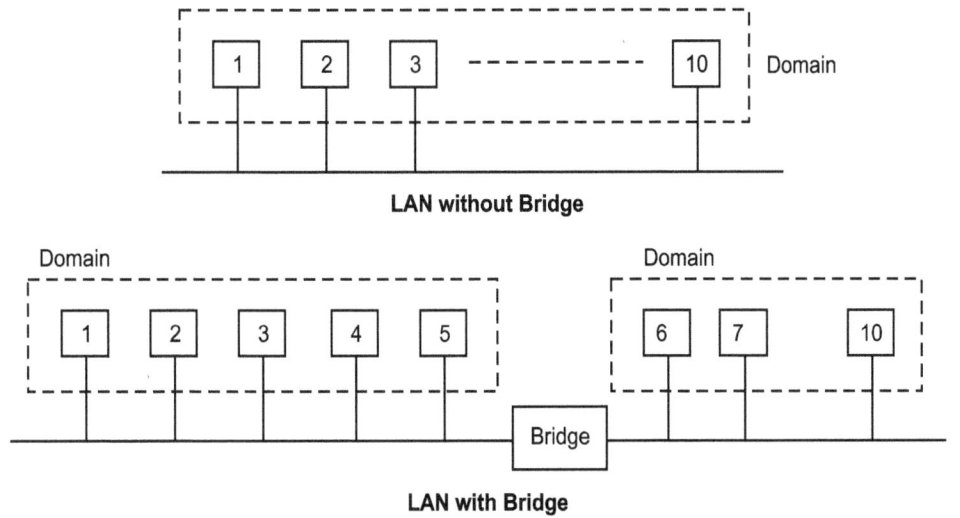

Fig. 6.38: Bridged ethernet

Another advantage is number of nodes in collision domain are reduced and hence probability of collision reduces by 50%.

6.10.2 Switched Ethernet

If we divide the number of nodes in the LAN, there is improvement in bandwidth efficiency. We can have only single node in each network. If there are N nodes in LAN, there will be N networks. It is called switched LAN as shown below. The collision domain is also divided into N domains.

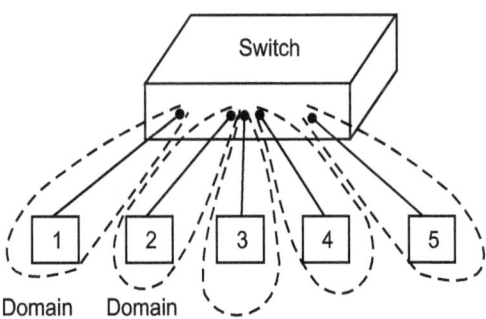

Fig. 6.39: Switched ethernet

The bandwidth will be shared between station and the switch (i.e. 5 Mbps each).

Full Duplex Ethernet:

In half duplex a station can either send or receive. In full duplex mode Ethernet, send and receive operations can be done simultaneously. The capacity of each domain is doubled because of this. Two links will be used in such configuration.

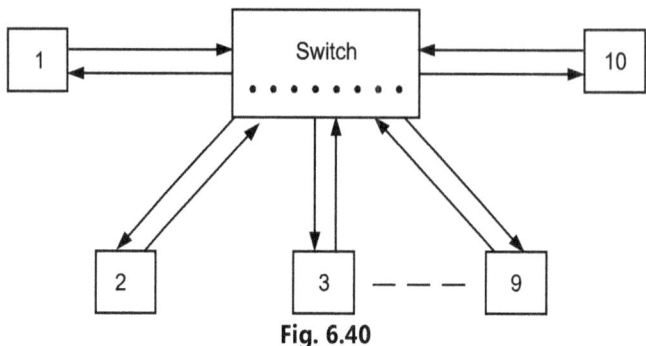

Fig. 6.40

In this mode, there is need of CSMA/CD, since each station is independent. The new layer called MAC control layer is added between LLC sublayer and MAC sublayer to provide flow control and error control in full-duplex switched Ethernet.

6.11 Fast Ethernet

Fast Ethernet (100BASE-T) offers a speed increase ten times that of the 10BaseT Ethernet specification, while preserving such qualities as frame format, MAC mechanisms, and MTU. Such similarities allow the use of existing 10BaseT applications and network management tools on Fast Ethernet networks. Officially, the 100BASE-T standard is IEEE 802.3u.

The goals of the Fast Ethernet are:
1. Upgrade the data rate to 100 Mbps
2. Keep address field 6 bytes.(48 bits)
3. Keep Same frame format
4. Have compatibility with Standard Ethernet
5. Keep Minimum and Maximum Frame size same.

Like Ethernet, 100BASE-T is based on the CSMA/CD LAN access method. Actually there is no need of CSMA/CD for full duplex Fast Ethernet.

Physical Layer:

Fast Ethernet can have two topologies: (i) Point-to-Point topology (ii) Star topology.

The encoding scheme used in Standard Ethernet is Manchester encoding. It is not suitable for higher data rates as it requires more bandwidth. For 100 Mbps data rate we require 200-Mbaud bandwidth. 4B/5B block encoding is used followed by Manchester line encoding.

There are several different cabling schemes that can be used with 100BASE-T, including:
- 100BASE-TX: Two pairs of high-quality twisted-pair wires.
- 100BASE-T4: Four pairs of normal-quality twisted-pair wires.
- 100BASE-FX: Fiber optic cables.

The Fast Ethernet specifications include mechanisms for Auto-Negotiation of the media speed. This makes it possible for vendors to provide dual-speed Ethernet interfaces that can be installed and run at either 10-Mbps or 100-Mbps automatically.

The IEEE identifiers include three pieces of information. The first item, "100", stands for the media speed of 100-Mbps. The "BASE" stands for "baseband," which is a type of signaling. Baseband signaling simply means that Ethernet signals are the only signals carried over the media system.

The third part of the identifier provides an indication of the segment type. The "T4" segment type is a twisted-pair segment that uses four pairs of telephone-grade twisted-pair wire. The "TX" segment type is a twisted-pair segment that uses two pairs of wires and is based on the data grade twisted-pair physical medium standard developed by ANSI. The "FX" segment type is a fiber optic link segment based on the fiber optic physical medium standard developed by ANSI and that uses two strands of fiber cable. The TX and FX medium standards are collectively known as 100BASE-X.

The 100BASE-TX and 100BASE-FX media standards used in Fast Ethernet are both adopted from physical media standards first developed by ANSI, the American National Standards Institute. The ANSI physical media standards were originally developed for the Fiber Distributed Data Interface (FDDI) LAN standard (ANSI standard X3T9.5), and are widely used in FDDI LANs.

Protocol Structure - Fast Ethernet: 100 Mbps Ethernet (IEEE 802.3u) The basic IEEE 802.3 Ethernet MAC Data Frame for 10/100 Mbps Ethernet

Number of bytes	7	1	2/6	2/6	2	612 <= n <= 1500	4 bytes
Name of field	Pre	SFD	DA	SA	Length/Type	Data unit + pad	FCS

- **Preamble (PRE)** - 7 bytes. The PRE is an alternating pattern of ones and zeros that tells receiving stations that a frame is coming, and that provides a means to synchronize the frame-reception portions of receiving physical layers with the incoming bit stream.
- **Start-of-frame delimiter (SFD)** - 1 byte. The SFD is an alternating pattern of ones and zeros, ending with two consecutive 1-bits indicating that the next bit is the left-most bit in the left-most byte of the destination address.

- **Destination address (DA)** - 6 bytes. The DA field identifies which station(s) should receive the frame.
- **Source addresses (SA)** - 6 bytes. The SA field identifies the sending station.
- **Length/Type** - 2 bytes. This field indicates either the number of MAC-client data bytes that are contained in the data field of the frame, or the frame type ID if the frame is assembled using an optional format.
- **Data** - Is a sequence of n bytes ($612 \leq n \leq 1500$) of any value. Note that since transmission speed has increased from 10 Mbps to 100 Mbps, frame transmission time reduces by factor of 10. Hence, minimum frame size increases by a factor of 10 to 640.
- **Frame check sequence (FCS)** - 4 bytes. This sequence contains a 32-bit Cyclic Redundancy Check (CRC) value, which is created by the sending MAC and is recalculated by the receiving MAC to check for damaged frames.

Following table gives Comparison of Physical Layer Implementation of Fast Ethernet.

Table 6.6: Summary of Fast Ethernet Implementations

Characteristics	100Base-TX	100Base-FX	100Base-T4
Media used	Cat 5 UTP/STP	Optical Fiber	Cat 4 UTP
Max Length	100 m	100 m	100 m
Block Encoding	4B/5B	4B/5B	-
Line coding technique	Split phase Manchester	NRZ-I	8B/6T

Gigabit (1000 Mbps) Ethernet

Ethernet protocols refer to the family of Local-Area Network (LAN) covered by the IEEE 802.3 standard. The Gigabit Ethernet is based on the Ethernet protocol, but increased speed tenfold over the fast Ethernet, using shorter frames with carrier extension. It is published as the IEEE 802.3z and 802.3ab, supplement to the IEEE 802.3 base standards.

The goals of the Gigabit Ethernet are:
1. Upgrade the data rate to 1 Gbps
2. Keep address field 6 bytes. (48-bits)
3. Keep Same frame format
4. Have compatibility with Standard Ethernet
5. Keep Minimum and Maximum Frame size same.
6. To Support autonegotiation as defined in Fast Ethernet

The Gigabit Ethernet standards are fully compatible with Ethernet and Fast Ethernet installations. It retains Carrier Sense Multiple Access/Collision Detection (CSMA/CD) as the access method. It supports full-duplex as well as half duplex modes of operation.

Single-mode and multi mode fiber and short-haul coaxial cable, and twisted pair cables are supported. The Gigabit Ethernet architecture is displayed in Fig. 6.41.

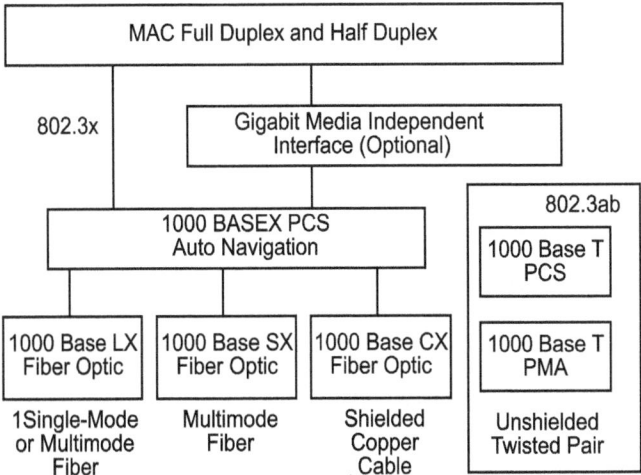

Fig. 6.41: Gigabit ethernet architecture

The IEEE 802.3z defines the Gigabit Ethernet over fiber and cable, which has a physical media standard 1000Base-X (1000BaseSX - short wave covers up to 500 m, and 1000BaseLX - long wave covers up to 5 km). The IEEE 802.3ab defines the Gigabit Ethernet over the unshielded twisted pair wire (1000Base-T covers up to 75m).

The Gigabit interface converter (GBIC) allows network managers to configure each gigabit port on a port-by-port basis for short-wave (SX), long-wave (LX), long-haul (LH), and copper physical interfaces (CX). LH GBICs extended the single-mode fiber distance from the standard 5 km to 10 km.

Mac Sublayer:
The Mac sublayer for Gigabit Ethernet had to be modified to achieve data rate of 1 Gbps. Two approaches of medium accesses are possible with Gigabit Ethernet (i) Half Duplex and (ii) Full Duplex. In Full duplex mode, a central switch is connected to all computers or other switches. Buffer is available at input port of switches to store data before transmission. CSMA/CD is not required because there is no collision. The maximum length of cable is decided by signal attenuation.

In Half duplex mode, hub is used and acts as common cable. Collision can occur and hence CSMA/CD is required. Maximum length of network in this approach is dependent on minimum frame size. There are three methods to decide this viz. traditional, carrier extension, and frame bursting.

In traditional approach, the frame length is retained same as standard Ethernet i.e. 512 bits. The slot time will be 512/1Gbps=0.512 microsec. This will reduce maximum length also by 100 times i.e. 25 m. This is suitable for single room size network.

In carrier extension approach, minimum frame size is made 512 bytes. Padding will be required for frames less than this length. This will increase the maximum length by 8 times i.e. 200 m but this technique will be inefficient if there are more short frames during transmission.

Frame bursting is used to avoid padding in case of short length frames. Multiple frames are sent instead of adding extension to each frame.

Physical Layer:
It is more complex than Standard or Fast Ethernet in case of Gigabit Ethernet. There are two topologies for connection of stations. They are i) Point-to-point ii) Star. The star topology can be with hub or switch.

NRZ encoder, decoder is used as it requires less bandwidth compared to Manchester. But for synchronization 8B/10B block encoding, decoding is used.

Protocol Structure - Gigabit (1000 Mbps) Ethernet
1000Base-X has a minimum frame size of 416 bytes, and 1000Base-T has a minimum frame size of 520 bytes. An extension field is used to fill the frames that are shorter than the minimum length.

Number of bytes	7	1	6	6	2	494 <= n <=1500	4	Variable
Name of field	Pre	SFD	DA	SA	Length/Type	Data unit + pad	FCS	Ext

- **Preamble (PRE)** - 7 bytes. The PRE is an alternating pattern of ones and zeros that tells receiving stations that a frame is coming, and that provides a means to synchronize the frame-reception portions of receiving physical layers with the incoming bit stream.
- **Start-of-frame delimiter (SFD)** - 1 byte. The SFD is an alternating pattern of ones and zeros, ending with two consecutive 1-bits indicating that the next bit is the left-most bit in the left-most byte of the destination address.
- **Destination address (DA)** - 6 bytes. The DA field identifies which station(s) should receive the frame.
- **Source addresses (SA)** - 6 bytes. The SA field identifies the sending station.
- **Length/Type** - 2 bytes. This field indicates either the number of MAC-Client Data Bytes that are contained in the data field of the frame, or the frame type ID if the frame is assembled using an optional format.

- **Data** - Is a sequence of n bytes (494 <= n <=1500) of any value.
- **Frame check sequence (FCS)** - 4 bytes. This sequence contains a 32-bit cyclic redundancy check (CRC) value, which is created by the sending MAC and is recalculated by the receiving MAC to check for damaged frames.
- **Ext** - extension, which is an non-data variable extension field for frames that are shorter than the minimum length.

Following table gives Comparison of Physical Layer Implementation of Gigabit Ethernet.

Table 6.7: Summary of Gigabit Ethernet Implementations

Characteristics	1000Base-SX	1000Base-LX	1000Base-CX	1000Base-T
Media used	Optical Fiber Short wave	Optical Fiber Short wave	STP	Cat 5 UTP
Max Length	550 m	5000 m	25 m	100 m
Number of Wires	2	2	2	4
Block Encoding	8B/10B	8B/10B	8B/10B	-
Line coding technique	NRZ	NRZ	NRZ	4D-PAM5

6.12 Introduction to Network

1. It is fastest growing technologies. Thus, wired networks are being replaced by wireless networks in office buildings, college campus and many public places like airport, railway stations etc.
2. Classification of wireless networks is given as:

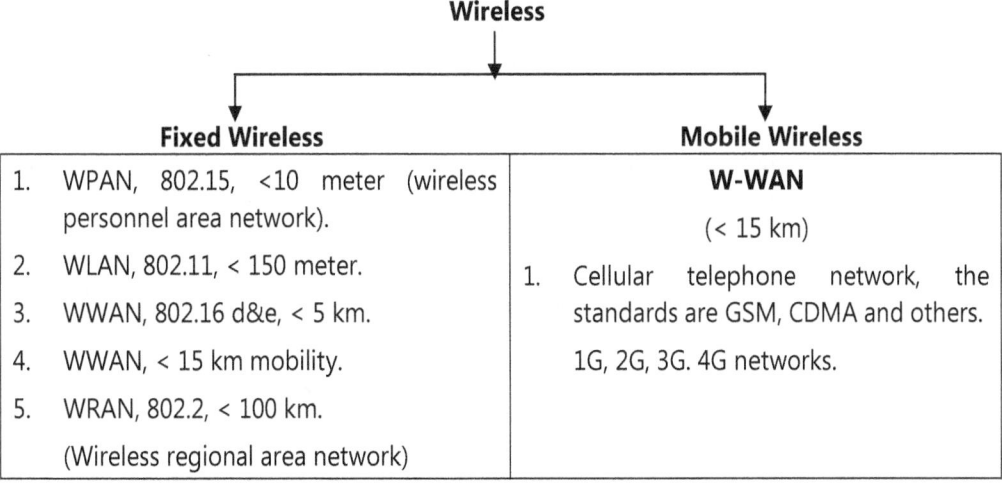

3. Following are the advantages of wireless communication.

(a) Mobility

(b) Reliability

- Fewer wires and connectors translates to fewer problems.
- The downtime due to cable faults in wired networks is eliminated.

(c) Ease of installation.

(d) Affordability (cost decreases).

(e) Scalability - Systems are easily configured and rearranged to accommodate more users.

(f) Installation flexibility - Wireless can go where wire cannot go.

6.12.1 Typical Wireless Network

Networks are widely used in both the business and consumer landscapes.

1. In the corporate environment, LANs are commonly used to share resources, including electronic files and devices such as printers.

2. These LANs are generally connected to other networks via WANs and the Internet to facilitate global data access.

3. In healthcare, LANs are used in the clinical environment to provide information such as patient's medical records and drug formularies for doctors and nurses.

Wireless networks provide the next step in utility and convenience for many industries, including health care.

1. In general, wireless networks provide the power and freedom of mobility, with the setbacks of reduced speed and unpolished functions (as compared to wired networks).

2. While wireless networks have existed for decades, only the recent boom of handheld and mobile devices has spurred the demand necessary to create robust networks.

If a home has more than one computer, then installing a computer network is a smart decision.

1. Networks allow you to share an Internet connection and files among multiple PC's.

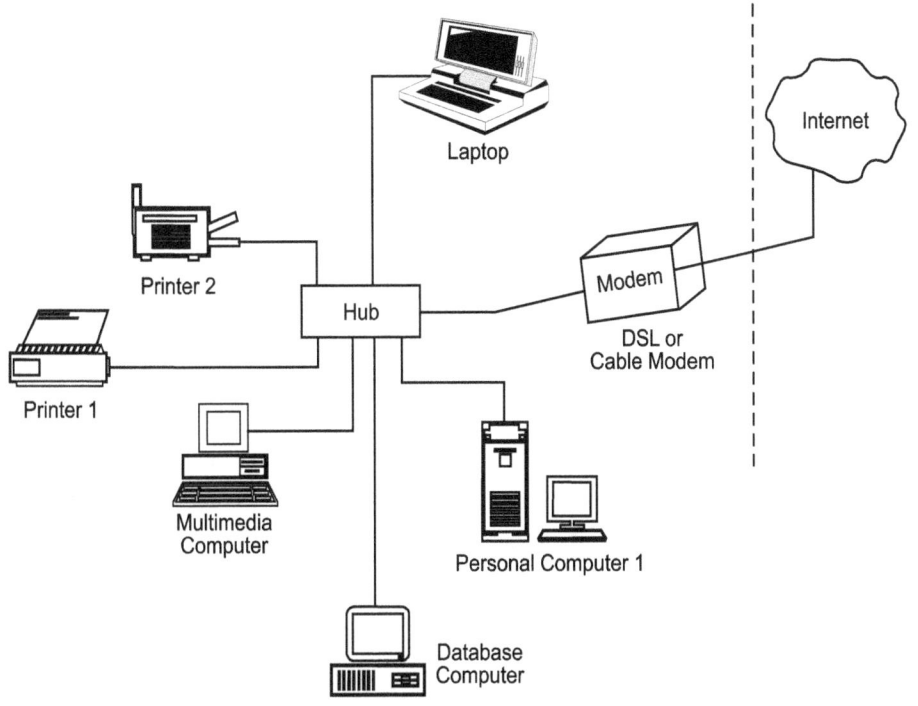

Fig. 6.42: Typical home computer network (wired)

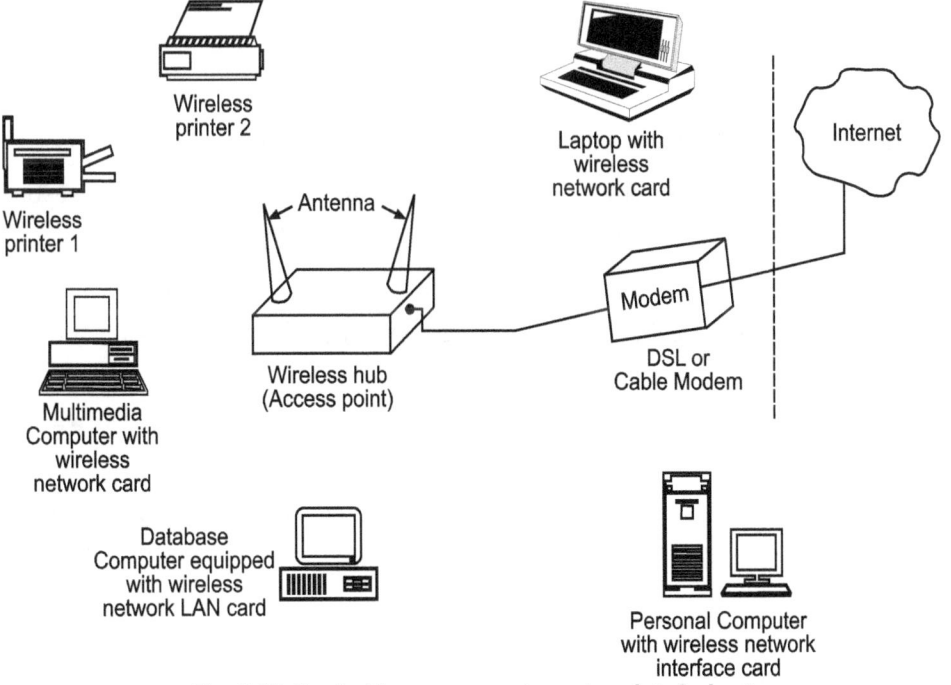

Fig. 6.43: Typical home computer network (wireless)

2. More importantly, they save time and money, and make using your computer equipment much more enjoyable for everyone in the office as well as in family.
3. Lets consider the networking for the home, but all information given here applies to networking for a small business as well.
4. Setting-up a home network is the simplest way to get the most out of your computer equipment.
5. And as your family grows or you add additional computers, expansion is no problem. Best of all, creating a network is easier than you might think.

The key benefits of networking a home include :
- Sharing a high-speed Internet connection - without anyone having to sign-off, and without having another phone line installed.
- Playing games head-to-head on different computers from different rooms.
- Sharing an expensive resource like the colour photo printer in office without having to interrupt any office work.
- Everyone in the family can share files from every PC in the house - no need to put files onto floppy or zip discs and swap them.

To go wireless or wired? That is the question. A wireless set-up uses radio waves, while wired networks communicate through data cables. Both systems have their own advantages and disadvantages.

The following points decide whether to go for wired or wireless networks:
- **Range:** The range of the network is an important consideration while using a network.
- **Throughput:** The amount of data transferable using devices is important.
- **Integrity:** The network should have a stable form of communication. The robust designs of technology should provide data integrity performance equal to or better than other technologies.
- **Inter-operability:** Device should provide the ability to connect to wired or wireless LAN with ease.
- **Scalability:** Networks can be designed to be extremely simple or quite complex. Networks should support large number of nodes and/or large physical areas to boost or extend coverage.
- **Simplicity of installation and use:** Users should need very little new information to take advantage of LANs to be used. It should be simple and easy to install.

- **Security:** Because network technology has roots in military applications and banking applications, security has long been a design criterion for network technology.
- **Power requirement for networks:** End-user products should be designed to run with less power and accordingly the networking technique will be decided.
- **Safety:** The used technology should be safe for human and nature. Network must meet stringent government and industry regulations for safety.

6.13 IEEE 802.11

1. IEEE has defined the specifications for a wireless LAN, called as IEEE 802.11, which covers the data link layer and physical layer.
2. IEEE 802.11 networks are also known as Wi-Fi networks.
3. We will cover following things in IEEE 802.11 networks.
(a) Architecture of IEEE 802.11.
(b) MAC sublayer of IEEE 802.11.
(c) Addressing mechanism in IEEE 802.11.
(d) Physical layer of IEEE 802.11.

6.14 Architecture of IEEE 802.11

1. The standard defines two kinds of services:
(a) Basic Service Set (BSS).
(b) Extended Service Set (ESS).

6.14.1 Basic Service Set

1. IEEE 802.11 defines the BSS as the building block of a WLAN.
2. A BSS is made of following:
(a) Stationary or mobile wireless stations.
(b) An optional central base station (access point-AP).
3. In this standard, there are two sets available.
(a) BSS (Basic Service Set).
(b) ESS (Extended Service Set).
4. The typical BSS is as shown in Figure 6.44.

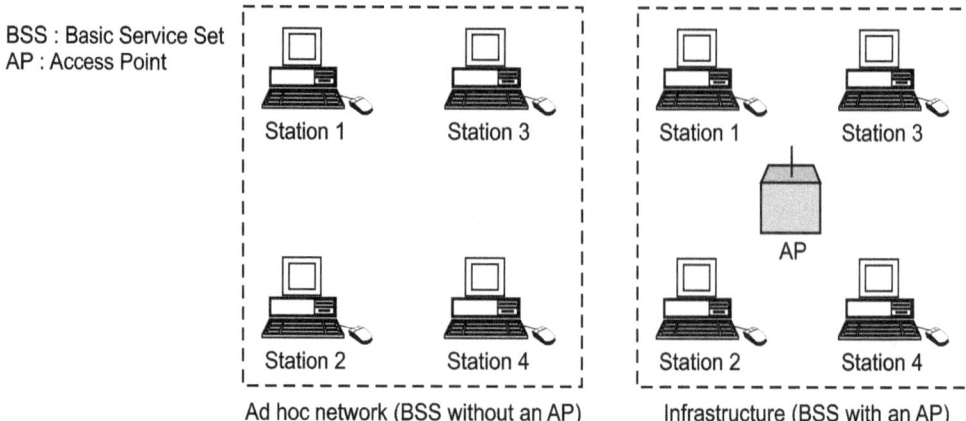

Fig. 6.44; Typical BSS

5. The BSS without an AP is a stand-alone network and cannot send data to other BSSs. This type of architecture is also known as ad-hoc architecture.
6. In this architecture station communicates with each other without the need of an AP.
7. A BSS with an AP is called as an infrastructure network.
8. The typical ESS (Extended Service Cost) is shown in Fig. 6.45.

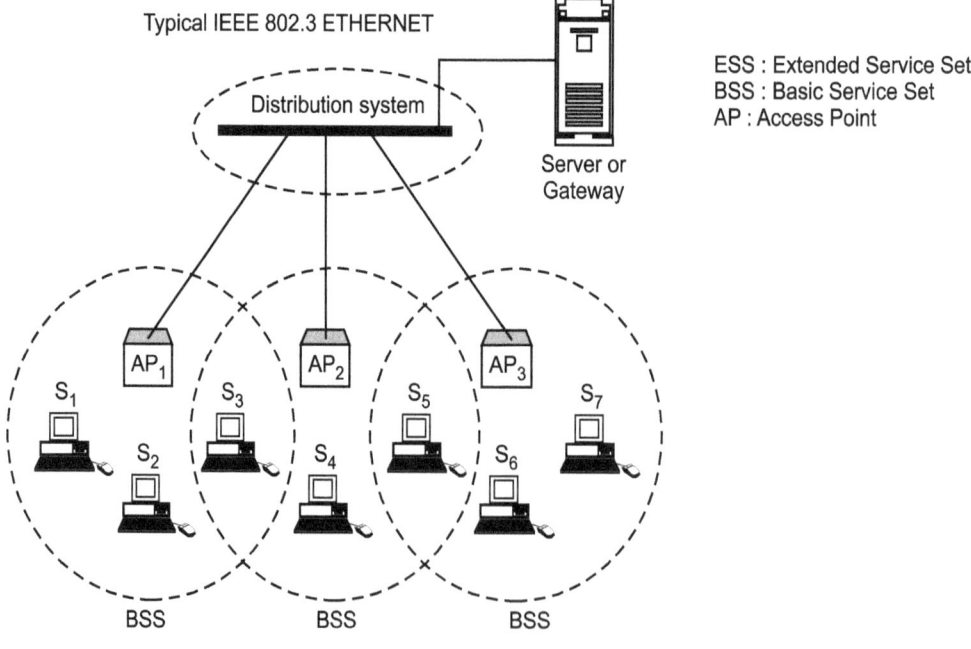

Fig. 6.45: Typical ESS (Extended Service Set)

9. An ESS is made up of two or more BSSs with APs.
10. In this, BSSs are connected with each other through a distribution system, which is nothing but a wired LAN.
11. The APs in the BSSs are connected using Distribution System.
12. Distribution system can be wired IEEE Ethernet LAN like IEEE 802.3.
13. ESS uses two types of stations:
(a) Mobile
(b) Stationary.
14. The mobile stations are normal stations inside a BSS.
15. The stationary stations are AP stations that are part of a wired LAN.
16. When BSSs are connected using distribution system, then S_2 can communicate with S_4 station without use of an AP.
17. However, usually, communication between two stations, S_2 and S_4 in two different BSSs usually occurs via. APs (i.e. AP_1 and AP_2). (This concept is applicable in cellular mobile communication).
18. There are three types of stations defined by 802.11, based on their mobility in WLAN.
(a) No-transition mobility.
(b) BSS-transition mobility.
(c) ESS-transition mobility.
19. The station with **No-transition mobility** is either stationary (not moving) or moving only inside a specific BSS.
20. A station with **BSS-transition mobility** can move from one BSS to other BSS, but the movement is confined inside one ESS.
21. A station with **ESS-transition mobility** can move from one ESS to another ESS.

6.15 MAC Sublayer in IEEE 802.11

1. IEEE 802.11 defines two MAC sublayers.
(a) DCF (Distributed Co-ordination Function).
(b) PCF (Point Co-ordination Function).
2. The relationship between the two MAC sublayers, LLC sublayer and physical layer is shown in Fig. 6.46.

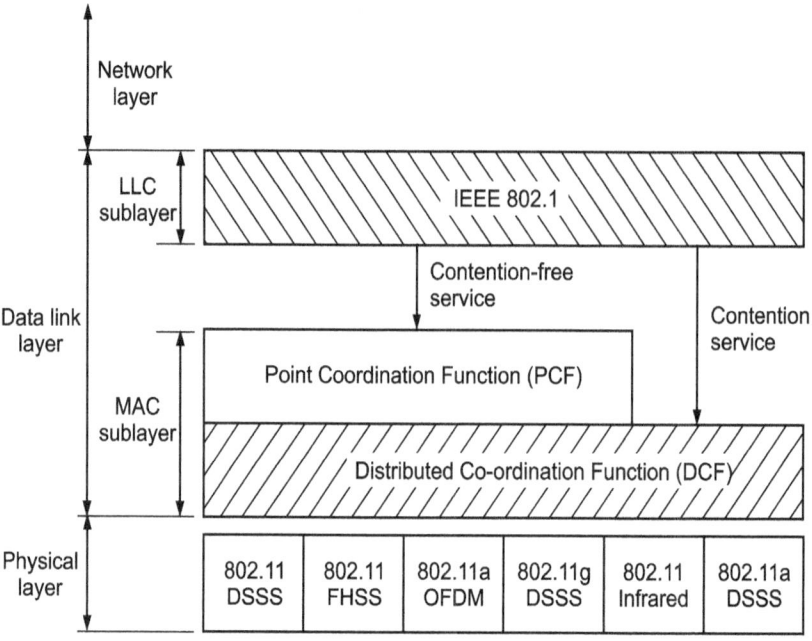

Fig. 6.46: IEEE 802.11 MAC layers detail

6.15.1 DCF (Distributed Co-ordination Function)

1. DCF uses CSMA/CA as the access method.
2. WLANs cannot implement CSMA/CD for three reasons.

    (a) For collision detection a station must be able to send data and receive collision signals at the same time (i.e. simultaneously). This increases cost (costly stations) and bandwidth requirement increases.

    (b) Collision may not be detected because of "Hidden station problem".

(c) If the distance between stations is greater, signal fading could prevent a station at one end from hearing a collision at the other end.

3. The process flowchart for CSMA/CA used for WLAN is given in Fig. 6.47.

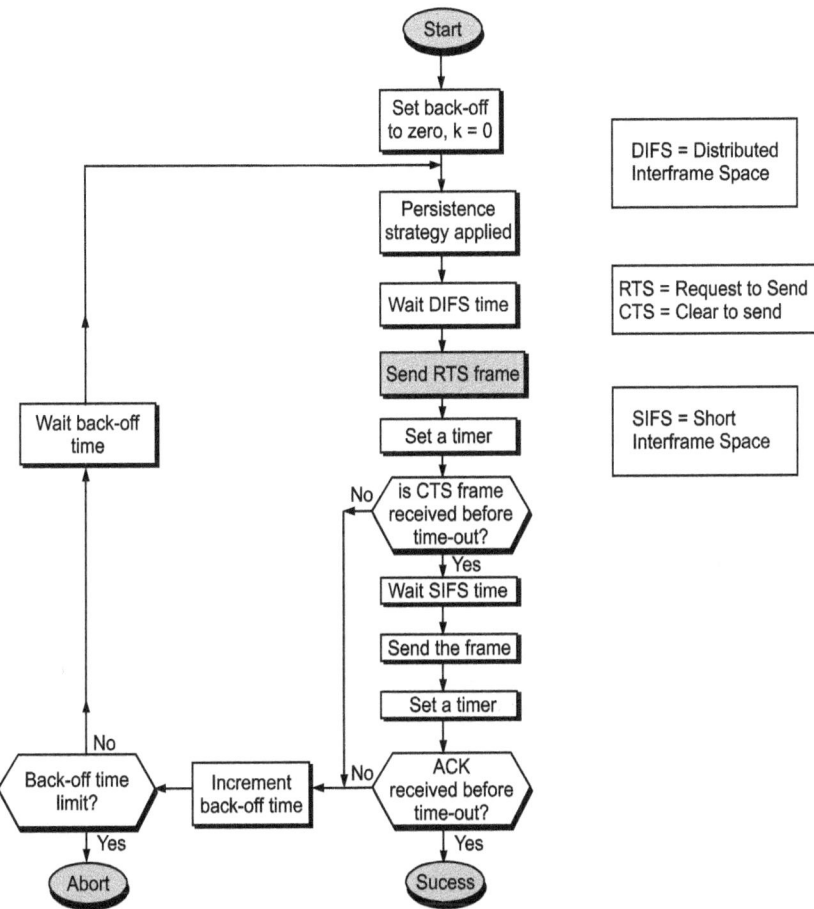

Fig. 6.47: Flow chart for CSMA/CA of WLAN system

4. The "frame exchange time line diagram" is shown in Fig. 6.48.

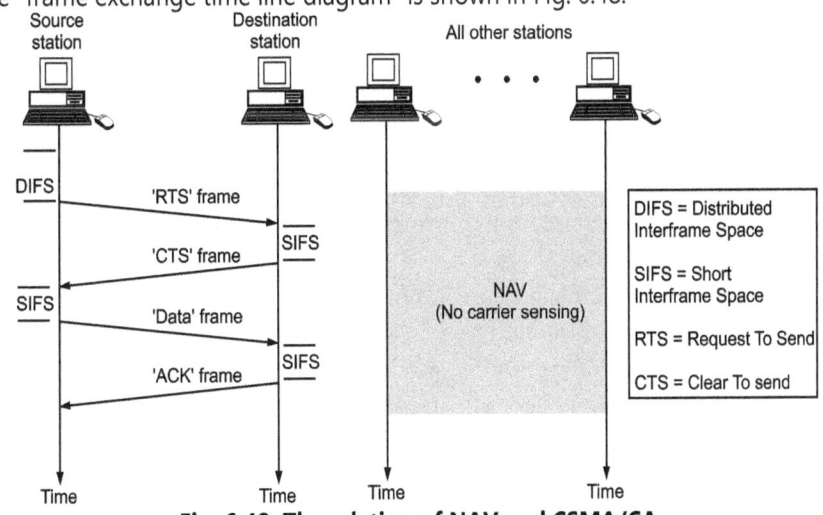

Fig. 6.48: The relation of NAV and CSMA/CA

5. In CSMA/CA flowchart, following are the steps:
(a) Before transmitting (sending) a frame, the source station senses the medium by checking the level of energy at the carrier frequency.
- Channel uses persistence strategy with back-off until the channel is idle.
- After the station is found to be idle, the station waits for a period of time called the DIFS, then the station sends a control frame called as RTS.
(b) After receiving RTS and waiting a period of time called the SIFS, the destination station sends a control frame, known as CTS, to source station. Thus, control frame CTS, indicates that the destination station is ready to receive data.
(c) The source station sends the data after waiting an amount of time equals to SIFS time.
(d) Thus, destination station, after waiting an amount of time equal to SIFS time, it sends an acknowledgement to show that the frame has been received. ACK is needed in this CSMA/CA protocol because the station does not have any means to check for the successful arrival of its data at the destination.

6. **The NAV (Network Allocation Vector)**
- The collision avoidance aspect of this protocol is accomplished by the feature i.e. Network Allocation Vector (NAV).
- Each station, before sensing the physical medium to see if it is idle, first checks its NAV to see if it has expired.

7. **Collision During Handshaking**
- When RTS or CTS control frames are in transition, this period is called as handshaking period.
- If there is a collision during this handshaking period, two or more stations may try to send RTS frames at the same time.
- These control frames may collide.
- However, because there is no mechanism for collision detection, the sender assumes there has been a collision if it has not received a CTS control frame from the receiver end.
- Thus, back-off strategy is then employed and the sender tries again.

6.15.2 Point Co-ordination Function (PCF)

1. PCF is an optional access method that can be implemented in an infrastructure network mode. (Not in adhoc mode).
2. It is implemented on top of DCF layer. It is mostly used in time sensitive transmission.
3. PCF has centralized and contention free polling access method.
4. AP performs polling for computer stations that are capable of being polled. The computer stations are polled one after another, sending any data they have to use the AP.
5. To give priority to PCF over DCF, following set of interframe spaces has been defined.

(a) PIFS (PCF IFS).
(b) SIFS (SIFS is same as that in DCF).
6. PIFS is always shorter than DIFS. This means IF AP wants to use PCF and computer station wants to use DCF at same time, then AP has priority.
7. PCF has priority over DCF, because of which computer stations that only use DCF may not gain access to the medium. To avoid (prevent) this, repetition interval has been designed to cover both contention free (PCF) and contention based (DCF) traffic.
8. The repetition interval which is repeated continuously and start with a special control frame, known as beacon frame.
9. When computer stations listens the beacon frame, they start their Network Allocation Vector (NAV) for the duration of the contention free period of the repetition interval.

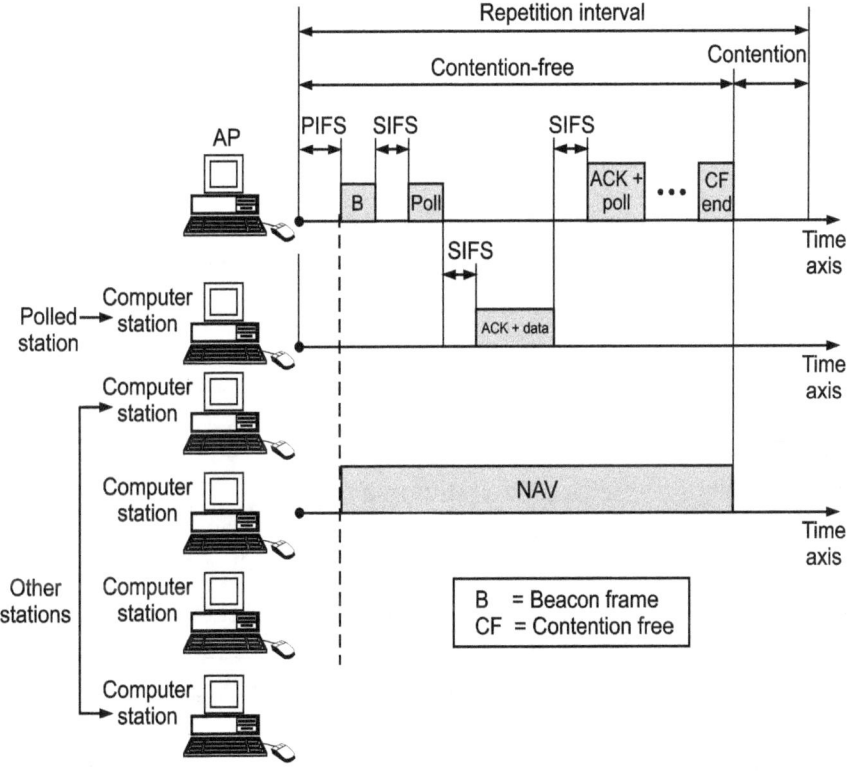

Fig. 6.49: Typical example of repetition interval

10. Thus, Point Controller (PC) can send a poll frame, receive data, send an ACK, receive an ACK or do any combination of these process, during the repetition interval.
11. For these processes IEEE 802.11 network uses piggybacking technique.

12. Thus, finally at the end of the contention free period, the Point Controller (PC) sends contention free end (CF end) frame to allow the contention based stations to use the medium.
13. In wireless environment, if noise corrupts the frame then it has to be transmitted. Thus, due to which MAC protocol recommends fragmentation process. Thus, fragmentation means division of large frame into smaller ones. It is more efficient and convenient to resend a small frame than a large one.

6.15.3 Frame Format

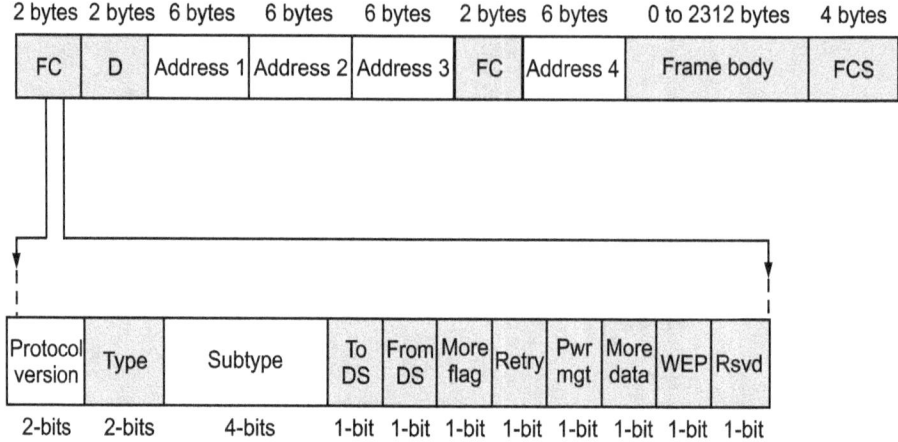

Fig. 6.50: Frame format of IEEE 802.11 WLAN

1. **FC (Frame Control):**
It defines type of frame and some control information.
2. The Table 7.1 describes the subfields of frame control in detail.

Table 6.9: Subfields in FC field (FC)

Field	Explanation
Version	Current version is 0.
Type	Type of information: Management (00), Control (01), or data (10).
Subtype	Subtype of each type (RTS, CTS or ACK).
To DS	Later explained.
From DS	Later explained.
More flag	When set to 1, means more fragments
Retry	When set to 1, means retransmitted frame.
Pwr mgt	When set to 1, means station is in power management mode.
More data	When set to 1, means station has more data to send.
WEP	Wired equivalent privacy (encryption implemented for security).
Rsvd	Reserved.

3. **D:** D defines duration of the transmission that is used to set the value of Network Allocation Vector (NAV). In one control frame, this field defines the ID of the frame.
4. **Address:** There are 4-address fields Address 1, 2, 3 and 4.
5. **Sequence Control (SC):** It defines the sequence number of the frame to be used in flow control process.
6. **Frame body:** It contains information based on the type and the subtype defined in frame control (FC) field.
7. **FCS:** Frame check sequence field contains a CRC-32 error detection sequence.

6.15.4 Frame Types

1. IEEE 802.11 has following categories of frame.
(a) Management frames.
(b) Control frames.
(c) Data frames.
2. Management frames are used for initial communication between computer stations and access points.
3. Control frames are used for accessing the channel and acknowledging frames. The RTS and CTS or ACK control frames are given.

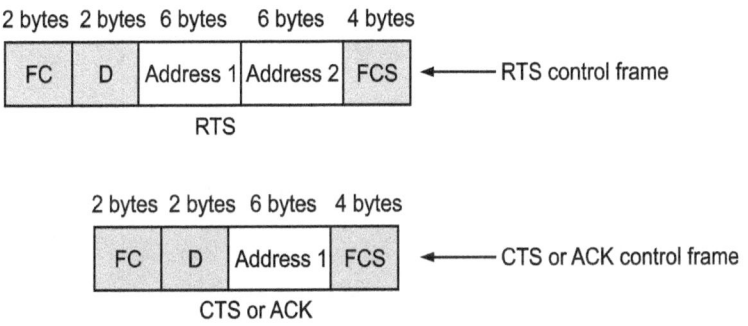

Fig. 6.51: RTS, CTS or ACK control frames

4. Data frames: Data frames are used for carrying data and control information in wireless communication.
5. Addressing mechanism table is shown as follows.

Table 6.10: Addresses used in WLAN

To DS	From DS	Address 1	Address 2	Address 3	Address 4
0	0	Destination	Source	BSS ID	N/A (NIL)
0	1	Destination	Sending AP	Source	N/A (NIL)
1	0	Receiving AP	Source	Destination	N/A (NIL)
1	1	Receiving AP	Sending AP	Destination	Source

6.15.5 Hidden Station Problem

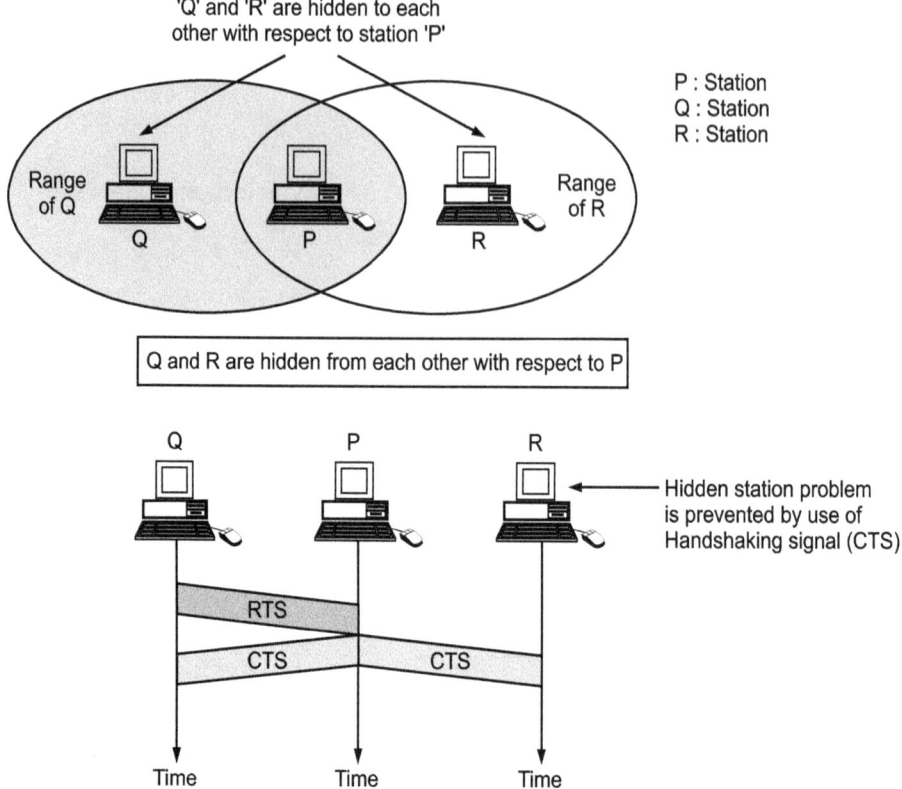

Fig. 6.52: Hidden station problem and prevention

1. In the given scenario, station 'R' is outside the transmission range of 'Q' and station 'Q' is outside the transmission range of 'R'. Also station 'P' is in area covered by both 'Q' and 'R'. Thus, 'P' can hear any signal transmitted by 'Q' or 'R'.
2. Assume that station 'Q' is sending data to station 'P.
3. In the middle of this transmission, station 'R' also has data to send to station 'P'.
4. However, station 'R' is out of 'Q' stations range and transmission from 'Q' can not reach 'R'.
5. Therefore, 'R' thinks the medium is free.
6. Station 'R' sends its data to 'P', which results in a collision at 'P' because this station is receiving data from both 'Q' and 'C'.
7. In this case, we say that stations 'Q' and 'R' are hidden from each other w.r.t. 'P'.
8. Hidden stations can reduce the capacity of the network because of the possibility of collision.
9. The solution to the hidden station problem is the use of the handshake frames (CTS and RTS) that we have discussed.

10. The RTS message from 'Q' reaches 'P' but not 'R'.
11. However, because both 'Q' and 'R' are within the range of 'P', the CTS message, which contains the duration of data transmission from 'Q' to 'P' reaches 'R'.
12. Station 'R' knows that some hidden station is using the channel and refrains from transmitting until that duration is over.
13. Thus, CTS frame in CSMA/CA handshake can prevent collision from a hidden computer station.

6.15.6 Exposed Station Problem

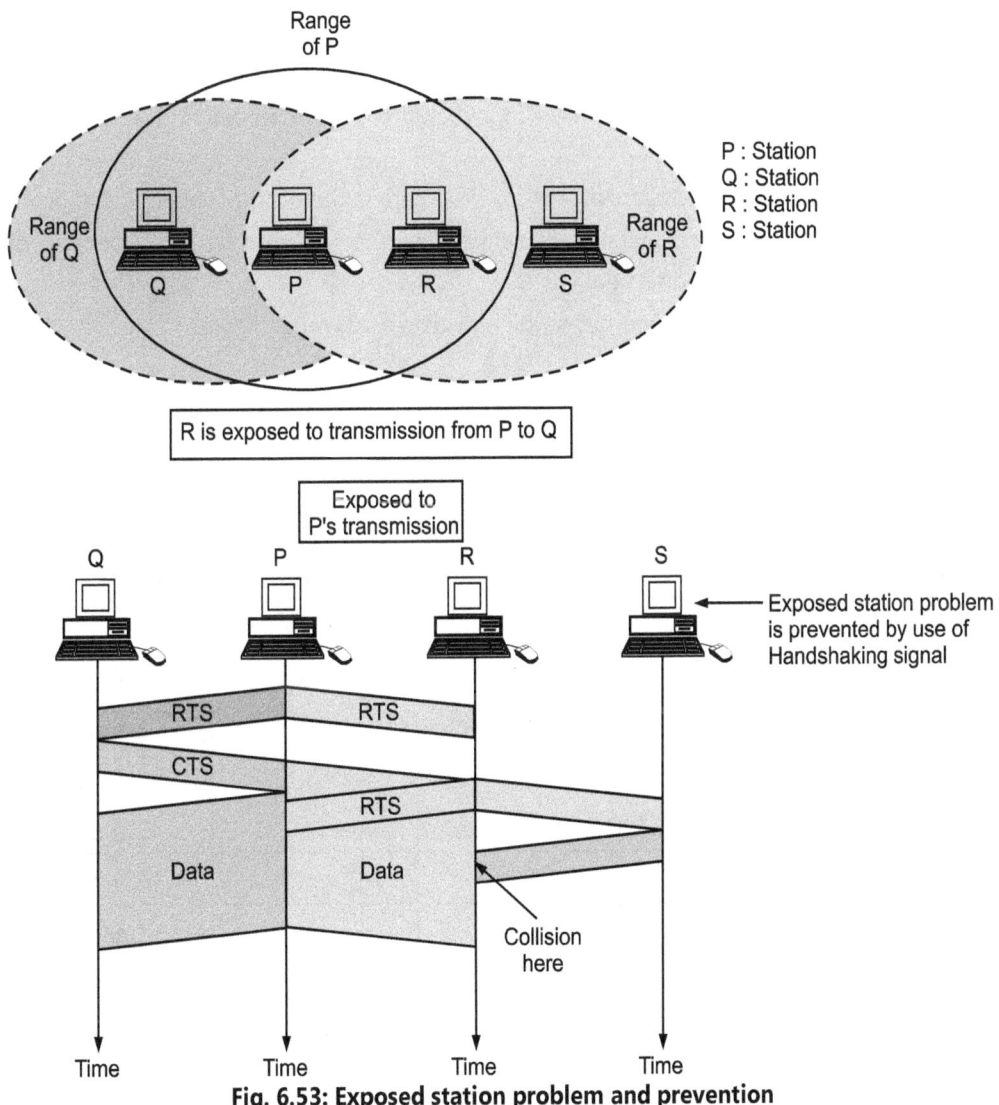

Fig. 6.53: Exposed station problem and prevention

1. In this problem, a station refrains (hold back) from using a channel when it is available.
2. Station 'P' is transmitting to station 'Q'. Station 'R' has some data to send to station 'S', which can be sent without interfering with the transmission from 'P' to 'Q'.
3. However, station 'R' is exposed to transmission from 'P', it listens (hears) what 'P' is sending and thus hold back from sending.
4. In other words, 'R' is too conservative and wastes the capacity of the channel.
5. The handshaking messages RTS and CTS can not help in this case.
6. Station 'R' hears the RTS from 'P', but does not hear the CTS from 'Q'.
7. Station 'R', after hearing the RTS from 'P', can wait for a time so that CTS from 'Q' reaches 'P'. It then sends an RTS to 'S' to show that it needs to communicate with 'S'.
8. Both station 'Q' and 'P' may hear this RTS, but station 'P' is in the sending state, not the receiving state.
9. The station 'Q' however, responds with a CTS. There is the main problem. If station 'P' has started sending its data, station 'R' cannot hear the CTS from station 'S' because of the collision. It cannot send its data to 'S'.
10. It remains exposed until 'P' finishes sending its data as shown in figure.

6.16 Physical Layer in IEEE 802.11

Table 6.12

IEEE	Technique	Band	Modulation	Rate (Mbps)
802.11	FHSS	2.4 GHz	FSK	1 and 2
	DSSS	2.4 GHz	PSK	1 and 2
	IR-A	215 THz - 430 THz	PPM	1 and 2
	IR-B	100 THz - 215 THz	PPM	1 and 2
	IR-C	100 THz - 300 THz	PPM	1 and 2
802.11a	OFDM	5.725 GHz	PSK or QAM	6 to 54
802.11b	DSSS	2.4 GHz	PSK	5.5 and 11
802.11g	OFDM	2.4 GHz	DBPSK/DQPSK	22 and 54

1. Infrared operates in 100 THz to 430 THz in the band of IR-A, IR-B and IR-C.
2. All other implementations operate in ISM (Industrial Scientific and Medical) band.
3. The ISM band ranges are given as follows.

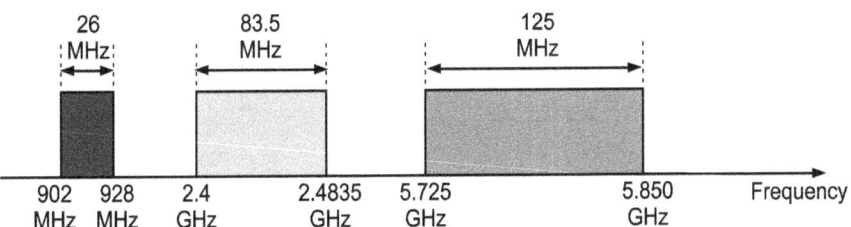

Fig. 6.54: ISM band (frequency bands) are unlicensed band

4. In the table given 'PPM' modulation is pulse position modulation. DBPSK is Differential BPSK.

6.16.1 IEEE 802.11 FHSS

1. IEEE 802.11 FHSS uses the Frequency Hopping Spread Spectrum (FHSS) technique.
2. It uses 2.4 GHz ISM band for data communication.
3. This 2.4 GHz band is divided into 79 subbands of 1 MHz. Also some guard bands are also added.
4. The PN sequence generator (or Pseudo random number generator) selects the hopping sequence in FHSS.
5. The modulation technique used is two level FSK or four level FSK (frequency shift keying).
6. The baud rate for FSK is 1 or 2 bits/baud.
7. The resultant data rate is 1 or 2 Mbps.

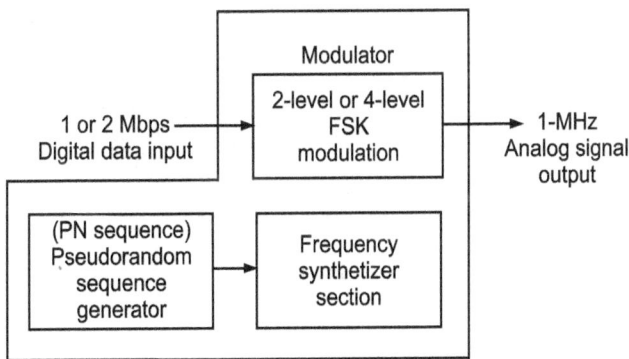

Fig. 6.55: IEEE 802.11 FHSS physical layer

6.16.2 IEEE 802.11 DSSS

1. IEEE 802.11 DSSS uses the Direct Sequence Spread Spectrum (DSSS) technique.
2. DSSS uses 2.4 GHz ISM band for data communication.
3. The modulation technique used is PSK (Phase Shift Keying).
4. The baud rate for PSK is 1 Mbaud/sec.

5. The IEEE 802.11 DSSS, PSK system allows 1 or 2 bits/baud (i.e. BPSK or QPSK).
6. The resultant data rate is 1 or 2 Mbps.

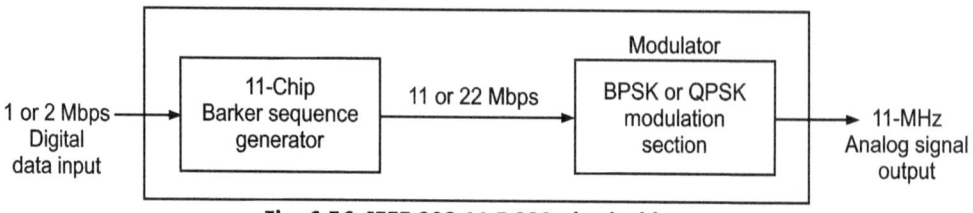

Fig. 6.56: IEEE 802.11 DSSS physical layer

6.16.3 IEEE Infrared

1. The recommended division of infrared radiation into the following three bands:
   (a) IR-A (700 nm-1400 nm) (215 THz-430 THz).
   (b) IR-B (1400 nm-3000 nm) (100 THz-215 THz).
   (c) IR-C (3000 nm-1 mm) (300 GHz-100 THz).
2. IEEE 802.,11 infrared uses infrared light in the range of 800 to 950 nm.
3. The modulation used in this standard in Pulse Position Modulation (PPM).
4. For 1 Mbps data rate, 4-bit sequence if first mapped into a 16-bit sequence in which only one bit is set to '1' and the rest of the bits are set to '0'.
5. For 2 Mbps data rate, 2-bit sequence is first mapped into a 4-bit sequence in which only one bit is set to '1' and the rest of the bits are set to '0'.
6. Mapped sequences are then converted to optical signals. The presence of light specifies 1 and absence of light specifies '0'.

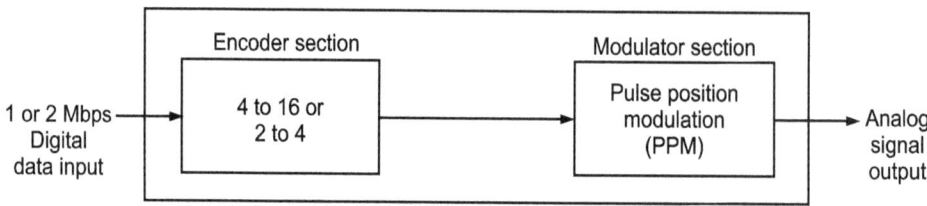

Fig. 6.57: IEEE 802.11: Infrared physical layer

6.16.4 EEE 802.11a – OFDM

1. The IEEE 802.11a – OFDM explains the orthogonal frequency - division multiplexing method for signal generation.
2. It uses 5 GHz ISM band for data communication.
3. This OFDM is similar to FDM (Frequency Division Multiplexing) method except one. The sub-bands are used by one source at a given time in OFDM.
4. Sources content with one another at the layer - 2 (Data Link Layer) for channel access.

5. The band is divided into 52 sub-bands, with 48 sub-bands or sending 48 groups of bits at a time and remaining 4 sub-bands are used for control information.
6. This scheme is similar to ADSL technology where Band is divided into sub-bands which reduces the effects of interference.
7. If sub-bands are used randomly, security increases considerably in wireless communication.
8. OFDM uses PSK and QAM modulation techniques as digital continuous wave modulation.
9. If PSK modulation is used data rate is 18 mbps and if QAM modulation is used then data rate is 54 mbps.

6.16.5 IEEE 802.11b – DSSS

1. The IEEE 802.11b – DSSS explains the High Rate - Direct Sequence Spread Spectrum (HR-DSSS) method for signal generation.
2. It uses 2.4 GHz ISM band for data communication.
3. The HR-DSSS is similar to DSSS except for the encoding method, which is known as Complementary Code Keying (CCK) technique.
4. CCK encoding technique encodes 4 or 8 bits to one CCK symbol.
5. To backward compatible with DSSS, HR-DSSS defines four data rates:
   (a) 1 mbps
   (b) 2 mbps
   (c) 5.5 mbps
   (d) 11 mbps
6. The 1 mbps and 2 mbps data rates uses same modulation techniques as DSSS i.e. PSK (Phase Shift Keying).
7. The 5.5 mbps version uses BPSK modulation and transmits at 1.375 Mbaud/sec. with 4-bit CCK encoding technique.
8. The 11 mbps version uses QPSK modulation and transmits at 1.375 mbps with 8-bit CCK encoding technique.

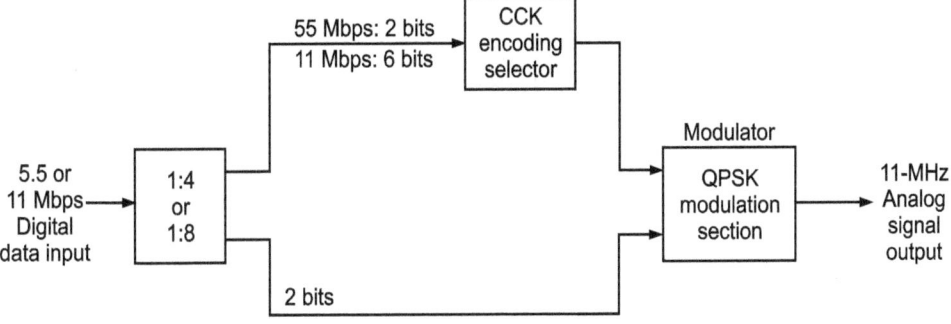

Fig. 6.58: IEEE 802.11b – DSSS physical layer

6.16.6 IEEE 802.11g

1. IEEE 802.11g specification defines forward error correction as added feature compared to its backward compatible standard 802.11b.
2. It uses OFDM technique in 2.4 GHz ISM band.
3. It uses DBPSK and DQPSK modulation technique.
4. It gives 22 and 54 Mbps as data rate output.
5. Despite its major acceptance, 802.11g suffers from the same interference as 802.11b in the already crowded 2.4 GHz range.
6. Devices operating in this range include microwave ovens, Bluetooth devices, baby monitors and digital cordless telephones, which can lead to interference issues.
7. Additionally, the success of the standard has caused usage/density problems related to crowding in urban areas.
8. To prevent interference there are only three non-overlapping usable channels 1.6, 11 and 25 MHz separation in US and 1, 5, 9 and 20 MHz separation in Europe.
9. Even with such separation, some interference due to side lobes exists, though it is considerably weaker.

SUMMARY

- Both analog and digital information can be encoded as either analog or digital signals. The particular encoding that is chosen depends on the media and communications facilities available and the requirements to be met. For example, to transmit digital information over an analog telephone line, a modem is used to convert the digital data into analog form. Similarly, there is an increasing use of digital facilities, and voice signals must be encoded in digital form to be transmitted on these digital facilities.

- To make efficient use of high-speed telecommunications lines, some form of multiplexing is used. Multiplexing allows several-transmission sources to share a larger transmission capacity. The two common forms of multiplexing are frequency-division multiplexing (FDM) and time-division multiplexing (TI M).

- Public telephone and telecommunications networks have evolved from an all-analog technology to one that is increasingly digital. Digital carrier standards specify a time-division multiplexed structure for transmission within the network.

The functions performed by an ISDN can be defined by the services that it support-s' and the functions visible at the user-network interface. Among the most important defining characteristics of ISDN are the following:

- **Transmission structure:** ISDN offers a service structured as a set of channels. The B channel is a user channel that supports circuit-switched, semipermanent, and packet-switched use. The D channel supports user-network control signaling and packet switching. The two standard transmission offerings are the basic service, consisting of two B channels and one D channel, and the primary service, consisting of 24 or 31 B channels and one D channel.

- **User-network interface configurations:** The user-network interface is defined in terms of reference points and functional groupings. This approach provides for standardized interfaces that facilitate the use of equipment from multiple vendors and that simplify access to ISDN.
- **Protocol architecture:** The interaction between ISDN and a subscriber can be described within the context of the OSI protocol reference model. Essentially, the ISDN recommendations deal with layers 1 to 3 of that model. A physical layer specification covers both basic and primary access for all channels. For the D channel, LAID is defined at the data link layer, and Q.931 (call control) and the X.25 packet level (packet-mode service on the D channel) are specified for the network ' vel. For the B channel, ISDN supports the use of X.25 and LAMB for packet-mode service and also provides I.465/V.120 as a common optional data link mechanism.
- **ISDN connections:** ISDN provides four types of service for end-to-end communication: circuit-switched calls over a B or H channel, semipermanent connections over a B or H channel, packet-switched calls over a B or H channel, and packet-switched calls over the D channel.
- **Addressing:** Addressing refers to the way in which a calling user specifies the called user so that the network can perform routing and delivery functions. ISDN makes use of a number scheme based on E.164 and can interwork with non-ISDN numbers to allow Interworking of ISDN with other networks.
- **Interworking:** Interworking refers to the capability for an ISDN subscriber to establish a connection to a subscriber on a non-ISDN network. The most important such networks are public switched telephone networks (analog networks), circuit-switched public data networks (X.21 networks), and packet-switched public data networks (X.25 networks).

EXERCISE

1. Write notes on services provided by ISDN.
2. What are the different types of ISDN terminals?
3. List out different non-ISDN terminals.
4. Write detail note on ISDN devices.
5. Explain ISDN PRI service in detail.
6. Write short note on characteristics of B and D channels.
7. Write a short note on "ISDN equipment and interface terminology".
8. Explain "ISDN protocol stack" in detail.
9. What is Ethernet?
10. State various forms of Ethernet based on data rate.

11. Explain standard Ethernet and frame format of standard ethernet.
12. What is bridged ethernet?
13. What is switched ethernet?
14. Explain various physical layer implementations of 10 Mbps Ethernet.
15. What is Fast Ethernet? Give its frame format.
16. What is Gigabit Ethernet? Give its frame format.
17. What are the different features of WLAN?
18. What are the different advantages of wireless network?
19. Which points decides whether to go for wired or wireless networks.
20. Draw and explain architecture of IEEE 802.11.
21. Explain what is BSS and ESS.
22. Draw and explain MAC sublayer in IEEE 802.11.
23. Write short note on:
    (a) DCF, (b) PCF, (c) Frame format of WLAN
24. Explain the following:
    (a) Hidden station problem
    (b) Exposed station problem
    (c) Physical layer in IEEE 802.11